DIOGENES LAERTIUS
I

LCL 184

DIOGENES LAERTIUS

LIVES OF EMINENT PHILOSOPHERS

WITH AN ENGLISH TRANSLATION BY

R. D. HICKS

VOLUME I

HARVARD UNIVERSITY PRESS

CAMBRIDGE, MASSACHUSETTS

LONDON, ENGLAND

First published 1925
Reprinted 1938, 1942, 1950, 1959, 1966
Reprinted with new introductory material 1972
Reprinted 1991, 1995

ISBN 0-674-99203-2

Printed in Great Britain by St Edmundsbury Press Ltd,
Bury St Edmunds, Suffolk, on acid-free paper.
Bound by Hunter & Foulis Ltd, Edinburgh, Scotland.

CONTENTS

CONTENTS

FOREWORD

TO REPRINT OF 1972

In issuing for the Loeb Classical Library another reprint of our first volume of Diogenes Laertius, contributed first in 1925 by that remarkable man R. D. Hicks, we have availed ourselves of the kindness and scholarship of Herbert S. Long, Professor of Classics in Case Western Reserve University, Cleveland, Ohio, who has provided an appreciation of Hicks, a new appraisal of Diogenes Laertius, and an up-to-date bibliography. For all this we thank him.—E. H. Warmington, Editor, L.C.L.

January 1972

PREFACE

BY HERBERT S. LONG

In 1925 the Loeb Classical Library published its first edition of Diogenes Laertius with an Introduction, text and translation by Robert Drew Hicks, a Fellow of Trinity College, Cambridge, and well known for his work on ancient philosophy, which included editions of Aristotle's *Politics* (1894) and *De Anima* (1907), and the book "Stoic and Epicurean" (1910), as well as a number of articles. After some hesitation, since several scholars had announced that they were working on or planning critical editions of Diogenes, in whole or in part, Hicks decided to complete his own edition in the belief that "the text of the biographies is hardly likely to undergo radical reconstruction." He accordingly prepared "an eclectic text based largely on the Didot edition, . . . confident that, whatever the less important parts may lose or gain by later revision, the text of what is most valuable, namely the fragments, will undergo little alteration, failing the discovery of fresh MS. material." Hicks accompanied his eclectic text with a delightfully readable version that hits off Diogenes' various manners, now serious and straightforward, now banal and fatuous, to a T.

Cobet's Didot edition unfortunately had no *apparatus criticus*. It was thus not immediately clear that

xi

PREFACE

Cobet placed great reliance on one MS., F, and that he emended freely—though one might have expected a notable producer of *variae lectiones* to do just that. When the first critical edition [a] of the entire text was finally published in 1964, those particular characteristics of Cobet's text were either eliminated or made visible by an *apparatus*; more MSS. were examined and used; and the indirect tradition, unusually extensive in Diogenes, was more fully exploited. Still the latest editor would claim no more than to have made a beginning at editing an author who is deceptively simple. Further progress will likely come, not from the MSS., but from careful study of the sense of the text—a large undertaking for an author embodying so many and such disparate quoted materials as Diogenes.

Hicks, it turns out, was quite right: the text of the biographies has not undergone "radical" reconstruction. The changes *vis-à-vis* Cobet's edition have been many and small, for the most part. Yet the basis of the text is considerably altered. Cobet preferred F and tended to distrust B, as his practice shows. Hicks went so far as to state: "There is substantial agreement that . . . the scribe of . . . the Borbonicus . . . did not know Greek." All detailed descriptions of B, it is true, note the extraordinary frequency of itacism in that MS.; but itacism proves a *knowledge* of Greek, if not of orthography. Mss. written by scribes ignorant of the language they were transcribing are, it seems, extremely rare. The Rev. Professor B. M. Metzger of the Princeton Theological Seminary has pointed out to me one

[a] [By Professor Long himself in the series of Oxford Classical Texts.—E.H.W.]

PREFACE

instance, the only one known to him among all the
MSS. of the New Testament in various languages :
viz., the Codex Koridethi (=Theta) of the Gospels,
a MS. whose scribe was a Georgian who may have
known some Greek, but who drew rather than wrote
his Greek letters. (This unusual MS. was fully described and discussed in an article by Kirsopp Lake
and Robert P. Blake in the *Harvard Theological
Review*, xvi (1923), especially pp. 267-286.) Such was
not the scribe of B, a MS. that sometimes enables us,
in cruces, to get behind the speciously smooth text
provided by F.

There were two English versions of Diogenes prior
to Hicks' : an awkward sounding, literal, frequently
incorrect version by C. D. Yonge (Bohn, 1853) ; and
a late-17th-century translation by ten persons, now
merely quaint. Hicks owed nothing to these versions
but the inspiration to make a good one. In his
Preface he praised the German of Apelt (1921) and
Bignone's Italian translation of Book X (1920).
Since then there have appeared two other complete
translations of high quality, both provided with
many helpful notes : an Italian by Marcello Gigante
(1962), and a Rumanian by Professor C. I. Balmuș
with Introduction and notes by the late Professor
Aram Frenkian (1963).

Readers of the final paragraph of Hicks' Preface
may have felt that he thanked unusually many
persons for help of various sorts. His contemporaries
did not need to be told that he was blind. Born in
1850, in 1868 he entered Trinity College Cambridge,
where he had a distinguished undergraduate career
and where he remained as Fellow and Lecturer in
Classics. In 1896 he married Bertha Mary Heath, a

classicist herself, who had studied at Girton College
and held an M.A. in classics of the University of
London. Between 1898 and 1900 Hicks became
totally blind. He nevertheless continued his career,
publishing most of his major works after 1900, and
serving on various Cambridge examining boards.
He employed a number of secretaries and also received help from friends, some of whom are named
in the Prefaces to his various books. But his chief
aid was always his wife, whose part in the production
of his scholarly works can now be known to few.
Hicks died on the 9th of March, 1929. His career
is an extraordinary example of personal determina-
tion supported by the devoted and selfless assistance
of his wife, brother-in-law, and a remarkable circle
of loyal friends. For most of these facts I am indebted
to Hicks' son, the Rev. W. Francis Hicks of Cambridge, by a letter of 11th September, 1971.

INTRODUCTION

BY HERBERT S. LONG

DIOGENES LAERTIUS, as he is now generally called, is rarely named in ancient works, and even so his name appears in several forms. He is called Laertius Diogenes regularly in the mss. of his book, by Sopater in Photius, *Biblioth.* 161, and in "Suidas" (the Suda), *s.v.* τετραλογία : in earlier modern scholarly works this was the customary form of his name. The order Diogenes Laertius occurs, so it appears, only in Stephanus of Byzantium, *s.v.* Δρυΐδαι (in only part of the mss.), and in a lemma to *Anthologia Palatina*, vii. 95. Eustathius on *Iliad* M. 153 refers to him as Laertes ; Stephanus Byz. *s.v.* 'Ενετοί calls him plain Diogenes in a passage that has been taken to refer to our Diogenes and used to emend ii. 113 *sub fin*. Stephanus, *s.v.* Χολλεῖδαι, refers to him as Διογένης ὁ Λαερτιεύς, implying that he was a native of some town, perhaps Laerte in Caria or Laerte(s) in Cilicia, two of the ancient world's most unknown places : this explanation of his name and origin was generally accepted from the Renaissance until the 18th century. Stahr, in Smith's *Dictionary of Greek and Roman Biography*, suggested that Diogenes' ancestors included one who had for a patron a member of the Roman family of the Laertii. The favourite modern theory, however, is that of

xv

Wilamowitz [a] that Laertius was a learned nickname of a type familiar in post-classical times, invented to distinguish this Diogenes from the many others, and based upon the Homeric formula διογενὲς Λαερτιάδη used in addressing Odysseus.

All that we know of his life is what can be deduced from his own book. His date, for example, can be estimated only by what he included or left out. He has been variously dated in every century A.D. from the first to the fourth.[b] He clearly wrote before ca. A.D. 500, since Sopater cited him. The latest philosophers whom he mentions appear to be Theodosius the Sceptic, Sextus Empiricus and Saturninus, all of the third century A.D. He does not refer to Neo-Pythagoreanism nor—a more striking omission—to Neo-Platonism, although at least part of his work was intended for a woman who was an ardent Platonist (iii. 47). On the basis of these somewhat tenuous arguments Delatte [c] dated Diogenes ca. A.D. 225–250.

In addition to his history of philosophy, Diogenes quotes 49 of his own epigrams on 43 different philosophers, and implies (i. 39) that he had published a separate collection of his verses called Πάμμετρος ("Poems in All Metres") in at least two books, for he cites the first book. The extant poems are so wretched as fully to justify von Gutschmid's [d] thanks to Apollo and the Muses for allowing the collection as a whole to vanish.

[a] *Philologische Untersuchungen*, iii. 163 and *Hermes*, xxxiv, p. 629.
[b] Bibliography in M. Trevissoi, "D. L., L'età in cui visse," *Rivista di storia antica*, 12 (1908), pp. 482-505.
[c] P. 6. For works referred to by author's name only, see the Selected Bibliography.
[d] *Kleine Schriften*, i, p. 188, n. 1.

INTRODUCTION

Diogenes obviously was well educated; but his treatment of philosophy is such that we cannot make out what school he belonged to, nor even whether he ever studied philosophy seriously and on a level above that of general education, of which he clearly considered philosophy a most important part.[a] His approach is biographical and literary, not truly philosophic, so that "Philosophers' Lives" is a more fitting short title for the book than some others. His account of Plato, one of his longest (Book III), clearly shows how superficial and unreliable he was,[b] even when writing for a Platonist. A number of scholars have regarded him as an Epicurean because of the length and value of his account of Epicurus (Book X); but its high quality as a source comes from the fact that Diogenes, for whatever reason, quoted very extensively from Epicurus' own writings. He has in common with the Sceptics an openness to and impartiality towards the views of all schools, which he describes with more or less equal care—or indifference. The phrase Ἀπολλωνίδης ὁ Νικαεὺς ὁ παρ' ἡμῶν (ix. 109), which has sometimes been taken (as by Schwartz in RE, col. 761) to prove Diogenes a Sceptic, would only do so if (a) we were certain that Apollonides himself was a Sceptic, and (b) the phrase ὁ παρ' ἡμῶν had to mean "member of our school." Neither of these conditions holds beyond doubt, however. Diogenes' apparent impartiality is as likely to come from philosophic indifference as from Sceptic principles. It seems impossible to demonstrate that Diogenes was a confirmed adherent of *any* school to the exclusion of all others. The tone

[a] ii. 79-80 quote dicta of Aristippus illustrating this attitude.   [b] Hope, pp. 204-208.

of his work as a whole suits better a man of the world who happened to be interested in philosophers, but more as men and writers than as philosophers in a technical sense.[a] If he gives a full account of Sceptic doctrines and carries the succession of that school later than of any other, it is probably because he enjoyed juggling paradoxes, the more outrageous, the better. There are numbers of first-person references in Diogenes, but they are surprisingly unrevealing : the majority of them merely state how he adjusted the source materials that were available to him by finding other information, as in ii. 59 or viii. 53. The cross references backwards and forwards are almost all correct. Diogenes seldom expresses any personal opinion on a philosophical matter, and then he does so without heat except at x. 3-12, where he unexpectedly rises to a passionate defence of Epicurus, which may, to be sure, have come from Epicurean sources. The rather motley, fluctuating impression produced by Diogenes' book as a whole derives, not particularly from his own personality, but from the huge and variegated mass of source materials that he transmits to us. His own personality is as elusive as that of a *florilegium* ; yet much can be learned about his interests and the tastes of his audience by observing the types of material that he chose to include.

The title of Diogenes' work appears in the MSS. in various lengthy forms, of which that in P is typical : Λαερτίου Διογένους βίοι καὶ γνῶμαι τῶν ἐν φιλοσοφίᾳ εὐδοκιμησάντων καὶ τῶν ἑκάστῃ αἱρέσει ἀρεσκόντων ἐν ἐπιτόμῳ συναγωγή ("Laertius Diogenes' Lives and Opinions of Those Who Were Distinguished in

[a] So Delatte, p. 39.

INTRODUCTION

Philosophy and Succinct Collection of the Doctrines Acceptable to Each School "). Citations usually shorten the title to such a form as φιλοσόφων βίοι, "Philosophers' Lives," which, since it emphasizes the biographical aspect of the work, more truly represents Diogenes' interest.

Diogenes has acquired an importance out of all proportion to his merits because the loss of many primary sources and of the earlier secondary compilations has accidentally left him the chief continuous source for the history of Greek philosophy. In the late Middle Ages Diogenes' book was already the basis of what then passed for history of philosophy, as we see from such a work as the very popular and widely distributed *De vita et moribus philosophorum* of Walter Burley (1275–?1345). The use of Diogenes as the skeleton for histories of ancient philosophy passed away gradually in modern times, but his name still appears often in footnotes, as in W. K. C. Guthrie's *History of Greek Philosophy* ; for Diogenes is a veritable tissue of quotations from all sorts of authors and on most conceivable, and some inconceivable, aspects of philosophers' lives. Richard Hope counted 1,186 explicit references to 365 books by about 250 authors, as well as more than 350 anonymous references : that is, an average of nearly three references to a page of the Oxford Classical Text edition. Much of this quoted material is trivial, merely amusing, or probably false ; but some of it is very valuable. Hence the importance of Diogenes. In any given passage he is as useful and reliable as the source he happens to be quoting at that exact moment.

Diogenes arranged his work as follows. He began

with a general introduction or Prologue (i. 1-21) on
non-Greek philosophies, questions concerning the
arrangement of the work, and an account of the
Sages (i. 22-122), whom he distinguished from
philosophers proper. He then gave his lives of the
philosophers arranged in two "successions" (διαδοχαί),
a method of treatment developed in essence by
Theophrastus and then fully by Sotion of Alexandria.

 A. Ionian Succession : Pre-Socratics to Socrates
  (ii. 1-47), where it branched in three—
   1. Plato, Middle and New Academies to
    Clitomachus (iii, iv).
   2. Antisthenes, Cynics and Stoics to Chrysippus
    (vi, vii).
   3. (Plato), Aristotle, Theophrastus (v).
 B. Italian Succession : Pherecydes, Pythagoras,
  Eleatics, Atomists to Epicurus (viii) ; followed
  by philosophers who did not found successions
  (ix, x).

This arrangement scatters the Pre-Socratics in Books
I, II, VIII and IX. Diogenes insists in the Prologue
(i. 16) that the Sceptics were a philosophical school,
but they are not fitted into any of the successions,
though they receive elaborate treatment in Book IX.

 It is a curious fact that all four of these successions
end in the first century A.D., whereas the Sceptics
were carried down to much nearer Diogenes' own
day (Aenesidemus, Favorinus, Menodotus). This
imbalance reflects the dates of his chief sources, and
does not necessarily result from his being a Sceptic.
He may also have preferred them as a subject because
their teachings were startling, since one of his chief
aims was obviously to entertain.

 In our MSS. Book VII, though the longest, is in-

complete, leaving off in the middle of a title in the
list of Chrysippus' works ; but the old table of
contents found at the beginning of MS. P lists 20
other Stoics, ending with Cornutus, whose lives were
once included in the book. Otherwise, the work
seems finished as we have it (*cf.* x. 138), though capable of infinite expansion by digressions of the same
sort as abound already ; as is true also of Aelian,
Aulus Gellius or any other miscellany, not to mention Herodotus, a more respectable writer whose work
sought digressions. Many of the anecdotes Diogenes tells about philosophers have to do with proofs of
eminence [a] ; but, in the last analysis, any good story
will do, whether true, probable, possible, or patently
false.

While Diogenes cites hundreds of sources, certain
ones were clearly his favourites, and many of these
not the most learned : such writers as Antigonus of
Carystus, Antisthenes of Rhodes, Apollodorus the
chronologist, Demetrius and Diocles of Magnesia,
Heraclides Lembus, Hermippus, Hieronymus of
Rhodes, Hippobotus, Neanthes of Cyzicus, Pamphila,
Favorinus. Most of these authors come from either
the third and second centuries B.C. or the first century
A.D. ; between these dates there is a rather notice-
able lack of both sources and references to historical
events, a lacuna reflecting Diogenes' choice of his
main sources.

The biographical material tends to fall under certain rubrics which are identified by Delatte [b] as
follows :

1. origin ;
2. education, philosophical training, travels ;

    [a] Hope, pp. 115-122.   [b] Pp. 54 f.

3. place in a succession, or founding of a school ;
4. character and temperament, illustrated by anecdotes and sayings ;
5. important events of his life ;
6. anecdotes about his death, epigrams ;
7. chronological data, including *floruit* ;
8. works ;
9. doctrines ;
10. documents (last will, letters) ;
11. other men of the same name ;
12. miscellaneous notes, such as lists of followers, jibes in comic or satiric poets, inventions, political activity.

The fourth item of this list is especially likely to be fully developed—giving a good indication of Diogenes' and his audience's tastes—under the following sub-headings : costume, physical characteristics, temperament, moral character, love affairs (especially if scandalous), eating habits and daily routine, literary appraisal, plus quantities of anecdotes intended to be edifying, amusing, or characteristic.[a]

It is difficult to say where Diogenes obtained his doxographic summaries, some of the longest of which (Plato, Aristotle, Epicurus) appear in connection with lists of works. Close analysis reveals that these summaries do not necessarily come straight from the appropriate school of philosophy, but may reach us by a most devious route, undergoing distortion in the process : *e.g.*, Aristotle's doctrines are viewed through Stoic eyes. No doxographic information in Diogenes can be accepted on his authority alone, but must be tested against texts and fragments of the philosopher, or at least by inherent

---

[a] Delatte, pp. 54-63 ; Hope, pp. 144-168.

probability and general consonance with the philosopher's other known doctrines.

Another type of material abundant in Diogenes consists of apophthegms, which tend to fall into types [a] : for instance, 120 or more sayings are presented as answers to questions, and either embody doctrines in a pithy form or, more usually, demonstrate how quick-witted the philosopher was at repartee. It is obvious that Diogenes and presumably his audience greatly appreciated bright sayings. This interest is, of course, a measure of Diogenes' value as a historian of philosophy. There were collections of such apophthegms, existing both as separate works and as parts of biographies. The specific history of most such sayings would be quite impossible to trace, any more than one could determine who first asked, "When did you stop beating your wife?" The range of Diogenes' puns and anecdotes is very wide : some are edifying and some are risqué, some are vulgar, and some puns are outrageous enough for even a Victorian taste.

In 1904 Herbert Richards expressed a judgement on Diogenes [b] to which we can still subscribe : "The man was foolish enough, but the book is of extreme value for the history, especially the literary history, of Greek philosophy." Diogenes was obviously industrious, and most persons who know his work would also agree that he was basically honest [c] : when he states that he had revised his main source of the moment, [d] he probably had. But he was utterly

---

[a] Hope, pp. 171 ff.   [b] *Classical Review*, xviii, p. 340.

[c] So Schwartz in *RE*, cols. 761, 763 ; and Hicks in his Introduction to the first Loeb edition, pp. xiv-xv.

[d] Passages listed by Delatte, p. 11.

uncritical, for he would cite any type of author for any sort of information, as Hope's elaborate study [a] proves. For example, statements on astronomy are drawn from Eudemus (a good source), but also from Favorinus, Parmenides, Theophrastus, Hesiod (by way of Zeno, though the original was available to Diogenes), Euripides, Callimachus' *Iambi* and Timon of Phlius. Diogenes clearly drew most of his material from secondary and tertiary sources, epitomes of summaries of digests, so that his sources often come in nests, two and three deep. He used an already existing mountain of erudition (much of it of a low order), and piled on a few more items himself. On the same point he will cite sources regardless of whether they repeat one another, contradict one another, or fail to jibe significantly. He sank beneath the immense mass of material that he tried to use : *e.g.*, viii. 19 cites Aristotle for a small point in a long passage all drawn ultimately from Aristotle.[b] Expressions of personal opinion are rare and timid, lost among his thousands of filing cards. But he wrote to please an uncritical audience of worldlings, and should not be blamed if he often fails to satisfy a critical student of Greek philosophy. Sometimes, almost or quite by accident, he preserves material that we regard as valuable. At the same time he is usually sprightly, and often entertaining.

The first parts of Diogenes to be printed were the lives of Aristotle and Theophrastus, included in the Aldine Aristotle of 1497. The *editio princeps* of the whole Greek text was published by Froben at Basel in 1533, apparently on the basis of a MS. very like

[a] Pp. 59-97.
[b] Delatte, pp. 44 and 117 ff. with the testimonia there cited.

the extant Codex Lobkowicensis (=z), an inferior
MS. The Bibliography lists other important editions
and commentaries, of which Huebner's (1828–1833)
was the last before Lachmann systematized and
disseminated (for it would be wrong to say, invented)
modern methods of textual criticism. Cobet's Didot
edition of 1850 was based on new collations, but
contained no *apparatus*. The earliest truly critical
editions, therefore, were of parts of the text. The
first attempt at a critical edition of the entire text
appeared only in 1964.

The problem of the stemma of the MSS. and of their
relation to the very extensive indirect tradition,
which includes quotations in Hesychius of Miletus,
"Suidas" and others, two sizes of an epitome, and
several Latin versions, has been well set forth by
Artur Biedl. It is the latest editor's opinion that the
stemma of the MSS. known to us is so contaminated
that simple, clear lines of descent cannot be found
or represented in the usual form of an inverted
family tree. Certain MSS. (B, F, P) have long been
known to bring us closer to what Diogenes wrote,
but few of the others can be identified as copies of
known MSS. and so eliminated ; even Q, demon-
strably a copy of P, must still be used to determine
readings of P when it was less damaged than it now
is. On the other hand, all the known MSS. of the
complete text are descended from a single ancestor,
for they all lack the end of Book VII.

The relationship of the Latin versions to the
Greek text requires further investigation. It is
unfortunate that Biedl's death in 1950 put a pre-
mature end to his study of this extremely complex
problem, on which he was the only real expert.

INTRODUCTION

Besides the relatively late Latin version by Thomas Aldobrandini (1594), there was an earlier one made by Ambrogio Traversari, published about 1472, but made before February, 1432—for there is a dated MS. And long before that, there existed one or more medieval Latin versions, from which quotations survive in such works as Walter Burley's, referred to above. No one, I suppose, would maintain that Burley knew Greek ; hence we are left with the question when and where the Latin translation was made that Burley used so extensively in his own book. Valentin Rose [a] showed that one Henricus Aristippus (a Greek, to judge by the name Aristippus), who lived in Sicily in the 12th century, had translated at least some of Diogenes into Latin. Earlier than that, there are 10th-century MSS. of a work entitled *Tractatus de dictis philosophorum* showing a knowledge of Diogenes. Only an extensive search of medieval documents referring to the Greek philosophers could begin to show how many medieval Latin versions there were, and what their affiliations are to the known Greek MSS., including the epitomes. This investigation, useful as it could be for medieval studies, might prove to contribute exactly nothing of value for the text of Diogenes We shall only know if it is done. More improvement in Diogenes' text is likely to be made at the present time by careful study and interpretation of the text itself.

[a] In *Hermes*, i (1866), pp. 367-397.

SELECTED BIBLIOGRAPHY

A. Greek mss.

Listed in Artur Biedl, *Zur Textgeschichte des Laertios Diogenes : Das grosse Exzerpt* Φ, Città del Vaticano, 1955 ("Studi e Testi," 184), pp. 110-111 ; and in *Diogenis Laertii Vitae Philosophorum* ; recognovit H. S. Long, Oxonii, 1964 (" Oxford Classical Text "), Vol. I, p. xx.

More elaborate description by Edgar Martini in "Analecta Laertiana," *Leipziger Studien zur classischen Philologie,* 19 (1899), pp. 78-103.

B. Latin Versions

Laertii Diogenis de vitis . . . eorum qui in philosophia claruerunt libri x, T. Aldobrandino interprete, Romae, 1594 ; 1664 ; 1692.

Laertii Diogenis vitae et sententiae eorum qui in philosophia probati fuerunt, Romae, 1472 (?)=the Latin version of Ambrosius Traversarius Camaldulensis, made before 1432.

On the medieval Latin versions see Biedl, *op. cit.*, pp. 44-46 ; Valentin Rose, " Die Lücke in Diogenes Laertius und der alte Übersetzer," *Hermes,* 1 (1866), pp. 367-397 ; John A. Stigall, " The Manuscript Tradition of the *De Vita et Moribus Philosophorum* of Walter Burley," *Medievalia et Humanistica,* fasc. 11 (1957), pp. 44-57, with a list of 105 mss. of Burley's work, to which at least 21 more are added in the unpub-

SELECTED BIBLIOGRAPHY

lished Incipit Catalogue (chiefly the work of the Rev.
Philotheus Boehner, O.F.M. ?) in the Franciscan Institute of St. Bonaventure University, St. Bonaventure, N.Y.

C. EDITIONS OF THE GREEK TEXT

1. Parts published before the *editio princeps* of the whole
   Lives of Aristotle and Theophrastus in Vol. III of the
   Aldine Aristotle, 1497.

   Life of Xenophon in the Juntine Xenophon of 1527 (the
   2nd edition).

2. Complete Greek text

   Hieronymus Frobenius et Nicolaus Episcopius studiosis
   S.P.D., apud Frobenium, Basel, 1533 (the *editio
   princeps*).

   *Diogenis Laertii De vitis, dogm. et apophtheg. eorum qui
   in Philosophia claruerunt, libri x*, in aedibus H.
   Stephani (Geneva), 1570, with the Latin version of
   Ambrosius. Beginning with the edition of 1593, Stephanus included the useful Notes of Isaac Casaubon.

   *Laertii Diogenis De vitis dogmatis et apophthegmatis
   eorum qui in philosophia claruerunt*, London, 1664 :
   the Pearson edition, including the notes of Aldobrandini, Stephanus, Isaac and Méric Casaubon and
   Ménage.

   Diogenes Laertius de vitis . . ., ed. H. G. Huebnerus,
   2 vols., Leipzig, 1828 and 1831 ; and *Commentarii
   in Diogenem Laertium*, 2 vols., Leipzig, 1830 and
   1833, with the notes of the Casaubons, Ménage and
   J. Kühn.

   Diogenis Laertii Vitae Philosophorum, ed. C. G. Cobet,
   Paris, 1850.

   The Oxford Classical Text, listed above under A.

3. Parts of the Greek text, in order of publication

   I. Bywater, *Heracliti Ephesii reliquiae*, Oxford, 1877.

   I. Bywater, Ἀριστοτέλους βίος ἐκ τῶν Λαερτίου, Oxford,
   1879.

SELECTED BIBLIOGRAPHY

C. **Wachsmuth,** *Sillographorum Graecorum reliquiae,* 2 vols., Leipzig, 1885.

H. Usener, *Epicurea,* Leipzig, 1887.

H. Diels, *Poetarum philosophorum fragmenta,* **Berlin,** 1901.

I. ab Arnim, *Stoicorum veterum fragmenta,* 3 vols., Leipzig, 1903-1905.

H. Diels, *Fragmente der Vorsokratiker,* Berlin, 1904 *et seqq.*

H. Breitenbach *et al., Diogenis Laertii vita Platonis,* Basel, 1907.

A. Delatte, *La Vie de Pythagore de Diogène Laërce,* Bruxelles, 1922.

P. von der Mühll, *Epicuri epistulae tres et ratae sententiae,* Leipzig, 1922.

C. Bailey, *Epicurus,* Oxford, 1926.

F. Wehrli, *Die Schule des Aristoteles,* Basel, 1944 *et seqq.*

I. Düring, *Aristotle in the Ancient Biographical Tradition,* Göteborg, 1957, pp. 29-56.

D. Studies

1. On the MSS. and stemma : Martini, Biedl, and Oxford Classical Text, pp. vi-ix, as above.
2. A. Pauly, G. Wissowa, W. Kroll, *Real-Encyklopädie der classischen Altertumswissenschaft,* Berlin, 1894 *et seqq.*: art. on Diogenes (40) by Schwartz in vol. 9 (1903), cols. 738-763.
3. Elaborate introduction by A. Delatte to his edition of the life of Pythagoras, pp. 5-100 : under C.3.
4. Introduction by R. D. Hicks to the first edition in the Loeb series, Vol. I, pp. ix-xliii, London, 1925.
5. Richard Hope, *The Book of Diogenes Laertius,* New York, 1930.

E. Translations

German : *Diogenes Laertius : Leben und Meinungen be-*

rühmter Philosophen, übersetzt und erläutert von Otto
Apelt, 2 vols., Leipzig, 1921.

Italian : *Diogene Laerzio : Vite dei filosofi,* a cura di
Marcello Gigante, Bari, 1962.

Rumanian : *Diogenes Laertios : Despre Vieţile şi doc-
trinele Filozofilor,* Traducere . . . de . . . C. I. Balmuş,
Bucuresti, 1963. The latter two have extensive notes.

DIOGENES LAERTIUS

TESTIMONIA

Stephanus Byzantinus (ὁ ἐθνικογράφος)

s.v. Δρυίδαι.　Ἔθνος Γαλατικόν, φιλόσοφον, ὡς Λαέρτιος Διογένης
ἐν φιλοσόφῳ ἱστορίᾳ.
[Proem, §§ 1 and 6.]
(Λαέρτιος Διογένης codd. Palat. et Vossianus :
Διογένης Λαέρτιος alii codd.)

s.v. Ἐνετοί.　. . . Ἔστι καὶ πόλις Ἐνετός, ἀφ᾽ ἧς ἦν Μύρμηξ ὁ
διαλεκτικὸς φιλόσοφος, ὡς Διογένης ἐν δευτέρῳ
φιλοσόφου ἱστορίας.
[ii. 113.]

s.v. Χολλεῖδαι.　Δῆμος τῆς Λεοντίδος φυλῆς.　ὁ δημότης Χολλείδης,
Διογένης δ᾽ ὁ Λαερτιεὺς ἐν τρίτῳ φιλοσόφου
ἱστορίας Χολλειδεύς φησι.
[iii. 41.]

Suidas ex Hesychio

Gaisford's index has some 180 articles under Diogenes
Laertius.　In none of them does he appear to be named,
and the coincidence between the illustrative quotations in
Suidas and the text of D. L. may be explained by the
supposition that Hesychius drew these extracts from the
original authorities.　The following samples exemplify both
the general agreement and the occasional divergence of
the mss. of Suidas and D. L.

593 B. Ἀρχή.　Ἀρχαὶ τῶν ὅλων δύο, τὸ ποιοῦν, καὶ τὸ πάσχον.
τὸ μὲν οὖν πάσχον εἶναι τὴν ἄποιον οὐσίαν, τὴν ὕλην·
τὸ ποιοῦν δὲ τὸν ἐν αὐτῇ λόγον, τὸν θεόν.　διαφέρουσι
[*v.l.* διαφέρειν] δὲ ἀρχαὶ καὶ στοιχεῖα ⟨τῷ⟩ τὰς μὲν
εἶναι ἀγενήτους καὶ ἀφθάρτους· τὰ δὲ στοιχεῖα κατὰ
τὴν ἐκπύρωσιν φθείρεσθαι, ἀλλὰ καὶ τῷ ἀσωμάτους
μὲν εἶναι τὰς ἀρχὰς καὶ ἀμόρφους. τὰ δὲ μεμορφῶ-
σθαι.
[vii. 134.]

ἀσωμάτους] σώματα D. L.

xxxii

SELECTED TESTIMONIES

Druids.—A philosophic caste among the Gauls : so Laertius
Diogenes in his philosophic history.
[D. L. Proem, §§ 1 and 6.]

Eneti.—. . . There is also a city Enetus, whence came
Myrmex, the dialectical philosopher, according to
Diogenes in the second book of his philosophic history.
[D. L. ii. 113.]

Cholleidae.—A deme or hamlet of the tribe Leontis. A
member of the deme is called a Cholleidean, but
Diogenes the Laertian in the third book of his philosophic history uses the term Cholleideus.
[D. L. iii. 41.]

SUIDAS FROM HESYCHIUS

593 B. *Beginning* [*i.e.* Principle].—" . . . There are two
principles in the universe, the active and the passive.
The passive principle then is a substance without
quality, *i.e.* matter, whereas the active is the reason
inherent in this substance, that is God. . . . There is
a difference between principles and elements, because
the former are without generation or destruction,
whereas the elements are destroyed when all things
are resolved into fire. Moreover, the principles are
incorporeal and formless, while the elements have been
endowed with form." [D. L. vii. 134.]

854 D. Γυμνορρύπαροι.   Οἱ σοφισταί.
   Ἦσαν δὲ περὶ αὐτοῦ γυμνορρύπαροί τινες.
   [D. L. vii. 16.]

2150 C. Κόνιον.   Βοτάνη δηλητήριος· διὰ τοῦ ὂ μικροῦ διὰ τὸ μέτρον τοῦ στίχου.

   Πρὸς γὰρ Ἀθηναίων κόνιον μὲν ἁπλῶς σὺ ἐδέξω,
   αὐτοὶ δ' ἐξέπιον τοῦτο τεῷ στόματι.
   [D. L. ii. 46.]

   In the ordinary text of D. L. the reading is κώνειον ἁπλῶς μὲν ἐδέξω, with a weak caesura in the fourth foot.

2565 A. Ναυτικῶς δανείζειν.   Φασὶ Ζήνωνα ὑπὲρ τὰ χίλια τάλαντα ἔχοντα ἐλθεῖν εἰς τὴν Ἑλλάδα καὶ ταῦτα δανείζειν ναυτικῶς.   [D. L. vii. 13.]

3413 D. *s.v.* Στωικοί.   Ζήνων ὁ Κιτιεὺς ἀνακάμπτων ἐν τῃ ποικίλῃ στοᾷ καὶ Πεισιανακτείᾳ καλουμένῃ ὕστερον δὲ ἀπὸ τῆς γραφῆς τοῦ ζωγράφου Πολυγνώτου ποικίλῃ κληθείσῃ, διετίθετο τοὺς λόγους. ἐπὶ τῶν λ´ πολιτῶν πρὸς τοῖς χιλίοις τετρακόσιοι ἀνῄρηντο ἐν αὐτῷ. προσῇεσαν δὴ λοιπὸν ἀκούοντες αὐτοῦ, καὶ διὰ τοῦτο Στωικοὶ ἐκλήθησαν καὶ οἱ ἀπ' αὐτοῦ ὁμοίως, πρότερον Ζηνώνειοι καλούμενοι.   [D. L. vii. 5.]

   λοιπόν] πολλοί D. L.

3467 C. Σύστασις καὶ συσταθῆναι.   Ὁμοδίαιτον καὶ φίλον γενέσθαι. ἐλθόντα δι' ἀπορίαν ὑπὸ Πλάτωνος παροφθῆναι, ὑπὸ δ' Ἀριστίππου συσταθῆναι.   [D. L. ii. 61.]

PHOTIUS, *Bibliotheca*, 161 (p. 103 A, l. 18 ; 103 B, l. 41, Bekker)

Ἀνεγνώσθησαν ἐκλογαὶ διάφοροι ἐν βιβλίοις ιβ´ Σωπάτρου σοφιστοῦ· συνείλεκται δὲ αὐτῷ τὸ βιβλίον ἐκ πολλῶν καὶ διαφόρων ἱστοριῶν καὶ γραμμάτων. . . .

[In Sopater's 6th book.] Καὶ ταῦτα μὲν ὡς ἀπὸ Ῥούφου, σύγκειται δὲ αὐτῷ καὶ ἐκ τῶν Δαμοστράτου ἁλιευτικῶν δευτέρου λόγου καὶ ἐκ τῶν Λαερτίου Διογένους Φιλοσόφων βίων βιβλίου πρώτου καὶ πέμπτου ἐννάτου τε καὶ δεκάτου·

TESTIMONIA

854 D. *Ragamuffins.*—The sophists.

> " And he had about him certain ragamuffins."
>
> [D. L. vii. 16.]

2150 C. *Hemlock.*—A poisonous herb, the form of the word with Omicron in place of Omega being due to metrical exigency.

> " For when thou didst frankly take the hemlock at the hands of the Athenians, they themselves drained it as it passed thy lips."   [D. L. ii. 46.]

2565 A. *Lending on bottomry.*—" It is said that Zeno had more than a thousand talents when he came to Greece, and that he lent this money on bottomry."
>
> [D. L. vii. 13.]

3413 D. *Stoics.*—Zeno of Citium, " passing up and down in the painted colonnade, which is also called the colonnade of Pisianax, but which later received its name, the ' Painted Colonnade,' from the painting of Polygnotus, used to discourse.   In the time of the Thirty, fourteen hundred citizens were put to death there. Hither, then, people came in after time to hear Zeno, and this is why they were known as men of the Stoa, or Stoics ; and the same name was given his followers who had formerly been known as Zenonians."
>
> [D. L. vii. 5.]

3467 C. *Association and intimacy* : to become messmates and friends. [They say that] having come [thither] through want, he was neglected by Plato but admitted to intimacy by Aristippus.   [D. L. ii. 61.]

PHOTIUS

" Various Extracts " in twelve books by Sopater the sophist were read [by me].   His book was put together from many different histories and writings. . . .

[In Book VI.]   Thus much from Rufus.   He compiled it from the second book of the treatise of Damostratus on Angling, and from the first, fifth, ninth, and tenth books of the *Lives of Philosophers* by Laertius

DIOGENES LAERTIUS

ἐν οἷς τὰ περὶ τῶν φιλοσόφων διέξεισιν, ὅθεν τε τὸ φιλοσοφίας ἱερὸν χρῆμα τὴν ἀρχὴν ἔφυ καὶ ὅπως ἤκμασε, τίνες τε τίνων αἱρέσεων ἀρχηγοὶ καὶ προστάται κατέστησαν, τίνας τε εἶχον ἐρασταὶ καὶ τίνας ἀντιτέχνους τίνες, ποῖόν τε ἕκαστος αὐτῶν ἐπεδείκνυτο ἦθος, καὶ πόθεν εἷλκε τὸ γένος καὶ οἷον τὸ ἐξ ἀρχῆς ἐπιτήδευμα καὶ πότε καιροῦ ἤκμασε.

EUSTATHIUS, *Comm. in Iliadem*, M 153
(vol. iii. p. 103 Stallbaum)

Τὸ δὲ κομπεῖν καὶ ἐπὶ σκευῶν ἤχου λέγεται· κομπεῖν γοῦν χύτραν ἢ λοπάδα φησὶν ὁ Λαέρτης ἐν τοῖς τῶν σοφιστῶν βίοις· ἔνθα καὶ ζητεῖται, καθὰ καὶ παρὰ τῷ κωμικῷ, τίς ἡ τῆς χύτρας καὶ τῆς λοπάδος διαφορά.

TZETZES, *Chil.* ii. 995-1000 (Hist. 61, περὶ Δημοκρίτου)

'Επιγραμματογράφος τέ τις γράφει τὸ τοῦ Ἅιδου·
καὶ τίς ἔφυ σοφὸς ὧδε; τίς ἔργον ἔρεξε τοσοῦτον,
ὅσσον ὁ παντοδαὴς μήνυσε Δημόκριτος ;
ὃς θάνατον παρεόντα τρί' ἤματα δώμασιν ἔσχε
καὶ θερμοῖς ἄρτων ἀσθμασιν ἐξένισεν.

Est Diogenis Laert. lib. ix. (p. 657 ed. Casaubon) : *Anthol.* tom. i. p. 237 ed. Tauchn. (ed. J. Kiessling, Leipsic, 1826). In marg. cod. A appositum est nomen ὁ Διογενιανός.

The preceding context (ll. 991-995) is :

τοῦτον τὸν Δημόκριτον πάνσοφον ὑπηργμένον
ἄλλα μυρία λέγουσι δρᾶσαι τῶν τεραστίων,
καί γε τὸν Ἅιδην κατασχεῖν τρεῖς ὅλας ἐφ' ἡμέρας
ἄρτων θερμοῖς ἐν ἀσθμασι τοῦτον ξενοδοχοῦντα.
πολλοί φασι τὰ τοῦ ἀνδρὸς καὶ Κῷος Ἱπποκράτης.

TESTIMONIA

Diogenes, in which he relates the fortunes of the philosophers, whence that sacred thing philosophy arose and how it flourished, who were constituted heads and chiefs of the various sects, what admirers and rivals they had respectively, what were their several characters, whence each came, what was his original profession, and at what time he flourished.

EUSTATHIUS

The verb κομπεῖν is used of the ringing noise of utensils. At all events Laertes in his *Lives of the Sages* [or *Sophists*] applies the word to jars and dishes. Hence the question is raised, as also by the comic poet, what is the difference between a pot and a pan.

[D. L. ii. 78, vi. 30.]

TZETZES

996. A writer of epigrams writes about Death: " Pray who was so wise, who wrought so vast a work as the omniscient Democritus achieved ? When Death drew near, for three days he kept him in his house, and regaled him with the steam of hot loaves."

[D. L. ix. 43.]

991-995. This wondrous wise Democritus, they say, did countless other marvels. Death himself for three whole days he kept at bay, receiving him with the hot steam of loaves. The man's deeds are told by many, and by Hippocrates of Cos.

ΔΙΟΓΕΝΟΥΣ ΛΑΕΡΤΙΟΥ

ΒΙΩΝ ΚΑΙ ΓΝΩΜΩΝ ΤΩΝ ΕΝ ΦΙΛΟΣΟΦΙΑΙ ΕΥΔΟΚΙΜΗΣΑΝΤΩΝ ΤΩΝ ΕΙΣ ΔΕΚΑ ΤΟ ΠΡΩΤΟΝ

ΠΡΟΟΙΜΙΟΝ

1 Τὸ τῆς φιλοσοφίας ἔργον ἔνιοί φασιν ἀπὸ βαρβάρων ἄρξαι. γεγενῆσθαι γὰρ παρὰ μὲν Πέρσαις Μάγους, παρὰ δὲ Βαβυλωνίοις ἢ Ἀσσυρίοις Χαλδαίους, καὶ Γυμνοσοφιστὰς παρ᾽ Ἰνδοῖς, παρά τε Κελτοῖς καὶ Γαλάταις τοὺς καλουμένους Δρυΐδας καὶ Σεμνοθέους, καθά φησιν Ἀριστοτέλης ἐν τῷ Μαγικῷ καὶ Σωτίων ἐν τῷ εἰκοστῷ τρίτῳ τῆς Διαδοχῆς. Φοίνικά τε γενέσθαι Μῶχον, καὶ Θρᾷκα Ζάμολξιν, καὶ Λίβυν Ἄτλαντα.

Αἰγύπτιοι μὲν γὰρ Νείλου γενέσθαι παῖδα Ἥφαιστον, ὃν ἄρξαι φιλοσοφίας, ἧς τοὺς προ-
2 εστῶτας ἱερέας εἶναι καὶ προφήτας. ἀπὸ δὲ τούτου εἰς Ἀλέξανδρον τὸν Μακεδόνα ἐτῶν εἶναι μυριάδας τέσσαρας καὶ ὀκτακισχίλια ὀκτακόσια ἑξήκοντα τρία· ἐν οἷς ἡλίου μὲν ἐκλείψεις γενέσθαι τριακοσίας ἑβδομήκοντα τρεῖς, σελήνης δὲ ὀκτακοσίας τριάκοντα δύο.

---

[a] The alteration of the numeral from 23 to 13 is supported by what little we know of Sotion's work. It was from a similar source that Clement of Alexandria must have taken

2

DIOGENES LAERTIUS

LIVES AND OPINIONS OF EMINENT PHILOSOPHERS IN TEN BOOKS

BOOK I

PROLOGUE

THERE are some who say that the study of philosophy had its beginning among the barbarians. They urge that the Persians have had their Magi, the Babylonians or Assyrians their Chaldaeans, and the Indians their Gymnosophists ; and among the Celts and Gauls there are the people called Druids or Holy Ones, for which they cite as authorities the *Magicus* of Aristotle and Sotion in the twenty-third [a] book of his *Succession of Philosophers*. Also they say that Mochus was a Phoenician, Zamolxis a Thracian, and Atlas a Libyan.

If we may believe the Egyptians, Hephaestus was the son of the Nile, and with him philosophy began, priests and prophets being its chief exponents. Hephaestus lived 48,863 years before Alexander of Macedon, and in the interval there occurred 373 solar and 832 lunar eclipses.

what we find in *Strom.* i. 71 concerning Chaldaeans, Druids, Magians, Gymnosophists, and other barbarian philosophers.

Ἀπὸ δὲ τῶν Μάγων, ὧν ἄρξαι Ζωροάστρην τὸν Πέρσην, Ἑρμόδωρος μὲν ὁ Πλατωνικὸς ἐν τῷ Περὶ μαθημάτων φησὶν εἰς τὴν Τροίας ἅλωσιν ἔτη γεγονέναι πεντακισχίλια· Ξάνθος δὲ ὁ Λυδὸς εἰς τὴν Ξέρξου διάβασιν ἀπὸ τοῦ Ζωροάστρου ἑξακισχίλιά φησι, καὶ μετ' αὐτὸν γεγονέναι πολλούς τινας Μάγους κατὰ διαδοχήν, Ὀστάνας καὶ Ἀστραμψύχους καὶ Γωβρύας καὶ Παζάτας, μέχρι τῆς τῶν Περσῶν ὑπ' Ἀλεξάνδρου καταλύσεως.

8   Λανθάνουσι δ' αὑτοὺς τὰ τῶν Ἑλλήνων κατορθώματα, ἀφ' ὧν μὴ ὅτι γε φιλοσοφία, ἀλλὰ καὶ γένος ἀνθρώπων ἦρξε, βαρβάροις προσάπτοντες. ἰδοὺ γοῦν παρὰ μὲν Ἀθηναίοις γέγονε Μουσαῖος, παρὰ δὲ Θηβαίοις Λίνος. καὶ τὸν μὲν Εὐμόλπου παῖδά φασι, ποιῆσαι δὲ Θεογονίαν καὶ Σφαῖραν πρῶτον· φάναι τε ἐξ ἑνὸς τὰ πάντα γίνεσθαι καὶ εἰς ταὐτὸν ἀναλύεσθαι. τοῦτον τελευτῆσαι Φαληροῖ, καὶ αὐτῷ ἐπιγεγράφθαι τόδε τὸ ἐλεγεῖον·

Εὐμόλπου φίλον υἱὸν ἔχει τὸ Φαληρικὸν οὖδας,
Μουσαῖον, φθιμένου σῶμ', ὑπὸ τῷδε τάφῳ.

ἀπὸ δὲ τοῦ πατρὸς τοῦ Μουσαίου καὶ Εὐμολπίδαι καλοῦνται παρ' Ἀθηναίοις.

4   Τὸν δὲ Λίνον παῖδα εἶναι Ἑρμοῦ καὶ Μούσης Οὐρανίας· ποιῆσαι δὲ κοσμογονίαν, ἡλίου καὶ σελήνης πορείαν, καὶ ζώων καὶ καρπῶν γενέσεις. τούτῳ ἀρχὴ τῶν ποιημάτων ἥδε·

ἦν ποτέ τοι χρόνος οὗτος, ἐν ᾧ ἅμα πάντ' ἐπεφύκει.

ὅθεν λαβὼν Ἀναξαγόρας πάντα ἔφη χρήματα
4

I. 2-4. PROLOGUE

The date of the Magians, beginning with Zoroaster the Persian, was 5000 years before the fall of Troy, as given by Hermodorus the Platonist in his work on mathematics ; but Xanthus the Lydian reckons 6000 years from Zoroaster to the expedition of Xerxes, and after that event he places a long line of Magians in succession, bearing the names of Ostanas, Astrampsychos, Gobryas, and Pazatas, down to the conquest of Persia by Alexander.

These authors forget that the achievements which they attribute to the barbarians belong to the Greeks, with whom not merely philosophy but the human race itself began. For instance, Musaeus is claimed by Athens, Linus by Thebes. It is said that the former, the son of Eumolpus, was the first to compose a genealogy of the gods and to construct a sphere, and that he maintained that all things proceed from unity and are resolved again into unity. He died at Phalerum, and this is his epitaph[a] :

> Musaeus, to his sire Eumolpus dear,
> In Phalerean soil lies buried here ;

and the Eumolpidae at Athens get their name from the father of Musaeus.

Linus again was (so it is said) the son of Hermes and the Muse Urania. He composed a poem describing the creation of the world, the courses of the sun and moon, and the growth of animals and plants. His poem begins with the line :

> Time was when all things grew up at once ;

and this idea was borrowed by Anaxagoras when he

---

[a] *Anth. Pal.* vii. 615.

γεγονέναι ὁμοῦ, νοῦν δὲ ἐλθόντα αὐτὰ διακοσμῆσαι.
τὸν δὲ Λίνον τελευτῆσαι ἐν Εὐβοίᾳ τοξευθέντα ὑπ’
Ἀπόλλωνος, καὶ αὐτῷ ἐπιγεγράφθαι·

ἥδε[1] Λίνον Θηβαῖον ἐδέξατο γαῖα θανόντα,
Μούσης Οὐρανίης υἱὸν ἐϋστεφάνου.

καὶ ὧδε μὲν ἀφ’ Ἑλλήνων ἦρξε φιλοσοφία, ἧς καὶ
αὐτὸ τὸ ὄνομα τὴν βάρβαρον ἀπέστραπται προσ-
ηγορίαν.

5 Οἱ δὲ τὴν εὕρεσιν διδόντες ἐκείνοις παράγουσι
καὶ Ὀρφέα τὸν Θρᾷκα, λέγοντες φιλόσοφον γεγονέναι καὶ εἶναι ἀρχαιότατον. ἐγὼ δέ, εἰ τὸν περὶ
θεῶν ἐξαγορεύσαντα τοιαῦτα χρὴ φιλόσοφον καλεῖν
οὐκ οἶδα, ⟨οὐδὲ⟩[2] τίνα δεῖ προσαγορεύειν τὸν πᾶν
τὸ ἀνθρώπειον πάθος ἀφειδοῦντα τοῖς θεοῖς προσ-
τρῖψαι, καὶ τὰ σπανίως ὑπό τινων ἀνθρώπων
αἰσχρουργούμενα τῷ τῆς φωνῆς ὀργάνῳ. τοῦτον
δὲ ὁ μὲν μῦθος ὑπὸ γυναικῶν ἀπολέσθαι φησί· τὸ
δ’ ἐν Δίῳ τῆς Μακεδονίας ἐπίγραμμα, κεραυνω-
θῆναι αὐτόν, λέγον οὕτως·

Θρήϊκα χρυσολύρην τῇδ’ Ὀρφέα Μοῦσαι ἔθαψαν,
ὃν κτάνεν ὑψιμέδων Ζεὺς ψολόεντι βέλει.

6 Οἱ δὲ φάσκοντες ἀπὸ βαρβάρων ἄρξαι φιλοσοφίαν καὶ τὸν τρόπον παρ’ ἑκάστοις αὐτῆς ἐκ-
τίθενται· καί φασι τοὺς μὲν Γυμνοσοφιστὰς καὶ
Δρυΐδας αἰνιγματωδῶς ἀποφθεγγομένους φιλο-
σοφῆσαι, σέβειν θεοὺς καὶ μηδὲν κακὸν δρᾶν καὶ
ἀνδρείαν ἀσκεῖν. τοὺς γοῦν Γυμνοσοφιστὰς καὶ

---

[1] ἥδε] ὧδε Anth. Pal. vii. 616.
[2] οὐδὲ addidit Apelt.

declared that all things were originally together
until Mind came and set them in order.   Linus died
in Euboea, slain by the arrow of Apollo, and this is
his epitaph[a]:

> Here Theban Linus, whom Urania bore,
> The fair-crowned Muse, sleeps on a foreign shore.

And thus it was from the Greeks that philosophy
took its rise : its very name refuses to be translated
into foreign speech.

But those who attribute its invention to barbarians
bring forward Orpheus the Thracian, calling him a
philosopher of whose antiquity there can be no
doubt.   Now, considering the sort of things he said
about the gods, I hardly know whether he ought to
be called a philosopher ; for what are we to make of
one who does not scruple to charge the gods with
all human suffering, and even the foul crimes wrought
by the tongue amongst a few of mankind ?   The
story goes that he met his death at the hands of
women ; but according to the epitaph at Dium in
Macedonia he was slain by a thunderbolt ; it runs
as follows[b]:

> Here have the Muses laid their minstrel true,
> The Thracian Orpheus whom Jove's thunder slew.

But the advocates of the theory that philosophy
took its rise among the barbarians go on to explain
the different forms it assumed in different countries.
As to the Gymnosophists and Druids we are told
that they uttered their philosophy in riddles, bidding
men to reverence the gods, to abstain from wrong-
doing, and to practise courage.   That the Gymno-

[a] *Anth. Pal.* vii. 616.   [b] *Anth. Plan.* ii. 99.

θανάτου καταφρονεῖν φησι Κλείταρχος ἐν τῇ
δωδεκάτῃ· τοὺς δὲ Χαλδαίους περὶ ἀστρονομίαν
καὶ πρόρρησιν ἀσχολεῖσθαι· τοὺς δὲ Μάγους περί
τε θεραπείας θεῶν διατρίβειν καὶ θυσίας καὶ εὐχάς,
ὡς αὐτοὺς μόνους ἀκουομένους. ἀποφαίνεσθαί τε
περί τε οὐσίας θεῶν καὶ γενέσεως, οὓς καὶ πῦρ
εἶναι καὶ γῆν καὶ ὕδωρ· τῶν δὲ ξοάνων κατα-
γινώσκειν, καὶ μάλιστα τῶν λεγόντων ἄρρενας
7 εἶναι θεοὺς καὶ θηλείας. περί τε δικαιοσύνης
λόγους ποιεῖσθαι, καὶ ἀνόσιον ἡγεῖσθαι πυρὶ
θάπτειν· καὶ ὅσιον νομίζειν μητρὶ ἢ θυγατρὶ μί-
γνυσθαι, ὡς ἐν τῷ εἰκοστῷ τρίτῳ φησὶν ὁ Σωτίων·
ἀσκεῖν τε μαντικὴν καὶ πρόρρησιν, καὶ θεοὺς
αὐτοῖς ἐμφανίζεσθαι λέγοντας. ἀλλὰ καὶ εἰδώλων
πλήρη εἶναι τὸν ἀέρα, κατ᾽ ἀπόρροιαν ὑπ᾽ ἀναθυ-
μιάσεως εἰσκρινομένων ταῖς ὄψεσι τῶν ὀξυδερκῶν·
προκοσμήματά τε καὶ χρυσοφορίας ἀπαγορεύειν.
τούτων δὲ ἐσθὴς μὲν λευκή, στιβὰς δὲ εὐνή, καὶ
λάχανον τροφή, τυρός τε καὶ ἄρτος εὐτελής, καὶ
κάλαμος ἡ βακτηρία, ᾧ κεντοῦντες, φασί, τοῦ
τυροῦ ἀνῃροῦντο καὶ ἀπήσθιον.

8 Τὴν δὲ γοητικὴν μαγείαν οὐδ᾽ ἔγνωσαν, φησὶν
Ἀριστοτέλης ἐν τῷ Μαγικῷ καὶ Δείνων ἐν τῇ
πέμπτῃ τῶν Ἱστοριῶν· ὃς καὶ μεθερμηνευόμενόν
φησι τὸν Ζωροάστρην ἀστροθύτην εἶναι· φησὶ δὲ

---

[a] Compare Pliny, N.H. xx. 11. 242 : Zoroaster lived in
the wilderness on cheese (cf. Yasht, xxii. 18 "Spring butter
is the ambrosia of the blessed "). For fuller comments on
§§ 7-9 see J. H. Moulton's Early Zoroastrianism, pp.
410-418.

[b] This popular etymology, though wide-spread, is
erroneous, the true form of the prophet's name being
Zarathustra, almost certainly derived from zarath="old"

sophists at all events despise even death itself is
affirmed by Clitarchus in his twelfth book; he also
says that the Chaldaeans apply themselves to
astronomy and forecasting the future; while the
Magi spend their time in the worship of the gods,
in sacrifices and in prayers, implying that none but
themselves have the ear of the gods. They pro-
pound their views concerning the being and origin
of the gods, whom they hold to be fire, earth, and
water; they condemn the use of images, and
especially the error of attributing to the divinities
difference of sex. They hold discourse of justice,
and deem it impious to practise cremation; but
they see no impiety in marriage with a mother or
daughter, as Sotion relates in his twenty-third book.
Further, they practise divination and forecast the
future, declaring that the gods appear to them in
visible form. Moreover, they say that the air is
full of shapes which stream forth like vapour and
enter the eyes of keen-sighted seers. They prohibit
personal ornament and the wearing of gold. Their
dress is white, they make their bed on the ground,
and their food is vegetables, cheese,[a] and coarse
bread; their staff is a reed and their custom is, so
we are told, to stick it into the cheese and take up
with it the part they eat.

With the art of magic they were wholly un-
acquainted, according to Aristotle in his *Magicus*
and Dinon in the fifth book of his *History* Dinon
tells us that the name Zoroaster, literally interpreted,
means "star-worshipper" [b]; and Hermodorus agrees

(a Zend stem, parallel to γέροντ-) and *ustra*="camel."
Cf. J. H. Moulton, *op. cit.* p. 426, and, for star-lore in the
Avesta, *ib.* p. 210.

τοῦτο καὶ ὁ Ἑρμόδωρος. Ἀριστοτέλης δ' ἐν
πρώτῳ Περὶ φιλοσοφίας καὶ πρεσβυτέρους εἶναι
τῶν Αἰγυπτίων· καὶ δύο κατ' αὐτοὺς εἶναι ἀρχάς,
ἀγαθὸν δαίμονα καὶ κακὸν δαίμονα· καὶ τῷ μὲν
ὄνομα εἶναι Ζεὺς καὶ Ὠρομάσδης, τῷ δὲ Ἅδης
καὶ Ἀρειμάνιος. φησὶ δὲ τοῦτο καὶ Ἕρμιππος ἐν
τῷ πρώτῳ περὶ Μάγων καὶ Εὔδοξος ἐν τῇ Περιόδῳ
καὶ Θεόπομπος ἐν τῇ ὀγδόῃ τῶν Φιλιππικῶν·
9 ὃς καὶ ἀναβιώσεσθαι κατὰ τοὺς Μάγους φησὶ τοὺς
ἀνθρώπους καὶ ἀθανάτους ἔσεσθαι, καὶ τὰ ὄντα
ταῖς αὐτῶν ἐπικλήσεσι διαμενεῖν. ταῦτα δὲ καὶ
Εὔδημος ὁ Ῥόδιος ἱστορεῖ. Ἑκαταῖος δὲ καὶ
γενητοὺς τοὺς θεοὺς εἶναι κατ' αὐτούς. Κλέαρχος δὲ ὁ Σολεὺς ἐν τῷ Περὶ παιδείας καὶ τοὺς
Γυμνοσοφιστὰς ἀπογόνους εἶναι τῶν Μάγων φησίν·
ἔνιοι δὲ καὶ τοὺς Ἰουδαίους ἐκ τούτων εἶναι. πρὸς
τούτοις καταγινώσκουσιν Ἡροδότου οἱ τὰ περὶ
Μάγων γράψαντες· μὴ γὰρ ἂν εἰς τὸν ἥλιον βέλη
Ξέρξην ἀκοντίσαι, μηδ' εἰς τὴν θάλασσαν πέδας
καθεῖναι, θεοὺς ὑπὸ τῶν Μάγων παραδεδομένους.
τὰ μέντοι ἀγάλματα εἰκότως καθαιρεῖν.

10 Τὴν δὲ τῶν Αἰγυπτίων φιλοσοφίαν εἶναι τοιαύτην
περί τε θεῶν καὶ ὑπὲρ δικαιοσύνης. φάσκειν τε
ἀρχὴν μὲν εἶναι τὴν ὕλην, εἶτα τὰ τέσσαρα στοιχεῖα
ἐξ αὐτῆς διακριθῆναι, καὶ ζῷα παντοῖα ἀπο-

ᵃ In this clause the word ἐπικλήσεσι is usually taken as
equivalent to ὀνόμασι (names). The meaning then would
be : " What exists now will exist hereafter under its own
present name." Diels would alter ἐπικλήσεσι to περικυ-
κλήσεσι, thus obtaining something very like the Heraclitean
union of opposites : " the things which are will continue to
be through all their revolutions." But ἐπίκλησις like
ἐπικαλεῖσθαι can be used of prayer, and there is some

with him in this. Aristotle in the first book of his
dialogue *On Philosophy* declares that the Magi are
more ancient than the Egyptians ; and further, that
they believe in two principles, the good spirit and
the evil spirit, the one called Zeus or Oromasdes,
the other Hades or Arimanius. This is confirmed
by Hermippus in his first book about the Magi,
Eudoxus in his *Voyage round the World*, and Theopompus in the eighth book of his *Philippica*. The
last-named author says that according to the Magi
men will live in a future life and be immortal, and
that the world will endure through their invocations.[a]
This is again confirmed by Eudemus of Rhodes.
But Hecataeus relates that according to them the
gods are subject to birth. Clearchus of Soli in his
tract *On Education* further makes the Gymnosophists
to be descended from the Magi ; and some trace
the Jews also to the same origin. Furthermore,
those who have written about the Magi criticize
Herodotus. They urge that Xerxes would never
have cast javelins at the sun nor have let down
fetters into the sea, since in the creed of the Magi
sun and sea are gods. But that statues of the
gods should be destroyed by Xerxes was natural
enough.

The philosophy of the Egyptians is described as
follows so far as relates to the gods and to justice.
They say that matter was the first principle, next
the four elements were derived from matter, and
thus living things of every species were produced.

evidence that Avestan religion fully recognized the efficacy
of prayers and spells. The testimony of Theopompus, who
wrote in the fourth century, to the Zoroastrian doctrine of
immortality is regarded by J. H. Moulton as specially
important : *cf. Early Zoroastrianism*, pp. 177 *sq.* and 416.

τελεσθῆναι. θεοὺς δ' εἶναι ἥλιον καὶ σελήνην, τὸν
μὲν Ὄσιριν, τὴν δ' Ἶσιν καλουμένην· αἰνίττεσθαί
τε αὐτοὺς διά τε κανθάρου καὶ δράκοντος καὶ
ἱέρακος καὶ ἄλλων, ὥς φησι Μανέθως ἐν τῇ τῶν
Φυσικῶν ἐπιτομῇ καὶ Ἑκαταῖος ἐν τῇ πρώτῃ Περὶ
τῆς Αἰγυπτίων φιλοσοφίας. κατασκευάζειν δὲ
<καὶ> ἀγάλματα καὶ τεμένη τῷ μὴ εἰδέναι τὴν
11 τοῦ θεοῦ μορφήν. τὸν κόσμον γενητὸν καὶ φθαρτὸν
καὶ σφαιροειδῆ· τοὺς ἀστέρας πῦρ εἶναι, καὶ τῇ
τούτων κράσει τὰ ἐπὶ γῆς γίνεσθαι· σελήνην ἐκ-
λείπειν εἰς τὸ σκίασμα τῆς γῆς ἐμπίπτουσαν· τὴν
ψυχὴν καὶ ἐπιδιαμένειν καὶ μετεμβαίνειν· ὑετοὺς
κατὰ ἀέρος τροπὴν ἀποτελεῖσθαι· τά τε ἄλλα
φυσιολογεῖν, ὡς Ἑκαταῖός τε καὶ Ἀρισταγόρας
ἱστοροῦσιν. ἔθεσαν δὲ καὶ νόμους ὑπὲρ δικαιοσύνης, οὓς εἰς Ἑρμῆν ἀνήνεγκαν· καὶ τὰ εὔχρηστα
τῶν ζῴων θεοὺς ἐδόξασαν. λέγουσι δὲ καὶ ὡς
αὐτοὶ γεωμετρίαν τε καὶ ἀστρολογίαν καὶ ἀρι-
θμητικὴν ἀνεῦρον. καὶ τὰ μὲν περὶ τῆς εὑρέσεως
ὧδε ἔχει.

12 Φιλοσοφίαν δὲ πρῶτος ὠνόμασε Πυθαγόρας καὶ
ἑαυτὸν φιλόσοφον, ἐν Σικυῶνι διαλεγόμενος Λέοντι
τῷ Σικυωνίων τυράννῳ ἢ Φλιασίων, καθά φησιν
Ἡρακλείδης ὁ Ποντικὸς ἐν τῇ Περὶ τῆς ἄπνου·
μηδένα γὰρ εἶναι σοφὸν [ἄνθρωπον] ἀλλ' ἢ θεόν.
θᾶττον δὲ ἐκαλεῖτο σοφία, καὶ σοφὸς ὁ ταύτην
ἐπαγγελλόμενος, ὃς εἴη ἂν κατ' ἀκρότητα ψυχῆς
ἀπηκριβωμένος, φιλόσοφος δὲ ὁ σοφίαν ἀσπαζό-
μενος. οἱ δὲ σοφοὶ καὶ σοφισταὶ ἐκαλοῦντο· καὶ

---

[a] This is confirmed by Clement, *Strom.* i. 61, who also
repeats (*Strom.* i. 24) the statement that σοφιστής = σοφός.

The sun and the moon are gods bearing the names of Osiris and Isis respectively ; they make use of the beetle, the dragon, the hawk, and other creatures as symbols of divinity, according to Manetho in his *Epitome of Physical Doctrines*, and Hecataeus in the first book of his work *On the Egyptian Philosophy*. They also set up statues and temples to these sacred animals because they do not know the true form of the deity. They hold that the universe is created and perishable, and that it is spherical in shape. They say that the stars consist of fire, and that, according as the fire in them is mixed, so events happen upon earth ; that the moon is eclipsed when it falls into the earth's shadow ; that the soul survives death and passes into other bodies ; that rain is caused by change in the atmosphere ; of all other phenomena they give physical explanations, as related by Hecataeus and Aristagoras. They also laid down laws on the subject of justice, which they ascribed to Hermes ; and they deified those animals which are serviceable to man. They also claimed to have invented geometry, astronomy, and arithmetic. Thus much concerning the invention of philosophy.

But the first to use the term, and to call himself a philosopher or lover of wisdom, was Pythagoras ; [a] for, said he, no man is wise, but God alone. Heraclides of Pontus, in his *De mortua*, makes him say this at Sicyon in conversation with Leon, who was the prince of that city or of Phlius. All too quickly the study was called wisdom and its professor a sage, to denote his attainment of mental perfection ; while the student who took it up was a philosopher or lover of wisdom. Sophists was another name for

13

οὐ μόνον, ἀλλὰ καὶ οἱ ποιηταὶ σοφισταί, καθὰ καὶ
Κρατῖνος ἐν 'Αρχιλόχοις τοὺς περὶ Ὅμηρον καὶ
Ἡσίοδον ἐπαινῶν οὕτως καλεῖ.

13 Σοφοὶ δὲ ἐνομίζοντο οἵδε· Θαλῆς, Σόλων, Περίανδρος, Κλεόβουλος, Χείλων, Βίας, Πιττακός.
τούτοις προσαριθμοῦσιν 'Ανάχαρσιν τὸν Σκύθην,
Μύσωνα τὸν Χηνέα, Φερεκύδην τὸν Σύριον,
'Επιμενίδην τὸν Κρῆτα· ἔνιοι δὲ καὶ Πεισίστρατον
τὸν τύραννον. καὶ οἱ μὲν σοφοί.

Φιλοσοφίας δὲ δύο γεγόνασιν ἀρχαί, ἥ τε ἀπὸ
'Αναξιμάνδρου καὶ ἡ ἀπὸ Πυθαγόρου· τοῦ μὲν
Θαλοῦ διακηκοότος, Πυθαγόρου δὲ Φερεκύδης καθηγήσατο. καὶ ἐκαλεῖτο ἡ μὲν 'Ιωνική, ὅτι Θαλῆς
'Ίων ὤν, Μιλήσιος γάρ, καθηγήσατο 'Αναξιμάνδρου·
ἡ δὲ 'Ιταλικὴ ἀπὸ Πυθαγόρου, ὅτι τὰ πλεῖστα
14 κατὰ τὴν 'Ιταλίαν ἐφιλοσόφησεν. καταλήγει δὲ
ἡ μὲν εἰς Κλειτόμαχον καὶ Χρύσιππον καὶ Θεόφραστον [ἡ 'Ιωνική]· ἡ δὲ 'Ιταλικὴ εἰς 'Επίκουρον.
Θαλοῦ μὲν γὰρ 'Αναξίμανδρος, οὗ 'Αναξιμένης,
οὗ 'Αναξαγόρας, οὗ 'Αρχέλαος, οὗ Σωκράτης ὁ
τὴν ἠθικὴν εἰσαγαγών· οὗ οἵ τε ἄλλοι Σωκρατικοὶ
καὶ Πλάτων ὁ τὴν ἀρχαίαν 'Ακαδημείαν συ-
στησάμενος· οὗ Σπεύσιππος καὶ Ξενοκράτης, οὗ
Πολέμων, οὗ Κράντωρ καὶ Κράτης, οὗ 'Αρκεσίλαος
ὁ τὴν μέσην 'Ακαδημείαν εἰσηγησάμενος· οὗ Λακύδης

---

[a] Compare Clem. Alex. Strom. i. 59. His authority
includes another candidate for admission to the Seven,
Acusilaus of Argos, but makes no mention of Pisistratus.

[b] See iv. 59-61, where Lacydes is made the founder of
the New Academy, although other authorities, e.g. Sext.

the wise men, and not only for philosophers but for the poets also. And so Cratinus when praising Homer and Hesiod in his *Archilochi* gives them the title of sophist.

The men who were commonly regarded as sages were the following : Thales, Solon, Periander, Cleobulus, Chilon, Bias, Pittacus. To these are added Anacharsis the Scythian, Myson of Chen, Pherecydes of Syros, Epimenides the Cretan ; and by some even Pisistratus the tyrant. So much for the sages or wise men.[a]

But philosophy, the pursuit of wisdom, has had a twofold origin ; it started with Anaximander on the one hand, with Pythagoras on the other. The former was a pupil of Thales, Pythagoras was taught by Pherecydes. The one school was called Ionian, because Thales, a Milesian and therefore an Ionian, instructed Anaximander ; the other school was called Italian from Pythagoras, who worked for the most part in Italy. And the one school, that of Ionia, terminates with Clitomachus and Chrysippus and Theophrastus, that of Italy with Epicurus. The succession passes from Thales through Anaximander, Anaximenes, Anaxagoras, Archelaus, to Socrates, who introduced ethics or moral philosophy ; from Socrates to his pupils the Socratics, and especially to Plato, the founder of the Old Academy ; from Plato, through Speusippus and Xenocrates, the succession passes to Polemo, Crantor, and Crates, Arcesilaus, founder of the Middle Academy, Lacydes,[b]

Emp. *Pyrrh. Hyp.* i. 220, say the Third or New Academy began with Carneades. But the claim of Lacydes is supported by *Ind. Acad.* pp. 76. 37 *sq.* Mekler, and the article *s.v.* in Suidas, which comes from Hesychius.

ὁ τὴν νέαν Ἀκαδημείαν φιλοσοφήσας· οὗ Καρνεάδης,
οὗ Κλειτόμαχος. καὶ ὧδε μὲν εἰς Κλειτόμαχον.

15 Εἰς δὲ Χρύσιππον οὕτω καταλήγει· Σωκράτους
Ἀντισθένης, οὗ Διογένης ὁ κύων, οὗ Κράτης ὁ
Θηβαῖος, οὗ Ζήνων ὁ Κιτιεύς, οὗ Κλεάνθης, οὗ
Χρύσιππος. εἰς δὲ Θεόφραστον οὕτως· Πλάτωνος
Ἀριστοτέλης, οὗ Θεόφραστος. καὶ ἡ μὲν Ἰωνικὴ
τοῦτον καταλήγει τὸν τρόπον.

Ἡ δὲ Ἰταλικὴ οὕτω· Φερεκύδους Πυθαγόρας, οὗ
Τηλαύγης ὁ υἱός, οὗ Ξενοφάνης, οὗ Παρμενίδης,
οὗ Ζήνων ὁ Ἐλεάτης, οὗ Λεύκιππος, οὗ Δημόκριτος, οὗ πολλοὶ μέν, ἐπ' ὀνόματος δὲ Ναυσιφάνης
[καὶ Ναυκύδης], ὧν Ἐπίκουρος.

16 Τῶν δὲ φιλοσόφων οἱ μὲν γεγόνασι δογματικοί,
οἱ δ' ἐφεκτικοί· δογματικοὶ μὲν ὅσοι περὶ τῶν
πραγμάτων ἀποφαίνονται ὡς καταληπτῶν· ἐφ-
εκτικοὶ δὲ ὅσοι ἐπέχουσι περὶ αὐτῶν ὡς ἀκατα-
λήπτων. καὶ οἱ μὲν αὐτῶν κατέλιπον ὑπομνήματα,
οἱ δ' ὅλως οὐ συνέγραψαν, ὥσπερ κατά τινας Σωκράτης, Στίλπων, Φίλιππος, Μενέδημος, Πύρρων,
Θεόδωρος, Καρνεάδης, Βρύσων· κατά τινας Πυθαγόρας, Ἀρίστων ὁ Χῖος, πλὴν ἐπιστολῶν ὀλίγων·
οἱ δὲ ἀνὰ ἓν σύγγραμμα· Μέλισσος, Παρμενίδης,
Ἀναξαγόρας· πολλὰ δὲ Ζήνων, πλείω Ξενοφάνης,
πλείω Δημόκριτος, πλείω Ἀριστοτέλης, πλείω
Ἐπίκουρος, πλείω Χρύσιππος.

ᵃ This succession (Pythagoras, Telauges, Xenophanes,
Parmenides) does not exactly agree with what is said in
the lives of Xenophanes and Parmenides, ix. 18, 21, where
Parmenides, not Xenophanes, is made a pupil of the Pyth-
agoreans. The arrangement followed in i. 12-15 treats the
Italian school as a true succession, whereas in Book IX.

founder of the New Academy, Carneades, and Clitomachus. This line brings us to Clitomachus.

There is another which ends with Chrysippus, that is to say by passing from Socrates to Antisthenes, then to Diogenes the Cynic, Crates of Thebes, Zeno of Citium, Cleanthes, Chrysippus. And yet again another ends with Theophrastus ; thus from Plato it passes to Aristotle, and from Aristotle to Theophrastus. In this manner the school of Ionia comes to an end.

In the Italian school the order of succession is as follows : first Pherecydes, next Pythagoras, next his son Telauges, then Xenophanes, Parmenides,[a] Zeno of Elea, Leucippus, Democritus, who had many pupils, in particular Nausiphanes [and Naucydes], who were teachers of Epicurus.

Philosophers may be divided into dogmatists and sceptics : all those who make assertions about things assuming that they can be known are dogmatists ; while all who suspend their judgement on the ground that things are unknowable are sceptics. Again, some philosophers left writings behind them, while others wrote nothing at all, as was the case according to some authorities with Socrates, Stilpo, Philippus, Menedemus, Pyrrho, Theodorus, Carneades, Bryson ; some add Pythagoras and Aristo of Chios, except that they wrote a few letters. Others wrote no more than one treatise each, as Melissus, Parmenides, Anaxagoras. Many works were written by Zeno, more by Xenophanes, more by Democritus, more by Aristotle, more by Epicurus, and still more by Chrysippus.

many of them are regarded as sporadic thinkers, according to the view expressed in viii. 91.

17 Τῶν δὲ φιλοσόφων οἱ μὲν ἀπὸ πόλεων προσ-
ηγορεύθησαν, ὡς οἱ Ἡλιακοὶ καὶ Μεγαρικοὶ καὶ
Ἐρετρικοὶ καὶ Κυρηναϊκοί· οἱ δὲ ἀπὸ τόπων, ὡς οἱ
Ἀκαδημαϊκοὶ καὶ Στωϊκοί. καὶ ἀπὸ συμπτωμάτων
δέ, ὡς οἱ Περιπατητικοί, καὶ ἀπὸ σκωμμάτων, ὡς
οἱ Κυνικοί· οἱ δὲ ἀπὸ διαθέσεων, ὡς οἱ Εὐδαι-
μονικοί· τινὲς ἀπὸ οἰήσεως, ὡς οἱ Φιλαλήθεις καὶ
Ἐλεγκτικοὶ καὶ Ἀναλογητικοί· ἔνιοι δ' ἀπὸ τῶν
διδασκάλων, ὡς οἱ Σωκρατικοὶ καὶ Ἐπικούρειοι,
καὶ τὰ ὅμοια. καὶ οἱ μὲν ἀπὸ τῆς περὶ φύσιν
πραγματείας φυσικοί· οἱ δ' ἀπὸ τῆς περὶ τὰ ἤθη
σχολῆς ἠθικοί· διαλεκτικοὶ δὲ ὅσοι περὶ τὴν τῶν
λόγων τερθρείαν καταγίνονται.

18 Μέρη δὲ φιλοσοφίας τρία, φυσικόν, ἠθικόν, δια-
λεκτικόν· φυσικὸν μὲν τὸ περὶ κόσμου καὶ τῶν ἐν
αὐτῷ· ἠθικὸν δὲ τὸ περὶ βίου καὶ τῶν πρὸς ἡμᾶς·
διαλεκτικὸν δὲ τὸ ἀμφοτέρων τοὺς λόγους πρε-
σβεῦον. καὶ μέχρι μὲν Ἀρχελάου τὸ φυσικὸν ἦν
εἶδος· ἀπὸ δὲ Σωκράτους, ὡς προείρηται, τὸ
ἠθικόν· ἀπὸ δὲ Ζήνωνος τοῦ Ἐλεάτου τὸ διαλεκτικόν. τοῦ δὲ ἠθικοῦ γεγόνασιν αἱρέσεις δέκα,
Ἀκαδημαϊκή, Κυρηναϊκή, Ἡλιακή, Μεγαρική,
Κυνική, Ἐρετρική, Διαλεκτική, Περιπατητική,
Στωϊκή, Ἐπικούρειος.

19 Ἀκαδημαϊκῆς μὲν οὖν τῆς ἀρχαίας προέστη
Πλάτων, τῆς μέσης Ἀρκεσίλαος, τῆς νέας Λακύδης·
Κυρηναϊκῆς Ἀρίστιππος ὁ Κυρηναῖος, Ἡλιακῆς
Φαίδων ὁ Ἠλεῖος, Μεγαρικῆς Εὐκλείδης Μεγα-
ρεύς, Κυνικῆς Ἀντισθένης Ἀθηναῖος, Ἐρετρικῆς

Some schools took their name from cities, as the Elians and the Megarians, the Eretrians and the Cyrenaics ; others from localities, as the Academics and the Stoics ; others from incidental circumstances, as the Peripatetics ; others again from derisive nick-names, as the Cynics ; others from their tempera-ments, as the Eudaemonists or Happiness School ; others from a conceit they entertained, as Truth-lovers, Refutationists, and Reasoners from Analogy ; others again from their teachers, as Socratics, Epicureans, and the like ; some take the name of Physicists from their investigation of nature, others that of Moralists because they discuss morals ; while those who are occupied with verbal jugglery are styled Dialecticians.

Philosophy has three parts, physics, ethics, and dialectic or logic. Physics is the part concerned with the universe and all that it contains ; ethics that concerned with life and all that has to do with us ; while the processes of reasoning employed by both form the province of dialectic. Physics flourished down to the time of Archelaus ; ethics, as we have said, started with Socrates ; while dialectic goes as far back as Zeno of Elea. In ethics there have been ten schools : the Academic, the Cyrenaic, the Elian, the Megarian, the Cynic, the Eretrian, the Dialectic, the Peripatetic, the Stoic, and the Epicurean.

The founders of these schools were : of the Old Academy, Plato ; of the Middle Academy, Arcesilaus ; of the New Academy, Lacydes ; of the Cyrenaic, Aristippus of Cyrene ; of the Elian, Phaedo of Elis ; of the Megarian, Euclides of Megara ; of the Cynic, Antisthenes of Athens ; of the Eretrian, Menedemus

Μενέδημος Ἐρετριεύς, Διαλεκτικῆς Κλειτόμαχος Καρχηδόνιος, Περιπατητικῆς Ἀριστοτέλης Σταγειρίτης, Στωϊκῆς Ζήνων Κιτιεύς· ἡ δὲ Ἐπικούρειος ἀπ᾽ αὐτοῦ κέκληται Ἐπικούρου.

Ἱππόβοτος δ᾽ ἐν τῷ Περὶ αἱρέσεων ἐννέα φησὶν αἱρέσεις καὶ ἀγωγὰς εἶναι· πρώτην Μεγαρικήν, δευτέραν Ἐρετρικήν, τρίτην Κυρηναϊκήν, τετάρτην Ἐπικούρειον, πέμπτην Ἀννικέρειον, ἕκτην Θεοδώρειον, ἑβδόμην Ζηνώνειον τὴν καὶ Στωϊκήν, ὀγδόην Ἀκαδημαϊκὴν τὴν ἀρχαίαν, ἐνάτην Περι-
20 πατητικήν· οὔτε δὲ Κυνικήν, οὔτε Ἠλιακήν, οὔτε Διαλεκτικήν. τὴν μὲν γὰρ Πυρρώνειον οὐδ᾽ οἱ πλείους προσποιοῦνται διὰ τὴν ἀσάφειαν· ἔνιοι δὲ κατά τι μὲν αἵρεσιν εἶναί φασιν αὐτήν, κατά τι δὲ οὔ. δοκεῖ δὲ αἵρεσις εἶναι. αἵρεσιν μὲν γὰρ λέγομεν τὴν λόγῳ τινὶ κατὰ τὸ φαινόμενον ἀκολουθοῦσαν ἢ δοκοῦσαν ἀκολουθεῖν· καθ᾽ ὃ εὐλόγως ἂν αἵρεσιν τὴν Σκεπτικὴν καλοῖμεν. εἰ δὲ αἵρεσιν νοοῖμεν πρόσκλισιν δόγμασιν ἀκολουθίαν ἔχουσιν, οὐκέτ᾽ ἂν προσαγορεύοιτο αἵρεσις· οὐ γὰρ ἔχει δόγματα. αἵδε μὲν ἀρχαὶ καὶ διαδοχαὶ καὶ τοσαῦτα μέρη καὶ τόσαι φιλοσοφίας αἱρέσεις.

21 Ἔτι δὲ πρὸ ὀλίγου καὶ ἐκλεκτική τις αἵρεσις εἰσήχθη ὑπὸ Ποτάμωνος τοῦ Ἀλεξανδρέως, ἐκλεξα-

---

[a] The separation of the followers of Anniceris from the Cyrenaic school was made by the author whom Clement of Alexandria followed in ii. 130. This author may have been Antiochus of Ascalon. Strabo x. 837 *s.f.* supports the same view: Ἀννίκερις ὁ δοκῶν ἐπανορθῶσαι τὴν Κυρηναϊκὴν αἵρεσιν, καὶ παραγαγεῖν ἀντ᾽ αὐτῆς τὴν Ἀννικερείαν.

[b] *Cf.* the distinction drawn by Sextus Empiricus in *Pyrrh. Hyp.* i. 16, 17. If by rules for conduct dogmas are implied, then the Pyrrhonians are not a sect, *i.e.* a dogmatic school.

[c] Certainly not the same ᴀs the person mentioned by

of Eretria ; of the Dialectical school, Clitomachus of Carthage ; of the Peripatetic, Aristotle of Stagira ; of the Stoic, Zeno of Citium ; while the Epicurean school took its name from Epicurus himself.

Hippobotus in his work *On Philosophical Sects* declares that there are nine sects or schools, and gives them in this order : (1) Megarian, (2) Eretrian, (3) Cyrenaic, (4) Epicurean, (5) Annicerean,[a] (6) Theodorean, (7) Zenonian or Stoic, (8) Old Academic, (9) Peripatetic. He passes over the Cynic, Elian, and Dialectical schools ; for as to the Pyrrhonians, so indefinite are their conclusions that hardly any authorities allow them to be a sect ; some allow their claim in certain respects, but not in others. It would seem, however, that they are a sect, for we use the term of those who in their attitude to appearance follow or seem to follow some principle ; and on this ground we should be justified in calling the Sceptics a sect. But if we are to understand by " sect " a bias in favour of coherent positive doctrines, they could no longer be called a sect,[b] for they have no positive doctrines. So much for the beginnings of philosophy, its subsequent developments, its various parts, and the number of the philosophic sects.

One word more : not long ago an Eclectic school was introduced by Potamo of Alexandria,[c] who

Porphyry in his *Life of Plotinus*, 9, 11, for Polemo, not Potamo, is the correct form of the name in that place. Potamo is said by Suidas (*s.v.* Ποτάμων 'Αλ.) to have lived shortly before and contemporary with Augustus, whence it follows that Diogenes has taken without alteration a statement by an earlier writer who might truthfully say " not long ago " of the reign of Augustus. Suidas, whose article αἵρεσις agrees closely with our text, naturally omits πρὸ ὀλίγου.

μένου τὰ ἀρέσκοντα ἐξ ἑκάστης τῶν αἱρέσεων.
ἀρέσκει δ' αὐτῷ, καθά φησιν ἐν τῇ Στοιχειώσει,
κριτήρια τῆς ἀληθείας εἶναι· τὸ μὲν ὡς ὑφ' οὗ
γίνεται ἡ κρίσις, τουτέστι τὸ ἡγεμονικόν· τὸ δὲ
ὡς δι' οὗ, οἷον τὴν ἀκριβεστάτην φαντασίαν.
ἀρχάς τε τῶν ὅλων τήν τε ὕλην καὶ τὸ ποιοῦν,
ποιότητά τε καὶ τόπον· ἐξ οὗ γὰρ καὶ ὑφ' οὗ καὶ
ποίῳ καὶ ἐν ᾧ. τέλος δὲ εἶναι ἐφ' ὃ πάντα ἀναφέρεται, ζωὴν κατὰ πᾶσαν ἀρετὴν τελείαν, οὐκ ἄνευ
τῶν τοῦ σώματος κατὰ φύσιν καὶ τῶν ἐκτός.

Λεκτέον δὲ περὶ αὐτῶν τῶν ἀνδρῶν, καὶ πρῶτόν
γε περὶ Θαλοῦ.

Κεφ. α'. ΘΑΛΗΣ

22 Ἦν τοίνυν ὁ Θαλῆς, ὡς μὲν Ἡρόδοτος καὶ
Δοῦρις καὶ Δημόκριτός φασι, πατρὸς μὲν Ἐξαμύου,
μητρὸς δὲ Κλεοβουλίνης, ἐκ τῶν Θηλιδῶν,[1] οἵ εἰσι
Φοίνικες, εὐγενέστατοι τῶν ἀπὸ Κάδμου καὶ
Ἀγήνορος. ⟨ἦν δὲ τῶν ἑπτὰ σοφῶν⟩, καθὰ καὶ
Πλάτων φησί· καὶ πρῶτος σοφὸς ὠνομάσθη ἄρχοντος Ἀθήνησι Δαμασίου, καθ' ὃν καὶ οἱ ἑπτὰ σοφοὶ
ἐκλήθησαν, ὥς φησι Δημήτριος ὁ Φαληρεὺς ἐν τῇ
τῶν ἀρχόντων Ἀναγραφῇ. ἐπολιτογραφήθη δὲ ἐν
Μιλήτῳ, ὅτε ἦλθε σὺν Νείλεῳ ἐκπεσόντι Φοινίκης·
ὡς δ' οἱ πλείους φασίν, ἰθαγενὴς Μιλήσιος ἦν καὶ
γένους λαμπροῦ.

---

[1] Θηλιδῶν] Νηλιδῶν Bywater.

---

[a] Nelidae, if Bywater's emendation is correct.
[b] 582 B.C.

made a selection from the tenets of all the existing sects. As he himself states in his *Elements of Philosophy*, he takes as criteria of truth (1) that by which the judgement is formed, namely, the ruling principle of the soul; (2) the instrument used, for instance the most accurate perception. His universal principles are matter and the efficient cause, quality, and place; for that out of which and that by which a thing is made, as well as the quality with which and the place in which it is made, are principles. The end to which he refers all actions is life made perfect in all virtue, natural advantages of body and environment being indispensable to its attainment.

It remains to speak of the philosophers themselves, and in the first place of Thales.

Chapter 1. THALES (*floruit circa* 585 B.C., the date of the eclipse)

Herodotus, Duris, and Democritus are agreed that Thales was the son of Examyas and Cleobulina, and belonged to the Thelidae *a* who are Phoenicians, and among the noblest of the descendants of Cadmus and Agenor. As Plato testifies, he was one of the Seven Sages. He was the first to receive the name of Sage, in the archonship of Damasias *b* at Athens, when the term was applied to all the Seven Sages, as Demetrius of Phalerum mentions in his *List of Archons*. He was admitted to citizenship at Miletus when he came to that town along with Nileos, who had been expelled from Phoenicia. Most writers, however, represent him as a genuine Milesian and of a distinguished family.

23 Μετὰ δὲ τὰ πολιτικὰ τῆς φυσικῆς ἐγένετο θεωρίας. καὶ κατά τινας μὲν σύγγραμμα κατέλιπεν οὐδέν· ἡ γὰρ εἰς αὐτὸν ἀναφερομένη Ναυτικὴ ἀστρολογία Φώκου λέγεται εἶναι τοῦ Σαμίου. Καλλίμαχος δ' αὐτὸν οἶδεν εὑρετὴν τῆς ἄρκτου τῆς μικρᾶς, λέγων ἐν τοῖς Ἰάμβοις οὕτως·

> καὶ τῆς ἁμάξης ἐλέγετο σταθμήσασθαι
> τοὺς ἀστερίσκους, ᾗ πλέουσι Φοίνικες.

κατά τινας δὲ μόνα δύο συνέγραψε, Περὶ τροπῆς καὶ Ἰσημερίας, τὰ ἄλλ' ἀκατάληπτα εἶναι δοκιμάσας. δοκεῖ δὲ κατά τινας πρῶτος ἀστρολογῆσαι καὶ ἡλιακὰς ἐκλείψεις καὶ τροπὰς προειπεῖν, ὥς φησιν Εὔδημος ἐν τῇ περὶ τῶν Ἀστρολογουμένων ἱστορίᾳ· ὅθεν αὐτὸν καὶ Ξενοφάνης καὶ Ἡρόδοτος θαυμάζει. μαρτυρεῖ δ' αὐτῷ καὶ Ἡράκλειτος καὶ Δημόκριτος.

24 Ἔνιοι δὲ καὶ αὐτὸν πρῶτον εἰπεῖν φασιν ἀθανάτους τὰς ψυχάς· ὧν ἐστι Χοιρίλος ὁ ποιητής. πρῶτος δὲ καὶ τὴν ἀπὸ τροπῆς ἐπὶ τροπὴν πάροδον εὗρε, καὶ πρῶτος τὸ τοῦ ἡλίου μέγεθος ⟨τοῦ ἡλιακοῦ κύκλου ὥσπερ καὶ τὸ τῆς σελήνης μέγεθος⟩ τοῦ σεληναίου ἑπτακοσιοστὸν καὶ εἰκοστὸν μέρος ἀπεφήνατο κατά τινας. πρῶτος δὲ καὶ τὴν ὑστάτην ἡμέραν τοῦ μηνὸς τριακάδα εἶπε. πρῶτος δὲ καὶ περὶ φύσεως διελέχθη, ὥς τινες.

Ἀριστοτέλης δὲ καὶ Ἱππίας φασὶν αὐτὸν καὶ τοῖς ἀψύχοις μεταδιδόναι ψυχῆς, τεκμαιρόμενον ἐκ τῆς λίθου τῆς μαγνήτιδος καὶ τοῦ ἠλέκτρου.

ᵃ Cf. Simplicius, In Phys. i. 23, 29-33 D.
ᵇ Greek mariners steered by the Great Bear, the Phoenicians by the Little Bear, as Ovid states, Tristia, iv. 3. 1, 2.

After engaging in politics he became a student of nature. According to some he left nothing in writing; for the *Nautical Astronomy* [a] attributed to him is said to be by Phocus of Samos. Callimachus knows him as the discoverer of the Ursa Minor; for he says in his *Iambics*:

> Who first of men the course made plain
> Of those small stars we call the Wain,
> Whereby Phoenicians sail the main.[b]

But according to others he wrote nothing but two treatises, one *On the Solstice* and one *On the Equinox*, regarding all other matters as incognizable. He seems by some accounts to have been the first to study astronomy,[c] the first to predict eclipses of the sun and to fix the solstices; so Eudemus in his *History of Astronomy*. It was this which gained for him the admiration of Xenophanes and Herodotus and the notice of Heraclitus and Democritus.

And some, including Choerilus the poet, declare that he was the first to maintain the immortality of the soul. He was the first to determine the sun's course from solstice to solstice, and according to some the first to declare the size of the sun to be one seven hundred and twentieth part of the solar circle, and the size of the moon to be the same fraction of the lunar circle. He was the first to give the last day of the month the name of Thirtieth, and the first, some say, to discuss physical problems.

Aristotle[d] and Hippias affirm that, arguing from the magnet and from amber, he attributed a soul or life even to inanimate objects. Pamphila states that,

---

[c] See Sir T. L. Heath, *Aristarchus of Samos*, pp. 12-23.
[d] *De anima*, A 2, 405 a 19.

παρά τε Αἰγυπτίων γεωμετρεῖν μαθόντα φησὶ
Παμφίλη πρῶτον καταγράψαι κύκλου τὸ τρίγωνον
25 ὀρθογώνιον, καὶ θῦσαι βοῦν. οἱ δὲ Πυθαγόραν
φασίν, ὧν ἐστιν Ἀπολλόδωρος ὁ λογιστικός.
οὗτος προήγαγεν ἐπὶ πλεῖστον, ἅ φησι Καλλίμαχος
ἐν τοῖς Ἰάμβοις Εὔφορβον εὑρεῖν τὸν Φρύγα, οἷον
" σκαληνὰ καὶ τρίγωνα " καὶ ὅσα γραμμικῆς
ἔχεται θεωρίας.[a]

Δοκεῖ δὲ καὶ ἐν τοῖς πολιτικοῖς ἄριστα βεβου-
λεῦσθαι. Κροίσου γοῦν πέμψαντος πρὸς Μιλησίους
ἐπὶ συμμαχίᾳ ἐκώλυσεν· ὅπερ Κύρου κρατήσαντος
ἔσωσε τὴν πόλιν. καὶ αὐτὸς δέ φησιν, ὡς Ἡρακλείδης ἱστορεῖ, μονήρη αὐτὸν γεγονέναι καὶ ἰδια-
26 στήν. ἔνιοι δὲ καὶ γῆμαι αὐτὸν καὶ Κύβισθον υἱὸν
σχεῖν· οἱ δὲ ἄγαμον μεῖναι, τῆς δὲ ἀδελφῆς τὸν
υἱὸν θέσθαι. ὅτε καὶ ἐρωτηθέντα διὰ τί οὐ τεκνο-
ποιεῖ, " διὰ φιλοτεκνίαν " εἰπεῖν. καὶ λέγουσιν
ὅτι τῆς μητρὸς ἀναγκαζούσης αὐτὸν γῆμαι, " [νὴ
Δία]," ἔλεγεν, " οὐδέπω καιρός." εἶτα, ἐπειδὴ
παρήβησεν ἐγκειμένης, εἰπεῖν, " οὐκέτι καιρός."
φησὶ δὲ καὶ Ἱερώνυμος ὁ Ῥόδιος ἐν τῷ δευτέρῳ
Τῶν σποράδην ὑπομνημάτων, ὅτι βουλόμενος
δεῖξαι ῥᾴδιον εἶναι πλουτεῖν, φορᾶς μελλούσης
ἐλαιῶν ἔσεσθαι, προνοήσας ἐμισθώσατο τὰ ἐλαιουρ-
γεῖα καὶ πάμπλειστα συνεῖλε χρήματα.[c]

27 Ἀρχὴν δὲ τῶν πάντων ὕδωρ ὑπεστήσατο, καὶ
τὸν κόσμον ἔμψυχον καὶ δαιμόνων πλήρη. τάς τε

---

[a] *i.e.* a theory concerned with lines, γραμμαί, which of
course include curves as well as straight lines.
[b] Namely, in a dialogue. *Cf.* viii. 4.
[c] Because, having created a monopoly, he could charge
what he pleased. See Aristotle's version of the story, *Pol.*
i. 11, 1259 a 6-18.

having learnt geometry from the Egyptians, he was
the first to inscribe a right-angled triangle in a circle,
whereupon he sacrificed an ox. Others tell this tale
of Pythagoras, amongst them Apollodorus the arith-
metician. (It was Pythagoras who developed to
their furthest extent the discoveries attributed by
Callimachus in his *Iambics* to Euphorbus the
Phrygian, I mean " scalene triangles " and whatever
else has to do with theoretical geometry.[a])

Thales is also credited with having given excellent
advice on political matters. For instance, when
Croesus sent to Miletus offering terms of alliance,
he frustrated the plan ; and this proved the salvation
of the city when Cyrus obtained the victory. Heraclides makes Thales himself [b] say that he had always
lived in solitude as a private individual and kept
aloof from State affairs. Some authorities say that
he married and had a son Cybisthus ; others that
he remained unmarried and adopted his sister's son,
and that when he was asked why he had no children
of his own he replied " because he loved children."
The story is told that, when his mother tried to
force him to marry, he replied it was too soon, and
when she pressed him again later in life, he replied
that it was too late. Hieronymus of Rhodes in the
second book of his *Scattered Notes* relates that, in
order to show how easy it is to grow rich, Thales,
foreseeing that it would be a good season for olives,
rented all the oil-mills and thus amassed a fortune.[c]

His doctrine was that water is the universal
primary substance, and that the world is animate
and full of divinities. He is said to have discovered

ὥρας τοῦ ἐνιαυτοῦ φασιν αὐτὸν εὑρεῖν καὶ εἰς
τριακοσίας ἑξήκοντα πέντε ἡμέρας διελεῖν.

Οὐδεὶς δὲ αὐτοῦ καθηγήσατο, πλὴν ὅτι εἰς
Αἴγυπτον ἐλθὼν τοῖς ἱερεῦσι συνδιέτριψεν. ὁ δὲ
Ἱερώνυμος καὶ ἐκμετρῆσαί φησιν αὐτὸν τὰς πυρα-
μίδας ἐκ τῆς σκιᾶς, παρατηρήσαντα ὅτε ἡμῖν
ἰσομεγέθης ἐστίν. συνεβίω δὲ καὶ Θρασυβούλῳ
τῷ Μιλησίων τυράννῳ, καθά φησι Μινύης.

Τὰ δὲ περὶ τὸν τρίποδα φανερὰ τὸν εὑρεθέντα
ὑπὸ τῶν ἁλιέων καὶ διαπεμφθέντα τοῖς σοφοῖς ὑπὸ
28 τοῦ δήμου τῶν Μιλησίων. φασὶ γὰρ Ἰωνικούς
τινας νεανίσκους βόλον ἀγοράσαι παρὰ Μιλησίων
ἁλιέων. ἀνασπασθέντος δὲ τοῦ τρίποδος ἀμφισβή-
τησις ἦν, ἕως οἱ Μιλήσιοι ἔπεμψαν εἰς Δελφούς·
καὶ ὁ θεὸς ἔχρησεν οὕτως·

ἔκγονε Μιλήτου, τρίποδος πέρι Φοῖβον ἐρωτᾷς;
τίς σοφίῃ πάντων πρῶτος, τούτου τρίποδ᾽ αὐδῶ.

διδοῦσιν οὖν Θαλῇ· ὁ δὲ ἄλλῳ καὶ ἄλλος ἄλλῳ ἕως
Σόλωνος. ὁ δὲ ἔφη σοφίᾳ πρῶτον εἶναι τὸν θεὸν
καὶ ἀπέστειλεν εἰς Δελφούς. ταῦτα δὴ ὁ Καλλίμαχος ἐν τοῖς Ἰάμβοις ἄλλως ἱστορεῖ, παρὰ
Μαιανδρίου λαβὼν τοῦ Μιλησίου. Βαθυκλέα γάρ
τινα Ἀρκάδα φιάλην καταλιπεῖν καὶ ἐπισκῆψαι
" δοῦναι τῶν σοφῶν ὀνήϊστῳ." ἐδόθη δὴ Θαλῇ
29 καὶ κατὰ περίοδον πάλιν Θαλῇ· ὁ δὲ τῷ Δ ιδυμεῖ

---

* *Anth. Plan.* vi. 51.
* Or in prose: " Offspring of Miletus, do you ask Phoebus
concerning the tripod ? Whoso in wisdom is of all the first,
to him the tripod I adjudge."
* Although disguised as Leandrius, the writer meant is
Maeandrius, who is known (*Inscr. Gr.* no. 2905) to have

the seasons of the year and divided it into 365 days.

He had no instructor, except that he went to Egypt and spent some time with the priests there. Hieronymus informs us that he measured the height of the pyramids by the shadow they cast, taking the observation at the hour when our shadow is of the same length as ourselves. He lived, as Minyas relates, with Thrasybulus, the tyrant of Miletus.

The well-known story of the tripod found by the fishermen and sent by the people of Miletus to all the Wise Men in succession runs as follows. Certain Ionian youths having purchased of the Milesian fishermen their catch of fish, a dispute arose over the tripod which had formed part of the catch. Finally the Milesians referred the question to Delphi, and the god gave an oracle in this form ᵃ :

> Who shall possess the tripod ? Thus replies
> Apollo : " Whosoever is most wise." ᵇ

Accordingly they give it to Thales, and he to another, and so on till it comes to Solon, who, with the remark that the god was the most wise, sent it off to Delphi. Callimachus in his *Iambics* has a different version of the story, which he took from Maeandrius of Miletus.ᶜ It is that Bathycles, an Arcadian, left at his death a bowl with the solemn injunction that it " should be given to him who had done most good by his wisdom." So it was given to Thales, went the round of all the sages, and came back to Thales again. And he sent it

written a local history of Miletus. Such histories, c:g. of Sicyon, Megara, Samos, Naxos, Argolis, Epirus, Thessaly, abounded in the Alexandrian age.

Ἀπόλλωνι ἀπέστειλεν, εἰπὼν οὕτω κατὰ τὸν Καλλίμαχον·

Θαλῆς με τῷ μεδεῦντι Νείλεω δήμου
δίδωσι, τοῦτο δὶς λαβὼν ἀριστεῖον.

τὸ δὲ πεζὸν οὕτως ἔχει· "Θαλῆς Ἐξαμύου Μιλήσιος Ἀπόλλωνι Δελφινίῳ Ἑλλήνων ἀριστεῖον δὶς λαβών." ὁ δὲ περιενεγκὼν τὴν φιάλην τοῦ Βαθυκλέους παῖς Θυρίων ἐκαλεῖτο, καθά φησιν Ἔλευσις ἐν τῷ Περὶ Ἀχιλλέως καὶ Ἀλέξων ὁ Μύνδιος ἐν ἐνάτῳ Μυθικῶν.

Εὔδοξος δ' ὁ Κνίδιος καὶ Εὐάνθης ὁ Μιλήσιός φασι τῶν Κροίσου τινὰ φίλων λαβεῖν παρὰ τοῦ βασιλέως ποτήριον χρυσοῦν, ὅπως δῷ τῷ σοφωτάτῳ τῶν Ἑλλήνων· τὸν δὲ δοῦναι Θαλῇ.

30 Καὶ περιελθεῖν εἰς Χίλωνα, ὃν πυνθάνεσθαι τοῦ Πυθίου τίς αὐτοῦ σοφώτερος· καὶ τὸν ἀνελεῖν[1] Μύσωνα, περὶ οὗ λέξομεν. (τοῦτον οἱ περὶ τὸν Εὔδοξον ἀντὶ Κλεοβούλου τιθέασι, Πλάτων δ' ἀντὶ Περιάνδρου.) περὶ αὐτοῦ δὴ τάδε ἀνεῖλεν[2] ὁ Πύθιος·

Οἰταῖόν τινα φημὶ Μύσων' ἐνὶ Χηνὶ γενέσθαι
σοῦ μᾶλλον πραπίδεσσιν ἀρηρότα πευκαλίμῃσιν.

ὁ δ' ἐρωτήσας ἦν Ἀνάχαρσις. Δαΐμαχος δ' ὁ Πλατωνικὸς καὶ Κλέαρχος φιάλην ἀποσταλῆναι ὑπὸ Κροίσου Πιττακῷ καὶ οὕτω περιενεχθῆναι.

---

[1] ἀνειπεῖν vulg.: corr. H. Richards.
[2] ἀνεῖπεν vulg.: corr. H. Richards.

* Anth. Plan. vi. 40.

to Apollo at Didyma, with this dedication, according to Callimachus :

> Lord of the folk of Neleus' line,
> Thales, of Greeks adjudged most wise,
> Brings to thy Didymaean shrine
> His offering, a twice-won prize.

But the prose inscription is :

Thales the Milesian, son of Examyas [dedicates this] to Delphinian Apollo after twice winning the prize from all the Greeks.

The bowl was carried from place to place by the son of Bathycles, whose name was Thyrion, so it is stated by Eleusis in his work *On Achilles*, and Alexo the Myndian in the ninth book of his *Legends*.

But Eudoxus of Cnidos and Euanthes of Miletus agree that a certain man who was a friend of Croesus received from the king a golden goblet in order to bestow it upon the wisest of the Greeks ; this man gave it to Thales, and from him it passed to others and so to Chilon.

Chilon laid the question " Who is a wiser man than I ? " before the Pythian Apollo, and the god replied " Myson." Of him we shall have more to say presently. (In the list of the Seven Sages given by Eudoxus, Myson takes the place of Cleobulus ; Plato also includes him by omitting Periander.) The answer of the oracle respecting him was as follows [a] :

> Myson of Chen in Oeta ; this is he
> Who for wiseheartedness surpasseth thee :

and it was given in reply to a question put by Anacharsis. Daïmachus the Platonist and Clearchus allege that a bowl was sent by Croesus to Pittacus and began the round of the Wise Men from him.

"Ανδρων δ' ἐν τῷ Τρίποδι 'Αργείους ἆθλον
ἀρετῆς τῷ σοφωτάτῳ τῶν 'Ελλήνων τρίποδα θεῖναι·
κριθῆναι δὲ 'Αριστόδημον Σπαρτιάτην, ὃν παρα-
31 χωρῆσαι Χίλωνι. μέμνηται τοῦ 'Αριστοδήμου καὶ
'Αλκαῖος οὕτως·

> ὡς γὰρ δή ποτ' 'Αριστόδαμόν φασ' οὐκ ἀπάλαμνον
>   ἐν Σπάρτᾳ λόγον
> εἰπεῖν· χρήματ' ἀνήρ, πενιχρὸς δ' οὐδεὶς πέλετ'
>   ἐσλός.

ἔνιοι δέ φασιν ὑπὸ Περιάνδρου Θρασυβούλῳ τῷ
Μιλησίων τυράννῳ πλοῖον ἔμφορτον ἀποσταλῆναι·
τοῦ δὲ περὶ τὴν Κῷαν θάλασσαν ναυαγήσαντος,
ὕστερον εὑρεθῆναι πρός τινων ἁλιέων τὸν τρίποδα.
Φανόδικος δὲ περὶ τὴν 'Αθηναίων θάλασσαν
εὑρεθῆναι καὶ ἀνενεχθέντα εἰς ἄστυ γενομένης
32 ἐκκλησίας Βίαντι πεμφθῆναι· διὰ τί δέ, ἐν τῷ περὶ
Βίαντος λέξομεν.

"Αλλοι φασὶν ἡφαιστότευκτον εἶναι αὐτὸν καὶ
δοθῆναι πρὸς τοῦ θεοῦ Πέλοπι γαμοῦντι· αὖθίς τε
εἰς Μενέλαον ἐλθεῖν καὶ σὺν τῇ 'Ελένῃ ἁρπασθέντα
ὑπ' 'Αλεξάνδρου ῥιφῆναι εἰς τὴν Κῷαν θάλασσαν
πρὸς τῆς Λακαίνης, εἰπούσης ὅτι περιμάχητος
ἔσται. χρόνῳ δὲ Λεβεδίων τινῶν αὐτόθι γρῖφον
ὠνησαμένων καταληφθῆναι καὶ τὸν τρίποδα, μαχομένων δὲ πρὸς τοὺς ἁλιέας γενέσθαι τὴν ἄνοδον
ἕως τῆς Κῶ· καὶ ὡς οὐδὲν ἤνυτον, τοῖς Μιλησίοις
μητροπόλει οὔσῃ μηνύουσιν. οἱ δ' ἐπειδὴ διαπρε-
σβευόμενοι ἠλογοῦντο, πρὸς τοὺς Κῴους πολεμοῦσι.
καὶ πολλῶν ἑκατέρωθεν πιπτόντων ἐκπίπτει χρη-

ᵃ Andron of Ephesus (§ 119) is known to have written
in the life-time (or at least before the death) of Theopompus,

I. 30–32. THALES

The story told by Andron [a] in his work on *The Tripod* is that the Argives offered a tripod as a prize of virtue to the wisest of the Greeks ; Aristodemus of Sparta was adjudged the winner but retired in favour of Chilon. Aristodemus is mentioned by Alcaeus thus [b] :

> Surely no witless word was this of the Spartan, I deem,
> "Wealth is the worth of a man ; and poverty void of esteem."

Some relate that a vessel with its freight was sent by Periander to Thrasybulus, tyrant of Miletus, and that, when it was wrecked in Coan waters, the tripod was afterwards found by certain fishermen. However, Phanodicus declares it to have been found in Athenian waters and thence brought to Athens. An assembly was held and it was sent to Bias ; for what reason shall be explained in the life of Bias.

There is yet another version, that it was the work of Hephaestus presented by the god to Pelops on his marriage. Thence it passed to Menelaus and was carried off by Paris along with Helen and was thrown by her into the Coan sea, for she said it would be a cause of strife. In process of time certain people of Lebedus, having purchased a catch of fish thereabouts, obtained possession of the tripod, and, quarrelling with the fishermen about it, put in to Cos, and, when they could not settle the dispute, reported the fact to Miletus, their mother - city. The Milesians, when their embassies were disregarded, made war upon Cos ; many fell on both sides, and an oracle pronounced that the tripod

who is accused of having plagiarized from *The Tripod* : Eusebius, *Praep. Ev.* x. 3, 7.
  [b] Fr. 49 Bergk ; *cf. Schol.* Pindar, *Isthm.* ii. 17.

σμὸς δοῦναι τῷ σοφωτάτῳ· καὶ ἀμφότεροι συνήνεσαι
Θαλῇ. ὁ δὲ μετὰ τὴν περίοδον τῷ Διδυμεῖ τίθησιν
33 Ἀπόλλωνι. Κῴοις μὲν οὖν τοῦτον ἐχρήσθη τὸν
τρόπον·

οὐ πρότερον λήξει νεῖκος Μερόπων καὶ Ἰώνων,
πρὶν τρίποδα χρύσειον, ὃν Ἥφαιστος βάλε πόντῳ,
ἐκ πόλιος πέμψητε καὶ ἐς δόμον ἀνδρὸς ἵκηται,
ὃς σοφὸς ᾖ τά ἐόντα τά τ’ ἐσσόμενα πρό τ’ ἐόντα.

Μιλησίοις δέ·

ἔκγονε Μιλήτου, τρίποδος πέρι Φοῖβον ἐρωτᾷς;

καὶ ὡς προείρηται. καὶ τόδε μὲν οὕτως.
Ἕρμιππος δ’ ἐν τοῖς Βίοις εἰς τοῦτον ἀναφέρει
τὸ λεγόμενον ὑπό τινων περὶ Σωκράτους. ἔφασκε
γάρ, φασί, τριῶν τούτων ἕνεκα χάριν ἔχειν τῇ
Τύχῃ· πρῶτον μὲν ὅτι ἄνθρωπος ἐγενόμην καὶ οὐ
θηρίον, εἶτα ὅτι ἀνὴρ καὶ οὐ γυνή, τρίτον ὅτι Ἕλλην
34 καὶ οὐ βάρβαρος. λέγεται δ’ ἀγόμενος ὑπὸ γραὸς
ἐκ τῆς οἰκίας, ἵνα τὰ ἄστρα κατανοήσῃ, εἰς βόθρον
ἐμπεσεῖν καὶ αὐτῷ ἀνοιμώξαντι φάναι τὴν γραῦν·
“ σὺ γάρ, ὦ Θαλῆ, τὰ ἐν ποσὶν οὐ δυνάμενος ἰδεῖν
τὰ ἐπὶ τοῦ οὐρανοῦ οἴει γνώσεσθαι; ” οἶδε δ’ αὐτὸν
ἀστρονομούμενον καὶ Τίμων, καὶ ἐν τοῖς Σίλλοις
ἐπαινεῖ αὐτὸν λέγων·

οἷόν θ’ ἑπτὰ Θάλητα σοφῶν σοφὸν ἀστρονόμημα.

Τὰ δὲ γεγραμμένα ὑπ’ αὐτοῦ φησι Λόβων ὁ
Ἀργεῖος εἰς ἔπη τείνειν διακόσια. ἐπιγεγράφθαι δ’
αὐτοῦ ἐπὶ τῆς εἰκόνος τόδε·

34

should be given to the wisest; both parties to the dispute agreed upon Thales. After it had gone the round of the sages, Thales dedicated it to Apollo of Didyma. The oracle which the Coans received was on this wise :

> Hephaestus cast the tripod in the sea ;
> Until it quit the city there will be
> No end to strife, until it reach the seer
> Whose wisdom makes past, present, future clear.

That of the Milesians beginning " Who shall possess the tripod ? " has been quoted above. So much for this version of the story.

Hermippus in his *Lives* refers to Thales the story which is told by some of Socrates, namely, that he used to say there were three blessings for which he was grateful to Fortune : " first, that I was born a human being and not one of the brutes ; next, that I was born a man and not a woman ; thirdly, a Greek and not a barbarian." It is said that once, when he was taken out of doors by an old woman in order that he might observe the stars, he fell into a ditch, and his cry for help drew from the old woman the retort, " How can you expect to know all about the heavens, Thales, when you cannot even see what is just before your feet ? " Timon too knows him as an astronomer, and praises him in the *Silli* where he says [a] :

> Thales among the Seven the sage astronomer.

His writings are said by Lobon of Argos to have run to some two hundred lines. His statue is said to bear this inscription [b] :

[a] Fr. 23 Diels.
[b] *Anth. Pal.* vii. 83.

τόνδε Θαλῆν Μίλητος Ἰὰς θρέψασ' ἀνέδειξεν
ἀστρολόγων πάντων πρεσβύτατον σοφίᾳ.

25 Τῶν τε ἀδομένων αὐτοῦ τάδε εἶναι·

οὔ τι τὰ πολλὰ ἔπη φρονίμην ἀπεφήνατο δόξαν·
ἕν τι μάτευε σοφόν,
ἕν τι κεδνὸν αἱροῦ·
δήσεις γὰρ ἀνδρῶν κωτίλων γλώσσας ἀπεραντο-
λόγους.

Φέρεται δὲ καὶ ἀποφθέγματα αὐτοῦ τάδε·

πρεσβύτατον τῶν ὄντων θεός· ἀγένητον γάρ.
κάλλιστον κόσμος· ποίημα γὰρ θεοῦ.
μέγιστον τόπος· ἅπαντα γὰρ χωρεῖ.
τάχιστον νοῦς· διὰ παντὸς γὰρ τρέχει.
ἰσχυρότατον ἀνάγκη· κρατεῖ γὰρ πάντων.
σοφώτατον χρόνος· ἀνευρίσκει γὰρ πάντα.

οὐδὲν ἔφη τὸν θάνατον διαφέρειν τοῦ ζῆν. "σὺ οὖν,"
ἔφη τις, "διὰ τί οὐκ ἀποθνήσκεις;" "ὅτι," ἔφη,
36 "οὐδὲν διαφέρει." πρὸς τὸν πυθόμενον τί πρότερον
γεγόνοι, νὺξ ἢ ἡμέρα, "ἡ νύξ," ἔφη, "μιᾷ ἡμέρᾳ
πρότερον." ἠρώτησέ τις αὐτὸν εἰ λήθοι θεοὺς
ἄνθρωπος ἀδικῶν· "ἀλλ' οὐδὲ διανοούμενος," ἔφη.
πρὸς τὸν μοιχὸν ἐρόμενον εἰ ὀμόσειε μὴ μεμοι-
χευκέναι, "οὐ χεῖρον," ἔφη, "μοιχείας ἐπιορκία."
ἐρωτηθεὶς τί δύσκολον, ἔφη, "τὸ ἑαυτὸν γνῶναι·"
τί δὲ εὔκολον, "τὸ ἄλλῳ ὑποθέσθαι·" τί ἥδιστον,
"τὸ ἐπιτυγχάνειν·" τί τὸ θεῖον, "τὸ μήτε ἀρχὴν
ἔχον μήτε τελευτήν." τί δὲ καινὸν εἴη τεθεαμένος

I. 34–36. THALES

Pride of Miletus and Ionian lands,
Wisest astronomer, here Thales stands.

Of songs still sung these verses belong to him:

Many words do not declare an understanding heart.
Seek one sole wisdom.
Choose one sole good.
For thou wilt check the tongues of chatterers prating
without end.

Here too are certain current apophthegms assigned
to him :

Of all things that are, the most ancient is God, for he is
uncreated.
The most beautiful is the universe, for it is God's workman-
ship.
The greatest is space, for it holds all things.
The swiftest is mind, for it speeds everywhere.
The strongest, necessity, for it masters all.
The wisest, time, for it brings everything to light.

He held there was no difference between life and
death. " Why then," said one, " do you not die? "
" Because," said he, " there is no difference." To
the question which is older, day or night, he
replied : " Night is the older by one day." Some
one asked him whether a man could hide an evil
deed from the gods : " No," he replied, " nor yet
an evil thought." To the adulterer who inquired if
he should deny the charge upon oath he replied that
perjury was no worse than adultery. Being asked
what is difficult, he replied, " To know oneself."
" What is easy? " " To give advice to another."
" What is most pleasant? " " Success." " What
is the divine? " " That which has neither beginning
nor end." To the question what was the strangest

ἔφη· "γέροντα τύραννον." πῶς ἄν τις ἀτυχίαν
ῥᾷστα φέροι, "εἰ τοὺς ἐχθροὺς χεῖρον πράσσοντας
βλέποι·" πῶς ἂν ἄριστα καὶ δικαιότατα βιώσαιμεν,
"ἐὰν ἃ τοῖς ἄλλοις ἐπιτιμῶμεν, αὐτοὶ μὴ δρῶμεν·"
37 τίς εὐδαίμων, "ὁ τὸ μὲν σῶμα ὑγιής, τὴν δὲ ψυχὴν
εὔπορος, τὴν δὲ φύσιν εὐπαίδευτος." φίλων παρόντων καὶ ἀπόντων μεμνῆσθαί φησι· μὴ τὴν ὄψιν
καλλωπίζεσθαι, ἀλλὰ τοῖς ἐπιτηδεύμασιν εἶναι
καλόν. "μὴ πλούτει," φησί, "κακῶς, μηδὲ δια-
βαλλέτω σε λόγος πρὸς τοὺς πίστεως κεκοινωνη-
κότας." "οὓς ἂν ἐράνους εἰσενέγκῃς," φησί,
"τοῖς γονεῦσιν, τοὺς αὐτοὺς προσδέχου καὶ παρὰ
τῶν τέκνων." τὸν Νεῖλον εἶπε πληθύειν ἀνα-
κοπτομένων τῶν ῥευμάτων ὑπὸ τῶν ἐτησίων ἐναντίων ὄντων.

Φησὶ δ' Ἀπολλόδωρος ἐν τοῖς Χρονικοῖς γεγενῆσθαι αὐτὸν κατὰ τὸ πρῶτον ἔτος τῆς τριακοστῆς
38 πέμπτης [ἐνάτης?] Ὀλυμπιάδος. ἐτελεύτησε δ'
ἐτῶν ἑβδομήκοντα ὀκτώ, (ἤ, ὡς Σωσικράτης φησίν,
ἐνενήκοντα)· τελευτῆσαι γὰρ ἐπὶ τῆς πεντηκοστῆς
ὀγδόης Ὀλυμπιάδος, γεγονότα κατὰ Κροῖσον, ᾧ
καὶ τὸν Ἅλυν ὑποσχέσθαι ἄνευ γεφύρας περᾶσαι,
τὸ ῥεῖθρον παρατρέψαντα.

Γεγόνασι δὲ καὶ ἄλλοι Θαλαῖ, καθά φησι Δημήτριος ὁ Μάγνης ἐν τοῖς Ὁμωνύμοις, πέντε·

ῥήτωρ Καλλατιανός, κακόζηλος·
ζωγράφος Σικυώνιος, μεγαλοφυής·
τρίτος ἀρχαῖος πάνυ, κατὰ Ἡσίοδον καὶ Ὅμηρον
καὶ Λυκοῦργον·
τέταρτος οὗ μέμνηται Δοῦρις ἐν τῷ Περὶ
ζωγραφίας·

thing he had ever seen, his answer was, "An aged tyrant." "How can one best bear adversity?" "If he should see his enemies in worse plight." "How shall we lead the best and most righteous life?" "By refraining from doing what we blame in others." "What man is happy?" "He who has a healthy body, a resourceful mind and a docile nature." He tells us to remember friends, whether present or absent; not to pride ourselves upon outward appearance, but to study to be beautiful in character. "Shun ill-gotten gains," he says. "Let not idle words prejudice thee against those who have shared thy confidence." "Whatever provision thou hast made for thy parents, the same must thou expect from thy children." He explained the overflow of the Nile as due to the etesian winds which, blowing in the contrary direction, drove the waters upstream.

Apollodorus in his *Chronology* places his birth in the first year of the 35th Olympiad [640 B.C.]. He died at the age of 78 (or, according to Sosicrates, of 90 years); for he died in the 58th Olympiad, being contemporary with Croesus, whom he undertook to take across the Halys without building a bridge, by diverting the river.

There have lived five other men who bore the name of Thales, as enumerated by Demetrius of Magnesia in his *Dictionary of Men of the Same Name*:

1. A rhetorician of Callatia, with an affected style.
2. A painter of Sicyon, of great gifts.
3. A contemporary of Hesiod, Homer and Lycurgus, in very early times.
4. A person mentioned by Duris in his work *On Painting*.

πέμπτος νεώτερος, ἄδοξος, οὗ μνημονεύει Διονύσιος ἐν Κριτικοῖς.

39 Ὁ δ' οὖν σοφὸς ἐτελεύτησεν ἀγῶνα θεώμενος
γυμνικὸν ὑπό τε καύματος καὶ δίψους καὶ ἀσθενείας,
ἤδη γηραιός. καὶ αὐτοῦ ἐπιγέγραπται τῷ μνή-
ματι·

ἦ ὀλίγον τόδε σᾶμα — τὸ δὲ κλέος οὐρανόμακες —
τῶ πολυφροντίστω τοῦτο Θάλητος ὅρη.

ἔστι καὶ παρ' ἡμῖν ἐς αὐτὸν ἐν τῷ πρώτῳ τῶν
Ἐπιγραμμάτων ἢ Παμμέτρῳ τόδε τὸ ἐπίγραμμα·

γυμνικὸν αὖ ποτ' ἀγῶνα θεώμενον, ἠέλιε Ζεῦ,
τὸν σοφὸν ἄνδρα Θαλῆν ἥρπασας ἐκ σταδίου.
αἰνέω ὅττι μιν ἐγγὺς ἀπήγαγες· ἦ γὰρ ὁ πρέσβυς
οὐκέθ' ὁρᾶν ἀπὸ γῆς ἀστέρας ἠδύνατο.

40 Τούτου ἐστὶν τὸ Γνῶθι σαυτόν, ὅπερ Ἀντισθένης ἐν ταῖς Διαδοχαῖς Φημονόης εἶναί φησιν,
ἐξιδιοποιήσασθαι δὲ αὐτὸ Χίλωνα.

Περὶ δὴ τῶν ἑπτά—ἄξιον γὰρ ἐνταῦθα καθολικῶς
κἀκείνων ἐπιμνησθῆναι—λόγοι φέρονται τοιοῦτοι.
Δάμων ὁ Κυρηναῖος, γεγραφὼς Περὶ τῶν φιλοσόφων, πᾶσιν ἐγκαλεῖ, μάλιστα δὲ τοῖς ἑπτά.
Ἀναξιμένης δέ φησι πάντας ἐπιθέσθαι ποιητικῇ·
ὁ δὲ Δικαίαρχος οὔτε σοφοὺς οὔτε φιλοσόφους
φησὶν αὐτοὺς γεγονέναι, συνετοὺς δέ τινας καὶ

40

5. An obscure person in more recent times who
    is mentioned by Dionysius in his *Critical
    Writings*.

Thales the Sage died as he was watching an athletic
contest from heat, thirst, and the weakness incident
to advanced age. And the inscription on his tomb
is [a] :

> Here in a narrow tomb great Thales lies ;
> Yet his renown for wisdom reached the skies.

I may also cite one of my own, from my first book,
Epigrams in Various Metres [b] :

> As Thales watched the games one festal day
> The fierce sun smote him, and he passed away ;
> Zeus, thou didst well to raise him ; his dim eyes
> Could not from earth behold the starry skies.[c]

To him belongs the proverb " Know thyself,"
which Antisthenes in his *Successions of Philosophers*
attributes to Phemonoë, though admitting that it
was appropriated by Chilon.

This seems the proper place for a general notice of
the Seven Sages, of whom we have such accounts
as the following. Damon of Cyrene in his *History
of the Philosophers* carps at all sages, but especially
the Seven. Anaximenes remarks that they all
applied themselves to poetry ; Dicaearchus that
they were neither sages nor philosophers, but merely

---

[a] *Anth. Pal.* vii. 84.
[b] *Anth. Pal.* vii. 85.
[c] In plain prose : " As the wise Thales was one day
watching the contest of the racers, thou, O Sun-god, O Zeus,
didst snatch him from the stadium. I praise thee for re-
moving him to be near thee ; for verily the old man could
no more discern the stars from earth."

41

νομοθετικούς. Ἀρχέτιμος δὲ ὁ Συρακούσιος ὁμι-
λίαν αὐτῶν ἀναγέγραφε παρὰ Κυψέλῳ, ᾗ καὶ αὐτός
φησι παρατυχεῖν· Ἔφορος δὲ παρὰ Κροίσῳ πλὴν
Θαλοῦ. φασὶ δέ τινες καὶ ἐν Πανιωνίῳ καὶ ἐν
41 Κορίνθῳ καὶ ἐν Δελφοῖς συνελθεῖν αὐτούς. δια-
φωνοῦνται δὲ καὶ αἱ ἀποφάσεις αὐτῶν καὶ ἄλλου
ἄλλο φασίν, ὡς ἐκεῖνο·

ἦν Λακεδαιμόνιος Χίλων σοφός, ὃς τάδ' ἔλεξε·
'' μηδὲν ἄγαν· καιρῷ πάντα πρόσεστι καλά.''

στασιάζεται δὲ καὶ περὶ τοῦ ἀριθμοῦ αὐτῶν.
Μαιάνδριος μὲν γὰρ ἀντὶ Κλεοβούλου καὶ Μύσωνος
Λεώφαντον Γοργιάδα, Λεβέδιον ἢ Ἐφέσιον, ἐγ-
κρίνει καὶ Ἐπιμενίδην τὸν Κρῆτα· Πλάτων δὲ ἐν
Πρωταγόρᾳ Μύσωνα ἀντὶ Περιάνδρου· Ἔφορος
δὲ ἀντὶ Μύσωνος Ἀνάχαρσιν· οἱ δὲ καὶ Πυθαγόραν
προσγράφουσιν. Δικαίαρχος δὲ τέσσαρας ὡμολο-
γημένους ἡμῖν παραδίδωσι, Θαλῆν, Βίαντα, Πιττακόν, Σόλωνα. ἄλλους δὲ ὀνομάζει ἕξ, ὧν ἐκλέξασθαι τρεῖς, Ἀριστόδημον, Πάμφυλον, Χίλωνα
Λακεδαιμόνιον, Κλεόβουλον, Ἀνάχαρσιν, Περίανδρον. ἔνιοι προστιθέασιν Ἀκουσίλαον Κάβα ἢ
42 Σκάβρα Ἀργεῖον. Ἕρμιππος δ' ἐν τῷ Περὶ
τῶν σοφῶν ἑπτακαίδεκά φησιν, ὧν τοὺς ἑπτὰ
ἄλλους ἄλλως αἱρεῖσθαι· εἶναι δὲ Σόλωνα, Θαλῆν,
Πιττακόν, Βίαντα, Χίλωνα, ‹Μύσωνα›, Κλεό-

---

* The opinion of Dicaearchus thus expressed is correct.
With the exception of Thales, no one whose life is contained
in Book I. has any claim to be styled a philosopher. The
tradition of the Seven Wise Men and of their meeting at
some court, whether of a native tyrant like Periander
or of a foreign prince like Croesus, was used by Plato
(*Protag.* 343 A) and, largely through his influence, grew into

shrewd men with a turn for legislation.[a] Archetimus
of Syracuse describes their meeting at the court of
Cypselus, on which occasion he himself happened to
be present ; for which Ephorus substitutes a meeting
without Thales at the court of Croesus. Some make
them meet at the Pan-Ionian festival, at Corinth,
and at Delphi. Their utterances are variously reported, and are attributed now to one now to the
other, for instance the following [b] :

> Chilon of Lacedaemon's words are true :
> Nothing too much ; good comes from measure due.

Nor is there any agreement how the number is made
up ; for Maeandrius, in place of Cleobulus and Myson,
includes Leophantus, son of Gorgiadas, of Lebedus
or Ephesus, and Epimenides the Cretan in the list ;
Plato in his *Protagoras* admits Myson and leaves
out Periander ; Ephorus substitutes Anacharsis
for Myson ; others add Pythagoras to the Seven.
Dicaearchus hands down four names fully recognized :
Thales, Bias, Pittacus and Solon ; and appends the
names of six others, from whom he selects three :
Aristodemus, Pamphylus, Chilon the Lacedaemonian,
Cleobulus, Anacharsis, Periander. Others add Acusilaus, son of Cabas or Scabras, of Argos. Hermippus
in his work *On the Sages* reckons seventeen, from
which number different people make different selec-
tions of seven. They are : Solon, Thales, Pittacus,
Bias, Chilon, Myson, Cleobulus, Periander, Ana-

---

[a] romantic legend, the result being late biographies, collections of apophthegms, and letters attributed to various
authors, *e.g.* the apophthegms of Demetrius of Phalerum.
Diogenes Laertius swallows all this as true ; modern criticism
rejects it all as forgery.
[b] *Anth. Plan.* iv. 22.

βουλον, Περίανδρον, Ἀνάχαρσιν, Ἀκουσίλαον,
Ἐπιμενίδην, Λεώφαντον, Φερεκύδην, Ἀριστόδη-
μον, Πυθαγόραν, Λᾶσον Χαρμαντίδου ἢ Σισυμ-
βρίνου, ἢ ὡς Ἀριστόξενος Χαβρίνου, Ἑρμιονέα,
Ἀναξαγόραν. Ἱππόβοτος δὲ ἐν τῇ Τῶν φιλοσόφων
ἀναγραφῇ· Ὀρφέα, Λίνον, Σόλωνα, Περίανδρον,
Ἀνάχαρσιν, Κλεόβουλον, Μύσωνα, Θαλῆν Βίαντα,
Πιττακόν, Ἐπίχαρμον, Πυθαγόραν.

Φέρονται δὲ καὶ τοῦ Θαλοῦ ἐπιστολαὶ αἵδε·

Θαλῆς Φερεκύδει

43 " Πυνθάνομαί σε πρῶτον Ἰώνων μέλλειν λόγους
ἀμφὶ τῶν θείων χρημάτων ἐς τοὺς Ἕλληνας
φαίνειν. καὶ τάχα μὲν ἡ γνώμη τοι δικαίη ἐς τὸ
ξυνὸν καταθέσθαι γραφὴν ἢ ἐφ᾽ ὁποιοισοῦν ἐπι-
τρέπειν χρῆμα ἐς οὐδὲν ὄφελος. εἰ δή τοι ἥδιον,
ἐθέλω γενέσθαι λεσχηνευτὴς περὶ ὅτέων γράφεις·
καὶ ἢν κελεύῃς, παρὰ σὲ ἀφίξομαι ἐς Σῦρον. ἢ
γὰρ ἂν οὐ φρενήρεες εἴημεν ἐγώ τε καὶ Σόλων
ὁ Ἀθηναῖος, εἰ πλώσαντες μὲν ἐς Κρήτην κατὰ τὴν
τῶν κεῖθι ἱστορίην, πλώσαντες δὲ ἐς Αἴγυπτον
ὁμιλήσοντες τοῖς ἐκεῖ ὅσοι ἱερέες τε καὶ ἀστρο-
λόγοι, παρὰ σὲ δὲ μὴ [πλώσαιμεν]. ἥξει γὰρ
44 καὶ ὁ Σόλων, ἢν ἐπιτρέπῃς. σὺ μέντοι χωρο-
φιλέων ὀλίγα φοιτέεις ἐς Ἰωνίην, οὐδέ σε ποθὴ
ἴσχει ἀνδρῶν ξείνων· ἀλλά, ὡς ἔλπομαι, ἑνὶ μούνῳ
χρήματι πρόσκεαι τῇ γραφῇ. ἡμέες δὲ οἱ μηδὲν
γράφοντες περιχωρέομεν τήν τε Ἑλλάδα καὶ
Ἀσίην."

44

charsis, Acusilaus, Epimenides, Leophantus, Phere-
cydes, Aristodemus, Pythagoras, Lasos, son of
Charmantides or Sisymbrinus, or, according to
Aristoxenus, of Chabrinus, born at Hermione, Anax-
agoras. Hippobotus in his *List of Philosophers*
enumerates : Orpheus, Linus, Solon, Periander,
Anacharsis, Cleobulus, Myson, Thales, Bias, Pittacus,
Epicharmus, Pythagoras.

Here follow the extant letters of Thales.

Thales to Pherecydes

" I hear that you intend to be the first Ionian to
expound theology to the Greeks. And perhaps it
was a wise decision to make the book common property without taking advice, instead of entrusting it
to any particular persons whatsoever, a course which
has no advantages. However, if it would give you
any pleasure, I am quite willing to discuss the subject of your book with you ; and if you bid me
come to Syros I will do so. For surely Solon of
Athens and I would scarcely be sane if, after having
sailed to Crete to pursue our inquiries there, and
to Egypt to confer with the priests and astronomers,
we hesitated to come to you. For Solon too will
come, with your permission. You, however, are so
fond of home that you seldom visit Ionia and have
no longing to see strangers, but, as I hope, apply
yourself to one thing, namely writing, while we,
who never write anything, travel all over Hellas
and Asia."

Θαλῆς Σόλωνι

" Ὑπαποστὰς ἐξ Ἀθηνέων δοκέεις ἄν μοι ἁρμο-
διώτατα ἐν Μιλήτῳ οἶκον ποιέεσθαι παρὰ τοῖς
ἀποίκοις ὑμέων· καὶ γὰρ ἐνθαῦτά τοι δεινὸν οὐδέν.
εἰ δὲ ἀσχαλήσεις ὅτι καὶ Μιλήσιοι τυραννεόμεθα—
ἐχθαίρεις γὰρ πάντας αἰσυμνήτας—ἀλλὰ τέρποι᾽
ἂν σὺν τοῖς ἑτάροις ἡμῖν καταβιούς. ἐπέστειλε
δέ τοι καὶ Βίης ἥκειν ἐς Πριήνην· σὺ δὲ εἰ προσ-
ηνέστερόν τοι τὸ Πριηνέων ἄστυ, κεῖθι οἰκέειν,
καὶ αὐτοὶ παρὰ σὲ οἰκήσομεν."

Κεφ. β΄. ΣΟΛΩΝ

45 Σόλων Ἐξηκεστίδου Σαλαμίνιος πρῶτον μὲν
τὴν σεισάχθειαν εἰσηγήσατο Ἀθηναίοις· τὸ δὲ ἦν
λύτρωσις σωμάτων τε καὶ κτημάτων. καὶ γὰρ
ἐπὶ σώμασιν ἐδανείζοντο καὶ πολλοὶ δι᾽ ἀπορίαν
ἐθήτευον. ἑπτὰ δὴ ταλάντων ὀφειλομένων αὐτῷ
πατρῴων συνεχώρησε πρῶτος καὶ τοὺς λοιποὺς τὸ
ὅμοιον προὔτρεψε πρᾶξαι. καὶ οὗτος ὁ νόμος
ἐκλήθη σεισάχθεια· φανερὸν δὲ διὰ τί.
    Ἔπειτα τοὺς λοιποὺς νόμους ἔθηκεν, οὓς μακρὸν
ἂν εἴη διεξιέναι, καὶ ἐς τοὺς ἄξονας κατέθετο.

46 Τὸ δὲ μέγιστον, τῆς πατρίδος αὐτοῦ [Σαλαμῖνος]
ἀμφισβητουμένης ὑπό τε Ἀθηναίων καὶ Μεγαρέων
καὶ πολλάκις τῶν Ἀθηναίων ἐπταικότων ἐν τοῖς
πολέμοις καὶ ψηφισαμένων εἴ τις ἔτι συμβουλεύσοι
περὶ Σαλαμῖνος μάχεσθαι, θανάτῳ ζημιοῦσθαι, οὗτος
μαίνεσθαι προσποιησάμενος καὶ στεφανωσάμενος
εἰσέπαισεν εἰς τὴν ἀγοράν· ἔνθα τοῖς Ἀθηναίοις
ἀνέγνω διὰ κήρυκος τὰ συντείνοντα περὶ Σαλα-

Thales to Solon

" If you leave Athens, it seems to me that you could most conveniently set up your abode at Miletus, which is an Athenian colony ; for there you incur no risk. If you are vexed at the thought that we are governed by a tyrant, hating as you do all absolute rulers, you would at least enjoy the society of your friends. Bias wrote inviting you to Priene ; and if you prefer the town of Priene for a residence, I myself will come and live with you."

CHAPTER 2. SOLON (archon 594 B.C.)

Solon, the son of Execestides, was born at Salamis. His first achievement was the σεισάχθεια or Law of Release, which he introduced at Athens ; its effect was to ransom persons and property. For men used to borrow money on personal security, and many were forced from poverty to become serfs or day-labourers. He then first renounced his claim to a debt of seven talents due to his father, and encouraged others to follow his example. This law of his was called σεισάχθεια, and the reason is obvious.

He next went on to frame the rest of his laws, which would take time to enumerate, and inscribed them on the revolving pillars.

His greatest service was this : Megara and Athens laid rival claims to his birthplace Salamis, and after many defeats the Athenians passed a decree punishing with death any man who should propose a renewal of the Salaminian war. Solon, feigning madness, rushed into the Agora with a garland on his head ; there he had his poem on Salamis read to

μῖνος ἐλεγεῖα καὶ παρώρμησεν αὐτούς. καὶ αὖθις
πρὸς τοὺς Μεγαρέας ἐπολέμησαν καὶ ἐνίκων διὰ
47 Σόλωνα. ἦν δὲ τὰ ἐλεγεῖα τὰ μάλιστα καθ-
αψάμενα τῶν Ἀθηναίων τάδε·

εἴην δὴ τότ' ἐγὼ Φολεγάνδριος ἢ Σικινίτης
ἀντί γ' Ἀθηναίου, πατρίδ' ἀμειψάμενος.
αἶψα γὰρ ἂν φάτις ἥδε μετ' ἀνθρώποισι γένοιτο·
Ἀττικὸς οὗτος ἀνὴρ τῶν Σαλαμιναφετῶν.

εἶτα·

ἴομεν εἰς Σαλαμῖνα μαχησόμενοι περὶ νήσου
ἱμερτῆς χαλεπόν τ' αἶσχος ἀπωσόμενοι.

ἔπεισε δὲ αὐτοὺς καὶ τὴν ἐν Θρᾴκῃ Χερρόνησον
48 προσκτήσασθαι. ἵνα δὲ μὴ δοκοίη βίᾳ μόνον,
ἀλλὰ καὶ δίκῃ τὴν Σαλαμῖνα κεκτῆσθαι, ἀνασκάψας
τινὰς τάφους ἔδειξε τοὺς νεκροὺς πρὸς ἀνατολὰς
ἐστραμμένους, ὡς ἦν ἔθος θάπτειν Ἀθηναίοις·
ἀλλὰ καὶ αὐτοὺς τοὺς τάφους πρὸς ἕω βλέποντας
καὶ ἀπὸ τῶν δήμων τοὺς χρηματισμοὺς ἐγκεχα-
ραγμένους, ὅπερ ἦν ἴδιον Ἀθηναίων. ἔνιοι δέ
φασι καὶ ἐγγράψαι αὐτὸν εἰς τὸν κατάλογον τοῦ
Ὁμήρου μετὰ τὸν

Αἴας δ' ἐκ Σαλαμῖνος ἄγεν δυοκαίδεκα νῆας—

στῆσε δ' ἄγων, ἵν' Ἀθηναίων ἵσταντο φάλαγγες.

49 Τοῦ δὴ λοιποῦ προσεῖχον αὐτῷ ὁ δῆμος καὶ ἡδέως

ᵃ Fr. 2 Bergk. ᵇ Ib. 3.
ᶜ If these words are pressed, they contradict the precise
statement in Plutarch's *Life of Solon* (c. 10) that the
Athenians buried their dead to face the setting sun; *cf.*
Aelian, *Var. Hist.* v. 14. The Mycenaean graves with two
exceptions showed the dead with their heads to the east and

the Athenians by the herald and roused them to
fury. They renewed the war with the Megarians
and, thanks to Solon, were victorious. These were
the lines which did more than anything else to
inflame the Athenians [a]:

> Would I were citizen of some mean isle
> Far in the Sporades! For men shall smile
> And mock me for Athenian: " Who is this?"
> " An Attic slave who gave up Salamis ";

and [b]

> Then let us fight for Salamis and fair fame,
> Win the beloved isle, and purge our shame!

He also persuaded the Athenians to acquire the
Thracian Chersonese. And lest it should be thought
that he had acquired Salamis by force only and not
of right, he opened certain graves and showed that
the dead were buried with their faces to the east,
as was the custom of burial among the Athenians;
further, that the tombs themselves faced the east,[c]
and that the inscriptions graven upon them named
the deceased by their demes, which is a style peculiar
to Athens. Some authors assert that in Homer's
catalogue of the ships after the line [d]:

> Ajax twelve ships from Salamis commands,

Solon inserted one of his own:

> And fixed their station next the Athenian bands.

Thereafter the people looked up to him, and
their feet to the west. Sir W. Ridgeway (*Early Age of
Greece*, c. 7) assumes that Plutarch and Aelian are right
and Diogenes either mistaken or inaccurate in his mode of
expression. A view has been put forward that there was no
uniform orientation in early times (see H. J. Rose, *Classical
Review*, xxxiv. p. 141 *sq.*).

[d] *Il.* ii. 557.

κἂν τυραννεῖσθαι ἤθελον πρὸς αὐτοῦ· ὁ δ' οὐχ
εἴλετο, ἀλλὰ καὶ Πεισίστρατον τὸν συγγενῆ, καθά
φησι Σωσικράτης, προαισθόμενος τὸ ἐφ' ἑαυτῷ
διεκώλυσεν. ᾄξας γὰρ εἰς τὴν ἐκκλησίαν μετὰ
δόρατος καὶ ἀσπίδος προεῖπεν αὐτοῖς τὴν ἐπίθεσιν
τοῦ Πεισιστράτου· καὶ οὐ μόνον, ἀλλὰ καὶ βοηθεῖν
ἕτοιμος εἶναι, λέγων ταῦτα· " ἄνδρες Ἀθηναῖοι,
τῶν μὲν σοφώτερος, τῶν δὲ ἀνδρειότερός εἰμι·
σοφώτερος μὲν τῶν τὴν ἀπάτην τοῦ Πεισιστράτου
μὴ συνιέντων, ἀνδρειότερος δὲ τῶν ἐπισταμένων
μέν, διὰ δέος δὲ σιωπώντων." καὶ ἡ βουλή,
Πεισιστρατίδαι ὄντες, μαίνεσθαι ἔλεγον αὐτόν·
ὅθεν εἶπε ταυτί·

δείξει δὴ μανίην μὲν ἐμὴν βαιὸς χρόνος ἀστοῖς,
δείξει, ἀληθείης ἐς μέσον ἐρχομένης.

50 τὰ δὲ περὶ τῆς τοῦ Πεισιστράτου τυραννίδος
ἐλεγεῖα προλέγοντος αὐτοῦ ταῦτα ἦν·

ἐκ νεφέλης φέρεται χιόνος μένος ἠδὲ χαλάζης·
βροντή τ' ἐκ λαμπρῆς γίγνεται ἀστεροπῆς·
ἀνδρῶν δ' ἐκ μεγάλων πόλις ὄλλυται· ἐς δὲ μονάρχου
δῆμος ἀϊδρίῃ δουλοσύνην ἔπεσεν.

Ἤδη δὲ αὐτοῦ κρατοῦντος οὐ πείθων ἔθηκε τὰ
ὅπλα πρὸ τοῦ στρατηγείου καὶ εἰπών, " ὦ πατρίς,
βεβοήθηκά σοι καὶ λόγῳ καὶ ἔργῳ," ἀπέπλευσεν
εἰς Αἴγυπτον καὶ εἰς Κύπρον, καὶ πρὸς Κροῖσον
ἦλθεν. ὅτε καὶ ἐρωτηθεὶς ὑπ' αὐτοῦ, " τίς σοι
δοκεῖ εὐδαίμων;" " Τέλλος," ἔφη, " Ἀθηναῖος
καὶ Κλέοβις καὶ Βίτων" καὶ τὰ θρυλούμενα.

would gladly have had him rule them as tyrant ; he refused, and, early perceiving the designs of his kinsman Pisistratus (so we are told by Sosicrates), did his best to hinder them. He rushed into the Assembly armed with spear and shield, warned them of the designs of Pisistratus, and not only so, but declared his willingness to render assistance, in these words : " Men of Athens, I am wiser than some of you and more courageous than others : wiser than those who fail to understand the plot of Pisistratus, more courageous than those who, though they see through it, keep silence through fear." And the members of the council, who were of Pisistratus' party, declared that he was mad : which made him say the lines [a] :

> A little while, and the event will show
> To all the world if I be mad or no.

That he foresaw the tyranny of Pisistratus is proved by a passage from a poem of his [b] :

> On splendid lightning thunder follows straight,
> Clouds the soft snow and flashing hail-stones bring ;
> So from proud men comes ruin, and their state
> Falls unaware to slavery and a king.

When Pisistratus was already established, Solon, unable to move the people, piled his arms in front of the generals' quarters, and exclaimed, " My country, I have served thee with my word and sword ! " Thereupon he sailed to Egypt and to Cyprus, and thence proceeded to the court of Croesus. There Croesus put the question, " Whom do you consider happy ? " and Solon replied, " Tellus of Athens, and Cleobis and Biton," and went on in words too familiar to be quoted here.

[a] Fr. 10 Bergk.   [b] Fr. 9 Bergk.

51 Φασὶ δέ τινες ὅτι κοσμήσας ἑαυτὸν ὁ Κροῖσος
παντοδαπῶς καὶ καθίσας εἰς τὸν θρόνον ἤρετο αὐτὸν
εἴ τι θέαμα κάλλιον τεθέαται· ὁ δέ '' ἀλεκτρυόνας,
εἶπε, καὶ φασιανοὺς καὶ ταῶς· φυσικῷ γὰρ ἄνθει
κεκόσμηνται καὶ μυρίῳ καλλίονι.'' ἐκεῖθέν τε
ἀπαλλαγεὶς ἐγένετο ἐν Κιλικίᾳ, καὶ πόλιν συν-
ῴκισεν ἣν ἀπ' αὐτοῦ Σόλους ἐκάλεσεν· ὀλίγους τέ
τινας τῶν Ἀθηναίων ἐγκατῴκισεν, οἳ τῷ χρόνῳ
τὴν φωνὴν ἀποξενωθέντες σολοικίζειν ἐλέχθησαν.
καὶ εἰσιν οἱ μὲν ἔνθεν Σολεῖς, οἱ δ' ἀπὸ Κύπρου
Σόλιοι. ὅτε δὲ τὸν Πεισίστρατον ἔμαθεν ἤδη
τυραννεῖν, τάδε ἔγραψε πρὸς τοὺς Ἀθηναίους·

52 εἰ δὲ πεπόνθατε δεινὰ δι' ὑμετέρην κακότητα,
    μή τι θεοῖς τούτων μοῖραν ἐπαμφέρετε.
    αὐτοὶ γὰρ τούτους ηὐξήσατε, ῥύσια δόντες,
    καὶ διὰ ταῦτα κακὴν ἴσχετε δουλοσύνην.
    ὑμέων δ' εἷς μὲν ἕκαστος ἀλώπεκος ἴχνεσι βαίνει,
    σύμπασιν δ' ὑμῖν κοῦφος ἔνεστι νόος.
    εἰς γὰρ γλῶσσαν ὁρᾶτε καὶ εἰς ἔπη αἱμύλου ἀνδρός,
    εἰς ἔργον δ' οὐδὲν γιγνόμενον βλέπετε.

καὶ οὗτος μὲν ταῦτα. Πεισίστρατος δ' αὐτῷ
φεύγοντι τοῦτον ἐπέστειλε τὸν τρόπον·

Πεισίστρατος Σόλωνι

53 '' Οὔτε μόνος Ἑλλήνων τυραννίδι ἐπεθέμην, οὔτε
οὐ προσῆκόν μοι, γένους ὄντι τῶν Κοδριδῶν.
ἀνέλαβον γὰρ ἐγὼ ἃ ὀμόσαντες Ἀθηναῖοι παρέξειν
Κόδρῳ τε καὶ τῷ ἐκείνου γένει, ἀφείλοντο. τά
τε ἄλλα ἁμαρτάνω οὐδὲν ἢ περὶ θεοὺς ἢ περὶ ἀν-
θρώπους· ἀλλὰ καθότι σὺ διέθηκας τοὺς θεσμοὺς

I. 51–53. SOLON

There is a story that Croesus in magnificent array sat himself down on his throne and asked Solon if he had ever seen anything more beautiful. " Yes," was the reply, " cocks and pheasants and peacocks ; for they shine in nature's colours, which are ten thousand times more beautiful." After leaving that place he lived in Cilicia and founded a city which he called Soli after his own name. In it he settled some few Athenians, who in process of time corrupted the purity of Attic and were said to " solecize." Note that the people of this town are called Solenses, the people of Soli in Cyprus Solii. When he learnt that Pisistratus was by this time tyrant, he wrote to the Athenians on this wise *a* :

If ye have suffered sadly through your own wickedness, lay not the blame for this upon the gods. For it is you yourselves who gave pledges to your foes and made them great ; this is why you bear the brand of slavery. Every one of you treadeth in the footsteps of the fox, yet in the mass ye have little sense. Ye look to the speech and fair words of a flatterer, paying no regard to any practical result.

Thus Solon. After he had gone into exile Pisistratus wrote to him as follows :

Pisistratus to Solon

" I am not the only man who has aimed at a tyranny in Greece, nor am I, a descendant of Codrus, unfitted for the part. That is, I resume the privileges which the Athenians swore to confer upon Codrus and his family, although later they took them away. In everything else I commit no offence against God or man ; but I leave to the Athenians the management

a Fr. 11 Bergk.

'Αθηναίοις, ἐπιτρέπω πολιτεύειν. καὶ ἄμεινόν γε
πολιτεύουσιν ἢ κατὰ δημοκρατίαν· οὐκ ἐῶ γὰρ
οὐδένα ὑβρίζειν· καὶ ὁ τύραννος ἐγὼ οὐ πλέον τι
φέρομαι τἀξιώματος καὶ τῆς τιμῆς· ὁποῖα δὲ καὶ
τοῖς πρόσθεν βασιλεῦσιν ἦν τὰ ῥητὰ γέρα. ἀπάγει
δὲ ἕκαστος 'Αθηναίων τοῦ αὐτοῦ κλήρου δεκάτην,
οὐκ ἐμοί, ἀλλ' ὁπόθεν ἔσται ἀναλοῦν εἴς τε θυσίας
δημοτελεῖς καὶ εἴ τι ἄλλο τῶν κοινῶν καὶ ἢν [ὁ]
πόλεμος ἡμᾶς καταλάβῃ.

54 " Σοὶ δ' ἐγὼ οὔτι μέμφομαι μηνύσαντι τὴν ἐμὴν
διάνοιαν. εὐνοίᾳ γὰρ τῆς πόλεως μᾶλλον ἢ κατὰ
τὸ ἐμὸν ἔχθος ἐμήνυες· ἔτι τε ἀμαθίᾳ τῆς ἀρχῆς,
ὁποίαν τινὰ ἐγὼ καταστήσομαι. ἐπεὶ μαθὼν τάχ'
ἂν ἠνέσχου καθισταμένου, οὐδ' ἔφυγες. ἐπάνιθι
τοίνυν οἴκαδε, πιστεύων μοι καὶ ἀνωμότῳ, ἄχαρι
μηδὲν πείσεσθαι Σόλωνα ἐκ Πεισιστράτου. ἴσθι
γὰρ μηδ' ἄλλον τινὰ πεπονθέναι τῶν ἐμοὶ ἐχθρῶν.
εἰ δὲ ἀξιώσεις τῶν ἐμῶν φίλων εἷς εἶναι, ἔσῃ ἀνὰ
πρώτους· οὐ γάρ τι ἐν σοὶ ἐνορῶ δολερὸν ἢ ἄπιστον·
εἴτε ἄλλως 'Αθήνησιν οἰκεῖν, ἐπιτετράψεται. ἡμῶν
δὲ οὕνεκα μὴ ἐστέρησο τῆς πατρίδος."

55 Ταῦτα μὲν Πεισίστρατος. Σόλων δὲ ὅρον ἀνθρωπίνου βίου φησὶν ἔτη ἑβδομήκοντα.

Δοκεῖ δὲ καὶ κάλλιστα νομοθετῆσαι· ἐάν τις μὴ
τρέφῃ τοὺς γονέας, ἄτιμος ἔστω· ἀλλὰ καὶ ὁ τὰ
πατρῷα κατεδηδοκὼς ὁμοίως. καὶ ὁ ἀργὸς ὑπεύ-

of their affairs according to the ordinances established by you. And they are better governed than they would be under a democracy ; for I allow no one to extend his rights, and though I am tyrant I arrogate to myself no undue share of reputation and honour, but merely such stated privileges as belonged to the kings in former times. Every citizen pays a tithe of his property, not to me but to a fund for defraying the cost of the public sacrifices or any other charges on the State or the expenditure on any war which may come upon us.

"I do not blame you for disclosing my designs ; you acted from loyalty to the city, not through any enmity to me, and further, in ignorance of the sort of rule which I was going to establish ; since, if you had known, you would perhaps have tolerated me and not gone into exile. Wherefore return home, trusting my word, though it be not sworn, that Solon will suffer no harm from Pisistratus. For neither has any other enemy of mine suffered ; of that you may be sure. And if you choose to become one of my friends, you will rank with the foremost, for I see no trace of treachery in you, nothing to excite mistrust ; or if you wish to live at Athens on other terms, you have my permission. But do not on my account sever yourself from your country.

So far Pisistratus. To return to Solon : one of his sayings is that 70 years are the term of man's life.

He seems to have enacted some admirable laws ; for instance, if any man neglects to provide for his parents, he shall be disfranchised ; moreover there is a similar penalty for the spendthrift who runs through his patrimony. Again, not to have a settled

θυνος ἔστω παντὶ τῷ βουλομένῳ γράφεσθαι. Λυσίας
δ' ἐν τῷ κατὰ Νικίου Δράκοντά φησι γεγραφέναι
τὸν νόμον, Σόλωνα δὲ τὸν ἡταιρηκότα εἴργειν τοῦ
βήματος. συνέστειλε δὲ καὶ τὰς τιμὰς τῶν ἐν
ἀγῶσιν ἀθλητῶν, Ὀλυμπιονίκῃ μὲν τάξας πεντακοσίας δραχμάς, Ἰσθμιονίκῃ δὲ ἑκατόν, καὶ ἀνὰ
λόγον ἐπὶ τῶν ἄλλων. ἀπειρόκαλον γὰρ τὸ ἐξ-
αίρειν τὰς τούτων τιμάς, ἀλλὰ μόνων ἐκείνων τῶν
ἐν πολέμοις τελευτησάντων, ὧν καὶ τοὺς υἱοὺς
δημοσίᾳ τρέφεσθαι καὶ παιδεύεσθαι.

56 Ὅθεν καὶ ἐζήλουν πολλοὶ καλοὶ κἀγαθοὶ γίνεσθαι
κατὰ πόλεμον· ὡς Πολύζηλος, ὡς Κυνέγειρος, ὡς
Καλλίμαχος, ὡς σύμπαντες οἱ Μαραθωνομάχοι·
ἔτι τε Ἁρμόδιος καὶ Ἀριστογείτων καὶ Μιλτιάδης
καὶ μυρίοι ὅσοι. ἀθληταὶ δὲ καὶ ἀσκούμενοι πολυ-
δάπανοι, καὶ νικῶντες ἐπιζήμιοι καὶ στεφανοῦνται
κατὰ τῆς πατρίδος μᾶλλον ἢ κατὰ τῶν ἀνταγωνι-
στῶν· γέροντές τε γενόμενοι κατὰ τὸν Εὐριπίδην

τρίβωνες ἐκλιπόντες οἴχονται κρόκας.

ὅπερ συνιδὼν ὁ Σόλων μετρίως αὐτοὺς ἀπεδέξατο.
κάλλιστον δὲ κἀκεῖνο· τὸν ἐπίτροπον τῇ τῶν ὀρφανῶν μητρὶ μὴ συνοικεῖν, μηδ' ἐπιτροπεύειν, εἰς
ὃν ἡ οὐσία ἔρχεται τῶν ὀρφανῶν τελευτησάντων.
57 κἀκεῖνο· δακτυλιογλύφῳ μὴ ἐξεῖναι σφραγῖδα
φυλάττειν τοῦ πραθέντος δακτυλίου· καὶ ἐὰν ἕνα
ὀφθαλμὸν ἔχοντος ἐκκόψῃ τις, ἀντεκκόπτειν τοὺς
δύο. ἃ μὴ ἔθου, μὴ ἀνέλῃ· εἰ δὲ μή, θάνατος ἡ

---

[a] *Autolycus*, Fr. 1, l. 12 Nauck, *T.G.F.*[2], *Eur.* 282.
[b] This censure of athletes recurs Diod. Sic. ix. 2. 3 f. It
was probably a commonplace κεφάλαιον in some earlier life
of Solon.

occupation is made a crime for which any one may, if he pleases, impeach the offender.   Lysias, however, in his speech against Nicias ascribes this law to Draco, and to Solon another depriving open profligates of the right to speak in the Assembly.   He curtailed the honours of athletes who took part in the games, fixing the allowance for an Olympic victor at 500 drachmae, for an Isthmian victor at 100 drachmae, and proportionately in all other cases.   It was in bad taste, he urged, to increase the rewards of these victors, and to ignore the exclusive claims of those who had fallen in battle, whose sons ought, moreover, to be maintained and educated by the State.

The effect of this was that many strove to acquit themselves as gallant soldiers in battle, like Polyzelus, Cynegirus, Callimachus and all who fought at Marathon ; or again like Harmodius and Aristogiton, and Miltiades and thousands more.   Athletes, on the other hand, incur heavy costs while in training, do harm when successful, and are crowned for a victory over their country rather than over their rivals, and when they grow old they, in the words of Euripides,[a]

Are worn threadbare, cloaks that have lost the nap ;

and Solon, perceiving this, treated them with scant respect.[b]   Excellent, too, is his provision that the guardian of an orphan should not marry the mother of his ward, and that the next heir who would succeed on the death of the orphans should be disqualified from acting as their guardian.   Furthermore, that no engraver of seals should be allowed to retain an impression of the ring which he has sold, and that the penalty for depriving a one-eyed man of his single eye should be the loss of the offender's two eyes.   A deposit shall not be removed except by the

57

ζημία. τῷ ἄρχοντι, ἐὰν μεθύων ληφθῇ, θάνατον εἶναι τὴν ζημίαν.

Τά τε Ὁμήρου ἐξ ὑποβολῆς γέγραφε ῥαψῳδεῖσθαι, οἷον ὅπου ὁ πρῶτος ἔληξεν, ἐκεῖθεν ἄρχεσθαι τὸν ἐχόμενον. μᾶλλον οὖν Σόλων Ὅμηρον ἐφώτισεν ἢ Πεισίστρατος, ὥς φησι Διευχίδας ἐν πέμπτῳ Μεγαρικῶν. ἦν δὲ μάλιστα τὰ ἔπη ταυτί· "οἳ δ᾽ ἄρ᾽ Ἀθήνας εἶχον" καὶ τὰ ἑξῆς.

58 Πρῶτος δὲ Σόλων τὴν τριακάδα ἔνην καὶ νέαν ὠνόμασε. καὶ πρῶτος τὴν συναγωγὴν τῶν ἐννέα ἀρχόντων ἐποίησεν εἰς τὸ συνειπεῖν, ὡς Ἀπολλόδωρός φησιν ἐν δευτέρῳ Περὶ νομοθετῶν. ἀλλὰ καὶ τῆς στάσεως γενομένης οὔτε μετὰ τῶν ἐξ ἄστεος, οὔτε μετὰ τῶν πεδιέων, ἀλλ᾽ οὐδὲ μετὰ τῶν παράλων ἐτάχθη.

Ἔλεγε δὲ τὸν μὲν λόγον εἴδωλον εἶναι τῶν ἔργων· βασιλέα δὲ τὸν ἰσχυρότατον τῇ δυνάμει. τοὺς δὲ νόμους τοῖς ἀραχνίοις ὁμοίους· καὶ γὰρ ἐκεῖνα, ἐὰν μὲν ἐμπέσῃ τι κοῦφον καὶ ἀσθενές, στέγειν· ἐὰν δὲ μεῖζον, διακόψαν οἴχεσθαι. ἔφασκέ τε σφραγίζεσθαι τὸν μὲν λόγον σιγῇ, τὴν δὲ 59 σιγὴν καιρῷ. ἔλεγε δὲ τοὺς παρὰ τοῖς τυράννοις δυναμένους παραπλησίους εἶναι ταῖς ψήφοις ταῖς ἐπὶ τῶν λογισμῶν. καὶ γὰρ ἐκείνων ἑκάστην ποτὲ μὲν πλείω σημαίνειν, ποτὲ δὲ ἥττω· καὶ τούτων τοὺς τυράννους ποτὲ μὲν ἕκαστον μέγαν ἄγειν καὶ λαμπρόν, ποτὲ δὲ ἄτιμον. ἐρωτηθεὶς διὰ τί κατὰ πατροκτόνου νόμον οὐκ ἔθηκε,

depositor himself, on pain of death. That the magistrate found intoxicated should be punished with death.

He has provided that the public recitations of Homer shall follow in fixed order [a] : thus the second reciter must begin from the place where the first left off. Hence, as Dieuchidas says in the fifth book of his *Megarian History*, Solon did more than Pisistratus to throw light on Homer. The passage in Homer more particularly referred to is that beginning " Those who dwelt at Athens . . ." [b]

Solon was the first to call the 30th day of the month the Old-and-New day, and to institute meetings of the nine archons for private conference, as stated by Apollodorus in the second book of his work *On Legislators*. When civil strife began, he did not take sides with those in the city, nor with the plain, nor yet with the coast section.

One of his sayings is : Speech is the mirror of action ; and another that the strongest and most capable is king. He compared laws to spiders' webs, which stand firm when any light and yielding object falls upon them, while a larger thing breaks through them and makes off. Secrecy he called the seal of speech, and occasion the seal of secrecy. He used to say that those who had influence with tyrants were like the pebbles employed in calculations ; for, as each of the pebbles represented now a large and now a small number, so the tyrants would treat each one of those about them at one time as great and famous, at another as of no account. On being asked why he had not framed any law against parricide,

---

[a] Or " in succession," though this is rather ἐξ ὑποδοχῆς. In Plato, *Hipparchus* 228 в, the same thing is expressed by ἐξ ὑπολήψεως ἐφεξῆς. [b] *Iliad* ii. 546.

"διὰ τὸ ἀπελπίσαι," ἔφη. πῶς τε ἥκιστ' ἂν
ἀδικοῖεν οἱ ἄνθρωποι, "εἰ ὁμοίως," ἔφη, "ἄχθοιντο
τοῖς ἀδικουμένοις οἱ μὴ ἀδικούμενοι." καὶ "τὸν
μὲν κόρον ὑπὸ τοῦ πλούτου γεννᾶσθαι, τὴν δὲ
ὕβριν ὑπὸ τοῦ κόρου." ἠξίωσέ τε Ἀθηναίους
τὰς ἡμέρας κατὰ σελήνην ἄγειν. καὶ Θέσπιν
ἐκώλυσε τραγῳδίας διδάσκειν, ὡς ἀνωφελῆ τὴν
60 ψευδολογίαν. ὅτ' οὖν Πεισίστρατος ἑαυτὸν κατ-
έτρωσεν, ἐκεῖθεν ἔφη ταῦτα φῦναι. τοῖς τε ἀνθρώποις συνεβούλευσεν, ὥς φησιν Ἀπολλόδωρος ἐν
τῷ Περὶ τῶν φιλοσόφων αἱρέσεων, τάδε· καλο-
κἀγαθίαν ὅρκου πιστοτέραν ἔχε. μὴ ψεύδου. τὰ
σπουδαῖα μελέτα. φίλους μὴ ταχὺ κτῶ· οὓς δ'
ἂν κτήσῃ μὴ ἀποδοκίμαζε. ἄρχε πρῶτον μαθὼν
ἄρχεσθαι. συμβούλευε μὴ τὰ ἥδιστα, ἀλλὰ τὰ
ἄριστα. νοῦν ἡγεμόνα ποιοῦ. μὴ κακοῖς ὁμίλει.
θεοὺς τίμα, γονέας αἰδοῦ. φασὶ δ' αὐτὸν καὶ
Μιμνέρμου γράψαντος,

αἲ γὰρ ἄτερ νούσων τε καὶ ἀργαλέω νμελε-
    δωνέων
ἐξηκονταέτη μοῖρα κίχοι θανάτου,

61 ἐπιτιμῶντα αὐτῷ εἰπεῖν·

ἀλλ' εἴ μοι κἂν νῦν ἔτι πείσεαι, ἔξελε τοῦτον·
μηδὲ μέγαιρ' ὅτι σεῦ λῷον ἐπεφρασάμην·
καὶ μεταποίησον, Λιγυαστάδη, ὧδε δ' ἄειδε·
ὀγδωκονταέτη μοῖρα κίχοι θανάτου.

Τῶν δὲ ᾀδομένων αὐτοῦ ἐστι τάδε·

πεφυλαγμένος ἄνδρα ἕκαστον, ὅρα
μὴ κρυπτὸν ἔχθος ἔχων κραδίῃ,

60

he replied that he hoped it was unnecessary. Asked how crime could most effectually be diminished, he replied, " If it caused as much resentment in those who are not its victims as in those who are," adding, " Wealth breeds satiety, satiety outrage." He required the Athenians to adopt a lunar month. He prohibited Thespis from performing tragedies on the ground that fiction was pernicious. When therefore Pisistratus appeared with self-inflicted wounds, Solon said, " This comes from acting tragedies." His counsel to men in general is stated by Apollodorus in his work on the *Philosophic Sects* as follows : Put more trust in nobility of character than in an oath. Never tell a lie. Pursue worthy aims. Do not be rash to make friends and, when once they are made, do not drop them. Learn to obey before you command. In giving advice seek to help, not to please, your friend. Be led by reason. Shun evil company. Honour the gods, reverence parents. He is also said to have criticized the couplet of Mimnermus :

> Would that by no disease, no cares opprest,
> I in my sixtieth year were laid to rest ;

and to have replied thus [a] :

> Oh take a friend's suggestion, blot the line,
> Grudge not if my invention better thine ;
> Surely a wiser wish were thus expressed,
> At eighty years let me be laid to rest.

Of the songs sung this is attributed to Solon [b] :

Watch every man and see whether, hiding hatred in his

[a] Fr. 20 Bergk.
[b] Fr. 42 Bergk.

φαιδρῷ προσενέπῃ προσώπῳ,
γλῶσσα δέ οἱ διχόμυθος
ἐκ μελανῆς φρενὸς γεγωνῇ.

Γέγραφε δὲ δῆλον μὲν ὅτι τοὺς νόμους, καὶ δημη-
γορίας καὶ εἰς ἑαυτὸν ὑποθήκας, ἐλεγεῖα, καὶ τὰ
περὶ Σαλαμῖνος καὶ τῆς Ἀθηναίων πολιτείας ἔπη
πεντακισχίλια, καὶ ἰάμβους καὶ ἐπῳδούς.

62 Ἐπὶ δὲ τῆς εἰκόνος αὐτοῦ ἐπιγέγραπται τάδε·

ἡ Μήδων ἄδικον παύσασ' ὕβριν, ἥδε Σόλωνα
τόνδε τεκνοῖ Σαλαμὶς θεσμοθέτην ἱερόν.

Ἤκμαζε μὲν οὖν περὶ τὴν τεσσαρακοστὴν ἕκτην
Ὀλυμπιάδα, ἧς τῷ τρίτῳ ἔτει ἦρξεν Ἀθήνησι,
καθά φησι Σωσικράτης· ὅτε καὶ τίθησι τοὺς νόμους.
ἐτελεύτησε δ' ἐν Κύπρῳ βιοὺς ἔτη ὀγδοήκοντα,
τοῦτον ἐπισκήψας τοῖς ἰδίοις τὸν τρόπον, ἀπο-
κομίσαι αὐτοῦ τὰ ὀστᾶ εἰς Σαλαμῖνα καὶ τεφρώσαν-
τας εἰς τὴν χώραν σπεῖραι. ὅθεν καὶ Κρατῖνος
ἐν τοῖς Χείρωσί φησιν, αὐτὸν ποιῶν λέγοντα·

οἰκῶ δὲ νῆσον, ὡς μὲν ἀνθρώπων λόγος,
ἐσπαρμένος κατὰ πᾶσαν Αἴαντος πόλιν.

63 Ἔστι δὲ καὶ ἡμέτερον ἐπίγραμμα ἐν τῇ προειρημένῃ Παμμέτρῳ, ἔνθα καὶ περὶ πάντων τῶν
τελευτησάντων ἐλλογίμων διείλεγμαι παντὶ μέτρῳ
καὶ ῥυθμῷ, ἐπιγράμμασι καὶ μέλεσιν, ἔχον οὕτως·

σῶμα μὲν ἦρε Σόλωνος ἐν ἀλλοδαπῇ Κύπριον πῦρ·
ὀστέ' ἔχει Σαλαμίς, ὧν κόνις ἀστάχυες.
ψυχὴν δ' ἄξονες εὐθὺς ἐς οὐρανὸν ἤγαγον· εὖ γὰρ
θῆκε νόμους ἀστοῖς ἄχθεα κουφότατα.

heart, he speaks with friendly countenance, and his tongue rings with double speech from a dark soul.

He is undoubtedly the author of the laws which bear his name ; of speeches, and of poems in elegiac metre, namely, counsels addressed to himself, on Salamis and on the Athenian constitution, five thousand lines in all, not to mention poems in iambic metre and epodes.

His statue has the following inscription [a] :

> At Salamis, which crushed the Persian might,
> Solon the legislator first saw light.

He flourished, according to Sosicrates, about the 46th Olympiad, in the third year of which he was archon at Athens [b]; it was then that he enacted his laws. He died in Cyprus at the age of eighty. His last injunctions to his relations were on this wise : that they should convey his bones to Salamis and, when they had been reduced to ashes, scatter them over the soil. Hence Cratinus in his play, *The Chirons*, makes him say [c] :

> This is my island home ; my dust, men say,
> Is scattered far and wide o'er Ajax' land.

An epigram of my own is also contained in the collection of *Epigrams in Various Metres* mentioned above, where I have discoursed of all the illustrious dead in all metres and rhythms, in epigrams and lyrics. Here it is [d] :

> Far Cyprian fire his body burnt ; his bones,
> Turned into dust, made grain at Salamis :
> Wheel-like, his pillars bore his soul on high ;
> So light the burden of his laws on men.

---

[a] *Anth. Pal.* vii. 86.   [b] 594 B.C.
[c] Fr. 5 Meineke, *C.G.F.* ii. 149.
[d] *Anth. Pal.* vii. 87.

Ἀπεφθέγξατο δέ, φασί, Μηδὲν ἄγαν. καὶ αὐτόν
φησι Διοσκουρίδης ἐν τοῖς Ἀπομνημονεύμασιν,
ἐπειδὴ δακρύοι τὸν παῖδα τελευτήσαντα, ὃν ἡμεῖς
οὐ παρειλήφαμεν, πρὸς τὸν εἰπόντα, " ἀλλ' οὐδὲν
ἀνύτεις," εἰπεῖν, " δι' αὐτὸ δὲ τοῦτο δακρύω,
ὅτι οὐδὲν ἀνύτω."

Φέρονται δὲ αὐτοῦ καὶ ἐπιστολαὶ αἵδε·

64

Σόλων Περιάνδρῳ

" Ἀπαγγέλλεις μοι πολλούς τοι ἐπιβουλεύειν.
σὺ δὲ εἰ μὲν μέλλεις ἐκποδὼν ἅπαντας ποιήσεσθαι,
οὐκ ἂν φθάνοις. ἐπιβουλεύσειε δ' ἄν τις καὶ
τῶν ἀνυπόπτων, ὁ μὲν δεδιὼς περὶ αὑτῷ, ὁ δὲ
σοῦ καταγνούς, οὐκ ἔσθ' ὅ τι οὐκ ὀρρωδοῦντος·
κἂν τῇ πόλει χάριν κατάθοιτο ἐξευρών, ἣν μὴ
ὕποπτος εἴης. ἄριστον μὲν οὖν ἀπέχεσθαι, ἵνα
τῆς αἰτίας ἀπαλλαγῇς. εἰ δὲ πάντως τυραννη-
τέον, φροντίζειν ὅπως τὴν ἀλλοδαπὴν δύναμιν
μείζονα ἕξεις τῶν ἐν τῇ πόλει, καὶ οὐδεὶς ἔτι τοι
δεινός, μηδὲ σὺ ἐκποδών τινα ποιοῦ."

Σόλων Ἐπιμενίδῃ

" Οὔτε οἱ ἐμοὶ θεσμοὶ ἄρα Ἀθηναίους ἐπιπολὺ
ὀνήσειν ἔμελλον, οὔτε σὺ καθήρας τὴν πόλιν
ὤνησας. τό τε γὰρ θεῖον καὶ οἱ νομοθέται οὐ
καθ' ἑαυτὰ δύνανται ὀνῆσαι τὰς πόλεις, οἱ δὲ ἀεὶ
τὸ πλῆθος ἄγοντες ὅπως ἂν γνώμης ἔχωσιν. οὕτω
δὲ καὶ τὸ θεῖον καὶ οἱ νόμοι, εὖ μὲν ἀγόντων, εἰσὶν
ὠφέλιμοι· κακῶς δὲ [ἀγόντων], οὐδὲν ὠφελοῦσιν.

64

I. 63–64. SOLON

It is said that he was the author of the apophthegm "Nothing too much," *Ne quid nimis*. According to Dioscurides in his *Memorabilia*, when he was weeping for the loss of his son, of whom nothing more is known, and some one said to him, "It is all of no avail," he replied, "That is why I weep, because it is of no avail."

The following letters are attributed to Solon:

Solon to Periander

"You tell me that many are plotting against you. You must lose no time if you want to get rid of them all. A conspirator against you might arise from a quite unexpected quarter, say, one who had fears for his personal safety or one who disliked your timorous dread of anything and everything. He would earn the gratitude of the city who found out that you had no suspicion. The best course would be to resign power, and so be quit of the reproach. But if you must at all hazards remain tyrant, endeavour to make your mercenary force stronger than the forces of the city. Then you have no one to fear, and need not banish any one."

Solon to Epimenides

"It seems that after all I was not to confer much benefit on Athenians by my laws, any more than you by purifying the city. For religion and legislation are not sufficient in themselves to benefit cities; it can only be done by those who lead the multitude in any direction they choose. And so, if things are going well, religion and legislation are beneficial; if not, they are of no avail.

65 "Οὐδ' οἱ ἐμοὶ ἀμείνους εἰσὶ καὶ ὅσα ἐγὼ ἐνο-
μοθέτησα. οἱ δ' ἐπιτρέποντες τὸ ξυνὸν ἔβλα-
πτον, οἳ οὐκ ἐγένοντο ἐμποδὼν Πεισιστράτῳ
ἐπιθέσθαι τυραννίδι. οὐδ' ἐγὼ προλέγων πιστὸς
ἦν. ἐκεῖνος δὲ πιστότερος κολακεύων Ἀθηναίους
ἐμοῦ ἀληθεύοντος. ἐγὼ δὴ θέμενος πρὸ τοῦ
στρατηγείου τὰ ὅπλα εἶπον τῶν μὲν μὴ αἰσθα-
νομένων Πεισίστρατον τυραννησείοντα εἶναι ξυνε-
τώτερος, τῶν δὲ ὀκνούντων ἀμύνεσθαι ἀλκιμώ-
τερος. οἱ δὲ μανίαν Σόλωνος κατεγίγνωσκον.
τελευτῶν δὲ ἐμαρτυράμην, " ὦ πατρίς, οὗτος
μὲν Σόλων ἕτοιμός τοι καὶ λόγῳ καὶ ἔργῳ ἀμύνειν·
τοῖς δ' αὖ καὶ μαίνεσθαι δοκῶ. ὥστε ἄπειμί
τοι ἐκ μέσου ὁ μόνος ἐχθρὸς Πεισιστράτου· οἱ
δὲ καὶ δορυφορούντων αὐτόν εἴ τι βούλονται."
ἴσθι γὰρ τὸν ἄνδρα, ὦ ἑταῖρε, δεινότατα ἁψάμενον
66 τῆς τυραννίδος. ἤρξατο μὲν δημαγωγεῖν· εἶτα δὲ
ἑαυτῷ τραύματα ποιήσας, παρελθὼν ἐπ' Ἡλιαίαν
ἐβόα φάμενος πεπονθέναι ταῦτα ὑπὸ τῶν ἐχθρῶν·
καὶ φύλακας ἠξίου παρασχεῖν οἱ τετρακοσίους
τοὺς νεωτάτους. οἱ δὲ ἀνηκουστήσαντές μου
παρέσχον τοὺς ἄνδρας. οὗτοι δὲ ἦσαν κορυνη-
φόροι. καὶ μετὰ τοῦτο τὸν δῆμον κατέλυσεν.
ἦ μάτην ἔσπευδον ἀπαλλάξαι τοὺς πένητας αὐτῶν
τῆς θητείας, οἵ γε δὴ νῦν ξύμπαντες ἑνὶ δουλεύουσι
Πεισιστράτῳ."

Σόλων Πεισιστράτῳ

" Πιστεύω μηδὲν κακὸν ἐκ σοῦ πείσεσθαι. καὶ
γὰρ πρὸ τῆς τυραννίδος φίλος σοὶ ἦν, καὶ νῦν οὐ

"Nor are my laws nor all my enactments any better; but the popular leaders did the commonwealth harm by permitting licence, and could not hinder Pisistratus from setting up a tyranny. And, when I warned them, they would not believe me. He found more credit when he flattered the people than I when I told them the truth. I laid my arms down before the generals' quarters and told the people that I was wiser than those who did not see that Pisistratus was aiming at tyranny, and more courageous than those who shrank from resisting him. They, however, denounced Solon as mad. And at last I protested : " My country, I, Solon, am ready to defend thee by word and deed ; but some of my countrymen think me mad. Wherefore I will go forth out of their midst as the sole opponent of Pisistratus ; and let them, if they like, become his bodyguard." For you must know, my friend, that he was beyond measure ambitious to be tyrant. He began by being a popular leader ; his next step was to inflict wounds on himself and appear before the court of the Heliaea, crying out that these wounds had been inflicted by his enemies ; and he requested them to give him a guard of 400 young men. And the people without listening to me granted him the men, who were armed with clubs. And after that he destroyed the democracy. It was in vain that I sought to free the poor amongst the Athenians from their condition of serfdom, if now they are all the slaves of one master, Pisistratus."

Solon to Pisistratus

"I am sure that I shall suffer no harm at your hands ; for before you became tyrant I was your

μᾶλλον διάφορος ἢ τῶν ἄλλων τις Ἀθηναίων
ὅτῳ μὴ ἀρέσκει τυραννίς. εἴτε δὲ ὑφ' ἑνὸς ἄρχεσθαι ἄμεινον αὐτοῖς, εἴτε δημοκρατεῖσθαι, πεπεί-
87 σθω ᾗ ἑκάτερος γιγνώσκει. καὶ σὲ φημὶ πάντων
τυράννων εἶναι βέλτιστον. ἐπανήκειν δέ μοι Ἀθήναζε οὐ καλῶς ἔχον ὁρῶ, μή μέ τις μέμψηται,
εἰ διαθεὶς Ἀθηναίοις ἰσοπολιτείαν, καὶ παρὸν
τυραννεῖν αὐτὸς οὐκ ἀξιώσας, νῦν ἐπανελθὼν
ἀρεσκοίμην οἷς σὺ πράσσεις."

Σόλων Κροίσῳ

"'Ἀγαμαί σε τῆς περὶ ἡμᾶς φιλοφροσύνης· καὶ
νὴ τὴν Ἀθηνᾶν, εἰ μὴ περὶ παντός μοι ἦν οἰκεῖν
ἐν δημοκρατίᾳ, ἐδεξάμην ἂν μᾶλλον τὴν δίαιταν
ἔχειν ἐν τῇ παρὰ σοὶ βασιλείᾳ ἢ Ἀθήνησι, τυραν-
νοῦντος βιαίως Πεισιστράτου. ἀλλὰ καὶ ἡδίων
ἡμῖν ἡ βιοτή, ἔνθα πᾶσι τὰ δίκαια καὶ ἴσα. ἀφίξομαι δ' οὖν παρὰ σέ, σπεύδων τοι ξένος γενέσθαι."

Κεφ. γ'. ΧΙΛΩΝ

68 Χίλων Δαμαγήτου Λακεδαιμόνιος. οὗτος ἐποίησεν ἐλεγεῖα εἰς ἔπη διακόσια, καὶ ἔφασκε πρόνοιαν περὶ τοῦ μέλλοντος λογισμῷ καταληπτὴν
εἶναι ἀνδρὸς ἀρετήν. πρός τε τὸν ἀδελφὸν δυσφοροῦντα ὅτι μὴ ἔφορος ἐγένετο, αὐτοῦ ὄντος,
"ἐγὼ μὲν γὰρ ἐπίσταμαι," εἶπεν, "ἀδικεῖσθαι,
σὺ δὲ οὔ." γέγονε δὲ ἔφορος κατὰ τὴν πεντηκοστὴν πέμπτην Ὀλυμπιάδα· Παμφίλη δέ φησι
κατὰ τὴν ἕκτην. καὶ πρῶτον ἔφορον γενέσθαι
ἐπὶ Εὐθυδήμου, ὥς φησι Σωσικράτης. καὶ πρῶ-
68

friend, and now I have no quarrel with you beyond that of every Athenian who disapproves of tyranny. Whether it is better for them to be ruled by one man or to live under a democracy, each of us must decide for himself upon his own judgement. You are, I admit, of all tyrants the best; but I see that it is not well for me to return to Athens. I gave the Athenians equality of civil rights; I refused to become tyrant when I had the opportunity; how then could I escape censure if I were now to return and set my approval on all that you are doing?"

Solon to Croesus

"I admire you for your kindness to me; and, by Athena, if I had not been anxious before all things to live in a democracy, I would rather have fixed my abode in your palace than at Athens, where Pisistratus is setting up a rule of violence. But in truth to live in a place where all have equal rights is more to my liking. However, I will come and see you, for I am eager to make your acquaintance."

CHAPTER 3. CHILON (c. 560 B.C.)

Chilon, son of Damagetas, was a Lacedaemonian. He wrote a poem in elegiac metre some 200 lines in length; and he declared that the excellence of a man is to divine the future so far as it can be grasped by reason. When his brother grumbled that he was not made ephor as Chilon was, the latter replied, " I know how to submit to injustice and you do not." He was made ephor in the 55th Olympiad; Pamphila, however, says the 56th. He first became ephor, according to Sosicrates, in the archonship of Euthy-

τος εἰσηγήσατο ἐφόρους τοῖς βασιλεῦσι παρα-
ζευγνύναι· Σάτυρος δὲ Λυκοῦργον.

Οὗτος, ὥς φησιν Ἡρόδοτος ἐν τῇ πρώτῃ, Ἱππο-
κράτει θυομένῳ ἐν Ὀλυμπίᾳ, τῶν λεβήτων αὐτομάτων ζεσάντων, συνεβούλευσεν ἢ μὴ γῆμαι, ἤ, εἰ
ἔχοι γυναῖκα, ἐκπέμψαι καὶ παῖδας ἀπείπασθαι.
69 φασὶ δ' αὐτὸν καὶ Αἰσώπου[1] πυθέσθαι, ὁ Ζεὺς τί
εἴη ποιῶν· τὸν δὲ φάναι, "τὰ μὲν ὑψηλὰ ταπει-
νῶν, τὰ δὲ ταπεινὰ ὑψῶν." ἐρωτηθεὶς τίνι διαφέρουσιν οἱ πεπαιδευμένοι τῶν ἀπαιδεύτων, ἔφη,
"ἐλπίσιν ἀγαθαῖς." τί δύσκολον, "τὸ τὰ ἀπόρρητα σιωπῆσαι, καὶ σχολὴν εὖ διαθέσθαι, καὶ
ἀδικούμενον [δύνασθαι] φέρειν." προσέταττε δὲ
καὶ ταῦτα· γλώττης κρατεῖν, καὶ μάλιστα ἐν
συμποσίῳ. μὴ κακολογεῖν τοὺς πλησίον· εἰ δὲ
70 μή, ἀκούσεσθαι ἐφ' οἷς λυπήσεσθαι. μὴ ἀπει-
λεῖν μηδενί· γυναικῶδες γάρ. ταχύτερον ἐπὶ τὰς
ἀτυχίας τῶν φίλων ἢ ἐπὶ τὰς εὐτυχίας πορεύεσθαι.
γάμον εὐτελῆ ποιεῖσθαι. τὸν τεθνηκότα μὴ κακολογεῖν. γῆρας τιμᾶν. φυλάττειν ἑαυτόν. ζημίαν
αἱρεῖσθαι μᾶλλον ἢ κέρδος αἰσχρόν· ἡ μὲν γὰρ
ἅπαξ ἐλύπησε, τὸ δὲ διὰ παντός. ἀτυχοῦντι μὴ
ἐπεγγελᾶν. ἰσχυρὸν ὄντα πρᾷον εἶναι, ὅπως οἱ
πλησίον αἰδῶνται μᾶλλον ἢ φοβῶνται. μανθάνειν
τῆς αὑτοῦ οἰκίας καλῶς προστατεῖν. τὴν γλῶτταν
μὴ προτρέχειν τοῦ νοῦ. θυμοῦ κρατεῖν. μαντικὴν

_____

[1] αὑτοῦ . . . Αἴσωπον Reiske.

_____

[a] There seems to be some confusion in these extracts.
Possibly Diogenes Laertius found among his materials some
such note as this: Χίλων τῶν ἑπτὰ σοφῶν πρῶτος ἔφορος,
and connected it with the date as given by Sosicrates,

demus. He first proposed the appointment of ephors as auxiliaries to the kings, though Satyrus says this was done by Lycurgus.[a]

As Herodotus relates in his first Book, when Hippocrates was sacrificing at Olympia and his cauldrons boiled of their own accord, it was Chilon who advised him not to marry, or, if he had a wife, to divorce her and disown his children. The tale is also told that he inquired of Aesop what Zeus was doing and received the answer : " He is humbling the proud and exalting the humble." Being asked wherein lies the difference between the educated and the uneducated, Chilon answered, " In good hope." What is hard ? " To keep a secret, to employ leisure well, to be able to bear an injury." These again are some of his precepts : To control the tongue, especially at a banquet. Not to abuse our neighbours, for if you do, things will be said about you which you will regret. Do not use threats to any one ; for that is womanish. Be more ready to visit friends in adversity than in prosperity. Do not make an extravagant marriage. *De mortuis nil nisi bonum.* Honour old age. Consult your own safety. Prefer a loss to a dishonest gain : the one brings pain at the moment, the other for all time. Do not laugh at another's misfortune. When strong, be merciful, if you would have the respect, not the fear, of your neighbours. Learn to be a wise master in your own house. Let not your tongue outrun your thought. Control anger. Do not hate divina-

namely, the archonship of Euthydemus, meticulously correcting this date from Pamphila. But he seems to have mistaken the meaning of πρῶτος ἔφορος and to have rashly inferred from it that it was Chilon who introduced the ephorate.

μὴ ἐχθαίρειν. μὴ ἐπιθυμεῖν ἀδυνάτων. ἐν ὁδῷ
μὴ σπεύδειν. λέγοντα μὴ κινεῖν τὴν χεῖρα· μα-
νικὸν γάρ. νόμοις πείθεσθαι. ἡρεμίᾳ χρῆσθαι.

71 Τῶν δὲ ᾀδομένων αὐτοῦ μάλιστα εὐδοκίμησεν
ἐκεῖνο· '' ἐν λιθίναις ἀκόναις ὁ χρυσὸς ἐξετάζεται,
διδοὺς βάσανον φανεράν· ἐν δὲ χρυσῷ ἀνδρῶν
ἀγαθῶν τε κακῶν τε νοῦς ἔδωκ' ἔλεγχον.'' φασὶ
δ' αὐτόν ποτε γηραιὸν ἤδη ὄντα εἰπεῖν, ὡς οὐδὲν
συνειδείη ἄνομον ἑαυτῷ ἐν τῷ βίῳ· διστάζειν
δὲ περὶ ἑνός. κρίνων γάρ ποτε φίλῳ δίκην αὐτὸς
μὲν κατὰ τὸν νόμον, τὸν δὲ φίλον πείσειεν ἀπο-
δικάσαι αὐτοῦ, ἵνα ἀμφότερα καὶ τὸν νόμον καὶ
τὸν φίλον τηρήσαι.

Ἐνδοξότατος δὲ μάλιστα παρὰ τοῖς Ἕλλησιν
ἐγένετο προειπὼν περὶ Κυθήρων τῆς νήσου τῆς
Λακωνικῆς. καταμαθὼν γὰρ τὴν φύσιν αὐτῆς,
'' εἴθε,'' ἔφη, '' μὴ ἐγεγόνει, ἢ γενομένη κατ-
72 εβυθίσθη.'' καὶ εὖ προὐνοήσατο. Δημάρατος μὲν
γὰρ φυγὰς ὢν Λακεδαιμονίων Ξέρξῃ συνεβούλευσε
τὰς ναῦς συνέχειν ἐν τῇ νήσῳ· κἂν ἑαλώκει ἡ
Ἑλλάς, εἰ ἐπείσθη Ξέρξης. ὕστερόν τε Νικίας
ἐπὶ τῶν Πελοποννησιακῶν καταστρεψάμενος τὴν
νῆσον, φρουρὰν ἐγκατέστησεν Ἀθηναίων, καὶ πάμ-
πολλα τοὺς Λακεδαιμονίους κακὰ διέθηκε.

Βραχυλόγος τε ἦν· ὅθεν καὶ Ἀρισταγόρας ὁ
Μιλήσιος τοῦτον τὸν τρόπον Χιλώνειον καλεῖ.
. . . Βράγχου δὲ εἶναι, ὃς τὸ ἱερὸν ἔκτισε τὸ ἐν
Βραγχίδαις. ἦν δὲ γέρων περὶ τὴν πεντηκοστὴν
δευτέραν Ὀλυμπιάδα, ὅτε Αἴσωπος ὁ λογοποιὸς

tion. Do not aim at impossibilities. Let no one see you in a hurry. Gesticulation in speaking should be avoided as a mark of insanity. Obey the laws. Be restful.

Of his songs the most popular is the following: "By the whetstone gold is tried, giving manifest proof; and by gold is the mind of good and evil men brought to the test." He is reported to have said in his old age that he was not aware of having ever broken the law throughout his life; but on one point he was not quite clear. In a suit in which a friend of his was concerned he himself pronounced sentence according to the law, but he persuaded his colleague who was his friend to acquit the accused, in order at once to maintain the law and yet not to lose his friend.

He became very famous in Greece by his warning about the island of Cythera off the Laconian coast. For, becoming acquainted with the nature of the island, he exclaimed: "Would it had never been placed there, or else had been sunk in the depths of the sea." And this was a wise warning; for Demaratus, when an exile from Sparta, advised Xerxes to anchor his fleet off the island; and if Xerxes had taken the advice Greece would have been conquered. Later, in the Peloponnesian war, Nicias reduced the island and placed an Athenian garrison there, and did the Lacedaemonians much mischief.

He was a man of few words; hence Aristagoras of Miletus calls this style of speaking Chilonean. . . . is of Branchus, founder of the temple at Branchidae. Chilon was an old man about the 52nd Olympiad, when Aesop the fabulist was flourishing. According

ἤκμαζεν. ἐτελεύτησε δ', ὥς φησιν Ἕρμιππος, ἐν
Πίσῃ, τὸν υἱὸν Ὀλυμπιονίκην ἀσπασάμενος πυγμῆς.
ἔπαθε δὲ τοῦτο ὑπερβολῇ τε χαρᾶς καὶ ἀσθενείᾳ
πολυετίας. καὶ αὐτὸν πάντες οἱ κατὰ τὴν πανήγυριν ἐντιμότατα παρέπεμψαν.

Ἔστι δὲ καὶ εἰς τοῦτον ἐπίγραμμα ἡμῶν·

73 Φωσφόρε, σοί, Πολύδευκες, ἔχω χάριν, οὕνεκεν υἱὸς
Χίλωνος πυγμῇ χλωρὸν ἕλεν κότινον.
εἰ δ' ὁ πατὴρ στεφανοῦχον ἰδὼν τέκνον ἤμυσεν ἡσθείς,
οὐ νεμεσητόν· ἐμοὶ τοῖος ἴτω θάνατος.

ἐπὶ δὲ τῆς εἰκόνος αὐτοῦ ἐπιγέγραπται τόδε·

τόνδε δοριστέφανος Σπάρτα Χίλων' ἐφύτευσεν,
ὃς τῶν ἑπτὰ σοφῶν πρῶτος ἔφυ σοφίᾳ.

ἀπεφθέγξατο, " ἐγγύα, πάρα δ' ἄτα." ἔστιν
αὐτοῦ καὶ ἐπιστόλιον τόδε·

Χίλων Περιάνδρῳ

" Ἐπιστέλλεις ἐμὶν ἐκστρατείαν ἐπὶ ἐκδάμως,
ὡς αὐτός κα ἐξέρποις· ἐγὼν δὲ δοκέω καὶ τὰ
οἰκῆα σφαλερὰ ἦμεν ἀνδρὶ μονάρχῳ, καὶ τῆνον
τυράννων εὐδαιμονίζω ὅστις κα οἴκοι ἐξ αὐτὸς
αὑτῶ κατθάνῃ."

Κεφ. δ'. ΠΙΤΤΑΚΟΣ

74 Πιττακὸς Ὑρραδίου Μυτιληναῖος. φησὶ δὲ Δοῦρις τὸν πατέρα αὐτοῦ Θρᾷκα εἶναι. οὗτος μετὰ
τῶν Ἀλκαίου γενόμενος ἀδελφῶν Μέλαγχρον

to Hermippus, his death took place at Pisa, just after he had congratulated his son on an Olympic victory in boxing. It was due to excess of joy coupled with the weakness of a man stricken in years. And all present joined in the funeral procession.

I have written an epitaph on him also, which runs as follows [a] :

> I praise thee, Pollux, for that Chilon's son
> By boxing feats the olive chaplet won.
> Nor at the father's fate should we repine ;
> He died of joy ; may such a death be mine.

The inscription on his statue runs thus [b] :

> Here Chilon stands, of Sparta's warrior race,
> Who of the Sages Seven holds highest place.

His apophthegm is : " Give a pledge, and suffer for it." A short letter is also ascribed to him.

Chilon to Periander

" You tell me of an expedition against foreign enemies, in which you yourself will take the field. In my opinion affairs at home are not too safe for an absolute ruler ; and I deem the tyrant happy who dies a natural death in his own house."

Chapter 4.   PITTACUS (*c.* 600 B.C.)

Pittacus was the son of Hyrrhadius and a native of Mitylene. Duris calls his father a Thracian. Aided by the brothers of Alcaeus he overthrew

---

[a] *Anth. Pal.* vii. 88.   [b] *Anth. Pal.* ix. 596.

καθεῖλε τὸν τῆς Λέσβου τύραννον· καὶ περὶ τῆς
Ἀχιλείτιδος χώρας μαχομένων Ἀθηναίων καὶ
Μυτιληναίων ἐστρατήγει μὲν αὐτός, Ἀθηναίων
δὲ Φρύνων παγκρατιαστὴς Ὀλυμπιονίκης. συν-
έθετο δὴ μονομαχῆσαι πρὸς αὐτόν· καὶ δίκτυον
ἔχων ὑπὸ τὴν ἀσπίδα λαθραίως περιέβαλε τὸν
Φρύνωνα, καὶ κτείνας ἀνεσώσατο τὸ χωρίον.
ὕστερον μέντοι φησὶν Ἀπολλόδωρος ἐν τοῖς
Χρονικοῖς διαδικασθῆναι τοὺς Ἀθηναίους περὶ
τοῦ χωρίου πρὸς τοὺς Μυτιληναίους, ἀκούοντος
τῆς δίκης Περιάνδρου, ὃν καὶ τοῖς Ἀθηναίοις
προσκρῖναι.

75 Τότε δ᾽ οὖν τὸν Πιττακὸν ἰσχυρῶς ἐτίμησαν
οἱ Μυτιληναῖοι, καὶ τὴν ἀρχὴν ἐνεχείρισαν
αὐτῷ. ὁ δὲ δέκα ἔτη κατασχὼν καὶ εἰς τάξιν
ἀγαγὼν τὸ πολίτευμα, κατέθετο τὴν ἀρχήν, καὶ
δέκα ἐπεβίω ἄλλα. καὶ χώραν αὐτῷ ἀπένειμαν
οἱ Μυτιληναῖοι· ὁ δὲ ἱερὰν ἀνῆκεν, ἥτις νῦν
Πιττάκειος καλεῖται. Σωσικράτης δέ φησιν ὅτι
ὀλίγον ἀποτεμόμενος ἔφη τὸ ἥμισυ τοῦ παντὸς
πλεῖον εἶναι. ἀλλὰ καὶ Κροίσου διδόντος χρήματα οὐκ ἐδέξατο, εἰπὼν ἔχειν ὧν ἐβούλετο
διπλάσια· ἄπαιδος γὰρ τἀδελφοῦ τελευτήσαντος
κεκληρονομηκέναι.

76 Παμφίλη δέ φησιν ἐν τῷ δευτέρῳ τῶν Ὑπομνημάτων, ὡς τὸν υἱὸν αὐτοῦ Τυρραῖον καθήμενον
ἐπὶ κουρείου ἐν Κύμῃ χαλκεύς τις πέλεκυν ἐμβαλὼν
ἀνέλοι. τῶν δὲ Κυμαίων πεμψάντων τὸν φονέα
τῷ Πιττακῷ, μαθόντα καὶ ἀπολύσαντα εἰπεῖν,
" συγγνώμη μετανοίας κρείσσων." Ἡράκλειτος δὲ

Melanchrus, tyrant of Lesbos; and in the war
between Mitylene and Athens for the territory of
Achileis he himself had the chief command on the
one side, and Phrynon, who had won an Olympic
victory in the pancratium, commanded the Athenians.
Pittacus agreed to meet him in single combat; with
a net which he concealed beneath his shield he en-
tangled Phrynon, killed him, and recovered the
territory. Subsequently, as Apollodorus states in
his *Chronology*, Athens and Mitylene referred their
claims to arbitration. Periander heard the appeal
and gave judgement in favour of Athens.

At the time, however, the people of Mitylene
honoured Pittacus extravagantly and entrusted him
with the government. He ruled for ten years
and brought the constitution into order, and then
laid down his office. He lived another ten years
after his abdication and received from the people
of Mitylene a grant of land, which he dedicated
as sacred domain; and it bears his name to this
day Sosicrates relates that he cut off a small
portion for himself and pronounced the half to be
more than the whole. Furthermore, he declined
an offer of money made him by Croesus, saying
that he had twice as much as he wanted; for his
brother had died without issue and he had inherited
his estate.

Pamphila in the second book of her *Memorabilia*
narrates that, as his son Tyrraeus sat in a barber's
shop in Cyme, a smith killed him with a blow from
an axe. When the people of Cyme sent the murderer
to Pittacus, he, on learning the story, set him at
liberty and declared that " It is better to pardon
now than to repent later." Heraclitus, however, says

φησιν, Ἀλκαῖον ὑποχείριον λαβόντα καὶ ἀπολύσαντα φάναι, "συγγνώμη τιμωρίας κρείσσων."

Νόμους δὲ ἔθηκε· τῷ μεθύοντι, ἐὰν ἁμάρτῃ,
διπλῆν εἶναι τὴν ζημίαν· ἵνα μὴ μεθύωσι, πολλοῦ
κατὰ τὴν νῆσον οἴνου γινομένου. εἶπέ τε " χαλεπὸν
ἐσθλὸν ἔμμεναι·" οὗ καὶ Σιμωνίδης μέμνηται
λέγων· " ἄνδρ' ἀγαθὸν ἀλαθέως γενέσθαι χαλεπόν,
77 τὸ Πιττάκειον." μέμνηται αὐτοῦ καὶ Πλάτων ἐν
Πρωταγόρᾳ· " ἀνάγκᾳ δ' οὐδὲ θεοὶ μάχονται." καὶ
" ἀρχὴ ἄνδρα δείκνυσιν." ἐρωτηθεὶς δέ ποτε τί
ἄριστον, "τὸ παρὸν εὖ ποιεῖν." καὶ ὑπὸ Κροίσου τίς
ἀρχὴ μεγίστη, " ἡ τοῦ ποικίλου," ἔφη, " ξύλου,"
σημαίνων τὸν νόμον. ἔλεγε δὲ καὶ τὰς νίκας ἄνευ
αἵματος ποιεῖσθαι. ἔφη δὲ καὶ πρὸς τὸν Φωκαϊκὸν
φάσκοντα δεῖν ζητεῖν ἄνθρωπον σπουδαῖον, " ἂν
λίαν," ἔφη, " ζητῇς, οὐχ εὑρήσεις." καὶ πρὸς
τοὺς πυνθανομένους τί εὐχάριστον, " χρόνος," ἔφη·
ἀφανές, " τὸ μέλλον"· πιστόν, " γῆ"· ἄπιστον,
" θάλασσα." ἔλεγέ τε συνετῶν ἀνδρῶν, πρὶν γενέ-
78 σθαι τὰ δυσχερῆ, προνοῆσαι ὅπως μὴ γένηται·
ἀνδρείων δέ, γενόμενα εὖ θέσθαι. ὃ μέλλεις
πράττειν, μὴ πρόλεγε· ἀποτυχὼν γὰρ γελασθήσῃ.
ἀτυχίαν μὴ ὀνειδίζειν, νέμεσιν αἰδούμενον. παρα-
καταθήκην λαβόντα ἀποδοῦναι. φίλον μὴ λέγειν
κακῶς, ἀλλὰ μηδὲ ἐχθρόν. εὐσέβειαν ἀσκεῖν.
σωφροσύνην φιλεῖν. ἀλήθειαν ἔχειν, πίστιν, ἐμπει-
ρίαν, ἐπιδεξιότητα, ἑταιρίαν, ἐπιμέλειαν.

---

that it was Alcaeus whom he set at liberty when he had got him in his power, and that what he said was : " Mercy is better than vengeance."

Among the laws which he made is one providing that for any offence committed in a state of intoxication the penalty should be doubled ; his object was to discourage drunkenness, wine being abundant in the island. One of his sayings is, " It is hard to be good," which is cited by Simonides in this form : " Pittacus's maxim, ' Truly to become a virtuous man is hard.' " Plato also cites him in the *Protagoras* [a] : " Even the gods do not fight against necessity." Again, " Office shows the man." Once, when asked what is the best thing, he replied, " To do well the work in hand." And, when Croesus inquired what is the best rule, he answered, " The rule of the shifting wood," by which he meant the law. He also urged men to win bloodless victories. When the Phocaean said that we must search for a good man, Pittacus rejoined, " If you seek too carefully, you will never find him." He answered various inquiries thus : " What is agreeable ? " " Time." " Obscure ? " " The future." " Trustworthy ? " " The earth." " Untrustworthy ? " " The sea." " It is the part of prudent men," he said, " before difficulties arise, to provide against their arising ; and of courageous men to deal with them when they have arisen." Do not announce your plans beforehand ; for, if they fail, you will be laughed at. Never reproach any one with a misfortune, for fear of Nemesis. Duly restore what has been entrusted to you. Speak no ill of a friend, nor even of an enemy. Practise piety. Love temperance. Cherish truth, fidelity, skill, cleverness, sociability, carefulness.

79

Τῶν δὲ ἀδομένων αὐτοῦ μάλιστα εὐδοκίμησε τάδε·

ἔχοντα χρὴ τόξα καὶ ἰοδόκον φαρέτρην
στείχειν ποτὶ φῶτα κακόν.
πιστὸν γὰρ οὐδὲν γλῶσσα διὰ στόματος
λαλεῖ διχόθυμον ἔχουσα
κραδίη νόημα.

79 ἐποίησε δὲ καὶ ἐλεγεῖα ἔπη ἑξακόσια, καὶ ὑπὲρ νόμων καταλογάδην τοῖς πολίταις.

Ἤκμαζε μὲν οὖν περὶ τὴν τεσσαρακοστὴν δευτέραν Ὀλυμπιάδα· ἐτελεύτησε δ᾽ ἐπὶ Ἀριστομένους τῷ τρίτῳ ἔτει τῆς πεντηκοστῆς δευτέρας Ὀλυμπιάδος, βιοὺς ὑπὲρ ἔτη ἑβδομήκοντα, [ἤδη γηραιός]. καὶ αὐτῷ ἐπὶ τοῦ μνήματος ἐπιγέγραπται τόδε·

οἰκείοις δακρύοις ἁ γειναμένα κατακλαίει
    Πιττακὸν ἥδ᾽ ἱερὰ Λέσβος ἀποφθίμενον.

ἀπόφθεγμα αὐτοῦ· καιρὸν γνῶθι.

Γέγονε δὲ καὶ ἕτερος Πιττακὸς νομοθέτης, ὥς φησι Φαβωρῖνος ἐν Ἀπομνημονευμάτων πρώτῳ καὶ Δημήτριος ἐν Ὁμωνύμοις, ὃς καὶ μικρὸς προσηγορεύθη.

Τὸν δ᾽ οὖν σοφὸν λέγεταί ποτε νεανίσκῳ συμβουλευομένῳ περὶ γάμου ταῦτα εἰπεῖν, ἅ φησι Καλλίμαχος ἐν τοῖς ἐπιγράμμασι·

80 ξεῖνος Ἀταρνείτης τις ἀνήρετο Πιττακὸν οὕτω
    τὸν Μυτιληναῖον, παῖδα τὸν Ὑρραδίου·
ἄττα γέρον, δοιός με καλεῖ γάμος· ἡ μία μὲν δὴ
    νύμφη καὶ πλούτῳ καὶ γενεῇ κατ᾽ ἐμέ·
ἡ δ᾽ ἑτέρη προβέβηκε. τί λώϊον; εἰ δ᾽ ἄγε σύν μοι
    βούλευσον, ποτέρην εἰς ὑμέναιον ἄγω.

Of his songs the most popular is this:

> With bow and well-stored quiver
> We must march against our foe,
> Words of his tongue can no man trust,
> For in his heart there is a deceitful thought.

He also wrote poems in elegiac metre, some 600 lines, and a prose work *On Laws* for the use of the citizens.

He was flourishing about the 42nd Olympiad. He died in the archonship of Aristomenes, in the third year of the 52nd Olympiad,[a] having lived more than seventy years, to a good old age. The inscription on his monument runs thus [b]:

> Here holy Lesbos, with a mother's woe,
> Bewails her Pittacus whom death laid low.

To him belongs the apophthegm, "Know thine opportunity."

There was another Pittacus, a legislator, as is stated by Favorinus in the first book of his *Memorabilia*, and by Demetrius in his work on *Men of the Same Name*. He was called the Less.

To return to the Sage: the story goes that a young man took counsel with him about marriage, and received this answer, as given by Callimachus in his Epigrams [c]:

A stranger of Atarneus thus inquired of Pittacus, the son
   of Hyrrhadius:
Old sire, two offers of marriage are made to me; the one
   bride is in wealth and birth my equal;
The other is my superior. Which is the better? Come now
   and advise me which of the two I shall wed.

<hr/>

[a] 570 B.C. [b] *Anth. Plan.* ii. 3.
      [c] *Anth. Pal.* vii. 89.

εἶπεν· ὁ δὲ σκίπωνα, γεροντικὸν ὅπλον, ἀείρας,
ἤνιδε, κεῖνοί σοι πᾶν ἐρέουσιν ἔπος.
οἱ δ' ἄρ' ὑπὸ πληγῇσι θοὰς βέμβικας ἔχοντες
ἔστρεφον εὐρείη παῖδες ἐνὶ τριόδῳ.
κείνων ἔρχεο, φησί, μετ' ἴχνια. χὼ μὲν ἐπέστη
πλησίον· οἱ δ' ἔλεγον· τὴν κατὰ σαυτὸν ἔλα.
ταῦτ' ἀΐων ὁ ξεῖνος ἐφείσατο μείζονος οἴκου
δράξασθαι, παίδων κληδόνα[1] συνθέμενος.
τὴν δ' ὀλίγην ὡς κεῖνος ἐς οἰκίον ἤγετο νύμφην.
οὕτω καὶ σύ, Δίων, τὴν κατὰ σαυτὸν ἔλα.

81 δοκεῖ δ' ἐκ διαθέσεως αὐτὰ εἰρηκέναι. εὐ-
γενεστέρα γὰρ αὐτῷ οὖσα ἡ γυνή, ἐπειδήπερ ἦν
Δράκοντος ἀδελφὴ τοῦ Πενθίλου, σφόδρα κατ-
εσοβαρεύετο αὐτοῦ.

Τοῦτον Ἀλκαῖος σαράποδα μὲν καὶ σάραπον
ἀποκαλεῖ διὰ τὸ πλατύπουν εἶναι καὶ ἐπισύρειν
τὼ πόδε· χειροπόδην δὲ διὰ τὰς ἐν τοῖς ποσὶ
ῥαγάδας, ἃς χειράδας ἐκάλουν· γαύρηκα δὲ ὡς
εἰκῆ γαυριῶντα· φύσκωνα δὲ καὶ γάστρωνα ὅτι
παχὺς ἦν· ἀλλὰ μὴν καὶ ζοφοδορπίδαν ὡς ἄλυχνον·
ἀγάσυρτον δὲ ὡς ἐπισεσυρμένον καὶ ῥυπαρόν.
τούτῳ γυμνασία ἦν σῖτον ἀλεῖν, ὥς φησι Κλέαρχος
ὁ φιλόσοφος.

Καὶ αὐτοῦ ἐστιν ἐπιστόλιον τοιόνδε·

Πιττακὸς Κροίσῳ

" Κέλεαί με ἱκνέεσθαι ἐς Λυδίην, ὅπως σοι τὸν
ὄλβον ἴδοιμι· ἐγὼ δὲ καὶ μὴ ὀρεὶς πέπεισμαι τὸν
Ἀλυάττεω παῖδα τῶν βασιλήων πολυχρυσότατον
πέλειν. οὐδέν τε πλέον ἄμμιν ἱκομένοις ἐς Σάρδις·

[1] κληδόνι vulg.

So spake he. But Pittacus, raising his staff, an old man's
    weapon, said, " See there, yonder boys will tell you the
    whole tale."
The boys were whipping their tops to make them go fast
    and spinning them in a wide open space.
" Follow in their track," said he. So he approached near,
    and the boys were saying, "Keep to your own sphere."
When he heard this, the stranger desisted from aiming at
    the lordlier match, assenting to the warning of the boys.
And, even as he led home the humble bride, so do you,
    Dion, keep to your own sphere.

The advice seems to have been prompted by his
situation. For he had married a wife superior in
birth to himself : she was the sister of Draco, the
son of Penthilus, and she treated him with great
haughtiness.

Alcaeus nicknamed him σαράπους and σάραπος
because he had flat feet and dragged them in walking ; also " Chilblains," because he had chapped feet,
for which their word was χειράς ; and Braggadocio,
because he was always swaggering ; Paunch and
Potbelly, because he was stout ; a Diner-in-the-Dark,
because he dispensed with a lamp ; and the Sloven,
because he was untidy and dirty. The exercise he
took was grinding corn, as related by Clearchus the
philosopher.

The following short letter is ascribed to him :

Pittacus to Croesus

" You bid me come to Lydia in order to see your
prosperity : but without seeing it I can well believe
that the son of Alyattes is the most opulent of kings.
There will be no advantage to me in a journey to

χρυσοῦ γὰρ οὐ δεύμεθα, ἀλλὰ πέπαμαι ἄρκια καὶ
τοῖς ἐμοῖς ἑτάροις. ἔμπας δ' ἵξομαι, ὡς ἀνδρὶ
ξείνῳ γενοίμην τοι συνόμιλος."

Κεφ. ε΄. ΒΙΑΣ

82 Βίας Τευτάμου Πριηνεύς, προκεκριμένος τῶν
ἑπτὰ ὑπὸ Σατύρου. τοῦτον οἱ μὲν πλούσιον,
Δοῦρις δὲ πάροικόν φησι γεγονέναι. Φανόδικος
δὲ κόρας αἰχμαλώτους λυτρωσάμενον Μεσσηνίας
θρέψαι τε ὡς θυγατέρας καὶ προῖκας ἐπιδοῦναι
καὶ εἰς τὴν Μεσσήνην ἀποστεῖλαι τοῖς πατράσιν
αὐτῶν. χρόνῳ δὲ ἐν ταῖς Ἀθήναις, ὡς προείρηται,
τοῦ τρίποδος εὑρεθέντος ὑπὸ τῶν ἁλιέων, τοῦ
χαλκοῦ, ἐπιγραφὴν ἔχοντος " τῷ σοφῷ," Σάτυρος
μέν φησι παρελθεῖν τὰς κόρας—οἱ δὲ τὸν πατέρα
αὐτῶν, ὡς καὶ Φανόδικος—εἰς τὴν ἐκκλησίαν,
καὶ εἰπεῖν τὸν Βίαντα σοφόν, διηγησαμένας τὰ
καθ' ἑαυτάς. καὶ ἀπεστάλη ὁ τρίπους· καὶ ὁ
Βίας ἰδὼν ἔφη τὸν Ἀπόλλωνα σοφὸν εἶναι, οὐδὲ
83 προσήκατο. οἱ δὲ λέγουσιν ἐν Θήβαις τῷ Ἡρα-
κλεῖ αὐτὸν ἀναθεῖναι, ἐπεὶ ἀπόγονος ἦν Θηβαίων
ἀποικίαν εἰς Πριήνην στειλάντων, ὥσπερ καὶ Φανό-
δικός φησι.

Λέγεται δὲ καὶ Ἀλυάττου πολιορκοῦντος
Πριήνην τὸν Βίαντα πιήναντα δύο ἡμιόνους
ἐξελάσαι εἰς τὸ στρατόπεδον· τὸν δὲ συνιδόντα
καταπλαγῆναι τὸ μέχρι καὶ ἀλόγων διατείνειν
αὐτῶν τὴν εὐθενίαν. καὶ ἐβουλήθη σπείσασθαι,

Sardis, for I am not in want of money, and my possessions are sufficient for my friends as well as myself. Nevertheless, I will come, to be entertained by you and to make your acquaintance."

CHAPTER 5. BIAS (c. 570 B.C.)

Bias, the son of Teutames, was born at Priene, and by Satyrus is placed at the head of the Seven Sages. Some make him of a wealthy family, but Duris says he was a labourer living in the house. Phanodicus relates that he ransomed certain Messenian maidens captured in war and brought them up as his daughters, gave them dowries, and restored them to their fathers in Messenia. In course of time, as has been already related, the bronze tripod with the inscription " To him that is wise " having been found at Athens by the fishermen, the maidens according to Satyrus, or their father according to other accounts, including that of Phanodicus, came forward into the assembly and, after the recital of their own adventures, pronounced Bias to be wise. And thereupon the tripod was dispatched to him ; but Bias, on seeing it, declared that Apollo was wise, and refused to take the tripod. But others say that he dedicated it to Heracles in Thebes, since he was a descendant of the Thebans who had founded a colony at Priene ; and this is the version of Phanodicus.

A story is told that, while Alyattes was besieging Priene, Bias fattened two mules and drove them into the camp, and that the king, when he saw them, was amazed at the good condition of the citizens actually extending to their beasts of burden. And he decided

καὶ εἰσέπεμψεν ἄγγελον. Βίας δὲ σωροὺς ψάμ-
μου χέας καὶ ἄνωθεν σῖτον περιχέας ἔδειξε
τῷ ἀνθρώπῳ· καὶ τέλος μαθὼν ὁ Ἀλυάττης
εἰρήνην ἐσπείσατο πρὸς τοὺς Πριηνέας. θᾶττον
δ' αὐτῷ πέμψαντι πρὸς τὸν Βίαντα ἵνα ἥκοι παρ'
αὐτόν, " ἐγὼ δέ," φησίν, " Ἀλυάττῃ κελεύω
84 κρόμμυα ἐσθίειν, [ἴσον τῷ κλαίειν]." λέγεται
δὲ καὶ δίκας δεινότατος γεγονέναι εἰπεῖν. ἐπ'
ἀγαθῷ μέντοι τῇ τῶν λόγων ἰσχύι προσεχρῆτο.
ὅθεν καὶ Δημόδικος ὁ Λέριος τοῦτο αἰνίττεται λέγων·

ἢν τύχῃς κρίνων δικάζευ τὴν Πριηνίην δίκην·

καὶ Ἱππῶναξ· " ἃ καὶ δικάζεσθαι Βίαντος τοῦ
Πριηνέως κρεῖσσον."

Τοῦτον οὖν καὶ ἐτελεύτα τὸν τρόπον. δίκην
γὰρ ὑπέρ τινος λέξας ἤδη ὑπέργηρως ὑπάρχων,
μετὰ τὸ καταπαῦσαι τὸν λόγον ἀπέκλινε τὴν
κεφαλὴν εἰς τοὺς τοῦ τῆς θυγατρὸς υἱοῦ κόλπους·
εἰπόντος δὲ καὶ τοῦ ἐξ ἐναντίας καὶ τῶν δικαστῶν τὴν ψῆφον ἐνεγκόντων τῷ ὑπὸ τοῦ Βίαντος
βοηθουμένῳ, λυθέντος τοῦ δικαστηρίου νεκρὸς ἐν
85 τοῖς κόλποις εὑρέθη. καὶ αὐτὸν μεγαλοπρεπῶς
ἔθαψεν ἡ πόλις, καὶ ἐπέγραψαν·

κλεινοῖς ἐν δαπέδοισι Πριήνης φύντα καλύπτει
ἥδε Βίαντα πέτρη, κόσμον Ἴωσι μέγαν.

ἀλλὰ καὶ ἡμεῖς·

τῇδε Βίαντα κέκευθα, τὸν ἀτρέμας ἤγαγεν Ἑρμῆς
εἰς Ἀΐδην, πολιῷ γήραϊ νιφόμενον.
εἶπε γάρ, εἶπε δίκην ἑτάρου τινός· εἶτ' ἀποκλινθεὶς
παιδὸς ἐς ἀγκαλίδας μακρὸν ἔτεινεν ὕπνον.

86

to make terms and sent a messenger. But Bias piled up heaps of sand with a layer of corn on the top, and showed them to the man, and finally, on being informed of this, Alyattes made a treaty of peace with the people of Priene. Soon afterwards, when Alyattes sent to invite Bias to his court, he replied, " Tell Alyattes, from me, to make his diet of onions," that is, to weep. It is also stated that he was a very effective pleader ; but he was accustomed to use his powers of speech to a good end. Hence it is to this that Demodicus of Leros makes reference in the line :

If you happen to be prosecuting a suit, plead as they do at Priene ;

and Hipponax thus : " More powerful in pleading causes than Bias of Priene." [a]

This was the manner of his death. He had been pleading in defence of some client in spite of his great age. When he had finished speaking, he reclined his head on his grandson's bosom. The opposing counsel made a speech, the judges voted and gave their verdict in favour of the client of Bias, who, when the court rose, was found dead in his grandson's arms. The city gave him a magnificent funeral and inscribed on his tomb [b] :

Here Bias of Priene lies, whose name
Brought to his home and all Ionia fame.

My own epitaph is [c] :

Here Bias rests. A quiet death laid low
The aged head which years had strewn with snow.
His pleading done, his friend preserved from harms,
A long sleep took him in his grandson's arms.

[a] P. 79 Bergk ; Strabo xiv. p. 636.
[b] *Anth. Pal.* vii. 90.　　[c] *Anth. Pal.* vii. 91.

Ἐποίησε δὲ περὶ Ἰωνίας, τίνα μάλιστα ἂν τρόπον εὐδαιμονοίη, εἰς ἔπη δισχίλια. τῶν δὲ ᾀδομένων αὐτοῦ εὐδοκίμησε τάδε·

ἀστοῖσιν ἄρεσκε πᾶσιν. ἐν πόλει* αἴκε μένῃς·
πλείσταν γὰρ ἔχει χάριν· αὐθάδης δὲ τρόπος πολλάκι
βλαβερὰν ἐξέλαμψεν ἄταν.

86 καὶ τὸ μὲν ἰσχυρὸν γενέσθαι τῆς φύσεως ἔργον· τὸ δὲ λέγειν δύνασθαι τὰ συμφέροντα τῇ πατρίδι ψυχῆς ἴδιον καὶ φρονήσεως. εὐπορίαν δὲ χρημάτων πολλοῖς καὶ διὰ τύχην περιγίνεσθαι. ἔλεγε δὲ ἀτυχῆ εἶναι τὸν ἀτυχίαν μὴ φέροντα· καὶ νόσον ψυχῆς τὸ τῶν ἀδυνάτων ἐρᾶν, ἀλλοτρίων δὲ κακῶν ἀμνημόνευτον εἶναι. ἐρωτηθεὶς τί δυσχερές, τὴν "ἐπὶ τὸ χεῖρον," ἔφη, "μεταβολὴν εὐγενῶς ἐνεγκεῖν." συμπλέων ποτὲ ἀσεβέσι, χειμαζομένης τῆς νεὼς κἀκείνων τοὺς θεοὺς ἐπικαλουμένων, "σιγᾶτε," ἔφη, "μὴ αἴσθωνται ὑμᾶς ἐνθάδε πλέοντας." ἐρωτηθεὶς ὑπὸ ἀσεβοῦς ἀνθρώπου τί ποτέ ἐστιν εὐσέβεια, ἐσίγα. τοῦ δὲ τὴν αἰτίαν τῆς σιγῆς πυθομένου, "σιωπῶ," ἔφη, "ὅτι περὶ τῶν οὐδέν σοι προσηκόντων πυνθάνῃ."

87 Ἐρωτηθεὶς τί γλυκὺ ἀνθρώποις, "ἐλπίς," ἔφη. ἥδιον ἔλεγε δικάζειν μεταξὺ ἐχθρῶν ἢ φίλων· τῶν μὲν γὰρ φίλων πάντως ἐχθρὸν ἔσεσθαι τὸν ἕτερον, τῶν δὲ ἐχθρῶν τὸν ἕτερον φίλον. ἐρωτηθεὶς τί ποιῶν ἄνθρωπος τέρπεται, ἔφη, "κερδαίνων."

88

He wrote a poem of 2000 lines on Ionia and the manner of rendering it prosperous. Of his songs the most popular is the following :

Find favour with all the citizens . . .
   . . . in whatever state you dwell.
For this earns most gratitude ;
   the headstrong spirit often flashes forth with harmful bane.

The growth of strength in man is nature's work ; but to set forth in speech the interests of one's country is the gift of soul and reason. Even chance brings abundance of wealth to many. He also said that he who could not bear misfortune was truly unfortunate ; that it is a disease of the soul to be enamoured of things impossible of attainment ; and that we ought not to dwell upon the woes of others. Being asked what is difficult, he replied, " Nobly to endure a change for the worse." He was once on a voyage with some impious men ; and, when a storm was encountered, even they began to call upon the gods for help. " Peace ! " said he, " lest they hear and become aware that you are here in the ship." When an impious man asked him to define piety, he was silent ; and when the other inquired the reason, " I am silent," he replied, " because you are asking questions about what does not concern you."

Being asked " What is sweet to men," he answered, " Hope." He said he would rather decide a dispute between two of his enemies than between two of his friends ; for in the latter case he would be certain to make one of his friends his enemy, but in the former case he would make one of his enemies his friend. Asked what occupation gives a man most pleasure, he replied, " Making

ἔλεγέ τε τὸν βίον οὕτω μετρεῖν ὡς καὶ πολὺν καὶ
ὀλίγον χρόνον βιωσομένους, καὶ φιλεῖν ὡς μισή-
σοντας· τοὺς γὰρ πλείστους εἶναι κακούς. συνεβούλευέ τε ὧδε· βραδέως ἐγχείρει τοῖς πραττο-
μένοις· ὃ δ᾽ ἂν ἕλῃ, βεβαίως τηρῶν διάμενε. μὴ
88 ταχὺ λάλει· μανίαν γὰρ ἐμφαίνει. φρόνησιν ἀγάπα.
περὶ θεῶν λέγε, ὡς εἰσίν. ἀνάξιον ἄνδρα μὴ
ἐπαίνει διὰ πλοῦτον. πείσας λαβέ, μὴ βιασά-
μενος. ὅ τι ἂν ἀγαθὸν πράττῃς, εἰς θεοὺς ἀνά-
πεμπε. ἐφόδιον ἀπὸ νεότητος εἰς γῆρας ἀνα-
λάμβανε σοφίαν· βεβαιότερον γὰρ τοῦτο τῶν
ἄλλων κτημάτων.

Μέμνηται τοῦ Βίαντος καὶ Ἱππῶναξ, ὡς προείρηται, καὶ ὁ δυσάρεστος Ἡράκλειτος μάλιστα
αὐτὸν ἐπήνεσε γράψας· " ἐν Πριήνῃ Βίας ἐγένετο
ὁ Τευτάμεω, οὗ πλέων λόγος ἢ τῶν ἄλλων." καὶ
οἱ Πριηνεῖς δὲ αὐτῷ τέμενος καθιέρωσαν τὸ
Τευτάμειον λεγόμενον. ἀπεφθέγξατο· οἱ πλεῖ-
στοι κακοί.

Κεφ. ϛ´. ΚΛΕΟΒΟΥΛΟΣ

89 Κλεόβουλος Εὐαγόρου Λίνδιος, ὡς δὲ Δοῦρις,
Κάρ· ἔνιοι δὲ εἰς Ἡρακλέα ἀναφέρειν τὸ γένος
αὐτόν· ῥώμῃ δὲ καὶ κάλλει διαφέρειν, μετασχεῖν τε
τῆς ἐν Αἰγύπτῳ φιλοσοφίας. γενέσθαι τε αὐτῷ
θυγατέρα Κλεοβουλίνην, αἰνιγμάτων ἑξαμέτρων
ποιήτριαν, ἧς μέμνηται καὶ Κρατῖνος ἐν τῷ ὁμω-
νύμῳ δράματι, πληθυντικῶς ἐπιγράψας. ἀλλὰ καὶ
τὸ ἱερὸν τῆς Ἀθηνᾶς ἀνανεώσασθαι αὐτὸν κτισθὲν
90

money." He advised men to measure life as if they had both a short and a long time to live; to love their friends as if they would some day hate them, the majority of mankind being bad. Further, he gave this advice: Be slow to set about an enterprise, but persevere in it steadfastly when once it is undertaken. Do not be hasty of speech, for that is a sign of madness. Cherish wisdom. Admit the existence of the gods. If a man is unworthy, do not praise him because of his wealth. Gain your point by persuasion, not by force. Ascribe your good actions to the gods. Make wisdom your provision for the journey from youth to old age; for it is a more certain support than all other possessions.

Bias is mentioned by Hipponax as stated above, and Heraclitus, who is hard to please, bestows upon him especial praise in these words [a]: " In Priene lived Bias, son of Teutames, a man of more consideration than any." And the people of Priene dedicated a precinct to him, which is called the Teutameum. His apophthegm is : Most men are bad.

CHAPTER 6   CLEOBULUS (c. 600 B.C.)

Cleobulus, the son of Euagoras, was born at Lindus, but according to Duris he was a Carian. Some say that he traced his descent back to Heracles, that he was distinguished for strength and beauty, and was acquainted with Egyptian philosophy. He had a daughter Cleobuline, who composed riddles in hexameters; she is mentioned by Cratinus, who gives one of his plays her name, in the plural form Cleobulinae. He is also said to have rebuilt the temple of Athena which was founded by Danaus.

[a] P. 39 D, 112 B.

91

ὑπὸ Δαναοῦ. οὗτος ἐποίησεν ᾄσματα καὶ γρίφους
εἰς ἔπη τρισχίλια.

Καὶ τὸ ἐπίγραμμά τινες τὸ ἐπὶ Μίδᾳ τοῦτόν
φασι ποιῆσαι·

χαλκῆ παρθένος εἰμί, Μίδα δ' ἐπὶ σήματι κεῖμαι.
ἔστ' ἂν ὕδωρ τε νάῃ καὶ δένδρεα μακρὰ τεθήλῃ,
90   ἠέλιός τ' ἀνιὼν λάμπῃ, λαμπρά τε σελήνη,
καὶ ποταμοί γε ῥέωσιν, ἀνακλύζῃ δὲ θάλασσα,
αὐτοῦ τῇδε μένουσα πολυκλαύτῳ ἐπὶ τύμβῳ,
ἀγγελέω παριοῦσι, Μίδας ὅτι τῇδε τέθαπται.

φέρουσι δὲ μαρτύριον Σιμωνίδου ᾆσμα, ὅπου φησί

τίς κεν αἰνήσειε νόῳ πίσυνος
Λίνδου ναέταν Κλεόβουλον
ἀενάοις ποταμοῖς
ἄνθεσί τ' εἰαρινοῖς
ἀελίου τε φλογὶ χρυσέας τε σελάνας
καὶ θαλασσαίαισι δίνῃς
ἀντιθέντα μένος στάλας;
ἅπαντα γάρ ἐστι θεῶν ἥσσω· λίθον δὲ
καὶ βρότεοι παλάμαι θραύοντι· μωροῦ
φωτὸς ἅδε βουλά.

οὐ γὰρ εἶναι Ὁμήρου τὸ ἐπίγραμμα, πολλοῖς ἔτεσι
προέχοντος, φασί, τοῦ Μίδα.

Φέρεται δ' αὐτοῦ ἐν τοῖς Παμφίλης Ὑπομνήμασι
καὶ αἴνιγμα τοῖον·

91   εἷς ὁ πατήρ, παῖδες δυοκαίδεκα. τῶν δὲ ἑκάστῳ
παῖδες δὶς τριάκοντα διάνδιχα εἶδος ἔχουσαι·
αἱ μὲν λευκαὶ ἔασιν ἰδεῖν, αἱ δ' αὖτε μέλαιναι·
ἀθάνατοι δέ τ' ἐοῦσαι, ἀποφθινύθουσιν ἅπασαι.

ἔστι δὲ ὁ ἐνιαυτός.
92

He was the author of songs and riddles, making some 3000 lines in all.

The inscription on the tomb of Midas is said by some to be his [a] :

I am a maiden of bronze and I rest upon Midas's tomb. So long as water shall flow and tall trees grow, and the sun shall rise and shine, and the bright moon, and rivers shall run and the sea wash the shore, here abiding on his tear-sprinkled tomb I shall tell the passers-by—Midas is buried here.

The evidence they adduce is a poem of Simonides in which he says [b] :

Who, if he trusts his wits, will praise Cleobulus the dweller at Lindus for opposing the strength of a column to ever-flowing rivers, the flowers of spring, the flame of the sun, and the golden moon and the eddies of the sea ? But all things fall short of the might of the gods ; even mortal hands break marble in pieces ; this is a fool's devising.

The inscription cannot be by Homer, because he lived, they say, long before Midas.

The following riddle of Cleobulus is preserved in Pamphila's collection [c] :

One sire there is, he has twelve sons, and each of these has twice thirty daughters different in feature ; some of the daughters are white, the others again are black ; they are immortal, and yet they all die.

And the answer is, " The year."

[a] *Anth. Pal.* vii. 153.
[b] Fr. 57 Bergk.
[c] *Anth. Pal.* xiv. 101 ; Stob. *Ecl. Phys.* i. 99. 15 W.

Τῶν δὲ ἀδομένων αὐτοῦ εὐδοκίμησε τάδε·
Ἀμουσία τὸ πλέον μέρος ἐν βροτοῖσι, λόγων τε
πλῆθος· ἀλλ' ὁ καιρὸς ἀρκέσει. φρόνει τι κεδνόν.
μὴ μάταιος ἄχαρις γινέσθω. ἔφη δὲ δεῖν συνοι-
κίζειν τὰς θυγατέρας, παρθένους μὲν τὴν ἡλικίαν,
τὸ δὲ φρονεῖν γυναῖκας· ὑποδεικνὺς ὅτι δεῖ παιδεύεσθαι καὶ τὰς παρθένους. ἔλεγέ τε τὸν φίλον δεῖν
εὐεργετεῖν, ὅπως μᾶλλον ᾖ φίλος· τὸν δὲ ἐχθρὸν
φίλον ποιεῖν. φυλάσσεσθαι γὰρ τῶν μὲν φίλων
92 τὸν ψόγον, τῶν δὲ ἐχθρῶν τὴν ἐπιβουλήν. καὶ ὅταν
τις ἐξίῃ τῆς οἰκίας, ζητείτω πρότερον τί μέλλει
πράσσειν· καὶ ὅταν εἰσέλθῃ πάλιν, ζητείτω τί
ἔπραξε. συνεβούλευέ τε εὖ τὸ σῶμα ἀσκεῖν·
φιλήκοον εἶναι μᾶλλον ἢ φιλόλαλον· [φιλομαθῆ
μᾶλλον ἢ ἀμαθῆ·] γλῶσσαν εὔφημον ἴσχειν· ἀρετῆς
οἰκεῖον εἶναι, κακίας ἀλλότριον· ἀδικίαν φεύγειν·
πόλει τὰ βέλτιστα συμβουλεύειν· ἡδονῆς κρατεῖν·
βίᾳ μηδὲν πράττειν· τέκνα παιδεύειν· ἐχθρὰν
διαλύειν. γυναικὶ μὴ φιλοφρονεῖσθαι, μηδὲ μάχεσθαι, ἀλλοτρίων παρόντων· τὸ μὲν γὰρ ἄνοιαν, τὸ
δὲ μανίαν σημαίνειν. οἰκέτην παρ' οἶνον μὴ
κολάζειν, δοκεῖν γὰρ ἂν παροινεῖν. γαμεῖν ἐκ τῶν
ὁμοίων· ἂν γὰρ ἐκ τῶν κρειττόνων λάβῃς, φησί,
93 δεσπότας κτήσῃ τοὺς συγγενέας. μὴ ἐπεγγελᾶν
τοῖς σκωπτομένοις· ἀπεχθήσεσθαι γὰρ τούτοις.
εὐτυχῶν μὴ ἴσθι ὑπερήφανος· ἀπορήσας μὴ ταπει-
νοῦ. τὰς μεταβολὰς τῆς τύχης γενναίως ἐπίστασο
φέρειν.

---

[a] These moral precepts are similar to those of Stobaeus in
the *Florilegium*, *e.g.* i. 172.

Of his songs the most popular are : It is want of taste that reigns most widely among mortals and multitude of words ; but due season will serve. Set your mind on something good. Do not become thoughtless or rude. He said that we ought to give our daughters to their husbands maidens in years but women in wisdom ; thus signifying that girls need to be educated as well as boys. Further, that we should render a service to a friend to bind him closer to us, and to an enemy in order to make a friend of him. For we have to guard against the censure of friends and the intrigues of enemies. When anyone leaves his house, let him first inquire what he means to do ; and on his return let him ask himself what he has effected. Moreover, he advised men to practise bodily exercise ; to be listeners rather than talkers ; to choose instruction rather than ignorance ; to refrain from ill-omened words ; to be friendly to virtue, hostile to vice ; to shun injustice ; to counsel the state for the best ; not to be overcome by pleasure ; to do nothing by violence ; to educate their children ; to put an end to enmity. Avoid being affectionate to your wife, or quarrelling with her, in the presence of strangers ; for the one savours of folly, the other of madness. Never correct a servant over your wine, for you will be thought to be the worse for wine. Mate with one of your own rank ; for if you take a wife who is superior to you, her kinsfolk will become your masters. When men are being bantered, do not laugh at their expense, or you will incur their hatred. Do not be arrogant in prosperity ; if you fall into poverty, do not humble yourself. Know how to bear the changes of fortune with nobility.[a]

Ἐτελεύτησε δὲ γηραιός, ἔτη βιοὺς ἑβδομήκοντα· καὶ αὐτῷ ἐπεγράφη·

ἄνδρα σοφὸν Κλεόβουλον ἀποφθίμενον καταπενθεῖ
ἥδε πάτρα Λίνδος πόντῳ ἀγαλλομένη.

Ἀπεφθέγξατο· μέτρον ἄριστον. καὶ Σόλωνι ἐπέστειλεν οὕτω·

Κλεόβουλος Σόλωνι

" Πολλοὶ μέν τιν ἔασιν ἔταροι καὶ οἶκος πάντῃ· φαμὶ δὲ ἐγὼν ποτανεστάταν ἐσεῖσθαι Σόλωνι τὰν Λίνδον δαμοκρατεομέναν. καὶ ἁ νᾶσος πελαγία, ἔνθα οἰκέοντι οὐδὲν δεινὸν ἐκ Πεισιστράτω. καὶ τοὶ ἔταροι δὲ ἑκαστόθεν πὰρ τὺ βασοῦνται."

Κεφ. ζ΄. ΠΕΡΙΑΝΔΡΟΣ

94 Περίανδρος Κυψέλου Κορίνθιος ἀπὸ τοῦ τῶν Ἡρακλειδῶν γένους. οὗτος γήμας Λυσίδην, ἣν αὐτὸς Μέλισσαν ἐκάλει, τὴν Προκλέους τοῦ Ἐπιδαυρίων τυράννου καὶ Ἐρισθενείας τῆς Ἀριστοκράτους παιδός, ἀδελφῆς δὲ τοῦ Ἀριστοδήμου θυγατέρα, οἳ σχεδὸν πάσης Ἀρκαδίας ἐπῆρξαν, ὥς φησιν Ἡρακλείδης ὁ Ποντικὸς ἐν τῷ Περὶ ἀρχῆς, παῖδας ἐξ αὐτῆς ἐποίησε δύο, Κύψελον καὶ Λυκόφρονα· τὸν μὲν νεώτερον συνετόν, τὸν δὲ πρεσβύτερον ἄφρονα. χρόνῳ δὴ ὑπ᾽ ὀργῆς βαλὼν ὑποβάθρῳ ἢ λακτίσας τὴν γυναῖκα ἔγκυον οὖσαν ἀπέκτεινε, πεισθεὶς διαβολαῖς παλλακίδων, ἃς ὕστερον ἔκαυσε.

Τόν τε παῖδα ἀπεκήρυξεν εἰς Κέρκυραν, λυπού-

He died at the ripe age of seventy ; and the in-scription over him is [a] :

Here the wise Rhodian, Cleobulus, sleeps,
And o'er his ashes sea-proud Lindus weeps.

His apophthegm was : Moderation is best. And he wrote to Solon the following letter :

Cleobulus to Solon

" You have many friends and a home wherever you go ; but the most suitable for Solon will, say I, be Lindus, which is governed by a democracy. The island lies on the high seas, and one who lives here has nothing to fear from Pisistratus. And friends from all parts will come to visit you."

CHAPTER 7. PERIANDER (tyrant 625–585 B.C.)

Periander, the son of Cypselus, was born at Corinth, of the family of the Heraclidae. His wife was Lysida, whom he called Melissa. Her father was Procles, tyrant of Epidaurus, her mother Eristheneia, daughter of Aristocrates and sister of Aristodemus, who together reigned over nearly the whole of Arcadia, as stated by Heraclides of Pontus in his book *On Government*. By her he had two sons, Cypselus and Lycophron, the younger a man of intelligence, the elder weak in mind. However, after some time, in a fit of anger, he killed his wife by throwing a footstool at her, or by a kick, when she was preg-nant, having been egged on by the slanderous tales of concubines, whom he afterwards burnt alive.

When the son whose name was Lycophron grieved

* *Anth. Pal.* vii. 618.

μενον ἐπὶ τῇ μητρί, ᾧ ὄνομα Λυκόφρων. ἤδη δὲ
95 ἐν γήρᾳ καθεστὼς μετεπέμπετο αὐτὸν ὅπως παρα-
λάβοι τὴν τυραννίδα· ὃν φθάσαντες οἱ Κερκυραῖοι
διεχρήσαντο. ὅθεν ὀργισθεὶς ἔπεμψε τοὺς παῖδας
αὐτῶν πρὸς Ἀλυάττην ἐπ᾽ ἐκτομῇ· προσχούσης δὲ
τῆς νεὼς Σάμῳ, ἱκετεύσαντες τὴν Ἥραν ὑπὸ τῶν
Σαμίων διεσώθησαν.

Καὶ ὃς ἀθυμήσας ἐτελεύτησεν, ἤδη γεγονὼς
ἔτη ὀγδοήκοντα. Σωσικράτης δέ φησι πρότερον
Κροίσου τελευτῆσαι αὐτὸν ἔτεσι τεσσαράκοντα καὶ
ἑνί, πρὸ τῆς τεσσαρακοστῆς ἐνάτης Ὀλυμπιάδος.
τοῦτον Ἡρόδοτος ἐν τῇ πρώτῃ ξένον φησὶν εἶναι
Θρασυβούλῳ τῷ Μιλησίων τυράννῳ.

96 Φησὶ δὲ Ἀρίστιππος ἐν πρώτῳ Περὶ παλαιᾶς
τρυφῆς περὶ αὐτοῦ τάδε, ὡς ἄρα ἐρασθεῖσα ἡ
μήτηρ αὐτοῦ Κράτεια συνῆν αὐτῷ λάθρα· καὶ ὃς
ἥδετο. φανεροῦ δὲ γενομένου βαρὺς πᾶσιν ἐγένετο
διὰ τὸ ἀλγεῖν ἐπὶ τῇ φωρᾷ. ἀλλὰ καὶ Ἔφορος
ἱστορεῖ ὡς εὔξαιτο, εἰ νικήσειεν Ὀλύμπια τεθρ-
ίππῳ, χρυσοῦν ἀνδριάντα ἀναθεῖναι. νικήσας δὲ
καὶ ἀπορῶν χρυσίου, κατά τινα ἑορτὴν ἐπιχώριον
κεκοσμημένας ἰδὼν τὰς γυναῖκας πάντα ἀφείλετο
τὸν κόσμον, καὶ ἔπεμψε τὸ ἀνάθημα.

Λέγουσι δέ τινες ὡς θελήσας αὐτοῦ τὸν τάφον
μὴ γνωσθῆναι, τοιοῦτόν τι ἐμηχανήσατο. δυσὶν
ἐκέλευσε νεανίσκοις, δείξας τινὰ ὁδόν, ἐξελθεῖν
νύκτωρ, καὶ τὸν ἀπαντήσαντα ἀνελεῖν καὶ θάψαι·
ἔπειτα βαδίζειν ἄλλους τε κατὰ τούτων τέτταρας,

ᵃ 584–580 B.C.

ᵇ An unsavoury work by a scandal-monger who, to judge
from the fragment of bk. iv., bore a grudge against philosophers, especially Academics: cf. Wilamowitz, *Antigonos
von Karystos*, pp. 48 ff.

for his mother, he banished him to Corcyra. And when well advanced in years he sent for his son to be his successor in the tyranny ; but the Corcyraeans put him to death before he could set sail. Enraged at this, he dispatched the sons of the Corcyraeans to Alyattes that he might make eunuchs of them ; but, when the ship touched at Samos, they took sanctuary in the temple of Hera, and were saved by the Samians.

Periander lost heart and died at the age of eighty. Sosicrates' account is that he died forty-one years before Croesus, just before the 49th Olympiad.[a] Herodotus in his first book says that he was a guest-friend of Thrasybulus, tyrant of Miletus.

Aristippus in the first book of his work *On the Luxury of the Ancients* [b] accuses him of incest with his own mother Crateia, and adds that, when the fact came to light, he vented his annoyance in indiscriminate severity. Ephorus records his vow that, if he won the victory at Olympia in the chariot-race, he would set up a golden statue. When the victory was won, being in sore straits for gold, he despoiled the women of all the ornaments which he had seen them wearing at some local festival. He was thus enabled to send the votive offering.

There is a story that he did not wish the place where he was buried to be known, and to that end contrived the following device. He ordered two young men to go out at night by a certain road which he pointed out to them ; they were to kill the man they met and bury him. He afterwards ordered four more to go in pursuit of the two, kill them and bury them ; again, he dispatched a larger

καὶ ἀνελόντας θάψαι· πάλιν τε κατὰ τούτων
πλείονας. καὶ οὕτως αὐτὸς τοῖς πρώτοις ἐντυχὼν
ἀνηρέθη. Κορίνθιοι δὲ ἐπί τι κενοτάφιον ἐπέγραψαν αὐτῷ τόδε·

97 πλούτου καὶ σοφίης πρύτανιν πατρὶς ἥδε Κόρινθος
     κόλποις ἀγχίαλος γῆ Περίανδρον ἔχει.

ἔστι καὶ ἡμῶν·

μή ποτε λυπήσῃ σε τὸ μή σε τυχεῖν τινος· ἀλλὰ
τέρπεο πᾶσιν ὁμῶς οἷσι δίδωσι θεός.
καὶ γὰρ ἀθυμήσας ὁ σοφὸς Περίανδρος ἀπέσβη,
οὕνεκεν οὐκ ἔτυχεν πρήξιος ἧς ἔθελεν.

Τούτου ἐστὶ καὶ τὸ Μηδὲν χρημάτων ἕνεκα πράτ-
τειν· δεῖν γὰρ τὰ κερδαντὰ κερδαίνειν. ἐποίησε
δὲ καὶ ὑποθήκας εἰς ἔπη δισχίλια. εἶπέ τε τοὺς
μέλλοντας ἀσφαλῶς τυραννήσειν τῇ εὐνοίᾳ δορυ-
φορεῖσθαι, καὶ μὴ τοῖς ὅπλοις. καί ποτε ἐρωτηθεὶς
διὰ τί τυραννεῖ, ἔφη, "ὅτι καὶ τὸ ἑκουσίως ἀπο-
στῆναι καὶ τὸ ἀφαιρεθῆναι κίνδυνον φέρει." ἔλεγε
δὲ καὶ τάδε· καλὸν ἡσυχία· ἐπισφαλὲς προπέτεια·
κέρδος αἰσχρόν· * δημοκρατία κρεῖττον τυραννίδος·
αἱ μὲν ἡδοναὶ φθαρταί, αἱ δὲ τιμαὶ ἀθάνατοι·
98 εὐτυχῶν μὲν μέτριος ἴσθι, δυστυχῶν δὲ φρόνιμος·
φίλοις εὐτυχοῦσι καὶ ἀτυχοῦσιν ὁ αὐτὸς ἴσθι· ὃ ἂν
ὁμολογήσῃς, διατήρει· λόγων ἀπορρήτων ἐκφορὰν
μὴ ποιοῦ· μὴ μόνον τοὺς ἁμαρτάνοντας, ἀλλὰ καὶ
τοὺς μέλλοντας κόλαζε.

Οὗτος πρῶτος δορυφόρους ἔσχε, καὶ τὴν ἀρχὴν
εἰς τυραννίδα μετέστησε· καὶ οὐκ εἴα ἐν ἄστει
ζῆν τοὺς βουλομένους, καθά φησιν Ἔφορος καὶ

number in pursuit of the four. Having taken these measures, he himself encountered the first pair and was slain. The Corinthians placed the following inscription upon a cenotaph [a] :

> In mother earth here Periander lies,
> The prince of sea-girt Corinth rich and wise.

My own epitaph on him is [b] :

> Grieve not because thou hast not gained thine end,
> But take with gladness all the gods may send ;
> Be warned by Periander's fate, who died
> Of grief that one desire should be denied.

To him belongs the maxim : Never do anything for money ; leave gain to trades pursued for gain. He wrote a didactic poem of 2000 lines. He said that those tyrants who intend to be safe should make loyalty their bodyguard, not arms. When some one asked him why he was tyrant, he replied, " Because it is as dangerous to retire voluntarily as to be dispossessed." Here are other sayings of his : Rest is beautiful. Rashness has its perils. Gain is ignoble. Democracy is better than tyranny. Pleasures are transient, honours are immortal. Be moderate in prosperity, prudent in adversity. Be the same to your friends whether they are in prosperity or in adversity. Whatever agreement you make, stick to it. Betray no secret. Correct not only the offenders but also those who are on the point of offending.

He was the first who had a bodyguard and who changed his government into a tyranny, and he would let no one live in the town without his permission, as we know from Ephorus and Aristotle.

[a] *Anth. Pal.* vii. 619.   [b] *Anth. Pal.* vii. 620.

Ἀριστοτέλης, ἤκμαζε δὲ περὶ τὴν τριακοστὴν ὀγδόην Ὀλυμπιάδα, καὶ ἐτυράννησεν ἔτη τετταράκοντα.

Σωτίων δὲ καὶ Ἡρακλείδης καὶ Παμφίλη ἐν τῷ πέμπτῳ τῶν Ὑπομνημάτων δύο φασὶ Περιάνδρους γεγονέναι, τὸν μὲν τύραννον, τὸν δὲ σοφὸν καὶ 99 Ἀμβρακιώτην. τοῦτο καὶ Νεάνθης φησὶν ὁ Κυζικηνός, ἀνεψιούς τε εἶναι ἀλλήλοις. καὶ Ἀριστοτέλης μὲν τὸν Κορίνθιόν φησιν εἶναι τὸν σοφόν· Πλάτων δὲ οὔ φησι.

Τούτου ἐστί· Μελέτη τὸ πᾶν. ἤθελε δὲ καὶ τὸν Ἰσθμὸν διορύξαι.

Φέρεται δὲ αὐτοῦ καὶ ἐπιστολή·

Περίανδρος τοῖς σοφοῖς

"Πολλὰ χάρις τῷ Πυθοῖ Ἀπόλλωνι τοῦ εἰς ἓν ἐλθόντας εὑρεῖν. ἀξοῦντί τε καὶ ἐς Κόρινθον ταὶ ἐμαὶ ἐπιστολαί. ἐγὼν δὲ ὑμᾶς ἀποδέχομαι, ὡς ἴστε αὐτοί, ὅτι δαμοτικώτατα. πεύθομαι ὡς πέρυτι ἐγένετο ὑμῶν ἁλία παρὰ τὸν Λυδὸν ἐς Σάρδεις. ἤδη ὦν μὴ ὀκνεῖτε καὶ παρ' ἐμὲ φοιτῆν τὸν Κορίνθου τύραννον. ὑμᾶς γὰρ καὶ ἄσμενοι ὄψονται Κορίνθιοι φοιτεῦντας ἐς οἶκον τὸν Περιάνδρου."

Περίανδρος Προκλεῖ

100 "Ἐμὶν μὲν ἀκούσιον τᾶς δάμαρτος τὸ ἄγος· τὺ δὲ ἑκὼν τῷ παιδί με ἄπο θυμοῦ ποιήσαις ἀδικεῖς. ἢ ὦν παῦσον τὰν ἀπήνειαν τῶ παιδός, ἢ ἐγὼν τὺ

---

[a] Periander is mentioned in the *Politics* of Aristotle (v. 4, 1304 a 32), but not as one of the Seven Wise Men. In Plato's *Protagoras*, 343 A, where the Seven Wise Men are

102

He flourished about the 38th Olympiad and was tyrant for forty years.

Sotion and Heraclides and Pamphila in the fifth book of her *Commentaries* distinguish two Perianders, one a tyrant, the other a sage who was born in Ambracia. Neanthes of Cyzicus also says this, and adds that they were near relations. And Aristotle [a] maintains that the Corinthian Periander was the sage ; while Plato denies this.

His apophthegm is : Practice makes perfect. He planned a canal across the Isthmus.

A letter of his is extant :

Periander to the Wise Men

" Very grateful am I to the Pythian Apollo that I found you gathered together ; and my letters will also bring you to Corinth, where, as you know, I will give you a thoroughly popular reception. I learn that last year you met in Sardis at the Lydian court. Do not hesitate therefore to come to me, the ruler of Corinth. The Corinthians will be pleased to see you coming to the house of Periander."

Periander to Procles

" The murder of my wife was unintentional ; but yours is deliberate guilt when you set my son's heart against me. Either therefore put an end to my son's harsh treatment, or I will revenge myself

enumerated, Periander's name is omitted, his place being taken by Myson. It would almost seem as if Diogenes Laertius knew of some passage in Aristotle in which Periander was called one of the Seven, though no such passage is extant.

ἀμυνοῦμαι. καὶ γὰρ δὴν καὶ αὐτὸς ποινὰς ἔτισα
τὶν τᾷ θυγατρί, συγκατακαύσαις αὐτᾷ τὰ πασᾶν
Κορινθιᾶν εἵματα.''

Ἔγραψε δὲ αὐτῷ καὶ Θρασύβουλος οὕτω·

Θρασύβουλος Περιάνδρῳ

''Τῷ μὲν κήρυκι σεῦ οὐδὲν ὑπεκρινάμην· ἀγαγὼν
δὲ αὐτὸν ἐς λήϊον, τοὺς ὑπερφυέας τῶν ἀσταχύων
ῥάβδῳ παίων ἀπεθέριζον, ὁμαρτέοντος ἐκείνου.
καί σοι ἀναγγελέει εἰ ἐπέροιο, ὅ τι μευ ἀκούσειεν
ἢ ἴδοι. σὺ δὲ ποίει οὕτως, ἤν γ' ἐθέλῃς καρτύνασθαι
τὴν αἰσυμνητίην· τοὺς ἐξόχους τῶν πολιτέων ἐξ-
αίρειν, ἤν τέ τις ἐχθρός τοι φαίνηται, ἤν τε μή.
ὕποπτος γὰρ ἀνδρὶ αἰσυμνήτῃ καὶ τῶν τις ἑτάρων.''

Κεφ. η΄. ΑΝΑΧΑΡΣΙΣ Ο ΣΚΥΘΗΣ

101 Ἀνάχαρσις ὁ Σκύθης Γνούρου μὲν ἦν υἱός,
ἀδελφὸς δὲ Καδουΐδα τοῦ Σκυθῶν βασιλέως,
μητρὸς δὲ Ἑλληνίδος· διὸ καὶ δίγλωττος ἦν.
οὗτος ἐποίησε τῶν τε παρὰ τοῖς Σκύθαις νομίμων
καὶ τῶν παρὰ τοῖς Ἕλλησιν, εἰς εὐτέλειαν βίου καὶ
τὰ κατὰ τὸν πόλεμον ἔπη ὀκτακόσια. παρέσχε δὲ
καὶ ἀφορμὴν παροιμίας διὰ τὸ παρρησιαστὴς εἶναι,
τὴν ἀπὸ Σκυθῶν ῥῆσιν.

Λέγει δὲ αὐτὸν Σωσικράτης ἐλθεῖν εἰς Ἀθήνας
κατὰ τὴν τεσσαρακοστὴν ἑβδόμην Ὀλυμπιάδα
ἐπὶ ἄρχοντος Εὐκράτους. Ἕρμιππος δὲ πρὸς
τὴν Σόλωνος οἰκίαν ἀφικόμενον τῶν θεραπόντων
τινὶ κελεῦσαι μηνῦσαι ὅτι παρείη πρὸς αὐτὸν
Ἀνάχαρσις, καὶ βούλοιτο αὐτὸν θεάσασθαι, ξένος
102 τε, εἰ οἷόν τε, γενέσθαι. καὶ ὁ θεράπων εἰσ-

on you. For long ago I made expiation to you for your daughter by burning on her pyre the apparel of all the women of Corinth."

There is also a letter written to him by Thrasybulus, as follows :

Thrasybulus to Periander

" I made no answer to your herald ; but I took him into a cornfield, and with a staff smote and cut off the over-grown ears of corn, while he accompanied me. And if you ask him what he heard and what he saw, he will give his message. And this is what you must do if you want to strengthen your absolute rule : put to death those among the citizens who are pre-eminent, whether they are hostile to you or not. For to an absolute ruler even a friend is an object of suspicion."

Chapter 8. ANACHARSIS

Anacharsis the Scythian was the son of Gnurus and brother of Caduidas, king of Scythia. His mother was a Greek, and for that reason he spoke both languages. He wrote on the institutions of the Greeks and the Scythians, dealing with simplicity of life and military matters, a poem of 800 lines. So outspoken was he that he furnished occasion for a proverb, " To talk like a Scythian."

Sosicrates makes him come to Athens about the 47th Olympiad [a] in the archonship of Eucrates. Hermippus relates that on his arrival at the house of Solon he told one of the servants to announce that Anacharsis had come and was desirous of seeing him and, if possible, of becoming his guest. The

* 591–588 B.C.

αγγείλας ἐκελεύσθη ὑπὸ τοῦ Σόλωνος εἰπεῖν αὐτῷ,
ὅτιπερ ἐν ταῖς ἰδίαις πατρίσι ξένους ποιοῦνται.
ἔνθεν ὁ ᾿Ανάχαρσις ἑλὼν ἔφη νῦν αὐτὸν ἐν τῇ
πατρίδι εἶναι καὶ προσήκειν αὐτῷ ξένους ποιεῖσθαι.
ὁ δὲ καταπλαγεὶς τὴν ἑτοιμότητα εἰσέφρησεν αὐτὸν
καὶ μέγιστον φίλον ἐποιήσατο.

Μετὰ χρόνον δὲ παραγενόμενος εἰς τὴν Σκυθίαν
καὶ δοκῶν τὰ νόμιμα παραλύειν τῆς πατρίδος πολὺς
ὢν ἐν τῷ ἑλληνίζειν, τοξευθεὶς ἐν κυνηγεσίῳ πρὸς
τἀδελφοῦ τελευτᾷ, εἰπὼν διὰ μὲν τὸν λόγον ἐκ τῆς
῾Ελλάδος σωθῆναι, διὰ δὲ τὸν φθόνον ἐν τῇ οἰκείᾳ
ἀπολέσθαι. ἔνιοι δὲ τελετὰς ῾Ελληνικὰς ἐπιτελοῦντα
διαχρησθῆναι.

Καὶ ἔστιν ἡμῶν εἰς αὐτόν·

103 ἐς Σκυθίην ᾿Ανάχαρσις ὅτ᾿ ἤλυθε, πολλὰ πλανηθεὶς
πάντας ἔπειθε βιοῦν ἤθεσιν ῾Ελλαδικοῖς.
τὸν δ᾿ ἔτι μῦθον ἄκραντον ἐνὶ στομάτεσσιν ἔχοντα
πτηνὸς ἐς ἀθανάτους ἥρπασεν ὦκα δόναξ.

Οὗτος τὴν ἄμπελον εἶπε τρεῖς φέρειν βότρυς· τὸν
πρῶτον ἡδονῆς· τὸν δεύτερον μέθης· τὸν τρίτον
ἀηδίας. θαυμάζειν δὲ ἔφη πῶς παρὰ τοῖς ῞Ελλησιν
ἀγωνίζονται μὲν οἱ τεχνῖται, κρίνουσι δὲ οἱ μὴ
τεχνῖται. ἐρωτηθεὶς πῶς οὐκ ἂν γένοιτό τις
φιλοπότης, " εἰ πρὸ ὀφθαλμῶν," εἶπεν, " ἔχοι τὰς
τῶν μεθυόντων ἀσχημοσύνας." θαυμάζειν τε ἔλεγε
πῶς οἱ ῞Ελληνες νομοθετοῦντες κατὰ τῶν ὑβρι-
ζόντων, τοὺς ἀθλητὰς τιμῶσιν ἐπὶ τῷ τύπτειν

servant delivered his message and was ordered by Solon to tell him that men as a rule choose their guests from among their own countrymen. Then Anacharsis took him up and said that he was now in his own country and had a right to be entertained as a guest. And Solon, struck with his ready wit, admitted him into his house and made him his greatest friend.

After a while Anacharsis returned to Scythia, where, owing to his enthusiasm for everything Greek, he was supposed to be subverting the national institutions, and was killed by his brother while they were out hunting together. When struck by the arrow he exclaimed, " My reputation carried me safe through Greece, but the envy it excited at home has been my ruin." In some accounts it is said that he was slain while performing Greek rites.

Here is my own epitaph upon him [a] :

> Back from his travels Anacharsis came,
> To hellenize the Scythians all aglow ;
> Ere half his sermon could their minds inflame,
> A wingèd arrow laid the preacher low.

It was a saying of his that the vine bore three kinds of grapes : the first of pleasure, the next of intoxication, and the third of disgust. He said he wondered why in Greece experts contend in the games and non-experts award the prizes. Being asked how one could avoid becoming a toper, he answered, " By keeping before your eyes the disgraceful exhibition made by the drunkard." Again, he expressed surprise that the Greek lawgivers should impose penalties on wanton outrage, while they honour athletes for bruising one another. After

---

[a] *Anth. Pal.* vii. 92.

ἀλλήλους. μαθὼν τέτταρας δακτύλους εἶναι τὸ
πάχος τῆς νεώς, τοσοῦτον ἔφη τοῦ θανάτου τοὺς
πλέοντας ἀπέχειν.

104 Τὸ ἔλαιον μανίας φάρμακον ἔλεγε διὰ τὸ
ἀλειφομένους τοὺς ἀθλητὰς ἐπιμαίνεσθαι ἀλλήλοις. πῶς, ἔλεγεν, ἀπαγορεύοντες τὸ ψεύδεσθαι
ἐν ταῖς καπηλείαις φανερῶς ψεύδονται; καὶ
θαυμάζειν φησὶ πῶς Ἕλληνες ἀρχόμενοι μὲν
ἐν μικροῖς πίνουσι, πλησθέντες δὲ ἐν μεγάλοις.
ἐπιγράφεται δὲ αὐτοῦ ταῖς εἰκόσι· "γλώσσης,
γαστρός, αἰδοίων κρατεῖν." ἐρωτηθεὶς εἰ εἰσὶν ἐν
Σκύθαις αὐλοί, εἶπεν, "ἀλλ᾽ οὐδὲ ἄμπελοι." ἐρωτηθεὶς τίνα τῶν πλοίων εἰσὶν ἀσφαλέστερα, ἔφη,
"τὰ νενεωλκημένα." καὶ τοῦτο ἔφη θαυμασιώ-
τατον ἑωρακέναι παρὰ τοῖς Ἕλλησιν, ὅτι τὸν μὲν
καπνὸν ἐν τοῖς ὄρεσι καταλείπουσι, τὰ δὲ ξύλα εἰς
τὴν πόλιν κομίζουσιν. ἐρωτηθεὶς πότεροι πλείους
εἰσίν, οἱ ζῶντες ἢ οἱ νεκροί, ἔφη, "τοὺς οὖν
πλέοντας ποῦ τίθης;" ὀνειδιζόμενος ὑπὸ Ἀττικοῦ
ὅτι Σκύθης ἐστίν, ἔφη, "ἀλλ᾽ ἐμοῦ μὲν ὄνειδος ἡ
105 πατρίς, σὺ δὲ τῆς πατρίδος." ἐρωτηθεὶς τί ἐστιν ἐν
ἀνθρώποις ἀγαθόν τε καὶ φαῦλον, ἔφη, "γλῶσσα."
κρεῖττον ἔλεγεν ἕνα φίλον ἔχειν πολλοῦ ἄξιον ἢ
πολλοὺς μηδενὸς ἀξίους. τὴν ἀγορὰν ὡρισμένον
ἔφη τόπον εἰς τὸ ἀλλήλους ἀπατᾶν καὶ πλεονεκτεῖν.
ὑπὸ μειρακίου παρὰ πότον ὑβρισθεὶς ἔφη, "μειράκιον, ἐὰν νέος ὢν τὸν οἶνον οὐ φέρῃς, γέρων
γενόμενος ὕδωρ οἴσεις."

---

* *i.e.* in the form of charcoal.   *Cf.* A. S. Ferguson in
Class. Rev. vol. xxxi. p. 97.

ascertaining that the ship's side was four fingers' breadth in thickness, he remarked that the passengers were just so far from death.

Oil he called a drug which produced madness, because the athletes when they anoint themselves with it are maddened against each other. How is it, he asked, that the Greeks prohibit falsehood and yet obviously tell falsehoods in retail trade ? Nor could he understand why at the beginning of their feasts they drink from small goblets and when they are " full " from large ones. The inscription on his statues is : " Bridle speech, gluttony, and sensuality." Being asked if there were flutes in Scythia, he replied, " No, nor yet vines." To the question what vessels were the safest his reply was, " Those which have been hauled ashore." And he declared the strangest thing he had seen in Greece to be that they leave the smoke on the mountains and convey the fuel into the city.*a* When some one inquired which were more in number, the living or the dead, he rejoined, " In which category, then, do you place those who are on the seas ? " When some Athenian reproached him with being a Scythian, he replied, " Well, granted that my country is a disgrace to me, you are a disgrace to your country." To the question, "What among men is both good and bad ? " his answer was " The tongue." He said it was better to have one friend of great worth than many friends worth nothing at all. He defined the market as a place set apart where men may deceive and overreach one another. When insulted by a boy over the wine he said, " If you cannot carry your liquor when you are young, boy, you will be a water carrier when you are old."

Εὗρε δ' εἰς τὸν βίον ἄγκυράν τε καὶ κεραμικὸν τροχόν, ὥς τινες.

Καὶ ἐπέστειλεν ὧδε·

Ἀνάχαρσις Κροίσῳ

" Ἐγώ, βασιλεῦ Λυδῶν, ἀφῖγμαι εἰς τὴν τῶν Ἑλλήνων, διδαχθησόμενος ἤθη τὰ τούτων καὶ ἐπιτηδεύματα. χρυσοῦ δ' οὐδὲ δέομαι, ἀλλ' ἀπόχρη με ἐπανήκειν ἐς Σκύθας ἄνδρα ἀμείνονα. ἥκω γοῦν ἐς Σάρδεις, πρὸ μεγάλου ποιούμενος ἐν γνώμῃ τοι γενέσθαι."

Κεφ. θ'. ΜΥΣΩΝ

106 Μύσων Στρύμωνος, ὥς φησι Σωσικράτης Ἕρμιππον παρατιθέμενος, τὸ γένος Χηνεύς, ἀπὸ κώμης τινὸς Οἰταϊκῆς ἢ Λακωνικῆς, σὺν τοῖς ἑπτὰ καταριθμεῖται. φασὶ δὲ αὐτὸν καὶ τυράννου πατρὸς εἶναι. λέγεται δὴ πρός τινος Ἀναχάρσιδος πυνθανομένου εἴ τις αὐτοῦ σοφώτερος εἴη, τὴν Πυθίαν ἀνελεῖν[1] ἅπερ προείρηται ἐν τῷ Θαλοῦ βίῳ ὑπὲρ Χίλωνος·

Οἰταῖόν τινά φημι Μύσων' ἐνὶ Χηνὶ γενέσθαι
σοῦ μᾶλλον πραπίδεσσιν ἀρηρότα πευκαλίμῃσι.

πολυπραγμονήσαντα δὲ ἐλθεῖν εἰς τὴν κώμην καὶ εὑρεῖν αὐτὸν θέρους ἐχέτλην ἀρότρῳ προσαρμόττοντα, καὶ εἰπεῖν, " ἀλλ', ὦ Μύσων, οὐχ ὥρα νῦν ἀρότρου." " καὶ μάλα," εἶπεν, " ὥστε ἐπι-
107 σκευάζειν." ἄλλοι δὲ τὸν χρησμὸν οὕτως ἔχειν φασί, " Ἠτεῖόν τινά φημι·" καὶ ζητοῦσι τί ἐστιν

[1] ἀνειπεῖν vulg. : corr. H. Richards.

According to some he was the inventor of the anchor and the potter's wheel.

To him is attributed the following letter :

Anacharsis to Croesus

" I have come, O King of the Lydians, to the land of the Greeks to be instructed in their manners and pursuits. And I am not even in quest of gold, but am well content to return to Scythia a better man. At all events here I am in Sardis, being greatly desirous of making your acquaintance."

CHAPTER 9. MYSON (c. 600 B.C.)

Myson was the son of Strymon, according to Sosicrates, who quotes Hermippus as his authority, and a native of Chen, a village in the district of Oeta or Laconia ; and he is reckoned one of the Seven Sages. They say that his father was a tyrant. We are told by some one that, when Anacharsis inquired if there were anyone wiser than himself, the Pythian priestess gave the response which has already been quoted in the Life of Thales as her reply to a question by Chilon [a] :

> Myson of Chen in Oeta ; this is he
> Who for wiseheartedness surpasseth thee.

His curiosity aroused, Anacharsis went to the village in summer time and found him fitting a share to a plough and said, " Myson, this is not the season for the plough." " It is just the time to repair it," was the reply. Others cite the first line of the oracle differently, " Myson of Chen in Etis," and inquire what

[a] *Anth. Plan.* vi. 40.

ὁ Ἠτεῖος. Παρμενίδης μὲν οὖν δῆμον εἶναι
Λακωνικῆς, ὅθεν εἶναι τὸν Μύσωνα. Σωσικράτης
δ' ἐν Διαδοχαῖς, ἀπὸ μὲν πατρὸς Ἠτεῖον εἶναι, ἀπὸ
δὲ μητρὸς Χηνέα. Εὐθύφρων δ' ὁ Ἡρακλείδου
τοῦ Ποντικοῦ, Κρῆτά φησιν εἶναι· Ἠτείαν γὰρ
πόλιν εἶναι Κρήτης. Ἀναξίλαος δ' Ἀρκάδα.
Μέμνηται δ' αὐτοῦ καὶ Ἱππῶναξ εἰπών·

καὶ Μύσων ὃν Ὠπόλλων
ἀνεῖλεν ἀνδρῶν σωφρονέστατον πάντων.

Ἀριστόξενος δέ φησιν ἐν τοῖς σποράδην οὐ πόρρω
Τίμωνος αὐτὸν καὶ Ἀπημάντου γεγονέναι· μισ-
108 ανθρωπεῖν γάρ. ὀφθῆναι γοῦν ἐν Λακεδαίμονι
μόνον ἐπ' ἐρημίας γελῶντα· ἄφνω δέ τινος ἐπι-
στάντος καὶ πυθομένου διὰ τί μηδενὸς παρόντος
γελᾷ, φάναι, " δι' αὐτὸ τοῦτο." φησὶ δ' Ἀριστόξενος ὅτι ἔνθεν καὶ ἄδοξος ἦν, ὅτι μηδὲ πόλεως,
ἀλλὰ κώμης, καὶ ταῦτα ἀφανοῦς. ὅθεν διὰ τὴν
ἀδοξίαν αὐτοῦ καὶ τὰ αὐτοῦ τινας Πεισιστράτῳ
περιθεῖναι τῷ τυράννῳ, χωρὶς Πλάτωνος τοῦ
φιλοσόφου. μέμνηται γὰρ αὐτοῦ καὶ οὗτος ἐν τῷ
Πρωταγόρᾳ, ἀντὶ Περιάνδρου θεὶς αὐτόν.

Ἔφασκε δὲ μὴ ἐκ τῶν λόγων τὰ πράγματα,
ἀλλ' ἐκ τῶν πραγμάτων τοὺς λόγους ζητεῖν· οὐ
γὰρ ἕνεκα τῶν λόγων τὰ πράγματα συντελεῖσθαι,
ἀλλ' ἕνεκα τῶν πραγμάτων τοὺς λόγους.

Κατέστρεψε δὲ βιοὺς ἔτη ἑπτὰ καὶ ἐννενήκοντα.

" Myson of Etis " means. Parmenides indeed explains that Etis is a district in Laconia to which Myson belonged. Sosicrates in his *Successions of Philosophers* makes him belong to Etis on the father's side and to Chen on the mother's. Euthyphro, the son of Heraclides of Pontus, declares that he was a Cretan, Eteia being a town in Crete. Anaxilaus makes him an Arcadian.

Myson is mentioned by Hipponax, the words being [a] :

> And Myson, whom Apollo's self proclaimed
> Wisest of all men.

Aristoxenus in his *Historical Gleanings* says he was not unlike Timon and Apemantus, for he was a misanthrope. At any rate he was seen in Lacedaemon laughing to himself in a lonely spot ; and when some one suddenly appeared and asked him why he laughed when no one was near, he replied, " That is just the reason." And Aristoxenus says that the reason why he remained obscure was that he belonged to no city but to a village and that an unimportant one. Hence because he was unknown, some writers, but not Plato the philosopher, attributed to Pisistratus the tyrant what properly belonged to Myson. For Plato mentions him in the *Protagoras*,[b] reckoning him as one of the Seven instead of Periander.

He used to say we should not investigate facts by the light of arguments, but arguments by the light of facts ; for the facts were not put together to fit the arguments, but the arguments to fit the facts.

He died at the age of ninety-seven.

---

[a] Fr. 45 Bergk.　　　　　[b] 343 A.

Κεφ. ι΄. ΕΠΙΜΕΝΙΔΗΣ

109 Ἐπιμενίδης, καθά φησι Θεόπομπος καὶ ἄλλοι συχνοί, πατρὸς μὲν ἦν Φαιστίου, οἱ δὲ Δωσιάδα οἱ δὲ Ἀγησάρχου· Κρὴς τὸ γένος ἀπὸ Κνωσοῦ, καθέσει τῆς κόμης τὸ εἶδος παραλλάσσων. οὗτός ποτε πεμφθεὶς παρὰ τοῦ πατρὸς εἰς ἀγρὸν ἐπὶ πρόβατον, τῆς ὁδοῦ κατὰ μεσημβρίαν ἐκκλίνας ὑπ᾽ ἄντρῳ τινὶ κατεκοιμήθη ἑπτὰ καὶ πεντήκοντα ἔτη. διαναστὰς δὲ μετὰ ταῦτα ἐζήτει τὸ πρόβατον, νομίζων ἐπ᾽ ὀλίγον κεκοιμῆσθαι. ὡς δὲ οὐχ εὕρισκε, παρεγένετο εἰς τὸν ἀγρόν, καὶ μετεσκευασμένα πάντα καταλαβὼν καὶ παρ᾽ ἑτέρῳ τὴν κτῆσιν, πάλιν ἧκεν εἰς ἄστυ διαπορούμενος. κἀκεῖ δὲ εἰς τὴν ἑαυτοῦ εἰσιὼν οἰκίαν περιέτυχε τοῖς πυνθανομένοις τίς εἴη, ἕως τὸν νεώτερον ἀδελφὸν εὑρὼν τότε ἤδη γέροντα ὄντα, πᾶσαν 110 ἔμαθε παρ᾽ ἐκείνου τὴν ἀλήθειαν. γνωσθεὶς δὲ παρὰ τοῖς Ἕλλησι θεοφιλέστατος εἶναι ὑπελήφθη.

Τότε καὶ Ἀθηναίοις [τότε] λοιμῷ κατεχομένοις ἔχρησεν ἡ Πυθία καθῆραι τὴν πόλιν· οἱ δὲ πέμπουσι ναῦν τε καὶ Νικίαν τὸν Νικηράτου εἰς Κρήτην, καλοῦντες τὸν Ἐπιμενίδην. καὶ ὃς ἐλθὼν Ὀλυμπιάδι τεσσαρακοστῇ ἕκτῃ ἐκάθηρεν αὐτῶν τὴν πόλιν καὶ ἔπαυσε τὸν λοιμὸν τοῦτον τὸν τρόπον. λαβὼν πρόβατα μέλανά τε καὶ λευκὰ ἤγαγε πρὸς τὸν Ἄρειον πάγον· κἀκεῖθεν εἴασεν ἰέναι οἷ βούλοιντο, προστάξας τοῖς ἀκολούθοις ἔνθα ἂν κατακλίνοι αὐτῶν ἕκαστον, θύειν τῷ προσήκοντι θεῷ· καὶ οὕτω λῆξαι τὸ κακόν. ὅθεν ἔτι καὶ νῦν ἔστιν εὑρεῖν κατὰ τοὺς δήμους τῶν

ᵃ 595–592 B.C.

Chapter 10. EPIMENIDES (*c.* 600 B.C.)

Epimenides, according to Theopompus and many other writers, was the son of Phaestius ; some, however, make him the son of Dosiadas, others of Agesarchus. He was a native of Cnossos in Crete, though from wearing his hair long he did not look like a Cretan. One day he was sent into the country by his father to look for a stray sheep, and at noon he turned aside out of the way, and went to sleep in a cave, where he slept for fifty-seven years. After this he got up and went in search of the sheep, thinking he had been asleep only a short time. And when he could not find it, he came to the farm, and found everything changed and another owner in possession. Then he went back to the town in utter perplexity ; and there, on entering his own house, he fell in with people who wanted to know who he was. At length he found his younger brother, now an old man, and learnt the truth from him. So he became famous throughout Greece, and was believed to be a special favourite of heaven.

Hence, when the Athenians were attacked by pestilence, and the Pythian priestess bade them purify the city, they sent a ship commanded by Nicias, son of Niceratus, to Crete to ask the help of Epimenides. And he came in the 46th Olympiad,[a] purified their city, and stopped the pestilence in the following way. He took sheep, some black and others white, and brought them to the Areopagus ; and there he let them go whither they pleased, instructing those who followed them to mark the spot where each sheep lay down and offer a sacrifice to the local divinity. And thus, it is said, the plague was stayed. Hence even to this day altars may be

115

Ἀθηναίωι βωμοὺς ἀνωνύμους, ὑπόμνημα τῆς τότε γενομένης ἐξιλάσεως. οἱ δὲ τὴν αἰτίαν εἰπεῖν τοῦ λοιμοῦ τὸ Κυλώνειον ἄγος σημαίνειν τε τὴν ἀπαλλαγήν· καὶ διὰ τοῦτο ἀποθανεῖν δύο νεανίας, Κρατῖνον καὶ Κτησίβιον, καὶ λυθῆναι τὴν συμφοράν.

111 Ἀθηναῖοι δὲ τάλαντον ἐψηφίσαντο δοῦναι αὐτῷ καὶ ναῦν τὴν ἐς Κρήτην ἀπάξουσαν αὐτόν. ὁ δὲ τὸ μὲν ἀργύριον οὐ προσήκατο· φιλίαν δὲ καὶ συμμαχίαν ἐποιήσατο Κνωσίων καὶ Ἀθηναίων.

Καὶ ἐπανελθὼν ἐπ' οἴκου μετ' οὐ πολὺ μετ-ήλλαξεν, ὥς φησι Φλέγων ἐν τῷ Περὶ μακροβίων, βιοὺς ἔτη ἑπτὰ καὶ πεντήκοντα καὶ ἑκατόν· ὡς δὲ Κρῆτες λέγουσιν, ἑνὸς δέοντα τριακόσια· ὡς δὲ Ξενοφάνης ὁ Κολοφώνιος ἀκηκοέναι φησί, τέτταρα πρὸς τοῖς πεντήκοντα καὶ ἑκατόν.

Ἐποίησε δὲ Κουρήτων καὶ Κορυβάντων γένεσιν καὶ Θεογονίαν, ἔπη πεντακισχίλια, Ἀργοῦς ναυ-πηγίαν τε καὶ Ἰάσονος εἰς Κόλχους ἀπόπλουν 112 ἔπη ἑξακισχίλια πεντακόσια. συνέγραψε δὲ καὶ καταλογάδην Περὶ θυσιῶν καὶ τῆς ἐν Κρήτῃ πολιτείας καὶ Περὶ Μίνω καὶ Ῥαδαμάνθυος εἰς ἔπη τετρακισχίλια. ἱδρύσατο δὲ καὶ παρ' Ἀθη-ναίοις τὸ ἱερὸν τῶν Σεμνῶν, ὥς φησι Λόβων ὁ Ἀργεῖος ἐν τῷ Περὶ ποιητῶν. λέγεται δὲ καὶ πρῶτος οἰκίας καὶ ἀγροὺς καθῆραι καὶ ἱερὰ ἱδρύ-σασθαι. εἰσὶ δ' οἳ μὴ κοιμηθῆναι αὐτὸν λέγουσιν, ἀλλὰ χρόνον τινὰ ἐκπατῆσαι ἀσχολούμενον περὶ ῥιζοτομίαν.

---

[a] These long poems may have been written by Lobon himself on the Hesiodic model ; or Lobon may merely have affirmed their existence in his treatise *On Poets*.

found in different parts of Attica with no name inscribed upon them, which are memorials of this atonement. According to some writers he declared the plague to have been caused by the pollution which Cylon brought on the city and showed them how to remove it. In consequence two young men, Cratinus and Ctesibius, were put to death and the city was delivered from the scourge.

The Athenians voted him a talent in money and a ship to convey him back to Crete. The money he declined, but he concluded a treaty of friendship and alliance between Cnossos and Athens.

So he returned home and soon afterwards died. According to Phlegon in his work *On Longevity* he lived one hundred and fifty-seven years; according to the Cretans two hundred and ninety-nine years. Xenophanes of Colophon gives his age as 154, according to hearsay.

He wrote a poem *On the Birth of the Curetes and Corybantes* and a *Theogony*,[a] 5000 lines in all; another on the building of the Argo and Jason's voyage to Colchis in 6500 lines. He also compiled prose works *On Sacrifices and the Cretan Constitution*, also *On Minos and Rhadamanthus*, running to about 4000 lines. At Athens again he founded the temple of the Eumenides, as Lobon of Argos tells us in his work *On Poets*. He is stated to have been the first who purified houses and fields, and the first who founded temples. Some are found to maintain that he did not go to sleep but withdrew himself [b] for a while, engaged in gathering simples.

---

[b] This is the meaning of ἐκπατεῖν in three other passages, iv. 19, ix. 3, 63, in the last of which it is glossed by ἐρημάζειν, as if the sage were a recluse, a lover of solitude.

Φέρεται δ' αὐτοῦ καὶ ἐπιστολὴ πρὸς Σόλωνα τὸν νομοθέτην, περιέχουσα πολιτείαν ἣν διέταξε Κρησὶ Μίνως. ἀλλὰ Δημήτριος ὁ Μάγνης ἐν τοῖς περὶ ὁμωνύμων ποιητῶν τε καὶ συγγραφέων διελέγχειν πειρᾶται τὴν ἐπιστολὴν ὡς νεαρὰν καὶ μὴ τῇ Κρητικῇ φωνῇ γεγραμμένην, Ἀτθίδι δὲ καὶ ταύτῃ νέᾳ. ἐγὼ δὲ καὶ ἄλλην εὗρον ἐπιστολὴν ἔχουσαν οὕτως·

Ἐπιμενίδης Σόλωνι

113 " Θάρρει, ὦ ἑταῖρε. αἰ γὰρ ἔτι θητευόντεσσιν Ἀθηναίοις καὶ μὴ εὐνομημένοις ἐπεθήκατο Πεισίστρατος, εἶχέ κα τὰν ἀρχὰν ἀεί, ἀνδραποδιξάμενος τὼς πολιήτας· νῦν δὲ οὐ κακῶς ἄνδρας δουλῶται· τοὶ μεμναμένοι τᾶς Σόλωνος μανύσιος ἀλγιόντι πεδ' αἰσχύνας οὐδὲ ἀνεξοῦνται τυραννούμενοι. ἀλλ' αἴ κα Πεισίστρατος ⟨αὐτὸς⟩ κατασχέθη τὰν πόλιν, οὐ μὰν ἐς παῖδάς γε τήνω ἔλπομαι τὸ κράτος ἵξεσθαι· δυσμάχανον γὰρ ἀνθρώπως ἐλευθεριάξαντας ἐν τεθμοῖς ἀρίστοις δούλως ἦμεν. τὺ δὲ μὴ ἀλᾶσθαι, ἀλλ' ἕρπε ἐς Κρήτην ποθ' ἀμέ. τουτᾶ γὰρ οὐκ ἐσεῖταί τιν δεινὸς ὁ μόναρχος· αἰ δέ πη ἐπ' ἀλατείᾳ ἐγκύρσωντί τοι τοὶ τήνω φίλοι, δειμαίνω μή τι δεινὸν πάθῃς.''

114 Καὶ οὗτος μὲν ὧδε. φησὶ δὲ Δημήτριός τινας ἱστορεῖν ὡς λάβοι παρὰ Νυμφῶν ἔδεσμά τι καὶ φυλάττοι ἐν χηλῇ βοός· προσφερόμενός τε κατ' ὀλίγον μηδεμιᾷ κενοῦσθαι ἀποκρίσει μηδὲ ὀφθῆναί ποτε ἐσθίων. μέμνηται αὐτοῦ καὶ Τίμαιος ἐν τῇ δευτέρᾳ. λέγουσι δέ τινες ὅτι Κρῆτες αὐτῷ

118

There is extant a letter of his to Solon the law-giver, containing a scheme of government which Minos drew up for the Cretans. But Demetrius of Magnesia, in his work on poets and writers of the same name, endeavours to discredit the letter on the ground that it is late and not written in the Cretan dialect but in Attic, and New Attic too. However, I have found another letter by him which runs as follows:

Epimenides to Solon

"Courage, my friend. For if Pisistratus had attacked the Athenians while they were still serfs and before they had good laws, he would have secured power in perpetuity by the enslavement of the citizens. But, as it is, he is reducing to subjection men who are no cowards, men who with pain and shame remember Solon's warning and will never endure to be under a tyrant. But even should Pisistratus himself hold down the city, I do not expect that his power will be continued to his children; for it is hard to contrive that men brought up as free men under the best laws should be slaves. But, instead of going on your travels, come quietly to Crete to me; for here you will have no monarch to fear, whereas, if some of his friends should fall in with you while you are travelling about, I fear you may come to some harm.'

This is the tenor of the letter. But Demetrius reports a story that he received from the Nymphs food of a special sort and kept it in a cow's hoof; that he took small doses of this food, which was entirely absorbed into his system, and he was never seen to eat. Timaeus mentions him in his second book. Some writers say that the Cretans sacrifice to him

119

θύουσιν ὡς θεῷ· φασὶ γὰρ καὶ <προ>γνωστι-
κώτατον γεγονέναι. ἰδόντα γοῦν τὴν Μουνιχίαν
παρ' Ἀθηναίοις ἀγνοεῖν φάναι αὐτοὺς ὅσων κακῶν
αἴτιον ἔσται τοῦτο τὸ χωρίον αὐτοῖς· ἐπεὶ κἂν
τοῖς ὀδοῦσιν αὐτὸ διαφορῆσαι· ταῦτα ἔλεγε τοσού-
τοις πρότερον χρόνοις. λέγεται δὲ ὡς καὶ πρῶτος
αὐτὸν Αἰακὸν λέγοι, καὶ Λακεδαιμονίοις προείποι
τὴν ὑπ' Ἀρκάδων ἅλωσιν προσποιηθῆναί τε
πολλάκις ἀναβεβιωκέναι.

115 Θεόπομπος δ' ἐν τοῖς Θαυμασίοις, κατασκευά-
ζοντος αὐτοῦ τὸ τῶν Νυμφῶν ἱερὸν ῥαγῆναι
φωνὴν ἐξ οὐρανοῦ, "Ἐπιμενίδη, μὴ Νυμφῶν,
ἀλλὰ Διός·" Κρησί τε προειπεῖν τὴν Λακεδαιμονίων ἧτταν ὑπ' Ἀρκάδων, καθάπερ προείρηται·
καὶ δὴ καὶ ἐλήφθησαν πρὸς Ὀρχομενῷ.

Γηρᾶσαί τ' ἐν τοσαύταις ἡμέραις αὐτὸν ὅσαπερ
ἔτη κατεκοιμήθη· καὶ γὰρ τοῦτό φησι Θεόπομπος. Μυρωνιανὸς δὲ ἐν Ὁμοίοις φησὶν ὅτι
Κούρητα αὐτὸν ἐκάλουν Κρῆτες· καὶ τὸ σῶμα
αὐτοῦ φυλάττουσι Λακεδαιμόνιοι παρ' ἑαυτοῖς
κατά τι λόγιον, ὥς φησι Σωσίβιος ὁ Λάκων.

Γεγόνασι δὲ καὶ Ἐπιμενίδαι ἄλλοι δύο, ὅ τε
γενεαλόγος καὶ τρίτος ὁ Δωρίδι γεγραφὼς περὶ
Ῥόδου.

Κεφ. ια΄. ΦΕΡΕΚΥΔΗΣ

116 Φερεκύδης Βάβυος Σύριος, καθά φησιν Ἀλέξανδρος ἐν Διαδοχαῖς, Πιττακοῦ διακήκοεν. τοῦτόν

as a god; for they say that he had superhuman foresight. For instance, when he saw Munichia, at Athens, he said the Athenians did not know how many evils that place would bring upon them; for, if they did, they would destroy it even if they had to do so with their teeth. And this he said so long before the event. It is also stated that he was the first to call himself Aeacus; that he foretold to the Lacedaemonians their defeat by the Arcadians; and that he claimed that his soul had passed through many incarnations.

Theopompus relates in his *Mirabilia* that, as he was building a temple to the Nymphs, a voice came from heaven: " Epimenides, not a temple to the Nymphs but to Zeus," and that he foretold to the Cretans the defeat of the Lacedaemonians by the Arcadians, as already stated; and in very truth they were crushed at Orchomenus.

And he became old in as many days as he had slept years; for this too is stated by Theopompus. Myronianus in his *Parallels* declares that the Cretans called him one of the Curetes. The Lacedaemonians guard his body in their own keeping in obedience to a certain oracle; this is stated by Sosibius the Laconian.

There have been two other men named Epimenides, namely, the genealogist and another who wrote in Doric Greek about Rhodes.

CHAPTER 11.   PHERECYDES (*flor. c.* 540 B.C.)

Pherecydes, the son of Babys, and a native of Syros according to Alexander in his *Successions of Philosophers*, was a pupil of Pittacus. Theopompus

φησι Θεόπομπος πρῶτον περὶ φύσεως καὶ θεῶν
γράψαι.

Πολλὰ δὲ καὶ θαυμάσια λέγεται περὶ αὐτοῦ.
καὶ γὰρ παρὰ τὸν αἰγιαλὸν τῆς Σάμου περι-
πατοῦντα καὶ ναῦν οὐριοδρομοῦσαν ἰδόντα εἰπεῖν
ὡς οὐ μετὰ πολὺ καταδύσεται· καὶ ἐν ὀφθαλμοῖς
αὐτοῦ καταδῦναι. καὶ ἀνιμηθέντος ἐκ φρέατος
ὕδατος πιόντα προειπεῖν, ὡς εἰς τρίτην ἡμέραν
ἔσοιτο σεισμός, καὶ γενέσθαι. ἀνιόντα τε ἐξ
Ὀλυμπίας εἰς Μεσσήνην τῷ ξένῳ Περιλάῳ συμβουλεῦσαι ἐξοικῆσαι μετὰ τῶν οἰκείων· καὶ τὸν
μὴ πεισθῆναι, Μεσσήνην δὲ ἑαλωκέναι.

117 Καὶ Λακεδαιμονίοις εἰπεῖν μήτε χρυσὸν τιμᾶν
μήτε ἄργυρον, ὥς φησι Θεόπομπος ἐν Θαυμασίοις·
προστάξαι δὲ αὐτῷ ὄναρ τοῦτο τὸν Ἡρακλέα, ὃν
καὶ τῆς αὐτῆς νυκτὸς τοῖς βασιλεῦσι κελεῦσαι
Φερεκύδῃ πείθεσθαι. ἔνιοι δὲ Πυθαγόρᾳ περι-
άπτουσι ταῦτα.

Φησὶ δ' Ἕρμιππος πολέμου συνεστῶτος Ἐφεσίοις
καὶ Μάγνησι βουλόμενον τοὺς Ἐφεσίους νικῆσαι
πυθέσθαι τινὸς παριόντος πόθεν εἴη, τοῦ δ' εἰπόντος
" ἐξ Ἐφέσου," " ἕλκυσόν με τοίνυν, ἔφη, τῶν
σκελῶν καὶ θὲς εἰς τὴν τῶν Μαγνήτων χώραν,
καὶ ἀπάγγειλόν σου τοῖς πολίταις μετὰ τὸ νικῆσαι
αὐτόθι με θάψαι· ἐπεσκηφέναι τε ταῦτα Φερε-
118 κύδην." ὁ μὲν <οὖν> ἀπήγγειλεν· οἱ δὲ μετὰ
μίαν ἐπελθόντες κρατοῦσι τῶν Μαγνήτων, καὶ
τόν τε Φερεκύδην μεταλλάξαντα θάπτουσιν αὐτόθι
καὶ μεγαλοπρεπῶς τιμῶσιν. ἔνιοι δέ φασιν

tells us that he was the first who wrote in Greek on nature and the gods.

Many wonderful stories are told about him. He was walking along the beach in Samos and saw a ship running before the wind; he exclaimed that in no long time she would go down, and, even as he watched her, down she went. And as he was drinking water which had been drawn up from a well he predicted that on the third day there would be an earthquake; which came to pass. And on his way from Olympia he advised Perilaus, his host in Messene, to move thence with all belonging to him; but Perilaus could not be persuaded, and Messene was afterwards taken.[a]

He bade the Lacedaemonians set no store by gold or silver, as Theopompus says in his *Mirabilia*. He told them he had received this command from Heracles in a dream; and the same night Heracles enjoined upon the kings to obey Pherecydes. But some fasten this story upon Pythagoras.

Hermippus relates that on the eve of war between Ephesus and Magnesia he favoured the cause of the Ephesians, and inquired of some one passing by where he came from, and on receiving the reply "From Ephesus," he said, "Drag me by the legs and place me in the territory of Magnesia; and take a message to your countrymen that after their victory they must bury me there, and that this is the last injunction of Pherecydes." The man gave the message; a day later the Ephesians attacked and defeated the Magnesians; they found Pherecydes dead and buried him on the spot with great honours. Another

---

[a] These stories no doubt come from Theopompus, whose work on *Marvels* is cited in the next paragraph.

ἐλθόντα εἰς Δελφοὺς ἀπὸ τοῦ Κωρυκίου ὄρους
αὐτὸν δισκῆσαι. Ἀριστόξενος δ' ἐν τῷ Περὶ
Πυθαγόρου καὶ τῶν γνωρίμων αὐτοῦ φησι νοσήσαντα αὐτὸν ὑπὸ Πυθαγόρου ταφῆναι ἐν Δήλῳ.
οἱ δὲ φθειριάσαντα τὸν βίον τελευτῆσαι· ὅτε καὶ
Πυθαγόρου παραγενομένου καὶ πυνθανομένου, πῶς
διακέοιτο, διαβαλόντα τῆς θύρας τὸν δάκτυλον
εἰπεῖν, "χροῖ δῆλα"· καὶ τοὐντεῦθεν παρὰ τοῖς
φιλολόγοις ἡ λέξις ἐπὶ τῶν χειρόνων τάττεται,
οἱ δ' ἐπὶ τῶν βελτίστων χρώμενοι διαμαρτά-
119 νουσιν. ἔλεγέ τε ὅτι οἱ θεοὶ τὴν τράπεζαν θυωρὸν
καλοῦσιν.

Ἄνδρων δ' ὁ Ἐφέσιός φησι δύο γεγονέναι
Φερεκύδας Συρίους, τὸν μὲν ἀστρολόγον, τὸν
δὲ θεολόγον υἱὸν Βάβυος, ᾧ καὶ Πυθαγόραν
σχολάσαι. Ἐρατοσθένης δ' ἕνα μόνον, καὶ ἕτερον
Ἀθηναῖον, γενεαλόγον.

Σώζεται δὲ τοῦ Συρίου τό τε βιβλίον ὃ συνέγραψεν, οὗ ἡ ἀρχή· "Ζὰς μὲν καὶ Χρόνος ἦσαν
ἀεὶ καὶ Χθονίη· Χθονίῃ δὲ ὄνομα ἐγένετο Γῆ,
ἐπειδὴ αὐτῇ Ζὰς γῆν γέρας διδοῖ." σώζεται δὲ
καὶ ἡλιοτρόπειον ἐν Σύρῳ τῇ νήσῳ.

Φησὶ δὲ Δοῦρις ἐν τῷ δευτέρῳ τῶν Ὡρῶν
ἐπιγεγράφθαι αὐτῷ τὸ ἐπίγραμμα τόδε·

120 τῆς σοφίης πάσης ἐν ἐμοὶ τέλος· ἢν δέ τι πλεῖον,
Πυθαγόρῃ τὠμῷ λέγε ταῦθ', ὅτι πρῶτος ἁπάντων
ἔστιν ἀν' Ἑλλάδα γῆν· οὐ ψεύδομαι ὧδ' ἀγορεύων.

Ἴων δ' ὁ Χῖός φησιν περὶ αὐτοῦ·

124

version is that he came to Delphi and hurled himself down from Mount Corycus. But Aristoxenus in his work *On Pythagoras and his School* affirms that he died a natural death and was buried by Pythagoras in Delos ; another account again is that he died of a verminous disease, that Pythagoras was also present and inquired how he was, that he thrust his finger through the doorway and exclaimed, " My skin tells its own tale," a phrase subsequently applied by the grammarians as equivalent to " getting worse," although some wrongly understand it to mean " all is going well." He maintained that the divine name for " table " is θυωρός, or that which takes care of offerings.

Andron of Ephesus says that there were two natives of Syros who bore the name of Pherecydes : the one was an astronomer, the other was the son of Babys and a theologian, teacher of Pythagoras. Eratosthenes, however, says that there was only one Pherecydes of Syros, the other Pherecydes being an Athenian and a genealogist.

There is preserved a work by Pherecydes of Syros, a work which begins thus : " Zeus and Time and Earth were from all eternity, and Earth was called Γῆ because Zeus gave her earth (γῇ) as guerdon (γέρας)." His sun-dial is also preserved in the island of Syros.

Duris in the second book of his *Horae* gives the inscription on his tomb as follows [a] :

> All knowledge that a man may have had I ;
> Yet tell Pythagoras, were more thereby,
> That first of all Greeks is he ; I speak no lie.

Ion of Chios says of him [b] :

[a] *Anth. Pal.* vii. 93.   [b] Fr. 4 Bergk.

ὡς ὁ μὲν ἠνορέῃ τε κεκασμένος ἠδὲ καὶ αἰδοῖ
καὶ φθίμενος ψυχῇ τερπνὸν ἔχει βίοτον,
εἴπερ Πυθαγόρης ἐτύμως ὁ σοφὸς περὶ πάντων
ἀνθρώπων γνώμας ᾔδεε κἀξέμαθεν.

Ἔστι καὶ ἡμῶν οὕτως ἔχον τῷ μέτρῳ τῷ
Φερεκρατείῳ·

> τὸν κλεινὸν Φερεκύδην,
> ὃν τίκτει ποτὲ Σῦρος,
> ἐς φθεῖρας λόγος ἐστὶν
> ἀλλάξαι τὸ πρὶν εἶδος,
> θεῖναί τ' εὐθὺ κελεύειν
> Μαγνήτων, ἵνα νίκην
> δοίη τοῖς Ἐφέσοιο
> γενναίοις πολιήταις.
> ἦν γὰρ χρησμός, ὃν ᾔδει
> μοῦνος, τοῦτο κελεύων·
> καὶ θνήσκει παρ' ἐκείνοις.
> ἦν οὖν τοῦτ' ἄρ' ἀληθές·
> ἦν ᾖ τις σοφὸς ὄντως,
> καὶ ζῶν ἐστιν ὄνησις,
> χὤταν μηδὲν ὑπάρχῃ.

121

Γέγονε δὲ κατὰ τὴν πεντηκοστὴν καὶ ἐνάτην
Ὀλυμπιάδα. καὶ ἐπέστειλεν ὧδε·

Φερεκύδης Θαλῇ

122 " Εὖ θνήσκοις ὅταν τοι τὸ χρεὼν ἥκῃ. νοῦσός με
καταλελάβηκε δεδεγμένον τὰ παρὰ σέο γράμματα.
φθειρῶν ἔβρυον πᾶς καί με εἶχεν ἠπίαλος. ἐπέ-
έσκηψα δ' ὧν τοῖσιν οἰκιήτησιν, ἐπήν με καθά-
ψωσιν, ἐς σὲ τὴν γραφὴν ἐνεῖκαι. σὺ δὲ ἢν δοκι-

126

I. 120–122. PHERECYDES

> With manly worth endowed and modesty,
> Though he be dead, his soul lives happily,
> If wise Pythagoras indeed saw light
> And read the destinies of men aright.

There is also an epigram of my own in the Phere-cratean metre [a] :

> The famous Pherecydes, to whom Syros gave birth, when his former beauty was consumed by vermin, gave orders that he should be taken straight to the Magnesian land in order that he might give victory to the noble Ephesians. There was an oracle, which he alone knew, enjoining this : and there he died among them. It seems then it is a true tale : if anyone is truly wise, he brings blessings both in his lifetime and when he is no more.

He lived in the 59th Olympiad. He wrote the following letter :

Pherecydes to Thales [b]

" May yours be a happy death when your time comes. Since I received your letter, I have been attacked by disease. I am infested with vermin and subject to a violent fever with shivering fits. I have therefore given instructions to my servants to carry my writing to you after they have buried me. I would like you to publish it, provided that you and

---

[a] *Anth. Plan.* iii. 128.
[b] This forgery is easily analysed. There is the tradition of the malady which proved fatal to Pherecydes (*cf.* Porphyry, *Vit. Pyth.* § 55), with the anecdote of his protruding his finger through the door. There is also an allusion to the alleged obscurity of the work on the gods which passed current as written by him.

μώσῃς σὺν τοῖς ἄλλοις σοφοῖς, οὕτω μιν φῆνον·
ἢν δὲ οὐ δοκιμώσητε, μὴ φήνῃς. ἐμοὶ μὲν γὰρ
οὔκω ἥνδανεν. ἔστι δὲ οὐκ ἀτρεκηίη πρηγμάτων
οὐδ' ὑπίσχομαι τἀληθὲς εἰδέναι· ἄσσα δ' ἂν ἐπι-
λέγῃ θεολογέων· τὰ ἄλλα χρὴ νοέειν· ἅπαντα
γὰρ αἰνίσσομαι. τῇ δὲ νούσῳ πιεζόμενος ἐπὶ
μᾶλλον οὔτε τῶν τινα ἰητρῶν οὔτε τοὺς ἑταίρους
ἐσιέμην· προεστεῶσι δὲ τῇ θύρῃ καὶ εἰρομένοις
ὁκοῖόν τι εἴη, διεὶς δάκτυλον ἐκ τῆς κληίθρης
ἔδειξ' ἂν ὡς ἔβρυον τοῦ κακοῦ. καὶ προεῖπα
αὐτοῖσι ἥκειν ἐς τὴν ὑστεραίην ἐπὶ τὰς Φερε-
κύδεω ταφάς.''

Καὶ οὗτοι μὲν οἱ κληθέντες σοφοί, οἷς τινες
καὶ Πεισίστρατον τὸν τύραννον προσκαταλέγουσι.
λεκτέον δὲ περὶ τῶν φιλοσόφων· καὶ πρῶτόν γε
ἀρκτέον ἀπὸ τῆς Ἰωνικῆς φιλοσοφίας, ἧς καθηγήσατο Θαλῆς, οὗ διήκουσεν Ἀναξίμανδρος.

the other sages approve of it, and not otherwise. For I myself am not yet satisfied with it. The facts are not absolutely correct, nor do I claim to have discovered the truth, but merely such things as one who inquires about the gods picks up. The rest must be thought out, for mine is all guess-work. As I was more and more weighed down with my malady, I did not permit any of the physicians or my friends to come into the room where I was, but, as they stood before the door and inquired how I was, I thrust my finger through the keyhole and showed them how plague-stricken I was ; and I told them to come to-morrow to bury Pherecydes."

So much for those who are called the Sages, with whom some writers also class Pisistratus the tyrant. I must now proceed to the philosophers and start with the philosophy of Ionia. Its founder was Thales, and Anaximander was his pupil.

B

Κεφ. α'. ΑΝΑΞΙΜΑΝΔΡΟΣ

1 Ἀναξίμανδρος Πραξιάδου Μιλήσιος. οὗτος ἔφα
σκεν ἀρχὴν καὶ στοιχεῖον τὸ ἄπειρον, οὐ διορίζων
ἀέρα ἢ ὕδωρ ἢ ἄλλο τι. καὶ τὰ μὲν μέρη μετα
βάλλειν, τὸ δὲ πᾶν ἀμετάβλητον εἶναι. μέσην τε
τὴν γῆν κεῖσθαι, κέντρου τάξιν ἐπέχουσαν οὖσαν
σφαιροειδῆ· τήν τε σελήνην ψευδοφαῆ, καὶ ἀπὸ
ἡλίου φωτίζεσθαι, ἀλλὰ καὶ τὸν ἥλιον οὐκ ἐλάτ
τονα τῆς γῆς, καὶ καθαρώτατον πῦρ.

Εὗρεν δὲ καὶ γνώμονα πρῶτος καὶ ἔστησεν
ἐπὶ τῶν σκιοθήρων ἐν Λακεδαίμονι, καθά φησι
Φαβωρῖνος ἐν Παντοδαπῇ ἱστορίᾳ, τροπάς τε
καὶ ἰσημερίας σημαίνοντα, καὶ ὡροσκοπεῖα κατ
2 εσκεύασε. καὶ γῆς καὶ θαλάσσης περίμετρον πρῶ
τος ἔγραψεν, ἀλλὰ καὶ σφαῖραν κατεσκεύασε.

Τῶν δὲ ἀρεσκόντων αὐτῷ πεποίηται κεφαλαιώδη
τὴν ἔκθεσιν, ᾗ που περιέτυχεν καὶ Ἀπολλόδωρος
ὁ Ἀθηναῖος· ὃς καί φησιν αὐτὸν ἐν τοῖς Χρονικοῖς
τῷ δευτέρῳ ἔτει τῆς πεντηκοστῆς ὀγδόης Ὀλυμ

---

^a With this Life Diels (*Dox. Gr.* p. 133) compares Hippolytus (*Ref. Haer.* i. 6), Plutarch (*Strom.* 2), Aëtius, i. 3. 3 ;
iii. 11. 1 ; iii. 10. 2 ; ii. 11. 5 ; ii. 20. 1 ; ii. 24. 2 ; ii. 29. 1 ;
ii. 21. 1 ; iii. 15. 6 ; v. 19. 4, which go back to Theophrastus,
Phys. Opin. Fr. 2.

BOOK II

Chapter 1. ANAXIMANDER [a] (611–546 b.c.)

ANAXIMANDER, the son of Praxiades, was a native of Miletus. He laid down as his principle and element that which is unlimited without defining it as air or water or anything else. He held that the parts undergo change, but the whole is unchangeable; that the earth, which is of spherical shape, lies in the midst, occupying the place of a centre; that the moon, shining with borrowed light, derives its illumination from the sun; further, that the sun is as large as the earth and consists of the purest fire.[b]

He was the first inventor of the gnomon and set it up for a sundial in Lacedaemon,[c] as is stated by Favorinus in his *Miscellaneous History*, in order to mark the solstices and the equinoxes; he also constructed clocks to tell the time. He was the first to draw on a map the outline of land and sea, and he constructed a globe as well.

His exposition of his doctrines took the form of a summary which no doubt came into the hands, among others, of Apollodorus of Athens. He says in his *Chronology* that in the second year of the 58th

[b] These astronomical discoveries belong properly to Anaxagoras.

[c] But see Herodotus ii. 109, who makes the Babylonians the inventors.

131

πιάδος ἐτῶν εἶναι ἑξήκοντα τεττάρων καὶ μετ'
ὀλίγον τελευτῆσαι, ἀκμάσαντά πη μάλιστα κατὰ
Πολυκράτην τὸν Σάμου τύραννον. τούτου φασὶν
ᾄδοντος καταγελάσαι τὰ παιδάρια, τὸν δὲ μαθόντα
φάναι, '' βέλτιον οὖν ἡμῖν ᾀστέον διὰ τὰ παιδάρια.''

Γέγονε δὲ καὶ ἄλλος Ἀναξίμανδρος ἱστορικός,
καὶ αὐτὸς Μιλήσιος τῇ Ἰάδι γεγραφώς.

Κεφ. β΄. ΑΝΑΞΙΜΕΝΗΣ

3 Ἀναξιμένης Εὐρυστράτου Μιλήσιος ἤκουσει
Ἀναξιμάνδρου. ἔνιοι δὲ καὶ Παρμενίδου φασὶν
ἀκοῦσαι αὐτόν. οὗτος ἀρχὴν ἀέρα εἶπε καὶ τὸ
ἄπειρον. κινεῖσθαι δὲ τὰ ἄστρα οὐχ ὑπὸ γῆν,
ἀλλὰ περὶ γῆν. κέχρηταί τε λέξει Ἰάδι ἁπλῇ
καὶ ἀπερίττῳ.

Καὶ γεγένηται μέν, καθά φησιν Ἀπολλόδωρος,
περὶ τὴν Σάρδεων ἅλωσιν, ἐτελεύτησε δὲ τῇ
ἑξηκοστῇ τρίτῃ Ὀλυμπιάδι.

Γεγόνασι δὲ καὶ ἄλλοι δύο Λαμψακηνοί, ῥήτωρ
καὶ ἱστορικός, ὃς ἀδελφῆς υἱὸς ἦν τοῦ ῥήτορος
τοῦ τὰς Ἀλεξάνδρου πράξεις γεγραφότος.

Οὗτος δὴ ὁ φιλόσοφος καὶ ἐπέστειλεν ὧδε

Ἀναξιμένης Πυθαγόρῃ

4 '' Θαλῆς Ἐξαμύου ἐπὶ γήρως οὐκ εὐπότμως οἴ-
χεται· εὐφρόνης, ὥσπερ ἐώθει, ἅμα τῇ ἀμφιπόλῳ

---

a 547–546 B.C.

b There is a chronological difficulty in this statement of
Diogenes, for Polycrates of Samos died in 522. The difficulty, however, disappears if the statement be taken to refer
not to Anaximander but to Pythagoras.

c Diels (*op. cit.* p. 135) compares Hippolytus, *Ref. Haer.*

Olympiad[a] Anaximander was sixty-four, and that he died not long afterwards. Thus he flourished almost at the same time as Polycrates the tyrant of Samos.[b] There is a story that the boys laughed at his singing, and that, when he heard of it, he rejoined, " Then to please the boys I must improve my singing."

There is another Anaximander, also of Miletus, a historian who wrote in the Ionic dialect.

Chapter 2. ANAXIMENES[c] (*flor. c.* 546 B.C.)

Anaximenes, the son of Eurystratus, a native of Miletus, was a pupil of Anaximander. According to some, he was also a pupil of Parmenides. He took for his first principle air or that which is unlimited. He held that the stars move round the earth but do not go under it. He writes simply and unaffectedly in the Ionic dialect.

According to Apollodorus he was contemporary with the taking of Sardis and died in the 63rd Olympiad.[d]

There have been two other men named Anaximenes, both of Lampsacus, the one a rhetorician who wrote on the achievements of Alexander, the other, the nephew of the rhetorician, who was a historian.

Anaximenes the philosopher wrote the following letters :

Anaximenes to Pythagoras

" Thales, the son of Examyas, has met an unkind fate in his old age. He went out from the court of

i. 7. 1 ; Plutarch, *Strom.* 3 ; Aëtius, i. 3. 4 ; iii. 15. 8 ; ii. 13. 10 ; ii. 16. 6 ; iii. 4. 1 ; iii. 3. 1 ; iii. 5. 10 ; iii. 14. 3, ultimately from Theophrastus, *Phys. Opin.* Fr. 2.
   [d] 528–525 B.C.

προϊὼν ἐκ τοῦ αὐλίου τὰ ἄστρα ἐθεῖτο· καί—οὐ γὰρ
ἐς μνήμην ἔθετο—θηεύμενος ἐς τὸ κρημνῶδες ἐκβὰς
καταπίπτει. Μιλησίοισι μέν νυν ὁ αἰθερολόγος ἐν
τοιῷδε κεῖται τέλει. ἡμέες δὲ οἱ λεσχηνευταὶ αὐτοί
τε μεμνώμεθα τοῦ ἀνδρός, οἵ τε ἡμέων παῖδές τε καὶ
λεσχηνευταί, ἐπιδεξιοίμεθα δ' ἔτι τοῖς ἐκείνου λόγοις.
ἀρχὴ μέντοι παντὸς τοῦ λόγου Θαλῇ ἀνακείσθω."

Καὶ πάλιν·

Ἀναξιμένης Πυθαγόρῃ

5 " Εὐβουλότατος ἦς ἡμέων, μεταναστὰς ἐκ Σάμου
ἐς Κρότωνα, ἐνθάδε εἰρηνέεις. οἱ δὲ Αἰακέος παῖδες
ἄλαστα κακὰ ἔρδουσι καὶ Μιλησίους οὐκ ἐπιλείπουσι
αἰσυμνῆται. δεινὸς δὲ ἡμῖν καὶ ὁ Μήδων βασιλεύς,
οὐκ ἤν γε ἐθέλωμεν δασμοφορέειν· ἀλλὰ μέλλουσι δὴ
ἀμφὶ τῆς ἐλευθερίης ἁπάντων Ἴωνες Μήδοις κατ-
ίστασθαι ἐς πόλεμον· καταστᾶσι δὲ οὐκέτι ἐλπὶς ἡμῖν
σωτηρίης. κῶς ἂν οὖν Ἀναξιμένης ἐν θυμῷ ἔτι
ἔχοι αἰθερολογέειν, ἐν δείματι ἐὼν ὀλέθρου ἢ δου-
λοσύνης; σὺ δὲ εἶ καταθύμιος μὲν Κροτωνιήτῃσι,
καταθύμιος δὲ καὶ τοῖσι ἄλλοισι Ἰταλιώτῃσι·
φοιτέουσι δέ τοι λεσχηνευταὶ καὶ ἐκ Σικελίης."

Κεφ. γ΄. ΑΝΑΞΑΓΟΡΑΣ

6 Ἀναξαγόρας Ἡγησιβούλου ἢ Εὐβούλου Κλαζομένιος. οὗτος ἤκουσεν Ἀναξιμένους, καὶ πρῶτος
τῇ ὕλῃ νοῦν ἐπέστησεν, ἀρξάμενος οὕτω τοῦ συγ-

ª Diels (*Dox. Gr.* p. 137) compares Hippolytus, *Ref.*
Haer. i. 8. 1-11 ; Aëtius, i. 3. 5 ; iv. 1. 3 ; ii. 20. 6 ; ii. 21. 3 ;
ii. 28. 5 ; ii. 29. 7 ; ii. 23. 2 ; ii. 25. 9 ; iii. 1. 5 ; iii. 2. 2 ;
iii. 2. 9 ; iii. 3. 4 ; iii. 15. 14 ; v. 7. 4, and Theophrastus, *Phys.*

his house at night, as was his custom, with his maid-servant to view the stars, and, forgetting where he was, as he gazed, he got to the edge of a steep slope and fell over. In such wise have the Milesians lost their astronomer. Let us who were his pupils cherish his memory, and let it be cherished by our children and pupils ; and let us not cease to entertain one another with his words. Let all our discourse begin with a reference to Thales."

And again :

Anaximenes to Pythagoras

" You were better advised than the rest of us when you left Samos for Croton, where you live in peace. For the sons of Aeaces work incessant mischief, and Miletus is never without tyrants. The king of the Medes is another terror to us, not indeed so long as we are willing to pay tribute ; but the Ionians are on the point of going to war with the Medes to secure their common freedom, and once we are at war we have no more hope of safety. How then can Anaximenes any longer think of studying the heavens when threatened with destruction or slavery ? Meanwhile you find favour with the people of Croton and with the other Greeks in Italy ; and pupils come to you even from Sicily."

CHAPTER 3. ANAXAGORAS [a] (500–428 B.C.)

Anaxagoras, the son of Hegesibulus or Eubulus, was a native of Clazomenae. He was a pupil of Anaximenes, and was the first who set mind above

Opin. Fr. 4. For Anaxagoras as astronomer see Sir T. L. Heath, *Aristarchus of Samos*, pp. 78-85.

γράμματος, ὅ ἐστιν ἡδέως καὶ μεγαλοφρόνως ἡρμη-
νευμένον· " πάντα χρήματα ἦν ὁμοῦ· εἶτα νοῦς ἐλθὼν
αὐτὰ διεκόσμησε." παρὸ καὶ Νοῦς ἐπεκλήθη, καί
φησι περὶ αὐτοῦ Τίμων ἐν τοῖς Σίλλοις οὕτω·

καί που 'Αναξαγόρην φάσ' ἔμμεναι, ἄλκιμον ἥρω
Νοῦν, ὅτι δὴ νόος αὐτῷ, ὃς ἐξαπίνης ἐπεγείρας
πάντα συνεσφήκωσεν ὁμοῦ τεταραγμένα πρόσθεν.

Οὗτος εὐγενείᾳ καὶ πλούτῳ διαφέρων ἦν, ἀλλὰ
καὶ μεγαλοφροσύνῃ, ὅς γε τὰ πατρῷα παρεχώρησε
7 τοῖς οἰκείοις. αἰτιαθεὶς γὰρ ὑπ' αὐτῶν ὡς ἀμελῶν,
" τί οὖν," ἔφη, " οὐχ ὑμεῖς ἐπιμελεῖσθε;" καὶ
τέλος ἀπέστη καὶ περὶ τὴν τῶν φυσικῶν θεωρίαν ἦν
οὐ φροντίζων τῶν πολιτικῶν. ὅτε καὶ πρὸς τὸν
εἰπόντα, " οὐδέν σοι μέλει τῆς πατρίδος;" " εὐ-
φήμει," ἔφη, " ἐμοὶ γὰρ καὶ σφόδρα μέλει τῆς
πατρίδος," δείξας τὸν οὐρανόν.

Λέγεται δὲ κατὰ τὴν Ξέρξου διάβασιν εἴκοσιν ἐτῶν
εἶναι, βεβιωκέναι δὲ ἑβδομήκοντα δύο. φησὶ δ'
'Απολλόδωρος ἐν τοῖς Χρονικοῖς γεγενῆσθαι αὐτὸν
τῇ ἑβδομηκοστῇ 'Ολυμπιάδι, τεθνηκέναι δὲ τῷ
πρώτῳ ἔτει τῆς ὀγδοηκοστῆς ὀγδόης. ἤρξατο δὲ
φιλοσοφεῖν 'Αθήνησιν ἐπὶ Καλλίου, ἐτῶν εἴκοσιν ὤν,
ὥς φησι Δημήτριος ὁ Φαληρεὺς ἐν τῇ τῶν 'Αρχόντων
ἀναγραφῇ, ἔνθα καί φασιν αὐτὸν ἐτῶν διατρῖψαι
τριάκοντα.

8 Οὗτος ἔλεγε τὸν ἥλιον μύδρον εἶναι διάπυρον καὶ
μείζω τῆς Πελοποννήσου· οἱ δέ φασι Τάνταλον· τὴν
δὲ σελήνην οἰκήσεις ἔχειν, ἀλλὰ καὶ λόφους καὶ

---

[a] Fr. 24 D.   [b] 500–497 B.C.   [c] 428 B.C.
[d] i.e. 456 B.C.; but possibly the year 480 is meant, when
Calliades was archon.

matter, for at the beginning of his treatise, which is composed in attractive and dignified language, he says, " All things were together ; then came Mind and set them in order." This earned for Anaxagoras himself the nickname of Nous or Mind, and Timon in his *Silli* says of him [a] :

> Then, I ween, there is Anaxagoras, a doughty champion, whom they call Mind, because forsooth his was the mind which suddenly woke up and fitted closely together all that had formerly been in a medley of confusion.

He was eminent for wealth and noble birth, and furthermore for magnanimity, in that he gave up his patrimony to his relations. For, when they accused him of neglecting it, he replied, " Why then do you not look after it ? " And at last he went into retirement and engaged in physical investigation without troubling himself about public affairs. When some one inquired, " Have you no concern in your native land ? " " Gently," he replied, " I am greatly concerned with my fatherland," and pointed to the sky.

He is said to have been twenty years old at the invasion of Xerxes and to have lived seventy-two years. Apollodorus in his *Chronology* says that he was born in the 70th Olympiad,[b] and died in the first year of the 88th Olympiad.[c] He began to study philosophy at Athens in the archonship of Callias [d] when he was twenty ; Demetrius of Phalerum states this in his list of archons ; and at Athens they say he remained for thirty years.

He declared the sun to be a mass of red-hot metal and to be larger than the Peloponnesus, though others ascribe this view to Tantalus ; he declared that there were dwellings on the moon, and moreover

φάραγγας. ἀρχὰς δὲ τὰς ὁμοιομερείας· καθάπερ
γὰρ ἐκ τῶν ψηγμάτων λεγομένων τὸν χρυσὸν συνεστάναι, οὕτως ἐκ τῶν ὁμοιομερῶν μικρῶν σωμάτων
τὸ πᾶν συγκεκρίσθαι. καὶ νοῦν μὲν ἀρχὴν κινήσεως·
τῶν δὲ σωμάτων τὰ μὲν βαρέα τὸν κάτω τόπον,
⟨ὡς τὴν γῆν⟩, τὰ δὲ κοῦφα τὸν ἄνω ἐπισχεῖν, ὡς τὸ
πῦρ· ὕδωρ δὲ καὶ ἀέρα τὸν μέσον. οὕτω γὰρ ἐπὶ τῆς
γῆς πλατείας οὔσης τὴν θάλασσαν ὑποστῆναι, δια-
9 τμισθέντων ὑπὸ τοῦ ἡλίου τῶν ὑγρῶν. τὰ δ᾽ ἄστρα
κατ᾽ ἀρχὰς μὲν θολοειδῶς ἐνεχθῆναι, ὥστε κατὰ
κορυφὴν τῆς γῆς τὸν ἀεὶ φαινόμενον εἶναι πόλον,
ὕστερον δὲ τὴν ἔγκλισιν λαβεῖν. καὶ τὸν γαλαξίαν
ἀνάκλασιν εἶναι φωτὸς ⟨τῶν ὑπὸ⟩ ἡλίου μὴ κατα-
λαμπομένων [τῶν] ἄστρων. τοὺς δὲ κομήτας σύν-
οδον πλανητῶν φλόγας ἀφιέντων· τούς τε διάττον-
τας οἷον σπινθῆρας ἀπὸ τοῦ ἀέρος ἀποπάλλεσθαι.
ἀνέμους γίγνεσθαι λεπτυνομένου τοῦ ἀέρος ὑπὸ
τοῦ ἡλίου. βροντὰς σύγκρουσιν νεφῶν· ἀστρα-
πὰς ἔκτριψιν νεφῶν· σεισμὸν ὑπονόστησιν ἀέρος
εἰς γῆν.

Ζῷα γίγνεσθαι ἐξ ὑγροῦ καὶ θερμοῦ καὶ γεώδους,
ὕστερον δὲ ἐξ ἀλλήλων· καὶ ἄρρενα μὲν ἀπὸ τῶν
δεξιῶν, θήλεα δὲ ἀπὸ τῶν ἀριστερῶν.

10 Φασὶ δ᾽ αὐτὸν προειπεῖν τὴν περὶ Αἰγὸς ποταμοὺς
γενομένην τοῦ λίθου πτῶσιν, ὃν εἶπεν ἐκ τοῦ ἡλίου
πεσεῖσθαι. ὅθεν καὶ Εὐριπίδην, μαθητὴν ὄντα
αὐτοῦ, χρυσέαν βῶλον εἰπεῖν τὸν ἥλιον ἐν τῷ Φαέ-
θοντι. ἀλλὰ καὶ εἰς Ὀλυμπίαν ἐλθόντα ἐν δερμα-

---

[a] This version agrees with Pliny, *Nat. Hist.* ii. 149
"celebrant Graeci Anaxagoram Clazomenium Olympiadis
septuagesimae octavae secundo anno praedixisse caelestium
litterarum scientia quibus diebus saxum casurum esset e sole."

hills and ravines. He took as his principles the homoeomeries or homogeneous molecules ; for just as gold consists of fine particles which are called gold-dust, so he held the whole universe to be compounded of minute bodies having parts homogeneous to themselves. His moving principle was Mind ; of bodies, he said, some, like earth, were heavy, occupying the region below, others, light like fire, held the region above, while water and air were intermediate in position. For in this way over the earth, which is flat, the sea sinks down after the moisture has been evaporated by the sun. In the beginning the stars moved in the sky as in a revolving dome, so that the celestial pole which is always visible was vertically overhead ; but subsequently the pole took its inclined position. He held the Milky Way to be a reflection of the light of stars which are not shone upon by the sun ; comets to be a conjunction of planets which emit flames ; shooting-stars to be a sort of sparks thrown off by the air. He held that winds arise when the air is rarefied by the sun's heat ; that thunder is a clashing together of the clouds, lightning their violent friction ; an earthquake a subsidence of air into the earth.

Animals were produced from moisture, heat, and an earthy substance ; later the species were propagated by generation from one another, males from the right side, females from the left.

There is a story that he predicted the fall of the meteoric stone at Aegospotami, which he said would fall from the sun.[a] Hence Euripides, who was his pupil, in the *Phaëthon* calls the sun itself a " golden clod." [b] Furthermore, when he went to Olympia,

* Nauck, *T.G.F.*[2], *Eur.* 783.

τίνῳ καθίσαι, ὡς μέλλοντος ὕσειν· καὶ γενέσθαι.
πρός τε τὸν εἰπόντα, εἰ τὰ ἐν Λαμψάκῳ ὄρη ἔσται
ποτὲ θάλαττα, φασὶν εἰπεῖν, " ἐάν γε ὁ χρόνος μὴ
ἐπιλίπῃ." ἐρωτηθείς ποτε εἰς τί γεγέννηται, " εἰς
θεωρίαν," ἔφη, " ἡλίου καὶ σελήνης καὶ οὐρανοῦ."
πρὸς τὸν εἰπόντα, " ἐστερήθης Ἀθηναίων," " οὐ μὲν
οὖν," ἔφη, " ἀλλ' ἐκεῖνοι ἐμοῦ." ἰδὼν τὸν Μαυσώ-
λου τάφον ἔφη, " τάφος πολυτελὴς λελιθωμένης
11 ἐστὶν οὐσίας εἴδωλον." πρὸς τὸν δυσφοροῦντα ὅτι
ἐπὶ ξένης τελευτᾷ, " πανταχόθεν," ἔφη, " ὁμοία ἐστὶν
ἡ εἰς ἅδου κατάβασις."

Δοκεῖ δὲ πρῶτος, καθά φησι Φαβωρῖνος ἐν Παντοδαπῇ ἱστορίᾳ, τὴν Ὁμήρου ποίησιν ἀποφήνασθαι
εἶναι περὶ ἀρετῆς καὶ δικαιοσύνης· ἐπὶ πλεῖον δὲ
προστῆναι τοῦ λόγου Μητρόδωρον τὸν Λαμψακηνόν,
γνώριμον ὄντα αὐτοῦ, ὃν καὶ πρῶτον σπουδάσαι τοῦ
ποιητοῦ περὶ τὴν φυσικὴν πραγματείαν. πρῶτος
δὲ Ἀναξαγόρας καὶ βιβλίον ἐξέδωκε συγγραφῆς.
φησὶ δὲ Σιληνὸς ἐν τῇ πρώτῃ τῶν Ἱστοριῶν ἐπὶ
12 ἄρχοντος Δημύλου[1] λίθον ἐξ οὐρανοῦ πεσεῖν· τὸν δὲ
Ἀναξαγόραν εἰπεῖν ὡς ὅλος ὁ οὐρανὸς ἐκ λίθων

---

[1] Δη⟨μοτίωνος⟩ μύλου Diels.

---

[a] Anaxagoras, whose death falls in the fifth century,
circa 428–425 B.C., could not possibly have seen the famous
Mausoleum erected by Artemisia, the widow of Mausolus,
not earlier than 350 B.C. Mausolus ruled over Caria, according to Diodorus, from 377 to 353. The apophthegm is
therefore either wrongly attributed to Anaxagoras or, if
genuine, must have been uttered on some other occasion.

[b] From Plutarch's Life of Nicias, c. 23, and Clement of
Alexandria (*Strom.* i. 78, p. 364 P.), διὰ γραφῆς (for which
Diels conjectures ⟨μετὰ⟩ διαγραφῆς) ἐκδοῦναι βιβλίον ἱστοροῦσιν,
the inference seems to be that Anaxagoras was credited

he sat down wrapped in a sheep-skin cloak as if it were going to rain; and the rain came. When some one asked him if the hills at Lampsacus would ever become sea, he replied, "Yes, it only needs time." Being asked to what end he had been born, he replied, "To study sun and moon and heavens." To one who inquired, "You miss the society of the Athenians?" his reply was, "Not I, but they miss mine." When he saw the tomb of Mausolus, he said, "A costly tomb is an image of an estate turned into stone." [a] To one who complained that he was dying in a foreign land, his answer was, "The descent to Hades is much the same from whatever place we start."

Favorinus in his *Miscellaneous History* says Anaxagoras was the first to maintain that Homer in his poems treats of virtue and justice, and that this thesis was defended at greater length by his friend Metrodorus of Lampsacus, who was the first to busy himself with Homer's physical doctrine. Anaxagoras was also the first to publish a book with diagrams. [b] Silenus [c] in the first book of his *History* gives the archonship of Demylus [d] as the date when the meteoric stone fell, and says that Anaxagoras declared the whole firmament to be made of stones; that the

with diagrams as well as text, διδασκαλία καὶ γραφή. Laertius, if the text is sound, is much too vague; and some translate "was the first to bring out a book written by himself."

[c] Silenus of Calatia, who served in the Hannibalic war, wrote a History quoted by Cicero, Livy and Pliny; also a work on Sicily, *F.H.G.* iii. 100.

[d] We know no archon Demylus. Various dates are suggested by critics; the years of (1) Demotion, archon 470, (2) Lysistratus, 467, (3) Diphilus, 442 B.C. The letters -μυλου may not be part of the archon's name but a distinct word, calling the meteor a " millstone," *i.e.* in size.

συγκέοιτο· τῇ σφοδρᾷ δὲ περιδινήσει συνεστάναι καὶ
ἀνεθέντα κατενεχθήσεσθαι.

Περὶ δὲ τῆς δίκης αὐτοῦ διάφορα λέγεται. Σωτίων μὲν γάρ φησιν ἐν τῇ Διαδοχῇ τῶν φιλοσόφων
ὑπὸ Κλέωνος αὐτὸν ἀσεβείας κριθῆναι, διότι τὸν
ἥλιον μύδρον ἔλεγε διάπυρον· ἀπολογησαμένου δὲ
ὑπὲρ αὐτοῦ Περικλέους τοῦ μαθητοῦ, πέντε ταλάντοις ζημιωθῆναι καὶ φυγαδευθῆναι. Σάτυρος δ' ἐν
τοῖς Βίοις ὑπὸ Θουκυδίδου φησὶν εἰσαχθῆναι τὴν
δίκην, ἀντιπολιτευομένου τῷ Περικλεῖ· καὶ οὐ μόνον
ἀσεβείας, ἀλλὰ καὶ μηδισμοῦ· καὶ ἀπόντα κατα-
13 δικασθῆναι θανάτῳ. ὅτε καὶ ἀμφοτέρων αὐτῷ προσ-
αγγελέντων, τῆς τε καταδίκης καὶ τῆς τῶν παίδων
τελευτῆς, εἰπεῖν περὶ μὲν τῆς καταδίκης, ὅτι ἄρα
"κἀκείνων κἀμοῦ πάλαι ἡ φύσις κατεψηφίσατο,"
περὶ δὲ τῶν παίδων, ὅτι " ᾔδειν αὐτοὺς θνητοὺς
γεννήσας." οἱ δ' εἰς Σόλωνα τοῦτ' ἀναφέρουσιν,
ἄλλοι εἰς Ξενοφῶντα. τοῦτον δὲ καὶ θάψαι ταῖς
ἰδίαις χερσὶν αὐτοὺς Δημήτριός φησιν ὁ Φαληρεὺς ἐν
τῷ Περὶ γήρως. Ἕρμιππος δ' ἐν τοῖς Βίοις φησὶν
ὅτι καθείρχθη ἐν τῷ δεσμωτηρίῳ τεθνηξόμενος.
Περικλῆς δὲ παρελθὼν εἶπεν εἴ τι ἔχουσιν ἐγκαλεῖν
αὐτῷ κατὰ τὸν βίον· οὐδὲν δὲ εἰπόντων, " καὶ μὴν
ἐγώ," ἔφη, " τούτου μαθητής εἰμι· μὴ οὖν διαβολαῖς
ἐπαρθέντες ἀποκτείνητε τὸν ἄνθρωπον, ἀλλ' ἐμοὶ
πεισθέντες ἄφετε." καὶ ἀφείθη· οὐκ ἐνεγκὼν δὲ
14 τὴν ὕβριν ἑαυτὸν ἐξήγαγεν. Ἱερώνυμος δ' ἐν τῷ
δευτέρῳ Τῶν σποράδην ὑπομνημάτων φησὶν ὅτι ὁ
Περικλῆς παρήγαγεν αὐτὸν ἐπὶ τὸ δικαστήριον, δι-

---

* This version of the story agrees with that of Plutarch
in his Life of Lysander, § 12 λέγεται δὲ . . . τοῦ παντός.

rapidity of rotation caused it to cohere; and that if this were relaxed it would fall.[a]

Of the trial of Anaxagoras different accounts are given. Sotion in his *Succession of the Philosophers* says that he was indicted by Cleon on a charge of impiety, because he declared the sun to be a mass of red-hot metal; that his pupil Pericles defended him, and he was fined five talents and banished. Satyrus in his *Lives* says that the prosecutor was Thucydides, the opponent of Pericles, and the charge one of treasonable correspondence with Persia as well as of impiety; and that sentence of death was passed on Anaxagoras by default. When news was brought him that he was condemned and his sons were dead, his comment on the sentence was, " Long ago nature condemned both my judges and myself to death "; and on his sons, " I knew that my children were born to die." Some, however, tell this story of Solon, and others of Xenophon. That he buried his sons with his own hands is asserted by Demetrius of Phalerum in his work *On Old Age*. Hermippus in his *Lives* says that he was confined in the prison pending his execution; that Pericles came forward and asked the people whether they had any fault to find with him in his own public career; to which they replied that they had not. " Well," he continued, " I am a pupil of Anaxagoras; do not then be carried away by slanders and put him to death. Let me prevail upon you to release him." So he was released; but he could not brook the indignity he had suffered and committed suicide. Hieronymus in the second book of his *Scattered Notes* states that Pericles brought him into court so weak and wasted from illness that he owed his

ερρυηκότα καὶ λεπτὸν ὑπὸ νόσου, ὥστε ἐλέῳ μᾶλλον
ἢ κρίσει ἀφεθῆναι. καὶ τὰ μὲν περὶ τῆς δίκης
αὐτοῦ τοσαῦτα.

Ἔδοξε δέ πως καὶ Δημοκρίτῳ ἀπεχθῶς ἐσχηκέναι
ἀποτυχὼν τῆς πρὸς αὐτὸν κοινολογίας. καὶ τέλος
ἀποχωρήσας εἰς Λάμψακον αὐτόθι κατέστρεψεν.
ὅτε καὶ τῶν ἀρχόντων τῆς πόλεως ἀξιούντων τί βούλεται αὐτῷ γενέσθαι, φάναι, " τοὺς παῖδας ἐν ᾧ ἂν
ἀποθάνῃ μηνὶ κατ' ἔτος παίζειν συγχωρεῖν." καὶ
15 φυλάττεται τὸ ἔθος καὶ νῦν. τελευτήσαντα δὴ αὐτὸν ἔθαψαν ἐντίμως οἱ Λαμψακηνοὶ καὶ ἐπέγραψαν·

ἐνθάδε, πλεῖστον ἀληθείας ἐπὶ τέρμα περήσας
οὐρανίου κόσμου, κεῖται Ἀναξαγόρας.

Ἔστι καὶ ἡμῶν εἰς αὐτόν·

ἠέλιον πυρόεντα μύδρον ποτὲ φάσκεν ὑπάρχειν,
καὶ διὰ τοῦτο θανεῖν μέλλεν Ἀναξαγόρας·
ἀλλ' ὁ φίλος Περικλῆς μὲν ἐρύσατο τοῦτον, ὁ δ'
αὑτὸν
ἐξάγαγεν βιότου μαλθακίῃ σοφίης.

Γεγόνασι δὲ καὶ ἄλλοι τρεῖς Ἀναξαγόραι, ὧν [ἐν
οὐδενὶ πάντα, ἀλλ'] ὁ μὲν ἦν ῥήτωρ Ἰσοκράτειος·
ὁ δ' ἀνδριαντοποιός, οὗ μέμνηται Ἀντίγονος·
ἄλλος γραμματικὸς Ζηνοδότειος.

Κεφ. δ΄. ΑΡΧΕΛΑΟΣ

16 Ἀρχέλαος Ἀθηναῖος ἢ Μιλήσιος, πατρὸς Ἀπολ-

---

[a] In ix. 34, 35 the statement that Democritus was hostile
to Anaxagoras and criticized his doctrines is ascribed to
Favorinus, and, as the motive alleged is similar, Favorinus
may also be the source of the statement of ii. 14.

acquittal not so much to the merits of his case as to the sympathy of the judges. So much then on the subject of his trial.

He was supposed to have borne Democritus a grudge because he had failed to get into communication with him.[a] At length he retired to Lampsacus and there died. And when the magistrates of the city asked if there was anything he would like done for him, he replied that he would like them to grant an annual holiday to the boys in the month in which he died; and the custom is kept up to this day. So, when he died, the people of Lampsacus gave him honourable burial and placed over his grave the following inscription [b] :

> Here Anaxagoras, who in his quest
> Of truth scaled heaven itself, is laid to rest.

I also have written an epigram upon him [c] :

> The sun's a molten mass,
> Quoth Anaxagoras :
> This is his crime, his life must pay the price.
> Pericles from that fate
> Rescued his friend too late ;
> His spirit crushed, by his own hand he dies.

There have been three other men who bore the name of Anaxagoras [of whom no other writer gives a complete list]. The first was a rhetorician of the school of Isocrates ; the second a sculptor, mentioned by Antigonus ; the third a grammarian, pupil of Zenodotus.

Chapter 4. ARCHELAUS [d] (c. 450 B.C.)

Archelaus, the son of Apollodorus, or as some say

[b] *Anth. Pal.* vii. 94.   [c] *Anth. Pal.* vii. 95.
[d] Diels (*Dox. Gr.* p. 139) compares Hippolytus, *Ref. Haer.* i. 9. 1-5 ; Aëtius, i. 3. 6 ; Theophrastus, *Phys. Opin.* Fr. 4.

λοδώρου, ὡς δέ τινες, Μίδωνος, μαθητὴς Ἀναξαγόρου, διδάσκαλος Σωκράτους. οὗτος πρῶτος ἐκ
τῆς Ἰωνίας τὴν φυσικὴν φιλοσοφίαν μετήγαγεν
Ἀθήναζε, καὶ ἐκλήθη φυσικός, παρὸ καὶ ἔληξεν
ἐν αὐτῷ ἡ φυσικὴ φιλοσοφία, Σωκράτους τὴν
ἠθικὴν εἰσαγαγόντος. ἔοικεν δὲ καὶ οὗτος ἅψασθαι
τῆς ἠθικῆς. καὶ γὰρ περὶ νόμων πεφιλοσόφηκε
καὶ καλῶν καὶ δικαίων· παρ' οὗ λαβὼν Σωκράτης
τῷ αὐξῆσαι εἰς τὸ[1] ⟨ἄκρον⟩ εὑρεῖν ὑπελήφθη.
ἔλεγε δὲ δύο αἰτίας εἶναι γενέσεως, θερμὸν καὶ
ψυχρόν. καὶ τὰ ζῷα ἀπὸ τῆς ἰλύος γεννηθῆναι·
καὶ τὸ δίκαιον εἶναι καὶ τὸ αἰσχρὸν οὐ φύσει, ἀλλὰ
νόμῳ.

17 Ὁ δὲ λόγος αὐτῷ οὕτως ἔχει. τηκόμενόν φησι
τὸ ὕδωρ ὑπὸ τοῦ θερμοῦ, καθὸ μὲν εἰς τὸ ⟨κάτω
διὰ τὸ⟩ πυρῶδες συνίσταται, ποιεῖν γῆν· καθὸ δὲ
περιρρεῖ, ἀέρα γεννᾶν. ὅθεν ἡ μὲν ὑπὸ τοῦ ἀέρος,
ὁ δὲ ὑπὸ τῆς τοῦ πυρὸς περιφορᾶς κρατεῖται.
γεννᾶσθαι δέ φησι τὰ ζῷα ἐκ θερμῆς τῆς γῆς καὶ
ἰλὺν παραπλησίαν γάλακτι οἷον τροφὴν ἀνείσης·
οὕτω δὴ καὶ τοὺς ἀνθρώπους ποιῆσαι. πρῶτος δὲ
εἶπε φωνῆς γένεσιν τὴν τοῦ ἀέρος πλῆξιν. τὴν δὲ
θάλατταν ἐν τοῖς κοίλοις διὰ τῆς γῆς ἠθουμένην
συνεστάναι. μέγιστον τῶν ἄστρων τὸν ἥλιον, καὶ
τὸ πᾶν ἄπειρον.

Γεγόνασι δὲ καὶ ἄλλοι τρεῖς Ἀρχέλαοι· ὁ
χωρογράφος τῆς ὑπὸ Ἀλεξάνδρου πατηθείσης

---

[1] εἰς τὸ] αὐτὸς Emperius.

[a] οὗτος. This statement is not really applicable to
Archelaus. Clement of Alexandria in *Strom.* i. 63 under-
stood it of Anaxagoras : μεθ' οὗ [Anaximenes] Ἀναξαγόρας
Ἡγησιβούλου Κλαζομένιος. οὗτος μετήγαγεν ἀπὸ τῆς Ἰωνίας
Ἀθήναζε τὴν διατριβήν.

146

of Midon, was a citizen of Athens or of Miletus; he was a pupil of Anaxagoras, who [a] first brought natural philosophy from Ionia to Athens. Archelaus was the teacher of Socrates. He was called the physicist inasmuch as with him natural philosophy came to an end, as soon as Socrates had introduced ethics. It would seem that Archelaus himself also treated of ethics, for he has discussed laws and goodness and justice; Socrates took the subject from him and, having improved it to the utmost, was regarded as its inventor. Archelaus laid down that there were two causes of growth or becoming, heat and cold; that living things were produced from slime; and that what is just and what is base depends not upon nature but upon convention.

His theory is to this effect. Water is melted by heat and produces on the one hand earth in so far as by the action of fire it sinks and coheres, while on the other hand it generates air in so far as it overflows on all sides. Hence the earth is confined by the air, and the air by the circumambient fire. Living things, he holds, are generated from the earth when it is heated and throws off slime of the consistency of milk to serve as a sort of nourishment, and in this same way the earth produced man. He was the first who explained the production of sound as being the concussion of the air, and the formation of the sea in hollow places as due to its filtering through the earth. He declared the sun to be the largest of the heavenly bodies and the universe to be unlimited.

There have been three other men who bore the name of Archelaus: the topographer who described the countries traversed by Alexander; the author

γῆς, ὁ τὰ Ἰδιοφυῆ ποιήσας, ἄλλος τεχνογράφος ῥήτωρ.

Κεφ. ε΄. ΣΩΚΡΑΤΗΣ

18 Σωκράτης Σωφρονίσκου μὲν ἦν υἱὸς λιθουργοῦ καὶ Φαιναρέτης μαίας, ὡς καὶ Πλάτων ἐν Θεαιτήτῳ φησίν, Ἀθηναῖος, τῶν δήμων Ἀλωπεκῆθεν. ἐδόκει δὲ συμποιεῖν Εὐριπίδῃ· ὅθεν Μνησίμαχος οὕτω φησί,

Φρύγες ἐστὶ καινὸν δρᾶμα τοῦτ᾽ Εὐριπίδου,
      . . . ᾧ καὶ Σωκράτης
τὰ φρύγαν᾽ ὑποτίθησι.

καὶ πάλιν, " Εὐριπίδας σωκρατογόμφους." καὶ Καλλίας Πεδήταις·

A. Τί δὴ σὺ σεμνὴ καὶ φρονεῖς οὕτω μέγα;
B. Ἔξεστι γάρ μοι· Σωκράτης γὰρ αἴτιος.

Ἀριστοφάνης Νεφέλαις·

Εὐριπίδῃ δ᾽ ὁ τὰς τραγῳδίας ποιῶν
τὰς περιλαλούσας οὗτός ἐστι, τὰς σοφάς.

19 Ἀκούσας δὲ Ἀναξαγόρου κατά τινας, ἀλλὰ καὶ Δάμωνος, ὡς Ἀλέξανδρος ἐν Διαδοχαῖς, μετὰ τὴν ἐκείνου καταδίκην διήκουσεν Ἀρχελάου τοῦ φυσικοῦ· οὗ καὶ παιδικὰ γενέσθαι φησὶν Ἀριστόξενος. Δοῦρις δὲ καὶ δουλεῦσαι αὐτὸν καὶ ἐργάσασθαι λίθους· εἶναί τε αὐτοῦ καὶ τὰς ἐν ἀκροπόλει Χάριτας ἔνιοί φασιν, ἐνδεδυμένας οὔσας. ὅθεν καὶ Τίμωνα ἐν τοῖς Σίλλοις εἰπεῖν·

---

[a] So Cobet for vulgate Mnesilochus, retained by Meineke, *C.G.F.* ii. 371.
[b] There is a pun in Φρύγες and φρύγανα (= firewood).
[c] Meineke, *C.G.F.* ii. 739.
[d] A mistake for Teleclides : see Meineke, *Comicorum Grae-*

of a treatise on Natural Curiosities; and lastly a rhetorician who wrote a handbook on his art.

CHAPTER 5. SOCRATES (469–399 B.C.)

Socrates was the son of Sophroniscus, a sculptor, and of Phaenarete, a midwife, as we read in the *Theaetetus* of Plato; he was a citizen of Athens and belonged to the deme Alopece. It was thought that he helped Euripides to make his plays; hence Mnesimachus [a] writes:

This new play of Euripides is *The Phrygians*; and Socrates provides the wood for frying.[b]

And again he calls Euripides " an engine riveted by Socrates." And Callias in *The Captives*[c]:

A. Pray why so solemn, why this lofty air?
B. I've every right; I'm helped by Socrates.

Aristophanes [d] in *The Clouds*:

'Tis he composes for Euripides
Those clever plays, much sound and little sense.

According to some authors he was a pupil of Anaxagoras, and also of Damon, as Alexander states in his *Successions of Philosophers*. When Anaxagoras was condemned, he became a pupil of Archelaus the physicist; Aristoxenus asserts that Archelaus was very fond of him. Duris makes him out to have been a slave and to have been employed on stonework, and the draped figures of the Graces on the Acropolis have by some been attributed to him. Hence the passage in Timon's *Silli*[e]:

corum Fragmenta, ii. p. 371 *sq*. Dindorf conjectured that τὰς σωκρατογόμφους belongs to the same passage of Teleclides' *Clouds* and might well follow σοφάς.
   [*] Fr. 25 D.

ἐκ δ' ἄρα τῶν ἀπέκλινεν ὁ λαξόος, ἐννομολέσχης,
Ἑλλήνων ἐπαοιδός, ἀκριβολόγους ἀποφήνας,
μυκτὴρ ῥητορόμυκτος, ὑπαττικὸς εἰρωνευτής.

ἦν γὰρ καὶ ἐν τοῖς ῥητορικοῖς δεινός, ὥς φησι
καὶ Ἰδομενεύς· ἀλλὰ καὶ οἱ τριάκοντα αὐτὸν ἐκώ-
20 λυσαν τέχνας διδάσκειν λόγων, ὥς φησι Ξενοφῶν.
καὶ Ἀριστοφάνης αὐτὸν κωμῳδεῖ ὡς τὸν ἥττω
λόγον κρείττω ποιοῦντα. καὶ γὰρ πρῶτος, ὥς
φησι Φαβωρῖνος ἐν Παντοδαπῇ ἱστορίᾳ, μετὰ τοῦ
μαθητοῦ Αἰσχίνου ῥητορεύειν ἐδίδαξε· λέγει δὲ
τοῦτο καὶ Ἰδομενεὺς ἐν τῷ περὶ τῶν Σωκρατικῶν.
καὶ πρῶτος περὶ βίου διελέχθη καὶ πρῶτος φιλοσόφων καταδικασθεὶς ἐτελεύτα. φησὶ δ' αὐτὸν
Ἀριστόξενος ὁ Σπινθάρου καὶ χρηματίσασθαι·
τιθέντα γοῦν τὸ βαλλόμενον κέρμα ἀθροίζειν· εἶτ'
ἀναλώσαντα πάλιν τιθέναι.

Κρίτωνα δ' ἀναστῆσαι αὐτὸν ἀπὸ τοῦ ἐργα-
στηρίου καὶ παιδεῦσαι τῆς κατὰ ψυχὴν χάριτος
21 ἐρασθέντα Δημήτριός φησιν ὁ Βυζάντιος. γνόντα
δὲ τὴν φυσικὴν θεωρίαν μηδὲν εἶναι πρὸς ἡμᾶς,
τὰ ἠθικὰ φιλοσοφεῖν ἐπί τε τῶν ἐργαστηρίων καὶ
ἐν τῇ ἀγορᾷ· κἀκεῖνα δὲ φάσκειν ζητεῖν,

ὅττι τοι ἐν μεγάροισι κακόν τ' ἀγαθόν τε τέτυκται.

πολλάκις δὲ βιαιότερον ἐν ταῖς ζητήσεσι διαλεγόμενον κονδυλίζεσθαι καὶ παρατίλλεσθαι, τὸ πλέον
τε γελᾶσθαι καταφρονούμενον· καὶ πάντα ταῦτα
φέρειν ἀνεξικάκως. ὅθεν καὶ λακτισθέντα, ἐπειδὴ

---

[a] Possibly the reference is to the same citation as in § 19
which Diogenes Laertius may have found independently in
two of his authorities. Diogenes himself notices the agreement between Favorinus and Idomeneus of Lampsacus, a

From these diverged the sculptor, a prater about laws, the enchanter of Greece, inventor of subtle arguments, the sneerer who mocked at fine speeches, half-Attic in his mock humility.

He was formidable in public speaking, according to Idomeneus ; moreover, as Xenophon tells us, the Thirty forbade him to teach the art of words. And Aristophanes attacks him in his plays for making the worse appear the better reason. For Favorinus in his *Miscellaneous History* says Socrates and his pupil Aeschines were the first to teach rhetoric ; and this is confirmed by Idomeneus in his work on the Socratic circle.[a] Again, he was the first who discoursed on the conduct of life, and the first philosopher who was tried and put to death. Aristoxenus, the son of Spintharus, says of him that he made money ; he would at all events invest sums, collect the interest accruing, and then, when this was expended, put out the principal again.

Demetrius of Byzantium relates that Crito removed him from his workshop and educated him, being struck by his beauty of soul ; that he discussed moral questions in the workshops and the market-place, being convinced that the study of nature is no concern of ours ; and that he claimed that his inquiries embraced

Whatso'er is good or evil in an house [b] ;

that frequently, owing to his vehemence in argument, men set upon him with their fists or tore his hair out ; and that for the most part he was despised and laughed at, yet bore all this ill-usage patiently. So much so that, when he had been kicked, and

much earlier author, for he was a disciple of Epicurus, whom he knew from 310 to 270 B.C.

[b] Hom. *Od.* iv. 392.

151

ἠνέσχετο, τινὸς θαυμάσαντος, εἰπεῖν, " εἰ δέ με
ὄνος ἐλάκτισε, δίκην ἂν αὐτῷ ἐλάγχανον; " καὶ
ταῦτα μὲν ὁ Δημήτριος.

22 Ἀποδημίας δὲ οὐκ ἐδεήθη, καθάπερ οἱ πλείους,
πλὴν εἰ μὴ στρατεύεσθαι ἔδει. τὸ δὲ λοιπὸν
αὐτόθι μένων φιλονεικότερον συνεζήτει τοῖς προσ-
διαλεγομένοις, οὐχ ὥστε ἀφελέσθαι τὴν δόξαν
αὐτούς, ἀλλ' ὥστε τὸ ἀληθὲς ἐκμαθεῖν πειρᾶ-
σθαι. φασὶ δ' Εὐριπίδην αὐτῷ δόντα τὸ
Ἡρακλείτου σύγγραμμα ἐρέσθαι, " τί δοκεῖ ; "
τὸν δὲ φάναι, " ἃ μὲν συνῆκα, γενναῖα· οἶμαι
δὲ καὶ ἃ μὴ συνῆκα· πλὴν Δηλίου γέ τινος δεῖται
κολυμβητοῦ."

Ἐπεμελεῖτο δὲ καὶ σωμασκίας, καὶ ἦν εὐέκτης.
ἐστρατεύσατο γοῦν εἰς Ἀμφίπολιν· καὶ Ξενοφῶντα
ἀφ' ἵππου πεσόντα ἐν τῇ κατὰ Δήλιον μάχῃ
23 διέσωσεν ὑπολαβών· ὅτε καὶ πάντων φευγόντων
Ἀθηναίων αὐτὸς ἠρέμα ἀνεχώρει, παρεπιστρε-
φόμενος ἡσυχῇ καὶ τηρῶν ἀμύνασθαι εἴ τίς οἱ
ἐπέλθοι. ἐστρατεύσατο δὲ καὶ εἰς Ποτίδαιαν διὰ
θαλάττης· πεζῇ γὰρ οὐκ ἐνῆν τοῦ πολέμου κωλύοντος. ὅτε καὶ μεῖναι διὰ νυκτὸς ὅλης ἐφ' ἑνὸς
σχήματος αὐτόν φασι, καὶ ἀριστεύσαντα αὐτόθι
παραχωρῆσαι Ἀλκιβιάδῃ τοῦ ἀριστείου· οὗ καὶ
ἐρασθῆναί φησιν αὐτὸν Ἀρίστιππος ἐν τετάρτῳ
Περὶ παλαιᾶς τρυφῆς. Ἴων δὲ ὁ Χῖος καὶ νέον

ᵃ The reason assigned for an expedition to Potidaea by
sea will not hold. Communications between Athens and
Thrace were, as a rule, made by sea. Moreover, the siege
of Potidaea began in 432 B.C., the year before the outbreak
of the Peloponnesian war. It has been suggested that the
words διὰ θαλάττης . . . κωλύοντος should properly follow
Ἰσθμόν eight lines lower down. If any Athenian wished to

some one expressed surprise at his taking it so quietly, Socrates rejoined, " Should I have taken the law of a donkey, supposing that he had kicked me ? " Thus far Demetrius.

Unlike most philosophers, he had no need to travel, except when required to go on an expedition. The rest of his life he stayed at home and engaged all the more keenly in argument with anyone who would converse with him, his aim being not to alter his opinion but to get at the truth. They relate that Euripides gave him the treatise of Heraclitus and asked his opinion upon it, and that his reply was, " The part I understand is excellent, and so too is, I dare say, the part I do not understand ; but it needs a Delian diver to get to the bottom of it."

He took care to exercise his body and kept in good condition. At all events he served on the expedition to Amphipolis ; and when in the battle of Delium Xenophon had fallen from his horse, he stepped in and saved his life. For in the general flight of the Athenians he personally retired at his ease, quietly turning round from time to time and ready to defend himself in case he were attacked. Again, he served at Potidaea, whither he had gone by sea, as land communications were interrupted by the war [a] ; and while there he is said to have remained a whole night without changing his position, and to have won the prize of valour. But he resigned it to Alcibiades, for whom he cherished the tenderest affection, according to Aristippus in the fourth book of his treatise *On the Luxury of the Ancients*. Ion of

attend the Isthmian games during the early part of the Peloponnesian war, it was probably safer not to risk the land journey owing to the bitter hostility of the Megarians.

ὄντα εἰς Σάμον σὺν Ἀρχελάῳ ἀποδημῆσαι· καὶ
Πυθώδε ἐλθεῖν Ἀριστοτέλης φησίν· ἀλλὰ καὶ εἰς
Ἰσθμόν, ὡς Φαβωρῖνος ἐν τῷ πρώτῳ τῶν Ἀπο-
μνημονευμάτων.

24 Ἦν δὲ καὶ ἰσχυρογνώμων καὶ δημοκρατικός,
ὡς δῆλον ἔκ τε τοῦ μὴ εἶξαι τοῖς περὶ Κριτίαν,
κελεύουσι Λέοντα τὸν Σαλαμίνιον, ἄνδρα πλούσιον, ἀγαγεῖν πρὸς αὐτούς, ὥστε ἀπολέσθαι· ἀλλὰ
καὶ μόνος ἀποψηφίσασθαι τῶν δέκα στρατηγῶν.
καὶ ἐνὸν αὐτῷ ἀποδρᾶναι τῆς εἱρκτῆς μὴ ἐθελῆσαι·
τοῖς τε κλαίουσιν αὐτὸν ἐπιπλῆξαι καὶ τοὺς καλ-
λίστους λόγους ἐκείνους δεδεμένον διαθέσθαι.

Αὐτάρκης τε ἦν καὶ σεμνός. καί ποτε Ἀλκιβιάδου, καθά φησι Παμφίλη ἐν τῷ ἑβδόμῳ τῶν
Ὑπομνημάτων, διδόντος αὐτῷ χώραν μεγάλην, ἵνα
ἐνοικοδομήσηται οἰκίαν, φάναι, '' καὶ εἰ ὑποδη-
μάτων ἔδει, καὶ βύρσαν μοι ἐδίδους, ἵν᾽ ἐμαυτῷ
ὑποδήματα ποιησαίμην, καταγέλαστος ἂν ἦν
25 λαβών.'' πολλάκις δ᾽ ἀφορῶν εἰς τὰ πλήθη τῶν
πιπρασκομένων ἔλεγε πρὸς αὑτόν, '' πόσων ἐγὼ
χρείαν οὐκ ἔχω.'' καὶ συνεχὲς ἐκεῖνα ἀνεφθέγγετο
τὰ ἰαμβεῖα·

τὰ δ᾽ ἀργυρώματ᾽ ἐστὶν ἥ τε πορφύρα
εἰς τοὺς τραγῳδοὺς χρήσιμ᾽, οὐκ εἰς τὸν βίον.

ὑπερεφρόνησε δὲ καὶ Ἀρχελάου τοῦ Μακεδόνος
καὶ Σκόπα τοῦ Κρανωνίου καὶ Εὐρυλόχου τοῦ
Λαρισσαίου, μήτε χρήματα προσέμενος παρ᾽ αὐτῶν,
μήτε παρ᾽ αὐτοὺς ἀπελθών. εὔτακτός τε ἦν τὴν

---

[a] Stobaeus, *Florilegium*, lvi. 15, attributes these and three
preceding lines to Philemon, the well-known poet of the New

Chios relates that in his youth he visited Samos in the company of Archelaus; and Aristotle that he went to Delphi ; he went also to the Isthmus, according to Favorinus in the first book of his *Memorabilia*.

His strength of will and attachment to the democracy are evident from his refusal to yield to Critias and his colleagues when they ordered him to bring the wealthy Leon of Salamis before them for execution, and further from the fact that he alone voted for the acquittal of the ten generals ; and again from the facts that when he had the opportunity to escape from the prison he declined to do so, and that he rebuked his friends for weeping over his fate, and addressed to them his most memorable discourses in the prison.

He was a man of great independence and dignity of character. Pamphila in the seventh book of her *Commentaries* tells how Alcibiades once offered him a large site on which to build a house ; but he replied, " Suppose, then, I wanted shoes and you offered me a whole hide to make a pair with, would it not be ridiculous in me to take it ? " Often when he looked at the multitude of wares exposed for sale, he would say to himself, " How many things I can do without ! " And he would continually recite the lines :

> The purple robe and silver's shine
> More fits an actor's need than mine.[a]

He showed his contempt for Archelaus of Macedon and Scopas of Cranon and Eurylochus of Larissa by refusing to accept their presents or to go to their court. He was so orderly in his way of life that on

Comedy. If Philemon wrote them, Socrates cannot have recited them, however well they express his temper.

δίαιταν οὕτως, ὥστε πολλάκις ᾿Αθήνησι λοιμῶν
γενομένων μόνος οὐκ ἐνόσησε.

26 Φησὶ δ᾿ ᾿Αριστοτέλης δύο γυναῖκας αὐτὸν ἀγα-
γέσθαι· προτέραν μὲν Ξανθίππην, ἐξ ἧς αὐτῷ
γενέσθαι Λαμπροκλέα· δευτέραν δὲ Μυρτώ, τὴν
᾿Αριστείδου τοῦ δικαίου θυγατέρα, ἣν καὶ ἄπροικον
λαβεῖν, ἐξ ἧς γενέσθαι Σωφρονίσκον καὶ Μενέ-
ξενον. οἱ δὲ προτέραν γῆμαι τὴν Μυρτώ φασιν·
ἔνιοι δὲ καὶ ἀμφοτέρας σχεῖν ὁμοῦ, ὧν ἐστι
Σάτυρός τε καὶ ῾Ιερώνυμος ὁ ῾Ρόδιος. φασὶ γὰρ
βουληθέντας ᾿Αθηναίους διὰ τὸ λειπανδρεῖν συν-
αυξῆσαι τὸ πλῆθος, ψηφίσασθαι γαμεῖν μὲν ἀστὴν
μίαν, παιδοποιεῖσθαι δὲ καὶ ἐξ ἑτέρας· ὅθεν τοῦτο
ποιῆσαι καὶ Σωκράτην.

27 ῏Ην δ᾿ ἱκανὸς καὶ τῶν σκωπτόντων [αὐτὸν]
ὑπερορᾶν. καὶ ἐσεμνύνετο ἐπὶ τῇ εὐτελείᾳ, μισθόν
τε οὐδένα εἰσεπράξατο. καὶ ἔλεγεν ἥδιστα ἐσθίων
ἥκιστα ὄψου προσδεῖσθαι· καὶ ἥδιστα πίνων ἥκιστα
τὸ μὴ παρὸν ποτὸν ἀναμένειν· καὶ ἐλαχίστων δεόμενος ἔγγιστα εἶναι θεῶν. τοῦτο δ᾿ ἐνέσται καὶ
παρὰ τῶν κωμῳδοποιῶν λαβεῖν, οἳ λανθάνουσιν
ἑαυτοὺς δι᾿ ὧν σκώπτουσιν ἐπαινοῦντες αὐτόν.
᾿Αριστοφάνης μὲν οὕτως·

δ ῶ τῆς μεγάλης ἐπιθυμήσας σοφίας ἄνθρωπε
δικαίως,
ὡς εὐδαίμων παρ᾿ ᾿Αθηναίοις καὶ τοῖς ῞Ελλησι
διάξεις.
εἰ γὰρ μνήμων καὶ φροντιστής, καὶ τὸ ταλαίπωρον
ἔνεστιν
ἐν τῇ γνώμῃ, κοὔτε τι κάμνεις οὔθ᾿ ἑστὼς οὔτε
βαδίζων,

several occasions when pestilence broke out in Athens he was the only man who escaped infection.

Aristotle says that he married two wives: his first wife was Xanthippe, by whom he had a son, Lamprocles; his second wife was Myrto, the daughter of Aristides the Just, whom he took without a dowry. By her he had Sophroniscus and Menexenus. Others make Myrto his first wife; while some writers, including Satyrus and Hieronymus of Rhodes, affirm that they were both his wives at the same time. For they say that the Athenians were short of men and, wishing to increase the population, passed a decree permitting a citizen to marry one Athenian woman and have children by another; and that Socrates accordingly did so.

He could afford to despise those who scoffed at him. He prided himself on his plain living, and never asked a fee from anyone. He used to say that he most enjoyed the food which was least in need of condiment, and the drink which made him feel the least hankering for some other drink; and that he was nearest to the gods in that he had the fewest wants. This may be seen from the Comic poets, who in the act of ridiculing him give him high praise. Thus Aristophanes [a]:

O man that justly desirest great wisdom, how blessed will be thy life amongst Athenians and Greeks, retentive of memory and thinker that thou art, with endurance of toil for thy character; never art thou weary whether standing or walk-

* *Clouds,* 412-417.

οὔτε ῥιγῶν ἄχθει λίαν, οὔτ᾽ ἀρίστων ἐπιθυμεῖς,
οἴνου τ᾽ ἀπέχει κἀδηφαγίας καὶ τῶν ἄλλων
ἀνοήτων.

28 Ἀμειψίας δ᾽ ἐν τρίβωνι παράγων αὐτὸν φησὶν
οὕτως·

Σώκρατες ἀνδρῶν βέλτιστ᾽ ὀλίγων, πολλῷ δὲ
ματαιόταθ᾽, ἥκεις
καὶ σὺ πρὸς ἡμᾶς. καρτερικός γ᾽ εἶ. πόθεν ἄν σοι
χλαῖνα γένοιτο;
Β. τουτὶ τὸ κακὸν κατ᾽ ἐπήρειαν τῶν σκυτοτόμων
γεγένηται.
Α. οὗτος μέντοι πεινῶν οὕτως οὐπώποτ᾽ ἔτλη
κολακεῦσαι.

τοῦτο δ᾽ αὐτοῦ τὸ ὑπεροπτικὸν καὶ μεγαλόφρον
ἐμφαίνει καὶ Ἀριστοφάνης λέγων οὕτως,

ὅτι βρενθύει τ᾽ ἐν ταῖσιν ὁδοῖς, καὶ τὠφθαλμὼ
παραβάλλεις,
κἀνυπόδητος κακὰ πόλλ᾽ ἀνέχει, κἂν ἡμῖν σεμνο-
προσωπεῖς.

καίτοι ἐνίοτε πρὸς τοὺς καιροὺς ἁρμοττόμενος καὶ
λαμπρὰ ἠμπίσχετο· καθάπερ ἐν τῷ Πλάτωνος
συμποσίῳ παρ᾽ Ἀγάθωνα βαδίζων.

29 Ἱκανὸς δ᾽ ἀμφότερα ἦν, καὶ προτρέψαι καὶ
ἀποτρέψαι. ὥσπερ τὸν Θεαίτητον περὶ ἐπιστήμης διαλεχθεὶς ἔνθεον ἀπέπεμψε, καθὰ καὶ
Πλάτων φησίν. Εὐθύφρονα δὲ τῷ πατρὶ γραψά-
μενον ξενοκτονίας δίκην περὶ ὁσίου τινὰ διαλεχθεὶς
ἀπήγαγε. καὶ τὸν Λύσιν δὲ ἠθικώτατον ἐποίησε
προτρέψας. ἦν γὰρ ἱκανὸς ἀπὸ τῶν πραγμάτων
τοὺς λόγους εὑρίσκειν. ἐνέτρεψε δὲ καὶ Λαμπρο-

ing, never numb with cold, never hungry for breakfast; from wine and from gross feeding and all other frivolities thou dost turn away.

Ameipsias too, when he puts him on the stage wearing a cloak, says[a] :

A. You come to join us, Socrates, worthiest of a small band and emptiest by far ! You are a robust fellow. Where can we get you a proper coat ?

B. Your sorry plight is an insult to the cobblers.

A. And yet, hungry as he is, this man has never stooped to flatter.

This disdainful, lofty spirit of his is also noticed by Aristophanes when he says[b] :

Because you stalk along the streets, rolling your eyes, and endure, barefoot, many a hardship, and gaze up at us [the clouds].

And yet at times he would even put on fine clothes to suit the occasion, as in Plato's *Symposium*,[c] where he is on his way to Agathon's house.

He showed equal ability in both directions, in persuading and dissuading men ; thus, after conversing with Theaetetus about knowledge, he sent him away, as Plato says, fired with a divine impulse ; but when Euthyphro had indicted his father for manslaughter, Socrates, after some conversation with him upon piety, diverted him from his purpose. Lysis, again, he turned, by exhortation, into a most virtuous character. For he had the skill to draw his arguments from facts. And when his son

[a] *Sc.* in the *Connus*, Meineke, *C.G.F.* i. 201 sq., ii. 703.
[b] *Clouds*, 362.   [c] 174 A.

κλέα τὸν υἱὸν τῇ μητρὶ ἀγριαινόμενον, ὥς που καὶ
Ξενοφῶν εἴρηκε. καὶ Γλαύκωνα μὲν τὸν Πλάτωνος
ἀδελφὸν θέλοντα πολιτεύεσθαι ἀπέστησε διὰ τὸ
ἀπείρως ἔχειν, ὥς φησι Ξενοφῶν· Χαρμίδην δὲ
τοὐναντίον ἔχοντα οἰκείως ἐπέστησεν.

30 Ἐπῆρε δὲ καὶ εἰς φρόνημα Ἰφικράτην τὸν
στρατηγόν, δείξας αὐτῷ τοῦ κουρέως Μειδίου
ἀλεκτρυόνας ἀντίον τῶν Καλλίου πτερυξαμένους.
καὶ αὐτὸν Γλαυκωνίδης ἠξίου τῇ πόλει περιποιεῖν
καθάπερ φασιανὸν ὄρνιν ἢ ταώ.

Ἔλεγε δὲ ὡς θαυμαστὸν πρόβατα μὲν ἕκαστον
εἰπεῖν ἂν ῥᾳδίως ὅσα ἔχει, φίλους δ' οὐκ ἂν ὀνο-
μάσαι ὁπόσους κέκτηται· οὕτως ὀλιγώρως ἔχειν
περὶ αὐτούς. ὁρῶν δ' Εὐκλείδην ἐσπουδακότα
περὶ τοὺς ἐριστικοὺς λόγους, "ὦ Εὐκλείδη," ἔφη,
"σοφισταῖς μὲν δυνήσῃ χρῆσθαι, ἀνθρώποις δὲ
οὐδαμῶς." ἄχρηστον γὰρ ᾤετο εἶναι τὴν περὶ
ταῦτα γλισχρολογίαν, ὡς καὶ Πλάτων ἐν Εὐθυδήμῳ
φησί.

31 Χαρμίδου τε οἰκέτας αὐτῷ διδόντος, ἵν' ἀπ'
αὐτῶν προσοδεύοιτο, οὐχ εἵλετο· καὶ τὸ κάλλος
ὑπερεῖδεν Ἀλκιβιάδου κατά τινας. καὶ ἐπῄνει
σχολὴν ὡς κάλλιστον κτημάτων, καθὰ καὶ Ξενοφῶν
ἐν Συμποσίῳ φησίν. ἔλεγε δὲ καὶ ἓν μόνον
ἀγαθὸν εἶναι, τὴν ἐπιστήμην, καὶ ἓν μόνον κακόν,
τὴν ἀμαθίαν· πλοῦτον δὲ καὶ εὐγένειαν οὐδὲν
σεμνὸν ἔχειν· πᾶν δὲ τοὐναντίον κακόν. εἰπόντος
γοῦν τινος αὐτῷ ὡς εἴη Ἀντισθένης μητρὸς

ᵃ *Mem.* iii. 7.

Lamprocles was violently angry with his mother, Socrates made him feel ashamed of himself, as I believe Xenophon has told us.   When Plato's brother Glaucon was desirous of entering upon politics, Socrates dissuaded him, as Xenophon relates, because of his want of experience ; but on the contrary he encouraged Charmides to take up politics because he had a gift that way.[a]

He roused Iphicrates the general to a martial spirit by showing him how the fighting cocks of Midias the barber flapped their wings in defiance of those of Callias.   Glauconides demanded that he should be acquired for the state as if he were some pheasant or peacock.

He used to say it was strange that, if you asked a man how many sheep he had, he could easily tell you the precise number ; whereas he could not name his friends or say how many he had, so slight was the value he set upon them.   Seeing Euclides keenly interested in eristic arguments, he said to him : " You will be able to get on with sophists, Euclides, but with men not at all."   For he thought there was no use in this sort of hair-splitting, as Plato shows us in the *Euthydemus*.

Again, when Charmides offered him some slaves in order that he might derive an income from them, he declined the offer ; and according to some he scorned the beauty of Alcibiades.   He would extol leisure as the best of possessions, according to Xenophon in the *Symposium*.   There is, he said, only one good, that is, knowledge, and only one evil, that is, ignorance ; wealth and good birth bring their possessor no dignity, but on the contrary evil.   At all events, when some one told him that Antisthenes' mother

Θράττης, " σὺ δ᾽ ᾤου," ἔφη, " οὕτως ἂν γενναῖον ἐκ δυοῖν Ἀθηναίων γενέσθαι; " Φαίδωνα δὲ δι᾽ αἰχμαλωσίαν ἐπ᾽ οἰκήματος καθήμενον προσέταξε Κρίτωνι λυτρώσασθαι, καὶ φιλόσοφον ἀπειργάσατο.

32 Ἀλλὰ καὶ λυρίζειν ἐμάνθανεν ἤδη γηραιός,[1] μηδὲν λέγων ἄτοπον εἶναι ἅ τις μὴ οἶδεν ἐκμανθάνειν. ἔτι τε ὠρχεῖτο συνεχές, τῇ τοῦ σώματος εὐεξίᾳ λυσιτελεῖν ἡγούμενος τὴν τοιαύτην γυμνασίαν, ὡς καὶ Ξενοφῶν ἐν Συμποσίῳ φησίν. ἔλεγε δὲ καὶ προσημαίνειν τὸ δαιμόνιον τὰ μέλλοντα αὐτῷ· τό τε εὖ [ἄρχεσθαι] μικρὸν μὲν μὴ εἶναι, παρὰ μικρὸν δέ· καὶ εἰδέναι μὲν μηδὲν πλὴν αὐτὸ τοῦτο [εἰδέναι]. τούς τε τὰ πρώϊμα πολλοῦ ἐωνημένους ἀπογινώσκειν ἔλεγεν εἰς τὰς ὥρας ἐλθεῖν. καί ποτε ἐρωτηθείς, τίς ἀρετὴ νέου, " τὸ μηδὲν ἄγαν," εἶπεν. ἔφασκέ τε δεῖν γεωμετρεῖν μέχρι ἂν τις μέτρῳ δύνηται γῆν παραλαβεῖν καὶ παραδοῦναι.

33 Εὐριπίδου δ᾽ ἐν τῇ Αὔγῃ εἰπόντος περὶ ἀρετῆς,

κράτιστον εἰκῆ ταῦτ᾽ ἐᾶν ἀφειμένα,

ἀναστὰς ἐξῆλθε, φήσας γελοῖον εἶναι ἀνδράποδον μὲν μὴ εὑρισκόμενον ἀξιοῦν ζητεῖν, ἀρετὴν δ᾽ οὕτως ἐᾶν ἀπολωλέναι. ἐρωτηθεὶς πότερον γῆμαι ἢ μή, ἔφη, " ὃ ἂν αὐτῶν ποιήσῃς, μεταγνώσῃ." ἐλεγέ τε θαυμάζειν τῶν τὰς λιθίνας εἰκόνας κατα-

[1] ἤδη γηραιός] corr. Cobet : ὀτὲ καιρός vulg. : ὀτὲ ⟨οὐκέτι⟩ καιρός Reiske.

[a] This line, now found in Eur. Electra, 379, may have come into our text from the lost play Auge: cf. Nauck, T.G.F.[2], p. 437, s.v. ΑΥΓΗ.

was a Thracian, he replied, "Nay, did you expect a man so noble to have been born of two Athenian parents?" He made Crito ransom Phaedo who, having been taken prisoner in the war, was kept in degrading slavery, and so won him for philosophy.

Moreover, in his old age he learnt to play the lyre, declaring that he saw no absurdity in learning a new accomplishment. As Xenophon relates in the *Symposium*, it was his regular habit to dance, thinking that such exercise helped to keep the body in good condition. He used to say that his supernatural sign warned him beforehand of the future ; that to make a good start was no trifling advantage, but a trifle turned the scale ; and that he knew nothing except just the fact of his ignorance. He said that, when people paid a high price for fruit which had ripened early, they must despair of seeing the fruit ripen at the proper season. And, being once asked in what consisted the virtue of a young man, he said, " In doing nothing to excess." He held that geometry should be studied to the point at which a man is able to measure the land which he acquires or parts with.

On hearing the line of Euripides' play *Auge* where the poet says of virtue :

'Tis best to let her roam at will,[a]

he got up and left the theatre. For he said it was absurd to make a hue and cry about a slave who could not be found, and to allow virtue to perish in this way. Some one asked him whether he should marry or not, and received the reply, " Whichever you do you will repent it." He used to express his astonishment that the sculptors of marble statues

σκευαζομένων τοῦ μὲν λίθου προνοεῖν ὅπως ὁμοιό-
τατος ἔσται, αὐτῶν δ' ἀμελεῖν, ὡς μὴ ὁμοίους τῷ
λίθῳ φαίνεσθαι. ἠξίου δὲ καὶ τοὺς νέους συνεχὲς
κατοπτρίζεσθαι, ἵν' εἰ μὲν καλοὶ εἶεν, ἄξιοι γί-
γνοιντο· εἰ δ' αἰσχροί, παιδείᾳ τὴν δυσείδειαν
ἐπικαλύπτοιεν.

34 Καλέσας ἐπὶ δεῖπνον πλουσίους, καὶ τῆς Ξανθ-
ίππης αἰδουμένης ἔφη, " θάρρει· εἰ μὲν γὰρ
εἶεν μέτριοι, συμπεριενεχθεῖεν ἄν· εἰ δὲ φαῦλοι,
ἡμῖν αὐτῶν οὐδὲν μελήσει." ἔλεγέ τε τοὺς μὲν
ἄλλους ἀνθρώπους ζῆν ἵν' ἐσθίοιεν· αὐτὸς δὲ
ἐσθίειν ἵνα ζῴη. πρὸς τὸ οὐκ ἀξιόλογον πλῆθος
ἔφασκεν ὅμοιον εἴ τις τετράδραχμον ἓν ἀπο-
δοκιμάζων τὸν ἐκ τῶν τοιούτων σωρὸν ὡς δόκιμον
ἀποδέχοιτο. Αἰσχίνου δὲ εἰπόντος, " πένης εἰμὶ
καὶ ἄλλο μὲν οὐδὲν ἔχω, δίδωμι δέ σοι ἐμαυτόν,"
" ἆρ' οὖν," εἶπεν, " οὐκ αἰσθάνῃ τὰ μέγιστά μοι
διδούς;" τὸν ἀποδυσπετοῦντα ἐπὶ τῷ παρορᾶσθαι,
ὁπότε ἐπανέστησαν οἱ τριάκοντα, " ἆρα," ἔφη,
35 " μήτι σοι μεταμέλει;" πρὸς τὸν εἰπόντα, " θάνατόν
σου κατέγνωσαν Ἀθηναῖοι," " κἀκείνων," εἶπεν,
" ἡ φύσις." οἱ δὲ τοῦτ' Ἀναξαγόρου φασί. τῆς
γυναικὸς εἰπούσης, " ἀδίκως ἀποθνήσκεις," " σὺ
δέ," ἔφη, " δικαίως ἐβούλου;" ὄναρ δόξας τινὰ αὐτῷ
λέγειν,

ἤματί κεν τριτάτῳ Φθίην ἐρίβωλον ἵκοιο,

πρὸς Αἰσχίνην ἔφη, " εἰς τρίτην ἀποθανοῦμαι."
μέλλοντί τε αὐτῷ τὸ κώνειον πίεσθαι Ἀπολλόδωρος

---

* Hom. *Il.* ix. 363.
  ᵇ The proposal that Socrates should escape from prison
was attributed to Aeschines as well as to Crito (see below,
§ 60). The Homeric citation occurs in Plato's *Crito*, 44 ʙ.

should take pains to make the block of marble into a perfect likeness of a man, and should take no pains about themselves lest they should turn out mere blocks, not men. He recommended to the young the constant use of the mirror, to the end that handsome men might acquire a corresponding behaviour, and ugly men conceal their defects by education.

He had invited some rich men and, when Xanthippe said she felt ashamed of the dinner, " Never mind," said he, " for if they are reasonable they will put up with it, and if they are good for nothing, we shall not trouble ourselves about them." He would say that the rest of the world lived to eat, while he himself ate to live. Of the mass of men who do not count he said it was as if some one should object to a single tetradrachm as counterfeit and at the same time let a whole heap made up of just such pieces pass as genuine. Aeschines said to him, " I am a poor man and have nothing else to give, but I offer you myself," and Socrates answered, " Nay, do you not see that you are offering me the greatest gift of all ? " To one who complained that he was overlooked when the Thirty rose to power, he said, " You are not sorry for that, are you ? " To one who said, " You are condemned by the Athenians to die," he made answer, " So are they, by nature." But some ascribe this to Anaxagoras. When his wife said, " You suffer unjustly," he retorted, " Why, would you have me suffer justly ? " He had a dream that some one said to him[a] :

On the third day thou shalt come to the fertile fields of Phthia ;

and he told Aeschines, " On the third day I shall die." [b] When he was about to drink the hemlock,

165

ἱμάτιον ἐδίδου καλόν, ἵν' ἐκείνῳ ἐναποθάνοι· καὶ
ὅς, " τί δέ," ἔφη, " τὸ ἐμὸν ἱμάτιον ἐμβιῶναι μὲν
ἐπιτήδειον, ἐναποθανεῖν δὲ οὐχί ; " πρὸς τὸν
εἰπόντα, " κακῶς ὁ δεῖνά σε λέγει," " καλῶς γάρ,"
36 ἔφη, " λέγειν οὐκ ἔμαθε." στρέψαντος δὲ Ἀντισθένους τὸ διερρωγὸς τοῦ τρίβωνος εἰς τοὐμφανές,
" ὁρῶ σου," ἔφη, " διὰ τοῦ τρίβωνος τὴν κενοδοξίαν."
πρὸς τὸν εἰπόντα, " οὐ σοὶ λοιδορεῖται ὁ δεῖνα ; "
" οὐχί," ἔφη· " ἐμοὶ γὰρ οὐ πρόσεστι ταῦτα." ἔλεγε
δὲ τοῖς κωμικοῖς δεῖν ἐπίτηδες ἑαυτὸν διδόναι· εἰ
μὲν γάρ τι τῶν προσόντων λέξειαν, διορθώσονται·
εἰ δ' οὔ, οὐδὲν πρὸς ἡμᾶς. πρὸς Ξανθίππην
πρότερον μὲν λοιδοροῦσαν, ὕστερον δὲ καὶ περι-
χέασαν αὐτῷ, " οὐκ ἔλεγον," εἶπεν, " ὅτι Ξανθίππη
βροντῶσα καὶ ὕδωρ ποιήσει ; " πρὸς Ἀλκιβιάδην
εἰπόντα ὡς οὐκ ἀνεκτὴ ἡ Ξανθίππη λοιδοροῦσα,
" ἀλλ' ἔγωγ'," ἔφη, " συνείθισμαι, καθαπερεὶ καὶ
37 τροχιλίας ἀκούων συνεχές. καὶ σὺ μέν," εἶπε,
" χηνῶν βοώντων ἀνέχῃ." τοῦ δὲ εἰπόντος, " ἀλλά
μοι ᾠὰ καὶ νεοττοὺς τίκτουσι," " κἀμοί," φησί,
" Ξανθίππη παιδία γεννᾷ." ποτὲ αὐτῆς ἐν ἀγορᾷ
καὶ θοἰμάτιον περιελομένης συνεβούλευον οἱ γνώριμοι χερσὶν ἀμύνασθαι, " νὴ Δί'," εἶπεν, " ἵν' ἡμῶν
πυκτευόντων ἕκαστος ὑμῶν λέγῃ, εὖ Σώκρατες,
εὖ Ξανθίππη." ἔλεγε συνεῖναι τραχείᾳ γυναικὶ
καθάπερ οἱ ἱππικοὶ θυμοειδέσιν ἵπποις. " ἀλλ' ὡς
ἐκεῖνοι," φησί, " τούτων κρατήσαντες ῥᾳδίως τῶν
ἄλλων περιγίνονται, οὕτω κἀγὼ Ξανθίππῃ χρώμενος τοῖς ἄλλοις ἀνθρώποις συμπεριενεχθήσομαι."

Ταῦτα δὴ καὶ τοιαῦτα λέγων καὶ πράττων πρὸς

Apollodorus offered him a beautiful garment to die in: " What," said he, " is my own good enough to live in but not to die in?" When he was told that So-and-so spoke ill of him, he replied, " True, for he has never learnt to speak well." When Antisthenes turned his cloak so that the tear in it came into view, " I see," said he, " your vanity through your cloak." To one who said, "Don't you find so-and-so very offensive?" his reply was, " No, for it takes two to make a quarrel." We ought not to object, he used to say, to be subjects for the Comic poets, for if they satirize our faults they will do us good, and if not they do not touch us. When Xanthippe first scolded him and then drenched him with water, his rejoinder was, " Did I not say that Xanthippe's thunder would end in rain?" When Alcibiades declared that the scolding of Xanthippe was intolerable, " Nay, I have got used to it," said he, " as to the continued rattle of a windlass. And you do not mind the cackle of geese." " No," replied Alcibiades, " but they furnish me with eggs and goslings." " And Xanthippe," said Socrates, " is the mother of my children." When she tore his coat off his back in the market-place and his acquaintances advised him to hit back, " Yes, by Zeus," said he, " in order that while we are sparring each of you may join in with ' Go it, Socrates!' ' Well done, Xanthippe!'" He said he lived with a shrew, as horsemen are fond of spirited horses, " but just as, when they have mastered these, they can easily cope with the rest, so I in the society of Xanthippe shall learn to adapt myself to the rest of the world."

These and the like were his words and deeds, to

τῆς Πυθίας ἐμαρτυρήθη, Χαιρεφῶντι ἀνελούσης ἐκεῖνο δὴ τὸ περιφερόμενον,

ἀνδρῶν ἁπάντων Σωκράτης σοφώτατος.

38 ἀφ' οὗ δὴ καὶ ἐφθονήθη μάλιστα· καὶ δὴ καὶ ὅτι διήλεγχε τοὺς μέγα φρονοῦντας ἐφ' ἑαυτοῖς ὡς ἀνοήτους, καθάπερ ἀμέλει καὶ τὸν Ἄνυτον, ὡς καὶ ἐν τῷ Πλάτωνός ἐστι Μένωνι. οὗτος γὰρ οὐ φέρων τὸν ὑπὸ Σωκράτους χλευασμὸν πρῶτον μὲν ἐπήλειψεν αὐτῷ τοὺς περὶ Ἀριστοφάνην, ἔπειτα καὶ Μέλητον συνέπεισεν ἀπενέγκασθαι κατ' αὐτοῦ γραφὴν ἀσεβείας καὶ τῶν νέων διαφθορᾶς.

Ἀπηνέγκατο μὲν οὖν τὴν γραφὴν ὁ Μέλητος, εἶπε δὲ τὴν δίκην Πολύευκτος, ὥς φησι Φαβωρῖνος ἐν Παντοδαπῇ ἱστορίᾳ· συνέγραψε δὲ τὸν λόγον Πολυκράτης ὁ σοφιστής, ὥς φησιν Ἕρμιππος, ἢ Ἄνυτος, ὥς τινες· προητοίμασε δὲ πάντα Λύκων ὁ δημαγωγός.

39 Ἀντισθένης δ' ἐν ταῖς τῶν φιλοσόφων Διαδοχαῖς καὶ Πλάτων ἐν Ἀπολογίᾳ τρεῖς αὐτοῦ κατηγορῆσαί φασιν, Ἄνυτον καὶ Λύκωνα καὶ Μέλητον· τὸν μὲν Ἄνυτον ὡς ὑπὲρ τῶν δημιουργῶν καὶ τῶν πολιτικῶν ὀργιζόμενον· τὸν δὲ Λύκωνα ὑπὲρ τῶν ῥητόρων· καὶ τὸν Μέλητον ὑπὲρ τῶν ποιητῶν, οὓς ἅπαντας ὁ Σωκράτης διέσυρε. Φαβωρῖνος δέ φησιν ἐν τῷ πρώτῳ τῶν Ἀπομνημονευμάτων μὴ εἶναι ἀληθῆ τὸν λόγον τὸν Πολυκράτους κατὰ Σωκράτους· ἐν αὐτῷ γάρ, φησί, μνημονεύει τῶν ὑπὸ Κόνωνος τειχῶν ἀνασταθέντων, ἃ γέγονεν

---

[a] 95 A.

[b] The confusion in the last sentence of § 38 is due to the insertion in the wrong place of two extracts, one from

which the Pythian priestess bore testimony when she gave Chaerephon the famous response :

Of all men living Socrates most wise.

For this he was most envied ; and especially because he would take to task those who thought highly of themselves, proving them to be fools, as to be sure he treated Anytus, according to Plato's *Meno*.[a] For Anytus could not endure to be ridiculed by Socrates, and so in the first place stirred up against him Aristophanes and his friends ; then afterwards he helped to persuade Meletus to indict him on a charge of impiety and corrupting the youth.

The indictment was brought by Meletus, and the speech was delivered by Polyeuctus, according to Favorinus in his *Miscellaneous History*. The speech was written by Polycrates the sophist, according to Hermippus ; but some say that it was by Anytus. Lycon the demagogue had made all the needful preparations.[b]

Antisthenes in his *Successions of Philosophers*, and Plato in his *Apology*, say that there were three accusers, Anytus, Lycon and Meletus ; that Anytus was roused to anger on behalf of the craftsmen and politicians, Lycon on behalf of the rhetoricians, Meletus of the poets, all three of which classes had felt the lash of Socrates. Favorinus in the first book of his *Memorabilia* declares that the speech of Polycrates against Socrates is not authentic ; for he mentions the rebuilding of the walls by Conon, which

Favorinus and the other from Hermippus. When these are removed, the parts assigned to the three accusers, Meletus, Anytus and Lycon, become clear : ἀπηνέγκατο μὲν οὖν τὴν γραφὴν ὁ Μέλητος, εἶπε δὲ τὴν δίκην Ἄνυτος. προητοίμασε δὲ πάντα Λύκων ὁ δημαγωγός.

ἔτεσιν ἐξ τῆς τοῦ Σωκράτους τελευτῆς ὕστερον.
καὶ ἔστιν οὕτως ἔχον.

40 Ἡ δ' ἀντωμοσία τῆς δίκης τοῦτον εἶχε τὸν
τρόπον· ἀνάκειται γὰρ ἔτι καὶ νῦν, φησὶ Φαβωρῖνος,
ἐν τῷ Μητρῴῳ· "τάδε ἐγράψατο καὶ ἀντωμόσατο
Μέλητος Μελήτου Πιτθεὺς Σωκράτει Σωφρονίσκου
Ἀλωπεκῆθεν· ἀδικεῖ Σωκράτης, οὓς μὲν ἡ πόλις
νομίζει θεοὺς οὐ νομίζων, ἕτερα δὲ καινὰ δαιμόνια
εἰσηγούμενος· ἀδικεῖ δὲ καὶ τοὺς νέους διαφθείρων.
τίμημα θάνατος." ὁ δ' οὖν φιλόσοφος, Λυσίου
γράψαντος ἀπολογίαν αὐτῷ, διαναγνοὺς ἔφη, " καλὸς
μὲν ὁ λόγος, ὦ Λυσία, οὐ μὴν ἁρμόττων γ' ἐμοί."
δηλαδὴ γὰρ ἦν τὸ πλέον δικανικὸς ἢ ἐμφιλόσοφος.

41 εἰπόντος δὲ τοῦ Λυσίου, " πῶς, εἰ καλός ἐστιν ὁ
λόγος, οὐκ ἄν σοι ἁρμόττοι;" ἔφη, " οὐ γὰρ καὶ
ἱμάτια καλὰ καὶ ὑποδήματα εἴη ἂν ἐμοὶ ἀνάρμοστα;"

Κρινομένου δ' αὐτοῦ φησιν Ἰοῦστος ὁ Τιβεριεὺς
ἐν τῷ Στέμματι Πλάτωνα ἀναβῆναι ἐπὶ τὸ βῆμα
καὶ εἰπεῖν, " νεώτατος ὤν, ὦ ἄνδρες Ἀθηναῖοι,
τῶν ἐπὶ τὸ βῆμα ἀναβάντων·" τοὺς δὲ δικαστὰς
ἐκβοῆσαι, Κατάβα, κατάβα [τουτέστι κατάβηθι].
ὅτ' οὖν[1] καὶ κατεδικάσθη διακοσίαις ὀγδοήκοντα
μιᾷ πλείοσι ψήφοις τῶν ἀπολυουσῶν· καὶ τιμω-
μένων τῶν δικαστῶν τί χρὴ παθεῖν αὐτὸν ἢ
ἀποτῖσαι, πέντε καὶ εἴκοσιν ἔφη δραχμὰς ἀποτίσειν.
Εὐβουλίδης μὲν γάρ φησιν ἑκατὸν ὁμολογῆσαι·

42 θορυβησάντων δὲ τῶν δικαστῶν, " ἕνεκα μέν,"
εἶπε, " τῶν ἐμοὶ διαπεπραγμένων τιμῶμαι τὴν
δίκην τῆς ἐν πρυτανείῳ σιτήσεως."

Καὶ οἳ θάνατον αὐτοῦ κατέγνωσαν, προσθέντες
ἄλλας ψήφους ὀγδοήκοντα. καὶ δεθεὶς μετ' οὐ

----

[1] ὅτ' οὖν] ὁ δ' οὖν Richards.

did not take place till six years after the death of Socrates. And this is the case.

The affidavit in the case, which is still preserved, says Favorinus, in the *Metroön*, ran as follows : " This indictment and affidavit is sworn by Meletus, the son of Meletus of Pitthos, against Socrates, the son of Sophroniscus of Alopece : Socrates is guilty of refusing to recognize the gods recognized by the state, and of introducing other new divinities. He is also guilty of corrupting the youth. The penalty demanded is death." The philosopher then, after Lysias had written a defence for him, read it through and said : " A fine speech, Lysias ; it is not, however, suitable to me." For it was plainly more forensic than philosophical. Lysias said, " If it is a fine speech, how can it fail to suit you ? " " Well," he replied, " would not fine raiment and fine shoes be just as unsuitable to me ? "

Justus of Tiberias in his book entitled *The Wreath* says that in the course of the trial Plato mounted the platform and began : " Though I am the youngest, men of Athens, of all who ever rose to address you "—whereupon the judges shouted out, " Get down ! Get down ! " When therefore he was condemned by 281 votes more than those given for acquittal, and when the judges were assessing what he should suffer or what fine he should pay, he proposed to pay 25 drachmae. Eubulides indeed says he offered 100. When this caused an uproar among the judges, he said, " Considering my services, I assess the penalty at maintenance in the Prytaneum at the public expense."

Sentence of death was passed, with an accession of eighty fresh votes. He was put in prison, and a

πολλὰς ἡμέρας ἔπιε τὸ κώνειον, πολλὰ καλὰ
κἀγαθὰ διαλεχθείς, ἃ Πλάτων ἐν τῷ Φαίδωνί
φησιν. ἀλλὰ καὶ παιᾶνα κατά τινας ἐποίησεν,
οὗ ἡ ἀρχή·

Δήλι' Ἄπολλον χαῖρε, καὶ Ἄρτεμι, παῖδε κλεεινώ.

Διονυσόδωρος δέ φησι μὴ εἶναι αὐτοῦ τὸν παιᾶνα.
ἐποίησε δὲ καὶ μῦθον Αἰσώπειον οὐ πάνυ ἐπι-
τετευγμένως, οὗ ἡ ἀρχή·

Αἴσωπός ποτ' ἔλεξε Κορίνθιον ἄστυ νέμουσι,
μὴ κρίνειν ἀρετὴν λαοδίκῳ σοφίῃ.

43 Ὁ μὲν οὖν ἐξ ἀνθρώπων ἦν· Ἀθηναῖοι δ' εὐθὺς
μετέγνωσαν, ὥστε κλεῖσαι καὶ παλαίστρας καὶ
γυμνάσια. καὶ τοὺς μὲν ⟨ἄλλους⟩[1] ἐφυγάδευσαν,
Μελήτου δὲ θάνατον κατέγνωσαν· Σωκράτην δὲ
χαλκῇ εἰκόνι ἐτίμησαν, ἣν ἔθεσαν ἐν τῷ πομπείῳ,
Λυσίππου ταύτην ἐργασαμένου. Ἄνυτόν τε ἐπι-
δημήσαντα αὐθημερὸν ἐξεκήρυξαν Ἡρακλεῶται.
οὐ μόνον δ' ἐπὶ Σωκράτους Ἀθηναῖοι πεπόνθασι
τοῦτο, ἀλλὰ καὶ ἐπὶ πλείστων ὅσων. καὶ γὰρ
Ὅμηρον, καθά φησιν Ἡρακλείδης, πεντήκοντα
δραχμαῖς ὡς μαινόμενον ἐζημίωσαν, καὶ Τυρταῖον
παρακόπτειν ἔλεγον, καὶ Ἀστυδάμαντα πρότερον
44 τῶν περὶ Αἰσχύλον ἐτίμησαν εἰκόνι χαλκῇ. Εὐριπίδης δὲ καὶ ὀνειδίζει αὐτοῖς ἐν τῷ Παλαμήδει
λέγων· " ἐκάνετ' ἐκάνετε τὰν πάνσοφον τὰν οὐδὲν
ἀλγύνουσαν ἀηδόνα μουσᾶν." καὶ τάδε μὲν ὧδε.
Φιλόχορος δέ φησι προτελευτῆσαι τὸν Εὐριπίδην
τοῦ Σωκράτους.

---

[1] ⟨ἄλλους⟩ Richards.

few days afterwards drank the hemlock, after much
noble discourse which Plato records in the *Phaedo*.
Further, according to some, he composed a paean
beginning :

> All hail, Apollo, Delos' lord !
> Hail Artemis, ye noble pair !

Dionysodorus denies that he wrote the paean. He
also composed a fable of Aesop, not very skilfully,
beginning [a] :

> " Judge not, ye men of Corinth," Aesop cried,
> " Of virtue as the jury-courts decide."

So he was taken from among men ; and not long
afterwards the Athenians felt such remorse that they
shut up the training grounds and gymnasia. They
banished the other accusers but put Meletus to death ;
they honoured Socrates with a bronze statue, the
work of Lysippus, which they placed in the hall
of processions. And no sooner did Anytus visit
Heraclea than the people of that town expelled him
on that very day. Not only in the case of Socrates
but in very many others the Athenians repented in
this way. For they fined Homer (so says Heraclides [b])
50 drachmae for a madman, and said Tyrtaeus was
beside himself, and they honoured Astydamas before
Aeschylus and his brother poets with a bronze statue.
Euripides upbraids them thus in his *Palamedes* : " Ye
have slain, have slain, the all-wise, the innocent,
the Muses' nightingale." [c] This is one account ; but
Philochorus asserts that Euripides died before
Socrates.

[a] *Anth. Plan.* iv. 16.
[b] Most probably Heraclides of Pontus. This remarkable
assertion may have occurred in one of his dialogues, and
was perhaps not meant to be taken seriously.
[c] Nauck, *T.G.F.²*, *Eur.* 588.

Ἐγεννήθη δέ, καθά φησιν Ἀπολλόδωρος ἐν τοῖς Χρονικοῖς, ἐπὶ Ἀψεφίωνος ἐν τῷ τετάρτῳ ἔτει τῆς ἑβδομηκοστῆς ἑβδόμης Ὀλυμπιάδος, Θαργηλιῶνος ἕκτῃ, ὅτε καθαίρουσιν Ἀθηναῖοι τὴν πόλιν καὶ τὴν Ἄρτεμιν Δήλιοι γενέσθαι φασίν. ἐτελεύτησε δὲ τῷ πρώτῳ ἔτει τῆς ἐνενηκοστῆς πέμπτης Ὀλυμπιάδος, γεγονὼς ἐτῶν ἑβδομήκοντα. ταῦτά φησι καὶ Δημήτριος ὁ Φαληρεύς. ἔνιοι δὲ ἑξήκοντα ἐτῶν τελευτῆσαι αὐτόν φασιν.

45 Ἀμφότεροι δ᾽ ἤκουσαν Ἀναξαγόρου, καὶ οὗτος καὶ Εὐριπίδης, ὃς καὶ τῷ πρώτῳ ἔτει τῆς ἑβδομηκοστῆς πέμπτης Ὀλυμπιάδος ἐγεννήθη ἐπὶ Καλλιάδου.

Δοκεῖ δέ μοι καὶ περὶ τῶν φυσικῶν ὁ Σωκράτης διειλέχθαι· ὅπου γε καὶ περὶ προνοίας τινὰ διαλέγεται, καθά φησι καὶ Ξενοφῶν, καίτοι περὶ μόνων τῶν ἠθικῶν ποιεῖσθαι τοὺς λόγους αὐτὸν εἰπών. ἀλλὰ καὶ Πλάτων ἐν τῇ Ἀπολογίᾳ μνησθεὶς Ἀναξαγόρου καὶ ἄλλων τινῶν φυσικῶν, ἃ Σωκράτης ἀρνεῖται, περὶ τούτων αὐτὸς λέγει, καίπερ ἀνατιθεὶς πάντα Σωκράτει.

Φησὶ δ᾽ Ἀριστοτέλης μάγον τινὰ ἐλθόντα ἐκ Συρίας εἰς Ἀθήνας τά τε ἄλλα καταγνῶναι τοῦ Σωκράτους, καὶ δὴ καὶ βίαιον ἔσεσθαι τὴν τελευτὴν αὐτῷ.

46 Ἔστι δὲ καὶ ἡμῶν εἰς αὐτὸν οὕτω·

πῖνέ νυν ἐν Διὸς ὤν, ὦ Σώκρατες· ἦ σε γὰρ ὄντως
καὶ σοφὸν εἶπε θεός, καὶ θεὸς ἡ σοφίη.
πρὸς γὰρ Ἀθηναίων κώνειον ἁπλῶς σὺ ἐδέξω·
αὐτοὶ δ᾽ ἐξέπιον τοῦτο τεῷ στόματι.

Τούτῳ τις, καθά φησιν Ἀριστοτέλης ἐν τρίτῳ
174

II. 44–46. SOCRATES

He was born, according to Apollodorus in his *Chronology*, in the archonship of Apsephion, in the fourth year of the 77th Olympiad,[a] on the 6th day of the month of Thargelion, when the Athenians purify their city, which according to the Delians is the birthday of Artemis. He died in the first year of the 95th Olympiad [b] at the age of seventy. With this Demetrius of Phalerum agrees; but some say he was sixty when he died.

Both were pupils of Anaxagoras, I mean Socrates and Euripides, who was born in the first year of the 75th Olympiad in the archonship of Calliades.[c]

In my opinion Socrates discoursed on physics as well as on ethics, since he holds some conversations about providence, even according to Xenophon, who, however, declares that he only discussed ethics. But Plato, after mentioning Anaxagoras and certain other physicists in the *Apology*,[d] treats for his own part themes which Socrates disowned, although he puts everything into the mouth of Socrates.

Aristotle relates that a magician came from Syria to Athens and, among other evils with which he threatened Socrates, predicted that he would come to a violent end.

I have written verses about him too, as follows [e] :

Drink then, being in Zeus's palace, O Socrates ; for truly did the god pronounce thee wise, being wisdom himself ; for when thou didst frankly take the hemlock at the hands of the Athenians, they themselves drained it as it passed thy lips.

He was sharply criticized, according to Aristotle

---

[a] 469–468 B.C.   [b] 400–399 B.C.
[c] 480–479 B.C.   [d] 26 D.   [e] *Anth. Pal.* vii. 96.

Περὶ ποιητικῆς, ἐφιλονείκει Ἀντίλοχος Λήμνιος
καὶ Ἀντιφῶν ὁ τερατοσκόπος, ὡς Πυθαγόρᾳ
Κύλων Κροτωνιάτης· καὶ Σύαγρος Ὁμήρῳ ζῶντι,
ἀποθανόντι δὲ Ξενοφάνης ὁ Κολοφώνιος· καὶ
Κέρκωψ Ἡσιόδῳ ζῶντι, τελευτήσαντι δὲ ὁ προ-
ειρημένος Ξενοφάνης· καὶ Πινδάρῳ Ἀμφιμένης ὁ
Κῷος· Θάλητι δὲ Φερεκύδης καὶ Βίαντι Σάλαρος
Πριηνεύς· Πιττακῷ Ἀντιμενίδας καὶ Ἀλκαῖος,
Ἀναξαγόρᾳ Σωσίβιος, καὶ Σιμωνίδῃ Τιμοκρέων.

47 Τῶν δὲ διαδεξαμένων αὐτὸν τῶν λεγομένων
Σωκρατικῶν οἱ κορυφαιότατοι μὲν Πλάτων, Ξενοφῶν, Ἀντισθένης· τῶν δὲ φερομένων δέκα οἱ
διασημότατοι τέσσαρες, Αἰσχίνης, Φαίδων, Εὐκλείδης, Ἀρίστιππος. λεκτέον δὲ πρῶτον περὶ
Ξενοφῶντος, εἶτα περὶ Ἀντισθένους ἐν τοῖς
κυνικοῖς, ἔπειτα περὶ τῶν Σωκρατικῶν, εἶθ' οὕτω
περὶ Πλάτωνος, ἐπεὶ κατάρχει τῶν δέκα αἱρέσεων
καὶ τὴν πρώτην Ἀκαδημείαν αὐτὸς συνεστήσατο.
ἡ μὲν οὖν ἀκολουθία τοῦτον ἐχέτω τὸν τρόπον.

Γέγονε δὲ καὶ ἕτερος Σωκράτης, ἱστορικός,
περιήγησιν Ἄργους γεγραφώς· καὶ ἄλλος περιπατητικός, Βιθυνός· καὶ ἕτερος ἐπιγραμμάτων
ποιητής· καὶ ὁ Κῷος, ἐπικλήσεις θεῶν γεγραφώς.

Κεφ. ϛ'. ΞΕΝΟΦΩΝ

48 Ξενοφῶν Γρύλλου μὲν ἦν υἱός, Ἀθηναῖος, τῶν
δήμων Ἐρχιεύς· αἰδήμων δὲ καὶ εὐειδέστατος εἰς

---

[a] The text would perhaps be clearer if we transposed thus:
τῶν δὲ διαδεξαμένων αὐτὸν οἱ κορυφαιότατοι μὲν Πλάτων, Ξενοφῶν,
Ἀντισθένης. τῶν δὲ ⟨λεγομένων Σωκρατικῶν⟩ οἱ διασημότατοι
τέσσαρες, Αἰσχίνης, Φαίδων, Εὐκλείδης, Ἀρίστιππος κτλ. . . . .
εἶθ' οὕτω περὶ Πλάτωνος· ἐπεὶ κατάρχει τῶν ⟨φερομένων⟩ δέκα

in his third book *On Poetry*, by a certain Antilochus
of Lemnos, and by Antiphon the soothsayer, just as
Pythagoras was by Cylon of Croton, or as Homer
was assailed in his lifetime by Syagrus, and after his
death by Xenophanes of Colophon. So too Hesiod
was criticized in his lifetime by Cercops, and after
his death by the aforesaid Xenophanes ; Pindar by
Amphimenes of Cos ; Thales by Pherecydes ; Bias
by Salarus of Priene ; Pittacus by Antimenidas and
Alcaeus ; Anaxagoras by Sosibius ; and Simonides
by Timocreon.

Of those who succeeded him and were called
Socratics [a] the chief were Plato, Xenophon, Antisthenes, and of ten names on the traditional list the
most distinguished are Aeschines, Phaedo, Euclides,
Aristippus. I must first speak of Xenophon ;
Antisthenes will come afterwards among the Cynics ;
after Xenophon I shall take the Socratics proper, and
so pass on to Plato. With Plato the ten schools
begin : he was himself the founder of the First
Academy. This then is the order which I shall
follow.

Of those who bear the name of Socrates there is
one, a historian, who wrote a geographical work
upon Argos ; another, a Peripatetic philosopher of
Bithynia ; a third, a poet who wrote epigrams ;
lastly, Socrates of Cos, who wrote on the names of
the gods.

Chapter 6. XENOPHON (426 ?–354 B.C.)

Xenophon, the son of Gryllus, was a citizen of
Athens and belonged to the deme Erchia ; he was

αἱρέσεων. The division of moral philosophers into ten schools
was mentioned above, i. 18.

ὑπερβολήν. τούτῳ δὲ ἐν στενωπῷ φασιν ἀπαντήσαντα Σωκράτην διατεῖναι τὴν βακτηρίαν καὶ κωλύειν παριέναι, πυνθανόμενον ποῦ πιπράσκοιτο τῶν
προσφερομένων ἕκαστον· ἀποκριναμένου δὲ πάλιν
πυθέσθαι, ποῦ δὲ καλοὶ κἀγαθοὶ γίνονται ἄνθρωποι·
ἀπορήσαντος δέ, "ἕπου τοίνυν," φάναι, "καὶ
μάνθανε." καὶ τοὐντεῦθεν ἀκροατὴς Σωκράτους
ἦν. καὶ πρῶτος ὑποσημειωσάμενος τὰ λεγόμενα
εἰς ἀνθρώπους ἤγαγεν, Ἀπομνημονεύματα ἐπιγράψας. ἀλλὰ καὶ ἱστορίαν φιλοσόφων πρῶτος
ἔγραψε.

Καὶ αὐτόν φησιν Ἀρίστιππος ἐν τετάρτῳ Περὶ
43 παλαιᾶς τρυφῆς ἐρασθῆναι Κλεινίου· πρὸς ὃν καὶ
ταῦτα εἰπεῖν· "νῦν γὰρ ἐγὼ Κλεινίαν ἥδιον μὲν
θεῶμαι ἢ τἆλλα πάντα τὰ ἐν ἀνθρώποις καλά· τυφλὸς
δὲ τῶν ἄλλων πάντων δεξαίμην ἂν ἢ Κλεινίου ἑνὸς
ὄντος γενέσθαι· ἄχθομαι δὲ καὶ νυκτὶ καὶ ὕπνῳ,
ὅτι ἐκεῖνον οὐχ ὁρῶ· ἡμέρᾳ δὲ καὶ ἡλίῳ τὴν
μεγίστην χάριν οἶδα, ὅτι μοι Κλεινίαν ἀνα-
φαίνουσι."

Κύρῳ δὲ φίλος ἐγένετο τοῦτον τὸν τρόπον. ἦν
αὐτῷ συνήθης Πρόξενος ὄνομα, γένος Βοιώτιος,
μαθητὴς μὲν Γοργίου τοῦ Λεοντίνου, φίλος δὲ Κύρῳ.
οὗτος ἐν Σάρδεσι διατρίβων παρὰ τῷ Κύρῳ ἔπεμψεν
εἰς Ἀθήνας ἐπιστολὴν Ξενοφῶντι, καλῶν αὐτὸν ἵνα
γένηται Κύρῳ φίλος. ὁ δὲ τὴν ἐπιστολὴν δεικνύει
50 Σωκράτει καὶ σύμβουλον ᾑρεῖτο. καὶ ὃς ἀπέστειλεν
αὐτὸν εἰς Δελφοὺς χρησόμενον τῷ θεῷ. πείθεται
Ξενοφῶν· ἥκει παρὰ τὸν θεόν· πυνθάνεται οὐχὶ εἰ
χρὴ ἀπιέναι πρὸς Κῦρον, ἀλλ' ὅπως· ἐφ' ᾧ καὶ

a man of rare modesty and extremely handsome. The story goes that Socrates met him in a narrow passage, and that he stretched out his stick to bar the way, while he inquired where every kind of food was sold. Upon receiving a reply, he put another question, " And where do men become good and honourable ? " Xenophon was fairly puzzled ; " Then follow me," said Socrates, " and learn." From that time onward he was a pupil of Socrates. He was the first to take notes of, and to give to the world, the conversation of Socrates, under the title of *Memorabilia*. Moreover, he was the first to write a history of philosophers.

Aristippus, in the fourth book of his work *On the Luxury of the Ancients*, declares that he was enamoured of Clinias, and said in reference to him, " It is sweeter for me to gaze on Clinias than on all the fair sights in the world. I would be content to be blind to everything else if I could but gaze on him alone. I am vexed with the night and with sleep because I cannot see Clinias, and most grateful to the day and the sun for showing him to me."

He gained the friendship of Cyrus in the following way. He had an intimate friend named Proxenus, a Boeotian, a pupil of Gorgias of Leontini and a friend of Cyrus. Proxenus, while living in Sardis at the court of Cyrus, wrote a letter to Xenophon at Athens, inviting him to come and seek the friendship of Cyrus. Xenophon showed this letter to Socrates and asked his advice, which was that he should go to Delphi and consult the oracle. Xenophon complied and came into the presence of the god. He inquired, not *whether* he should go and seek service with Cyrus, but *in what way* he should do so. For

Σωκράτης αὐτὸν ᾐτιάσατο, συνεβούλευσε δὲ ἐξελθεῖν. καὶ ὃς γίνεται παρὰ Κύρῳ, καὶ τοῦ Προξένου φίλος οὐχ ἧττον ἦν αὐτῷ. τὰ μὲν οὖν ἄλλα τὰ κατὰ τὴν ἀνάβασιν γενόμενα καὶ τὴν κάθοδον ἱκανῶς αὐτὸς ἡμῖν διηγεῖται.[a] ἐχθρῶς δὲ διέκειτο πρὸς Μένωνα τὸν Φαρσάλιον παρὰ τὸν χρόνον τῆς ἀναβάσεως τὸν ξεναγόν· ὅτε καὶ λοιδορῶν αὐτὸν φησιν αὐτοῦ μείζοσι κεχρῆσθαι παιδικοῖς. ἀλλὰ καὶ Ἀπολλωνίδῃ τινὶ ὀνειδίζει τετρῆσθαι τὰ ὦτα.

51 Μετὰ δὲ τήν τ᾽ ἀνάβασιν καὶ τὰς ἐν τῷ Πόντῳ συμφορὰς καὶ τὰς παρασπονδήσεις τὰς Σεύθου τοῦ τῶν Ὀδρυσῶν βασιλέως ἧκεν εἰς Ἀσίαν πρὸς Ἀγησίλαον τὸν τῶν Λακεδαιμονίων βασιλέα, μισθοῦ τοὺς Κύρου στρατιώτας αὐτῷ παρασχών· φίλος τ᾽ ἦν εἰς ὑπερβολήν. παρ᾽ ὃν καιρὸν ἐπὶ Λακωνισμῷ φυγὴν ὑπ᾽ Ἀθηναίων κατεγνώσθη. γενόμενος δ᾽ ἐν Ἐφέσῳ καὶ χρυσίον ἔχων τὸ μὲν ἥμισυ Μεγαβύζῳ δίδωσι τῷ τῆς Ἀρτέμιδος ἱερεῖ φυλάττειν, ἕως ἂν ἐπανέλθοι· εἰ δὲ μή, ἄγαλμα ποιησάμενον ἀναθεῖναι τῇ θεῷ· τοῦ δὲ ἡμίσεος ἔπεμψεν εἰς Δελφοὺς ἀναθήματα. ἐντεῦθεν ἦλθεν εἰς τὴν Ἑλλάδα μετ᾽ Ἀγησιλάου, κεκλημένου εἰς τὸν πρὸς Θηβαίους πόλεμον· καὶ αὐτῷ προξενίαν ἔδοσαν οἱ Λακεδαιμόνιοι.

52 Ἐντεῦθεν ἐάσας τὸν Ἀγησίλαον ἧκεν εἰς Σκιλλοῦντα, χωρίον τῆς Ἠλείας ὀλίγον τῆς πόλεως ἀπέχον. εἵπετο δὲ αὐτῷ καὶ γύναιον ὄνομα Φιλησία, καθά φησι Δημήτριος ὁ Μάγνης, καὶ δύο υἱεῖς, Γρύλλος καὶ Διόδωρος, ὥς φησι Δείναρχος ἐν τῷ πρὸς

---

[a] *Anab.* iii. 1. 26-31.

this Socrates blamed him, yet at the same time he advised him to go. On his arrival at the court of Cyrus he became as warmly attached to him as Proxenus himself. We have his own sufficient narrative of all that happened on the expedition and on the return home. He was, however, at enmity with Meno of Pharsalus, the mercenary general, throughout the expedition, and, by way of abuse, charges him with having a favourite older than himself. Again, he reproaches one Apollonides with having had his ears bored.[a]

After the expedition and the misfortunes which overtook it in Pontus and the treacheries of Seuthes, the king of the Odrysians, he returned to Asia, having enlisted the troops of Cyrus as mercenaries in the service of Agesilaus, the Spartan king, to whom he was devoted beyond measure. About this time he was banished by the Athenians for siding with Sparta. When he was in Ephesus and had a sum of money, he entrusted one half of it to Megabyzus, the priest of Artemis, to keep until his return, or if he should never return, to apply to the erection of a statue in honour of the goddess. But the other half he sent in votive offerings to Delphi. Next he came to Greece with Agesilaus, who had been recalled to carry on the war against Thebes. And the Lacedaemonians conferred on him a privileged position.

He then left Agesilaus and made his way to Scillus, a place in the territory of Elis not far from the city. According to Demetrius of Magnesia he was accompanied by his wife Philesia, and, in a speech written for the freedman whom Xenophon prosecuted for neglect of duty, Dinarchus mentions that his two

181

Ξενοφῶντα ἀποστασίου, οἳ καὶ Διόσκουροι ἐπ-
εκαλοῦντο. ἀφικομένου δὲ τοῦ Μεγαβύζου κατὰ
πρόφασιν τῆς πανηγύρεως, κομισάμενος τὰ χρήματα χωρίον ἐπρίατο καὶ καθιέρωσε τῇ θεῷ, δι'
οὗ ποταμὸς ἔρρει Σελινοῦς, ὁμώνυμος τῷ ἐν Ἐφέσῳ.
τοὐντεῦθεν διετέλει κυνηγετῶν καὶ τοὺς φίλους
ἑστιῶν καὶ τὰς ἱστορίας συγγράφων. φησὶ δ' ὁ
Δείναρχος ὅτι καὶ οἰκίαν καὶ ἀγρὸν αὐτῷ ἔδοσαν
Λακεδαιμόνιοι.

53 Ἀλλὰ καὶ Φυλοπίδαν τὸν Σπαρτιάτην φασὶν αὐτῷ
πέμψαι αὐτόθι δωρεὰν ἀνδράποδα αἰχμάλωτα ἐκ
Δαρδάνου· καὶ τὸν διαθέσθαι αὐτὰ ὡς ἠβούλετο·
Ἠλείους τε στρατευσαμένους εἰς τὸν Σκιλλοῦντα
[καὶ] βραδυνόντων τῶν Λακεδαιμονίων ἐξελεῖν τὸ
χωρίον. ὅτε καὶ τοὺς υἱέας αὐτοῦ εἰς Λέπρεον
ὑπεξελθεῖν μετ' ὀλίγων οἰκετῶν, καὶ αὐτὸν Ξενοφῶντα εἰς τὴν Ἦλιν πρότερον, εἶτα [καὶ] εἰς
Λέπρεον πρὸς τοὺς παῖδας, κἀκεῖθεν σὺν αὐτοῖς εἰς
Κόρινθον διασωθῆναι καὶ αὐτόθι κατοικῆσαι. ἐν
τούτῳ δὲ ψηφισαμένων τῶν Ἀθηναίων βοηθεῖν
Λακεδαιμονίοις ἔπεμψε τοὺς παῖδας εἰς τὰς Ἀθήνας
54 στρατευσομένους ὑπὲρ τῶν Λακεδαιμονίων. καὶ
γὰρ ἐπεπαίδευντο αὐτόθι ἐν τῇ Σπάρτῃ, καθά φησι
Διοκλῆς ἐν τοῖς Βίοις τῶν φιλοσόφων. ὁ μὲν οὖν
Διόδωρος οὐδὲν ἐπιφανὲς πράξας ἐκ τῆς μάχης
ἀνασώζεται, καὶ αὐτῷ υἱὸς ὁμώνυμος γίνεται
τἀδελφῷ. ὁ δὲ Γρύλλος τεταγμένος κατὰ τοὺς ἱπ-
πέας—ἦν δὲ ἡ μάχη ἡ περὶ τὴν Μαντίνειαν—ἰσχυρῶς ἀγωνισάμενος ἐτελεύτησεν, ὥς φησιν Ἔφορος
ἐν τῇ πέμπτῃ καὶ εἰκοστῇ· Κηφισοδώρου μὲν ἱππ-

sons Gryllus and Diodorus, the Dioscuri as they were called, also went with him. Megabyzus having arrived to attend the festival, Xenophon received from him the deposit of money and bought and dedicated to the goddess an estate with a river running through, which bears the same name Selinus as the river at Ephesus. And from that time onward he hunted, entertained his friends, and worked at his histories without interruption. Dinarchus, however, asserts that it was the Lacedaemonians who gave him a house and land.

At the same time we are told that Phylopidas the Spartan sent to him at Scillus a present of captive slaves from Dardanus, and that he disposed of them as he thought fit, and that the Elians marched against Scillus, and owing to the slowness of the Spartans captured the place, whereupon his sons retired to Lepreum with a few of the servants, while Xenophon himself, who had previously gone to Elis, went next to Lepreum to join his sons, and then made his escape with them from Lepreum to Corinth and took up his abode there. Meanwhile the Athenians passed a decree to assist Sparta, and Xenophon sent his sons to Athens to serve in the army in defence of Sparta. According to Diocles in his *Lives of the Philosophers*, they had been trained in Sparta itself. Diodorus came safe out of the battle without performing any distinguished service, and he had a son of the same name (Gryllus) as his brother. Gryllus was posted with the cavalry and, in the battle which took place about Mantinea, fought stoutly and fell, as Ephorus relates in his twenty-fifth book, Cephisodorus being in command of the cavalry

αρχοῦντος, Ἡγησίλεω δὲ στρατηγοῦντος. ἐν ταύτῃ
τῇ μάχῃ καὶ Ἐπαμεινώνδας ἔπεσε. τηνικαῦτα δὴ
καὶ τὸν Ξενοφῶντά φασι θύειν ἐστεμμένον· ἀπ-
αγγελθέντος δ' αὐτῷ τοῦ θανάτου ἀποστεφανώσασθαι·
ἔπειτα μαθόντα ὅτι γενναίως, πάλιν ἐπιθέσθαι τὸν
55 στέφανον. ἔνιοι δὲ οὐδὲ δακρῦσαί φασιν αὐτὸν
ἀλλὰ * γὰρ εἰπεῖν, " ᾔδειν θνητὸν γεγεννηκώς."
φησὶ δ' Ἀριστοτέλης ὅτι ἐγκώμια καὶ ἐπιτάφιον
Γρύλλου μυρίοι ὅσοι συνέγραψαν, τὸ μέρος καὶ τῷ
πατρὶ χαριζόμενοι. ἀλλὰ καὶ Ἕρμιππος ἐν τῷ
περὶ Θεοφράστου καὶ Ἰσοκράτην φησὶ Γρύλλου
ἐγκώμιον γεγραφέναι. Τίμων δ' ἐπισκώπτει αὐτὸν
ἐν τούτοις·

ἀσθενική τε λόγων δυὰς ἢ τριὰς ἢ ἔτι πρόσσω,
οἷος Ξεινοφόων ἦτ' Αἰσχίνου οὐκ ἀπιθὴς <ἲς>
γράψαι. . . .

Καὶ ὁ μὲν βίος αὐτῷ τοιόσδε. ἤκμαζε δὲ κατὰ
τὸ τέταρτον ἔτος τῆς τετάρτης καὶ ἐνενηκοστῆς
Ὀλυμπιάδος, καὶ ἀναβέβηκε σὺν Κύρῳ ἐπὶ ἄρχοντος Ξεναινέτου ἑνὶ πρότερον ἔτει τῆς Σωκράτους
τελευτῆς.

56 Κατέστρεψε δέ, καθά φησι Κτησικλείδης[1] ὁ
Ἀθηναῖος ἐν τῇ τῶν ἀρχόντων καὶ Ὀλυμπιονικῶν
ἀναγραφῇ, ἔτει πρώτῳ τῆς πέμπτης καὶ ἑκατοστῆς
Ὀλυμπιάδος, ἐπὶ ἄρχοντος Καλλιδημίδου, ἐφ' οὗ
καὶ Φίλιππος ὁ Ἀμύντου Μακεδόνων ἦρξε. τέ-
θνηκε δ' ἐν Κορίνθῳ, ὥς φησι Δημήτριος ὁ Μάγνης,
ἤδη δηλαδὴ γηραιὸς ἱκανῶς· ἀνὴρ τά τ' ἄλλα
γεγονὼς ἀγαθὸς καὶ δὴ καὶ φίλιππος καὶ φιλο-
κύνηγος καὶ τακτικός, ὡς ἐκ τῶν συγγραμμάτων

---

[1] Στησικλείδης vulg.: corr. Wilamowitz.

and Hegesilaus commander-in-chief. In this battle Epaminondas also fell. On this occasion Xenophon is said to have been sacrificing, with a chaplet on his head, which he removed when his son's death was announced. But afterwards, upon learning that he had fallen gloriously, he replaced the chaplet on his head. Some say that he did not even shed tears, but exclaimed, "I knew my son was mortal." Aristotle mentions that there were innumerable authors of epitaphs and eulogies upon Gryllus, who wrote, in part at least, to gratify his father. Hermippus too, in his *Life of Theophrastus*, affirms that even Isocrates wrote an encomium on Gryllus. Timon, however, jeers at Xenophon in the lines [a] :

A feeble pair or triad of works, or even a greater number, such as would come from Xenophon or the might of Aeschines, that not unpersuasive writer.

Such was his life. He flourished in the fourth year of the 94th Olympiad,[b] and he took part in the expedition of Cyrus in the archonship of Xenaenetus in the year before the death of Socrates.

He died, according to Ctesiclides [c] of Athens in his list of archons and Olympic victors, in the first year of the 105th Olympiad, in the archonship of Callidemides,[d] the year in which Philip, the son of Amyntas, came to the throne of Macedon. He died at Corinth, as is stated by Demetrius of Magnesia, obviously at an advanced age. He was a worthy man in general, particularly fond of horses and hunting, an able tactician as is clear from his writings,

---

[a] Fr. 26 D.   [b] 401–400 B.C.
[c] Ctesiclides is known to us from Athenaeus, who cites his *Chronology*, vi. 272 c, x. 445 D. It may seem rash to intrude him here; but *cf.* iv. 5, where a similar error is certain.
[d] 360–359 B.C.

δῆλον· εὐσεβής τε καὶ φιλοθύτης καὶ ἱερεῖα δια-
γνῶναι ἱκανὸς καὶ Σωκράτην ζηλώσας ἀκριβῶς.

Συνέγραψε δὲ βιβλία πρὸς τὰ τετταράκοντα,
ἄλλων ἄλλως διαιρούντων·

57   Τήν τ' Ἀνάβασιν, ἧς κατὰ βιβλίον μὲν ἐποίησε
         προοίμιον, ὅλης δὲ οὔ· καὶ
      Κύρου Παιδείαν καὶ
      Ἑλληνικὰ καὶ
      Ἀπομνημονεύματα·
      Συμπόσιόν τε καὶ
      Οἰκονομικὸν καὶ
      Περὶ ἱππικῆς καὶ
      Κυνηγετικὸν καὶ
      Ἱππαρχικόν,
      Ἀπολογίαν τε Σωκράτους καὶ
      Περὶ πόρων καὶ
      Ἱέρωνα ἢ Τυραννικόν,
      Ἀγησίλαόν τε καὶ
      Ἀθηναίων καὶ Λακεδαιμονίων Πολιτείαν,

ἥν φησιν οὐκ εἶναι Ξενοφῶντος ὁ Μάγνης Δημήτριος. λέγεται δ' ὅτι καὶ τὰ Θουκυδίδου βιβλία
λανθάνοντα ὑφελέσθαι δυνάμενος αὐτὸς εἰς δόξαν
ἤγαγεν. ἐκαλεῖτο δὲ καὶ Ἀττικὴ Μοῦσα γλυκύ-
τητι τῆς ἑρμηνείας· ὅθεν καὶ πρὸς ἀλλήλους ζηλο-
τύπως εἶχον αὐτός τε καὶ Πλάτων, ὡς ἐν τῷ περὶ
Πλάτωνος λέξομεν.

58   Ἔστι δὲ καὶ εἰς τοῦτον ἡμῶν ἐπιγράμματα
τοῦτον ἔχοντα τὸν τρόπον·

         οὐ μόνον εἰς Πέρσας ἀνέβη Ξενοφῶν διὰ Κῦρον,
         ἀλλ' ἄνοδον ζητῶν ἐς Διὸς ἥτις ἄγοι.

pious, fond of sacrificing, and an expert in augury from the victims; and he made Socrates his exact model.

He wrote some forty books in all, though the division into books is not always the same, namely:

> The Anabasis, with a preface to each separate book but not one to the whole work.
> Cyropaedia.
> Hellenica.
> Memorabilia.
> Symposium.
> Oeconomicus.
> On Horsemanship.
> On Hunting.
> On the Duty of a Cavalry General.
> A Defence of Socrates.
> On Revenues.
> Hieron or Of Tyranny.
> Agesilaus.
> The Constitutions of Athens and Sparta.

Demetrius of Magnesia denies that the last of these works is by Xenophon. There is a tradition that he made Thucydides famous by publishing his history, which was unknown, and which he might have appropriated to his own use. By the sweetness of his narrative he earned the name of the Attic Muse. Hence he and Plato were jealous of each other, as will be stated in the chapter on Plato.

There is an epigram of mine on him also [a]:

> Up the steep path to fame toiled Xenophon
> In that long march of glorious memories;

----

[a] *Anth. Pal.* vii. 97.

παιδείης γὰρ ἑῆς Ἑλληνικὰ πράγματα δείξας,
ὡς καλὸν ἡ σοφίη μνήσατο Σωκράτεος.

ἄλλο, ὡς ἐτελεύτα·

εἰ καὶ σέ, Ξενοφῶν, Κραναοῦ Κέκροπός τε
πολῖται
φεύγειν κατέγνων, τοῦ φίλου χάριν Κύρου·
ἀλλὰ Κόρινθος ἔδεκτο φιλόξενος, ᾗ σὺ φιληδῶν
οὕτως ἀρέσκῃ· κεῖθι καὶ μένειν ἔγνως.

59 Εὗρον δ' ἀλλαχόθι ἀκμάσαι αὐτὸν περὶ τὴν ἐνάτην καὶ ὀγδοηκοστὴν Ὀλυμπιάδα σὺν τοῖς ἄλλοις
Σωκρατικοῖς, καὶ Ἴστρος φησὶν αὐτὸν φυγεῖν κατὰ
ψήφισμα Εὐβούλου, καὶ κατελθεῖν κατὰ ψήφισμα
τοῦ αὐτοῦ.

Γεγόνασι δὲ Ξενοφῶντες ἑπτά· πρῶτος αὐτὸς
οὗτος· δεύτερος Ἀθηναῖος, ἀδελφὸς Πυθοστράτου
τοῦ τὴν Θησηΐδα πεποιηκότος, γεγραφὼς ἄλλα τε
καὶ βίον Ἐπαμεινώνδου καὶ Πελοπίδου· τρίτος
ἰατρὸς Κῷος· τέταρτος ἱστορίαν Ἀννιβαϊκὴν γε-
γραφώς· πέμπτος μυθώδη τερατείαν πεπραγμα-
τευμένος· ἕκτος Πάριος, ἀγαλματοποιός· ἕβδομος
κωμῳδίας ἀρχαίας ποιητής.

Κεφ. ζ'. ΑΙΣΧΙΝΗΣ

60 Αἰσχίνης Χαρίνου τοῦ ἀλλαντοποιοῦ, οἱ δὲ Λυ-
σανίου, Ἀθηναῖος, ἐκ νέου φιλόπονος· διὸ καὶ
Σωκράτους οὐκ ἀπέστη. ὅθεν ἔλεγε, " μόνος ἡμᾶς
οἶδε τιμᾶν ὁ τοῦ ἀλλαντοποιοῦ." τοῦτον ἔφη

ᵃ Or in plain prose: " Not only for Cyrus's sake did
Xenophon go up to Persia, but because he sought the path
which leads to the abode of Zeus. For, having shown that

In deeds of Greece, how bright his lesson shone !
How fair was wisdom seen in Socrates ! [a]

There is another on the circumstances of his death [b] :

Albeit the countrymen of Cranaus and Cecrops condemned thee, Xenophon, to exile on account of thy friendship for Cyrus, yet hospitable Corinth welcomed thee, so well content with the delights of that city wast thou, and there didst resolve to take up thy rest.

In other authorities I find the statement that he flourished, along with the other Socratics, in the 89th Olympiad,[c] and Istrus affirms that he was banished by a decree of Eubulus and recalled by a decree of the same man.

There have been seven Xenophons : the first our subject himself ; the second an Athenian, brother of Pythostratus, who wrote the *Theseid*, and himself the author, amongst other works, of a biography of Epaminondas and Pelopidas ; the third a physician of Cos ; the fourth the author of a history of Hannibal ; the fifth an authority on legendary marvels ; the sixth a sculptor, of Paros ; the seventh a poet of the Old Comedy.

CHAPTER 7. AESCHINES (*c.* 400 B.C.)

Aeschines was the son of Charinus the sausage-maker, but others make his father's name Lysanias. He was a citizen of Athens, industrious from his birth up. For this reason he never quitted Socrates ; hence Socrates' remark, " Only the sausage-maker's son knows how to honour me." Idomeneus declared

the great deeds of Greece are the outcome of his training, he recalled what a beautiful thing was the wisdom of Socrates."
[b] *Anth. Pal.* vii. 98.
[c] This would be 424–420 B.C., a date obviously absurd as the *floruit* for either Xenophon or Plato.

Ἰδομενεὺς ἐν τῷ δεσμωτηρίῳ συμβουλεῦσαι **περὶ** τῆς φυγῆς Σωκράτει, καὶ οὐ Κρίτωνα· Πλάτωνα δέ, ὅτι ἦν Ἀριστίππῳ μᾶλλον φίλος, Κρίτωνι περιθεῖναι τοὺς λόγους. διεβάλλετο δ' ὁ Αἰσχίνης καὶ μάλισθ' ὑπὸ Μενεδήμου τοῦ Ἐρετριέως ὡς τοὺς πλείστους διαλόγους ὄντας Σωκράτους ὑποβάλλοιτο, λαμβάνων παρὰ Ξανθίππης· ὧν οἱ μὲν καλούμενοι ἀκέφαλοι σφόδρ' εἰσὶν ἐκλελυμένοι καὶ οὐκ ἐπιφαίνοντες τὴν Σωκρατικὴν εὐτονίαν· οὓς καὶ Πεισίστρατος ὁ Ἐφέσιος ἔλεγε μὴ εἶναι Αἰσχίνου.

61 καὶ τῶν ἑπτὰ δὲ τοὺς πλείστους Περσαῖός φησι Πασιφῶντος εἶναι τοῦ Ἐρετρικοῦ, εἰς τοὺς Αἰσχίνου δὲ κατατάξαι. ἀλλὰ καὶ τῶν Ἀντισθένους τόν τε μικρὸν Κῦρον καὶ τὸν Ἡρακλέα τὸν ἐλάσσω καὶ Ἀλκιβιάδην καὶ τοὺς τῶν ἄλλων δὲ ἐσκευώρηται. οἱ δ' οὖν τῶν Αἰσχίνου τὸ Σωκρατικὸν ἦθος ἀπομεμαγμένοι εἰσὶν ἑπτά· πρῶτος Μιλτιάδης, διὸ καὶ ἀσθενέστερόν πως ἔχει· Καλλίας, Ἀξίοχος, Ἀσπασία, Ἀλκιβιάδης, Τηλαύγης, Ῥίνων.

Φασὶ δ' αὐτὸν δι' ἀπορίαν ἐλθεῖν εἰς Σικελίαι πρὸς Διονύσιον, καὶ ὑπὸ μὲν Πλάτωνος παροφθῆναι, ὑπὸ δ' Ἀριστίππου συστῆναι· δόντα τέ τινας τῶν 62 διαλόγων δῶρα λαβεῖν. ἔπειτ' ἀφικόμενον Ἀθήναζε μὴ τολμᾶν σοφιστεύειν, εὐδοκιμούντων τότε τῶν περὶ Πλάτωνα καὶ Ἀρίστιππον. ἐμμίσθους δ' ἀκροάσεις ποιεῖσθαι· εἶτα συγγράφειν λόγους δικανικοὺς τοῖς ἀδικουμένοις· διὸ καὶ τὸν Τίμωνα εἰπεῖν ἐπ' αὐτοῦ " ἤτ' Αἰσχίνου οὐκ ἀπιθὴς ‹ἴς› γράψαι." φασὶ δ' αὐτῷ λέγειν Σωκράτην, ἐπειδή-

---

[a] Idomeneus, it may be conjectured, relied on some Socratic dialogue in which the part assigned by Plato to Crito was given to Aeschines.

that it was Aeschines, not Crito, who advised Socrates in the prison about making his escape,[a] but that Plato put the words into the mouth of Crito because Aeschines was more attached to Aristippus than to himself. It was said maliciously—by Menedemus of Eretria in particular—that most of the dialogues which Aeschines passed off as his own were really dialogues of Socrates obtained by him from Xanthippe. Those of them which are said to have no beginning (ἀκέφαλοι) are very slovenly and show none of the vigour of Socrates ; Pisistratus of Ephesus even denied that they were written by Aeschines. Persaeus indeed attributes the majority of the seven to Pasiphon of the school of Eretria, who inserted them among the dialogues of Aeschines. Moreover, Aeschines made use of the *Little Cyrus*, the *Lesser Heracles* and the *Alcibiades* of Antisthenes as well as dialogues by other authors. However that may be, of the writings of Aeschines those stamped with a Socratic character are seven, namely *Miltiades*, which for that reason is somewhat weak ; then *Callias*, *Axiochus*, *Aspasia*, *Alcibiades*, *Telauges*, and *Rhinon*.

They say that want drove him to Sicily to the court of Dionysius, and that Plato took no notice of him, but he was introduced to Dionysius by Aristippus, and on presenting certain dialogues received gifts from him. Afterwards on his return to Athens he did not venture to lecture owing to the popularity of Plato and Aristippus. But he took fees from pupils, and subsequently composed forensic speeches for aggrieved clients. This is the point of Timon's reference to him as " the might of Aeschines, that not unconvincing writer." They say that Socrates,

περ ἐπιέζετο ὑπὸ πενίας, παρ' ἑαυτοῦ δανείζεσθαι
τῶν σιτίων ὑφαιροῦντα. τούτου τοὺς διαλόγους
καὶ 'Αρίστιππος ὑπώπτευεν. ἐν γοῦν Μεγάροις
ἀναγινώσκοντος αὐτοῦ φασι σκῶψαι εἰπόντα,
" πόθεν σοι, λῃστά, ταῦτα; "

63 Φησὶ δὲ Πολύκριτος ὁ Μενδαῖος ἐν τῷ πρώτῳ
τῶν περὶ Διονύσιον ἄχρι τῆς ἐκπτώσεως συμβιῶναι
αὐτὸν τῷ τυράννῳ καὶ ἕως τῆς Δίωνος εἰς Συρα-
κούσας καθόδου, λέγων εἶναι σὺν αὐτῷ καὶ Καρκίνον
τὸν τραγῳδιοποιόν. φέρεται δὲ καὶ ἐπιστολὴ πρὸς
Διονύσιον Αἰσχίνου. ἦν δὲ καὶ ἐν τοῖς ῥητορικοῖς
ἱκανῶς γεγυμνασμένος· ὡς δῆλον ἔκ τε τῆς ἀπο-
λογίας τοῦ πατρὸς Φαίακος τοῦ στρατηγοῦ καὶ
Δίωνος. μάλιστα δὲ μιμεῖται Γοργίαν τὸν Λεον-
τῖνον. καὶ Λυσίας δὲ κατ' αὐτοῦ γέγραφε λόγον,
[περὶ] συκοφαντίας ἐπιγράψας· ἐξ ὧν δῆλον ὅτι καὶ
ῥητορικός τις ἦν. γνώριμος δ' αὐτοῦ φέρεται εἷς,
'Αριστοτέλης ὁ Μῦθος ἐπικληθείς.

64 Πάντων μέντοι τῶν Σωκρατικῶν διαλόγων
Παναίτιος ἀληθεῖς εἶναι δοκεῖ τοὺς Πλάτωνος,
Ξενοφῶντος, 'Αντισθένους, Αἰσχίνου· διστάζει δὲ
περὶ τῶν Φαίδωνος καὶ Εὐκλείδου, τοὺς δὲ ἄλλους
ἀναιρεῖ πάντας.

Γεγόνασι δ' Αἰσχίναι ὀκτώ· πρῶτος αὐτὸς οὗτος·
δεύτερος δ' ὁ τὰς τέχνας γεγραφὼς τὰς ῥητορικάς·
τρίτος ὁ ῥήτωρ ὁ κατὰ Δημοσθένην· τέταρτος
'Αρκάς, μαθητὴς 'Ισοκράτους· πέμπτος ὁ Μυτιληναῖος, ὃν καὶ ῥητορομάστιγα ἐκάλουν· ἕκτος Νεα-
πολίτης, φιλόσοφος 'Ακαδημαϊκός, Μελανθίου τοῦ
'Ροδίου μαθητὴς καὶ παιδικά· ἕβδομος Μιλήσιος,
πολιτικὸς συγγραφεύς· ὄγδοος ἀνδριαντοποιός.

seeing how he was pinched by poverty, advised him to borrow from himself by reducing his rations. Aristippus among others had suspicions of the genuineness of his dialogues. At all events, as he was reading one at Megara, Aristippus rallied him by asking, " Where did you get that, you thief ? "

Polycritus of Mende, in the first book of his *History of Dionysius*, says that he lived with the tyrant until his expulsion from Syracuse, and survived until the return of Dion, and that with him was Carcinus the tragic poet. There is also extant an epistle of Aeschines to Dionysius. That he had received a good rhetorical training is clear from his defence of the father of Phaeax the general, and from his defence of Dion. He is a close imitator of Gorgias of Leontini. Moreover, Lysias attacked him in a speech which he entitled " On dishonesty." And from this too it is clear that he was a rhetorician. A single disciple of his is mentioned, Aristotle, whose nickname was " Story."

Panaetius thinks that, of all the Socratic dialogues, those by Plato, Xenophon, Antisthenes and Aeschines are genuine ; he is in doubt about those ascribed to Phaedo and Euclides ; but he rejects the others one and all.

There are eight men who have borne the name of Aeschines: (1) our subject himself; (2) the author of handbooks of rhetoric; (3) the orator who opposed Demosthenes ; (4) an Arcadian, a pupil of Isocrates ; (5) a Mitylenean whom they used to call the " scourge of rhetoricians " ; (6) a Neapolitan, an Academic philosopher, a pupil and favourite of Melanthius of Rhodes; (7) a Milesian who wrote upon politics ; (8) a sculptor.

Κεφ. η΄. ΑΡΙΣΤΙΠΠΟΣ

65 Ἀρίστιππος τὸ μὲν γένος ἦν Κυρηναῖος, ἀφ-
ιγμένος δ᾽ Ἀθήναζε, καθά φησιν Αἰσχίνης, κατὰ
κλέος Σωκράτους. οὗτος σοφιστεύσας, ὥς φησι
Φανίας ὁ περιπατητικὸς ὁ Ἐρέσιος, πρῶτος τῶν
Σωκρατικῶν μισθοὺς εἰσεπράξατο καὶ ἀπέστειλε
χρήματα τῷ διδασκάλῳ. καί ποτε πέμψας αὐτῷ
μνᾶς εἴκοσι παλινδρόμους ἀπέλαβεν, εἰπόντος
Σωκράτους τὸ δαιμόνιον αὐτῷ μὴ ἐπιτρέπειν·
ἐδυσχέραινε γὰρ ἐπὶ τούτῳ. Ξενοφῶν τ᾽ εἶχε πρὸς
αὐτὸν δυσμενῶς· διὸ καὶ τὸν κατὰ τῆς ἡδονῆς λόγον
Σωκράτει κατ᾽ Ἀριστίππου περιτέθεικεν. οὐ μὴν
ἀλλὰ καὶ Θεόδωρος ἐν τῷ Περὶ αἱρέσεων ἐκάκισεν
αὐτὸν καὶ Πλάτων ἐν τῷ Περὶ ψυχῆς, ὡς ἐν ἄλλοις
εἰρήκαμεν.

66 Ἦν δὲ ἱκανὸς ἁρμόσασθαι καὶ τόπῳ καὶ χρόνῳ
καὶ προσώπῳ, καὶ πᾶσαν περίστασιν ἁρμοδίως
ὑποκρίνασθαι· διὸ καὶ παρὰ Διονυσίῳ τῶν ἄλλων
εὐδοκίμει μᾶλλον, ἀεὶ τὸ προσπεσὸν εὖ διατιθέ-
μενος. ἀπέλαυε μὲν γὰρ ἡδονῆς τῶν παρόντων,
οὐκ ἐθήρα δὲ πόνῳ τὴν ἀπόλαυσιν τῶν οὐ παρόντων·
ὅθεν καὶ Διογένης βασιλικὸν κύνα ἔλεγεν αὐτόν.
ὁ δὲ Τίμων παρέφαγεν ὡς θρυπτόμενον, οὑτωσί
πως εἰπών·

---

[a] *Mem.* ii. 1.

[b] In the Introduction to the *Phaedo*, 59 c, Aristippus is
said to have been in Aegina on the day when Socrates
drank the hemlock. How little this justifies the use of the
terms ἐκάκισεν and διαβάλλων may be seen from the previous statement in the *Phaedo* that Plato himself is said to
have been absent through illness on that occasion. Notice

Chapter 8. ARISTIPPUS (c. 435–350 b.c.)

Aristippus was by birth a citizen of Cyrene and, as Aeschines informs us, was drawn to Athens by the fame of Socrates. Having come forward as a lecturer or sophist, as Phanias of Eresus, the Peripatetic, informs us, he was the first of the followers of Socrates to charge fees and to send money to his master. And on one occasion the sum of twenty minae which he had sent was returned to him, Socrates declaring that the supernatural sign would not let him take it ; the very offer, in fact, annoyed him. Xenophon was no friend to Aristippus ; and for this reason he has made Socrates direct against Aristippus the discourse in which he denounces pleasure.[a] Not but what Theodorus in his work *On Sects* abuses him, and so does Plato in the dialogue *On the Soul*,[b] as has been shown elsewhere.

He was capable of adapting himself to place, time and person, and of playing his part appropriately under whatever circumstances. Hence he found more favour than anybody else with Dionysius, because he could always turn the situation to good account. He derived pleasure from what was present, and did not toil to procure the enjoyment of something not present Hence Diogenes called him the king's poodle [c] Timon, too, sneered at him for luxury in these words [d] :

that Diogenes Laertius refers to the Life of Plato as already written ; see iii. 36.

[c] Or " royal cynic." It is impossible to preserve the *double entendre* here, for κύων, dog, also means "cynic"; in fact the very name of that sect proclaims that they gloried in their dog-like attributes, especially in snarling and biting.

[d] Fr. 27 D.

οἷά τ' Ἀριστίππου τρυφερὴ φύσις ἀμφαφόωντος
ψεύδη.

τοῦτόν **φασί ποτε** κελεῦσαι πέρδικα πεντήκοντα
δραχμῶν ὠνηθῆναι· αἰτιασαμένου δέ τινος, " σὺ δ'
οὐκ ἄν," εἶπεν, " ὀβολοῦ τοῦτον ἐπρίω;" ἐπινεύσαντος δέ, " τοσοῦτον," ἔφη, " ἐμοὶ δύνανται αἱ
67 πεντήκοντα δραχμαί." Διονυσίου δέ ποτε τριῶν
ἑταιρῶν οὐσῶν μίαν ἐκλέξασθαι κελεύσαντος, τὰς
τρεῖς ἀπήγαγεν εἰπών, " οὐδὲ τῷ Πάριδι συνήνεγκε
μίαν προκρῖναι·" ἀπαγαγὼν μέντοι, φασίν, αὐτὰς
ἄχρι τοῦ θυρῶνος ἀπέλυσεν. οὕτως ἦν καὶ ἑλέσθαι
καὶ καταφρονῆσαι πολύς. διό ποτε Στράτωνα, οἱ
δὲ Πλάτωνα, πρὸς αὐτὸν εἰπεῖν, " σοὶ μόνῳ δέδοται
καὶ χλανίδα φορεῖν καὶ ῥάκος." Διονυσίου δὲ προσ-
πτύσαντος αὐτῷ ἠνέσχετο. μεμψαμένου δέ τινος,
" εἶτα οἱ μὲν ἁλιεῖς," εἶπεν, " ὑπομένουσι ῥαί-
νεσθαι τῇ θαλάττῃ, ἵνα κωβιὸν θηράσωσιν· ἐγὼ
δὲ μὴ ἀνάσχωμαι κράματι ῥανθῆναι, ἵνα βλέννοι
λάβω;"

68 Παριόντα ποτὲ αὐτὸν λάχανα πλύνων Διογένης
ἔσκωψε, καί φησιν,[1] " εἰ ταῦτα ἔμαθες προσφέρεσθαι, οὐκ ἂν τυράννων αὐλὰς ἐθεράπευες." ὁ δέ,
" καὶ σύ," εἶπεν, " εἴπερ ᾔδεις ἀνθρώποις ὁμιλεῖν,
οὐκ ἂν λάχανα ἔπλυνες." ἐρωτηθεὶς τί αὐτῷ περιγέγονεν ἐκ φιλοσοφίας, ἔφη, " τὸ δύνασθαι πᾶσι
θαρρούντως ὁμιλεῖν." ὀνειδιζόμενός ποτ' ἐπὶ τῷ
πολυτελῶς ζῆν, " εἰ τοῦτ'," ἔφη, " φαῦλον ἦν, οὐκ
ἂν ἐν ταῖς τῶν θεῶν ἑορταῖς ἐγίνετο." ἐρωτηθεὶς

---

[1] φησιν] "σύ" φησιν Richards : ἔφη " σύ Postgate.

---

[a] This alludes to his doctrine of sensation, sometimes
called " internal touch." Compare *infra* § 92, and more fully

Such was the delicate nature of Aristippus, who groped after error by touch.[a]

He is said to have ordered a partridge to be bought at a cost of fifty drachmae, and, when someone censured him, he inquired, " Would not you have given an obol for it ? " and, being answered in the affirmative, rejoined, " Fifty drachmae are no more to me." And when Dionysius gave him his choice of three courtesans, he carried off all three, saying, " Paris paid dearly for giving the preference to one out of three." And when he had brought them as far as the porch, he let them go. To such lengths did he go both in choosing and in disdaining. Hence the remark of Strato, or by some accounts of Plato, " You alone are endowed with the gift to flaunt in robes or go in rags." He bore with Dionysius when he spat on him, and to one who took him to task he replied, " If the fishermen let themselves be drenched with sea-water in order to catch a gudgeon, ought I not to endure to be wetted with negus in order to take a blenny ? "

Diogenes, washing the dirt from his vegetables, saw him passing and jeered at him in these terms, " If you had learnt to make these your diet, you would not have paid court to kings," to which his rejoinder was, " And if you knew how to associate with men, you would not be washing vegetables." Being asked what he had gained from philosophy, he replied, " The ability to feel at ease in any society." Being reproached for his extravagance, he said, " If it were wrong to be extravagant, it would not be in vogue at the festivals of the gods."

Sext. Emp. *Adv. mathem.* vii. 191. It has been paraphrased thus : " quae potuit tactu a falso discernere verum."

ποτε τί πλέον ἔχουσιν οἱ φιλόσοφοι, ἔφη, " ἐὰν
πάντες οἱ νόμοι ἀναιρεθῶσιν, ὁμοίως βιωσόμεθα."
69 ἐρωτηθεὶς ὑπὸ Διονυσίου διὰ τί οἱ μὲν φιλόσοφοι
ἐπὶ τὰς τῶν πλουσίων θύρας ἔρχονται, οἱ δὲ
πλούσιοι ἐπὶ τὰς τῶν φιλοσόφων οὐκέτι, ἔφη, " ὅτι
οἱ μὲν ἴσασιν ὧν δέονται, οἱ δ' οὐκ ἴσασιν." ὀνειδιζόμενός ποτ' ἐπὶ τῷ πολυτελῶς ζῆν ὑπὸ Πλάτωνος,
ἔφη, " ἆρα φαίνεταί σοι Διονύσιος ἀγαθός;" τοῦ
δ' ὁμολογήσαντος, " καὶ μήν," ἔφη, " ζῇ ἐμοῦ πολυ-
τελέστερον· ὥστ' οὐδὲν κωλύει καὶ πολυτελῶς καὶ
καλῶς ζῆν." ἐρωτηθεὶς τίνι διαφέρουσιν οἱ πεπαιδευμένοι τῶν ἀπαιδεύτων, ἔφη, " ὧπερ οἱ δεδα-
μασμένοι ἵπποι τῶν ἀδαμάστων." εἰσιών ποτε εἰς
ἑταίρας οἰκίαν, καὶ τῶν σὺν αὐτῷ μειρακίων τινὸς
ἐρυθριάσαντος, " οὐ τὸ εἰσελθεῖν," ἔφη, " χαλεπόν,
ἀλλὰ τὸ μὴ δύνασθαι ἐξελθεῖν."
70 Αἴνιγμά τινος αὐτῷ προτείναντος καὶ εἰπόντος,
" λῦσον," " τί, ὦ μάταιε," ἔφη, " λῦσαι θέλεις, ὃ
καὶ δεδεμένον ἡμῖν πράγματα παρέχει;" ἄμεινον
ἔφη ἐπαίτην ἢ ἀπαίδευτον εἶναι· οἱ μὲν γὰρ χρημάτων, οἱ δ' ἀνθρωπισμοῦ δέονται. λοιδορούμενός
ποτε ἀνεχώρει· τοῦ δ' ἐπιδιώκοντος εἰπόντος, " τί
φεύγεις;" " ὅτι," φησί, " τοῦ μὲν κακῶς λέγειν
σὺ τὴν ἐξουσίαν ἔχεις, τοῦ δὲ μὴ ἀκούειν ἐγώ."
εἰπόντος τινὸς ὡς ἀεὶ τοὺς φιλοσόφους βλέποι παρὰ
ταῖς τῶν πλουσίων θύραις, " καὶ γὰρ καὶ οἱ ἰατροί,"
φησί, " παρὰ ταῖς τῶν νοσούντων· ἀλλ' οὐ παρὰ
τοῦτό τις ἂν ἔλοιτο νοσεῖν ἢ ἰατρεύειν."

Being once asked what advantage philosophers have, he replied, " Should all laws be repealed, we shall go on living as we do now." When Dionysius inquired what was the reason that philosophers go to rich men's houses, while rich men no longer visit philosophers, his reply was that " the one know what they need while the other do not." When he was reproached by Plato for his extravagance, he inquired, " Do you think Dionysius a good man ? " and the reply being in the affirmative, " And yet," said he, " he lives more extravagantly than I do. So that there is nothing to hinder a man living extravagantly and well." To the question how the educated differ from the uneducated, he replied, " Exactly as horses that have been trained differ from untrained horses." One day, as he entered the house of a courtesan, one of the lads with him blushed, whereupon he remarked, " It is not going in that is dangerous, but being unable to go out."

Some one brought him a knotty problem with the request that he would untie the knot. " Why, you simpleton," said he, " do you want it untied, seeing that it causes trouble enough as it is ? " " It is better," he said, " to be a beggar than to be uneducated ; the one needs money, the others need to be humanized." One day that he was reviled, he tried to slip away ; the other pursued him, asking, " Why do you run away ? " " Because," said he, " as it is your privilege to use foul language, so it is my privilege not to listen." In answer to one who remarked that he always saw philosophers at rich men's doors, he said, " So, too, physicians are in attendance on those who are sick, but no one for that reason would prefer being sick to being a physician."

71 Εἰς Κόρινθον αὐτῷ πλέοντί ποτε καὶ χειμα-
ζομένῳ συνέβη ταραχθῆναι. πρὸς οὖν τὸν εἰπόντα,
"ἡμεῖς μὲν οἱ ἰδιῶται οὐ δεδοίκαμεν, ὑμεῖς δ' οἱ
φιλόσοφοι δειλιᾶτε," "οὐ γὰρ περὶ ὁμοίας," ἔφη,
"ψυχῆς ἀγωνιῶμεν ἑκάτεροι." σεμνυνομένου τινὸς
ἐπὶ πολυμαθείᾳ ἔφη, "ὥσπερ οὐχ οἱ τὰ πλεῖστα
ἐσθίοντες [καὶ γυμναζόμενοι] ὑγιαίνουσι μᾶλλον
τῶν τὰ δέοντα προσφερομένων, οὕτως οὐδὲ οἱ
πολλὰ ἀλλ' οἱ χρήσιμα ἀναγινώσκοντές εἰσι σπουδαῖοι." πρὸς τὸν ὑπὲρ αὐτοῦ λογογράφον δίκην
εἰπόντα καὶ νικήσαντα, ἔπειτα φάσκοντα πρὸς
αὐτόν, "τί σε ὤνησε Σωκράτης;" ἔφη, "τοῦτο,
τοὺς λόγους, οὓς εἶπας ὑπὲρ ἐμοῦ, ἀληθεῖς εἶναι."

72 Τὰ ἄριστα ὑπετίθετο τῇ θυγατρὶ Ἀρήτῃ, συνασκῶν
αὐτὴν ὑπεροπτικὴν τοῦ πλέονος εἶναι. ἐρωτηθεὶς
ὑπό τινος τί αὐτοῦ ὁ υἱὸς ἀμείνων ἔσται παιδευθείς,
"καὶ εἰ μηδὲν ἄλλο," εἶπεν, "ἐν γοῦν τῷ θεάτρῳ
οὐ καθεδεῖται λίθος ἐπὶ λίθῳ." συνιστάντος τινὸς
αὐτῷ υἱὸν ᾔτησε πεντακοσίας δραχμάς· τοῦ δ'
εἰπόντος, "τοσούτου δύναμαι ἀνδράποδον ὠνήσασθαι," "πρίω," ἔφη, "καὶ ἕξεις δύο." ἀργύριον
εἶπε παρὰ τῶν γνωρίμων λαμβάνειν, οὐχ ἵν' αὐτὸς
χρῷτο, ἀλλ' ἵν' ἐκεῖνοι εἰδεῖεν εἰς τίνα δεῖ χρῆσθαι
τοῖς ἀργυρίοις. ὀνειδιζόμενός ποτε ὅτι δίκην ἔχων
ἐμισθώσατο ῥήτορα, "καὶ γάρ," ἔφη, "ὅταν δεῖπνον
ἔχω, μάγειρον μισθοῦμαι."

73 Ἀναγκαζόμενός ποτε ὑπὸ Διονυσίου εἰπεῖν τι
τῶν ἐκ φιλοσοφίας, "γελοῖον," ἔφη, "εἰ τὸ λέγειν
μὲν παρ' ἐμοῦ μανθάνεις, τὸ δὲ πότε δεῖ λέγειν

It happened once that he set sail for Corinth and, being overtaken by a storm, he was in great consternation. Some one said, " We plain men are not alarmed, and are you philosophers turned cowards ? " To this he replied, " The lives at stake in the two cases are not comparable." When some one gave himself airs for his wide learning, this is what he said : " As those who eat most and take the most exercise are not better in health than those who restrict themselves to what they require, so too it is not wide reading but useful reading that tends to excellence." An advocate, having pleaded for him and won the case, thereupon put the question, " What good did Socrates do you ? " " Thus much," was the reply, " that what you said of me in your speech was true."

He gave his daughter Arete the very best advice, training her up to despise excess. He was asked by some one in what way his son would be the better for being educated. He replied, " If nothing more than this, at all events, when in the theatre he will not sit down like a stone upon stone." When some one brought his son as a pupil, he asked a fee of 500 drachmae. The father objected, " For that sum I can buy a slave." " Then do so," was the reply, " and you will have two." He said that he did not take money from his friends for his own use, but to teach them upon what objects their money should be spent. When he was reproached for employing a rhetorician to conduct his case, he made reply, " Well, if I give a dinner, I hire a cook."

Being once compelled by Dionysius to enunciate some doctrine of philosophy, " It would be ludicrous," he said, " that you should learn from me what to

σύ με διδάσκεις." ἐπὶ τούτῳ δὴ ἀγανακτήσαντα τὸν Διονύσιον ἔσχατον αὐτὸν κατακλῖναι· καὶ τόν, "ἐνδοξότερον," φάναι, "τὸν τόπον ἠθέλησας ποιῆσαι." αὐχοῦντός τινος ἐπὶ τῷ κολυμβᾶν, "οὐκ αἰσχύνῃ," εἶπεν, "ἐπὶ δελφῖνος ἔργοις ἀλαζονευόμενος;" ἐρωτηθείς ποτε τίνι διαφέρει ὁ σοφὸς τοῦ μὴ σοφοῦ, ἔφη, "εἰς ἀγνῶτας τοὺς δύο γυμνοὺς ἀπόστειλον, καὶ εἴσῃ." αὐχοῦντός τινος ἐπὶ τῷ πολλὰ πίνειν καὶ μὴ μεθύσκεσθαι, "τοῦτο καὶ ἡμίονος," φησί.

74 Πρὸς τὸν αἰτιώμενον ὅτι ἑταίρᾳ συνοικεῖ, "ἆρά γε," εἶπε, "μή τι διενέγκαι ⟨ἂν⟩ οἰκίαν λαβεῖν ἐν ᾗ πολλοί ποτε ᾤκησαν ἢ μηδείς," εἰπόντος δὲ οὔ, "τί δὲ πλεῦσαι ἐν νηῒ ᾗ μύριοι ποτὲ ἐνέπλευσαν ἢ μηδείς;" "οὐδαμῶς." "οὐδ' ἄρα γυναικί," ἔφη, "συνεῖναι ᾗ πολλοὶ κέχρηνται ἢ μηδείς." πρὸς τὸν αἰτιώμενον ὅτι Σωκράτους μαθητὴς ὢν ἀργύριον λαμβάνει, "καὶ μάλα," εἶπε· "καὶ γὰρ Σωκράτης, πεμπόντων αὐτῷ τινων καὶ σῖτον καὶ οἶνον, ὀλίγα λαμβάνων τὰ λοιπὰ ἀπέπεμπεν· εἶχε γὰρ ταμίας τοὺς πρώτους Ἀθηναίων, ἐγὼ δ' Εὐτυχίδην ἀργυρώνητον." ἐχρῆτο καὶ Λαΐδι τῇ ἑταίρᾳ, καθά 75 φησι Σωτίων ἐν τῷ δευτέρῳ τῶν Διαδοχῶν. πρὸς οὖν τοὺς μεμφομένους αὐτῷ ἔφη, "ἔχω [Λαΐδα], ἀλλ' οὐκ ἔχομαι· ἐπεὶ τὸ κρατεῖν καὶ μὴ ἡττᾶσθαι

say, and yet instruct me when to say it." At this, they say, Dionysius was offended and made him recline at the end of the table. And Aristippus said, "You must have wished to confer distinction on the last place." To some one who boasted of his diving, "Are you not ashamed," said he, "to brag of that which a dolphin can do?" Being asked on one occasion what is the difference between the wise man and the unwise, "Strip them both," said he, "and send them among strangers and you will know." To one who boasted that he could drink a great deal without getting drunk, his rejoinder was, "And so can a mule."

To one who accused him of living with a courtesan, he put the question, "Why, is there any difference between taking a house in which many people have lived before and taking one in which nobody has ever lived?" The answer being "No," he continued, "Or again, between sailing in a ship in which ten thousand persons have sailed before and in one in which nobody has ever sailed?" "There is no difference." "Then it makes no difference," said he, "whether the woman you live with has lived with many or with nobody." To the accusation that, although he was a pupil of Socrates, he took fees, his rejoinder was, "Most certainly I do, for Socrates, too, when certain people sent him corn and wine, used to take a little and return all the rest; and he had the foremost men in Athens for his stewards, whereas mine is my slave Eutychides." He enjoyed the favours of Laïs, as Sotion states in the second book of his *Successions of Philosophers*. To those who censured him his defence was, "I have Laïs, not she me; and it is not abstinence from

ἡδονῶν ἄριστον, οὐ τὸ μὴ χρῆσθαι." πρὸς τὸν
ὀνειδίσαντα αὐτῷ πολυτελῆ ὀψωνίαν ἔφη, " σὺ δ'
οὐκ ἂν τριωβόλου ταῦτ' ἐπρίω;" ὁμολογήσαντος
δέ, " οὐκέτι τοίνυν," ἔφη, " φιλήδονος ἐγώ, ἀλλὰ σὺ
φιλάργυρος." Σίμου ποτὲ τοῦ Διονυσίου ταμίου
πολυτελεῖς οἴκους αὐτῷ καὶ λιθοστρώτους δεικνύν-
τος—ἦν δὲ Φρὺξ καὶ ὄλεθρος—ἀναχρεμψάμενος
προσέπτυσε τῇ ὄψει· τοῦ δ' ἀγανακτήσαντος, " οὐκ
εἶχον," εἶπε, " τόπον ἐπιτηδειότερον."

76 Πρὸς Χαρώνδαν εἰπόντα, οἱ δὲ πρὸς Φαίδωνα, τίς
ὁ μεμυρισμένος; " ἐγώ," φησίν, " ὁ κακοδαίμων,
κἀμοῦ κακοδαιμονέστερος ὁ Περσῶν βασιλεύς.
ἀλλ' ὅρα μὴ ὡς οὐδὲν τῶν ἄλλων ζῴων παρὰ τοῦτό
τι ἐλαττοῦται, οὕτως οὐδ' ἂν ὁ ἄνθρωπος. κακοὶ
κακῶς δ' ἀπόλοιντο οἱ κίναιδοι, οἵτινες καλὸν ἡμῖν
ἄλειμμα διαβάλλουσιν." ἐρωτώμενος πῶς ἀπέθανε
Σωκράτης, ἔφη, " ὡς ἂν ἐγὼ εὐξαίμην." Πολυ-
ξένου ποτὲ τοῦ σοφιστοῦ εἰσελθόντος πρὸς αὐτὸν καὶ
θεασαμένου γυναῖκάς τε καὶ πολυτελῆ ὀψωνίαν,
ἔπειτα αἰτιασαμένου, μικρὸν διαλιπών, " δύνασαι,"
77 ἔφη, " καὶ σὺ σήμερον μεθ' ἡμῶν γενέσθαι;" τοῦ
δ' ἐπινεύσαντος, " τί οὖν," ἔφη, " ἐμέμφου; ἔοικας
γὰρ οὐ τὴν ὀψωνίαν ἀλλὰ τὸ ἀνάλωμα αἰτιᾶσθαι."
τοῦ δὲ θεράποντος ἐν ὁδῷ βαστάζοντος ἀργύριον
καὶ βαρυνομένου, ὥς φασιν οἱ περὶ τὸν Βίωνα ἐν
ταῖς Διατριβαῖς, " ἀπόχεε," ἔφη, " τὸ πλέον καὶ ὅσον
δύνασαι βάσταζε." πλέων ποτὲ ἐπεὶ τὸ σκάφος

pleasures that is best, but mastery over them without ever being worsted." To one who reproached him with extravagance in catering, he replied, " Wouldn't you have bought this if you could have got it for three obols ? " The answer being in the affirmative, " Very well, then," said Aristippus, " I am no longer a lover of pleasure, it is you who are a lover of money." One day Simus, the steward of Dionysius, a Phrygian by birth and a rascally fellow, was show-ing him costly houses with tesselated pavements, when Aristippus coughed up phlegm and spat in his face. And on his resenting this he replied, " I could not find any place more suitable."

When Charondas (or, as others say, Phaedo) in-quired, " Who is this who reeks with unguents ? " he replied, " It is I, unlucky wight, and the still more unlucky Persian king. But, as none of the other animals are at any disadvantage on that account, consider whether it be not the same with man. Confound the effeminates who spoil for us the use of good perfume." Being asked how Socrates died, he answered, " As I would wish to die myself." Poly-xenus the sophist once paid him a visit and, after having seen ladies present and expensive entertain-ment, reproached him with it later. After an in-terval Aristippus asked him, " Can you join us to-day ? " On the other accepting the invitation, Aristippus inquired, " Why, then, did you find fault ? For you appear to blame the cost and not the enter-tainment." When his servant was carrying money and found the load too heavy—the story is told by Bion in his *Lectures*—Aristippus cried, " Pour away the greater part, and carry no more than you can manage." Being once on a voyage, as soon as he

ἔγνω πειρατικόν, λαβὼν τὸ χρυσίον ἠρίθμει· ἔπειτα
εἰς θάλατταν ὡς μὴ θέλων παρακατέβαλε καὶ δῆθεν
ἀνώμωξεν. οἱ δὲ καὶ ἐπειπεῖν φασιν αὐτὸν ὡς
ἄμεινον ταῦτα δι᾽ Ἀρίστιππον ἢ διὰ ταῦτα Ἀρίστιππον ἀπολέσθαι. Διονυσίου ποτ᾽ ἐρομένου ἐπὶ
τί ἥκοι, ἔφη ἐπὶ τῷ μεταδώσειν ὧν ἔχοι, καὶ
78 μεταλήψεσθαι ὧν μὴ ἔχοι. ἔνιοι δ᾽ οὕτως ἀπο-
κρίνασθαι, "ὁπότε μὲν σοφίας ἐδεόμην, ἦκον παρὰ
τὸν Σωκράτην· νῦν δὲ χρημάτων δεόμενος παρὰ σὲ
ἥκω." κατεγίνωσκε τῶν ἀνθρώπων ὡς τὰ σκεύη
μὲν ἐν ταῖς ἀγορασίαις κομπούντων, τοὺς δὲ βίους
εἰκῇ δοκιμαζόντων· οἱ δὲ τοῦτο Διογένους φασί.
καὶ ποτε παρὰ πότον κελεύσαντος Διονυσίου
ἕκαστον ἐν πορφυρᾷ ἐσθῆτι ὀρχήσασθαι, τὸν μὲν
Πλάτωνα μὴ προσέσθαι, εἰπόντα·

 οὐκ ἂν δυναίμην θῆλυν ἐνδῦναι στολήν·

τὸν δ᾽ Ἀρίστιππον λαβόντα καὶ μέλλοντα ὀρχήσασθαι εὐστόχως εἰπεῖν·

καὶ γὰρ ἐν βακχεύμασιν
οὖσ᾽ ἥ γε σώφρων οὐ διαφθαρήσεται.

79   Δεόμενός ποτε ὑπὲρ φίλου Διονυσίου καὶ μὴ ἐπι-
τυγχάνων εἰς τοὺς πόδας αὐτοῦ ἔπεσε· πρὸς οὖν
τὸν ἐπισκώψαντα, "οὐκ ἐγώ," φησίν, "αἴτιος, ἀλλὰ
Διονύσιος ὁ ἐν τοῖς ποσὶ τὰς ἀκοὰς ἔχων." διατρίβων ἐν Ἀσίᾳ καὶ ληφθεὶς ὑπὸ Ἀρταφέρνου τοῦ
σατράπου πρὸς τὸν εἰπόντα, "καὶ ὧδε θαρρεῖς,"

discovered the vessel to be manned by pirates, he took out his money and began to count it, and then, as if by inadvertence, he let the money fall into the sea, and naturally broke out into lamentation. Another version of the story attributes to him the further remark that it was better for the money to perish on account of Aristippus than for Aristippus to perish on account of the money. Dionysius once asked him what he was come for, and he said it was to impart what he had and obtain what he had not. But some make his answer to have been, " When I needed wisdom, I went to Socrates ; now that I am in need of money, I come to you." He used to complain of mankind that in purchasing earthenware they made trial whether it rang true, but had no regular standard by which to judge life. Others attribute this remark to Diogenes. One day Dionysius over the wine commanded everybody to put on purple and dance. Plato declined, quoting the line [a] :

> I could not stoop to put on women's robes.

Aristippus, however, put on the dress and, as he was about to dance, was ready with the repartee :

> Even amid the Bacchic revelry
> True modesty will not be put to shame.[b]

He made a request to Dionysius on behalf of a friend and, failing to obtain it, fell down at his feet. And when some one jeered at him, he made reply, " It is not I who am to blame, but Dionysius who has his ears in his feet." He was once staying in Asia and was taken prisoner by Artaphernes, the satrap. " Can you be cheerful under these circumstances ? "

[a] Eur. *Bacch.* 836.   [b] *ib.* 317.

" πότε γάρ," εἶπεν, " ὦ μάταιε, θαρρήσαιμι ἂν
μᾶλλον ἢ νῦν, ὅτε μέλλω 'Αρταφέρνῃ διαλέξεσθαι; "
τοὺς τῶν ἐγκυκλίων παιδευμάτων μετασχόντας,
φιλοσοφίας δὲ ἀπολειφθέντας ὁμοίους ἔλεγεν εἶναι
τοῖς τῆς Πηνελόπης μνηστῆρσι· καὶ γὰρ ἐκείνους
Μελανθὼ μὲν καὶ Πολυδώραν καὶ τὰς ἄλλας
θεραπαίνας ἔχειν, πάντα δὲ μᾶλλον ἢ αὐτὴν τὴν
80 δέσποιναν δύνασθαι γῆμαι. τὸ δ' ὅμοιον καὶ
'Αρίστων· τὸν γὰρ 'Οδυσσέα καταβάντα εἰς ᾅδου
τοὺς μὲν νεκροὺς πάντας σχεδὸν ἑωρακέναι καὶ
συντετυχηκέναι, τὴν δὲ βασίλισσαν αὐτὴν μὴ
τεθεᾶσθαι.

'Ο δ' οὖν 'Αρίστιππος ἐρωτηθεὶς τίνα ἐστὶν ἃ
δεῖ τοὺς καλοὺς παῖδας μανθάνειν, ἔφη, " οἷς
ἄνδρες γενόμενοι χρήσονται." πρὸς τὸν εἰπόντα
ἐν αἰτίᾳ ὡς ἀπὸ Σωκράτους πρὸς Διονύσιον ἔλθοι,
" ἀλλὰ πρὸς Σωκράτην μέν," εἶπεν, " ἦλθον παιδείας
ἕνεκεν, πρὸς δὲ Διονύσιον παιδιᾶς." ἐξ ὁμιλίας
αὐτῷ χρηματισαμένῳ φησὶ Σωκράτης, " πόθεν
σοι τοσαῦτα; " καὶ ὅς, " ὅθεν σοι τὰ ὀλίγα."

81 Ἑταίρας εἰπούσης πρὸς αὐτόν, " ἐκ σοῦ κυῶ,"
" οὐ μᾶλλον," ἔφη, " γινώσκεις ἢ εἰ δι' ὁλοσχοίνων
ἰοῦσα ἔφασκες ὑπὸ τοῦδε κεκεντῆσθαι." ᾐτιάσατό
τις αὐτὸν τὸν υἱὸν ἀπορριπτοῦντα ὥσπερ οὐκ ἐξ
ἑαυτοῦ γεγονότα· καὶ ὅς, " καὶ τὸ φλέγμα," φησί,
" καὶ τοὺς φθεῖρας ἐξ ἡμῶν ἴσμεν γεννωμένους,
ἀλλ' ἀχρεῖα ὄντα ὡς πορρωτάτω ῥιπτοῦμεν."
ἐκδεξάμενος τὸ ἀργύριον παρὰ Διονυσίου, Πλάτωνος ἄραντος βιβλίον, πρὸς τὸν αἰτιασάμενον,

some one asked. " Yes, you simpleton," was the reply, " for when should I be more cheerful than now that I am about to converse with Artaphernes ? " Those who went through the ordinary curriculum, but in their studies stopped short at philosophy, he used to compare to the suitors of Penelope. For the suitors won Melantho, Polydora and the rest of the handmaidens, but were anything but successful in their wooing of the mistress. A similar remark is ascribed to Ariston. For, he said, when Odysseus went down into the under-world, he saw nearly all the dead and made their acquaintance, but he never set eyes upon their queen herself.

Again, when Aristippus was asked what are the subjects which handsome boys ought to learn, his reply was, " Those which will be useful to them when they are grown up." To the critic who censured him for leaving Socrates to go to Dionysius, his rejoinder was, " Yes, but I came to Socrates for education and to Dionysius for recreation." When he had made some money by teaching, Socrates asked him, " Where did you get so much ? " to which he replied, " Where you got so little."

A courtesan having told him that she was with child by him, he replied, " You are no more sure of this than if, after running through coarse rushes, you were to say you had been pricked by one in particular." Someone accused him of exposing his son as if it was not his offspring Whereupon he replied, " Phlegm, too, and vermin we know to be of our own begetting, but for all that, because they are useless, we cast them as far from us as possible." He received a sum of money from Dionysius at the same time that Plato carried off a book and, when

" ἐγὼ μὲν γάρ," εἶπεν, " ἀργυρίων, Πλάτων δὲ
βιβλίων ἐστὶν ἐνδεής." πρὸς τὸν εἰπόντα τίνος
ἕνεκα ἐλέγχεται παρὰ Διονυσίου, " οὗ ἕνεκα,"
φησίν, " οἱ ἄλλοι ἐλέγχουσιν."

82 Ἤιτει Διονύσιον ἀργύριον, καὶ ὅς, " ἀλλὰ μὴν
ἔφης οὐκ ἀπορήσειν τὸν σοφόν·" ὁ δ' ὑπολαβών,
" δός," εἶπε, " καὶ περὶ τούτου ζητῶμεν." δόντος
δέ, " ὁρᾷς," ἔφη, " ὅτι οὐκ ἠπόρηκα;" εἰπόντος
πρὸς αὐτὸν Διονυσίου·

> ὅστις γὰρ ὡς τύραννον ἐμπορεύεται,
> κείνου 'στὶ δοῦλος, κἂν ἐλεύθερος μόλῃ·

ὑπολαβών,

> οὐκ ἔστι δοῦλος, ἂν ἐλεύθερος μόλῃ.

τοῦτο Διοκλῆς φησιν ἐν τῷ Περὶ βίων φιλοσόφων·
ἄλλοι γὰρ εἰς Πλάτωνα ἀναφέρουσιν. ὀργισθεὶς
πρὸς Αἰσχίνην μετ' οὐ πολύ, " οὐ διαλλαχθησόμεθα,
οὐ παυσόμεθα," εἶπε, " ληροῦντες, ἀλλ' ἀναμενεῖς
ἕως ἂν ἐπὶ τῆς κύλικος ἡμᾶς διαλλάξῃ τις;" καὶ
83 ὅς, " ἄσμενος," ἔφη· " μνημόνευε τοίνυν," εἶπεν
ὁ Ἀρίστιππος, " ὅτι σοι πρότερος πρεσβύτερος
ὢν προσῆλθον." καὶ ὁ Αἰσχίνης, " εὖγε, νὴ τὴν
Ἥραν, εὐλόγως εἶπας, ἐπεὶ πολλῷ μου βελτίων
ὑπάρχεις· ἐγὼ μὲν γὰρ ἔχθρας, σὺ δὲ φιλίας
ἄρχεις." καὶ ταῦτα μὲν εἰς αὐτὸν ἀναφέρεται.

Γεγόνασι δ' Ἀρίστιπποι τέσσαρες· περὶ οὗ τε
ὁ λόγος καὶ δεύτερος ὁ τὰ περὶ Ἀρκαδίας γεγραφώς·

ᵃ Nauck, *T.G.F.*, *Soph.* 789.
ᵇ From a lost play of Sophocles : Plutarch, *De audiendis
poetis*, 12, p. 33 D, *Vita Pomp.* 78, p. 661 *s.f.*

he was twitted with this, his reply was,, " Well, I want money, Plato wants books." Some one asked him why he let himself be refuted by Dionysius. " For the same reason," said he, " as the others refute him."

Dionysius met a request of his for money with the words, " Nay, but you told me that the wise man would never be in want." To which he retorted, " Pay ! Pay ! and then let us discuss the question ; " and when he was paid, " Now you see, do you not," said he, " that I was not found wanting ? " Dionysius having repeated to him the lines :

> Whoso betakes him to a prince's court
> Becomes his slave, albeit of free birth,[a]

he retorted :

> If a free man he come, no slave is he. [b]

This is stated by Diocles in his work *On the Lives of Philosophers*; other writers refer the anecdotes to Plato. After getting in a rage with Aeschines, he presently addressed him thus : " Are we not to make it up and desist from vapouring, or will you wait for some one to reconcile us over the wine-bowl ? " To which he replied, " Agreed." " Then remember," Aristippus went on, " that, though I am your senior, I made the first approaches." Thereupon Aeschines said, " Well done, by Hera, you are quite right ; you are a much better man than I am. For the quarrel was of my beginning, you make the first move to friendship." Such are the repartees which are attributed to him.

There have been four men called Aristippus, (1) our present subject, (2) the author of a book about

τρίτος ὁ μητροδίδακτος, θυγατριδοῦς τοῦ πρώτου·
τέταρτος ὁ ἐκ τῆς νεωτέρας Ἀκαδημείας.

Τοῦ δὲ Κυρηναϊκοῦ φιλοσόφου φέρεται βιβλία
τρία μὲν ἱστορίας τῶν κατὰ Λιβύην, ἀπεσταλμένα
Διονυσίῳ· ἓν δὲ ἐν ᾧ διάλογοι πέντε καὶ εἴκοσιν,
οἱ μὲν Ἀτθίδι, οἱ δὲ Δωρίδι διαλέκτῳ γεγραμμένοι
οἵδε·

84 Ἀρτάβαζος.
Πρὸς τοὺς ναυαγούς.
Πρὸς τοὺς φυγάδας.
Πρὸς πτωχόν.
Πρὸς Λαΐδα.
Πρὸς Πῶρον.
Πρὸς Λαΐδα περὶ τοῦ κατόπτρου.
Ἑρμείας.
Ἐνύπνιον.
Πρὸς τὸν ἐπὶ τῆς κύλικος.
Φιλόμηλος.
Πρὸς τοὺς οἰκείους.
Πρὸς τοὺς ἐπιτιμῶντας ὅτι κέκτηται οἶνον παλαιὸν
    καὶ ἑταίρας.
Πρὸς τοὺς ἐπιτιμῶντας ὅτι πολυτελῶς ὀψωνεῖ.
Ἐπιστολὴ πρὸς Ἀρήτην τὴν θυγατέρα.
Πρὸς τὸν εἰς Ὀλυμπίαν γυμνάζοντα ἑαυτόν.
Ἐρώτησις.
Ἄλλη Ἐρώτησις.
Χρεία πρὸς Διονύσιον.
Ἄλλη ἐπὶ τῆς εἰκόνος.
Ἄλλη ἐπὶ τῆς Διονυσίου θυγατρός.
Πρὸς τὸν οἰόμενον ἀτιμάζεσθαι.
Πρὸς τὸν συμβουλεύειν ἐπιχειροῦντα.

Ἔνιοι δὲ καὶ διατριβῶν αὐτόν φασιν ἓξ γεγρα-

212

Arcadia, (3) the grandchild by a daughter of the first Aristippus, who was known as his mother's pupil, (4) a philosopher of the New Academy.

The following books by the Cyrenaic philosopher are in circulation : a history of Libya in three Books, sent to Dionysius ; one work containing twenty-five dialogues, some written in Attic, some in Doric, as follows :

Artabazus.
To the shipwrecked.
To the Exiles.
To a Beggar.
To Laïs.
To Porus.
To Laïs, On the Mirror.
Hermias.
A Dream.
To the Master of the Revels.
Philomelus.
To his Friends.
To those who blame him for his love of old wine
    and of women.
To those who blame him for extravagant living.
Letter to his daughter Arete.
To one in training for Olympia.
An Interrogatory.
Another Interrogatory.
An Occasional Piece to Dionysius.
Another, On the Statue.
Another, On the daughter of Dionysius.
To one who considered himself slighted.
To one who essayed to be a counsellor.

Some also maintain that he wrote six Books of

φέναι, οἱ δ' οὐδ' ὅλως γράψαι· ὧν ἐστι καὶ Σωσικράτης ὁ Ῥόδιος.

85 Κατὰ δὲ Σωτίωνα ἐν δευτέρῳ καὶ Παναίτιον ἔστιν αὐτῷ συγγράμματα τάδε·

Περὶ παιδείας.
Περὶ ἀρετῆς.
Προτρεπτικός.
Ἀρτάβαζος.
Ναυαγοί.
Φυγάδες.
Διατριβῶν ἕξ.
Χρειῶν τρία.
Πρὸς Λαΐδα.
Πρὸς Πῶρον.
Πρὸς Σωκράτην.
Περὶ τύχης.

Τέλος δ' ἀπέφαινε τὴν λείαν κίνησιν εἰς αἴσθησιν ἀναδιδομένην.

Ἡμεῖς δ' ἐπειδὴ τὸν βίον ἀνεγράψαμεν αὐτοῦ, φέρε νῦν διέλθωμεν τοὺς ἀπ' αὐτοῦ Κυρηναϊκούς, οἵ τινες ἑαυτοὺς οἱ μὲν Ἡγησιακούς, οἱ δὲ Ἀννικερείους, οἱ δὲ Θεοδωρείους προσωνόμαζον. οὐ μὴν ἀλλὰ καὶ τοὺς ἀπὸ Φαίδωνος, ὧν τοὺς κορυ-
86 φαιοτάτους Ἐρετρικούς. ἔχει δὲ οὕτως· Ἀριστίππου διήκουσεν ἡ θυγάτηρ Ἀρήτη καὶ Αἰθίοψ

---

[a] This sentence is a sort of preface to the valuable summary of Hedonistic tenets which occupies §§ 86-99 under four heads, Aristippus (86-93), Hegesias (93-96), Anniceris (96, 97), and Theodorus (97-99). *Cf.* note on i. 19 and Epiphanius (Diels, *Dox. Gr.* 591). It seems as if the sentence τέλος δὲ . . . ἀναδιδομένην ought to follow, not to precede, this preface. But before the doctrines comes a list of disciples, including Hegesias, Anniceris, and Theodorus, whose divergencies from Aristippus are noted below. The intrusion of Phaedo and

Essays; others, and among them Sosicrates of Rhodes, that he wrote none at all.

According to Sotion in his second book, and Panaetius, the following treatises are his:

On Education.
On Virtue.
Introduction to Philosophy.
Artabazus.
The Ship-wrecked.
The Exiles.
Six books of Essays.
Three books of Occasional Writings ($\chi\rho\epsilon\hat{\iota}\alpha\iota$).
To Laïs.
To Porus.
To Socrates.
On Fortune.

He laid down as the end the smooth motion resulting in sensation.

Having written his life, let me now proceed to pass in review the philosophers of the Cyrenaic school which sprang from him, although some call themselves followers of Hegesias, others followers of Anniceris, others again of Theodorus.[a] Not but what we shall notice further the pupils of Phaedo, the chief of whom were called the school of Eretria. The case stands thus. The disciples of Aristippus were his daughter Arete, Aethiops of Ptolemaïs,[b]

the Eretrians at this stage is certainly strange: it looks as if Diogenes Laertius jotted down a direction for his own future guidance.

[b] If the city was so named after a Ptolemy, it is impossible that one of its citizens could have been contemporary with the first Aristippus, the companion of Socrates. Even if Aristippus II. was the teacher of Aethiops the difficulty is not removed.

Πτολεμαεὺς καὶ Ἀντίπατρος Κυρηναῖος· Ἀρήτης
δὲ Ἀρίστιππος ὁ μητροδίδακτος ἐπικληθείς, οὗ
Θεόδωρος ὁ ἄθεος, εἶτα θεός· Ἀντιπάτρου δ' Ἐπι-
τιμίδης Κυρηναῖος, οὗ Παραιβάτης, οὗ Ἡγησίας
ὁ πεισιθάνατος καὶ Ἀννίκερις [ὁ Πλάτωνα λυτρω-
σάμενος].

Οἱ μὲν οὖν ἐπὶ τῆς ἀγωγῆς τῆς Ἀριστίππου
μείναντες καὶ Κυρηναϊκοὶ προσαγορευθέντες δό-
ξαις ἐχρῶντο τοιαύταις· δύο πάθη ὑφίσταντο,
πόνον καὶ ἡδονήν, τὴν μὲν λείαν κίνησιν, τὴν
37 ἡδονήν, τὸν δὲ πόνον τραχεῖαν κίνησιν. μὴ διαφέρειν τε ἡδονὴν ἡδονῆς, μηδὲ ἥδιόν τι εἶναι· καὶ
τὴν μὲν εὐδοκητὴν πᾶσι ζῴοις, τὸν δ' ἀποκρου-
στικόν. ἡδονὴν μέντοι τὴν τοῦ σώματος, ἣν καὶ
τέλος εἶναι, καθά φησι καὶ Παναίτιος ἐν τῷ Περὶ
τῶν αἱρέσεων, οὐ τὴν καταστηματικὴν ἡδονὴν
τὴν ἐπ' ἀναιρέσει ἀλγηδόνων καὶ οἷον ἀνοχλησίαν,
ἣν ὁ Ἐπίκουρος ἀποδέχεται καὶ τέλος εἶναί φησι.
δοκεῖ δ' αὐτοῖς καὶ τέλος εὐδαιμονίας διαφέρειν.
τέλος μὲν γὰρ εἶναι τὴν κατὰ μέρος ἡδονήν,
εὐδαιμονίαν δὲ τὸ ἐκ τῶν μερικῶν ἡδονῶν σύστημα,
αἷς συναριθμοῦνται καὶ αἱ παρῳχηκυῖαι καὶ αἱ
μέλλουσαι.

88 Εἶναί τε τὴν μερικὴν ἡδονὴν δι' αὑτὴν αἱρετήν·
τὴν δ' εὐδαιμονίαν οὐ δι' αὑτήν, ἀλλὰ διὰ τὰς κατὰ
μέρος ἡδονάς. πίστιν δ' εἶναι τοῦ τέλος εἶναι τὴν
ἡδονὴν τὸ ἀπροαιρέτως ἡμᾶς ἐκ παίδων ᾠκειῶσθαι
πρὸς αὐτήν, καὶ τυχόντας αὐτῆς μηθὲν ἐπιζητεῖν
μηθέν τε οὕτω φεύγειν ὡς τὴν ἐναντίαν αὐτῇ
ἀλγηδόνα. εἶναι δὲ τὴν ἡδονὴν ἀγαθὸν κἂν ἀπὸ
τῶν ἀσχημοτάτων γένηται, καθά φησιν Ἱππόβοτος
ἐν τῷ Περὶ αἱρέσεων. εἰ γὰρ καὶ ἡ πρᾶξις ἄτοπος

and Antipater of Cyrene. The pupil of Arete was Aristippus, who went by the name of mother-taught, and his pupil was Theodorus, known as the atheist, subsequently as " god." Antipater's pupil was Epitimides of Cyrene, his was Paraebates, and he had as pupils Hegesias, the advocate of suicide, and Anniceris, who ransomed Plato.

Those then who adhered to the teaching of Aristippus and were known as Cyrenaics held the following opinions. They laid down that there are two states, pleasure and pain, the former a smooth, the latter a rough motion, and that pleasure does not differ from pleasure nor is one pleasure more pleasant than another. The one state is agreeable and the other repellent to all living things. However, the bodily pleasure which is the end is, according to Panaetius in his work *On the Sects*, not the settled pleasure following the removal of pains, or the sort of freedom from discomfort which Epicurus accepts and maintains to be the end. They also hold that there is a difference between " end " and " happiness." Our end is particular pleasure, whereas happiness is the sum total of all particular pleasures, in which are included both past and future pleasures.

Particular pleasure is desirable for its own sake, whereas happiness is desirable not for its own sake but for the sake of particular pleasures. That pleasure is the end is proved by the fact that from our youth up we are instinctively attracted to it, and, when we obtain it, seek for nothing more, and shun nothing so much as its opposite, pain. Pleasure is good even if it proceed from the most unseemly conduct, as Hippobotus says in his work *On the Sects*. For even if the action be irregular,

εἴη, ἀλλ' οὖν ἡ ἡδονὴ δι' αὑτὴν αἱρετὴ καὶ ἀγαθόν.
89 ἡ δὲ τοῦ ἀλγοῦντος ὑπεξαίρεσις, ὡς εἴρηται παρ'
Ἐπικούρῳ, δοκεῖ αὐτοῖς μὴ εἶναι ἡδονή· οὐδὲ ἡ
ἀηδονία ἀλγηδών. ἐν κινήσει γὰρ εἶναι ἀμφότερα,
μὴ οὔσης τῆς ἀπονίας ἢ τῆς ἀηδονίας κινήσεως,
ἐπεὶ ἡ ἀπονία οἱονεὶ καθεύδοντός ἐστι κατάστασις.
δύνασθαι δέ φασι καὶ τὴν ἡδονήν τινας μὴ αἱρεῖσθαι
κατὰ διαστροφήν· οὐ πάσας μέντοι τὰς ψυχικὰς
ἡδονὰς καὶ ἀλγηδόνας ἐπὶ σωματικαῖς ἡδοναῖς
καὶ ἀλγηδόσι γίνεσθαι. καὶ γὰρ ἐπὶ ψιλῇ τῇ τῆς
πατρίδος εὐημερίᾳ ὥσπερ τῇ ἰδίᾳ χαρὰν ἐγγίνεσθαι.
ἀλλὰ μὴν οὐδὲ κατὰ μνήμην τῶν ἀγαθῶν ἢ προσ-
δοκίαν ἡδονήν φασιν ἀποτελεῖσθαι· ὅπερ ἤρεσκεν
90 Ἐπικούρῳ. ἐκλύεσθαι γὰρ τῷ χρόνῳ τὸ τῆς
ψυχῆς κίνημα. λέγουσι δὲ μηδὲ κατὰ ψιλὴν τὴν
ὅρασιν ἢ τὴν ἀκοὴν γίνεσθαι ἡδονάς. τῶν γοῦν
μιμουμένων θρήνους ἡδέως ἀκούομεν, τῶν δὲ κατ'
ἀλήθειαν ἀηδῶς. μέσας τε καταστάσεις ὠνόμαζον
ἀηδονίαν καὶ ἀπονίαν. πολὺ μέντοι τῶν ψυχικῶν
τὰς σωματικὰς ἀμείνους εἶναι, καὶ τὰς ὀχλήσεις
χείρους τὰς σωματικάς. ὅθεν καὶ ταύταις κολάζεσθαι μᾶλλον τοὺς ἁμαρτάνοντας. χαλεπώτερον
γὰρ τὸ πονεῖν, οἰκειότερον δὲ τὸ ἥδεσθαι ὑπελάμ-
βανον. ὅθεν καὶ πλείονα οἰκονομίαν περὶ θάτερον
ἐποιοῦντο. διὸ καὶ καθ' αὑτὴν αἱρετῆς οὔσης
τῆς ἡδονῆς τὰ ποιητικὰ ἐνίων ἡδονῶν ὀχληρὰ

still, at any rate, the resultant pleasure is desirable
for its own sake and is good.   The removal of
pain, however, which is put forward in Epicurus,
seems to them not to be pleasure at all, any more
than the absence of pleasure is pain.   For both
pleasure and pain they hold to consist in motion,
whereas absence of pleasure like absence of pain is
not motion, since painlessness is the condition of one
who is, as it were, asleep.   They assert that some
people may fail to choose pleasure because their
minds are perverted ; not all mental pleasures and
pains, however, are derived from bodily counter·
parts.   For instance, we take disinterested delight
in the prosperity of our country which is as real as
our delight in our own prosperity.   Nor again do they
admit that pleasure is derived from the memory or
expectation of good, which was a doctrine of Epicurus.
For they assert that the movement affecting the mind
is exhausted in course of time.   Again they hold
that pleasure is not derived from sight or from
hearing alone.   At all events, we listen with pleasure
to imitation of mourning, while the reality causes
pain.   They gave the names of absence of pleasure
and absence of pain to the intermediate conditions.
However, they insist that bodily pleasures are far
better than mental pleasures, and bodily pains far
worse than mental pains, and that this is the reason
why offenders are punished with the former.   For
they assumed pain to be more repellent, pleasure
more congenial.   For these reasons they paid more
attention to the body than to the mind.   Hence,
although pleasure is in itself desirable, yet they hold
that the things which are productive of certain
pleasures are often of a painful nature, the very

πολλάκις ἐναντιοῦσθαι· ὡς δυσκολώτατον αὐτοῖς φαίνεσθαι τὸν ἀθροισμὸν τῶν ἡδονῶν εὐδαιμονίαν ποιούντων.

91 Ἀρέσκει δ᾽ αὐτοῖς μήτε τὸν σοφὸν πάντα ἡδέως ζῆν, μήτε πάντα φαῦλον ἐπιπόνως, ἀλλὰ κατὰ τὸ πλεῖστον. ἀρκεῖ δὲ κἂν κατὰ μίαν τις προσπίπτουσαν ἡδέως ἐπανάγῃ. τὴν φρόνησιν ἀγαθὸν μὲν εἶναι λέγουσιν, οὐ δι᾽ ἑαυτὴν δὲ αἱρετήν, ἀλλὰ διὰ τὰ ἐξ αὐτῆς περιγινόμενα· τὸν φίλον τῆς χρείας ἕνεκα· καὶ γὰρ μέρος σώματος, μέχρις ἂν παρῇ, ἀσπάζεσθαι. τῶν ἀρετῶν ἐνίας καὶ περὶ τοὺς ἄφρονας συνίστασθαι. τὴν σωματικὴν ἄσκησιν συμβάλλεσθαι πρὸς ἀρετῆς ἀνάληψιν. τὸν σοφὸν μήτε φθονήσειν μήτε ἐρασθήσεσθαι ἢ δεισιδαιμονήσειν· γίνεσθαι γὰρ ταῦτα παρὰ κενὴν δόξαν. λυπήσεσθαι μέντοι καὶ φοβήσεσθαι· φυσικῶς γὰρ 92 γίνεσθαι. καὶ τὸν πλοῦτον δὲ ποιητικὸν ἡδονῆς εἶναι, οὐ δι᾽ αὐτὸν αἱρετὸν ὄντα.

Τά τε πάθη καταληπτά. ἔλεγον οὖν αὐτά, οὐκ ἀφ᾽ ὧν γίνεται. ἀφίσταντο δὲ καὶ τῶν φυσικῶν διὰ τὴν ἐμφαινομένην ἀκαταληψίαν· τῶν δὲ λογικῶν διὰ τὴν εὐχρηστίαν ἥπτοντο. Μελέαγρος δ᾽ ἐν τῷ δευτέρῳ Περὶ δοξῶν καὶ Κλειτόμαχος ἐν τῷ πρώτῳ Περὶ αἱρέσεων φασὶν αὐτοὺς ἄχρηστα ἡγεῖσθαι τό τε φυσικὸν μέρος καὶ τὸ διαλεκτικόν. δύνασθαι γὰρ καὶ εὖ λέγειν καὶ δεισιδαιμονίας ἐκτὸς εἶναι καὶ τὸν περὶ θανάτου φόβον ἐκφεύγειν τὸν ⟨τὸν⟩ περὶ ἀγαθῶν καὶ κακῶν λόγον ἐκμεμαθη- 93 κότα. μηδέν τε εἶναι φύσει δίκαιον ἢ καλὸν ἢ αἰσχρόν, ἀλλὰ νόμῳ καὶ ἔθει. ὁ μέντοι σπουδαῖος

opposite of pleasure ; so that to accumulate the pleasures which are productive of happiness appears to them a most irksome business.

They do not accept the doctrine that every wise man lives pleasantly and every fool painfully, but regard it as true for the most part only. It is sufficient even if we enjoy but each single pleasure as it comes. They say that prudence is a good, though desirable not in itself but on account of its consequences ; that we make friends from interested motives, just as we cherish any part of the body so long as we have it ; that some of the virtues are found even in the foolish ; that bodily training contributes to the acquisition of virtue ; that the sage will not give way to envy or love or superstition, since these weaknesses are due to mere empty opinion ; he will, however, feel pain and fear, these being natural affections ; and that wealth too is productive of pleasure, though not desirable for its own sake.

They affirm that mental affections can be known, but not the objects from which they come ; and they abandoned the study of nature because of its apparent uncertainty, but fastened on logical inquiries because of their utility. But Meleager in his second book *On Philosophical Opinions*, and Clitomachus in his first book *On the Sects*, affirm that they maintain Dialectic as well as Physics to be useless, since, when one has learnt the theory of good and evil, it is possible to speak with propriety, to be free from superstition, and to escape the fear of death. They also held that nothing is just or honourable or base by nature, but only by convention and custom. Nevertheless the good man will be deterred from

οὐδὲν ἄτοπον πράξει διὰ τὰς ἐπικειμένας ζημίας
καὶ δόξας· εἶναι δὲ τὸν σοφόν. προκοπήν τε
ἀπολείπουσι καὶ ἐν φιλοσοφίᾳ καὶ ἐν τοῖς ἄλλοις.
φασὶ δὲ καὶ λυπεῖσθαι ἄλλον ἄλλου μᾶλλον, καὶ
τὰς αἰσθήσεις μὴ πάντοτε ἀληθεύειν.

Οἱ δὲ Ἡγησιακοὶ λεγόμενοι σκοποὺς μὲν εἶχον
τοὺς αὐτούς, ἡδονὴν καὶ πόνον. μήτε δὲ χάριν τι
εἶναι μήτε φιλίαν μήτε εὐεργεσίαν, διὰ τὸ μὴ δι’
αὐτὰ ταῦτα αἱρεῖσθαι ἡμᾶς αὐτά, ἀλλὰ διὰ τὰς
χρείας αὐτάς, ὧν ἀπόντων μηδ’ ἐκεῖνα ὑπάρχειν.
94 τὴν εὐδαιμονίαν ὅλως ἀδύνατον εἶναι· τὸ μὲν γὰρ
σῶμα πολλῶν ἀναπεπλῆσθαι παθημάτων, τὴν δὲ
ψυχὴν συμπαθεῖν τῷ σώματι καὶ ταράττεσθαι,
τὴν δὲ τύχην πολλὰ τῶν κατ’ ἐλπίδα κωλύειν,
ὥστε διὰ ταῦτα ἀνύπαρκτον τὴν εὐδαιμονίαν εἶναι.
τήν τε ζωὴν καὶ τὸν θάνατον αἱρετόν. φύσει τ’
οὐδὲν ἡδὺ ἢ ἀηδὲς ὑπελάμβανον· διὰ δὲ σπάνιν ἢ
ξενισμὸν ἢ κόρον τοὺς μὲν ἥδεσθαι, τοὺς δ’ ἀηδῶς
ἔχειν. πενίαν καὶ πλοῦτον πρὸς ἡδονῆς λόγον
εἶναι οὐδέν· μὴ γὰρ διαφερόντως ἥδεσθαι τοὺς
πλουσίους ἢ τοὺς πένητας. δουλείαν ἐπίσης ἐλευ-
θερίᾳ ἀδιάφορον πρὸς ἡδονῆς μέτρον, καὶ εὐγένειαν
95 δυσγενείᾳ, καὶ δόξαν ἀδοξίᾳ. καὶ τῷ μὲν ἄφρονι
τὸ ζῆν λυσιτελὲς εἶναι· τῷ δὲ φρονίμῳ ἀδιάφορον.
τόν τε σοφὸν ἑαυτοῦ ἕνεκα πάντα πράξειν· οὐδένα
γὰρ ἡγεῖσθαι τῶν ἄλλων ἐπίσης ἄξιον αὑτῷ. κἂν
γὰρ τὰ μέγιστα δοκῇ παρά του καρποῦσθαι, μὴ

222

wrong-doing by the penalties imposed and the pre-
judices that it would arouse.   Further that the wise
man really exists.   They allow progress to be attain-
able in philosophy as well as in other matters.   They
maintain that the pain of one man exceeds that of
another, and that the senses are not always true and
trustworthy.

The school of Hegesias, as it is called, adopted the
same ends, namely pleasure and pain.   In their view
there is no such thing as gratitude or friendship or
beneficence, because it is not for themselves that we
choose to do these things but simply from motives
of interest, apart from which such conduct is nowhere
found.   They denied the possibility of happiness, for
the body is infected with much suffering, while the
soul shares in the sufferings of the body and is a
prey to disturbance, and fortune often disappoints.
From all this it follows that happiness cannot be
realized.   Moreover, life and death are each desirable
in turn.   But that there is anything naturally
pleasant or unpleasant they deny ; when some men
are pleased and others pained by the same objects,
this is owing to the lack or rarity or surfeit of such
objects.   Poverty and riches have no relevance to
pleasure ; for neither the rich nor the poor as such
have any special share in pleasure.   Slavery and
freedom, nobility and low birth, honour and dis-
honour, are alike indifferent in a calculation of
pleasure.   To the fool life is advantageous, while to
the wise it is a matter of indifference.   The wise man
will be guided in all he does by his own interests,
for there is none other whom he regards as equally
deserving.   For supposing him to reap the greatest
advantages from another, they would not be equal to

DIOGENES LAERTIUS

εἶναι ἀντάξια ὧν αὐτὸς παράσχῃ. ἀνήρουν δὲ καὶ
τὰς αἰσθήσεις ‹ὡς› οὐκ ἀκριβούσας τὴν ἐπίγνωσιν,
τῶν τ' εὐλόγως φαινομένων πάντα πράττειν.
ἔλεγον τὰ ἁμαρτήματα συγγνώμης τυγχάνειν·
οὐ γὰρ ἑκόντα ἁμαρτάνειν, ἀλλά τινι πάθει κατ-
ηναγκασμένον. καὶ μὴ μισήσειν, μᾶλλον δὲ μετα-
διδάξειν. τόν τε σοφὸν οὐχ οὕτω πλεονάσειν ἐν
τῇ τῶν ἀγαθῶν αἱρέσει, ὡς ἐν τῇ τῶν κακῶν φυγῇ,
τέλος τιθέμενον τὸ μὴ ἐπιπόνως ζῆν μηδὲ λυπηρῶς·
96 ὃ δὴ περιγίνεσθαι τοῖς ἀδιαφορήσασι περὶ τὰ ποιητικὰ τῆς ἡδονῆς.

Οἱ δ' Ἀννικέρειοι τὰ μὲν ἄλλα κατὰ ταὐτὰ
τούτοις· ἀπέλιπον δὲ καὶ φιλίαν ἐν βίῳ καὶ χάριν
καὶ πρὸς γονέας τιμὴν καὶ ὑπὲρ πατρίδος τι
πράξειν. ὅθεν διὰ ταῦτα, κἂν ὀχλήσεις ἀναδέξηται
ὁ σοφός, οὐδὲν ἧττον εὐδαιμονήσειν, κἂν ὀλίγα
ἡδέα περιγένηται αὐτῷ. τήν τε τοῦ φίλου εὐδαιμονίαν δι' αὐτὴν μὴ εἶναι αἱρετήν· μηδὲ γὰρ
αἰσθητὴν τῷ πέλας ὑπάρχειν· μὴ εἶναί τε αὐτάρκη
τὸν λόγον πρὸς τὸ θαρρῆσαι καὶ τῆς τῶν πολλῶν
δόξης ὑπεράνω γενέσθαι· δεῖν δ' ἀνεθίζεσθαι διὰ
τὴν ἐκ πολλοῦ συντραφεῖσαν ἡμῖν φαύλην διάθεσιν.
97 τόν τε φίλον μὴ διὰ τὰς χρείας μόνον ἀποδέχεσθαι,
ὧν ὑπολειπουσῶν μὴ ἐπιστρέφεσθαι ἀλλὰ καὶ
παρὰ τὴν γεγονυῖαν εὔνοιαν, ἧς ἕνεκα καὶ πόνους
ὑπομενεῖν. καίτοι τιθέμενον ἡδονὴν τέλος καὶ
ἀχθόμενον ἐπὶ τῷ στέρεσθαι αὐτῆς ὅμως ἑκουσίως
ὑπομενεῖν διὰ τὴν πρὸς τὸν φίλον στοργήν.

Οἱ δὲ Θεοδώρειοι κληθέντες τὴν μὲν ὀνομασίαν

what he contributes himself. They also disallow the claims of the senses, because they do not lead to accurate knowledge. Whatever appears rational should be done. They affirmed that allowance should be made for errors, for no man errs voluntarily, but under constraint of some suffering ; that we should not hate men, but rather teach them better. The wise man will not have so much advantage over others in the choice of goods as in the avoidance of evils, making it his end to live without pain of body or mind. This then, they say, is the advantage accruing to those who make no distinction between any of the objects which produce pleasure.

The school of Anniceris in other respects agreed with them, but admitted that friendship and gratitude and respect for parents do exist in real life, and that a good man will sometimes act out of patriotic motives. Hence, if the wise man receive annoyance, he will be none the less happy even if few pleasures accrue to him. The happiness of a friend is not in itself desirable, for it is not felt by his neighbour. Instruction is not sufficient in itself to inspire us with confidence and to make us rise superior to the opinion of the multitude. Habits must be formed because of the bad disposition which has grown up in us from the first. A friend should be cherished not merely for his utility—for, if that fails, we should then no longer associate with him—but for the good feeling for the sake of which we shall even endure hardships. Nay, though we make pleasure the end and are annoyed when deprived of it, we shall nevertheless cheerfully endure this because of our love to our friend.

The Theodoreans derived their name from Theo-

ἔσπασαν ἀπὸ Θεοδώρου τοῦ προγεγραμμένου,
καὶ δόγμασιν ἐχρήσαντο τοῖς αὐτοῦ. ἦν δ' ὁ
Θεόδωρος παντάπασιν ἀναιρῶν τὰς περὶ θεῶν
δόξας· καὶ αὐτοῦ περιετύχομεν βιβλίῳ ἐπιγεγραμ-
μένῳ Περὶ θεῶν, οὐκ εὐκαταφρονήτῳ· ἐξ οὗ φασιν
Ἐπίκουρον λαβόντα τὰ πλεῖστα εἰπεῖν.

98 Ἤκουσε δὲ καὶ Ἀννικέριδος ὁ Θεόδωρος καὶ
Διονυσίου τοῦ διαλεκτικοῦ, καθά φησιν Ἀντισθένης ἐν Φιλοσόφων διαδοχαῖς. τέλος δ' ὑπ-
ελάμβανε χαρὰν καὶ λύπην· τὴν μὲν ἐπὶ φρονήσει,
τὴν δ' ἐπὶ ἀφροσύνῃ· ἀγαθὰ δὲ φρόνησιν καὶ δικαιοσύνην, κακὰ δὲ τὰς ἐναντίας ἕξεις, μέσα δὲ ἡδονὴν
καὶ πόνον. ἀνῄρει δὲ καὶ φιλίαν, διὰ τὸ μήτ' ἐν
ἄφροσιν αὐτὴν εἶναι, μήτ' ἐν σοφοῖς. τοῖς μὲν
γὰρ τῆς χρείας ἀναιρεθείσης καὶ τὴν φιλίαν ἐκποδὼν εἶναι· τοὺς δὲ σοφοὺς αὐτάρκεις ὑπάρχοντας
μὴ δεῖσθαι φίλων. ἔλεγε δὲ καὶ εὔλογον εἶναι τὸν
σπουδαῖον ὑπὲρ τῆς πατρίδος μὴ ἐξαγαγεῖν αὐτόν·
οὐ γὰρ ἀποβαλεῖν τὴν φρόνησιν ἕνεκα τῆς τῶν
ἀφρόνων ὠφελείας.

99 Εἶναί τε πατρίδα τὸν κόσμον. κλέψειν τε καὶ
μοιχεύσειν καὶ ἱεροσυλήσειν ἐν καιρῷ· μηδὲν γὰρ
τούτων φύσει αἰσχρὸν εἶναι, τῆς ἐπ' αὐτοῖς δόξης
αἰρομένης, ἣ σύγκειται ἕνεκα τῆς τῶν ἀφρόνων
συνοχῆς. φανερῶς δὲ τοῖς ἐρωμένοις ἄνευ πάσης
ὑφοράσεως χρήσεσθαι τὸν σοφόν. διὸ καὶ τοιού-
τους λόγους ἠρώτα· " ἆρά γε γυνὴ γραμματικὴ
χρήσιμος ἂν εἴη παρ' ὅσον γραμματική ἐστι; "
" ναί." " καὶ παῖς καὶ νεανίσκος γραμματικὸς
χρήσιμος ἂν εἴη παρ' ὅσον γραμματικός ἐστι; "

dorus, who has already been mentioned, and adopted his doctrines. Theodorus was a man who utterly rejected the current belief in the gods. And I have come across a book of his entitled *Of the Gods* which is not contemptible. From that book, they say, Epicurus borrowed most of what he wrote on the subject.

Theodorus was also a pupil of Anniceris and of Dionysius the dialectician, as Antisthenes mentions in his *Successions of Philosophers*. He considered joy and grief to be the supreme good and evil, the one brought about by wisdom, the other by folly. Wisdom and justice he called goods, and their opposites evils, pleasure and pain being intermediate to good and evil. Friendship he rejected because it did not exist between the unwise nor between the wise ; with the former, when the want is removed, the friendship disappears, whereas the wise are self-sufficient and have no need of friends. It was reasonable, as he thought, for the good man not to risk his life in the defence of his country, for he would never throw wisdom away to benefit the unwise.

He said the world was his country. Theft, adultery, and sacrilege would be allowable upon occasion, since none of these acts is by nature base, if once you have removed the prejudice against them, which is kept up in order to hold the foolish multitude together. The wise man would indulge his passions openly without the least regard to circumstances. Hence he would use such arguments as this. " Is a woman who is skilled in grammar useful in so far as she is skilled in grammar ? " " Yes." " And is a boy or a youth skilled in grammar useful in so far as he is skilled in grammar ? " " Yes." " Again,

" ναί." " οὐκοῦν καὶ γυνὴ καλὴ χρησίμη ἂν εἴη
παρ' ὅσον καλή ἐστι, καὶ παῖς καὶ νεανίσκος καλὸς
χρήσιμος ἂν εἴη παρ' ὅσον καλός ἐστι;" "ναί."
" καὶ παῖς ἄρα καὶ νεανίσκος καλὸς πρὸς τοῦτ' ἂν
100 εἴη χρήσιμος πρὸς ὃ καλός ἐστι;" "ναί." "ἔστι
δὲ χρήσιμος πρὸς τὸ πλησιάζειν." ὧν δεδομένων
ἐπῆγεν· " οὐκοῦν εἴ τις πλησιασμῷ χρώμενος παρ'
ὅσον χρήσιμός ἐστιν, οὐ διαμαρτάνει· οὐδ' ἄρα εἰ
κάλλει χρήσαιτο παρ' ὅσον χρήσιμόν ἐστι, διαμαρ-
τήσεται." τοιαῦτα ἄττα διερωτῶν ἴσχυε τῷ λόγῳ.

Δοκεῖ δὲ θεὸς κληθῆναι, Στίλπωνος αὐτὸν
ἐρωτήσαντος οὕτως, " ἆρά γε, Θεόδωρε, ὃ φὴς
εἶναι, τοῦτο καὶ εἶ;" ἐπινεύσαντος δέ, " φὴς δ'
εἶναι θεόν;" τοῦ δ' ὁμολογήσαντος, " θεὸς εἶ
ἄρα," ἔφη. δεξαμένου δ' ἀσμένως, γελάσας φησίν,
" ἀλλ', ὦ μόχθηρε, τῷ λόγῳ τούτῳ καὶ κολοιὸς
ἂν ὁμολογήσειας εἶναι καὶ ἄλλα μυρία."

101 Ὁ δ' οὖν Θεόδωρος προσκαθίσας ποτὲ Εὐρυ-
κλείδῃ τῷ ἱεροφάντῃ, " λέγε μοι," ἔφη, " Εὐρυ-
κλείδη, τίνες εἰσὶν οἱ ἀσεβοῦντες περὶ τὰ μυστήρια."
εἰπόντος δ' ἐκείνου, " οἱ τοῖς ἀμυήτοις αὐτὰ
ἐκφέροντες," " ἀσεβεῖς ἄρα," ἔφη, " καὶ σύ, τοῖς
ἀμυήτοις διηγούμενος." καὶ μέντοι παρ' ὀλίγον
ἐκινδύνευσεν εἰς Ἄρειον ἀναχθῆναι πάγον, εἰ μὴ
Δημήτριος ὁ Φαληρεὺς αὐτὸν ἐρρύσατο. Ἀμφι-
κράτης δ' ἐν τῷ Περὶ ἐνδόξων ἀνδρῶν φησι κώνειον
αὐτὸν πιεῖν καταδικασθέντα.

102 Διατρίβων δὲ παρὰ Πτολεμαίῳ τῷ Λάγου
ἀπεστάλη ποθ' ὑπ' αὐτοῦ πρὸς Λυσίμαχον πρε-
σβευτής. ὅτε καὶ παρρησιαζομένῳ φησὶν ὁ Λυσί-
μαχος, " λέγε μοι, Θεόδωρε, οὐ σὺ εἶ ὁ ἐκπεσὼν
Ἀθήνηθεν;" καὶ ὅς, " ὀρθῶς ἀκήκοας· ἡ γὰρ τῶν

is a woman who is beautiful useful in so far as she is beautiful? And the use of beauty is to be enjoyed?" "Yes." When this was admitted, he would press the argument to the conclusion, namely, that he who uses anything for the purpose for which it is useful does no wrong. And by some such interrogatories he would carry his point.

He appears to have been called θεός (god) in consequence of the following argument addressed to him by Stilpo. "Are you, Theodorus, what you declare yourself to be?" To this he assented, and Stilpo continued, "And do you say you are god?" To this he agreed. "Then it follows that you are god." Theodorus accepted this, and Stilpo said with a smile, "But, you rascal, at this rate you would allow yourself to be a jackdaw and ten thousand other things."

However, Theodorus, sitting on one occasion beside Euryclides, the hierophant, began, "Tell me, Euryclides, who they are who violate the mysteries?" Euryclides replied, "Those who disclose them to the uninitiated." "Then you violate them," said Theodorus, "when you explain them to the uninitiated." Yet he would hardly have escaped from being brought before the Areopagus if Demetrius of Phalerum had not rescued him. And Amphicrates in his book *Upon Illustrious Men* says he was condemned to drink the hemlock.

For a while he stayed at the court of Ptolemy the son of Lagus, and was once sent by him as ambassador to Lysimachus. And on this occasion his language was so bold that Lysimachus said, "Tell me, are you not the Theodorus who was banished from Athens?" To which he replied, "Your in-

Ἀθηναίων πόλις οὐ δυναμένη με φέρειν, ὥσπερ ἡ
Σεμέλη τὸν Διόνυσον, ἐξέβαλε." πάλιν δ' εἰπόντος
τοῦ Λυσιμάχου, " [βλέπε] ὅπως μὴ παρέσῃ πρὸς
ἡμᾶς ἔτι," " οὐκ ἄν," ἔφη, " ἂν μὴ Πτολεμαῖος
ἀποστείλῃ." Μίθρου δὲ τοῦ διοικητοῦ τοῦ Λυσιμάχου παρεστῶτος καὶ εἰπόντος, " ἔοικας σὺ μὴ
μόνον θεοὺς ἀγνοεῖν ἀλλὰ καὶ βασιλέας," " πῶς,"
εἶπεν, " ἀγνοῶ, ὅπου γε καὶ θεοῖς σε ἐχθρὸν εἶναι
νομίζω;" φασὶ δέ ποτε ἐν Κορίνθῳ παρέρχεσθαι
αὐτὸν συχνοὺς ἐπαγόμενον μαθητάς, Μητροκλέα
δὲ τὸν κυνικὸν σκάνδικας πλύνοντα εἰπεῖν, " σὺ
ὁ σοφιστὴς οὐκ ἂν τοσούτων ἔχρῃζες μαθητῶν, εἰ
λάχανα ἔπλυνες·" τὸν δ' ὑπολαβόντ' εἰπεῖν, " καὶ
σὺ εἴπερ ἀνθρώποις ᾔδεις ὁμιλεῖν, οὐκ ἂν τούτοις
103 τοῖς λαχάνοις ἐχρῶ." τὸ ὅμοιον ἀναφέρεται, καθὰ
προείρηται, καὶ εἰς Διογένην καὶ Ἀρίστιππον.

Τοιοῦτος μὲν ὁ Θεόδωρος κἂν τούτοις. τελευ-
ταῖον δ' εἰς Κυρήνην ἀπελθὼν καὶ Μάγᾳ συμβιοὺς
ἐν πάσῃ τιμῇ διετέλει τυγχάνων. ἔνθεν τὸ πρῶτον
ἐκβαλλόμενος λέγεται χάριέν τι εἰπεῖν· ἔφη γάρ,
" καλῶς ποιεῖτε, ἄνδρες Κυρηναῖοι, ἐκ τῆς Λιβύης
εἰς τὴν Ἑλλάδα με ἐξορίζοντες."

Θεόδωροι δὲ γεγόνασιν εἴκοσι· πρῶτος Σάμιος,
υἱὸς Ῥοίκου. οὗτός ἐστιν ὁ συμβουλεύσας ἄνθρακας ὑποτιθέναι τοῖς θεμελίοις τοῦ ἐν Ἐφέσῳ
νεώ· καθύγρου γὰρ ὄντος τοῦ τόπου τοὺς ἄνθρακας
ἔφη τὸ ξυλῶδες ἀποβαλόντας αὐτὸ τὸ στερεὸν
ἀπαθὲς ἕξειν[1] ὕδατι. δεύτερος Κυρηναῖος, γεω-

---

[1] ἕξειν] corr. Richards : ἔχειν vulg.

ᵃ See § 68.

formation is correct, for, when Athens could not bear me any more than Semele could Dionysus, she cast me out." And upon Lysimachus adding, "Take care you do not come here again," "I never will," said he, "unless Ptolemy sends me." Mithras, the king's minister, standing by and saying, "It seems that you can ignore not only gods but kings as well," Theodorus replied, "How can you say that I ignore the gods when I regard you as hateful to the gods?" He is said on one occasion in Corinth to have walked abroad with a numerous train of pupils, and Metrocles the Cynic, who was washing chervil, remarked, "You, sophist that you are, would not have wanted all these pupils if you had washed vegetables." Thereupon Theodorus retorted, "And you, if you had known how to associate with men, would have had no use for these vegetables." A similar anecdote is told of Diogenes and Aristippus, as mentioned above.[a]

Such was the character of Theodorus and his surroundings. At last he retired to Cyrene, where he lived with Magas and continued to be held in high honour. The first time that he was expelled from Cyrene he is credited with a witty remark: "Many thanks,[b] men of Cyrene," said he, "for driving me from Libya into Greece."

Some twenty persons have borne the name of Theodorus: (1) a Samian, the son of Rhoecus. He it was who advised laying charcoal embers under the foundations of the temple in Ephesus; for, as the ground was very damp, the ashes, being free from woody fibre, would retain a solidity which is actually proof against moisture. (2) A Cyrenaean geometer,

---

[b] Or, if κακῶς is the right reading, "It is unkind of you." καλῶς is Stephanus's conjecture.

μέτρης οὗ διήκουσε Πλάτων· τρίτος ὁ προγεγραμ-
μένος φιλόσοφος· τέταρτος οὗ τὸ φωνασκικὸν
104 φέρεται βιβλίον πάγκαλον· πέμπτος ὁ περὶ τῶν
νομοποιῶν πεπραγματευμένος, ἀρξάμενος ἀπὸ
Τερπάνδρου· ἕκτος στωικός· ἕβδομος ὁ τὰ περὶ
Ῥωμαίων πεπραγματευμένος· ὄγδοος Συρακόσιος,
περὶ τακτικῶν γεγραφώς· ἔνατος Βυζάντιος, ἀπὸ
λόγων πολιτικῶν· δέκατος ὁμοίως, οὗ Ἀριστοτέλης μνημονεύει διὰ τῆς ἐπιτομῆς τῶν ῥητόρων·
ἑνδέκατος Θηβαῖος, ἀνδριαντοποιός· δωδέκατος
ζωγράφος, οὗ μέμνηται Πολέμων· τρισκαιδέκατος
ζωγράφος, Ἀθηναῖος, ὑπὲρ οὗ γράφει Μηνόδοτος·
τεσσαρεσκαιδέκατος Ἐφέσιος, ζωγράφος, οὗ μέμνηται Θεοφάνης ἐν τῷ περὶ γραφικῆς· πεντε-
καιδέκατος ποιητὴς ἐπιγραμμάτων· ἑκκαιδέκατος
γεγραφὼς περὶ ποιητῶν· ἑπτακαιδέκατος ἰατρός,
Ἀθηναίου μαθητής· ὀκτωκαιδέκατος Χῖος, φιλόσοφος στωικός· ἐννεακαιδέκατος Μιλήσιος, καὶ
αὐτὸς στωικὸς φιλόσοφος· εἰκοστὸς ποιητὴς τραγῳδίας.

Κεφ. θ΄. ΦΑΙΔΩΝ

105 Φαίδων Ἠλεῖος, τῶν εὐπατριδῶν, συνεάλω τῇ
πατρίδι καὶ ἠναγκάσθη στῆναι ἐπ’ οἰκήματος·
ἀλλὰ τὸ θύριον προστιθεὶς μετεῖχε Σωκράτους,
ἕως αὐτὸν λυτρώσασθαι τοὺς περὶ Ἀλκιβιάδην ἢ
Κρίτωνα προύτρεψε· καὶ τοὐντεῦθεν ἐλευθερίως
ἐφιλοσόφει. Ἱερώνυμος δ’ ἐν τῷ Περὶ ἐποχῆς
καθαπτόμενος δοῦλον αὐτὸν εἴρηκε. διαλόγους
δὲ συνέγραψε γνησίους μὲν Ζώπυρον, Σίμωνα,
καὶ δισταζόμενον Νικίαν, Μήδιον, ὃν φασί τινες

whose lectures Plato attended. (3) The philosopher above referred to. (4) The author of a fine work on practising the voice. (5) An authority upon musical composers from Terpander onwards. (6) A Stoic. (7) A writer upon the Romans. (8) A Syracusan who wrote upon Tactics. (9) A Byzantine, famous for his political speeches. (10) Another, equally famous, mentioned by Aristotle in his Epitome of Orators. (11) A Theban sculptor. (12) A painter, mentioned by Polemo. (13) An Athenian painter, of whom Menodotus writes. (14) An Ephesian painter, who is mentioned by Theophanes in his work upon painting. (15) A poet who wrote epigrams. (16) A writer on poets. (17) A physician, pupil of Athenaeus. (18) A Stoic philosopher of Chios. (19) A Milesian, also a Stoic philosopher (20) A tragic poet.

CHAPTER 9. PHAEDO

Phaedo was a native of Elis, of noble family, who on the fall of that city was taken captive and forcibly consigned to a house of ill-fame. But he would close the door and so contrive to join Socrates' circle, and in the end Socrates induced Alcibiades or Crito with their friends to ransom him ; from that time onwards he studied philosophy as became a free man. Hieronymus in his work *On Suspense of Judgement* attacks him and calls him a slave. Of the dialogues which bear his name the *Zopyrus* and *Simon* are genuine ; the *Nicias* is doubtful ; the *Medius* is said by some to be the work of Aeschines, while

Αἰσχίνου, οἱ δὲ Πολυαίνου· Ἀντίμαχον ἢ Πρε-
σβύτας· καὶ οὗτος διστάζεται· σκυτικοὺς λόγους·
καὶ τούτους τινὲς Αἰσχίνου φασί.

Διάδοχος δ' αὐτοῦ Πλείστανος Ἠλεῖος, καὶ
τρίτοι ἀπ' αὐτοῦ οἱ περὶ Μενέδημον τὸν Ἐρετριέα
καὶ Ἀσκληπιάδην τὸν Φλιάσιον, μετάγοντες ἀπὸ
Στίλπωνος. καὶ ἕως μὲν τούτων Ἠλιακοὶ προσηγορεύοντο, ἀπὸ δὲ Μενεδήμου Ἐρετρικοί· περὶ οὗ
λέξομεν ὕστερον διὰ τὸ καὶ αὐτὸν κατάρχειν
αἱρέσεως.

Κεφ. ι΄. ΕΥΚΛΕΙΔΗΣ

116 Εὐκλείδης ἀπὸ Μεγάρων τῶν πρὸς Ἰσθμῷ, ἢ
Γελῶος κατ' ἐνίους, ὥς φησιν Ἀλέξανδρος ἐν
Διαδοχαῖς. οὗτος καὶ τὰ Παρμενίδεια μετεχειρί-
ζετο, καὶ οἱ ἀπ' αὐτοῦ Μεγαρικοὶ προσηγορεύοντο,
εἶτ' ἐριστικοί, ὕστερον δὲ διαλεκτικοί, οὓς οὕτως
ὠνόμασε πρῶτος Διονύσιος ὁ Χαλκηδόνιος, διὰ
τὸ πρὸς ἐρώτησιν καὶ ἀπόκρισιν τοὺς λόγους
διατίθεσθαι. πρὸς τοῦτόν φησιν ὁ Ἑρμόδωρος
ἀφικέσθαι Πλάτωνα καὶ τοὺς λοιποὺς φιλοσόφους
μετὰ τὴν τοῦ Σωκράτους τελευτήν, δείσαντας τὴν
ὠμότητα τῶν τυράννων. οὗτος ἓν τὸ ἀγαθὸν
ἀπεφαίνετο πολλοῖς ὀνόμασι καλούμενον· ὁτὲ μὲν
γὰρ φρόνησιν, ὁτὲ δὲ θεόν, καὶ ἄλλοτε νοῦν καὶ τὰ
λοιπά. τὰ δ' ἀντικείμενα τῷ ἀγαθῷ ἀνήρει, μὴ
εἶναι φάσκων.

117 Ταῖς τε ἀποδείξεσιν ἐνίστατο οὐ κατὰ λήμματα,
ἀλλὰ κατ' ἐπιφοράν. καὶ τὸν διὰ παραβολῆς
λόγον ἀνήρει, λέγων ἤτοι ἐξ ὁμοίων αὐτὸν ἢ ἐξ

---

[a] So called to distinguish it from Megara Hyblaea, in
Sicily.

others ascribe it to Polyaenus ; the *Antimachus* or *The Elders* is also doubted ; the *Cobblers' Tales* are also by some attributed to Aeschines.

He was succeeded by Plistanus of Elis, and a generation later by Menedemus of Eretria and Asclepiades of Phlius, who came over from Stilpo's school. Till then the school was known as that of Elis, but from Menedemus onward it was called the Eretrian school. Of Menedemus we shall have to speak hereafter, because he too started a new school.

Chapter 10. EUCLIDES

Euclides was a native of Megara on the Isthmus,[c] or according to some of Gela, as Alexander states in his *Successions of Philosophers*. He applied himself to the writings of Parmenides, and his followers were called Megarians after him, then Eristics, and at a later date Dialecticians, that name having first been given to them by Dionysius of Chalcedon because they put their arguments into the form of question and answer. Hermodorus tells us that, after the death of Socrates, Plato and the rest of the philosophers came to him, being alarmed at the cruelty of the tyrants. He held the supreme good to be really one, though called by many names, sometimes wisdom, sometimes God, and again Mind, and so forth. But all that is contradictory of the good he used to reject, declaring that it had no existence.

When he impugned a demonstration, it was not the premises but the conclusion that he attacked. He rejected the argument from analogy, declaring that it must be taken either from similars or from

ἀνομοίων συνίστασθαι· καὶ εἰ μὲν ἐξ ὁμοίων, περὶ
αὐτὰ δεῖν μᾶλλον ἢ οἷς ὅμοιά ἐστιν ἀναστρέφεσθαι,
εἰ δ' ἐξ ἀνομοίων, παρέλκειν τὴν παράθεσιν. διὰ
ταῦτα δὲ καὶ περὶ αὐτοῦ ταῦτά φησι Τίμων,
προσπαρατρώγων καὶ τοὺς λοιποὺς Σωκρατικούς·

ἀλλ' οὔ μοι τούτων φλεδόνων μέλει, οὐδὲ γὰρ ἄλλου
οὐδενός, οὐ Φαίδωνος, ὅτις γένετ', οὐδ' ἐριδάντεω
Εὐκλείδεω, Μεγαρεῦσιν ὃς ἔμβαλε λύσσαν ἐρισμοῦ.

108 Διαλόγους δὲ συνέγραψεν ἕξ, Λαμπρίαν, Αἰσχίνην,
Φοίνικα, Κρίτωνα, Ἀλκιβιάδην, Ἐρωτικόν. τῆς
δ' Εὐκλείδου διαδοχῆς ἐστι καὶ Εὐβουλίδης ὁ
Μιλήσιος, ὃς καὶ πολλοὺς ἐν διαλεκτικῇ λόγους
ἠρώτησε, τόν τε ψευδόμενον καὶ τὸν διαλανθάνοντα
καὶ Ἠλέκτραν καὶ ἐγκεκαλυμμένον καὶ σωρίτην
καὶ κερατίνην καὶ φαλακρόν. περὶ τούτου φησί
τις τῶν κωμικῶν·

οὐριστικὸς δ' Εὐβουλίδης κερατίνας ἐρωτῶν
καὶ ψευδαλαζόσιν λόγοις τοὺς ῥήτορας κυλίων
ἀπῆλθ' ἔχων Δημοσθένους τὴν ῥωποπερπερήθραν.

ἐῴκει γὰρ αὐτοῦ καὶ Δημοσθένης ἀκηκοέναι καὶ
109 ῥωβικώτερος ὢν παύσασθαι. ὁ δ' Εὐβουλίδης καὶ
πρὸς Ἀριστοτέλην διεφέρετο, καὶ πολλὰ αὐτὸν δια-
βέβληκε.
Μεταξὺ δὲ ἄλλων ὄντων τῆς Εὐβουλίδου διαδοχῆς Ἀλεξῖνος ἐγένετο Ἠλεῖος, ἀνὴρ φιλονεικό-
τατος· διὸ καὶ Ἐλεγξῖνος ἐπεκλήθη. διεφέρετο
δὲ μάλιστα πρὸς Ζήνωνα. φησὶ δ' Ἕρμιππος
περὶ αὐτοῦ ὡς ἄρα ἀπελθὼν ἐκ τῆς Ἤλιδος εἰς
Ὀλυμπίαν αὐτόθι φιλοσοφοίη. τῶν δὲ μαθητῶν
αὐτοῦ πυνθανομένων διὰ τί τῇδε κατοικεῖ, φάναι

236

dissimilars. If it were drawn from similars, it is with these and not with their analogies that their arguments should deal ; if from dissimilars, it is gratuitous to set them side by side. Hence Timon says of him, with a side hit at the other Socratics as well[a] :

But I care not for these babblers, nor for anyone besides, not for Phaedo whoever he be, nor wrangling Euclides, who inspired the Megarians with a frenzied love of controversy.

He wrote six dialogues, entitled *Lamprias, Aeschines, Phoenix, Crito, Alcibiades,* and a *Discourse on Love.* To the school of Euclides belongs Eubulides of Miletus, the author of many dialectical arguments in an interrogatory form, namely, *The Liar, The Disguised, Electra, The Veiled Figure, The Sorites, The Horned One,* and *The Bald Head.* Of him it is said by one of the Comic poets[b] :

Eubulides the Eristic, who propounded his quibbles about horns and confounded the orators with falsely pretentious arguments, is gone with all the braggadocio of a Demosthenes.

Demosthenes was probably his pupil and thereby improved his faulty pronunciation of the letter R. Eubulides kept up a controversy with Aristotle and said much to discredit him.

Among other members the school of Eubulides included Alexinus of Elis, a man very fond of controversy, for which reason he was called Elenxinus. In particular he kept up a controversy with Zeno. Hermippus says of him that he left Elis and removed to Olympia, where he studied philosophy. His pupils inquired why he took up his abode here, and were

[a] Fr. 28 D.   [b] Meineke, *C.G.F.* iv. 618.

βούλεσθαι αἴρεσιν συστήσασθαι ἣν Ὀλυμπικὴν
κληθήσεσθαι. τοὺς δὲ καὶ τοῖς ἐφοδίοις θλιβομέ-
νους καὶ τὸ χωρίον νοσερὸν καταγνόντας ἀπελθεῖν,
καὶ τοῦ λοιποῦ διατρίβειν ἔρημον τὸν Ἀλεξῖνον
σὺν οἰκέτῃ μόνῳ· ἔπειτα μέντοι νηχόμενον ἐν τῷ
Ἀλφειῷ νυχθῆναι καλάμῳ καὶ οὕτω τελευτῆσαι.
110 Καὶ ἔστιν εἰς αὐτὸν ἡμῶν οὕτως ἔχον·

> οὐκ ἄρα μῦθος ἦν ἐκεῖνος εἰκαῖος,
>   ὡς ἀτυχής τις ἐὼν
> τὸν πόδα κολυμβῶν περιέπειρέ πως ἥλῳ.
>   καὶ γὰρ ὁ σεμνὸς ἀνήρ,
> πρὶν Ἀλφεόν ποτ᾽ ἐκπερᾶν, Ἀλεξῖνος
>   θνῆσκε νυγεὶς καλάμῳ.

γέγραφε δ᾽ οὐ μόνον πρὸς Ζήνωνα, ἀλλὰ καὶ ἄλλα
βιβλία καὶ πρὸς Ἔφορον τὸν ἱστοριογράφον.

Εὐβουλίδου δὲ καὶ Εὔφαντος γέγονε ⟨γνώριμος⟩
ὁ Ὀλύνθιος, ἱστορίας γεγραφὼς τὰς κατὰ τοὺς
χρόνους τοὺς ἑαυτοῦ. ἐποίησε δὲ καὶ τραγῳδίας
πλείους, ἐν αἷς εὐδοκίμει κατὰ τοὺς ἀγῶνας.
γέγονε δὲ καὶ Ἀντιγόνου τοῦ βασιλέως διδάσκαλος,
πρὸς ὃν καὶ λόγον γέγραφε Περὶ βασιλείας σφόδρα
εὐδοκιμοῦντα. τὸν βίον δὲ γήρᾳ κατέστρεψεν.
111 Εἰσὶ δὲ καὶ ἄλλοι διακηκοότες Εὐβουλίδου, ἐν οἷς
καὶ Ἀπολλώνιος ὁ Κρόνος, οὗ Διόδωρος Ἀμεινίου
Ἰασεύς, καὶ αὐτὸς Κρόνος ἐπίκλην, περὶ οὗ φησι
Καλλίμαχος ἐν ἐπιγράμμασιν·

> αὐτὸς ὁ Μῶμος
> ἔγραφεν ἐν τοίχοις, " ὁ Κρόνος ἐστὶ σοφός."

ἦν δὲ καὶ οὗτος διαλεκτικός, πρῶτος δόξας εὑρη-

told that it was his intention to found a school which should be called the Olympian school. But as their provisions ran short and they found the place unhealthy, they left it, and for the rest of his days Alexinus lived in solitude with a single servant. And some time afterwards, as he was swimming in the Alpheus, the point of a reed ran into him, and of this injury he died.

I have composed the following lines upon him [a]:

It was not then a vain tale that once an unfortunate man, while diving, pierced his foot somehow with a nail; since that great man Alexinus, before he could cross the Alpheus, was pricked by a reed and met his death.

He has written not only a reply to Zeno but other works, including one against Ephorus the historian.

To the school of Eubulides also belonged Euphantus of Olynthus, who wrote a history of his own times. He was besides a poet and wrote several tragedies, with which he made a great reputation at the festivals. He taught King Antigonus [b] and dedicated to him a work *On Kingship* which was very popular. He died of old age.

There are also other pupils of Eubulides, amongst them Apollonius surnamed Cronus. He had a pupil Diodorus, the son of Ameinias of Iasus, who was also nicknamed Cronus.[c] Callimachus in his *Epigrams* says of him:

Momus himself chalked up on the walls " Cronus is wise."

He too was a dialectician and was supposed to have been the first who discovered the arguments

---

[a] *Anth. Plan.* iii. 129.

[b] *i.e.* Antigonus Doson, born 262 B.C.   *Cf. F.H.G.* iii. 20.

[c] See Strabo xiv. 658, who says the nickname was transferred from the teacher to the more celebrated pupil.

κέναι τὸν ἐγκεκαλυμμένον καὶ κερατίνην λόγον
κατά τινας. οὗτος παρὰ Πτολεμαίῳ τῷ Σωτῆρι
διατρίβων λόγους τινὰς διαλεκτικοὺς ἠρωτήθη
πρὸς Στίλπωνος· καὶ μὴ δυνάμενος παραχρῆμα
διαλύσασθαι, ὑπὸ τοῦ βασιλέως τά τε ἄλλα ἐπ-
ετιμήθη καὶ δὴ καὶ Κρόνος ἤκουσεν ἐν σκώμματος
112 μέρει. ἐξελθὼν δὴ τοῦ συμποσίου καὶ λόγον
γράψας περὶ τοῦ προβλήματος ἀθυμίᾳ τὸν βίον
κατέστρεψε. καὶ ἔστιν ἡμῶν εἰς αὐτόν·

Κρόνε Διόδωρε, τίς σε δαιμόνων κακῇ
ἀθυμίῃ ξυνείρυσεν,
ἵν' αὐτὸς αὑτὸν ἐμβάλῃς εἰς Τάρταρον
Στίλπωνος οὐ λύσας ἔπη
αἰνιγματώδη; τοιγὰρ εὑρέθης Κρόνος
ἔξωθε τοῦ ῥῶ κάππα τε.

Τῶν δ' ἀπ' Εὐκλείδου ἐστὶ καὶ Ἰχθύας Μετάλλου,
ἀνὴρ γενναῖος, πρὸς ὃν καὶ Διογένης ὁ κυνικὸς
διάλογον πεποίηται· Κλεινόμαχός θ' ὁ Θούριος,
ὃς πρῶτος περὶ ἀξιωμάτων καὶ κατηγορημάτων
καὶ τῶν τοιούτων συνέγραψε· καὶ Στίλπων ὁ
Μεγαρεύς, διασημότατος φιλόσοφος, περὶ οὗ
λεκτέον.

Κεφ. ια΄. ΣΤΙΛΠΩΝ

113 Στίλπων Μεγαρεὺς τῆς Ἑλλάδος διήκουσε μὲν
τῶν ἀπ' Εὐκλείδου τινῶν· οἱ δὲ καὶ αὐτοῦ Εὐκλείδου ἀκοῦσαί φασιν αὐτόν, ἀλλὰ καὶ Θρασυμάχου
τοῦ Κορινθίου, ὃς ἦν Ἰχθύα γνώριμος, καθά φησιν
Ἡρακλείδης. τοσοῦτον δ' εὑρεσιλογίᾳ καὶ σοφι-
στείᾳ προῆγε τοὺς ἄλλους, ὥστε μικροῦ δεῆσαι

known as the " Veiled Figure " and the " Horned One." When he was staying with Ptolemy Soter, he had certain dialectical questions addressed to him by Stilpo, and, not being able to solve them on the spot, he was reproached by the king and, among other slights, the nickname Cronus was applied to him by way of derision. He left the banquet and, after writing a pamphlet upon the logical problem, ended his days in despondency. Upon him too I have written lines [a] :

> Diodorus Cronus, what sad fate
>   Buried you in despair,
> So that you hastened to the shades below,
>   Perplexed by Stilpo's quibbles?
> You would deserve your name of Cronus better
>   If C and R were gone.[b]

The successors of Euclides include Ichthyas, the son of Metallus, an excellent man, to whom Diogenes the Cynic has addressed one of his dialogues ; Clinomachus of Thurii, who was the first to write about propositions, predications and the like ; and Stilpo of Megara, a most distinguished philosopher, of whom we have now to treat.

Chapter 11. STILPO

Stilpo, a citizen of Megara in Greece, was a pupil of some of the followers of Euclides, although others make him a pupil of Euclides himself, and furthermore of Thrasymachus of Corinth, who was the friend of Ichthyas, according to Heraclides. And so far did he excel all the rest in inventiveness and sophistry that nearly the whole of Greece was attracted to

---

[a] *Anth. Plan.* vii. 19.   [b] Leaving ὄνος = " ass."

241

πᾶσαν τὴν Ἑλλάδα ἀφορῶσαν εἰς αὐτὸν μεγαρίσαι.
περὶ τούτου φησὶ Φίλιππος ὁ Μεγαρικὸς κατὰ
λέξιν οὕτω· '' παρὰ μὲν γὰρ Θεοφράστου Μητρόδωρον τὸν θεωρητικὸν καὶ Τιμαγόραν τὸν Γελῶιον
ἀπέσπασε, παρ' Ἀριστοτέλους δὲ τοῦ Κυρηναϊκοῦ
Κλείταρχον καὶ Σιμμίαν· ἀπὸ δὲ τῶν διαλεκτικῶν
Παιώνειον μὲν ἀπ' Ἀριστείδου, Δίφιλον δὲ τὸν
Βοσποριανὸν Εὐφάντου καὶ Μύρμηκα τὸν Ἐξ-
αινέτου παραγενομένους ὡς ἐλέγξοντας ἀμφοτέρους
114 ζηλωτὰς ἔσχε.'' χωρὶς τοίνυν τούτων Φρασίδημον
μὲν τὸν περιπατητικὸν καὶ φυσικῶν ἔμπειρον ὄντα
προσηγάγετο, καὶ τὸν ῥητορικὸν Ἄλκιμον, ἁπάντων
πρωτεύοντα τῶν ἐν τῇ Ἑλλάδι ῥητόρων, Κράτητά
τε καὶ ἄλλους πλείστους ὅσους ἐθήρασε· καὶ δὴ καὶ
Ζήνωνα τὸν Φοίνικα μετὰ τούτων ἀφείλετο.

Ἦν δὲ καὶ πολιτικώτατος.

Καὶ γυναῖκα ἠγάγετο· καὶ ἑταίρα συνῆν Νικαρέτῃ,
ὥς φησί που καὶ Ὀνήτωρ. καὶ θυγατέρα ἀκόλαστον ἐγέννησεν, ἣν ἔγημε γνώριμός τις αὐτοῦ Σιμμίας
Συρακόσιος. ταύτης οὐ κατὰ τρόπον βιούσης εἶπέ
τις πρὸς τὸν Στίλπωνα, ὡς καταισχύνοι αὐτόν· ὁ
δέ, '' οὐ μᾶλλον,'' εἶπεν, '' ἢ ἐγὼ ταύτην κοσμῶ.''

115 Ἀπεδέχετο δ' αὐτόν, φασί, καὶ Πτολεμαῖος ὁ
Σωτήρ. καὶ ἐγκρατὴς Μεγάρων γενόμενος ἐδίδου
τε ἀργύριον αὐτῷ καὶ παρεκάλει εἰς Αἴγυπτον
συμπλεῖν· ὁ δὲ μέτριον μέν τι τἀργυριδίου προσήκατο, ἀρνησάμενος δὲ τὴν ὁδὸν μετῆλθεν εἰς Αἴγιναν, ἕως ἐκεῖνος ἀπέπλευσεν. ἀλλὰ καὶ Δημήτριος
ὁ Ἀντιγόνου καταλαβὼν τὰ Μέγαρα τήν τε οἰκίαν
αὐτῷ φυλαχθῆναι καὶ πάντα τὰ ἁρπασθέντα
προὐνόησεν ἀποδοθῆναι. ὅτε καὶ βουλομένῳ παρ'
αὐτοῦ τῶν ἀπολωλότων ἀναγραφὴν λαβεῖν ἔφη

him and joined the school of Megara. On this let me cite the exact words of Philippus the Megarian philosopher : " for from Theophrastus he drew away the theorist Metrodorus and Timagoras of Gela, from Aristotle the Cyrenaic philosopher, Clitarchus, and Simmias ; and as for the dialecticians themselves, he gained over Paeonius from Aristides ; Diphilus of Bosphorus, the son of Euphantus, and Myrmex, the son of Exaenetus, who had both come to refute him, he made his devoted adherents." And besides these he won over Phrasidemus the Peripatetic, an accomplished physicist, and Alcimus the rhetorician, the first orator in all Greece ; Crates, too, and many others he got into his toils, and, what is more, along with these, he carried off Zeno the Phoenician.

He was also an authority on politics.

He married a wife, and had a mistress named Nicarete, as Onetor has somewhere stated. He had a profligate daughter, who was married to his friend Simmias of Syracuse. And, as she would not live by rule, some one told Stilpo that she was a disgrace to him. To this he replied, " Not so, any more than I am an honour to her."

Ptolemy Soter, they say, made much of him, and when he had got possession of Megara, offered him a sum of money and invited him to return with him to Egypt. But Stilpo would only accept a very moderate sum, and he declined the proposed journey, and removed to Aegina until Ptolemy set sail. Again, when Demetrius, the son of Antigonus, had taken Megara, he took measures that Stilpo's house should be preserved and all his plundered property restored to him. But when he requested that a schedule of the lost property should be drawn up,

μηδὲν τῶν οἰκείων ἀπολωλεκέναι· παιδείαν γὰρ μηδένα ἐξενηνοχέναι, τόν τε λόγον ἔχειν καὶ τὴν ἐπιστήμην.

116 Καὶ αὐτῷ διαλεχθεὶς περὶ ἀνθρώπων εὐεργεσίας οὕτως εἷλεν ὥστε προσέχειν αὐτῷ. τοῦτόν φασιν περὶ τῆς Ἀθηνᾶς τῆς τοῦ Φειδίου τοιοῦτόν τινα λόγον ἐρωτῆσαι· " ἆρά γε ἡ τοῦ Διὸς Ἀθηνᾶ θεός ἐστι; " φήσαντος δέ, " ναί," " αὕτη δέ γε," εἶπεν, " οὐκ ἔστι Διός, ἀλλὰ Φειδίου·" συγχωρουμένου δέ, " οὐκ ἄρα," εἶπε, " θεός ἐστιν." ἐφ' ᾧ καὶ εἰς Ἄρειον πάγον προσκληθέντα μὴ ἀρνήσασθαι, φάσκειν δ' ὀρθῶς διειλέχθαι· μὴ γὰρ εἶναι αὐτὴν θεόν, ἀλλὰ θεάν· θεοὺς δὲ εἶναι τοὺς ἄρρενας. καὶ μέντοι τοὺς Ἀρεοπαγίτας εὐθέως αὐτὸν κελεῦσαι τῆς πόλεως ἐξελθεῖν. ὅτε καὶ Θεόδωρον τὸν ἐπίκλην θεὸν ἐπισκώπτοντα εἰπεῖν, " πόθεν δὲ τοῦτ' ᾔδει Στίλπων; ἢ ἀνασύρας αὐτῆς τὸν κῆπον ἐθεάσατο; " ἦν δ' ἀληθῶς οὗτος μὲν θρασύτατος· Στίλπων δὲ κομψότατος.

117 Κράτητος τοίνυν αὐτὸν ἐρωτήσαντος εἰ οἱ θεοὶ χαίρουσι ταῖς προσκυνήσεσι καὶ εὐχαῖς, φασὶν εἰπεῖν, " περὶ τούτων μὴ ἐρώτα, ἀνόητε, ἐν ὁδῷ, ἀλλὰ μόνον." τὸ δ' αὐτὸ καὶ Βίωνα ἐρωτηθέντα εἰ θεοί εἰσιν εἰπεῖν·

οὐκ ἀπ' ἐμοῦ σκεδάσεις ὄχλον, ταλαπείριε πρέσβυ;

Ἦν δ' ὁ Στίλπων καὶ ἀφελὴς καὶ ἀνεπίπλαστος πρός τε τὸν ἰδιώτην εὔθετος. Κράτητος γοῦν ποτε τοῦ κυνικοῦ πρὸς μὲν τὸ ἐρωτηθὲν οὐκ ἀποκρινα-

Stilpo denied that he had lost anything which really belonged to him, for no one had taken away his learning, while he still had his eloquence and knowledge.

And conversing upon the duty of doing good to men he made such an impression on the king that he became eager to hear him. There is a story that he once used the following argument concerning the Athena of Phidias: " Is it not Athena the daughter of Zeus who is a goddess?" And when the other said " Yes," he went on, " But this at least is not by Zeus but by Phidias," and, this being granted, he concluded, " This then is not a god." For this he was summoned before the Areopagus; he did not deny the charge, but contended that the reasoning was correct, for that Athena was no god but a goddess; it was the male divinities who were gods. However, the story goes that the Areopagites ordered him to quit the city, and that thereupon Theodorus, whose nickname was Θεός, said in derision, " Whence did Stilpo learn this? and how could he tell whether she was a god or a goddess?" But in truth Theodorus was most impudent, and Stilpo most ingenious.

When Crates asked him whether the gods take delight in prayers and adorations, he is said to have replied, " Don't put such a question in the street, simpleton, but when we are alone!" It is said that Bion, when he was asked the same question whether there are gods, replied:

Will you not scatter the crowd from me, O much-enduring elder?

In character Stilpo was simple and unaffected, and he could readily adapt himself to the plain man. For instance, when Crates the Cynic did not answer the question put to him and only insulted the ques-

μένου, ἀποπαρδόντος δέ, " ἤδειν," ἔφη, " ὡς πάντα
118 μᾶλλον φθέγξῃ ἢ ἃ δεῖ." ἀλλὰ καὶ ἰσχάδα προτείναντος αὐτῷ ποτε καὶ ἐρώτημα, δεξάμενον
καταφαγεῖν· τοῦ δέ, " ὦ Ἡράκλεις," εἰπόντος,
" ἀπολώλεκα τὴν ἰσχάδα·" " οὐ μόνον," ἔφη,
" ἀλλὰ καὶ τὸ ἐρώτημα, οὗ ἦν ἀρραβὼν ἡ ἰσχάς."
πάλιν δὲ ἰδὼν τὸν Κράτητα χειμῶνος συγκεκαυ-
μένον, " ὦ Κράτης," εἶπε, " δοκεῖς μοι χρείαν ἔχειν
ἱματίου καινοῦ." [ὅπερ ἦν νοῦ καὶ ἱματίου.]
καὶ τὸν ἀχθεσθέντα παρῳδῆσαι εἰς αὐτὸν οὕτω·

καὶ μὴν Στίλπων' εἰσεῖδον χαλέπ' ἄλγε' ἔχοντα
ἐν Μεγάροις, ὅθι φασὶ Τυφωέος ἔμμεναι εὐνάς.
ἔνθα τ' ἐρίζεσκεν, πολλοὶ δ' ἀμφ' αὐτὸν ἑταῖροι·
τὴν δ' ἀρετὴν παρὰ γράμμα διώκοντες κατέτριβον.

119 Λέγεται δ' οὕτως Ἀθήνησιν ἐπιστρέψαι τοὺς ἀνθρώπους, ὥστ' ἀπὸ τῶν ἐργαστηρίων συνθεῖν ἵνα
αὐτὸν θεάσαιντο. καί τινος εἰπόντος, " Στίλπων,
θαυμάζουσί σε ὡς θηρίον," " οὐ μὲν οὖν," εἰπεῖν,
" ἀλλ' ὡς ἄνθρωπον ἀληθινόν." δεινὸς δ' ἄγαν ὢν
ἐν τοῖς ἐριστικοῖς ἀνῄρει καὶ τὰ εἴδη· καὶ ἔλεγε τὸν
λέγοντα ἄνθρωπον εἶναι μηδένα· οὔτε γὰρ τόνδε
εἶναι οὔτε τόνδε· τί γὰρ μᾶλλον τόνδε ἢ τόνδε; οὐδ'
ἄρα τόνδε. καὶ πάλιν· τὸ λάχανον οὐκ ἔστι τὸ
δεικνύμενον· λάχανον μὲν γὰρ ἦν πρὸ μυρίων ἐτῶν·
οὐκ ἄρα ἐστὶ τοῦτο λάχανον. φασὶ δ' αὐτὸν ὁμι-
λοῦντα Κράτητι μεταξὺ σπεῦσαι ἰχθῦς πρίασθαι·
τοῦ δ' ἐπισπωμένου καὶ φάσκοντος, " καταλείπεις
τὸν λόγον;" " οὐκ ἔγωγε," ἔφη, " ἀλλὰ τὸν μὲν

ᵃ The pun upon καινοῦ (" new ") and καὶ νοῦ (" mind as
well ") recurs vi. 3.
ᵇ *Anth. Plan.* Add. v. 13 b.

tioner, " I knew," said Stilpo, " that you would utter anything rather than what you ought." And once when Crates held out a fig to him when putting a question, he took the fig and ate it. Upon which the other exclaimed, " O Heracles, I have lost the fig," and Stilpo remarked, " Not only that but your question as well, for which the fig was payment in advance." Again, on seeing Crates shrivelled with cold in the winter, he said, " You seem to me, Crates, to want a new coat," *i.e.* to be wanting in sense as well.[a] And the other being annoyed replied with the following burlesque [b] :

> And Stilpo I saw enduring toilsome woes in Megara, where men say that the bed of Typhos is. There he would ever be wrangling, and many comrades about him, wasting time in the verbal pursuit of virtue.

It is said that at Athens he so attracted the public that people would run together from the workshops to look at him. And when some one said, " Stilpo, they stare at you as if you were some strange creature." " No, indeed," said he, " but as if I were a genuine man." And, being a consummate master of controversy, he used to demolish even the ideas, and say that he who asserted the existence of Man meant no individual ; he did not mean this man or that. For why should he mean the one more than the other ? Therefore neither does he mean this individual man. Again, " vegetable " is not what is shown to me, for vegetable existed ten thousand years ago. Therefore this is not vegetable. The story goes that while in the middle of an argument with Crates he hurried off to buy fish, and, when Crates tried to detain him and urged that he was leaving the argument, his answer was, " Not I. I

λόγον ἔχω, σὲ δὲ καταλείπω· ὁ μὲν γὰρ λόγος
περιμενεῖ, τὸ δ' ὄψον πεπράσεται."

120 Φέρονται δ' αὐτοῦ διάλογοι ἐννέα ψυχροί· Μόσχος,
'Αρίστιππος ἢ Καλλίας, Πτολεμαῖος, Χαιρε-
κράτης, Μητροκλῆς, 'Αναξιμένης, 'Επιγένης, Πρὸς
τὴν ἑαυτοῦ θυγατέρα, 'Αριστοτέλης. τούτου φησὶν
'Ηρακλείδης καὶ τὸν Ζήνωνα ἀκοῦσαι τὸν τῆς
στοᾶς κτίστην. γηραιὸν δὲ τελευτῆσαί φησιν
Ἕρμιππος, οἶνον προσενεγκάμενον ὅπως θᾶττον
ἀποθάνοι.

Ἔστι δὲ καὶ εἰς τοῦτον ἡμῶν·

τὸν Μεγαρέα Στίλπωνα, γιγνώσκεις δ' ἴσως,
γῆρας, ἔπειτα νόσος καθεῖλε, δύσμαχον ζυγόν·
ἀλλ' οἶνον εὗρε τῆς κακῆς συνωρίδος
φέρτερον ἡνίοχον· ‹χανδὸν› πιὼν γὰρ ἤλασεν.

προσεσκώφθη δὲ ὑπὸ Σωφίλου τοῦ κωμικοῦ ἐν
δράματι Γάμῳ·

Στίλπωνός ἐστι βύσμαθ' ὁ Χαρίνου λόγος.

Κεφ. ιβ'. ΚΡΙΤΩΝ

121 Κρίτων 'Αθηναῖος· οὗτος μάλιστα φιλοστοργό-
τατα διετέθη πρὸς Σωκράτην, καὶ οὕτως ἐπεμελεῖτο
αὐτοῦ, ὥστε μηδέποτ' ἐλλείπειν τι τῶν πρὸς τὴν
χρείαν. καὶ οἱ παῖδες δὲ αὐτοῦ διήκουσαν Σωκράτους, Κριτόβουλος, 'Ερμογένης, 'Επιγένης, Κτήσ-
ιππος. ὁ δ' οὖν Κρίτων διαλόγους γέγραφεν ἐν
ἑνὶ φερομένους βιβλίῳ ἑπτακαίδεκα, τοὺς ὑπο-
γεγραμμένους,

  Ὅτι οὐκ ἐκ τοῦ μαθεῖν οἱ ἀγαθοί.
  Περὶ τοῦ πλέον ἔχειν.

keep the argument though I am leaving you ; for the argument will remain, but the fish will soon be sold."

Nine dialogues of his are extant written in frigid style, *Moschus, Aristippus* or *Callias, Ptolemy, Chaere-crates, Metrocles, Anaximenes, Epigenes, To his Daughter, Aristotle.* Heraclides relates that Zeno, the founder of the Stoic school, was one of Stilpo's pupils [a] ; Hermippus that Stilpo died at a great age after taking wine to hasten his end.

I have written an epitaph on him also [b] :

Surely you know Stilpo the Megarian ; old age and then disease laid him low, a formidable pair. But he found in wine a charioteer too strong for that evil team ; he quaffed it eagerly and was borne along.

He was also ridiculed by Sophilus the Comic poet in his drama *The Wedding* [c] :

What Charinus says is just Stilpo's stoppers.

CHAPTER 12. CRITO

Crito was a citizen of Athens. He was most affectionate in his disposition towards Socrates, and took such care of him that none of his wants were left unsupplied. Further, his sons Critobulus, Hermogenes, Epigenes and Ctesippus were pupils of Socrates. Crito too wrote seventeen dialogues which are extant in a single volume under the titles :

That men are not made good by instruction.
Concerning superfluity.

[a] Compare the anecdote in vii. 24 from Apollonius of Tyre.
[b] *Anth Plan.* v. 42.
[c] Meineke, *C.G.F.* iv. 386, *s.v.* Diphilus.

Τί τὸ ἐπιτήδειον ἢ Πολιτικός.
Περὶ τοῦ καλοῦ.
Περὶ τοῦ κακουργεῖν.
Περὶ εὐθημοσύνης.
Περὶ τοῦ νόμου.
Περὶ τοῦ θείου.
Περὶ τεχνῶν.
Περὶ συνουσίας.
Περὶ σοφίας.
Πρωταγόρας ἢ Πολιτικός.
Περὶ γραμμάτων.
Περὶ ποιητικῆς, [περὶ τοῦ καλοῦ].
Περὶ τοῦ μαθεῖν.
Περὶ τοῦ γνῶναι ἢ Περὶ ἐπιστήμης.
Τί τὸ ἐπίστασθαι.

Κεφ. ιγ′. ΣΙΜΩΝ

122 Σίμων Ἀθηναῖος, σκυτοτόμος. οὗτος ἐρχομένου
Σωκράτους ἐπὶ τὸ ἐργαστήριον καὶ διαλεγομένου
τινά, ὧν ἐμνημόνευεν ὑποσημειώσεις ἐποιεῖτο· ὅθεν
σκυτικοὺς αὐτοῦ τοὺς διαλόγους καλοῦσιν. εἰσὶ
δὲ τρεῖς καὶ τριάκοντα ἐν ἑνὶ φερόμενοι βιβλίῳ·

Περὶ θεῶν.
Περὶ τοῦ ἀγαθοῦ.
Περὶ τοῦ καλοῦ.
Τί τὸ καλόν.
Περὶ δικαίου πρῶτον, δεύτερον.
Περὶ ἀρετῆς ὅτι οὐ διδακτόν.
Περὶ ἀνδρείας πρῶτον, δεύτερον, τρίτον.
Περὶ νόμου.
Περὶ δημαγωγίας.
Περὶ τιμῆς.

What is expedient, or The Statesman.
Of Beauty.
On Doing Ill.
On Tidiness.
On Law.
Of that which is Divine.
On Arts.
Of Society.
Of Wisdom.
Protagoras, or The Statesman.
On Letters.
Of Poetry.
Of Learning.
On Knowing, or On Science.
What is Knowledge.

Chapter 13. SIMON

Simon was a citizen of Athens and a cobbler. When Socrates came to his workshop and began to converse, he used to make notes of all that he could remember. And this is why people apply the term "leathern" to his dialogues. These dialogues are thirty-three in number, extant in a single volume:

Of the Gods.
Of the Good.
On the Beautiful.
What is the Beautiful.
On the Just: two dialogues.
Of Virtue, that it cannot be taught.
Of Courage: three dialogues.
On Law.
On Guiding the People.
Of Honour.

Περὶ ποιήσεως.
Περὶ εὐπαθείας.
Περὶ ἔρωτος.
Περὶ φιλοσοφίας
Περὶ ἐπιστήμης.
Περὶ μουσικῆς.
Περὶ ποιήσεως.
123   Τί τὸ καλόν.
Περὶ διδασκαλίας.
Περὶ τοῦ διαλέγεσθαι.
Περὶ κρίσεως.
Περὶ τοῦ ὄντος.
Περὶ ἀριθμοῦ.
Περὶ ἐπιμελείας.
Περὶ τοῦ ἐργάζεσθαι.
Περὶ φιλοκερδοῦς.
Περὶ ἀλαζονείας.
Περὶ τοῦ καλοῦ.

οἱ δέ,

Περὶ τοῦ βουλεύεσθαι.
Περὶ λόγου ἢ περὶ ἐπιτηδειότητος.
Περὶ κακουργίας.

Οὗτος, φασί, πρῶτος διελέχθη τοὺς λόγους τοὺς
Σωκρατικούς. ἐπαγγειλαμένου δὲ Περικλέους
θρέψειν αὐτὸν καὶ κελεύοντος ἀπιέναι πρὸς αὐτόν,
οὐκ ἂν ἔφη τὴν παρρησίαν ἀποδόσθαι.
124   Γέγονε δὲ καὶ ἄλλος Σίμων ῥητορικὰς τέχνας
γεγραφώς· καὶ ἕτερος ἰατρὸς κατὰ Σέλευκον τὸν
Νικάνορα· καί τις ἀνδριαντοποιός.

Of Poetry.
On Good Eating.
On Love.
On Philosophy.
On Knowledge.
On Music.
On Poetry.
What is the Beautiful
On Teaching.
On the Art of Conversation.
Of Judging.
Of Being.
Of Number.
On Diligence.
On Efficiency.
On Greed.
On Pretentiousness.
On the Beautiful.

Others are :

On Deliberation.
On Reason, or On Expediency.
On Doing Ill.

He was the first, so we are told, who introduced the Socratic dialogues as a form of conversation. When Pericles promised to support him and urged him to come to him, his reply was, " I will not part with my free speech for money."

There was another Simon, who wrote treatises *On Rhetoric* ; another, a physician, in the time of Seleucus Nicanor ; and a third who was a sculptor.

Κεφ. ιδ΄. ΓΛΑΥΚΩΝ

Γλαύκων Ἀθηναῖος· καὶ τούτου φέρονται ἐν ἑνὶ βιβλίῳ διάλογοι ἐννέα·

Φειδύλος.
Εὐριπίδης.
Ἀμύντιχος.
Εὐθίας.
Λυσιθείδης.
Ἀριστοφάνης.
Κέφαλος.
Ἀναξίφημος.
Μενέξενος.

φέρονται καὶ ἄλλοι δύο καὶ τριάκοντα, οἳ νοθεύονται.

Κεφ. ιε΄. ΣΙΜΜΙΑΣ

Σιμμίας Θηβαῖος· καὶ τούτου φέρονται ἐν ἑνὶ βιβλίῳ διάλογοι τρεῖς καὶ εἴκοσι·

Περὶ σοφίας.
Περὶ λογισμοῦ.
Περὶ μουσικῆς.
Περὶ ἐπῶν.
Περὶ ἀνδρείας.
Περὶ φιλοσοφίας.
Περὶ ἀληθείας.
Περὶ γραμμάτων.
Περὶ διδασκαλίας.
Περὶ τέχνης.
Περὶ τοῦ ἐπιστατεῖν.
Περὶ πρέποντος.
Περὶ αἱρετοῦ καὶ φευκτοῦ.
Περὶ φίλου.

Chapter 14. GLAUCON

Glaucon was a citizen of Athens. Nine dialogues of his are extant in a single volume :

> Phidylus.
> Euripides.
> Amyntichus.
> Euthias.
> Lysithides.
> Aristophanes.
> Cephalus.
> Anaxiphemus.
> Menexenus.

There are also extant thirty-two others, which **are** considered spurious.

Chapter 15. SIMMIAS

Simmias was a citizen of Thebes. Twenty-three dialogues of his are extant in a single volume :

> On Wisdom.
> On Reasoning.
> On Music.
> On Verses.
> Of Courage.
> On Philosophy.
> Of Truth.
> On Letters.
> On Teaching.
> On Art.
> On Government.
> Of that which is becoming.
> Of that which is to be chosen and avoided.
> On Friendship.

Περὶ τοῦ εἰδέναι.
Περὶ ψυχῆς.
Περὶ τοῦ εὖ ζῆν.
Περὶ δυνατοῦ.
Περὶ χρημάτων.
Περὶ ζωῆς.
Τί τὸ καλόν.
Περὶ ἐπιμελείας.
Περὶ ἔρωτος.

Κεφ. ιϛ΄. ΚΕΒΗΣ

125   Κέβης ὁ Θηβαῖος· καὶ τούτου φέρονται διάλογοι
τρεῖς·

Πίναξ.
Ἑβδόμη.
Φρύνιχος.

Κεφ. ιζ΄. ΜΕΝΕΔΗΜΟΣ

[Μενέδημος] Οὗτος τῶν ἀπὸ Φαίδωνος, Κλει-
σθένους τοῦ τῶν Θεοπροπιδῶν καλουμένων υἱός,
ἀνδρὸς εὐγενοῦς μέν, ἀρχιτέκτονος δὲ καὶ πένητος·
οἱ δὲ καὶ σκηνογράφον αὐτὸν εἶναί φασι καὶ μαθεῖν
ἑκάτερα τὸν Μενέδημον· ὅθεν γράψαντος αὐτοῦ
ψήφισμά τι καθήψατό τις Ἀλεξίνειος, εἰπὼν ὡς
οὔτε σκηνὴν οὔτε ψήφισμα προσήκει τῷ σοφῷ
γράφειν. πεμφθεὶς δὲ φρουρὸς ὁ Μενέδημος ὑπὸ
τῶν Ἐρετριέων εἰς Μέγαρα ἀνῆλθεν εἰς Ἀκαδήμειαν
πρὸς Πλάτωνα, καὶ θηραθεὶς κατέλιπε τὴν στρα-
126 τείαν. Ἀσκληπιάδου δὲ τοῦ Φλιασίου περισπά-
σαντος αὐτὸν ἐγένετο ἐν Μεγάροις παρὰ Στίλπωνι.

256

On Knowledge.
Of the Soul.
On a Good Life.
Of that which is possible.
On Money.
On Life.
What is the beautiful.
On Diligence.
On Love.

CHAPTER 16. CEBES

Cebes was a citizen of Thebes. Three dialogues
of his are extant :

The Tablet.
The Seventh Day.
Phrynichus.

CHAPTER 17. MENEDEMUS

Menedemus belonged to Phaedo's school ; he was
the son of Clisthenes, a member of the clan called
the Theopropidae, of good family, though a builder
and a poor man ; others say that he was a scene-
painter and that Menedemus learnt both trades.
Hence, when he had proposed a decree, a certain
Alexinius attacked him, declaring that the philosopher
was not a proper person to design either a scene or
a decree. When Menedemus was dispatched by
the Eretrians to Megara on garrison duty, he paid
a visit to Plato at the Academy and was so captivated
that he abandoned the service of arms. Asclepiades
of Phlius drew him away, and he lived at Megara
with Stilpo, whose lectures they both attended.

οὗπερ ἀμφότεροι διήκουσαν· κἀντεῦθεν πλεύσαντες εἰς Ἦλιν Ἀγχιπύλῳ καὶ Μόσχῳ τοῖς ἀπὸ Φαίδωνος παρέβαλον. καὶ μέχρι μὲν τούτων, ὡς προείρηται ἐν τῷ περὶ Φαίδωνος, Ἠλιακοὶ προσηγορεύοντο· Ἐρετρικοὶ δ' ἐκλήθησαν ἀπὸ τῆς πατρίδος τοῦ περὶ οὗ ὁ λόγος.

Φαίνεται δὴ ὁ Μενέδημος σεμνὸς ἱκανῶς γενέσθαι· ὅθεν αὐτὸν Κράτης παρῳδῶν φησι·

Φλιάσιόν τ' Ἀσκληπιάδην καὶ ταῦρον Ἐρέτρην.

ὁ δὲ Τίμων οὕτως·

ὄγκον ἀναστήσας ὠφρυωμένος ἀφροσιβόμβαξ.

127 οὕτω δ' ἦν σεμνὸς ὡς Εὐρύλοχον τὸν Κασανδρέα μετὰ Κλειππίδου Κυζικηνοῦ μειρακίου κληθέντα ὑπ' Ἀντιγόνου ἀντειπεῖν· φοβεῖσθαι γὰρ μὴ Μενέδημος αἴσθοιτο. ἦν γὰρ καὶ ἐπικόπτης καὶ παρρησιαστής. μειρακίου γοῦν καταθρασυνομένου εἶπε μὲν οὐδέν· λαβὼν δὲ κάρφος διέγραφεν εἰς τοὔδαφος περαινομένου σχῆμα· ἕως ὁρώντων πάντων συνὲν τὸ μειράκιον τὴν ὕβριν ἀπηλλάγη. Ἱεροκλέους δὲ τοῦ ἐπὶ τοῦ Πειραιῶς συνανακάμπτοντος αὐτῷ ἐν Ἀμφιαράου καὶ πολλὰ λέγοντος περὶ τῆς ἁλώσεως τῆς Ἐρετρίας, ἄλλο μὲν οὐδὲν εἶπεν, ἠρώτησε δὲ εἰς τί αὐτὸν Ἀντίγονος περαίνει.

128 Πρὸς δὲ τὸν θρασυνόμενον μοιχόν, "ἀγνοεῖς," ἔφη, "ὅτι οὐ μόνον κράμβη χυλὸν ἔχει χρηστόν, ἀλλὰ καὶ ῥαφανίς;" πρὸς δὲ τὸν νεώτερον κεκραγότα, "σκέψαι," ἔφη, "μή τι ὄπισθεν ἔχων λέληθας." Ἀντιγόνου δὲ συμβουλευομένου εἰ ἐπὶ κῶμον

─────────────

ᵃ Fr. 2 D.   ᵇ Fr. 29 D.

Thence they sailed to Elis, where they joined Anchipylus and Moschus of the school of Phaedo. Down to their time, as was stated in the Life of Phaedo, the school was called the Elian school. Afterwards it was called the Eretrian school, from the city to which my subject belonged.

It would appear that Menedemus was somewhat pompous. Hence Crates burlesques him thus *a* :

Asclepiades the sage of Phlius and the Eretrian bull;

and Timon as follows *b* :

A puffing, supercilious purveyor of humbug.

He was a man of such dignity that, when Eurylochus of Casandrea was invited by Antigonus to court along with Cleïppides, a youth of Cyzicus, he declined the invitation, being afraid that Menedemus would hear of it, so caustic and outspoken was he. When a young gallant would have taken liberties with him, he said not a word but picked up a twig and drew an insulting picture on the ground, until all eyes were attracted and the young man, perceiving the insult, made off. When Hierocles, who was in command of the Piraeus, walked up and down along with him in the shrine of Amphiaraus, and talked much of the capture of Eretria, he made no other reply beyond asking him what Antigonus's object was in treating him as he did. To an adulterer who was giving himself airs he said, " Do you not know that, if cabbage has a good flavour, so for that matter has radish ? " Hearing a youth who was very noisy, he said, " See what there is behind you." When Antigonus consulted him as to whether he should go to a rout, he sent

ἀφίκοιτο, σιωπήσας τἆλλα μόνον ἐκέλευσεν ἀπ-
αγγεῖλαι ὅτι βασιλέως υἱός ἐστι. πρὸς δὲ τὸν
ἀναίσθητον ἀναφέροντά τι αὐτῷ εἰκαίως, ἠρώτησεν
εἰ ἀγρὸν ἔχοι· φήσαντος δὲ καὶ πάμπλειστα κτή-
ματα, " πορεύου τοίνυν," ἔφη, " κἀκείνων ἐπι-
μελοῦ, μὴ συμβῇ σοι καὶ ταῦτα καταφθεῖραι καὶ
κομψὸν ἰδιώτην ἀποβαλεῖν." πρὸς δὲ τὸν πυθόμενον
εἰ γήμαι ὁ σπουδαῖος, ἔφη, " πότερον ἐγώ σοι
σπουδαῖος δοκῶ ἢ οὔ; " φήσαντος δ' εἶναι, " ἐγὼ
129 τοίνυν," εἶπε, " γεγάμηκα." πρὸς δὲ τὸν εἰπόντα
πολλὰ τὰ ἀγαθὰ ἐπύθετο πόσα τὸν ἀριθμὸν καὶ
εἰ νομίζοι πλείω τῶν ἑκατόν. μὴ δυνάμενος δὲ
τῶν καλούντων ἐπὶ δεῖπνόν τινος περιελεῖν τὴν
πολυτέλειαν, κληθείς ποτε οὐδὲν μὲν εἶπε· σιωπῶν
δ' αὐτὸν ἐνουθέτησε μόνας ἐλαίας προσενεγκά-
μενος. διὰ δὴ οὖν τὸ παρρησιαστικὸν τοῦτο
μικροῦ καὶ ἐκινδύνευσεν ἐν Κύπρῳ παρὰ Νικο-
κρέοντι σὺν Ἀσκληπιάδῃ τῷ φίλῳ. τοῦ γάρ τοι
βασιλέως ἐπιμήνιον ἑορτὴν τελοῦντος καὶ καλέ-
σαντος καὶ τούτους ὥσπερ τοὺς ἄλλους φιλοσόφους,
τὸν Μενέδημον εἰπεῖν ὡς εἰ καλὸν ἦν ἡ τῶν τοιούτων ἀνδρῶν συναγωγή, καθ' ἑκάστην ἡμέραν ἔδει
γίνεσθαι τὴν ἑορτήν· εἰ δ' οὔ, περιττῶς καὶ νῦν.
130 πρὸς δὲ τοῦτο ἀπαντήσαντος τοῦ τυράννου καὶ
εἰπόντος ὡς ταύτην τὴν ἡμέραν ἔχοι σχολάζουσαν
πρὸς τὸ διακούειν φιλοσόφων, ἔτι καὶ μᾶλλον
αὐστηρότερον ἐνέκειτο, δεικνὺς ἐπὶ τῆς θυσίας ὡς
χρὴ πάντα καιρὸν φιλοσόφων ἀκούειν· ὥστ' εἰ
μή τις αὐλητὴς αὐτοὺς διεπέμψατο, κἂν ἀπώλοντο.
ὅθεν χειμαζομένων ἐν τῷ πλοίῳ τὸν Ἀσκληπιάδην

260

a message to say no more than this, that he was the son of a king. When a stupid fellow related something to him with no apparent object, he inquired if he had a farm. And hearing that he had, and that there was a large stock of cattle on it, he said, " Then go and look after them, lest it should happen that they are ruined and a clever farmer thrown away." To one who inquired if the good man ever married, he replied, " Do you think me good or not ? " The reply being in the affirmative, he said, " Well, I am married." Of one who affirmed that there were many good things, he inquired how many, and whether he thought there were more than a hundred. Not being able to curb the extravagance of some one who had invited him to dinner, he said nothing when he was invited, but rebuked his host tacitly by confining himself to olives. However, on account of this freedom of speech he was in great peril in Cyprus with his friend Asclepiades when staying at the court of Nicocreon. For when the king held the usual monthly feast and invited these two along with the other philosophers, we are told that Menedemus said that, if the gathering of such men was a good thing, the feast ought to have been held every day ; if not, then it was superfluous even on the present occasion. The tyrant having replied to this by saying that on this day he had the leisure to hear philosophers, he pressed the point still more stubbornly, declaring, while the feast was going on, that any and every occasion should be employed in listening to philosophers. The consequence was that, if a certain flute-player had not got them away, they would have been put to death. Hence when they were in a storm in the boat

φασὶν εἰπεῖν ὡς ἡ μὲν τοῦ αὐλητοῦ εὐμουσία σέσωκεν αὐτούς, ἡ δὲ τοῦ Μενεδήμου παρρησία ἀπολώλεκεν.

Ἦν δέ, φασί, καὶ ἐκκλίτης καὶ τὰ τῆς σχολῆς ἀδιάφορος, οὔτε τάξιν γοῦν τινὰ ἦν παρ' αὐτῷ βλέπειν οὔτε βάθρα κύκλῳ διέκειτο, ἀλλ' οὗ ἂν ἕκαστος ἔτυχε περιπατῶν ἢ καθήμενος ἤκουε, καὶ 131 αὐτοῦ τοῦτον τὸν τρόπον διακειμένου. ἀγωνιάτης μέντοι, φασίν, ἦν ἄλλως καὶ φιλόδοξος ὥστε τὸ πρότερον τέκτονι συνοικοδομοῦντες αὐτός τε καὶ ὁ Ἀσκληπιάδης, ὁ μὲν Ἀσκληπιάδης ἐφαίνετο γυμνὸς ἐπὶ τοῦ τέγους τὸν πηλὸν παραφέρων, ὁ δὲ εἴ τιν' ἴδοι ἐρχόμενον, παρεκρύπτετο. ἐπεὶ δ' ἥψατο τῆς πολιτείας, οὕτως ἦν ἀγωνιάτης ὥστε καὶ τὸν λιβανωτὸν τιθεὶς διήμαρτε τοῦ θυμιατηρίου. καί ποτε Κράτητος περισταμένου αὐτὸν καὶ καθαπτομένου εἰς τὸ ὅτι πολιτεύεται, ἐκέλευσέ τισιν εἰς τὸ δεσμωτήριον αὐτὸν ἐμβαλεῖν· τὸν δὲ μηδὲν ἧττον τηρεῖν παριόντα καὶ ὑπερκύπτοντα Ἀγαμεμνόνειόν τε καὶ Ἡγησίπολιν ἀποκαλεῖν.

132 Ἦν δέ πως ἠρέμα καὶ δεισιδαιμονέστερος σὺν γοῦν Ἀσκληπιάδῃ κατ' ἄγνοιαν ἐν πανδοκείῳ ποτὲ κρεάτων ῥιπτουμένων φαγών, ἐπειδὴ μάθοι, ἐναντία τε καὶ ὠχρία· ἕως Ἀσκληπιάδης ἐπετίμησεν αὐτῷ ὡς οὐδὲν [εἰπὼν] ἠνώχλησεν αὐτὸν τὰ κρέα, ἀλλ' ἡ περὶ τούτων ὑπόνοια. τὰ δ' ἄλλα μεγαλόψυχος ἀνὴρ ἦν καὶ ἐλευθέριος. κατά τε τὴν ἕξιν τὴν σωματικὴν ἤδη καὶ πρεσβύτης ὑπάρχων οὐδὲν ἧττον ἀθλητοῦ στερεός τε καὶ ἐπι-

Asclepiades is reported to have said that the flute-player through good playing had proved their salvation when the free speech of Menedemus had been their undoing.

He shirked work, it is said, and was indifferent to the fortunes of his school. At least no order could be seen in his classes, and no circle of benches; but each man would listen where he happened to be, walking or sitting, Menedemus himself behaving in the same way. In other respects he is said to have been nervous and careful of his reputation; so much so that, when Menedemus himself and Asclepiades were helping a man who had formerly been a builder to build a house, whereas Asclepiades appeared stripped on the roof passing the mortar, Menedemus would try to hide himself as often as he saw anyone coming. After he took part in public affairs, he was so nervous that, when offering the frankincense, he would actually miss the censer. And once, when Crates stood about him and attacked him for meddling in politics, he ordered certain men to have Crates locked up. But Crates none the less watched him as he went by and, standing on tiptoe, called him a pocket Agamemnon and Hegesipolis.

He was also in a way rather superstitious. At all events once, when he was at an inn with Asclepiades and had inadvertently eaten some meat which had been thrown away, he turned sick and pale when he learnt the fact, until Asclepiades rebuked him, saying that it was not the meat which disturbed him but merely his suspicion of it. In all other respects he was magnanimous and liberal. In his habit of body, even in old age, he was as firm and sunburnt in appearance as any athlete, being stout and always

κεκαυμένος τὸ εἶδος, πίων τε καὶ τετριμμένος·
τὸ δὲ μέγεθος σύμμετρος, ὡς δῆλον ἐκ τοῦ εἰκονίου
τοῦ ἐν Ἐρετρίᾳ ἐν τῷ ἀρχαίῳ σταδίῳ. ἔστι γάρ,
ὡς ἐπίτηδες, παράγυμνον, τὰ πλεῖστα μέρη φαῖνον
τοῦ σώματος.

133 Ἦν δὲ καὶ φιλυπόδοχος καὶ διὰ τὸ νοσῶδες τῆς
Ἐρετρίας πλείω συνάγων συμπόσια· ἐν οἷς καὶ
ποιητῶν καὶ μουσικῶν. ἠσπάζετο δὲ καὶ Ἄρατον
καὶ Λυκόφρονα τὸν τῆς τραγῳδίας ποιητὴν καὶ
τὸν Ῥόδιον Ἀνταγόραν· μάλιστα δὲ πάντων
Ὁμήρῳ προσεῖχεν· εἶτα καὶ τοῖς μελικοῖς· ἔπειτα
Σοφοκλεῖ, καὶ δὴ καὶ Ἀχαιῷ, ᾧπερ καὶ τὸ δευ-
τερεῖον ἐν τοῖς Σατύροις, Αἰσχύλῳ δὲ τὸ πρωτεῖον
ἀπεδίδου. ὅθεν καὶ πρὸς τοὺς ἀντιπολιτευομένους
ταῦτα, φασί, προεφέρετο·

ἡλίσκετ' ἆρα καὶ πρὸς ἀσθενῶν ταχύς,
καὶ πρὸς χελώνης ἀετὸς βραχεῖ χρόνῳ.

134 ταῦτα δ' ἐστὶν Ἀχαιοῦ ἐκ τῆς σατυρικῆς Ὀμφάλης·
ὥστε πταίουσιν οἱ λέγοντες μηδὲν αὐτὸν ἀνεγνω-
κέναι πλὴν τῆς Μηδείας τῆς Εὐριπίδου, ἣν ἔνιοι
Νεόφρονος εἶναι τοῦ Σικυωνίου φασί.

Τῶν δὲ διδασκάλων τοὺς[1] περὶ Πλάτωνα καὶ
Ξενοκράτην, ἔτι τε Παραιβάτην τὸν Κυρηναῖον
κατεφρόνει, Στίλπωνα δ' ἐτεθαυμάκει· καί ποτε
ἐρωτηθεὶς περὶ αὐτοῦ ἄλλο μὲν οὐδὲν εἶπε πλὴν
ὅτι ἐλευθέριος. ἦν δὲ καὶ δυσκατανόητος ὁ Μενέδημος καὶ ἐν τῷ συνθέσθαι δυσανταγώνιστος·
ἐστρέφετό τε πρὸς πάντα καὶ εὑρεσιλόγει· ἐρι-
στικώτατός τε, καθά φησιν Ἀντισθένης ἐν Δια-

_____

[1] τούς] τῶν vulg. : corr. Reiske.

in the pink of condition ; in stature he was well-proportioned, as may be seen from the statuette in the ancient Stadium at Eretria. For it represents him, intentionally no doubt, almost naked, and displays the greater part of his body.

He was fond of entertaining and used to collect numerous parties about him because Eretria was unhealthy ; amongst these there would be parties of poets and musicians. He welcomed Aratus also and Lycophron the tragic poet, and Antagoras of Rhodes, but, above all, he applied himself to the study of Homer and, next, the Lyric poets ; then to Sophocles, and also to Achaeus, to whom he assigned the second place as a writer of satiric dramas, giving Aeschylus the first. Hence he quoted against his political opponents the following lines [a] :

> Ere long the swift is overtaken by the feeble,
> And the eagle by the tortoise,

which are from the *Omphale*, a satiric drama of Achaeus. Therefore it is a mistake to say that he had read nothing except the *Medea* of Euripides, which some have asserted to be the work of Neophron of Sicyon.

He despised the teachers of the school of Plato and Xenocrates as well as the Cyrenaic philosopher Paraebates. He had a great admiration for Stilpo ; and on one occasion, when he was questioned about him, he made no other answer than that he was a gentleman. Menedemus was difficult to see through, and in making a bargain it was difficult to get the better of him. He would twist and turn in every direction, and he excelled in inventing objections. He was a great controversialist, according to Anti-

---

[a] Nauck, *T.G.F.²*, *Achaeus*, 34.

δοχαῖς, ἦν. καὶ δὴ καὶ τόδε ἐρωτᾶν εἰώθει· " τὸ ἕτερον τοῦ ἑτέρου ἕτερόν ἐστι; " " ναί." " ἕτερον δέ ἐστι τὸ ὠφελεῖν τοῦ ἀγαθοῦ; " " ναί." " οὐκ ἄρα τὸ ὠφελεῖν ἀγαθόν ἐστιν."

135 Ἀνήρει δέ, φασί, καὶ τὰ ἀποφατικὰ τῶν ἀξιωμάτων, καταφατικὰ τιθείς· καὶ τούτων τὰ ἁπλᾶ προσδεχόμενος τὰ οὐχ ἁπλᾶ ἀνήρει, λέγω δὲ συνημμένα καὶ συμπεπλεγμένα. φησὶ δ' Ἡρακλείδης ἐν μὲν τοῖς δόγμασι Πλατωνικὸν εἶναι αὐτόν, διαπαίζειν δὲ τὰ διαλεκτικά· ὥστε Ἀλεξίνου ποτὲ ἐρωτήσαντος εἰ πέπαυται τὸν πατέρα τύπτων, " ἀλλ' οὔτ' ἔτυπτον," φάναι, " οὔτε πέπαυμαι." πάλιν τ' ἐκείνου λέγοντος ὡς ἐχρῆν εἰπόντα ναί ἢ οὔ λῦσαι τὴν ἀμφιβολίαν, " γελοῖον," εἶπε, " τοῖς ὑμετέροις νόμοις ἀκολουθεῖν, ἐξὸν ἐν πύλαις ἀντιβῆναι." Βίωνός τε ἐπιμελῶς κατατρέχοντος τῶν μάντεων, νεκροὺς αὐτὸν ἐπισφάττειν ἔλεγε.

136 Καί ποτέ τινος ἀκούσας ὡς μέγιστον ἀγαθὸν εἴη τὸ πάντων ἐπιτυγχάνειν ὧν τις ἐπιθυμεῖ, εἶπε, " πολὺ δὲ μεῖζον τὸ ἐπιθυμεῖν ὧν δεῖ." φησὶ δ' Ἀντίγονος ὁ Καρύστιος γράψαι αὐτὸν μηδὲν μηδὲ συντάξαι, ὥστε μηδ' ἐπὶ δόγματός τινος στηρίζειν. ἐν δὲ ταῖς ζητήσεσι, φησίν, ὧδε μάχιμος ἦν ὥστ' ὑπώπια φέρων ὑπῄει. ὅμως δ' οὖν τοιοῦτος ἐν τοῖς λόγοις ὑπάρχων ἐν τοῖς ἔργοις πρᾱότατος ἦν. Ἀλεξῖνον γοῦν πολλὰ καταπαίζων καὶ σκληρῶς ἐπισκώπτων, ὅμως αὐτὸν εὖ ἐποίησε τὴν γυναῖκα παραπέμψας ἐκ Δελφῶν ἕως Χαλκίδος,

sthenes in his *Successions of Philosophers*. In particular he was fond of using the following argument: " Is the one of two things different from the other ? " " Yes." " And is conferring benefits different from the good ? " " Yes." " Then to confer benefits is not good."

It is said that he disallowed negative propositions, converting them into affirmatives, and of these he admitted simple propositions only, rejecting those which are not simple, I mean hypothetical and complex propositions. Heraclides declares that, although in his doctrines he was a Platonist, yet he made sport of dialectic. So that, when Alexinus once inquired if he had left off beating his father, his answer was, " Why, I was not beating him and have not left off " ; and upon Alexinus insisting that he ought to have cleared up the ambiguity by a plain " Yes " or " No," " It would be absurd," he said, " for me to conform to your rules when I can stop you on the threshold." And when Bion persistently ran down the soothsayers, Menedemus said he was slaying the slain.

On hearing some one say that the greatest good was to get all you want, he rejoined, " To want the right things is a far greater good." Antigonus of Carystus asserts that he never wrote or composed anything, and so never held firmly by any doctrine. He adds that in discussing questions he was so pugnacious that he would only retire after he had been badly mauled. And yet, though he was so violent in debate, he was as mild as possible in his conduct. For instance, though he made sport of Alexinus and bantered him cruelly, he was nevertheless very kind to him, for, when his wife was afraid

εὐλαβουμένην τὰς κλωπείας τε καὶ τὰς καθ᾽ ὁδὸν
ληστείας.

137 Φίλος τε ἦν μάλιστα, ὡς δῆλον ἐκ τῆς πρὸς
Ἀσκληπιάδην συμπνοίας, οὐδέν τι διαφερούσης
τῆς Πυλάδου φιλοστοργίας. ἀλλὰ πρεσβύτερος
Ἀσκληπιάδης, ὡς λέγεσθαι ποιητὴν μὲν αὐτὸν
εἶναι, ὑποκριτὴν δὲ Μενέδημον. καί ποτέ φασιν
Ἀρχιπόλιδος τρισχιλίας αὐτοῖς διαγράψαντος στη-
ριζομένους περὶ τοῦ τίς δεύτερος ἀρεῖ, μηδέτερον
λαβεῖν. λέγεται δὲ καὶ γυναῖκας ἀγαγέσθαι αὐ-
τούς· ὧν τὴν μὲν θυγατέρα Ἀσκληπιάδην, τὴν δὲ
μητέρα Μενέδημον. κἀπειδὴ τελευτῆσαι τῷ Ἀσκληπιάδῃ τὸ γύναιον, λαβεῖν τὸ τοῦ Μενεδήμου·
ἐκεῖνόν τε, ἐπειδὴ προύστη τῆς πολιτείας, πλουσίαν
γῆμαι· οὐδὲν μέντοι ἧττον μιᾶς οὔσης οἰκίας
ἐπιτρέψαι τὸν Μενέδημον τὴν διοίκησιν τῇ προτέρᾳ
138 γυναικί. ὁ μέντοι Ἀσκληπιάδης προκατέστρεψεν
ἐν Ἐρετρίᾳ γηραιὸς ἤδη, συζήσας τῷ Μενεδήμῳ
σφόδρα εὐτελῶς ἀπὸ μεγάλων· ὅτε καὶ μετὰ
χρόνον ἐλθόντος ἐπὶ κῶμον ἐρωμένου τοῦ Ἀσκληπιάδου καὶ τῶν νεανίσκων ἀποκλειόντων αὐτόν,
ὁ Μενέδημος ἐκέλευσεν εἰσδέξασθαι, εἰπὼν ὅτι
Ἀσκληπιάδης αὐτῷ καὶ κατὰ γῆς ὢν τὰς θύρας
ἀνοίγει. ἦσαν δ᾽ οἱ σωματοποιήσαντες αὐτοὺς
Ἱππόνικός τε ὁ Μακεδὼν καὶ Ἀγήτωρ ὁ Λαμιεύς·
ὁ μὲν ἑκατέρῳ δοὺς τριάκοντα μνᾶς, ὁ δ᾽ Ἱππό-
νικος Μενεδήμῳ εἰς ἔκδοσιν τῶν θυγατέρων
δισχιλίας δραχμάς. ἦσαν δὲ τρεῖς, καθά φησιν
Ἡρακλείδης, ἐξ Ὠρωπίας αὐτῷ γυναικὸς γε-
γεννημέναι.

that on her journey she might be set upon and robbed, he gave her an escort from Delphi to Chalcis.

He was a very warm friend, as is shown by his affection for Asclepiades, which was hardly inferior to the devotion shown by Pylades. But, Asclepiades being the elder, it was said that he was the playwright and Menedemus the actor. They say that once, when Archipolis had given them a cheque for half a talent, they stickled so long over the point as to whose claim came second that neither of them got the money. It is said that they married a mother and her daughter; Asclepiades married the daughter and Menedemus the mother. But after the death of his own wife, Asclepiades took the wife of Menedemus; and afterwards the latter, when he became head of the state, married a rich woman as his second wife Nevertheless, as they kept one household, Menedemus entrusted his former wife with the care of his establishment. However, Asclepiades died first at a great age at Eretria, having lived with Menedemus economically, though they had ample means. Some time afterwards a favourite of Asclepiades, having come to a party and being refused admittance by the pupils, Menedemus ordered them to admit him, saying that even now, when under the earth, Asclepiades opened the door for him. It was Hipponicus the Macedonian and Agetor of Lamia who were their chief supporters; the one gave each of the two thirty minae, while Hipponicus furnished Menedemus with two thousand drachmae with which to portion his daughters. There were three of them according to Heraclides, his children by a wife who was a native of Oropus.

139 Τὰ δὲ συμπόσια τοῦτον ἐποιεῖτο τὸν τρόπον·
προηρίστα μετὰ δυοῖν ἢ τριῶν ἕως βραδέως ἦν τῆς
ἡμέρας· ἔπειτά τις ἐκάλει τοὺς παραγενομένους
καὶ αὐτοὺς ἤδη δεδειπνηκότας· ὥστ᾽ εἴ τις ἔλθοι
θᾶττον, ἀνακάμπτων ἐπυνθάνετο τῶν ἐξιόντων τί
εἴη παρακείμενον καὶ πῶς ἔχοι τὸ τοῦ χρόνου·
εἰ μὲν οὖν λαχάνιον ἢ ταρίχιον, ἀνεχώρουν· εἰ δὲ
κρεάδιον, εἰσῄεσαν. ἦν δὲ τοῦ μὲν θέρους ψίαθος
ἐπὶ τῶν κλινῶν, τοῦ δὲ χειμῶνος κώδιον· προσ-
κεφάλαιον αὐτῷ φέρειν ἔδει. τό τε περιαγόμενον
ποτήριον οὐ μεῖζον ἦν κοτυλιαίου· τράγημα θέρμος
ἢ κύαμος, ἔστι δ᾽ ὅτε καὶ τῶν ὡρίων ἄπιος ἢ ῥοιὰ
140 ἢ ὦχροι ἢ νὴ Δί᾽ ἰσχάδες. ἃ πάντα φησὶν ὁ
Λυκόφρων ἐν τοῖς πεποιημένοις σατύροις αὐτῷ,
οὓς Μενέδημος ἐπέγραψεν, ἐγκώμιον τοῦ φιλοσόφου
ποιήσας τὸ δρᾶμα· ὧν καί τινά ἐστι τοιαυτί·

ὡς ἐκ βραχείας δαιτὸς ἡ βαιὰ κύλιξ
αὐτοῖς κυκλεῖται πρὸς μέτρον, τράγημα δὲ
ὁ σωφρονιστὴς τοῖς φιληκόοις λόγος.

Τὰ μὲν οὖν πρῶτα κατεφρονεῖτο, κύων καὶ
λῆρος ὑπὸ τῶν Ἐρετριέων ἀκούων· ὕστερον δ᾽
ἐθαυμάσθη, ὥστε καὶ τὴν πόλιν ἐγχειρίσασθαι.
ἐπρέσβευσε δὲ καὶ πρὸς Πτολεμαῖον καὶ Λυσίμαχον, τιμώμενος πανταχοῦ· οὐ μὴν ἀλλὰ καὶ πρὸς
Δημήτριον. καὶ τῆς πόλεως διακόσια τάλαντα
τελούσης πρὸς ἔτος αὐτῷ, τὰ πεντήκοντα ἀφεῖλε·
πρὸς ὃν διαβληθεὶς ὡς τὴν πόλιν ἐγχειρίζων

---

* Nauck, *T.G.F.*² p. 818.

He used to give his parties in this fashion : he would breakfast beforehand with two or three friends and stay until it was late in the day. And in the next place some one would summon the guests who had arrived and who had themselves already dined, so that, if anyone came too soon, he would walk up and down and inquire from those who came out of the house what was on the table and what o'clock it was. If then it was only vegetables or salt fish, they would depart ; but if there was meat, they would enter the house. In the summer time a rush mat was put upon each couch, in winter time a sheepskin. The guest brought his own cushion. The loving-cup which was passed round was no larger than a pint cup. The dessert consisted of lupins or beans, sometimes of ripe fruit such as pears, pomegranates, a kind of pulse, or even dried figs. All of these facts are mentioned by Lycophron in his satiric drama entitled *Menedemus*, which was composed as a tribute to him. Here is a specimen of it [a] :

And after a temperate feast the modest cup was passed round with discretion, and their dessert was temperate discourse for such as cared to listen.

At first he was despised, being called a cynic and a humbug by the Eretrians. But afterwards he was greatly admired, so much so that they entrusted him with the government of the state. He was sent as envoy to Ptolemy and to Lysimachus, being honoured wherever he went. He was, moreover, envoy to Demetrius, and he caused the yearly tribute of two hundred talents which the city used to pay Demetrius to be reduced by fifty talents. And when he was accused to Demetrius of intriguing to hand over the city to Ptolemy, he defended

Πτολεμαίῳ, ἀπολογεῖται δι' ἐπιστολῆς ἧς ἡ ἀρχή·
141 '' Μενέδημος βασιλεῖ Δημητρίῳ χαίρειν. ἀκούω
πρὸς σὲ ἀνατεθῆναι περὶ ἡμῶν.'' λόγος δὲ δια-
βεβληκέναι αὐτὸν τῶν ἀντιπολιτευομένων τινὰ
Αἰσχύλον. δοκεῖ δ' ἐμβριθέστατα πρεσβεῦσαι πρὸς
Δημήτριον ὑπὲρ τοῦ 'Ωρωποῦ, ὡς καὶ Εὔφαντος
ἐν 'Ιστορίαις μνημονεύει. ἠγάπα δὲ αὐτὸν καὶ
'Αντίγονος καὶ μαθητὴν ἀνεκήρυττεν αὐτόν. καὶ
ἡνίκα ἐνίκα τοὺς βαρβάρους περὶ Λυσιμαχίαν,
γράφει ψήφισμα αὐτῷ Μενέδημος ἁπλοῦν τε καὶ
142 ἀκόλακον, οὗ ἡ ἀρχή· '' οἱ στρατηγοὶ καὶ οἱ
πρόβουλοι εἶπον. ἐπειδὴ βασιλεὺς 'Αντίγονος
μάχῃ νικήσας τοὺς βαρβάρους παραγίνεται εἰς τὴν
ἰδίαν, καὶ τὰ ἄλλα πάντα πράσσει κατὰ γνώμην·
ἔδοξε τῇ βουλῇ καὶ τῷ δήμῳ.''

Διὰ ταῦτα δὴ καὶ τὴν ἄλλην φιλίαν ὑποπτευθεὶς
προδιδόναι τὴν πόλιν αὐτῷ, διαβάλλοντος 'Αριστοδήμου ὑπεξῆλθε· καὶ διέτριβεν ἐν 'Ωρωπῷ ἐν
τῷ τοῦ 'Αμφιάρεω ἱερῷ· ἔνθα χρυσῶν ποτηρίων
ἀπολομένων, καθά φησιν 'Έρμιππος, δόγματι
κοινῷ τῶν Βοιωτῶν ἐκελεύσθη μετελθεῖν. ἐντεῦθεν ἀθυμήσας λαθραίως παρεισδὺς εἰς τὴν πατρίδα
καὶ τήν τε γυναῖκα καὶ τὰς θυγατέρας παρα-
λαβὼν πρὸς 'Αντίγονον ἐλθὼν ἀθυμίᾳ τὸν βίον
κατέστρεψε.

143 Φησὶ δ' 'Ηρακλείδης αὐτὸν πᾶν τοὐναντίον,
πρόβουλον γενόμενον τῶν 'Ερετριέων πολλάκις
ἐλευθερῶσαι τὴν πόλιν ἀπὸ τῶν τυράννων ἐπαγόμενον Δημήτριον· οὐκ ἂν δὴ οὖν προδοῦναι

himself in a letter which commences thus : " Menedemus to King Demetrius, greeting. I hear that
a report has reached you concerning me." There
is a tradition that one Aeschylus who belonged
to the opposite party had made these charges against
him. He seems to have behaved with the utmost
dignity in the embassy to Demetrius on the subject
of Oropus, as Euphantus relates in his *Histories*.
Antigonus too was much attached to him and used to
proclaim himself his pupil. And when he vanquished
the barbarians near the town of Lysimachia, Menedemus moved a decree in his honour in simple terms
and free from flattery, beginning thus : " On the
motion of the generals and the councillors—Whereas
King Antigonus is returning to his own country after
vanquishing the barbarians in battle, and whereas
in all his undertakings he prospers according to his
will, the senate and the people have decreed . . ."

On these grounds, then, and from his friendship for
him in other matters, he was suspected of betraying
the city to Antigonus, and, being denounced by
Aristodemus, withdrew from Eretria and stayed
awhile in Oropus in the temple of Amphiaraus.
And, because some golden goblets were missing
from the temple, he was ordered to depart by a
general vote of the Boeotians, as is stated by
Hermippus ; and thereupon in despair, after a secret
visit to his native city, he took with him his wife
and daughters and came to the court of Antigonus,
where he died of a broken heart.

Heraclides tells quite another story, that he was
made councillor of the Eretrians and more than once
saved the city from a tyranny by calling in Demetrius
—so then he would not be likely to betray the city

αὐτὸν 'Αντιγόνῳ τὴν πόλιν, ἀλλὰ διαβολὴν ἀναλαβεῖν ψευδῆ· φοιτᾶν τε πρὸς τὸν 'Αντίγονον καὶ βούλεσθαι ἐλευθερῶσαι τὴν πατρίδα· τοῦ δὲ μὴ εἴκοντος ὑπ' ἀθυμίας ἀσιτήσαντα ἑπτὰ ἡμέρας τὸν βίον μεταλλάξαι. τὰ ὅμοια τούτῳ καὶ 'Αντίγονος ὁ Καρύστιος ἱστορεῖ. μόνῳ δὲ Περσαίῳ διαπρύσιον εἶχε πόλεμον· ἐδόκει γὰρ 'Αντιγόνου βουλομένου τὴν δημοκρατίαν ἀποκαταστῆσαι τοῖς 144 'Ερετριεῦσι χάριν Μενεδήμου κωλῦσαι. διὸ καί ποτε παρὰ πότον ὁ Μενέδημος ἐλέγξας αὐτὸν τοῖς λόγοις τά τε ἄλλα ἔφη καὶ δὴ καὶ '' φιλόσοφος μὲν [τοι] τοιοῦτος, ἀνὴρ δὲ καὶ τῶν ὄντων καὶ τῶν γενησομένων κάκιστος.''

Ἐτελεύτα δὲ κατὰ τὸν Ἡρακλείδην τέταρτον καὶ ἑβδομηκοστὸν ἔτος βιούς. καὶ εἰς αὐτὸν ἡμῶν ἐστιν οὕτως ἔχον·

ἔκλυον, Μενέδημε, τεὸν μόρον, ὡς ἑκὼν ἀπέσβης
ἐν ἡμέρῃσιν ἑπτὰ μηδὲν ἐσθίων.
κᾆτ' ἔργον ἔρεξας Ἐρετρικόν, ἀλλ' ὅμως ἄνανδρον·
ἀψυχίη γὰρ ἡγεμὼν ἔπειγέ σε.

Καὶ οὗτοι μὲν οἱ Σωκρατικοὶ καὶ οἱ ἀπ' αὐτῶν. μετιτέον δὲ ἐπὶ Πλάτωνα τὸν τῆς 'Ακαδημείας κατάρξαντα, καὶ τοὺς ἀπ' αὐτοῦ, ὁπόσοι γεγόνασιν ἐλλόγιμοι.

to Antigonus, but was made the victim of a false charge; that he betook himself to Antigonus and was anxious to regain freedom for his country; that, as Antigonus would not give way, in despair he put an end to his life by abstaining from food for seven days. The account of Antigonus of Carystus is similar.[a] With Persaeus alone he carried on open warfare, for it was thought that, when Antigonus was willing for Menedemus's sake to restore to the Eretrians their democracy, Persaeus prevented him. Hence on one occasion over the wine Menedemus refuted Persaeus in argument and said, amongst other things, " Such he is as a philosopher but, as a man, the worst of all that are alive or to be born hereafter."

According to the statement of Heraclides he died in his seventy-fourth year. I have written the following epigram upon him[b]:

I heard of your fate, Menedemus, how, of your own free will, you expired by starving yourself for seven days, a deed right worthy of an Eretrian, but unworthy of a man; but despair was your leader and urged you on.

These then are the disciples of Socrates or their immediate successors. We must now pass to Plato, the founder of the Academy, and his successors, so far as they were men of reputation.

---

[a] Antigonus of Carystus (see Introd. p. xxiii) is the older authority, from whom Heraclides (probably Heraclides Lembos) directly or indirectly derived his information.

[b] *Anth. Plan.* v. 40.

Γ

ΠΛΑΤΩΝ

1 Πλάτων, Ἀρίστωνος καὶ Περικτιόνης — ἢ Πωτώνης, — Ἀθηναῖος, ἥτις τὸ γένος ἀνέφερεν εἰς Σόλωνα. τούτου γὰρ ἦν ἀδελφὸς Δρωπίδης, οὗ Κριτίας, οὗ Κάλλαισχρος, οὗ Κριτίας ὁ τῶν τριάκοντα καὶ Γλαύκων, οὗ Χαρμίδης καὶ Περικτιόνη, ἧς καὶ Ἀρίστωνος Πλάτων, ἕκτος ἀπὸ Σόλωνος. ὁ δὲ Σόλων εἰς Νηλέα καὶ Ποσειδῶνα ἀνέφερε τὸ γένος. φασὶ δὲ καὶ τὸν πατέρα αὐτοῦ ἀνάγειν εἰς Κόδρον τὸν Μελάνθου, οἵτινες ἀπὸ Ποσειδῶνος ἱστοροῦνται κατὰ Θρασύλον.

2 Σπεύσιππος δ' ἐν τῷ ἐπιγραφομένῳ Πλάτωνος περιδείπνῳ καὶ Κλέαρχος ἐν τῷ Πλάτωνος ἐγκωμίῳ καὶ Ἀναξιλαΐδης ἐν τῷ δευτέρῳ Περὶ φιλοσόφων φασίν, ὡς Ἀθήνησιν ἦν λόγος, ὡραίαν οὖσαν τὴν Περικτιόνην βιάζεσθαι τὸν Ἀρίστωνα καὶ μὴ τυγχάνειν· παυόμενόν τε τῆς βίας ἰδεῖν τὴν τοῦ Ἀπόλλωνος ὄψιν· ὅθεν καθαρὰν γάμου φυλάξαι ἕως τῆς ἀποκυήσεως.

Καὶ γίνεται Πλάτων, ὥς φησιν Ἀπολλόδωρος ἐν Χρονικοῖς, ὀγδόῃ καὶ ὀγδοηκοστῇ Ὀλυμπιάδι, Θαργηλιῶνος ἑβδόμῃ, καθ' ἣν Δήλιοι τὸν Ἀπόλλωνα
276

BOOK III

PLATO (427–347 B.C.)

PLATO was the son of Ariston and a citizen of Athens.
His mother was Perictione (or Potone), who traced
back her descent to Solon. For Solon had a brother,
Dropides ; he was the father of Critias, who was the
father of Callaeschrus, who was the father of Critias,
one of the Thirty, as well as of Glaucon, who was the
father of Charmides and Perictione. Thus Plato,
the son of this Perictione and Ariston, was in the
sixth generation from Solon. And Solon traced his
descent to Neleus and Poseidon. His father too is
said to be in the direct line from Codrus, the son of
Melanthus, and, according to Thrasylus, Codrus and
Melanthus also trace their descent from Poseidon.

Speusippus in the work entitled *Plato's Funeral
Feast*, Clearchus in his *Encomium on Plato*, and
Anaxilaïdes in his second book *On Philosophers*, tell
us that there was a story at Athens that Ariston
made violent love to Perictione, then in her bloom,
and failed to win her ; and that, when he ceased to
offer violence, Apollo appeared to him in a dream,
whereupon he left her unmolested until her child
was born.

Apollodorus in his *Chronology* fixes the date of
Plato's birth in the 88th Olympiad, on the seventh
day of the month Thargelion, the same day on which

γενέσθαι φασί. τελευτᾷ δὲ—ὥς φησιν Ἕρμιππος,
ἐν γάμοις δειπνῶν—τῷ πρώτῳ ἔτει τῆς ὀγδόης καὶ
ἑκατοστῆς Ὀλυμπιάδος, βιοὺς ἔτος ἓν πρὸς τοῖς
3 ὀγδοήκοντα. Νεάνθης δέ φησιν αὐτὸν τεττάρων
καὶ ὀγδοήκοντα τελευτῆσαι ἐτῶν. ἔστιν οὖν Ἰσοκράτους νεώτερος ἔτεσιν ἕξ· ὁ μὲν γὰρ ἐπὶ Λυσιμάχου, Πλάτων δὲ ἐπὶ Ἀμεινίου γέγονεν, ἐφ' οὗ
Περικλῆς ἐτελεύτησεν. ἦν δὲ τῶν δήμων Κολ-
λυτεύς, ὥς φησιν Ἀντιλέων ἐν δευτέρῳ Περὶ
χρόνων. καὶ ἐγεννήθη κατά τινας ἐν Αἰγίνῃ—ἐν
τῇ Φειδιάδου οἰκίᾳ τοῦ Θάλητος, ὥς φησι Φαβωρῖνος ἐν Παντοδαπῇ ἱστορίᾳ—τοῦ πατρὸς αὐτοῦ
μετὰ καὶ ἄλλων πεμφθέντος κληρούχου καὶ ἐπαν-
ελθόντος εἰς Ἀθήνας, ὁπόθ' ὑπὸ Λακεδαιμονίων
ἐξεβλήθησαν βοηθούντων Αἰγινήταις. ἀλλὰ καὶ
ἐχορήγησεν Ἀθήνησι Δίωνος ἀναλίσκοντος, ὥς
4 φησιν Ἀθηνόδωρος ἐν η' Περιπάτων. ἔσχε δ'
ἀδελφοὺς Ἀδείμαντον καὶ Γλαύκωνα καὶ ἀδελ-
φὴν Πωτώνην, ἐξ ἧς ἦν Σπεύσιππος.

Καὶ ἐπαιδεύθη μὲν γράμματα παρὰ Διονυσίῳ,
οὗ καὶ μνημονεύει ἐν τοῖς Ἀντερασταῖς. ἐγυμνά-
σατο δὲ παρὰ Ἀρίστωνι τῷ Ἀργείῳ παλαιστῇ·
ἀφ' οὗ καὶ Πλάτων διὰ τὴν εὐεξίαν μετωνομάσθη,
πρότερον Ἀριστοκλῆς ἀπὸ τοῦ πάππου καλούμενος
[ὄνομα], καθά φησιν Ἀλέξανδρος ἐν Διαδοχαῖς.
ἔνιοι δὲ διὰ τὴν πλατύτητα τῆς ἑρμηνείας οὕτως
ὀνομασθῆναι· ἢ ὅτι πλατὺς ἦν τὸ μέτωπον, ὥς φησι
Νεάνθης. εἰσὶ δ' οἳ καὶ παλαῖσαί φασιν αὐτὸν
Ἰσθμοῖ, καθὰ καὶ Δικαίαρχος ἐν πρώτῳ Περὶ

the Delians say that Apollo himself was born. He died, according to Hermippus, at a wedding feast, in the first year of the 108th Olympiad, in his eighty-first year.[a] Neanthes, however, makes him die at the age of eighty-four. He is thus seen to be six years the junior of Isocrates. For Isocrates was born in the archonship of Lysimachus,[b] Plato in that of Ameinias, the year of Pericles' death.[c] He belonged to the deme Collytus, as is stated by Antileon in his second book *On Dates*. He was born, according to some, in Aegina, in the house of Phidiades, the son of Thales, as Favorinus states in his *Miscellaneous History*, for his father had been sent along with others to Aegina to settle in the island, but returned to Athens when the Athenians were expelled by the Lacedaemonians, who championed the Aeginetan cause. That Plato acted as choregus at Athens, the cost being defrayed by Dion, is stated by Athenodorus in the eighth book of a work entitled *Walks*. He had two brothers, Adeimantus and Glaucon, and a sister, Potone, who was the mother of Speusippus.

He was taught letters in the school of Dionysius, who is mentioned by him in the *Rivals*. And he learnt gymnastics under Ariston, the Argive wrestler. And from him he received the name of Plato on account of his robust figure, in place of his original name which was Aristocles, after his grandfather, as Alexander informs us in his *Successions of Philosophers*. But others affirm that he got the name Plato from the breadth of his style, or from the breadth of his forehead, as suggested by Neanthes. Others again affirm that he wrestled in the Isthmian Games—this is stated by Dicaearchus in his first book *On Lives*—

[a] 427-347 B.C.   [b] 436-435 B.C.   [c] 429 B.C.

279

5 βίων, καὶ γραφικῆς ἐπιμεληθῆναι καὶ ποιήματα
γράψαι, πρῶτον μὲν διθυράμβους, ἔπειτα καὶ μέλη
καὶ τραγῳδίας. ἰσχνόφωνός τε, φασίν, ἦν, ὡς καὶ
Τιμόθεός φησιν ὁ ᾿Αθηναῖος ἐν τῷ Περὶ βίων.
λέγεται δ᾽ ὅτι Σωκράτης ὄναρ εἶδε κύκνου νεοττὸν
ἐν τοῖς γόνασιν ἔχειν, ὃν καὶ παραχρῆμα πτερο-
φυήσαντα ἀναπτῆναι ἡδὺ κλάγξαντα· καὶ μεθ᾽
ἡμέραν Πλάτων αὐτῷ συστῆναι, τὸν δὲ τοῦτον
εἰπεῖν εἶναι τὸν ὄρνιν.

᾿Εφιλοσόφει δὲ τὴν ἀρχὴν ἐν ᾿Ακαδημείᾳ, εἶτα
ἐν τῷ κήπῳ τῷ παρὰ τὸν Κολωνόν, ὥς φησιν
᾿Αλέξανδρος ἐν Διαδοχαῖς, καθ᾽ ῾Ηράκλειτον.
ἔπειτα μέντοι μέλλων ἀγωνιεῖσθαι τραγῳδίᾳ πρὸ
τοῦ Διονυσιακοῦ θεάτρου Σωκράτους ἀκούσας
κατέφλεξε τὰ ποιήματα εἰπών·

῞Ηφαιστε, πρόμολ᾽ ὧδε· Πλάτων νύ τι σεῖο χατίζει.

6 τοὐντεῦθεν δὴ γεγονώς, φασίν, εἴκοσιν ἔτη διήκουσε
Σωκράτους· ἐκείνου δ᾽ ἀπελθόντος προσεῖχε Κρα-
τύλῳ τε τῷ ῾Ηρακλειτείῳ καὶ ῾Ερμογένει τῷ τὰ
Παρμενίδου φιλοσοφοῦντι. εἶτα γενόμενος ὀκτὼ
καὶ εἴκοσιν ἔτη, καθά φησιν ῾Ερμόδωρος, εἰς
Μέγαρα πρὸς Εὐκλείδην σὺν καὶ ἄλλοις τισὶ
Σωκρατικοῖς ὑπεχώρησεν. ἔπειτα εἰς Κυρήνην
ἀπῆλθε πρὸς Θεόδωρον τὸν μαθηματικόν· κἀκεῖθεν
εἰς ᾿Ιταλίαν πρὸς τοὺς Πυθαγορικοὺς Φιλόλαον
καὶ Εὔρυτον. ἔνθεν τε εἰς Αἴγυπτον παρὰ τοὺς

---

[a] Compare Apuleius, *De Platone*, p. 64 Goldb. It has been
proposed to emend the next sentence by bracketing the words
ἐν ᾿Ακαδημείᾳ, εἶτα ἐν τῷ κήπῳ τῷ παρὰ τὸν Κολωνόν, as a
note inserted by Diogenes Laertius from a different author.

[b] Aelian (*V.H.* ii. 30) has πρὸ τῶν Διονυσίων, " before the
festival of Dionysus." [c] Hom. *Il.* xviii. 392.

and that he applied himself to painting and wrote poems, first dithyrambs, afterwards lyric poems and tragedies. He had, they say, a weak voice ; this is confirmed by Timotheus the Athenian in his book *On Lives.* It is stated that Socrates in a dream saw a cygnet on his knees, which all at once put forth plumage, and flew away after uttering a loud sweet note. And the next day Plato was introduced as a pupil, and thereupon he recognized in him the swan of his dream.[a]

At first he used to study philosophy in the Academy, and afterwards in the garden at Colonus (as Alexander states in his *Successions of Philosophers*), as a follower of Heraclitus. Afterwards, when he was about to compete for the prize with a tragedy, he listened to Socrates in front of the theatre of Dionysus,[b] and then consigned his poems to the flames, with the words [c] :

Come hither, O fire-god, Plato now has need of thee.[d]

From that time onward, having reached his twentieth year (so it is said), he was the pupil of Socrates. When Socrates was gone, he attached himself to Cratylus the Heraclitean, and to Hermogenes who professed the philosophy of Parmenides. Then at the age of twenty-eight, according to Hermodorus, he withdrew to Megara to Euclides, with certain other disciples of Socrates. Next he proceeded to Cyrene on a visit to Theodorus the mathematician, thence to Italy to see the Pythagorean philosophers Philolaus and Eurytus, and thence to Egypt to see

---

[a] ἔπειτα μέντοι . . . τι σεῖο χατίζει. It is suggested that this sentence also is an insertion by Diogenes, which interrupts the real sequence of the narrative.

προφήτας· οὗ φασι καὶ Εὐριπίδην αὐτῷ συν-
ακολουθῆσαι καὶ αὐτόθι νοσήσαντα πρὸς τῶν
ἱερέων ἀπολυθῆναι τῇ διὰ θαλάττης θεραπείᾳ·
ὅθεν που καὶ εἰπεῖν·

θάλασσα κλύζει πάντα τἀνθρώπων κακά.

7 ἀλλὰ καθ' Ὅμηρον φάναι ⟨περὶ⟩ πάντων ἀνθρώπων[1]
Αἰγυπτίους ἰατροὺς εἶναι. διέγνω δὴ ὁ Πλάτων
καὶ τοῖς Μάγοις συμμῖξαι· διὰ δὲ τοὺς τῆς Ἀσίας
πολέμους ἀπέστη. ἐπανελθὼν δὲ εἰς Ἀθήνας
διέτριβεν ἐν Ἀκαδημείᾳ. τὸ δ' ἐστὶ γυμνάσιον
προάστειον ἀλσῶδες ἀπό τινος ἥρωος ὀνομασθὲν
Ἑκαδήμου, καθὰ καὶ Εὔπολις ἐν Ἀστρατεύτοις
φησίν·

ἐν εὐσκίοις δρόμοισιν Ἑκαδήμου θεοῦ.

ἀλλὰ καὶ ὁ Τίμων εἰς τὸν Πλάτωνα λέγων φησί·

τῶν πάντων δ' ἡγεῖτο πλατίστακος, ἀλλ' ἀγορητὴς
ἡδυεπής, τέττιξιν ἰσογράφος, οἵ θ' Ἑκαδήμου
δένδρῳ ἐφεζόμενοι ὄπα λειριόεσσαν ἱᾶσιν.

8 πρότερον γὰρ διὰ τοῦ ε Ἑκαδήμεια ἐκαλεῖτο.
ὁ δ' οὖν φιλόσοφος καὶ Ἰσοκράτει φίλος ἦν. καὶ
αὐτῶν Πραξιφάνης ἀνέγραψε διατριβήν τινα περὶ
ποιητῶν γενομένην ἐν ἀγρῷ παρὰ Πλάτωνι ἐπι-
ξενωθέντος τοῦ Ἰσοκράτους. καὶ αὐτόν φησιν
Ἀριστόξενος τρὶς ἐστρατεῦσθαι, ἅπαξ μὲν εἰς
Τάναγραν, δεύτερον δὲ εἰς Κόρινθον, τρίτον ἐπὶ
Δηλίῳ· ἔνθα καὶ ἀριστεῦσαι. μίξιν τε ἐποιήσατο
τῶν τε Ἡρακλειτείων λόγων καὶ Πυθαγορικῶν

---

[1] πάντας ἀνθρώπους codd.

---

those who interpreted the will of the gods; and
Euripides is said to have accompanied him thither.
There he fell sick and was cured by the priests, who
treated him with sea-water, and for this reason he
cited the line [a]:

> The sea doth wash away all human ills.

Furthermore he said that, according to Homer,[b]
beyond all men the Egyptians were skilled in healing.
Plato also intended to make the acquaintance of the
Magians, but was prevented by the wars in Asia.
Having returned to Athens, he lived in the Academy,
which is a gymnasium outside the walls, in a grove
named after a certain hero, Hecademus, as is stated
by Eupolis in his play entitled *Shirkers* [c]:

> In the shady walks of the divine Hecademus.

Moreover, there are verses of Timon which refer to
Plato [d]:

> Amongst all of them Plato was the leader, a big fish, but
> a sweet-voiced speaker, musical in prose as the cicala who,
> perched on the trees of Hecademus, pours forth a strain as
> delicate as a lily.

Thus the original name of the place was Hecademy,
spelt with *e*. Now Plato was a friend of Isocrates.
And Praxiphanes makes them converse about poets
at a country-seat where Plato was entertaining
Isocrates. And Aristoxenus asserts that he went
on service three times, first to Tanagra, secondly
to Corinth, and thirdly at Delium, where also he
obtained the prize of valour. He mixed together
doctrines of Heraclitus, the Pythagoreans and

---

[c] Meineke, *C.G.F.* ii. 437. According to Suidas, *s.v.*
Εὔπολις, this play had a second title, Ἀνδρογύναι, by which
alone it is cited in *Etymol. Magnum.*

[d] Fr. 30 D.

καὶ Σωκρατικῶν· τὰ μὲν γὰρ αἰσθητὰ καθ᾽ Ἡρά-
κλειτον, τὰ δὲ νοητὰ κατὰ Πυθαγόραν, τὰ δὲ
πολιτικὰ κατὰ Σωκράτην ἐφιλοσόφει.

9 Λέγουσι δέ τινες, ὧν ἐστι καὶ Σάτυρος, ὅτι
Δίωνι ἐπέστειλεν εἰς Σικελίαν ὠνήσασθαι τρία
βιβλία Πυθαγορικὰ παρὰ Φιλολάου μνῶν ἑκατόν.
καὶ γὰρ ἐν εὐπορίᾳ, φασίν, ἦν παρὰ Διονυσίου
λαβὼν ὑπὲρ τὰ ὀγδοήκοντα τάλαντα, ὡς καὶ
Ὀνήτωρ φησὶν ἐν τῷ ἐπιγραφομένῳ " εἰ χρημα-
τιεῖται ὁ σοφός." πολλὰ δὲ καὶ παρ᾽ Ἐπιχάρμου
τοῦ κωμῳδιοποιοῦ προσωφέληται τὰ πλεῖστα
μεταγράψας, καθά φησιν Ἄλκιμος ἐν τοῖς πρὸς
Ἀμύνταν, ἅ ἐστι τέτταρα. ἔνθα καὶ ἐν τῷ πρώτῳ
φησὶ ταῦτα·

" Φαίνεται δὲ καὶ Πλάτων πολλὰ τῶν Ἐπιχάρμου
λέγων. σκεπτέον δέ· ὁ Πλάτων φησὶν αἰσθητὸν
μὲν εἶναι τὸ μηδέποτε ἐν τῷ ποιῷ μηδὲ ποσῷ
10 διαμένον ἀλλ᾽ ἀεὶ ῥέον καὶ μεταβάλλον, ὡς ἐξ ὧν
ἄν τις ἀνέλῃ τὸν ἀριθμόν, τούτων οὔτε ἴσων οὔτε
τινῶν οὔτε ποσῶν οὔτε ποιῶν ὄντων. ταῦτα δ᾽
ἐστὶν ὧν ἀεὶ γένεσις, οὐσία δὲ μηδέποτε πέφυκε.
νοητὸν δὲ ἐξ οὗ μηθὲν ἀπογίνεται μηδὲ προσγίνεται.
τοῦτο δ᾽ ἐστὶν ἡ τῶν ἀιδίων φύσις, ἣν ὁμοίαν τε
καὶ τὴν αὐτὴν ἀεὶ συμβέβηκεν εἶναι. καὶ μὴν ὅ γε
Ἐπίχαρμος περὶ τῶν αἰσθητῶν καὶ νοητῶν ἐναργῶς
εἴρηκεν·

— ἀλλ᾽ ἀεί τοι θεοὶ παρῆσαν χὑπέλιπον οὐ πώποκα,
τάδε δ᾽ ἀεὶ πάρεσθ᾽ ὁμοῖα διά τε τῶν αὐτῶν ἀεί.

---

[a] The genuineness of these fragments is doubted by
Wilamowitz, Rohde, and others; see Wilamowitz, *Platon*,
ii. 28 note 2, and on the other side Diels, note *ad loc.* (*Frag.
der Vorsok.* 13 B. 1-5).

Socrates. In his doctrine of sensible things he agrees with Heraclitus, in his doctrine of the intelligible with Pythagoras, and in political philosophy with Socrates.

Some authorities, amongst them Satyrus, say that he wrote to Dion in Sicily instructing him to purchase three Pythagorean books from Philolaus for 100 minae. For they say he was well off, having received from Dionysius over eighty talents. This is stated by Onetor in an essay upon the theme, "Whether a wise man will make money." Further, he derived great assistance from Epicharmus the Comic poet, for he transcribed a great deal from him, as Alcimus says in the essays dedicated to Amyntas, of which there are four. In the first of them he writes thus :

"It is evident that Plato often employs the words of Epicharmus.[a] Just consider. Plato asserts that the object of sense is that which never abides in quality or quantity, but is ever in flux and change. The assumption is that the things from which you take away number are no longer equal nor determinate, nor have they quantity or quality. These are the things to which becoming always, and being never, belongs. But the object of thought is something constant from which nothing is subtracted, to which nothing is added. This is the nature of the eternal things, the attribute of which is to be ever alike and the same. And indeed Epicharmus has expressed himself plainly about objects of sense and objects of thought.

a. But gods there always were ; never at any time were they wanting, while things in this world are always alike, and are brought about through the same agencies.

— ἀλλὰ λέγεται μὰν χάος πρᾶτον γενέσθαι τῶν
θεῶν.

— πῶς δέ κα; μὴ ἔχον γ᾽ ἀπὸ τίνος μηδ᾽ ἐς ὅ τι
πρᾶτον μόλοι.

— οὐκ ἄρ᾽ ἔμολε πρᾶτον οὐθέν; — οὐδὲ μὰ Δία
δεύτερον,

11   τῶνδέ γε ὦν ἁμὲς νῦν ὧδε λέγομες ἀλλ᾽ ἀεὶ
τάδ᾽ ἦν[1] . . .

αἰ πὸτ ἀριθμόν τις περισσόν, αἰ δὲ λῇς, πὸτ
ἄρτιον,

ποτθέμειν λῇ ψᾶφον ἢ καὶ τᾶν ὑπαρχουσᾶν
λαβεῖν,

ἦ δοκεῖ κά τοί γ᾽ ἔθ᾽ ωὑτὸς εἶμεν;—οὐκ ἐμίν
γα κά.

— οὐδὲ μὰν οὐδ᾽ αἰ ποτὶ μέτρον παχυαῖον
ποτθέμειν

λῇ τις ἕτερον μᾶκος ἢ τοῦ πρόσθ᾽ ἐόντος
ἀποταμεῖν,

ἔτι χ᾽ ὑπάρχοι κῆνο τὸ μέτρον; — οὐ γάρ.
— ὧδε νῦν ὅρη

καὶ τὸς ἀνθρώπως· ὁ μὲν γὰρ αὔξεθ᾽, ὁ δέ γα
μὰν φθίνει,

ἐν μεταλλαγᾷ δὲ πάντες ἐντὶ πάντα τὸν
χρόνον.

ὃ δὲ μεταλλάσσει κατὰ φύσιν κοὔποκ᾽ ἐν ταὐτῷ
μένει,

ἕτερον εἴη κα τόδ᾽ <ἀ>εὶ τῶ παρεξεστακότος.

καὶ τὺ δὴ κἀγὼ χθὲς ἄλλοι καί νυν ἄλλοι
τελέθομες

καὖθις ἄλλοι κοὔποχ᾽ ωὑτοὶ κατά <γα τοῦτον>
τὸν λόγον.''

---

[1] λέγω μέλλει τάδ᾽ εἶναι codd.: corr. Bergk.

B. Yet it is said that Chaos was the first-born of the gods.

A. How so? If indeed there was nothing out of which, or into which, it could come first.

B. What! Then did nothing come first after all?

A. No, by Zeus, nor second either, at least of the things which we are thus talking about now : on the contrary, they existed from all eternity. . . .

A. But suppose some one chooses to add a single pebble to a heap containing either an odd or an even number, whichever you please, or to take away one of those already there ; do you think the number of pebbles would remain the same?

B. Not I.

A. Nor yet, if one chooses to add to a cubit-measure another length,[a] or cut off some of what was there already, would the original measure still exist?

B. Of course not.

A. Now consider mankind in this same way. One man grows, and another again shrinks ; and they are all undergoing change the whole time. But a thing which naturally changes and never remains in the same state must ever be different from that which has thus changed. And even so you and I were one pair of men yesterday, are another to-day, and again will be another to-morrow, and will never remain ourselves, by this same argument."

---

[a] Or, reading στερρόν for ἕτερον, " a substantial length."

12 Ἔτι φησὶν ὁ Ἄλκιμος καὶ ταυτί· "φασὶν οἱ σοφοὶ τὴν ψυχὴν τὰ μὲν διὰ τοῦ σώματος αἰσθάνεσθαι οἷον ἀκούουσαν, βλέπουσαν, τὰ δ᾽ αὐτὴν καθ᾽ αὑτὴν ἐνθυμεῖσθαι μηδὲν τῷ σώματι χρωμένην· διὸ καὶ τῶν ὄντων τὰ μὲν αἰσθητὰ εἶναι, τὰ δὲ νοητά. ὧν ἕνεκα καὶ Πλάτων ἔλεγεν, ὅτι δεῖ τοὺς συνιδεῖν τὰς τοῦ παντὸς ἀρχὰς ἐπιθυμοῦντας πρῶτον μὲν αὐτὰς καθ᾽ αὑτὰς διελέσθαι τὰς ἰδέας, οἷον ὁμοιότητα καὶ μονάδα καὶ πλῆθος καὶ μέγεθος καὶ στάσιν καὶ κίνησιν· δεύτερον αὐτὸ καθ᾽ αὑτὸ τὸ **13** καλὸν καὶ ἀγαθὸν καὶ δίκαιον καὶ τὰ τοιαῦτα ὑποθέσθαι· τρίτον τῶν ἰδεῶν συνιδεῖν ὅσαι πρὸς ἀλλήλας εἰσίν, οἷον ἐπιστήμην ἢ μέγεθος ἢ δεσποτείαν (ἐνθυμουμένους ὅτι τὰ παρ᾽ ἡμῖν διὰ τὸ μετέχειν ἐκείνων ὁμώνυμα ἐκείνοις ὑπάρχει· λέγω δὲ οἷον δίκαια μὲν ὅσα τοῦ δικαίου, καλὰ δὲ ὅσα τοῦ καλοῦ). ἔστι δὲ τῶν εἰδῶν ἓν ἕκαστον ἀίδιόν τε καὶ νόημα καὶ πρὸς τούτοις ἀπαθές. [διὸ καί φησιν ἐν τῇ φύσει τὰς ἰδέας ἑστάναι καθάπερ παραδείγματα, τὰ δ᾽ ἄλλα ταύταις ἐοικέναι τούτων ὁμοιώματα καθεστῶτα.] ὁ τοίνυν Ἐπίχαρμος περί τε τοῦ ἀγαθοῦ καὶ περὶ τῶν ἰδεῶν οὕτω λέγει·

14 ἆρ᾽ ἔστιν αὔλησίς τι πρᾶγμα; — πάνυ μὲν οὖν.
— ἄνθρωπος οὖν αὔλησίς ἐστιν; — οὐδαμῶς.
— φέρ᾽ ἴδω, τί δ᾽ αὐλητάς; τίς εἶμέν τοι δοκεῖ;
ἄνθρωπος; ἢ οὐ γάρ; — πάνυ μὲν οὖν. — οὐκ
    οὖν δοκεῖς
οὕτως ἔχειν ⟨κα⟩ καὶ περὶ τἀγαθοῦ; τὸ μὲν

288

Again, Alcimus makes this further statement: "There are some things, say the wise, which the soul perceives through the body, as in seeing and hearing; there are other things which it discerns by itself without the aid of the body. Hence it follows that of existing things some are objects of sense and others objects of thought. Hence Plato said that, if we wish to take in at one glance the principles underlying the universe, we must first distinguish the ideas by themselves, for example, likeness, unity and plurality, magnitude, rest and motion; next we must assume the existence of beauty, goodness, justice and the like, each existing in and for itself; in the third place we must see how many of the ideas are relative to other ideas, as are knowledge, or magnitude, or ownership, remembering that the things within our experience bear the same names as those ideas because they partake of them; I mean that things which partake of justice are just, things which partake of beauty are beautiful. Each one of the ideas is eternal, it is a notion, and moreover is incapable of change. Hence Plato says that they stand in nature like archetypes, and that all things else bear a resemblance to the ideas because they are copies of these archetypes. Now here are the words of Epicharmus about the good and about the ideas:

A. Is flute-playing a thing?
B. Most certainly.
A. Is man then flute-playing?
B. By no means.
A. Come, let me see, what is a flute-player? Whom do you take him to be? Is he not a man?
B. Most certainly.
A. Well, don't you think the same would be the case with

ἀγαθόν τι πρᾶγμ' εἶμεν καθ' αὕθ', ὅστις δέ κα
εἰδῇ μαθὼν τήν', ἀγαθὸς ἤδη γίγνεται.
ὥσπερ γάρ ἐστ' αὔλησιν αὐλητὰς μαθὼν
ἢ ὄρχησιν ὀρχηστάς τις ἢ πλοκεὺς πλοκάν,
ἢ πᾶν γ' ὁμοίως τῶν τοιούτων ὅ τι τὺ λῇς,
οὔ χ' αὐτὸς εἴη χὰ τέχνα, τεχνικός γα μάν.

15 Πλάτων ἐν τῇ περὶ τῶν ἰδεῶν ὑπολήψει φησίν,
εἴπερ ἐστὶ μνήμη, τὰς ἰδέας ἐν τοῖς οὖσιν ὑπάρχειν
διὰ τὸ τὴν μνήμην ἠρεμοῦντός τινος καὶ μένοντος
εἶναι· μένειν δὲ οὐδὲν ἕτερον ἢ τὰς ἰδέας. 'τίνα
γὰρ ἂν τρόπον,' φησί, 'διεσῴζετο τὰ ζῷα μὴ τῆς
ἰδέας ἐφαπτόμενα καὶ πρὸς τοῦτο τὸν νοῦν φυσικὸν
εἰληφότα; νῦν δὲ μνημονεύει τῆς ὁμοιότητός τε
καὶ τροφῆς, ὁποία τις ἐστὶν αὐτοῖς, ἐνδεικνύμενα
διότι πᾶσι τοῖς ζῴοις ἔμφυτός ἐστιν ἡ τῆς ὁμοιό-
τητος θεωρία· διὸ καὶ τῶν ὁμοφύλων αἰσθάνεται.'
πῶς οὖν ὁ Ἐπίχαρμος;

16 Εὔμαιε, τὸ σοφόν ἐστιν οὐ καθ' ἓν μόνον,
ἀλλ' ὅσσα περ ζῇ, πάντα καὶ γνώμαν ἔχει.
καὶ γὰρ τὸ θῆλυ τᾶν ἀλεκτορίδων γένος,
αἰ λῇς καταμαθεῖν ἀτενές, οὐ τίκτει τέκνα
ζῶντ', ἀλλ' ἐπῴζει καὶ ποιεῖ ψυχὰν ἔχειν.
τὸ δὲ σοφὸν ἁ φύσις τόδ' οἶδεν ὡς ἔχει
μόνα· πεπαίδευται γὰρ αὐταύτας ὕπο.

καὶ πάλιν·

θαυμαστὸν οὐδὲν ἁμὲ ταῦθ' οὕτω λέγειν
καὶ ἀνδάνειν αὐτοῖσιν αὐτοὺς καὶ δοκεῖν
καλῶς πεφύκειν· καὶ γὰρ ἁ κύων κυνὶ
κάλλιστον εἶμεν φαίνεται καὶ βοῦς βοΐ,
ὄνος δ' ὄνῳ κάλλιστον, ὗς δέ θην ὑΐ."

the good ?   Is not the good in itself a thing ?   And does not he who has learnt that thing and knows it at once become good ?   For, just as he becomes a flute-player by learning flute-playing, or a dancer when he has learnt dancing, or a plaiter when he has learnt plaiting, in the same way, if he has learnt anything of the sort, whatever you like, he would not be one with the craft but he would be the craftsman.

Now Plato in conceiving his theory of Ideas says [a] : Since there is such a thing as memory, there must be ideas present in things, because memory is of something stable and permanent, and nothing is permanent except the ideas. ' For how,' he says, ' could animals have survived unless they had apprehended the idea and had been endowed by Nature with intelligence to that end ?   As it is, they remember similarities and what their food is like, which shows that animals have the innate power of discerning what is similar.   And hence they perceive others of their own kind.'   How then does Epicharmus put it ?

Wisdom is not confined, Eumaeus, to one kind alone, but all living creatures likewise have understanding.   For, if you will study intently the hen among poultry, she does not bring forth the chicks alive, but sits clucking on the eggs and wakens life in them.   As for this wisdom of hers, the true state of the case is known to Nature alone, for the hen has learnt it from herself.

And again :

It is no wonder then that we talk thus and are pleased with ourselves and think we are fine folk.   For a dog appears the fairest of things to a dog, an ox to an ox, an ass to an ass, and verily a pig to a pig.''

[a] *Cf. Phaedo*, 06 ʙ '' (I considered) whether it is blood or air or fire with which we think, or none of these things, but the brain which furnishes the senses of hearing and sight and smell, and from these arise memory and opinion, and from memory and opinion, when they have become stable, in the same way knowledge arises.''

291

DIOGENES LAERTIUS

17 Καὶ ταῦτα μὲν καὶ τὰ τοιαῦτα διὰ τῶν τεττάρων
βιβλίων παραπήγνυσιν ὁ Ἄλκιμος παρασημαίνων
τὴν ἐξ Ἐπιχάρμου Πλάτωνι περιγινομένην ὠφέλειαν. ὅτι δ' οὐδ' αὐτὸς Ἐπίχαρμος ἠγνόει τὴν
αὑτοῦ σοφίαν, μαθεῖν ἐστι κἀκ τούτων ἐν οἷς τὸν
ζηλώσοντα προμαντεύεται·

> ὡς δ' ἐγὼ δοκέω, — δοκέων γὰρ σάφα ἴσαμι
> τοῦθ' ὅτι
> τῶν ἐμῶν μνάμα ποκ' ἐσσεῖται λόγων τούτων ἔτι.
> καὶ λαβών τις αὐτὰ περιδύσας τὸ μέτρον ὃ νῦν
> ἔχει,
> εἷμα δοὺς καὶ πορφυροῦν λόγοισι ποικίλας καλοῖς
> δυσπάλαιστος ὢν τὸς ἄλλως εὐπαλαίστους ἀπο-
> φανεῖ.

18 Δοκεῖ δὲ Πλάτων καὶ τὰ Σώφρονος τοῦ μιμο-
γράφου βιβλία ἠμελημένα πρῶτος εἰς Ἀθήνας
διακομίσαι καὶ ἠθοποιῆσαι πρὸς αὐτόν· ἃ καὶ
εὑρεθῆναι ὑπὸ τῇ κεφαλῇ αὐτοῦ. τρὶς δὲ πέ-
πλευκεν εἰς Σικελίαν· πρῶτον μὲν κατὰ θέαν τῆς
νήσου καὶ τῶν κρατήρων, ὅτε καὶ Διονύσιος ὁ
Ἑρμοκράτους τύραννος ὢν ἠνάγκασεν ὥστε συμ-
μῖξαι αὐτῷ. ὁ δὲ διαλεγόμενος περὶ τυραννίδος
καὶ φάσκων ὡς οὐκ ἔστι τὸ τοῦ κρείττονος συμφέρον
αὐτὸ † μόνον, εἰ μὴ καὶ ἀρετῇ διαφέροι, προσέκρουσεν
αὐτῷ. ὀργισθεὶς γὰρ " οἱ λόγοι σου," φησί, " γερον-
19 τιῶσι," καὶ ὅς· " σοῦ¹ δέ γε τυραννιῶσιν." ἐντεῦθεν
ἀγανακτήσας ὁ τύραννος πρῶτον μὲν ἀνελεῖν
ὥρμησεν αὐτόν· εἶτα παρακληθεὶς ὑπὸ Δίωνος καὶ
Ἀριστομένους τοῦτο μὲν οὐκ ἐποίησε, παρέδωκε
δὲ αὐτὸν Πόλλιδι τῷ Λακεδαιμονίῳ κατὰ καιρὸν
διὰ πρεσβείαν ἀφιγμένῳ ὥστε ἀποδόσθαι. κά-

292

These and the like instances Alcimus notes through
four books, pointing out the assistance derived by
Plato from Epicharmus. That Epicharmus himself
was fully conscious of his wisdom can also be seen
from the lines in which he foretells that he will have
an imitator [a] :

And as I think—for when I think anything I know it full
well—that my words will some day be remembered ; some
one will take them and free them from the metre in which
they are now set, nay, will give them instead a purple robe,
embroidering it with fine phrases ; and, being invincible, he
will make every one else an easy prey.

Plato, it seems, was the first to bring to Athens
the mimes of Sophron which had been neglected,
and to draw characters in the style of that writer ;
a copy of the mimes, they say, was actually found
under his pillow. He made three voyages to Sicily,
the first time to see the island and the craters of
Etna : on this occasion Dionysius, the son of Hermo-
crates, being on the throne, forced him to become
intimate with him. But when Plato held forth on
tyranny and maintained that the interest of the
ruler alone was not the best end, unless he were
also pre-eminent in virtue, he offended Dionysius,
who in his anger exclaimed, " You talk like an old
dotard." " And you like a tyrant," rejoined Plato.
At this the tyrant grew furious and at first was bent
on putting him to death ; then, when he had been
dissuaded from this by Dion and Aristomenes, he
did not indeed go so far but handed him over to
Pollis the Lacedaemonian, who had just then arrived
on an embassy, with orders to sell him into slavery.

[a] This fragment (Fr. 6 D.), which has not the authority
of Alcimus, is generally condemned as spurious.

---

[1] σοῦ] οἱ σοί Richards.

κεῖνος ἀγαγὼν αὐτὸν εἰς Αἴγιναν ἐπίπρασκεν· ὅτε
καὶ Χάρμανδρος Χαρμανδρίδου ἐγράψατο αὐτῷ
δίκην θανάτου κατὰ τὸν παρ' αὐτοῖς τεθέντα νόμον,
τὸν πρῶτον ἐπιβάντα 'Αθηναίων τῇ νήσῳ ἄκριτον
ἀποθνήσκειν. ἦν δ' αὐτὸς ὁ θεὶς τὸν νόμον, καθά
φησι Φαβωρῖνος ἐν Παντοδαπῇ ἱστορίᾳ. εἰπόντος
δέ τινος, ἀλλὰ κατὰ παιδιάν, φιλόσοφον εἶναι τὸν
ἐπιβάντα, ἀπέλυσαν. ἔνιοι δέ φασι παραχθῆναι
αὐτὸν εἰς τὴν ἐκκλησίαν καὶ τηρούμενον μηδ'
ὁτιοῦν φθέγξασθαι, ἑτοίμως δὲ ἐκδέξασθαι τὸ
συμβαῖνον· οἱ δὲ ἀποκτεῖναι μὲν αὐτὸν οὐ διέγνωσαν,
πωλεῖν δὲ ἔκριναν τῷ τρόπῳ τῶν αἰχμαλώτων.

20 Λυτροῦται δὴ αὐτὸν κατὰ τύχην παρὼν 'Αννί-
κερις ὁ Κυρηναῖος εἴκοσι μνῶν — οἱ δὲ τριάκοντα
— καὶ ἀναπέμπει 'Αθήναζε πρὸς τοὺς ἑταίρους.
οἱ δ' εὐθὺς τἀργύριον ἐξέπεμψαν· ὅπερ οὐ προσήκατο εἰπὼν μὴ μόνους ἐκείνους ἀξίους εἶναι
Πλάτωνος κήδεσθαι. ἔνιοι δὲ καὶ Δίωνα ἀπο-
στεῖλαί φασι τὸ ἀργύριον καὶ τὸν μὴ προσέσθαι,
ἀλλὰ καὶ κηπίδιον αὐτῷ τὸ ἐν 'Ακαδημείᾳ πρίασθαι. τὸν μέντοι Πόλλιν λόγος ὑπό τε Χαβρίου
ἡττηθῆναι καὶ μετὰ ταῦτα ἐν Ἑλίκῃ καταποντω-
θῆναι τοῦ δαιμονίου μηνίσαντος διὰ τὸν φιλόσοφον,
ὡς καὶ Φαβωρῖνός φησιν ἐν πρώτῳ τῶν 'Απομνη-
21 μονευμάτων. οὐ μὴν ἡσύχαζεν ὁ Διονύσιος· μαθὼν
δὲ ἐπέστειλε Πλάτωνι μὴ κακῶς ἀγορεύειν αὐτόν.
καὶ ὃς ἀντεπέστειλε μὴ τοσαύτην αὐτῷ σχολὴν
εἶναι ὥστε Διονυσίου μεμνῆσθαι.

---

[a] In the tidal wave which swallowed up ten Lacedaemonian triremes in the great earthquake of 372 B.C. : Aelian,
Hist. animal. xi. 19.

And Pollis took him to Aegina and there offered him
for sale. And then Charmandrus, the son of Char-
mandrides, indicted him on a capital charge according
to the law in force among the Aeginetans, to the
effect that the first Athenian who set foot upon the
island should be put to death without a trial. This
law had been passed by the prosecutor himself,
according to Favorinus in his *Miscellaneous History*.
But when some one urged, though in jest, that the
offender was a philosopher, the court acquitted him.
There is another version to the effect that he was
brought before the assembly and, being kept under
close scrutiny, he maintained an absolute silence and
awaited the issue with confidence. The assembly
decided not to put him to death but to sell him just
as if he were a prisoner of war.

Anniceris the Cyrenaic happened to be present
and ransomed him for twenty minae—according to
others the sum was thirty minae—and dispatched
him to Athens to his friends, who immediately re-
mitted the money. But Anniceris declined it, saying
that the Athenians were not the only people worthy
of the privilege of providing for Plato. Others assert
that Dion sent the money and that Anniceris would
not take it, but bought for Plato the little garden
which is in the Academy. Pollis, however, is stated
to have been defeated by Chabrias and afterwards to
have been drowned at Helice,[a] his treatment of the
philosopher having provoked the wrath of heaven,
as Favorinus says in the first book of his *Memorabilia*.
Dionysius, indeed, could not rest. On learning the
facts he wrote and enjoined upon Plato not to speak
evil of him. And Plato replied that he had not the
leisure to keep Dionysius in his mind.

Δεύτερον πρὸς τὸν νεώτερον ἧκε Διονύσιον αἰτῶι γῆν καὶ ἀνθρώπους τοὺς κατὰ τὴν πολιτείαν αὐτοῦ ζησομένους· ὁ δὲ καίπερ ὑποσχόμενος οὐκ ἐποίησεν. ἔνιοι δέ φασι καὶ κινδυνεῦσαι αὐτὸν ὡς ἀναπείθοντα Δίωνα καὶ Θεοδόταν ἐπὶ τῇ τῆς νήσου ἐλευθερίᾳ· ὅτε καὶ Ἀρχύτας αὐτὸν ὁ Πυθαγορικὸς γράψας ἐπιστολὴν πρὸς Διονύσιον παρῃτήσατο καὶ διέσωσεν εἰς Ἀθήνας. ἔστι δὲ ἡ ἐπιστολὴ ἥδε·

" Ἀρχύτας Διονυσίῳ ὑγιαίνειν.

22 " Ἀπεστάλκαμέν τοι πάντες οἱ Πλάτωνος φίλοι τὼς περὶ Λαμίσκον τε καὶ Φωτίδαν ἀπολαμψούμεθα[1] τὸν ἄνδρα κὰτ τὰν πὰρ τὶν γενομέναν ὁμολογίαν. ὀρθῶς δέ κα ποιοῖς ἀμμιμνασκόμενος τήνας τᾶς σπουδᾶς, ἡνίκα πάντας ἀμὲ παρεκάλεις πὸτ τὰν Πλάτωνος ἄφιξιν ἀξιῶν προτρέπεσθαί τε αὐτὸν καὶ ἀναδέχεσθαι τά τε ἄλλα καὶ περὶ τὰν ἀσφάλειαν μένοντί τε καὶ ἀφορμίοντι. μέμνασο δὲ καὶ τῆνο ὅτι περὶ πολλῶ ἐποιήσω τὰν ἄφιξιν αὐτῶ καὶ ἀγάπης ἐκ τήνω τῶ χρόνω ὡς οὐδένα τῶν πὰρ τίν. αἰ δέ τις γέγονε τραχύτας, ἀνθρωπίζειν χρὴ κἀπο-διδόμεν ἀμὶν ἀβλαβῆ τὸν ἄνδρα. ταῦτα γὰρ ποιῶν δίκαια πραξεῖς καὶ ἀμὶν χαριξῇ."

23 Τρίτον ἦλθε διαλλάξων Δίωνα Διονυσίῳ· οὐ τυχὼν δὲ ἄπρακτος ἐπανῆλθεν εἰς τὴν πατρίδα. ἔνθα πολιτείας μὲν οὐχ ἥψατο, καίτοι πολιτικὸς ὢν ἐξ ὧν γέγραφεν. αἴτιον δὲ τὸ ἤδη τὸν δῆμον ἄλλοις πολιτεύμασιν ἐνειθίσθαι. φησὶ δὲ Παμφίλη ἐν τῷ πέμπτῳ καὶ εἰκοστῷ τῶν Ὑπομνημάτων

---

[1] ἢ ἀπολαμψούμενοι.

The second time he visited the younger Dionysius, requesting of him lands and settlers for the realization of his republic. Dionysius promised them but did not keep his word. Some say that Plato was also in great danger, being suspected of encouraging Dion and Theodotas in a scheme for liberating the whole island ; on this occasion Archytas the Pythagorean wrote to Dionysius, procured his pardon, and got him conveyed safe to Athens. The letter runs as follows :

"Archytas to Dionysius, wishing him good health.

"We, being all of us the friends of Plato, have sent to you Lamiscus and Photidas in order to take the philosopher away by the terms of the agreement made with you. You will do well to remember the zeal with which you urged us all to secure Plato's coming to Sicily, determined as you were to persuade him and to undertake, amongst other things, responsibility for his safety so long as he stayed with you and on his return. Remember this too, that you set great store by his coming, and from that time had more regard for him than for any of those at your court. If he has given you offence, it behoves you to behave with humanity and restore him to us unhurt. By so doing you will satisfy justice and at the same time put us under an obligation."

The third time he came to reconcile Dion and Dionysius, but, failing to do so, returned to his own country without achieving anything. And there he refrained from meddling with politics, although his writings show that he was a statesman. The reason was that the people had already been accustomed to measures and institutions quite different from his own. Pamphila in the twenty-fifth book of her

ὡς Ἀρκάδες καὶ Θηβαῖοι Μεγάλην πόλιν οἰκίζοντες
παρεκάλουν αὐτὸν νομοθέτην· ὁ δὲ μαθὼν ἴσον ἔχειν
οὐ θέλοντας οὐκ ἐπορεύθη. λόγος ὅτι καὶ Χαβρίᾳ
συνεῖπε τῷ στρατηγῷ φεύγοντι θανάτου μηδενὸς
24 τῶν πολιτῶν τοῦτο πρᾶξαι βουληθέντος. ὅτε καὶ
ἀνιόντι αὐτῷ εἰς τὴν ἀκρόπολιν σὺν τῷ Χαβρίᾳ
Κρωβύλος ὁ συκοφάντης ἀπαντήσας φησίν· '' ἄλλῳ
συναγορεύσων ἥκεις, ἀγνοῶν ὅτι καὶ σὲ τὸ Σωκράτους κώνειον ἀναμένει; '' τὸν δὲ φάναι· '' καὶ ὅτε
ὑπὲρ τῆς πατρίδος ἐστρατευόμην, ὑπέμενον τοὺς
κινδύνους, καὶ νῦν ὑπὲρ τοῦ καθήκοντος διὰ φίλον
ὑπομενῶ.''

Οὗτος πρῶτος ἐν ἐρωτήσει λόγον παρήνεγκεν,
ὥς φησι Φαβωρῖνος ἐν ὀγδόῃ Παντοδαπῆς ἱστορίας.
καὶ πρῶτος τὸν κατὰ τὴν ἀνάλυσιν τῆς ζητήσεως
τρόπον εἰσηγήσατο Λεωδάμαντι τῷ Θασίῳ. καὶ
πρῶτος ἐν φιλοσοφίᾳ ἀντίποδας ὠνόμασε καὶ
στοιχεῖον καὶ διαλεκτικὴν καὶ ποιότητα[1] καὶ τοῦ
ἀριθμοῦ τὸν προμήκη καὶ τῶν περάτων τὴν ἐπίπεδον
ἐπιφάνειαν καὶ θεοῦ πρόνοιαν.

25 Καὶ πρῶτος τῶν φιλοσόφων ἀντεῖπε πρὸς τὸν
λόγον τὸν Λυσίου τοῦ Κεφάλου ἐκθέμενος αὐτὸν
κατὰ λέξιν ἐν τῷ Φαίδρῳ. καὶ πρῶτος ἐθεώρησε
τῆς γραμματικῆς τὴν δύναμιν. πρῶτός τε ἀντ-
ειρηκὼς σχεδὸν ἅπασι τοῖς πρὸ αὐτοῦ, ζητεῖται διὰ
τί μὴ ἐμνημόνευσε Δημοκρίτου. τούτου φησὶ
Νεάνθης ὁ Κυζικηνὸς εἰς Ὀλύμπια ἀνιόντος τοὺς

---

[1] ποιήματα codd.: corr. Menagius.

---

^a Compare Aelian, *Var. Hist.* ii. 42.
^b The same statement that Plato made over to Leodamas
the analytical method occurs in Proclus, *On Eucl.* i. p. 211,

Memorabilia says that the Arcadians and Thebans, when they were founding Megalopolis, invited Plato to be their legislator ; but that, when he discovered that they were opposed to equality of possessions, he refused to go.[a] There is a story that he pleaded for Chabrias the general when he was tried for his life, although no one else at Athens would do so, and that, on this occasion, as he was going up to the Acropolis along with Chabrias, Crobylus the informer met him and said, " What, are you come to speak for the defence ? Don't you know that the hemlock of Socrates awaits you ? " To this Plato replied, " As I faced dangers when serving in the cause of my country, so I will face them now in the cause of duty for a friend."

He was the first to introduce argument by means of question and answer, says Favorinus in the eighth book of his *Miscellaneous History* ; he was the first to explain to Leodamas of Thasos the method of solving problems by analysis[b] ; and the first who in philosophical discussion employed the terms antipodes, element, dialectic, quality, oblong number, and, among boundaries, the plane superficies ; also divine providence.

He was also the first philosopher who controverted the speech of Lysias, the son of Cephalus, which he has set out word for word in the *Phaedrus*,[c] and the first to study the significance of grammar. And, as he was the first to attack the views of almost all his predecessors, the question is raised why he makes no mention of Democritus. Neanthes of Cyzicus says that, on his going to Olympia, the eyes of all

19-23 ed. Friedlein. See T. L. Heath, *Euclid*, vol. i. p. 36, also p. 134 note 1, and p. 137 ; vol. iii. p. 246.

[a] 230 E *sqq.*

Ἕλληνας ἅπαντας ἐπιστραφῆναι εἰς αὐτόν· ὅτε καὶ
Δίωνι συνέμιξε μέλλοντι στρατεύειν ἐπὶ Διονύσιον.
ἐν δὲ τῷ πρώτῳ τῶν Ἀπομνημονευμάτων Φαβω-
ρίνου φέρεται ὅτι Μιθραδάτης ὁ Πέρσης ἀνδριάντα
Πλάτωνος ἀνέθετο εἰς τὴν Ἀκαδήμειαν καὶ
ἐπέγραψε· " Μιθραδάτης Ὀροντοβάτου Πέρσης
Μούσαις εἰκόνα ἀνέθηκε Πλάτωνος, ἣν Σιλανίων
ἐποίησε."

26 Φησὶ δ' Ἡρακλείδης ὅτι νέος ὢν οὕτως ἦν
αἰδήμων καὶ κόσμιος ὥστε μηδέποτε ὀφθῆναι
γελῶν ὑπεράγαν· τοιοῦτος δ' ὢν ὅμως ἐσκώφθη καὶ
αὐτὸς ὑπὸ τῶν κωμικῶν. Θεόπομπος γοῦν ἐν
Ἡδυχάρει φησὶν οὕτως·

> ἓν γάρ ἐστιν οὐδὲ ἕν,
> τὼ δὲ δύο μόλις ἕν ἐστιν, ὥς φησι Πλάτων.

ἀλλὰ καὶ Ἀναξανδρίδης ἐν Θησεῖ·

> ὅτε τὰς μορίας ἔτρωγεν ὥσπερ⟨εὶ⟩ Πλάτων.

ἀλλὰ καὶ Τίμων οὑτωσὶ παραγραμματίζων αὐτόν·

> ὡς ἀνέπλασσε Πλάτων ⟨ὁ⟩ πεπλασμένα θαύ-
> ματα εἰδώς.

27 Ἄλεξις Μεροπίδι·

> εἰς καιρὸν ἥκεις· ὡς ἔγωγ' ἀπορουμένη
> ἄνω κάτω τε περιπατοῦσ' ὥσπερ Πλάτων
> σοφὸν οὐδὲν εὕρηκ', ἀλλὰ κοπιῶ τὰ σκέλη.

καὶ ἐν Ἀγκυλίωνι·

> λέγεις περὶ ὧν οὐκ οἶσθα· συγγενοῦ τρέχων
> Πλάτωνι καὶ γνώσῃ λίτρον καὶ κρόμμυον.

Ἄμφις Ἀμφικράτει·

the Greeks were turned towards him, and there he
met Dion, who was about to make his expedition
against Dionysius. In the first book of the *Memorabilia* of Favorinus there is a statement that
Mithradates the Persian set up a statue of Plato in
the Academy and inscribed upon it these words :
" Mithradates the Persian, the son of Orontobates,
dedicated to the Muses a likeness of Plato made by
Silanion."

Heraclides declares that in his youth he was so
modest and orderly that he was never seen to laugh
outright. In spite of this he too was ridiculed by the
Comic poets. At any rate Theopompus in his
Hedychares says [a] :

There is not anything that is truly one, even the number
two is scarcely one, according to Plato.

Moreover, Anaxandrides [b] in his *Theseus* says :

He was eating olives exactly like Plato.

Then there is Timon who puns on his name thus : [c]

As Plato placed strange platitudes.

Alexis again in the *Meropis* [d] :

You have come in the nick of time. For I am at my
wits' end and walking up and down, like Plato, and yet
have discovered no wise plan but only tired my legs.

And in the *Ancylion* [e] :

You don't know what you are talking about : run about
with Plato, and you'll know all about soap and onions.

Amphis,[f] too, in the *Amphicrates* says :

[a] Meineke, *C.G.F.* ii. 796.
[b] Comic poet ; *ib*. iii. 170.   [c] *Ib*. vi. 25.
[d] *Ib*. iii. 451.   [e] *Ib*. iii. 382.
[f] A poet of the Middle Comedy ; Meineke, *loc. cit*. iii. 302.

τὸ δ᾽ ἀγαθὸν ὅ τι ποτ᾽ ἐστίν, οὗ σὺ τυγχάνειν
μέλλεις διὰ ταύτην, ἧττον οἶδα τοῦτ᾽ ἐγώ,
ὦ δέσποτ᾽, ἢ τὸ Πλάτωνος ἀγαθόν.—πρόσεχε δή.

28 ἐν Δεξιδημίδη·

ὦ Πλάτων,
ὡς οὐδὲν οἶσθα[1] πλὴν σκυθρωπάζειν μόνον,
ὥσπερ κοχλίας σεμνῶς ἐπηρκὼς τὰς ὀφρῦς.

Κρατῖνος Ψευδυποβολιμαίῳ·

ἄνθρωπος εἶ δηλονότι καὶ ψυχὴν ἔχεις.
— κατὰ τὸν Πλάτων᾽ οὐκ οἶδα ⟨δ᾽⟩, ὑπονοῶ
δ᾽ ἔχειν.

Ἄλεξις Ὀλυμπιοδώρῳ·

σῶμα μὲν ὁμοῦ τὸ θνητὸν αὖον ἐγένετο,
τὸ δ᾽ ἀθάνατον ἐξῆξε[2] πρὸς τὸν ἀέρα.
— ταῦτ᾽ οὐ σχολὴ Πλάτωνος;

καὶ ἐν Παρασίτῳ·

ἢ μετὰ Πλάτωνος ἀδολεσχεῖν κατὰ μόνας.

χλευάζει δ᾽ αὐτὸν καὶ Ἀναξίλας Βοτρυλίωνι καὶ
Κίρκῃ καὶ Πλουσίαις.

29 Ἀρίστιππος δ᾽ ἐν τῷ τετάρτῳ Περὶ παλαιᾶς
τρυφῆς φησιν αὐτὸν Ἀστέρος μειρακίου τινὸς
ἀστρολογεῖν συνασκουμένου ἐρασθῆναι, ἀλλὰ καὶ
Δίωνος τοῦ προειρημένου — ἔνιοι καὶ Φαίδρου
φασί — δηλοῦν δὲ τὸν ἔρωτα αὐτοῦ τάδε τὰ
ἐπιγράμματα, ἃ καὶ πρὸς αὐτοῦ γενέσθαι εἰς
αὐτούς·

ἀστέρας εἰσαθρεῖς Ἀστὴρ ἐμός· εἴθε γενοίμην
οὐρανός, ὡς πολλοῖς ὄμμασιν εἰς σὲ βλέπω.

---

[1] ἦσθα codd. : ἦσθα edd. Basil.
[2] ἐξῆξε] ἐξῆρε codd. : corr. G. Hermann.

A. And as for the good, whatever that be, that you are likely to get on her account, I know no more about it, master, than I do of the good of Plato.

B. Just attend.

And in the *Dexidemides* [a]:

O Plato, all you know is how to frown with eyebrows lifted high like any snail.

Cratinus,[b] too, in *The False Changeling*:

A. Clearly you are a man and have a soul.

B. In Plato's words, I am not sure but suspect that I have.

And Alexis in the *Olympiodorus* [c]:

A. My mortal body withered up, my immortal part sped into the air.

B. Is not this a lecture of Plato's?

And in the *Parasite* [d]:

Or, with Plato, to converse alone.

Anaxilas,[e] again, in the *Botrylion*, and in *Circe* and *Rich Women*, has a gibe at him.

Aristippus in his fourth book *On the Luxury of the Ancients* says that he was attached to a youth named Aster, who joined him in the study of astronomy, as also to Dion who has been mentioned above, and, as some aver, to Phaedrus too. His passionate affection is revealed in the following epigrams which he is said to have written upon them [f]:

Star-gazing Aster, would I were the skies,
To gaze upon thee with a thousand eyes.

[a] Meineke, *C.G.F.* iii. 305.
[b] *Sc.* Cratinus Junior, of the Middle Comedy; Meineke, *C.G.F.* iii. 378.
[c] Meineke, *C.G.F.* iii. 455.   [d] *Ib.* iii. 468.
[e] Of the Middle Comedy; Meineke, iii. 342-352.
[f] *Anth. Pal.* vii. 669, 670.

καὶ ἄλλο·

δ   ἀστὴρ πρὶν μὲν ἔλαμπες ἐνὶ ζωοῖσιν Ἑῷος,
νῦν δὲ θανὼν λάμπεις Ἕσπερος ἐν φθιμένοις.

30 εἰς δὲ τὸν Δίωνα ὧδε·

δάκρυα μὲν Ἑκάβῃ τε καὶ Ἰλιάδεσσι γυναιξὶ
Μοῖραι ἐπέκλωσαν δὴ τότε γεινομέναις,
σοὶ δέ, Δίων, ῥέξαντι καλῶν ἐπινίκιον ἔργων
δαίμονες εὐροίας ἐλπίδας ἐξέχεαν.
κεῖσαι δ' εὐρυχόρῳ ἐν πατρίδι τίμιος ἀστοῖς,
ὦ ἐμὸν ἐκμήνας θυμὸν ἔρωτι Δίων.

31 τοῦτο καὶ ἐπιγεγράφθαι φησὶν ἐν Συρακούσαις ἐπὶ
τῷ τάφῳ.

Ἀλλὰ καὶ Ἀλέξιδος, φασίν, ἐρασθεὶς καὶ
Φαίδρου, καθὰ προείρηται, τοῦτον ἐποίησε τὸν
τρόπον·

νῦν, ὅτε μηδὲν Ἄλεξις ὅσον μόνον εἶφ' ὅτι καλός,
ὦπται καὶ πάντῃ πᾶς τις ἐπιστρέφεται.
θυμέ, τί μηνύεις κυσὶν ὀστέον; εἶτ' ἀνιήσῃ[1]
ὕστερον; οὐχ οὕτω Φαῖδρον ἀπωλέσαμεν;

ἔχειν τε Ἀρχεάνασσαν, εἰς ἣν καὶ αὐτὴν οὕτω
ποιῆσαι·

Ἀρχεάνασσαν ἔχω τὴν ἐκ Κολοφῶνος ἑταίραν,
ἧς καὶ ἐπὶ ῥυτίδων ἕζετο δριμὺς ἔρως.
ἆ δειλοὶ νεότητος ἀπαντήσαντες ἐκείνης
πρωτοπλόου, δι' ὅσης ἤλθετε πυρκαϊῆς.

32 ἀλλὰ καὶ εἰς Ἀγάθωνα·

τὴν ψυχὴν Ἀγάθωνα φιλῶν ἐπὶ χείλεσιν εἶχον·
ἦλθε γὰρ ἡ τλήμων ὡς διαβησομένη.

---

[1] ἀνιήσῃ] ἀνιήσεις codd.

304

And another :

> Among the living once the Morning Star,
> Thou shin'st, now dead, like Hesper from afar.

And he wrote thus upon Dion [a] :

> Tears from their birth the lot had been
> Of Ilium's daughters and their queen.
> By thee, O Dion, great deeds done
> New hopes and larger promise won.
> Now here thou liest gloriously,
> How deeply loved, how mourned by me.

This, they say, was actually inscribed upon his tomb at Syracuse.

Again, it is said that being enamoured of Alexis and Phaedrus, as before mentioned, he composed the following lines [b] :

Now, when Alexis is of no account, I have said no more than this. He is fair to see, and everywhere all eyes are turned upon him. Why, my heart, do you show the dogs a bone? And then will you smart for this hereafter? Was it not thus that we lost Phaedrus?

He is also credited with a mistress, Archeanassa, upon whom he wrote as follows [c] :

I have a mistress, fair Archeanassa of Colophon, on whose very wrinkles sits hot love. O hapless ye who met such beauty on its first voyage, what a flame must have been kindled in you!

There is another upon Agathon [d] :

While kissing Agathon, my soul leapt to my lips, as if fain, alas! to pass over to him.

[a] *Anth. Pal.* vii. 99.
[b] *Anth. Pal.* vii. 100.
[c] *Anth. Pal.* vii. 217.
[d] *Anth. Pal.* v. 78.

καὶ ἄλλο·

τῷ μήλῳ βάλλω σε· σὺ δ' εἰ μὲν ἑκοῦσα φιλεῖς με,
  δεξαμένη τῆς σῆς παρθενίης μετάδος,
εἰ δ' ἄρ' ὃ μὴ γίγνοιτο νοεῖς, τοῦτ' αὐτὸ λαβοῦσα
  σκέψαι τὴν ὥρην ὡς ὀλιγοχρόνιος.

‹καὶ ἄλλο›·

μῆλον ἐγώ. βάλλει με φιλῶν σέ τις· ἀλλ'
  ἐπίνευσον
Ξανθίππη· κἀγὼ καὶ σὺ μαραινόμεθα.

83 Φασὶ δὲ καὶ τὸ εἰς τοὺς Ἐρετριέας τοὺς σαγηνευ-
θέντας αὐτοῦ εἶναι·

Εὐβοίης γένος εἰμὲν Ἐρετρικόν, ἄγχι δὲ Σούσων
  κείμεθα. φεῦ, γαίης ὅσσον ἀφ' ἡμετέρης.

κἀκεῖνο·

ἁ Κύπρις Μούσαισι· " κοράσια, τὰν Ἀφροδίταν
  τιμᾶτ' ἢ τὸν Ἔρωτ' ὕμμιν ἐφοπλίσομαι."
αἱ Μοῦσαι ποτὶ Κύπριν· " " Ἄρει τὰ στωμύλα
  ταῦτα·
ἡμῖν οὐ πέτεται τοῦτο τὸ παιδάριον."

καὶ ἄλλο·

χρυσὸν ἀνὴρ εὑρὼν ἔλιπεν βρόχον· αὐτὰρ ὁ
  χρυσὸν
ὃν λίπεν οὐχ εὑρὼν ἧψεν ὃν εὗρε βρόχον.

34 Ἀλλά τοι Μόλων ἀπεχθῶς ἔχων πρὸς αὐτόν, " οὐ
τοῦτο," φησί, " θαυμαστὸν εἰ Διονύσιος ἐν Κορίνθῳ,
ἀλλ' εἰ Πλάτων ἐν Σικελίᾳ." ἔοικε δὲ καὶ Ξενοφῶν
πρὸς αὐτὸν ἔχειν οὐκ εὐμενῶς. ὥσπερ γοῦν
διαφιλονεικοῦντες τὰ ὅμοια γεγράφασι, Συμπόσιον,

---

^a *Anth. Pal.* v. 79.　　　　^b *Anth. Pal.* v. 80.

And another[a]:

I throw an apple to you and, if indeed you are willing to love me, then receive it and let me taste your virgin charms. But if you are otherwise minded, which heaven forbid, take this very apple and see how short-lived all beauty is.

And another[b]:

An apple am I, thrown by one who loves you. Nay, Xanthippe, give consent, for you and I are both born to decay.

It is also said that the epigram on the Eretrians, who were swept out of the country, was written by him[c]:

We are Eretrians by race, from Euboea, and lie near Susa. How far, alas, from our native land !

And again[d]:

> Thus Venus to the Muses spoke :
> Damsels, submit to Venus' yoke,
> Or dread my Cupid's arms.
> Those threats, the virgins nine replied,
> May weigh with Mars, but we deride
> Love's wrongs, or darts, or charms.

And again[e]:

> A certain person found some gold,
> Carried it off and, in its stead,
> Left a strong halter, neatly rolled.
> The owner found his treasure fled,
> And, daunted by his fortune's wreck,
> Fitted the halter to his neck.

Further, Molon, being his enemy, said, " It is not wonderful that Dionysius should be in Corinth, but rather that Plato should be in Sicily." And it seems that Xenophon was not on good terms with him. At any rate, they have written similar narratives as if out of rivalry with each other, a *Symposium*, a

[a] *Anth. Pal.* vii. 259.   [d] *Anth. Pal.* ix. 39.
[e] *Anth. Pal.* ix. 44.

Σωκράτους ἀπολογίαν, τὰ ἠθικὰ ἀπομνημονεύματα — εἶθ' ὁ μὲν Πολιτείαν, ὁ δὲ Κύρου παιδείαν.
καὶ ἐν τοῖς Νόμοις ὁ Πλάτων πλάσμα φησὶν εἶναι
τὴν παιδείαν αὐτοῦ· μὴ γὰρ εἶναι Κῦρον τοιοῦτον
— ἀμφότεροί τε Σωκράτους μνημονεύοντες, ἀλλή-
λων οὐδαμοῦ, πλὴν Ξενοφῶν Πλάτωνος ἐν τρίτῳ
35 Ἀπομνημονευμάτων. λέγεται δ' ὅτι καὶ Ἀντισθένης μέλλων ἀναγινώσκειν τι τῶν γεγραμμένων
αὐτῷ παρεκάλεσεν αὐτὸν παρατυχεῖν. καὶ πυθομένου, τί μέλλει ἀναγινώσκειν, εἶπεν ὅτι περὶ τοῦ
μὴ εἶναι ἀντιλέγειν· τοῦ δ' εἰπόντος· "πῶς οὖν σὺ
περὶ αὐτοῦ τούτου γράφεις;" καὶ διδάσκοντος ὅτι
περιτρέπεται, ἔγραψε διάλογον κατὰ Πλάτωνος
Σάθωνα ἐπιγράψας· ἐξ οὗ διετέλουν ἀλλοτρίως
ἔχοντες πρὸς ἀλλήλους. φασὶ δὲ καὶ Σωκράτην
ἀκούσαντα τὸν Λύσιν ἀναγινώσκοντος Πλάτωνος
" Ἡράκλεις," εἰπεῖν, " ὡς πολλά μου καταψεύδεθ'
ὁ νεανίσκος." οὐκ ὀλίγα γὰρ ὧν οὐκ εἴρηκε
Σωκράτης γέγραφεν ἀνήρ.

36 Εἶχε δὲ φιλέχθρως ὁ Πλάτων καὶ πρὸς Ἀρίστιππον. ἐν γοῦν τῷ Περὶ ψυχῆς διαβάλλων αὐτόν
φησιν ὅτι οὐ παρεγένετο Σωκράτει τελευτῶντι,
ἀλλ' ἐν Αἰγίνῃ ἦν καὶ σύνεγγυς. καὶ πρὸς Αἰσχίνην
δέ τινα φιλοτιμίαν εἶχε, φασίν, ὅτι δή περ καὶ
αὐτὸς εὐδοκίμει παρὰ Διονυσίῳ. ὃν ἐλθόντα δι'
ἀπορίαν ὑπὸ μὲν Πλάτωνος παροφθῆναι, ὑπὸ δ'
Ἀριστίππου συσταθῆναι. τούς τε λόγους οὓς
Κρίτωνι περιτέθεικεν ἐν τῷ δεσμωτηρίῳ περὶ τῆς
φυγῆς συμβουλεύοντι, φησὶν Ἰδομενεὺς εἶναι Αἰ-

Defence of Socrates, and their moral treatises or Memorabilia.[a] Next, the one wrote a *Republic,* the other a *Cyropaedia.* And in the *Laws* [b] Plato declares the story of the education of Cyrus to be a fiction, for that Cyrus did not answer to the description of him. And although both make mention of Socrates, neither of them refers to the other, except that Xenophon mentions Plato in the third book of his *Memorabilia.* It is said also that Antisthenes, being about to read publicly something that he had composed, invited Plato to be present. And on his inquiring what he was about to read, Antisthenes replied that it was something about the impossibility of contradiction. " How then," said Plato, " can you write on this subject ? " thus showing him that the argument refutes itself. Thereupon he wrote a dialogue against Plato and entitled it *Sathon.* After this they continued to be estranged from one another. They say that, on hearing Plato read the *Lysis,* Socrates exclaimed, " By Heracles, what a number of lies this young man is telling about me ! " For he has included in the dialogue much that Socrates never said.

Plato was also on bad terms with Aristippus. At least in the dialogue *Of the Soul* [c] he disparages him by saying that he was not present at the death of Socrates, though he was no farther off than Aegina. Again, they say that he showed a certain jealousy of Aeschines, because of his reputation with Dionysius, and that, when he arrived at the court, he was despised by Plato because of his poverty, but supported by Aristippus. And Idomeneus asserts that the arguments used by Crito, when in the prison he urges Socrates to escape, are really due to Aeschines,

DIOGENES LAERTIUS

σχίνου· τὸν δ' ἐκείνῳ περιθεῖναι διὰ τὴν πρὸς τοῦτον
δυσμένειαν.

37 Ἑαυτοῦ τε Πλάτων οὐδαμόθι τῶν ἑαυτοῦ
συγγραμμάτων μνήμην πεποίηται ὅτι μὴ ἐν τῷ
Περὶ ψυχῆς καὶ Ἀπολογίᾳ. φησὶ δ' Ἀριστοτέλης
τὴν τῶν λόγων ἰδέαν αὐτοῦ μεταξὺ ποιήματος
εἶναι καὶ πεζοῦ λόγου. τοῦτον μόνον παραμεῖναι
Πλάτωνι Φαβωρῖνός πού φησιν ἀναγινώσκοντι
τὸν Περὶ ψυχῆς, τοὺς δ' ἄλλους ἀναστῆναι πάντας.
ἔνιοί τε φασὶν ὅτι Φίλιππος ὁ Ὀπούντιος τοὺς
Νόμους αὐτοῦ μετέγραψεν ὄντας ἐν κηρῷ. τούτου
δὲ καὶ τὴν Ἐπινομίδα φασὶν εἶναι. Εὐφορίων δὲ
καὶ Παναίτιος εἰρήκασι πολλάκις ἐστραμμένην
εὑρῆσθαι τὴν ἀρχὴν τῆς Πολιτείας. ἣν Πολιτείαν
Ἀριστόξενός φησι πᾶσαν σχεδὸν ἐν τοῖς Πρωτ-
38 αγόρου γεγράφθαι Ἀντιλογικοῖς. λόγος δὲ πρῶτον γράψαι αὐτὸν τὸν Φαῖδρον· καὶ γὰρ ἔχειν
μειρακιῶδές τι τὸ πρόβλημα. Δικαίαρχος δὲ καὶ
τὸν τρόπον τῆς γραφῆς ὅλον ἐπιμέμφεται ὡς
φορτικόν.

Ὁ γοῦν Πλάτων λέγεται θεασάμενός τινα
κυβεύοντα αἰτιάσασθαι· τοῦ δὲ εἰπόντος ὡς ἐπὶ
μικροῖς, " ἀλλὰ τό γ' ἔθος," εἰπεῖν, " οὐ μικρόν."
ἐρωτηθεὶς εἰ ἀπομνημονεύματα αὐτοῦ ἔσται ὥσπερ
τῶν πρότερον ἀπεκρίνατο· " ὀνόματος δεῖ τυχεῖν
πρῶτον, εἶτα πολλὰ ἔσται." εἰσελθόντος ποτὲ
Ξενοκράτους εἶπε μαστιγῶσαι τὸν παῖδα· αὐτὸν
39 γὰρ μὴ δύνασθαι διὰ τὸ ὠργίσθαι. ἀλλὰ καὶ πρός
τινα τῶν παίδων, " μεμαστίγωσο ἄν," εἶπεν, " εἰ
μὴ ὠργιζόμην." ἐφ' ἵππου καθίσας εὐθέως κατέβη

---

[a] *Phaedo*, 59 B.　　　[b] 34 A.

and that Plato transferred them to Crito because of his enmity to Aeschines.

Nowhere in his writings does Plato mention himself by name, except in the dialogue *On the Soul* [a] and the *Apology*.[b] Aristotle remarks that the style of the dialogues is half-way between poetry and prose. And according to Favorinus, when Plato read the dialogue *On the Soul*, Aristotle alone stayed to the end ; the rest of the audience got up and went away. Some say that Philippus of Opus copied out the *Laws*, which were left upon waxen tablets, and it is said that he was the author of the *Epinomis*. Euphorion and Panaetius relate that the beginning of the *Republic* was found several times revised and rewritten, and the *Republic* itself Aristoxenus declares to have been nearly all of it included in the *Controversies* of Protagoras. There is a story that the *Phaedrus* was his first dialogue. For the subject has about it something of the freshness of youth. Dicaearchus, however, censures its whole style as vulgar.

A story is told that Plato once saw some one playing at dice and rebuked him. And, upon his protesting that he played for a trifle only, " But the habit," rejoined Plato, " is not a trifle." Being asked whether there would be any memoirs of him as of his predecessors, he replied, " A man must first make a name, and he will have no lack of memoirs." One day, when Xenocrates had come in, Plato asked him to chastise his slave, since he was unable to do it himself because he was in a passion. Further, it is alleged that he said to one of his slaves, " I would have given you a flogging, had I not been in a passion." Being mounted on horseback, he quickly

φήσας εὐλαβεῖσθαι μὴ ἱπποτυφίᾳ ληφθῇ. τοῖς μεθύουσι συνεβούλευε κατοπτρίζεσθαι· ἀποστήσεσθαι γὰρ τῆς τοιαύτης ἀσχημοσύνης. πίνειν δ' εἰς μέθην οὐδαμοῦ πρέπον ἔλεγε πλὴν ἐν ταῖς ἑορταῖς τοῦ καὶ τὸν οἶνον δόντος θεοῦ. καὶ τὸ πολλὰ δὲ καθεύδειν ἀπήρεσκεν αὐτῷ. ἐν γοῦν τοῖς Νόμοις φησί· " κοιμώμενος οὐδεὶς οὐδενὸς ἄξιος." εἶναί τε ἥδιον τῶν ἀκουσμάτων τὴν ἀλήθειαν· οἱ δὲ τὸ λέγειν τἀληθῆ. καὶ περὶ ἀληθείας
40 δ' ἐν τοῖς Νόμοις φησὶν οὕτως· " καλὸν μὲν ἡ ἀλήθεια, ὦ ξένε, καὶ μόνιμον· ἔοικε μὴν οὐ ῥᾴδιον <εἶναι> πείθειν." ἀλλὰ καὶ ἠξίου μνημόσυνον αὐτοῦ λείπεσθαι ἢ ἐν φίλοις ἢ ἐν βιβλίοις· ἐξετόπιζε καὶ αὐτὸς τὰ πλεῖστα, καθά τινες φασί.

Καὶ ἐτελεύτα μὲν ὃν εἴπομεν τρόπον Φιλίππου βασιλεύοντος ἔτος τρισκαιδέκατον, καθὰ καὶ Φαβωρῖνός φησιν Ἀπομνημονευμάτων τρίτῳ. ὑφ' οὗ καὶ ἐπιτιμηθῆναί φησιν αὐτὸν Θεόπομπος. Μυρωνιανὸς δ' ἐν Ὁμοίοις φησὶ Φίλωνα παροιμίας μνημονεύειν περὶ τῶν Πλάτωνος φθειρῶν, ὡς
41 οὕτως αὐτοῦ τελευτήσαντος. καὶ ἐτάφη ἐν τῇ Ἀκαδημείᾳ, ἔνθα τὸν πλεῖστον χρόνον διετέλεσε φιλοσοφῶν. ὅθεν καὶ Ἀκαδημαϊκὴ προσηγορεύθη ἡ ἀπ' αὐτοῦ αἵρεσις. καὶ παρεπέμφθη πανδημεὶ πρὸς τῶν αὐτόθι διαθέμενος τοῦτον τὸν τρόπον·

" Τάδε κατέλιπε Πλάτων καὶ διέθετο· τὸ ἐν

ᵃ 808 B.   ᵇ 663 E.

ᶜ The awkwardness of this last clause can be explained, but not excused, if we suppose that Diogenes Laertius got his citation of Theopompus from Favorinus.

ᵈ Cf. Hdt. vi. 39 τὸν ἀδελφεὸν δηλαδὴ ἐπιτιμέων.

got down again, declaring that he was afraid he would be infected with horse-pride. He advised those who got drunk to view themselves in a mirror ; for they would then abandon the habit which so disfigured them. To drink to excess was nowhere becoming, he used to say, save at the feasts of the god who was the giver of wine. He also disapproved of over - sleeping. At any rate in the *Laws*[a] he declares that " no one when asleep is good for anything." He also said that the truth is the pleasantest of sounds. Another version of this saying is that the pleasantest of all things is to speak the truth. Again, of truth he speaks thus in the *Laws*[b] : " Truth, O stranger, is a fair and durable thing. But it is a thing of which it is hard to persuade men." His wish always was to leave a memorial of himself behind, either in the hearts of his friends or in his books. He was himself fond of seclusion according to some authorities.

His death, the circumstances of which have already been related, took place in the thirteenth year of the reign of King Philip, as stated by Favorinus in the third book of his *Memorabilia*, and according to Theopompus[c] honours were paid to him at his death by Philip.[d] But Myronianus in his *Parallels* says that Philo mentions some proverbs that were in circulation about Plato's lice, implying that this was the mode of his death. He was buried in the Academy, where he spent the greatest part of his life in philosophical study. And hence the school which he founded was called the Academic school. And all the students there joined in the funeral procession. The terms of his will were as follows :

" These things have been left and devised by

DIOGENES LAERTIUS

Ἰφιστιαδῶν χωρίον, ᾧ γείτων βορρᾶθεν ἡ ὁδὸς ἡ
ἐκ τοῦ Κηφισιᾶσιν ἱεροῦ, νοτόθεν τὸ Ἡράκλειον
τὸ ἐν Ἰφιστιαδῶν, πρὸς ἡλίου δὲ ἀνιόντος Ἀρχέ-
στρατος Φρεάρριος, πρὸς ἡλίου δὲ δυομένου
Φίλιππος Χολλείδης· καὶ μὴ ἐξέστω τοῦτο μηδενὶ
μήτε ἀποδόσθαι μήτε ἀλλάξασθαι, ἀλλ' ἔστω Ἀδει-
42 μάντου τοῦ παιδίου εἰς τὸ δυνατόν· καὶ τὸ ἐν
Εἰρεσιδῶν χωρίον, ὃ παρὰ Καλλιμάχου ἐπριάμην,
ᾧ γείτων βορρᾶθεν Εὐρυμέδων Μυρρινούσιος,
νοτόθεν δὲ Δημόστρατος Ξυπεταιών, πρὸς ἡλίου
ἀνιόντος Εὐρυμέδων Μυρρινούσιος, πρὸς ἡλίου
δυομένου Κηφισός. ἀργυρίου μνᾶς τρεῖς. φιάλην
ἀργυρᾶν ἕλκουσαν ρξε΄, κυμβίον ἄγον με΄, δακτύλιον
χρυσοῦν καὶ ἐνώτιον χρυσοῦν ἄγοντα συνάμφω δ΄
δραχμάς, ὀβολοὺς γ΄. Εὐκλείδης ὁ λιθοτόμος
ὀφείλει μοι τρεῖς μνᾶς. Ἄρτεμιν ἀφίημι ἐλευθέραν.
οἰκέτας καταλείπω Τύχωνα Βίκταν Ἀπολλωνίδην
43 Διονύσιον. σκεύη ‹. . . . . .› τὰ γεγραμμένα, ὧν
ἔχει ἀντίγραφα Δημήτριος. ὀφείλω δ' οὐδενὶ
οὐθέν. ἐπίτροποι Λεωσθένης Σπεύσιππος Δημήτριος Ἡγίας Εὐρυμέδων Καλλίμαχος Θράσιππος.''

Καὶ διέθετο μὲν οὕτως. ἐπεγράφη δ' αὐτοῦ τῷ
τάφῳ ἐπιγράμματα τάδε· πρῶτον·

σωφροσύνῃ προφέρων θνητῶν ἤθει τε δικαίῳ
  ἐνθάδε δὴ κεῖται θεῖος Ἀριστοκλῆς·
εἰ δέ τις ἐκ πάντων σοφίης μέγαν ἔσχεν ἔπαινον
  τοῦτον ἔχει πλεῖστον καὶ φθόνος οὐχ ἕπεται.

44 ἕτερον δέ·

γαῖα μὲν ἐν κόλπῳ κρύπτει τόδε σῶμα Πλάτωνος,
  ψυχὴ δ' ἀθάνατον τάξιν ἔχει μακάρων

314

Plato : the estate in Iphistiadae, bounded on the
north by the road from the temple at Cephisia, on
the south by the temple of Heracles in Iphistiadae,
on the east by the property of Archestratus of
Phrearrhi, on the west by that of Philippus of
Chollidae : this it shall be unlawful for anyone to
sell or alienate, but it shall be the property of the
boy Adeimantus to all intents and purposes : the
estate in Eiresidae which I bought of Callimachus,
bounded on the north by the property of Eurymedon
of Myrrhinus, on the south by the property of
Demostratus of Xypete, on the east by that of
Eurymedon of Myrrhinus, and on the west by the
Cephisus ; three minae of silver ; a silver vessel
weighing 165 drachmas ; a cup weighing 45
drachmas ; a gold signet-ring and earring together
weighing four drachmas and three obols. Euclides
the lapidary owes me three minae. I enfranchise
Artemis. I leave four household servants, Tychon,
Bictas, Apollonides and Dionysius. Household
furniture, as set down in the inventory of which
Demetrius has the duplicate. I owe no one anything.
My executors are Leosthenes, Speusippus, Demetrius,
Hegias, Eurymedon, Callimachus and Thrasippus."

Such were the terms of his will. The following
epitaphs were inscribed upon his tomb [a] :

Here lies the god-like man Aristocles, eminent among men
for temperance and the justice of his character. And he, if
ever anyone, had the fullest meed of praise for wisdom, and
was too great for envy.

Next [b] :

Earth in her bosom here hides Plato's body, but his soul
hath its immortal station with the blest, Ariston's son,

[a] *Anth. Pal.* vii. 60.   [b] *Anth. Pal.* vii. 61.

υἱοῦ Ἀρίστωνος, τόν τις καὶ τηλόθι ναίων
τιμᾷ ἀνὴρ ἀγαθὸς θεῖον ἰδόντα βίον.

καὶ ἄλλο νεώτερον·

αἰετέ, τίπτε βέβηκας ὑπὲρ τάφον; ἢ τινος, εἰπέ,
ἀστερόεντα θεῶν οἶκον ἀποσκοπέεις;
—ψυχῆς εἰμι Πλάτωνος ἀποπταμένης ἐς Ὄλυμπον
εἰκών, σῶμα δὲ ‹γῆ› γηγενὲς Ἀτθὶς ἔχει.

45 ἔστι καὶ ἡμέτερον οὕτως ἔχον·

καὶ πῶς εἰ μὴ Φοῖβος ἀν' Ἑλλάδα φῦσε Πλάτωνα,
ψυχὰς ἀνθρώπων γράμμασιν ἠκέσατο;
καὶ γὰρ ὁ τοῦδε γεγὼς Ἀσκληπιός ἐστιν ἰητὴρ
σώματος, ὡς ψυχῆς ἀθανάτοιο Πλάτων.

καὶ ἄλλο, ὡς ἐτελεύτα·

Φοῖβος ἔφυσε βροτοῖς Ἀσκληπιὸν ἠδὲ Πλάτωνα,
τὸν μὲν ἵνα ψυχήν, τὸν δ' ἵνα σῶμα σάοι.
δαισάμενος δὲ γάμον πόλιν ἤλυθεν, ἣν ποθ' ἑαυτῷ
ἔκτισε καὶ δαπέδῳ Ζηνὸς ἐνιδρύσατο.

καὶ τὰ μὲν ἐπιγράμματα ταῦτα.

46 Μαθηταὶ δ' αὐτοῦ Σπεύσιππος Ἀθηναῖος, Ξενοκράτης Καλχηδόνιος, Ἀριστοτέλης Σταγειρίτης,
Φίλιππος Ὀπούντιος, Ἑστιαῖος Περίνθιος, Δίων
Συρακόσιος, Ἄμυκλος Ἡρακλεώτης, Ἔραστος
καὶ Κορίσκος Σκήψιοι, Τιμόλαος Κυζικηνός,
Εὐαίων Λαμψακηνός, Πύθων καὶ Ἡρακλείδης
Αἴνιοι, Ἱπποθάλης καὶ Κάλλιππος Ἀθηναῖοι,
Δημήτριος Ἀμφιπολίτης, Ἡρακλείδης Ποντικὸς
καὶ ἄλλοι πλείους, σὺν οἷς καὶ γυναῖκες δύο Λα-
σθένεια Μαντινικὴ καὶ Ἀξιοθέα Φλειασία ἢ καὶ
ἀνδρεῖα ἠμπίσχετο, ὥς φησι Δικαίαρχος. ἔνιοι
δὲ καὶ Θεόφραστον ἀκοῦσαί φασιν αὐτοῦ· καὶ

whom every good man, even if he dwell afar off, honours because he discerned the divine life.

And a third of later date [a]:

A. Eagle, why fly you o'er this tomb? Say, is your gaze fixed upon the starry house of one of the immortals?
B. I am the image of the soul of Plato, which has soared to Olympus, while his earth-born body rests in Attic soil.

There is also an epitaph of my own which runs thus [b]:

If Phoebus did not cause Plato to be born in Greece, how came it that he healed the minds of men by letters? As the god's son Asclepius is a healer of the body, so is Plato of the immortal soul.

And another on the manner of his death [c]:

Phoebus gave to mortals Asclepius and Plato, the one to save their souls, the other to save their bodies. From a wedding banquet he has passed to that city which he had founded for himself and planted in the sky.

Such then are his epitaphs.

His disciples were Speusippus of Athens, Xenocrates of Chalcedon, Aristotle of Stagira, Philippus of Opus, Hestiaeus of Perinthus, Dion of Syracuse, Amyclus of Heraclea, Erastus and Coriscus of Scepsus, Timolaus of Cyzicus, Euaeon of Lampsacus, Python and Heraclides of Aenus, Hippothales and Callippus of Athens, Demetrius of Amphipolis, Heraclides of Pontus, and many others, among them two women, Lastheneia of Mantinea and Axiothea of Phlius, who is reported by Dicaearchus to have worn men's clothes. Some say that Theophrastus too attended his lectures. Chamaeleon adds Hyper-

---

[a] *Anth. Pal.* vii. 62.   [b] *Anth. Pal.* vii. 108.
[c] *Anth. Pal.* vii. 109.

317

Ὑπερίδην τὸν ῥήτορα Χαμαιλέων φησὶ καὶ Λυ-
47 κοῦργον. ὁμοίως Πολέμων ἱστορεῖ. καὶ Δημοσθένην Σαβῖνος λέγει Μνησίστρατον Θάσιον παρατιθέμενος ἐν δ′ Μελετητικῆς ὕλης· καὶ εἰκός ἐστι.

Φιλοπλάτωνι δέ σοι δικαίως ὑπαρχούσῃ καὶ
παρ' ὁντινοῦν τὰ τοῦ φιλοσόφου δόγματα φιλο-
τίμως ζητούσῃ ἀναγκαῖον ἡγησάμην ὑπογράψαι
καὶ τὴν φύσιν τῶν λόγων καὶ τὴν τάξιν τῶν διαλόγων καὶ τὴν ἔφοδον τῆς ἐπαγωγῆς, ὡς οἷόν τε
στοιχειωδῶς καὶ ἐπὶ κεφαλαίων, πρὸς τὸ μὴ
ἀμοιρεῖν αὐτοῦ τῶν δογμάτων τὴν περὶ τοῦ βίου
συναγωγήν· γλαῦκα γὰρ εἰς 'Αθήνας, φασίν, εἰ
δέῃ σοι τὰ κατ' εἶδος διηγεῖσθαι.

48 Διαλόγους τοίνυν φασὶ πρῶτον γράψαι Ζήνωνα
τὸν 'Ελεάτην· 'Αριστοτέλης δὲ ἐν πρώτῳ Περὶ
ποιητῶν 'Αλεξαμενὸν Στυρέα ἢ Τήιον, ὡς καὶ
Φαβωρῖνος ἐν 'Απομνημονεύμασι. δοκεῖ δέ μοι
Πλάτων ἀκριβώσας τὸ εἶδος καὶ τὰ πρωτεῖα
δικαίως ἂν ὥσπερ τοῦ κάλλους οὕτω καὶ τῆς
εὑρέσεως ἀποφέρεσθαι. ἔστι δὲ διάλογος ⟨λόγος⟩
ἐξ ἐρωτήσεως καὶ ἀποκρίσεως συγκείμενος περί
τινος τῶν φιλοσοφουμένων καὶ πολιτικῶν μετὰ
τῆς πρεπούσης ἠθοποιίας τῶν παραλαμβανομένων
προσώπων καὶ τῆς κατὰ τὴν λέξιν κατασκευῆς.
διαλεκτικὴ δ' ἐστὶ τέχνη λόγων, δι' ἧς ἀνασκευά-
ζομέν τι ἢ κατασκευάζομεν ἐξ ἐρωτήσεως καὶ
ἀποκρίσεως τῶν προσδιαλεγομένων.

---

a Here begins the first of three appendices, being an
introduction to the study of the Platonic writings (47–66).
Freudenthal, in *Hell. Stud.* iii., has shown that the extant
fragment of the Πρόλογος of Albinus is similar and probably
derived from the same source. Albinus lived in the second
century A.D., for in 151–2 Galen was his pupil in Smyrna.

ides the orator and Lycurgus, and in this Polemo agrees. Sabinus makes Demosthenes his pupil, quoting, in the fourth book of his *Materials for Criticism*, Mnesistratus of Thasos as his authority. And it is not improbable.[a]

Now, as you are an enthusiastic Platonist, and rightly so, and as you eagerly seek out that philosopher's doctrines in preference to all others, I have thought it necessary to give some account of the true nature of his discourses, the arrangement of the dialogues, and the method of his inductive procedure, as far as possible in an elementary manner and in main outline, in order that the facts I have collected respecting his life may not suffer by the omission of his doctrines. For, in the words of the proverb, it would be taking owls to Athens, were I to give you of all people the full particulars.

They say that Zeno the Eleatic was the first to write dialogues. But, according to Favorinus in his *Memorabilia*, Aristotle in the first book of his dialogue *On Poets* asserts that it was Alexamenus of Styra or Teos. In my opinion Plato, who brought this form of writing to perfection, ought to be adjudged the prize for its invention as well as for its embellishment. A dialogue is a discourse consisting of question and answer on some philosophical or political subject, with due regard to the characters of the persons introduced and the choice of diction. Dialectic is the art of discourse by which we either refute or establish some proposition by means of question and answer on the part of the interlocutors.

The reader will note the careful style of the preface with its avoidance of hiatus. In x. 29 is a similar personal appeal to the reader.

49 Τοῦ δὴ <δια>λόγου τοῦ Πλατωνικοῦ δύ' εἰσὶν ἀνωτάτω χαρακτῆρες, ὅ τε ὑφηγητικὸς καὶ ὁ ζητητικός. διαιρεῖται δὲ ὁ ὑφηγητικὸς εἰς ἄλλους δύο χαρακτῆρας, θεωρηματικόν τε καὶ πρακτικόν. καὶ τῶν ὁ μὲν θεωρηματικὸς εἰς τὸν φυσικὸν καὶ λογικόν, ὁ δὲ πρακτικὸς εἰς τὸν ἠθικὸν καὶ πολιτικόν. τοῦ δὲ ζητητικοῦ καὶ αὐτοῦ δύο εἰσὶν οἱ πρῶτοι χαρακτῆρες, ὅ τε γυμναστικὸς καὶ ἀγωνιστικός. καὶ τοῦ μὲν γυμναστικοῦ μαιευτικός τε καὶ πειραστικός, τοῦ δὲ ἀγωνιστικοῦ ἐνδεικτικὸς καὶ ἀνατρεπτικός.

50 Οὐ λανθάνει δ' ἡμᾶς ὅτι τινὲς ἄλλως διαφέρειν τοὺς διαλόγους φασί—λέγουσι γὰρ αὐτῶν τοὺς μὲν δραματικούς, τοὺς δὲ διηγηματικούς, τοὺς δὲ μεικτούς—ἀλλ' ἐκεῖνοι μὲν τραγικῶς μᾶλλον ἢ φιλοσόφως τὴν διαφορὰν τῶν διαλόγων προσωνόμασαν. εἰσὶ δὲ τοῦ μὲν φυσικοῦ οἷον ὁ Τίμαιος· τοῦ δὲ λογικοῦ ὅ τε Πολιτικὸς καὶ ὁ Κρατύλος καὶ Παρμενίδης καὶ Σοφιστής· τοῦ δ' ἠθικοῦ ἥ τε Ἀπολογία καὶ ὁ Κρίτων καὶ Φαίδων καὶ Φαῖδρος καὶ τὸ Συμπόσιον Μενέξενός τε καὶ Κλειτοφῶν καὶ Ἐπιστολαὶ καὶ Φίληβος Ἵππαρχος Ἀντερασταί· τοῦ δὲ πολιτικοῦ ἥ τε Πολιτεία 51 καὶ οἱ Νόμοι καὶ ὁ Μίνως καὶ Ἐπινομὶς καὶ ὁ Ἀτλαντικός· τοῦ δὲ μαιευτικοῦ Ἀλκιβιάδαι Θεάγης Λύσις Λάχης· τοῦ δὲ πειραστικοῦ Εὐθύφρων Μένων Ἴων Χαρμίδης Θεαίτητος· τοῦ δὲ ἐνδεικτικοῦ ὡς ὁ Πρωταγόρας· καὶ τοῦ ἀνατρεπτικοῦ

320

Of the Platonic dialogues there are two most general types, the one adapted for instruction and the other for inquiry. And the former is further divided into two types, the theoretical and the practical. And of these the theoretical is divided into the physical and logical, and the practical into the ethical and political. The dialogue of inquiry also has two main divisions, the one of which aims at training the mind and the other at victory in controversy. Again, the part which aims at training the mind has two subdivisions, the one akin to the midwife's art, the other merely tentative. And that suited to controversy is also subdivided into one part which raises critical objections, and another which is subversive of the main position.

I am not unaware that there are other ways in which certain writers classify the dialogues. For some dialogues they call dramatic, others narrative, and others again a mixture of the two. But the terms they employ in their classification of the dialogues are better suited to the stage than to philosophy. Physics is represented by the *Timaeus*, logic by the *Statesman*, *Cratylus*, *Parmenides* and *Sophist*, ethics by the *Apology*, *Crito*, *Phaedo*, *Phaedrus* and *Symposium*, as well as by the *Menexenus*, *Clitophon*, the *Epistles*, *Philebus*, *Hipparchus* and the *Rivals*, and lastly politics by the *Republic*, the *Laws*, *Minos*, *Epinomis*, and the dialogue concerning Atlantis.[a] To the class of mental obstetrics belong the two *Alcibiades*, *Theages*, *Lysis* and *Laches*, while the *Euthyphro*, *Meno*, *Io*, *Charmides* and *Theaetetus* illustrate the tentative method. In the *Protagoras* is seen the method of critical objections; in the

* *i.e. Critias.*

Εὐθύδημος Γοργίας Ἱππίαι δύο. καὶ περὶ μὲν διαλόγου τί ποτέ ἐστι καὶ τίνες αὐτοῦ διαφοραί, <τοσαῦτα> ἀπόχρη λέγειν.

Ἐπεὶ δὲ πολλὴ στάσις ἐστὶ καὶ οἱ μέν φασιν αὐτὸν δογματίζειν, οἱ δ᾽ οὔ, φέρε καὶ περὶ τούτου διαλάβωμεν. αὐτὸ τοίνυν τὸ δογματίζειν ἐστὶ δόγματα τιθέναι ὡς τὸ νομοθετεῖν νόμους τιθέναι. δόγματα δὲ ἑκατέρως καλεῖται, τό τε δοξαζόμενον καὶ ἡ δόξα αὐτή.

52 Τούτων δὲ τὸ μὲν δοξαζόμενον πρότασίς ἐστιν, ἡ δὲ δόξα ὑπόληψις. ὁ τοίνυν Πλάτων περὶ μὲν ὧν κατείληφεν ἀποφαίνεται, τὰ δὲ ψευδῆ διελέγχει, περὶ δὲ τῶν ἀδήλων ἐπέχει. καὶ περὶ μὲν τῶν αὐτῷ δοκούντων ἀποφαίνεται διὰ τεττάρων προσώπων, Σωκράτους, Τιμαίου, τοῦ Ἀθηναίου ξένου, τοῦ Ἐλεάτου ξένου· εἰσὶ δ᾽ οἱ ξένοι οὐχ, ὥς τινες ὑπέλαβον, Πλάτων καὶ Παρμενίδης, ἀλλὰ πλάσματά ἐστιν ἀνώνυμα· ἐπεὶ καὶ τὰ Σωκράτους καὶ τὰ Τιμαίου λέγων Πλάτων δογματίζει. περὶ δὲ τῶν ψευδῶν ἐλεγχομένους εἰσάγει οἷον Θρασύμαχον καὶ Καλλικλέα καὶ Πῶλον Γοργίαν τε καὶ Πρωταγόραν, ἔτι Ἱππίαν καὶ Εὐθύδημον καὶ δὴ καὶ τοὺς ὁμοίους.

53 Ποιούμενος δὲ τὰς ἀποδείξεις πλείστῳ χρῆται τῷ τῆς ἐπαγωγῆς τρόπῳ, οὐ μὴν μονοτρόπῳ, ἀλλὰ διχῇ. ἔστι μὲν γὰρ ἐπαγωγὴ λόγος διά τινων ἀληθῶν τὸ ὅμοιον ἑαυτῷ ἀληθὲς οἰκείως ἐπιφέρων. δύο δὲ τῆς ἐπαγωγῆς εἰσι τρόποι, ὅ τε κατ᾽ ἐναντίωσιν καὶ ὁ ἐκ τῆς ἀκολουθίας. ὁ μὲν οὖν κατ᾽ ἐναντίωσίν ἐστιν ἐξ οὗ τῷ ἐρωτωμένῳ περὶ[1] πᾶσαν

[1] παρὰ Reiske.

[a] In the *Laws*.　　　[b] In the *Sophist* and the *Statesman*.

Euthydemus, *Gorgias*, and the two dialogues entitled
Hippias that of subversive argument.   So much then
for dialogue, its definition and varieties.

Again, as there is great division of opinion between
those who affirm and those who deny that Plato was
a dogmatist, let me proceed to deal with this further
question.   To be a dogmatist in philosophy is to lay
down positive dogmas, just as to be a legislator is
to lay down laws.   Further, under dogma two things
are included, the thing opined and the opinion itself.
Of these the former is a proposition, the latter a
conception.   Now where he has a firm grasp Plato
expounds his own view and refutes the false one,
but, if the subject is obscure, he suspends judgement.
His own views are expounded by four persons,
Socrates, Timaeus, the Athenian Stranger,[a] the
Eleatic Stranger.[b]   These strangers are not, as some
hold, Plato and Parmenides, but imaginary characters
without names,[c] for, even when Socrates and Timaeus
are the speakers, it is Plato's doctrines that are laid
down.   To illustrate the refutation of false opinions,
he introduces Thrasymachus, Callicles, Polus, Gorgias,
Protagoras, or again Hippias, Euthydemus and the
like.

In constructing his proofs he makes most use of
induction, not always in the same way, but under
two forms.   For induction is an argument which by
means of certain true premisses properly infers a
truth resembling them.   And there are two kinds of
induction, the one proceeding by way of contradiction, the other from agreement.   In the kind which
proceeds by contradiction the answer given to every
question will necessarily be the contrary of the

* That the Eleatic Stranger is not Parmenides is decisively
proved by *Soph.* 241 ᴇ.

ἀπόκρισιν ἀκολουθήσει τὸ ἐναντίον, οἷον· ὁ ἐμὸς
πατὴρ τῷ σῷ πατρὶ ἤτοι ἕτερός ἐστιν ἢ ὁ αὐτός.
εἰ μὲν οὖν ἕτερός ἐστι τοῦ ἐμοῦ πατρὸς ὁ σὸς
πατήρ, πατρὸς ἕτερος ὢν οὐκ ἂν εἴη πατήρ· εἰ δὲ
ὁ αὐτός ἐστι τῷ ἐμῷ πατρί, ὃ αὐτὸς ὢν τῷ ἐμῷ
54 πατρὶ ὁ ἐμὸς ἂν εἴη πατήρ. καὶ πάλιν· εἰ μή ἐστι
ζῷον ὁ ἄνθρωπος, λίθος ἂν εἴη ἢ ξύλον. οὐκ ἔστι
δὲ λίθος ἢ ξύλον· ἔμψυχον γάρ ἐστι καὶ ἐξ αὑτοῦ
κινεῖται· ζῷον ἄρα ἐστίν. εἰ δὲ ζῷόν ἐστι, ζῷον
δὲ καὶ ὁ κύων καὶ ὁ βοῦς, εἴη ἂν καὶ ὁ ἄνθρωπος
ζῷον ⟨ὢν⟩ καὶ κύων καὶ βοῦς. οὗτος μὲν ὁ τῆς
ἐπαγωγῆς κατ' ἐναντίωσιν καὶ μάχην τρόπος, ᾧ
ἐχρῆτο οὐ πρὸς τὸ δογματίζειν, ἀλλὰ πρὸς τὸ
διελέγχειν. ὁ δὲ τῆς ἀκολουθίας ἐστὶ διπλοῦς· ὁ
μὲν τὸ ἐπὶ μέρους ζητούμενον διὰ τοῦ ἐπὶ μέρους
ἀποδεικνύς, ὁ δὲ ⟨διὰ⟩ τοῦ καθόλου [διὰ τοῦ ἐπὶ
μέρους]. καὶ ἔστιν ὁ μὲν πρότερος ῥητορικός,
ὁ δὲ δεύτερος διαλεκτικός. οἷον ἐν τῷ προτέρῳ
ζητεῖται, εἰ ὅδε ἀπέκτεινεν. ἀπόδειξις τὸ εὑρῆσθαι αὐτὸν κατ' ἐκεῖνον τὸν χρόνον ἡμαγμένον.
55 ῥητορικὸς δ' ἐστὶν ὁ τρόπος τῆς ἐπαγωγῆς οὗτος,
ἐπειδὴ καὶ ἡ ῥητορικὴ περὶ τὰ ἐπὶ μέρους, οὐ τὰ
καθόλου τὴν πραγματείαν ἔχει. ζητεῖ γὰρ οὐ
περὶ αὐτοῦ τοῦ δικαίου, ἀλλὰ τῶν ἐπὶ μέρους
δικαίων. ὁ δὲ ἕτερός ἐστι διαλεκτικός, προαπο-
δειχθέντος τοῦ καθόλου διὰ τῶν ἐπὶ μέρους. οἷον
ζητεῖται, εἰ ἡ ψυχὴ ἀθάνατος καὶ εἰ ἐκ τῶν τεθνεώτων οἱ ζῶντες· ὅπερ ἀποδείκνυται ἐν τῷ Περὶ
ψυχῆς διά τινος καθολικοῦ, ὅτι ἐκ τῶν ἐναντίων
324

respondent's position, *e.g.* " My father is either other
than or the same as your father. If then your
father is other than my father, by being other than
a father he will not be a father. But if he is the
same as my father, then by being the same as my
father he will be my father." And again : " If
man is not an animal, he will be either a stick or a
stone. But he is not a stick or a stone ; for he is
animate and self-moved. Therefore he is an animal.
But if he is an animal, and if a dog or an ox is also
an animal, then man by being an animal will be a
dog and an ox as well." This is the kind of induction
which proceeds by contradiction and dispute, and
Plato used it, not for laying down positive doctrines
but for refutation. The other kind of induction by
agreement appears in two forms, the one proving
the particular conclusion under discussion from a
particular, the other proceeding by way of the universal [by means of particular facts]. The former is
suited to rhetoric, the latter to dialectic. For instance, under the first form the question is raised,
" Did so-and-so commit a murder ? " The proof is
that he was found at the time with stains of blood
on him. This is the rhetorical form of induction,
since rhetoric also is concerned with particular facts
and not with universals. It does not inquire about
justice in the abstract, but about particular cases of
justice. The other kind, where the general proposition is first established by means of particular
facts, is the induction of dialectic. For instance, the
question put is whether the soul is immortal, and
whether the living come back from the dead. And
this is proved in the dialogue *On the Soul* by means
of a certain general proposition, that opposites pro-

τὰ ἐναντία. καὶ αὐτὸ δὲ τὸ καθόλου **κατασκευά-**
ζεται ἔκ τινων ὄντων ἐπὶ μέρους· οἷον ὅτι τὸ
καθεύδειν ἐκ τοῦ ἐγρηγορέναι καὶ ἀνάπαλιν καὶ
τὸ μεῖζον ἐκ τοῦ μικροτέρου καὶ ἀνάπαλιν. τούτῳ
δὲ ἐχρῆτο εἰς τὴν τῶν ἑαυτῷ δοκούντων κατα-
σκευήν.

56 ῞Ωσπερ δὲ τὸ παλαιὸν ἐν τῇ τραγῳδίᾳ πρότερον
μὲν μόνος ὁ χορὸς διεδραμάτιζεν, ὕστερον δὲ
Θέσπις ἕνα ὑποκριτὴν ἐξεῦρεν ὑπὲρ τοῦ διανα-
παύεσθαι τὸν χορὸν καὶ δεύτερον Αἰσχύλος, τὸν δὲ
τρίτον Σοφοκλῆς καὶ συνεπλήρωσεν τὴν τραγῳδίαν,
οὕτως καὶ τῆς φιλοσοφίας ὁ λόγος πρότερον μὲν ἦν
μονοειδὴς ὡς ὁ φυσικός, δεύτερον δὲ Σωκράτης
προσέθηκε τὸν ἠθικόν, τρίτον δὲ Πλάτων τὸν
διαλεκτικὸν καὶ ἐτελεσιούργησε τὴν φιλοσοφίαν.
Θράσυλος δέ φησι καὶ κατὰ τὴν τραγικὴν τετραλογίαν ἐκδοῦναι αὐτὸν τοὺς διαλόγους, οἷον ἐκεῖνοι
τέτρασι δράμασιν ἠγωνίζοντο — Διονυσίοις, Λη-
ναίοις, Παναθηναίοις, Χύτροις — ὧν τὸ τέταρτον
ἦν Σατυρικόν· τὰ δὲ τέτταρα δράματα ἐκαλεῖτο
τετραλογία.

57 Εἰσὶ τοίνυν, φησίν, οἱ πάντες αὐτῷ γνήσιοι διάλογοι ἓξ καὶ πεντήκοντα, τῆς μὲν Πολιτείας εἰς
δέκα διαιρουμένης — ἣν καὶ εὑρίσκεσθαι σχεδὸν
ὅλην παρὰ Πρωταγόρᾳ ἐν τοῖς Ἀντιλογικοῖς φησι
Φαβωρῖνος ἐν Παντοδαπῆς ἱστορίας δευτέρῳ —
τῶν δὲ Νόμων εἰς δυοκαίδεκα. τετραλογίαι δὲ
ἐννέα, ἑνὸς βιβλίου χώραν ἐπεχούσης τῆς Πολιτείας καὶ ἑνὸς τῶν Νόμων. πρώτην μὲν οὖν
τετραλογίαν τίθησι τὴν κοινὴν ὑπόθεσιν ἔχουσαν·
παραδεῖξαι γὰρ βούλεται ὁποῖος ἂν εἴη ὁ τοῦ φιλο-

ceed from opposites. And the general proposition itself is established by means of certain propositions which are particular, as that sleep comes from waking and *vice versa*, the greater from the less and *vice versa*. This is the form which he used to establish his own views.

But, just as long ago in tragedy the chorus was the only actor, and afterwards, in order to give the chorus breathing space, Thespis devised a single actor, Aeschylus a second, Sophocles a third, and thus tragedy was completed, so too with philosophy : in early times it discoursed on one subject only, namely physics, then Socrates added the second subject, ethics, and Plato the third, dialectics, and so brought philosophy to perfection. Thrasylus says that he published his dialogues in tetralogies, like those of the tragic poets. Thus they contended with four plays at the Dionysia, the Lenaea, the Panathenaea and the festival of Chytri.[a] Of the four plays the last was a satiric drama ; and the four together were called a tetralogy.

Now, says Thrasylus, the genuine dialogues are fifty-six in all, if the *Republic* be divided into ten and the *Laws* into twelve. Favorinus, however, in the second book of his *Miscellaneous History* declares that nearly the whole of the *Republic* is to be found in a work of Protagoras entitled *Controversies.*[b] This gives nine tetralogies, if the *Republic* takes the place of one single work and the *Laws* of another. His first tetralogy has a common plan underlying it, for he wishes to describe what the life of the philosopher

[a] Pots.
[b] From iii. 37 we infer that Favorinus drew upon Aristoxenus for this wildly improbable assertion.

DIOGENES LAERTIUS

σόφου βίος. διπλαῖς τε χρῆται ταῖς ἐπιγραφαῖς
καθ' ἑκάστου τῶν βιβλίων, τῇ μὲν ἀπὸ τοῦ ὀνό-
58 ματος, τῇ δὲ ἀπὸ τοῦ πράγματος. ταύτης τῆς
τετραλογίας, ἥτις ἐστὶ πρώτη, ἡγεῖται Εὐθύφρων
ἢ περὶ ὁσίου· ὁ διάλογος δ' ἐστὶ πειραστικός·
δεύτερος Ἀπολογία Σωκράτους, ἠθικός· τρίτος
Κρίτων ἢ περὶ πρακτέου, ἠθικός· τέταρτος Φαίδων
ἢ περὶ ψυχῆς, ἠθικός. δευτέρα τετραλογία, ἧς
ἡγεῖται Κρατύλος ἢ περὶ ὀρθότητος ὀνομάτων,
λογικός· Θεαίτητος ἢ περὶ ἐπιστήμης, πειραστικός·
Σοφιστὴς ἢ περὶ τοῦ ὄντος, λογικός· Πολιτικὸς ἢ
περὶ βασιλείας, λογικός. τῆς τρίτης ἡγεῖται Παρμενίδης ἢ περὶ ἰδεῶν, λογικός· Φίληβος ἢ περὶ
ἡδονῆς, ἠθικός· Συμπόσιον ἢ περὶ ἀγαθοῦ, ἠθικός·
Φαῖδρος ἢ περὶ ἔρωτος, ἠθικός.
59 Τῆς τετάρτης ἡγεῖται Ἀλκιβιάδης ἢ περὶ ἀνθρώπου φύσεως, μαιευτικός· Ἀλκιβιάδης δεύτερος
ἢ περὶ εὐχῆς, μαιευτικός· Ἵππαρχος ἢ φιλοκερδής,
ἠθικός· Ἀντερασταὶ ἢ περὶ φιλοσοφίας, ἠθικός.
τῆς πέμπτης ἡγεῖται Θεάγης ἢ περὶ φιλοσοφίας,
μαιευτικός· Χαρμίδης ἢ περὶ σωφροσύνης, πειρα-
στικός· Λάχης ἢ περὶ ἀνδρείας, μαιευτικός· Λύσις
ἢ περὶ φιλίας, μαιευτικός. τῆς ἕκτης ἡγεῖται
Εὐθύδημος ἢ ἐριστικός, ἀνατρεπτικός· Πρωταγόρας ἢ σοφισταί, ἐνδεικτικός· Γοργίας ἢ περὶ
ῥητορικῆς, ἀνατρεπτικός· Μένων ἢ περὶ ἀρετῆς,
60 πειραστικός. τῆς ἑβδόμης ἡγοῦνται Ἱππίαι δύο
— α' ἢ περὶ τοῦ καλοῦ, β' ἢ περὶ τοῦ ψεύδους —
ἀνατρεπτικοί· Ἴων ἢ περὶ Ἰλιάδος, πειραστικός·
328

will be. To each of the works Thrasylus affixes a double title, the one taken from the name of the interlocutor, the other from the subject. This tetralogy, then, which is the first, begins with the *Euthyphro* or *On Holiness*, a tentative dialogue; the *Apology of Socrates*, an ethical dialogue, comes second; the third is *Crito* or *On what is to be done*, ethical; the fourth *Phaedo* or *On the Soul*, also ethical. The second tetralogy begins with *Cratylus* or *On Correctness of Names*, a logical dialogue, which is followed by *Theaetetus* or *On Knowledge*, tentative, the *Sophist* or *On Being*, a logical dialogue, the *Statesman* or *On Monarchy*, also logical. The third tetralogy includes, first, *Parmenides* or *On Ideas*, which is logical, next *Philebus* or *On Pleasure*, an ethical dialogue, the *Banquet* or *On the Good*, ethical, *Phaedrus* or *On Love*, also ethical.

The fourth tetralogy starts with *Alcibiades* or *On the Nature of Man*, an obstetric dialogue; this is followed by the second *Alcibiades* or *On Prayer*, also obstetric; then comes *Hipparchus* or *The Lover of Gain*, which is ethical, and *The Rivals* or *On Philosophy*, also ethical. The fifth tetralogy includes, first, *Theages* or *On Philosophy*, an obstetric dialogue, then *Charmides* or *On Temperance*, which is tentative, *Laches* or *On Courage*, obstetric, and *Lysis* or *On Friendship*, also obstetric. The sixth tetralogy starts with *Euthydemus* or *The Eristic*, a refutative dialogue, which is followed by *Protagoras* or *Sophists*, critical, *Gorgias* or *On Rhetoric*, refutative, and *Meno* or *On Virtue*, which is tentative. The seventh tetralogy contains, first, two dialogues entitled *Hippias*, the former *On Beauty*, the latter *On Falsehood*, both refutative; next *Ion* or *On the Iliad*, which is tentative,

Μενέξενος ἢ ἐπιτάφιος, ἠθικός. τῆς ὀγδόης ἡγεῖται
Κλειτοφῶν ἢ προτρεπτικός, ἠθικός· Πολιτεία ἢ
περὶ δικαίου, πολιτικός· Τίμαιος ἢ περὶ φύσεως,
φυσικός· Κριτίας ἢ ᾿Ατλαντικός, ἠθικός. τῆς
ἐνάτης ἡγεῖται Μίνως ἢ περὶ νόμου, πολιτικός·
Νόμοι ἢ περὶ νομοθεσίας, πολιτικός· ᾿Επινομὶς
ἢ νυκτερινὸς σύλλογος ἢ φιλόσοφος, πολιτικός·
61 ᾿Επιστολαὶ τρεισκαίδεκα, ἠθικαί — ἐν αἷς ἔγραφεν
εὖ πράττειν, ᾿Επίκουρος δὲ εὖ διάγειν, Κλέων
χαίρειν — πρὸς ᾿Αριστόδημον μία, πρὸς ᾿Αρχύταν
δύο, πρὸς Διονύσιον τέτταρες, πρὸς ῾Ερμίαν καὶ
῎Εραστον καὶ Κορίσκον μία, πρὸς Λεωδάμαντα
μία, πρὸς Δίωνα μία, πρὸς Περδίκκαν μία, πρὸς
τοὺς Δίωνος οἰκείους δύο. καὶ οὗτος μὲν οὕτω
διαιρεῖ καί τινες.

῎Ενιοι δέ, ὧν ἐστι καὶ ᾿Αριστοφάνης ὁ γραμματικός, εἰς τριλογίας ἕλκουσι τοὺς διαλόγους, καὶ
62 πρώτην μὲν τιθέασιν ἧς ἡγεῖται Πολιτεία Τίμαιος
Κριτίας· δευτέραν Σοφιστὴς Πολιτικὸς Κρατύλος·
τρίτην Νόμοι Μίνως ᾿Επινομίς· τετάρτην Θεαίτητος Εὐθύφρων ᾿Απολογία· πέμπτην Κρίτων
Φαίδων ᾿Επιστολαί. τὰ δ᾿ ἄλλα καθ᾿ ἓν καὶ
ἀτάκτως. ἄρχονται δὲ οἱ μέν, ὡς προείρηται, ἀπὸ
τῆς Πολιτείας· οἱ δ᾿ ἀπὸ ᾿Αλκιβιάδου τοῦ μείζονος·
οἱ δ᾿ ἀπὸ Θεάγους· ἔνιοι δὲ Εὐθύφρονος· ἄλλοι
Κλειτοφῶντος· τινὲς Τιμαίου· οἱ δ᾿ ἀπὸ Φαίδρου·
ἕτεροι Θεαιτήτου· πολλοὶ δὲ ⟨ἀπ᾿⟩ ᾿Απολογίας
τὴν ἀρχὴν ποιοῦνται. νοθεύονται δὲ τῶν διαλόγων
ὁμολογουμένως Μίδων ἢ ῾Ιπποτρόφος, ᾿Ερυξίας ἢ

and *Menexenus* or *The Funeral Oration*, which is ethical. The eighth tetralogy starts with *Clitophon* or *Introduction*, which is ethical, and is followed by the *Republic* or *On Justice*, political, *Timaeus* or *On Nature*, a physical treatise, and *Critias* or *Story of Atlantis*, which is ethical. The ninth tetralogy starts with *Minos* or *On Law*, a political dialogue, which is followed by the *Laws* or *On Legislation*, also political, *Epinomis* or *Nocturnal Council*, or *Philosopher*, political, and lastly the *Epistles*, thirteen in number, which are ethical. In these epistles his heading was " Welfare," as that of Epicurus was " A Good Life," and that of Cleon " All Joy." They comprise : one to Aristodemus, two to Archytas, four to Dionysius, one to Hermias, Erastus and Coriscus, one each to Leodamas, Dion and Perdiccas, and two to Dion's friends. This is the division adopted by Thrasylus and some others.

Some, including Aristophanes the grammarian, arrange the dialogues arbitrarily in trilogies. In the first trilogy they place the *Republic*, *Timaeus* and *Critias* ; in the second the *Sophist*, the *Statesman* and *Cratylus* ; in the third the *Laws*, *Minos* and *Epinomis* ; in the fourth *Theaetetus*, *Euthyphro* and the *Apology* ; in the fifth *Crito*, *Phaedo* and the *Epistles*. The rest follow as separate compositions in no regular order. Some critics, as has already been stated, put the *Republic* first, while others start with the greater *Alcibiades*, and others again with the *Theages* ; some begin with the *Euthyphro*, others with the *Clitophon* ; some with the *Timaeus*, others with the *Phaedrus* ; others again with the *Theaetetus*, while many begin with the *Apology*. The following dialogues are acknowledged to be spurious: the *Midon* or *Horse-*

Ἐρασίστρατος, Ἀλκυών, Ἀκέφαλοι ἢ Σίσυφος,
Ἀξίοχος, Φαίακες, Δημόδοκος, Χελιδών, Ἑβδόμη,
Ἐπιμενίδης· ὧν ἡ Ἀλκυὼν Λέοντός τινος εἶναι
δοκεῖ, καθά φησι Φαβωρῖνος ἐν τῷ πέμπτῳ τῶν
Ἀπομνημονευμάτων.

63 Ὀνόμασι δὲ κέχρηται ποικίλοις πρὸς τὸ μὴ
εὐσύνοπτον εἶναι τοῖς ἀμαθέσι τὴν πραγματείαν·
ἰδιαίτατα μὲν σοφίαν ἡγεῖται εἶναι τὴν τῶν νοητῶν
καὶ ὄντως ὄντων ἐπιστήμην, ἥν φησι περὶ θεὸν καὶ
ψυχὴν σώματος κεχωρισμένην. ἰδίᾳ δὲ σοφίαν καὶ
τὴν φιλοσοφίαν καλεῖ, ὄρεξιν οὖσαν τῆς θείας
σοφίας. κοινῶς δὲ λέγεται παρ' αὐτῷ σοφία καὶ
ἡ πᾶσα ἐμπειρία, οἷον ὅταν σοφὸν λέγῃ τὸν δημι-
ουργόν. χρῆται δὲ καὶ ἐπὶ διαφερόντως σημαι-
νομένων τοῖς αὐτοῖς ὀνόμασιν. ὁ γοῦν φαῦλος
λέγεται παρ' αὐτῷ καὶ ἐπὶ τοῦ ἁπλοῦ, ὡς καὶ
παρὰ Εὐριπίδῃ ἐν Λικυμνίῳ φέρεται ἐπὶ τοῦ
Ἡρακλέους οὑτωσί·

> φαῦλον, ἄκομψον, τὰ μέγιστ' ἀγαθόν,
> πᾶσαν ἐν ἔργῳ περιταμνόμενον
> σοφίαν, λέσχης ἀτρίβωνα.

64 χρῆται δὲ ὁ Πλάτων ἐνίοτε αὐτῷ καὶ ἐπὶ τοῦ
κακοῦ· ἔστι δ' ὅτε καὶ ἐπὶ τοῦ μικροῦ. πολλάκις
δὲ καὶ διαφέρουσιν ὀνόμασιν ἐπὶ τοῦ αὐτοῦ σημαινο-
μένου χρῆται. τὴν γοῦν ἰδέαν καὶ εἶδος ὀνομάζει
καὶ γένος καὶ παράδειγμα καὶ ἀρχὴν καὶ αἴτιον.
χρῆται δὲ καὶ ταῖς ἐναντίαις φωναῖς ἐπὶ τοῦ αὐτοῦ.
τὸ γοῦν αἰσθητὸν καὶ ὂν καλεῖ καὶ μὴ ὄν· ὂν μὲν

---

[a] *Cf.* Athenaeus xi. 506 c. The same statement about the
authorship of the *Alcyon* is attributed to Nicias of Nicaea.

[b] As *e.g. Theaet.* 147 c οἷον ἐν τῇ τοῦ πηλοῦ ἐρωτήσει
φαῦλόν **που καὶ** ἁπλοῦν εἰπεῖν ὅτι γῆ ὑγρῷ φυραθεῖσα πηλὸς ἂν

breeder, the *Eryxias* or *Erasistratus*, the *Alcyon*, the *Acephali* or *Sisyphus*, the *Axiochus*, the *Phaeacians*, the *Demodocus*, the *Chelidon*, the *Seventh Day*, the *Epimenides*. Of these the *Alcyon*[a] is thought to be the work of a certain Leon, according to Favorinus in the fifth book of his *Memorabilia*.

Plato has employed a variety of terms in order to make his system less intelligible to the ignorant. But in a special sense he considers wisdom to be the science of those things which are objects of thought and really existent, the science which, he says, is concerned with God and the soul as separate from the body. And especially by wisdom he means philosophy, which is a yearning for divine wisdom. And in a general sense all experience is also termed by him wisdom, *e.g.* when he calls a craftsman wise. And he applies the same terms with very different meanings. For instance, the word φαῦλος (slight, plain) is employed by him[b] in the sense of ἁπλοῦς (simple, honest), just as it is applied to Heracles in the *Licymnius* of Euripides in the following passage[c]:

Plain (φαῦλος), unaccomplished, staunch to do great deeds, unversed in talk, with all his store of wisdom curtailed to action.

But sometimes Plato uses this same word (φαῦλος) to mean what is bad, and at other times for what is small or petty. Again, he often uses different terms to express the same thing. For instance, he calls the Idea form (εἶδος), genus (γένος), archetype (παράδειγμα), principle (ἀρχή) and cause (αἴτιον). He also uses contrary expressions for the same thing. Thus he calls the sensible thing both existent and non-

εἴη, τὸ δ' ὅτου ἐὰν χαίρειν. *Cf. Rep.* 527 D οὐ πάνυ φαῦλον ἀλλὰ χαλεπὸν πιστεῦσαι. [c] Nauck, *T.G.F.*[2], Eur. 473.

333

διὰ τὸ γένεσιν αὐτοῦ εἶναι, μὴ ὂν δὲ διὰ τὴν συνεχῆ μεταβολήν. καὶ τὴν ἰδέαν οὔτε κινούμενον οὔτε μένον· καὶ ταὐτὸ καὶ ἕν καὶ πολλά. τὸ δ' αὐτὸ καὶ ἐπὶ πλειόνων εἴθισται ποιεῖν.

65 Ἔστι δὲ ἡ ἐξήγησις αὐτοῦ τῶν λόγων τριπλῆ· πρῶτον μὲν γὰρ ἐκδιδάξαι χρὴ ὅ τι ἐστὶν ἕκαστον τῶν λεγομένων· ἔπειτα, τίνος εἵνεκα λέλεκται, πότερα κατὰ προηγούμενον ἢ ἐν εἰκόνος μέρει, καὶ <εἰ> εἰς δογμάτων κατασκευὴν ἢ εἰς ἔλεγχον τοῦ προσδιαλεγομένου· τὸ δὲ τρίτον, εἰ ὀρθῶς λέλεκται.

Ἐπεὶ δὲ καὶ σημεῖά τινα τοῖς βιβλίοις αὐτοῦ παρατίθενται, φέρε καὶ περὶ τούτων τι εἴπωμεν. Χῖ λαμβάνεται πρὸς τὰς λέξεις καὶ τὰ σχήματα καὶ ὅλως τὴν Πλατωνικὴν συνήθειαν· διπλῆ πρὸς 66 τὰ δόγματα καὶ τὰ ἀρέσκοντα Πλάτωνι· Χῖ περιεστιγμένον πρὸς τὰς ἐκλογὰς καὶ καλλιγραφίας· διπλῆ περιεστιγμένη πρὸς τὰς ἐνίων διορθώσεις· ὀβελὸς περιεστιγμένος πρὸς τὰς εἰκαίους ἀθετήσεις· ἀντίσιγμα περιεστιγμένον πρὸς τὰς διττὰς χρήσεις καὶ μεταθέσεις τῶν γραφῶν· κεραύνιον πρὸς τὴν ἀγωγὴν τῆς φιλοσοφίας· ἀστερίσκος πρὸς τὴν συμφωνίαν τῶν δογμάτων· ὀβελὸς πρὸς τὴν ἀθέτησιν. τὰ μὲν σημεῖα ταῦτα καὶ τὰ βιβλία τοσαῦτα· ἅπερ Ἀντίγονός φησιν ὁ Καρύστιος ἐν τῷ Περὶ Ζήνωνος νεωστὶ ἐκδοθέντα εἴ τις ἤθελε διαναγνῶναι, μισθὸν ἐτέλει τοῖς κεκτημένοις.

67 Τὰ δὲ ἀρέσκοντα αὐτῷ ταῦτα ἦν. ἀθάνατον

---

[a] A wedge-shaped mark >, used in early papyri to denote a fresh paragraph.

[b] Here begins the second appendix περὶ τῶν Πλάτωνι ἀρεσκόντων, §§ 67-80. It should be observed that there is

existent, existent inasmuch as it comes into being, non-existent because it is continually changing. And he says the Idea is neither in motion nor at rest; that it is uniformly the same and yet both one and many. And it is his habit to do this in many more instances.

The right interpretation of his dialogues includes three things : first, the meaning of every statement must be explained; next, its purpose, whether it is made for a primary reason or by way of illustration, and whether to establish his own doctrines or to refute his interlocutor; in the third place it remains to examine its truth.

And since certain critical marks are affixed to his works let us now say a word about these. The cross X is taken to indicate peculiar expressions and figures of speech, and generally any idiom of Platonic usage ; the *diple* [a] (>) calls attention to doctrines and opinions characteristic of Plato ; the dotted cross (※) denotes select passages and beauties of style ; the dotted *diple* (⋗) editors' corrections of the text ; the dotted *obelus* (÷) passages suspected without reason ; the dotted antisigma (⊃·) repetitions and proposals for transpositions ; the *ceraunium* the philosophical school; the asterisk (✳) an agreement of doctrine ; the *obelus* (–) a spurious passage. So much for the critical marks and his writings in general. As Antigonus of Carystus says in his *Life of Zeno*, when the writings were first edited with critical marks, their possessors charged a certain fee to anyone who wished to consult them.

[b] The doctrines he approved are these. He held

absolutely no trace of Neo-Platonist tendencies. *Cf*. Plato, *Tim.* 42 E–43 A, 69 A.

ἔλεγε τὴν ψυχὴν καὶ πολλὰ μεταμφιεννυμένην
σώματα, ἀρχήν τε ἔχειν ἀριθμητικήν, τὸ δὲ σῶμα
γεωμετρικήν· ὡρίζετο δὲ αὐτὴν ἰδέαν τοῦ πάντῃ
διεστῶτος πνεύματος. αὐτοκίνητόν τε εἶναι καὶ
τριμερῆ· τὸ μὲν γὰρ αὐτῆς λογιστικὸν μέρος περὶ
τῇ κεφαλῇ καθιδρῦσθαι, τὸ δὲ θυμοειδὲς περὶ τῇ
καρδίᾳ, τὸ δὲ ἐπιθυμητικὸν περὶ τὸν ὀμφαλὸν καὶ
τὸ ἧπαρ συνίστασθαι.

68 Περιέχειν δὲ ἐκ τοῦ μέσου διὰ παντὸς κύκλῳ τὸ
σῶμα καὶ συνεστάναι ἐκ τῶν στοιχείων. διαιρε-
θεῖσάν τε κατὰ ἁρμονικὰ διαστήματα δύο κύκλους
ποιεῖν συνημμένους, ὧν τὸν ἐντὸς κύκλον ἑξαχῇ
τμηθέντα τοὺς ἅπαντας ἑπτὰ κύκλους ποιεῖν. καὶ
τοῦτον μὲν κατὰ διάμετρον κ‹ιν›εῖσθαι ἐπ' ἀριστερὰ
ἔσωθεν, τὸν δὲ κατὰ πλευρὰν ἐπὶ τὰ δεξιά. διὸ
καὶ κρατεῖν αὐτὸν ἕνα ὄντα· τὸν γὰρ ἕτερον ἔσωθεν
διῃρῆσθαι. καὶ τὸν μὲν εἶναι ταὐτοῦ, τοὺς δὲ
θατέρου, λέγων τὴν τῆς ψυχῆς κίνησιν εἶναι τὴν
[δὲ] τοῦ ὅλου καὶ τὰς τῶν πλανωμένων φοράς.

69 Οὕτω δ' ἐχούσης τῆς ἐκ μέσου τομῆς αὐτῇ
προσαρμοζομένης πρὸς τὰ ἔσχατα γινώσκειν τε τὰ
ὄντα καὶ ἐναρμόζειν διὰ τὸ ἔχειν ἐν αὐτῇ τὰ
στοιχεῖα κατὰ ἁρμονίαν. καὶ γίνεσθαι δόξαν μὲν
κατὰ τὸν θατέρου κύκλον ὀρθούμενον, ἐπιστήμην
δὲ κατὰ τὸν ταὐτοῦ. δύο δὲ τῶν πάντων ἀπέφηνεν
ἀρχάς, θεὸν καὶ ὕλην, ὃν καὶ νοῦν προσαγορεύει
καὶ αἴτιον. εἶναι δὲ τὴν ὕλην ἀσχημάτιστον καὶ
ἄπειρον, ἐξ ἧς γίνεσθαι τὰ συγκρίματα. ἀτάκτως

---

a Cf. Plato, *Tim.* 42 B *sqq.*, 90 E.
b Cf. Plato, *Tim.* 54 A *sqq.*
c Cf. Plato, *Tim.* 69 C *sqq.*, 89 E.
d Cf. Plato, *Tim.* 36 D–37 C.
e Cf. Plato, *Tim.* 50 D, E; 51 A.

that the soul is immortal, that by transmigration it puts on many bodies,[a] and that it has a numerical first principle, whereas the first principle of the body is geometrical [b]; and he defined soul as the idea of vital breath diffused in all directions. He held that it is self-moved and tripartite, the rational part of it having its seat in the head, the passionate part about the heart, while the appetitive is placed in the region of the navel and the liver.[c]

And from the centre outwards it encloses the body on all sides in a circle, and is compounded of elements, and, being divided at harmonic intervals, it forms two circles which touch one another twice ; and the interior circle, being slit six times over, makes seven circles in all. And this interior circle moves by way of the diagonal to the left, and the other by way of the side to the right. Hence also the one is supreme, being a single circle, for the other interior circle was divided ; the former is the circle of the Same, the latter that of the Other, whereby he means that the motion of the soul is the motion of the universe together with the revolutions of the planets.[d]

And the division from the centre to the circumference which is adjusted in harmony with the soul being thus determined, the soul knows that which is, and adjusts it proportionately because she has the elements proportionately disposed in herself. And when the circle of the Other revolves aright, the result is opinion ; but from the regular motion of the circle of the Same comes knowledge. He set forth two universal principles, God and matter, and he calls God mind and cause ; he held that matter is devoid of form and unlimited, and that composite things arise out of it [e] ; and that it was once in

δέ ποτε αὐτὴν κινουμένην ὑπὸ τοῦ θεοῦ φησιν εἰς
ἕνα συναχθῆναι τόπον τάξιν ἀταξίας κρείττονα
70 ἡγησαμένου. τραπέσθαι δὲ τὴν οὐσίαν ταύτην εἰς
τὰ τέτταρα στοιχεῖα, πῦρ, ὕδωρ, ἀέρα, γῆν· ἐξ ὧν
αὐτόν τε τὸν κόσμον καὶ τὰ ἐν αὐτῷ γεννᾶσθαι.
μόνην δὲ τὴν γῆν ἀμετάβολον εἶναί φησι, νομίζων
αἰτίαν τὴν τῶν σχημάτων διαφορὰν ἐξ ὧν σύγκειται.
τῶν μὲν γὰρ ἄλλων ὁμογενῆ φησιν εἶναι τὰ σχήματα — ἅπαντα γὰρ ἐξ ἑνὸς συγκεῖσθαι τοῦ
προμήκους τριγώνου — τῆς δὲ γῆς ἴδιον εἶναι τὸ
σχῆμα· πυρὸς μὲν γὰρ εἶναι στοιχεῖον πυραμίδα,
ἀέρος τὸ ὀκτάεδρον, ὕδατος τὸ εἰκοσάεδρον, γῆς
δὲ κύβον. ὅθεν μήτε γῆν εἰς ταῦτα μεταβάλλειν,
μήτε ταῦτα εἰς γῆν.

71 Οὐ διακεκρίσθαι δ' εἰς τοὺς οἰκείους τόπους
ἕκαστον, ὅτι ἡ περιφορὰ σφίγγουσα καὶ πρὸς τὸν
μέσον συνάγουσα συγκρίνει τὰ μικρά, τὰ δὲ
διακρίνει, τὰ μεγάλα. διόπερ τὰ εἴδη μεταβάλλοντα
καὶ τοὺς τόπους μεταβάλλειν.

Κόσμον τε εἶναι ἕνα γεννητόν, ἐπειδὴ καὶ αἰσθη-
τός ἐστιν ὑπὸ θεοῦ κατεσκευασμένος· ἔμψυχόν τε
εἶναι διὰ τὸ κρεῖττον εἶναι τοῦ ἀψύχου τὸ ἔμψυχον,
τοῦτο δὲ δημιούργημα ὑποκεῖσθαι τοῦ βελτίστου
αἰτίου. ἕνα τε αὐτὸν καὶ οὐκ ἄπειρον κατεσκευά-
σθαι, ὅτι καὶ τὸ ὑπόδειγμα ἓν ἦν ἀφ' οὗ αὐτὸν
ἐδημιούργησε· σφαιροειδῆ δὲ διὰ τὸ καὶ τὸν
72 γεννήσαντα τοιοῦτον ἔχειν σχῆμα. ἐκεῖνον μὲν
γὰρ περιέχειν τὰ ἄλλα ζῷα, τοῦτον δὲ τὰ σχήματα

---

[a] Cf. Plato, Tim. 30 A, 69 B.
[b] Cf. Plato, Tim. 58 A-C.
[c] Cf. Plato, Tim. 31 A, B ; 33 A ; 55 C, D ; 92 C.
[d] Cf. Plato, Tim. 30 B.

disorderly motion but, inasmuch as God preferred
order to disorder, was by him brought together in one
place.[a] This substance, he says, is converted into
the four elements, fire, water, air, earth, of which
the world itself and all that therein is are formed.
Earth alone of these elements is not subject to
change, the assumed cause being the peculiarity of
its constituent triangles. For he thinks that in all
the other elements the figures employed are homogeneous, the scalene triangle out of which they are
all put together being one and the same, whereas
for earth a triangle of peculiar shape is employed ;
the element of fire is a pyramid, of air an octahedron,
of water an icosahedron, of earth a cube. Hence
earth is not transmuted into the other three elements,
nor these three into earth.

But the elements are not separated each into its
own region of the universe, because the revolution
unites their minute particles, compressing and forcing
them together into the centre, at the same time as
it separates the larger masses. Hence as they change
their shapes, so also do they change the regions which
they occupy.[b]

And there is one created universe,[c] seeing that it
is perceptible to sense, which has been made by God.
And it is animate because that which is animate is
better than that which is inanimate.[d] And this
piece of workmanship is assumed to come from a
cause supremely good.[e] It was made one and not
unlimited because the pattern from which he made
it was one. And it is spherical because such is the
shape of its maker. For that maker contains the
other living things, and this universe the shapes of

---

[a] *Cf.* Plato, *Tim.* 30 A, B ; 55 C, D.

πάντων. λεῖον δὲ καὶ οὐδὲν ὄργανον ἔχοντα κύκλῳ
διὰ τὸ μηδεμίαν εἶναι χρῆσιν αὐτῶν. ἀλλὰ μὴν καὶ
ἄφθαρτον διαμένειν τὸν κόσμον διὰ τὸ μὴ διαλύεσθαι εἰς[1] τὸν θεόν. καὶ τῆς μὲν ὅλης γενέσεως
αἴτιον εἶναι τὸν θεόν, ὅτι πέφυκεν ἀγαθοποιὸν εἶναι
τὸ ἀγαθόν. τοῦ δὲ οὐρανοῦ τῆς γενέσεως τὸ
† αἴτιον· τοῦ γὰρ καλλίστου τῶν γεννητῶν τὸ
ἄριστον εἶναι τῶν νοητῶν αἴτιον. ὥστε ἐπεὶ
τοιοῦτος ὁ θεός, ὅμοιος δὲ τῷ ἀρίστῳ ὁ οὐρανὸς
κάλλιστός γε ὤν, οὐθενὶ ἂν ὅμοιος εἴη τῶν γεννητῶν
ἀλλ' ἢ τῷ θεῷ.

73 Συνεστάναι δὲ τὸν κόσμον ἐκ πυρός, ὕδατος,
ἀέρος, γῆς. ἐκ πυρὸς μέν, ὅπως ὁρατὸς ᾖ· ἐκ γῆς
δέ, ὅπως στερεός· ἐξ ὕδατος δὲ καὶ ἀέρος, ὅπως
ἀνάλογος — αἱ γὰρ τῶν στερεῶν δυνάμεις δύο
μεσότησιν ἀναλογοῦσιν ὡς ἐν γενέσθαι τὸ πᾶν — ἐξ
ἁπάντων δέ, ἵνα τέλειος καὶ ἄφθαρτος ᾖ.

Χρόνον τε γενέσθαι εἰκόνα τοῦ ἀϊδίου. κἀκεῖνον
μὲν ἀεὶ μένειν, τὴν δὲ τοῦ οὐρανοῦ φορὰν χρόνον
εἶναι· καὶ γὰρ νύκτα καὶ ἡμέραν καὶ μῆνα καὶ τὰ
τοιαῦτα πάντα χρόνου μέρη εἶναι. διόπερ ἄνευ
τῆς τοῦ κόσμου φύσεως οὐκ εἶναι χρόνον· ἅμα γὰρ
ὑπάρχειν αὐτῷ καὶ χρόνον εἶναι.

74 Πρὸς δὲ χρόνου γένεσιν ἥλιον καὶ σελήνην καὶ τὰ

---

[1] εἰς] ὡς Reiske: fort. ἐᾶν Basilienses.

---

[a] A perversion of *Tim.* 33 B. To that which is to com-
prehend all animals in itself that shape seems proper which
comprehends in itself all shapes. Diogenes Laertius opposes,
not universe and its shape, but maker and universe.
[b] *Cf.* Plato, *Tim.* 33 A–D ; 34 B ; 32 C ; 63 A.
[c] *Cf.* Plato, *Tim.* 32 C, 33 A ; 38 B ; 41 A, 43 D.
[d] *Cf.* Plato, *Tim.* 29 E–30 A ; 42 E.

them all.[a] It is smooth and has no organ all round because it has no need of organs. Moreover, the universe remains imperishable because it is not dissolved into the Deity.[b] And the creation as a whole is caused by God, because it is the nature of the good to be beneficent,[c] and the creation of the universe has the highest good for its cause. For the most beautiful of created things is due to the best of intelligible causes [d] ; so that, as God is of this nature, and the universe resembles the best in its perfect beauty, it will not be in the likeness of anything created, but only of God.

The universe is composed of fire, water, air and earth ; of fire in order to be visible ; of earth in order to be solid ; of water and air in order to be proportional.[e] For the powers represented by solids are connected by two mean proportionals in a way to secure the complete unity of the whole. And the universe was made of all the elements in order to be complete and indestructible.

Time was created as an image of eternity. And while the latter remains for ever at rest, time consists in the motion of the universe. For night and day and month and the like are all parts of time ; for which reason, apart from the nature of the universe, time has no existence. But so soon as the universe is fashioned time exists.[f]

And the sun and moon and planets were created

[e] Cf. Tim. 31 B–33 A. It would be more correct to say " in order that the bonds, the inserted terms (air and water), which unite fire to earth, may be proportional." " For the best of bonds is that which makes itself and the things which it binds as complete a unity as possible ; and the nature of proportion is to accomplish this most perfectly " (Tim. 31 c).
[f] Cf. Plato, Tim. 37 D–38 B.

πλανώμενα γενέσθαι. ὅπως δὲ διάδηλος τῶν ὡρῶν
ᾖ ἀριθμὸς καὶ μετάσχοι τὰ ζῷα ἀριθμοῦ, τὸ τοῦ
ἡλίου φῶς ἀνάψαι τὸν θεόν. εἶναι δὲ ἐν μὲν τῷ
ὑπὲρ γῆς κύκλῳ σελήνην, ἐν δὲ τῷ ἐχομένῳ ἥλιον,
ἐν δὲ τοῖς ἐπάνω τοὺς πλανήτας. ἔμψυχον δὲ
πάντως διὰ τὸ ἐμψύχῳ φορᾷ δεδέσθαι. ἵνα δὲ ὁ
κόσμος τελειωθῇ γενόμενος ὁμοίως τῷ νοητῷ ζῴῳ,
τὴν τῶν ἄλλων ζῴων γενέσθαι φύσιν. ἐπεὶ οὖν
ἐκεῖνο εἶχε, καὶ τὸν οὐρανὸν δεῖν ἔχειν. θεοὺς μὲν
οὖν ἔχειν τὸ πολὺ πυρίνους· εἶναι δὲ τρία γένη
75 τἆλλα, πτηνόν, ἔνυδρον, πεζόν. γῆν δὲ πρεσβυ-
τάτην μὲν εἶναι τῶν ἐν τῷ οὐρανῷ θεῶν· γενέσθαι
δὲ ὡς δημιούργημα νύκτα καὶ ἡμέραν ποιεῖν· οὖσαν
δ' ἐπὶ τοῦ μέσου κινεῖσθαι περὶ τὸ μέσον. ἐπεὶ δ'
αἰτίαι εἰσὶ δύο, τὰ μὲν διὰ νοῦ εἶναι, τὰ δ' ἐξ
ἀναγκαίας αἰτίας, φησί, λεκτέον. ταῦτα δ' ἐστὶν
ἀήρ, πῦρ, γῆ, ὕδωρ — καὶ οὐκ ὄντα μὲν στοιχεῖα
κατὰ ἀκρίβειαν, ἀλλὰ δεκτικά. ταῦτα δ' ἐκ τῶν
τριγώνων εἶναι συντιθεμένων καὶ διαλύεσθαι εἰς
ταῦτα· στοιχεῖα δ' αὐτῶν εἶναι τό τε πρόμηκες
τρίγωνον καὶ τὸ ἰσοσκελές.
76 Ἀρχὰς μὲν οὖν εἶναι καὶ αἴτια τὰ λεχθέντα δύο
ὧν μὲν παράδειγμα τὸν θεὸν καὶ τὴν ὕλην· ὅπερ
ἀνάγκη ἄμορφον εἶναι ὥσπερ καὶ ἐπὶ τῶν ἄλλων
δεκτικῶν. αἴτιον δὲ τούτων ἐξ ἀνάγκης εἶναι·
δεχόμενον γάρ πως τὰς ἰδέας γεννᾶν τὰς οὐσίας,
καὶ δι' ἀνομοιότητα δυνάμεως κινεῖσθαι καὶ κινού-

---

[a] Cf. Plato, *Tim.* 38 c–39 D.
[b] Cf. Plato, *Tim.* 30 c–31 B ; 39 c–40 A ; 41 B, C.
[c] Cf. Plato, *Tim.* 40 B, C.
[d] Cf. Plato, *Tim.* 46 D, E ; 47 E ; 48 A ; 68 E ; 69 A.
[e] Cf. Plato, *Tim.* 49 A *sqq.* ; 50 B–51 B ; 52 A, B.
[f] Cf. Plato, *Tim.* 53 c–55 c.

as means to the creation of time. And God kindled
the light of the sun in order that the number of the
seasons might be definite and in order that animals
might possess number. The moon is in the circle
immediately above the earth, and the sun in that
which is next beyond that, and in the circles above
come the planets. Further, the universe is an
animate being, for it is bound fast in animate movement.[a] And in order that the universe which had
been created in the likeness of the intelligible living
creature might be rendered complete, the nature
of all other animals was created. Since then its
pattern possesses them, the universe also ought to
have them. And thus it contains gods for the most
part of a fiery nature ; of the rest there are three
kinds, winged, aquatic and terrestrial.[b] And of all
the gods in heaven the earth is the oldest. And it
was fashioned to make night and day. And being
at the centre it moves round the centre.[c] And since
there are two causes, it must be affirmed, he says,
that some things are due to reason and others have
a necessary cause,[d] the latter being air, fire, earth
and water, which are not exactly elements but rather
recipients of form.[e] They are composed of triangles,
and are resolved into triangles. The scalene triangle and the isosceles triangle are their constituent
elements.[f]

The principles, then, and causes assumed are the
two above mentioned, of which God and matter are
the exemplar. Matter is of necessity formless like
the other recipients of form. Of all these there is
a necessary cause. For it somehow or other receives
the ideas and so generates substances, and it moves
because its power is not uniform, and, being in

μενον τὰ γινόμενα ἐξ αὑτῆς ἀντικινεῖν. ταῦτα δὲ
πρὶν μὲν ἀλόγως κινεῖσθαι καὶ ἀτάκτως, ἐπεὶ δὲ
ἤρξαντο συνιστάναι τὸν κόσμον, ἐκ τῶν ἐνδεχομένων ὑπὸ τοῦ θεοῦ συμμέτρως καὶ τεταγμένως
77 γενέσθαι. τὰς μὲν γὰρ αἰτίας καὶ πρὸ τῆς οὐρανο-
ποιίας δύο εἶναι καὶ τρίτην γένεσιν, ἀλλ' οὐ σαφεῖς,
ἴχνη δὲ μόνον καὶ ἀτάκτους· ἐπειδὴ δὲ ὁ κόσμος
ἐγένετο, λαβεῖν καὶ ταύτας τάξιν. ἐξ ἁπάντων δὲ
τῶν ὑπαρχόντων σωμάτων γενέσθαι τὸν οὐρανόν.
δοκεῖ δ' αὐτῷ τὸν θεὸν ὡς καὶ τὴν ψυχὴν ἀσώματον
εἶναι· οὕτω γὰρ μάλιστα φθορᾶς καὶ πάθους
ἀνεπίδεκτον ὑπάρχειν. τὰς δὲ ἰδέας ὑφίσταται,
καθὰ καὶ προείρηται, αἰτίας τινὰς καὶ ἀρχὰς τοῦ
τοιαῦτ' εἶναι τὰ φύσει συνεστῶτα, οἷάπερ ἐστὶν
αὐτά.

78 Περὶ δὲ ἀγαθῶν ἢ κακῶν τοιαῦτα ἔλεγε. τέλος
μὲν εἶναι τὴν ἐξομοίωσιν τῷ θεῷ. τὴν δ' ἀρετὴν
αὐτάρκη μὲν εἶναι πρὸς εὐδαιμονίαν. ὀργάνων δὲ
προσδεῖσθαι τῶν περὶ σῶμα πλεονεκτημάτων,
ἰσχύος, ὑγιείας, εὐαισθησίας, τῶν ὁμοίων· καὶ τῶν
ἐκτός, οἷον πλούτου καὶ εὐγενείας καὶ δόξης.
οὐδὲν δὲ ἧττον εὐδαίμονα ἔσεσθαι τὸν σοφόν, κἂν
ταῦτα μὴ παρῇ. πολιτεύσεσθαι αὖ καὶ γαμήσειν
καὶ τοὺς κειμένους νόμους οὐ παραβήσεσθαι· ἐκ
δὲ τῶν ἐνδεχομένων καὶ νομοθετήσειν τῇ ἑαυτοῦ
πατρίδι, ἐὰν μὴ τέλεον εὐπαραίτητα[1] ὁρᾷ τὰ πράγ-
79 ματα ἐν ὑπερβαλλούσῃ διαφθορᾷ δήμου. οἴεται
δὲ καὶ θεοὺς ἐφορᾶν τὰ ἀνθρώπινα καὶ δαίμονας
εἶναι. ἔννοιάν τε καλοῦ πρῶτος ἀπεφήνατο τὴν

---

[1] ἀπαραίτητα Casaubon.

ᵃ Cf. Plato, *Tim.* 52 D ; 53 B ; 57 C ; 69 B, C.
ᵇ Cf. Plato, *Tim.* 30 B ; 44 C.

motion, it in turn sets in motion those things which are generated from it. And these were at first in irrational and irregular motion, but after they began to frame the universe, under the conditions possible they were made by God symmetrical and regular. For the two causes existed even before the world was made, as well as becoming in the third place, but they were not distinct, merely traces of them being found, and in disorder. When the world was made, they too acquired order.[a] And out of all the bodies there are the universe was fashioned. He holds God, like the soul, to be incorporeal. For only thus is he exempt from change and decay. As already stated, he assumes the Ideas to be causes and principles whereby the world of natural objects is what it is.

On good and evil he would discourse to this effect. He maintained that the end to aim at is assimilation to God, that virtue is in itself sufficient for happiness, but that it needs in addition, as instruments for use, first, bodily advantages like health and strength, sound senses and the like, and, secondly, external advantages such as wealth, good birth and reputation. But the wise man will be no less happy even if he be without these things. Again, he will take part in public affairs, will marry, and will refrain from breaking the laws which have been made. And as far as circumstances allow he will legislate for his own country, unless in the extreme corruption of the people he sees that the state of affairs completely justifies his abstention. He thinks that the gods take note of human life [b] and that there are superhuman beings.[c] He was the first to define the notion of good as that which is bound up with

* *Cf.* Plato, *Tim.* 40 D.

ἐχομένην τοῦ ἐπαινετοῦ καὶ λογικοῦ καὶ χρησίμου
καὶ πρέποντος καὶ ἁρμόττοντος· ἅπερ πάντα ἔχεσθαι
τοῦ ἀκολούθου τῇ φύσει καὶ ὁμολογουμένου.

Διελέξατο δὲ καὶ περὶ ὀνομάτων ὀρθότητος·
ὥστε καὶ τὴν ἐπιστήμην τοῦ ὀρθῶς ἀποκρίνεσθαι
καὶ ἐρωτᾶν πρῶτον αὐτὸν διασυστῆσαι κατακόρως
χρησάμενον. ἐν δὲ τοῖς διαλόγοις καὶ τὴν δικαιοσύνην θεοῦ νόμον ὑπελάμβανεν ὡς ἰσχυροτέραν
προτρέψαι τὰ δίκαια πράττειν, ἵνα μὴ καὶ μετὰ
80 θάνατον δίκας ὑπόσχοιεν ὡς κακοῦργοι. ὅθεν καὶ
μυθικώτερος ἐνίοις ὑπελήφθη τοῖς συγγράμμασιν
ἐγκαταμίξας τὰς τοιαύτας διηγήσεις, ὅπως διὰ
†τοῦ ἀδήλου τρόπου τοῦ ἔχειν τὰ μετὰ τὸν θάνατον
οὕτως ἀπέχωνται τῶν ἀδικημάτων. καὶ ταῦτα
μὲν ἦν αὐτῷ τὰ ἀρέσκοντα.

Διῄρει δέ, φησὶν Ἀριστοτέλης, καὶ τὰ πράγματα
τοῦτον τὸν τρόπον. τῶν ἀγαθῶν ἐστι τὰ μὲν ἐν
ψυχῇ, τὰ δὲ ἐν σώματι, τὰ δὲ ἐκτός· οἷον ἡ μὲν
δικαιοσύνη καὶ ἡ φρόνησις καὶ ἡ ἀνδρεία καὶ ἡ
σωφροσύνη καὶ τὰ τοιαῦτα ἐν ψυχῇ· τὸ δὲ κάλλος
καὶ ἡ εὐεξία καὶ ἡ ὑγίεια καὶ ἡ ἰσχὺς ἐν σώματι·
οἱ δὲ φίλοι καὶ ἡ τῆς πατρίδος εὐδαιμονία καὶ ὁ
πλοῦτος ἐν τοῖς ἐκτός.

81 Τῶν ἀγαθῶν ἄρα τρία εἴδη ἐστί· τὰ μὲν ἐν ψυχῇ,
τὰ δὲ ἐν σώματι, τὰ δὲ ἐκτός. τῆς φιλίας τρία
εἴδη· ἡ μὲν γὰρ αὐτῆς ἐστι φυσική, ἡ δὲ ἑταιρική,
ἡ δὲ ξενική· φυσικὴν μὲν οὖν ταύτην λέγομεν, ἣν
οἱ γονεῖς πρὸς τὰ ἔκγονα ἔχουσι καὶ οἱ συγγενεῖς
πρὸς ἀλλήλους· ταύτης δὲ κεκλήρωται καὶ τἆλλα

ᵃ Cf. Plato, Tim. 42 B.

ᵇ The third appendix begins here, containing the διαιρέσεις
which are also attributed to Aristotle; see Rose, *Aristoteles*

whatever is praiseworthy and rational and useful and proper and becoming. And all these are bound up with that which is consistent and in accord with nature.

He also discoursed on the propriety of names, and indeed he was the first to frame a science for rightly asking and answering questions, having employed it himself to excess. And in the dialogues he conceived righteousness to be the law of God because it is stronger to incite men to do righteous acts, that malefactors may not be punished after death also. Hence to some he appeared too fond of myths. These narratives he intermingles with his works in order to deter men from wickedness, by reminding them how little they know of what awaits them [a] after death. Such, then, are the doctrines he approved.

He used also to divide things, according to Aristotle, in the following manner.[b] Goods are in the mind or in the body, or external. For example, justice, prudence, courage, temperance and such like are in the mind ; beauty, a good constitution, health and strength in the body ; while friends, the welfare of one's country and riches are amongst external things.

Thus there are three kinds of goods : goods of the mind, goods of the body and external goods. There are three species of friendship : one species is natural, another social, and another hospitable. By natural friendship we mean the affection which parents have for their offspring and kinsmen for each other. And other animals besides man have inherited this form.

Pseudepigraphus, pp. 679 *sqq.*, who gives a Christian recension. The original, the common source of Diogenes Laertius and the Christian writer, he refers vaguely to the Hellenistic age.

ζῷα. ἑταιρικὴν δὲ καλοῦμεν τὴν ἀπὸ συνηθείας
γινομένην καὶ μηδὲν προσήκουσαν γένει, ἀλλ' οἷον
ἡ Πυλάδου πρὸς Ὀρέστην. ἡ δὲ ξενικὴ φιλία ἡ
ἀπὸ συστάσεως καὶ διὰ γραμμάτων γινομένη πρὸς
τοὺς ξένους. τῆς ἄρα φιλίας ἡ μέν ἐστι φυσική,
ἡ δὲ ἑταιρική, ἡ δὲ ξενική· προστιθέασι δέ τινες
τετάρτην ἐρωτικήν.

82 Τῆς πολιτείας ἐστὶν εἴδη πέντε· τὸ μὲν γὰρ αὐτῆς
ἐστι δημοκρατικόν, ἄλλο δὲ ἀριστοκρατικόν, τρίτον
δὲ ὀλιγαρχικόν, τέταρτον βασιλικόν, πέμπτον
τυραννικόν. δημοκρατικὸν μὲν οὖν ἐστιν, ἐν αἷς
πόλεσι κρατεῖ τὸ πλῆθος καὶ τὰς ἀρχὰς καὶ τοὺς
νόμους δι' ἑαυτοῦ αἱρεῖται. ἀριστοκρατία δέ ἐστιν,
ἐν ᾗ μήθ' οἱ πλούσιοι μήθ' οἱ πένητες μήθ' οἱ
ἔνδοξοι ἄρχουσιν, ἀλλ' οἱ ἄριστοι τῆς πόλεως
προστατοῦσιν. ὀλιγαρχία δέ ἐστιν, ὅταν ἀπὸ
τιμημάτων αἱ ἀρχαὶ αἱρῶνται· ἐλάττους γάρ εἰσιν
οἱ πλούσιοι τῶν πενήτων. τῆς δὲ βασιλείας ἡ
μὲν κατὰ νόμον, ἡ δὲ κατὰ γένος ἐστίν. ἡ μὲν
οὖν ἐν Καρχηδόνι κατὰ νόμον· πωλητὴ γάρ ἐστιν.
83 ἡ δὲ ἐν Λακεδαίμονι καὶ Μακεδονίᾳ κατὰ γένος·
ἀπὸ γάρ τινος γένους ποιοῦνται τὴν βασιλείαν.
τυραννὶς δέ ἐστιν, ἐν ᾗ παρακρουσθέντες ἢ βια-
σθέντες ὑπό τινος ἄρχονται. τῆς ἄρα πολιτείας ἡ
μέν ἐστι δημοκρατία, ἡ δὲ ἀριστοκρατία, ἡ δὲ
ὀλιγαρχία, ἡ δὲ βασιλεία, ἡ δὲ τυραννίς.

Τῆς δὲ δικαιοσύνης ἐστὶν εἴδη τρία· ἡ μὲν γὰρ

---

[a] Plato probably refers to Carthage when he mentions
purchasable kingship, ὠνηταὶ βασιλεῖαι, amongst barbarians,
Rep. 544 D.   Aristotle repeats the epithet in his description
of the Carthaginian constitution, *Pol.* ii. 11, 1273 a 36.
Polybius says that at Carthage magistrates attain office, δῶρα

By the social form of friendship we mean that which
arises from intimacy and has nothing to do with
kinship; for instance, that of Pylades for Orestes.
The friendship of hospitality is that which is extended
to strangers owing to an introduction or letters of
recommendation. Thus friendship is either natural
or social or hospitable. Some add a fourth species,
that of love.

There are five forms of civil government : one form
is democratic, another aristocratic, a third oligarchic,
a fourth monarchic, a fifth that of a tyrant. The
democratic form is that in which the people has control and chooses at its own pleasure both magistrates
and laws. The aristocratic form is that in which the
rulers are neither the rich nor the poor nor the
nobles, but the state is under the guidance of the
best. Oligarchy is that form in which there is a
property-qualification for the holding of office ; for
the rich are fewer than the poor. Monarchy is
either regulated by law or hereditary. At Carthage
the kingship is regulated by law, the office being
put up for sale.[a] But the monarchy in Lacedaemon
and in Macedonia is hereditary, for they select the
king from a certain family. A tyranny is that form
in which the citizens are ruled either through fraud
or force by an individual. Thus civil government
is either democratic, aristocratic, oligarchic, or a
monarchy or a tyranny.

There are three species of justice. One is con-

φανερῶς διδόντες, vi. 56. 4.   This phrase is some help
towards an explanation, but whether it means open bribery
—possibly of the people, more probably of the Council—
or whether it refers to very large fees payable upon taking
office, it is not easy to determine. In either case wealth
would preponderate over merit.

αὐτῆς ἐστι περὶ θεούς, ἡ δὲ περὶ ἀνθρώπους, ἡ δὲ περὶ τοὺς ἀποιχομένους. οἱ μὲν γὰρ θύοντες κατὰ νόμους καὶ τῶν ἱερῶν ἐπιμελούμενοι δῆλον ὅτι περὶ θεοὺς εὐσεβοῦσιν· οἱ δὲ δάνεια ἀποδιδόντες καὶ παραθήκας δικαιοπραγοῦσι περὶ ἀνθρώπους· οἱ δὲ τῶν μνημείων ἐπιμελούμενοι δῆλον ὅτι περὶ τοὺς ἀποιχομένους. τῆς ἄρα δικαιοσύνης ἡ μὲν πρὸς θεούς ἐστιν, ἡ δὲ πρὸς ἀνθρώπους, ἡ δὲ περὶ τοὺς ἀποιχομένους.

84 Τῆς ἐπιστήμης εἴδη ἐστὶ τρία· τὸ μὲν γάρ ἐστι πρακτικόν, τὸ δὲ ποιητικόν, τὸ δὲ θεωρητικόν. ἡ μὲν οἰκοδομικὴ καὶ ναυπηγικὴ ποιητικαί εἰσιν· ἔστι γὰρ αὐτῶν ἰδεῖν ἔργον πεποιημένον. πολιτικὴ δὲ καὶ αὐλητικὴ καὶ κιθαριστικὴ καὶ αἱ τοιαῦται πρακτικαί· οὐ γάρ ἐστιν οὐδὲν ἰδεῖν †θετον αὐτῶν πεποιημένον, ἀλλὰ πράττουσί τι· ὁ μὲν γὰρ αὐλεῖ καὶ κιθαρίζει, ὁ δὲ πολιτεύεται. ἡ δὲ γεωμετρικὴ καὶ ἁρμονικὴ καὶ ἀστρολογικὴ θεωρητικαί· οὔτε γὰρ πράττουσιν οὔτε ποιοῦσιν οὐθέν· ἀλλ' ὁ μὲν γεωμέτρης θεωρεῖ πῶς πρὸς ἀλλήλας ἔχουσιν αἱ γραμμαί, ὁ δ' ἁρμονικὸς τοὺς φθόγγους, ὁ δ' ἀστρολογικὸς τὰ ἄστρα καὶ τὸν κόσμον. τῶν ἄρα ἐπιστημῶν αἱ μέν εἰσι θεωρητικαί, αἱ δὲ πρακτικαί, αἱ δὲ ποιητικαί.

85 Τῆς ἰατρικῆς ἐστιν εἴδη πέντε· ἡ μὲν φαρμακευτική, ἡ δὲ χειρουργική, ἡ δὲ διαιτητική, ἡ δὲ νοσογνωμονική, ἡ δὲ βοηθητική. ἡ μὲν φαρμακευτικὴ διὰ φαρμάκων ἰᾶται τὰς ἀρρωστίας, ἡ δὲ χειρουργικὴ διὰ τοῦ τέμνειν καὶ καίειν ὑγιάζει, ἡ δὲ διαιτητικὴ διὰ τοῦ διαιτᾶν ἀπαλλάττει τὰς ἀρρωστίας, ἡ δὲ νοσογνωμονικὴ διὰ τοῦ γνῶναι

cerned with gods, another with men, and the third with the departed. For those who sacrifice according to the laws and take care of the temples are obviously pious towards the gods. Those again who repay loans and restore what they have received upon trust act justly towards men. Lastly, those who take care of tombs are obviously just towards the departed. Thus one species of justice relates to the gods, another to men, while a third species is concerned with the departed.

There are three species of knowledge or science, one practical, another productive, and a third theoretical. For architecture and shipbuilding are productive arts, since the work produced by them can be seen. Politics and flute-playing, harp-playing and similar arts are practical. For nothing visible is produced by them; yet they do or perform something. In the one case the artist plays the flute or the harp, in the other the politician takes part in politics. Geometry and harmonics and astronomy are theoretical sciences. For they neither perform nor produce anything. But the geometer considers how lines are related to each other, the student of harmony investigates sounds, the astronomer stars and the universe. Thus some sciences are theoretical, others are practical, and others are productive.

There are five species of medicine: the first is pharmacy, the second is surgery, the third deals with diet and regimen, the fourth with diagnosis, the fifth with remedies. Pharmacy cures sickness by drugs, surgery heals by the use of knife and cautery, the species concerned with diet prescribes a regimen for the removal of disease, that concerned with diagnosis proceeds by determining the nature

τὸ ἀρρώστημα, ἡ δὲ βοηθητικὴ διὰ τοῦ βοηθῆσαι
εἰς τὸ παραχρῆμα ἀπαλλάττει τῆς ἀλγηδόνος.
τῆς ἄρα ἰατρικῆς ἡ μέν ἐστι φαρμακευτική, ἡ δὲ
χειρουργική, ἡ δὲ διαιτητική, ἡ δὲ βοηθητική, ἡ
δὲ νοσογνωμονική.

86 Νόμου διαιρέσεις δύο· ὁ μὲν γὰρ αὐτοῦ γεγραμμένος, ὁ δὲ ἄγραφος. ᾧ μὲν ἐν ταῖς πόλεσι πο-
λιτευόμεθα, γεγραμμένος ἐστίν. ὁ δὲ κατὰ ἔθη
γινόμενος οὗτος ἄγραφος καλεῖται· οἷον τὸ μὴ
γυμνὸν πορεύεσθαι εἰς τὴν ἀγορὰν μηδὲ γυναικεῖον
ἱμάτιον περιβάλλεσθαι. ταῦτα γὰρ οὐθεὶς νόμος
κωλύει, ἀλλ᾽ ὅμως οὐ πράττομεν διὰ τὸ ἀγράφῳ
νόμῳ κωλύεσθαι. τοῦ ἄρα νόμου ἐστὶν ὁ μὲν
γεγραμμένος, ὁ δὲ ἄγραφος.

Ὁ λόγος διαιρεῖται εἰς πέντε, ὧν εἷς μέν ἐστιν,
ὃν οἱ πολιτευόμενοι λέγουσιν ἐν ταῖς ἐκκλησίαις,
87 ὃς καλεῖται πολιτικός. ἑτέρα δὲ διαίρεσις λόγου,
ὃν οἱ ῥήτορες γράφουσιν †εἰς ἐπίδειξιν προφέρουσιν
εἰς ἐγκώμια καὶ ψόγους καὶ κατηγορίας· τὸ δὴ
τοιοῦτον εἶδός ἐστι ῥητορικόν. τρίτη δὲ διαίρεσις
λόγου, ὃν οἱ ἰδιῶται διαλέγονται πρὸς ἀλλήλους·
οὗτος δὴ ὁ τρόπος προσαγορεύεται ἰδιωτικός.
ἑτέρα δὲ διαίρεσις λόγου, ὃν οἱ κατὰ βραχὺ ἐρω-
τῶντες καὶ ἀποκρινόμενοι τοῖς ἐρωτῶσιν δια-
λέγονται· οὗτος δὲ καλεῖται ὁ λόγος διαλεκτικός.
πέμπτη δὲ διαίρεσις λόγου, ὃν οἱ τεχνῖται περὶ
τῆς ἑαυτῶν διαλέγονται τέχνης· ὃς δὴ καλεῖται
τεχνικός. τοῦ λόγου ἄρα τὸ μέν ἐστι πολιτικόν, τὸ
δὲ ῥητορικόν, τὸ δὲ ἰδιωτικόν, τὸ δὲ διαλεκτικόν, τὸ
δὲ τεχνικόν.

88 Ἡ μουσικὴ εἰς τρία διαιρεῖται· ἔστι γὰρ ἡ μὲν
διὰ τοῦ στόματος μόνον, οἷον ἡ ᾠδή· δεύτερον δὲ

of the ailment, that concerned with remedies by prescribing for the immediate removal of the pain. The species of medicine, then, are pharmacy, surgery, diet and regimen, diagnosis, prescription of remedies.

There are two divisions of law, the one written and the other unwritten. Written law is that under which we live in different cities, but that which has arisen out of custom is called unwritten law; for instance, not to appear in the market-place undressed or in women's attire. There is no statute forbidding this, but nevertheless we abstain from such conduct because it is prohibited by an unwritten law. Thus law is either written or unwritten.

There are five kinds of speech, of which one is that which politicians employ in the assemblies; this is called political speech. The second division is that which the rhetors employ in written compositions, whether composed for display or praise or blame, or for accusation. Hence this division is termed rhetorical. The third division of speech is that of private persons conversing with one another; this is called the mode of speech of ordinary life. Another division of speech is the language of those who converse by means of short questions and answers; this kind is called dialectical. The fifth division is the speech of craftsmen conversing about their own subjects; this is called technical language. Thus speech is either political, or rhetorical, or that of ordinary conversation, or dialectical, or technical.

Music has three divisions. One employs the mouth alone, like singing. The second employs both the

διὰ τοῦ στόματος καὶ τῶν χειρῶν, οἷον ἡ κιθαρῳδία·
τρίτον ἀπὸ τῶν χειρῶν μόνον, οἷον κιθαριστική.
τῆς ἄρα μουσικῆς ἐστι τὸ μὲν ἀπὸ τοῦ στόματος
μόνον, τὸ δ' ἀπὸ τοῦ στόματος καὶ τῶν χειρῶν,
τὸ δ' ἀπὸ τῶν χειρῶν.

Διαιρεῖται δὲ ἡ εὐγένεια εἰς εἴδη τέτταρα. ἓν
μέν, ἐὰν ὦσιν οἱ πρόγονοι καλοὶ κἀγαθοὶ καὶ δίκαιοι,
τοὺς ἐκ τούτων γεγεννημένους εὐγενεῖς φασιν
εἶναι. ἄλλο δέ, ἂν ὦσιν οἱ πρόγονοι δεδυναστευ-
κότες καὶ ἄρχοντες γεγενημένοι, τοὺς ἐκ τούτων
εὐγενεῖς φασιν εἶναι. ἄλλο δέ, ἂν ὦσιν οἱ πρόγονοι
ὀνομαστοί, οἷον ἀπὸ στρατηγίας, ἀπὸ στεφανιτῶν
ἀγώνων· καὶ γὰρ τοὺς ἐκ τούτων γεγεννημένους
89 εὐγενεῖς προσαγορεύομεν. ἄλλο εἶδος, ἐὰν αὐτός
τις ᾖ γεννάδας τὴν ψυχὴν καὶ μεγαλόψυχος· καὶ
τοῦτον εὐγενῆ φασι· καὶ τῆς γε εὐγενείας αὕτη
κρατίστη. τῆς ἄρα εὐγενείας τὸ μὲν ἀπὸ προ-
γόνων ἐπιεικῶν, τὸ δὲ δυναστῶν, τὸ δὲ ἐνδόξων,
τὸ δ' ἀπὸ τῆς αὑτοῦ καλοκαγαθίας.

Τὸ κάλλος διαιρεῖται εἰς τρία· ἓν μὲν γὰρ αὐτοῦ
ἐστιν ἐπαινετόν, οἷον ἡ διὰ τῆς ὄψεως εὐμορφία·
ἄλλο δὲ χρηστικόν, οἷον ὄργανον καὶ οἰκία καὶ
τὰ τοιαῦτα πρὸς χρῆσίν ἐστι καλά· τὸ δὲ πρὸς
νόμους καὶ ἐπιτηδεύματα καὶ τὰ τοιαῦτα, ⟨ἃ⟩
πρὸς ὠφέλειάν ἐστι καλά. τοῦ ἄρα κάλλους τὸ μέν
ἐστι πρὸς ἔπαινον, τὸ δὲ πρὸς χρῆσιν, τὸ δὲ
πρὸς ὠφέλειαν.

90 Ἡ ψυχὴ διαιρεῖται εἰς τρία· τὸ μὲν γὰρ αὐτῆς
ἐστι λογιστικόν, τὸ δὲ ἐπιθυμητικόν, τὸ δὲ θυμικόν.
τούτων δὲ τὸ μὲν λογιστικόν ἐστιν αἴτιον τοῦ
βουλεύεσθαί τε καὶ λογίζεσθαι καὶ διανοεῖσθαι καὶ
πάντων τῶν τοιούτων· τὸ δ' ἐπιθυμητικὸν μέρος

mouth and the hands, as is the case with the harper singing to his own accompaniment. The third division employs the hands alone; for instance, the music of the harp. Thus music employs either the mouth alone, or the mouth and the hands, or the hands alone.

Nobility has four divisions. First, when the ancestors are gentle and handsome and also just, their descendants are said to be noble. Secondly, when the ancestors have been princes or magistrates, their descendants are said to be noble. The third kind arises when the ancestors have been illustrious; for instance, through having held military command or through success in the national games. For then we call the descendants noble. The last division includes the man who is himself of a generous and high-minded spirit. He too is said to be noble. And this indeed is the highest form of nobility. Thus, of nobility, one kind depends on excellent ancestors, another on princely ancestors, a third on illustrious ancestors, while the fourth is due to the individual's own beauty and worth.

Beauty has three divisions. The first is the object of praise, as of form fair to see. Another is serviceable; thus an instrument, a house and the like are beautiful for use. Other things again which relate to customs and pursuits and the like are beautiful because beneficial. Of beauty, then, one kind is matter for praise, another is for use, and another for the benefit it procures.

The soul has three divisions. One part of it is rational, another appetitive, and a third irascible. Of these the rational part is the cause of purpose, reflection, understanding and the like. The appeti-

ἐστὶ τῆς ψυχῆς αἴτιον τοῦ ἐπιθυμεῖν φαγεῖν καὶ
τοῦ πλησιάσαι καὶ τῶν τοιούτων πάντων. τὸ δὲ
θυμικὸν μέρος αἴτιόν ἐστι τοῦ θαρρεῖν καὶ ἥδεσθαι
καὶ λυπεῖσθαι καὶ ὀργίζεσθαι. τῆς ἄρα ψυχῆς
ἐστι τὸ μὲν λογιστικόν, τὸ δὲ ἐπιθυμητικόν, τὸ δὲ
θυμικόν.

Τῆς τελείας ἀρετῆς εἴδη τέτταρα· ἓν μὲν φρόνησις, ἓν δὲ δικαιοσύνη, ἄλλο δ' ἀνδρεία, τέταρτον
91 σωφροσύνη. τούτων ἡ μὲν φρόνησις αἰτία τοῦ
πράττειν ὀρθῶς τὰ πράγματα· ἡ δὲ δικαιοσύνη τοῦ
ἐν ταῖς κοινωνίαις καὶ τοῖς συναλλάγμασι δικαιο-
πραγεῖν· ἡ δὲ ἀνδρεία τοῦ ἐν τοῖς κινδύνοις καὶ
φοβεροῖς μὴ ἐξίστασθαι ποιεῖν, ἀλλὰ μένειν· ἡ δὲ
σωφροσύνη τοῦ κρατεῖν τῶν ἐπιθυμιῶν καὶ ὑπὸ
μηδεμιᾶς ἡδονῆς δουλοῦσθαι, ἀλλὰ κοσμίως ζῆν.
τῆς ἀρετῆς ἄρα τὸ μέν ἐστι φρόνησις, ἄλλο δικαιοσύνη, τρίτον ἀνδρεία, τέταρτον σωφροσύνη.

Ἡ ἀρχὴ διαιρεῖται εἰς μέρη πέντε· ἓν μὲν εἰς τὸ
κατὰ νόμον, ἓν δὲ εἰς τὸ κατὰ φύσιν, ἓν δὲ εἰς τὸ
κατὰ ἔθος, τέταρτον εἰς τὸ κατὰ γένος, πέμπτον
92 δὲ κατὰ βίαν. οἱ μὲν οὖν ἐν ταῖς πόλεσιν ἄρχοντες
ὑπὸ τῶν πολιτῶν ἐπὰν αἱρεθῶσι, κατὰ νόμον
ἄρχουσιν· οἱ δὲ κατὰ φύσιν, οἱ ἄρρενες, οὐ μόνον
ἐν τοῖς ἀνθρώποις, ἀλλὰ καὶ ἐν τοῖς ἄλλοις ζῴοις·
ἐπὶ πολὺ γὰρ πανταχοῦ τὰ ἄρρενα τῶν θηλειῶν
ἄρχει. ἡ δὲ τοῦ κατὰ ἔθος ἀρχὴ τοιαύτη ἐστίν,
οἵαν οἱ παιδαγωγοὶ τῶν παίδων ἄρχουσι καὶ οἱ
διδάσκαλοι τῶν φοιτώντων. κατὰ γένος δὲ ἀρχὴ
τοιαύτη τις λέγεται, οἵαν οἱ Λακεδαιμόνιοι βασιλεῖς
ἄρχουσιν· ἀπὸ γὰρ γένους τινὸς ἡ βασιλεία. καὶ
ἐν Μακεδονίᾳ δὲ τὸν αὐτὸν τρόπον ἄρχουσι· καὶ
γὰρ ἐκεῖ ἀπὸ γένους ἡ βασιλεία καθίσταται. οἱ

tive part of the soul is the cause of desire of eating, sexual indulgence and the like, while the irascible part is the cause of courage, of pleasure and pain, and of anger. Thus one part of the soul is rational, another appetitive, and a third irascible.

Of perfect virtue there are four species : prudence, justice, bravery and temperance. Of these prudence is the cause of right conduct, justice of just dealing in partnerships and commercial transactions. Bravery is the cause which makes a man not give way but stand his ground in alarms and perils. Temperance causes mastery over desires, so that we are never enslaved by any pleasure, but lead an orderly life. Thus virtue includes first prudence, next justice, thirdly bravery, and lastly temperance.

Rule has five divisions, one that which is according to law, another according to nature, another according to custom, a fourth by birth, a fifth by force. Now the magistrates in cities when elected by their fellow-citizens rule according to law. The natural rulers are the males, not only among men, but also among the other animals ; for the males everywhere exert wide-reaching rule over the females. Rule according to custom is such authority as attendants exercise over children and teachers over their pupils. Hereditary rule is exemplified by that of the Lacedaemonian kings, for the office of king is confined to a certain family. And the same system is in force for the kingdom of Macedonia ; for there too the office of king goes by birth. Others have

δὲ βιασάμενοι ἢ παρακρουσάμενοι ἄρχουσιν ἀκόντων τῶν πολιτῶν· ἡ τοιαύτη ἀρχὴ κατὰ βίαν
λέγεται εἶναι. τῆς ἀρχῆς ἄρα ἐστὶ τὸ μὲν κατὰ
νόμον, τὸ δὲ κατὰ φύσιν, τὸ δὲ κατὰ ἔθος, τὸ δὲ
κατὰ γένος, τὸ δὲ κατὰ βίαν.

93 Τῆς ῥητορείας εἴδη ἐστὶν ἕξ. ὅταν μὲν γὰρ
κελεύωσι πολεμεῖν ἢ συμμαχεῖν πρός τινα, καλεῖται
τὸ τοιοῦτον εἶδος προτροπή. ὅταν δ' ἀξιῶσι μὴ
πολεμεῖν ⟨ἢ⟩ μὴ συμμαχεῖν, ἀλλ' ἡσυχίαν ἄγειν,
τὸ τοιοῦτον εἶδός ἐστιν ἀποτροπή. τρίτον εἶδος
τῆς ῥητορείας, ὅταν τις φάσκῃ ἀδικεῖσθαι ὑπό
τινος καὶ πολλῶν κακῶν αἴτιον ἀποφαίνῃ· τὸ δὴ
τοιοῦτον εἶδος κατηγορία ὀνομάζεται. τέταρτον
εἶδος τῆς ῥητορείας [ἀπολογία καλεῖται], ὅταν
ἀποφαίνῃ αὑτὸν μηθὲν ἀδικοῦντα μήτε ἄλλο ἄτοπον
μηθὲν πράττοντα· τὸ δὲ τοιοῦτον ἀπολογίαν καλοῦσι.

94 πέμπτον εἶδος ῥητορείας, ὅταν τις εὖ λέγῃ καὶ
ἀποφαίνῃ καλὸν κἀγαθόν· τὸ δὴ τοιοῦτον εἶδος
καλεῖται ἐγκώμιον. ἕκτον εἶδος, ὅταν τις ἀποφαίνῃ φαῦλον· τὸ δὲ τοιοῦτον εἶδος καλεῖται ψόγος.
τῆς ἄρα ῥητορείας ἐστὶ τὸ μὲν ἐγκώμιον, τὸ δὲ
ψόγος, τὸ δὲ προτροπή, τὸ δὲ ἀποτροπή, τὸ δὲ
κατηγορία, τὸ δὲ ἀπολογία.

Τὸ ὀρθῶς λέγειν διαιρεῖται εἰς τέτταρα· ἓν μὲν ἃ
δεῖ λέγειν, ἓν δὲ ὅσα δεῖ λέγειν, τρίτον πρὸς οὓς
δεῖ λέγειν, τέταρτον δὲ πηνίκα λέγειν δεῖ. ἃ μὲν
οὖν δεῖ λέγειν, ἃ μέλλει συμφέρειν τῷ λέγοντι καὶ
τῷ ἀκούοντι· τὸ δὲ ὅσα δεῖ λέγειν, μὴ πλείω μηδὲ
95 ἐλάττω τῶν ἱκανῶν. τὸ δὲ πρὸς οὓς δεῖ λέγειν,
ἄν τε πρὸς πρεσβυτέρους [ἁμαρτάνοντας] διαλέγῃ,

acquired power by force or fraud, and govern the citizens against their will; this kind of rule is called forcible. Thus rule is either by law, or by nature, or by custom, or by birth, or by force.

There are six kinds of rhetoric. For when the speakers urge war or alliance with a neighbouring state, that species of rhetoric is called persuasion. But when they speak against making war or alliance, and urge their hearers to remain at peace, this kind of rhetoric is called dissuasion. A third kind is employed when a speaker asserts that he is wronged by some one whom he makes out to have caused him much mischief; accusation is the name applied to the kind here defined. The fourth kind of rhetoric is termed defence; here the speaker shows that he has done no wrong and that his conduct is in no respect abnormal; defence is the term applied in such a case. A fifth kind of rhetoric is employed when a speaker speaks well of some one and proves him to be worthy and honourable; encomium is the name given to this kind. A sixth kind is that employed when the speaker shows some one to be unworthy; the name given to this is invective. Under rhetoric, then, are included encomium, invective, persuasion, dissuasion, accusation and defence.

Successful speaking has four divisions. The first consists in speaking to the purpose, the next to the requisite length, the third before the proper audience, and the fourth at the proper moment. The things to the purpose are those which are likely to be expedient for speaker and hearer. The requisite length is that which is neither more nor less than enough. To speak to the proper audience means this: in addressing persons older than yourself, the

ἁρμόττοντας δεῖ τοὺς λόγους διαλέγεσθαι ὡς
πρεσβυτέροις· ἄν τε πρὸς νεωτέρους, ἁρμόττοντας
δεῖ λέγεσθαι ὡς νεωτέροις. πηνίκα δὲ λέγειν ἐστί,
μήτε προτέρω μήτε ὑστέρω· εἰ δὲ μή, διαμαρτή-
σεσθαι καὶ οὐκ ὀρθῶς ἐρεῖν.

Ἡ εὐεργεσία διαιρεῖται εἰς τέτταρα· ἢ γὰρ
χρήμασιν ἢ σώμασιν ἢ ταῖς ἐπιστήμαις ἢ τοῖς
λόγοις. τοῖς μὲν οὖν χρήμασιν, ὅταν δεομένω
παραβοηθήσῃ τις εἰς χρημάτων λόγον εὐπορῆσαι·
τοῖς δὲ σώμασιν εὖ ποιοῦσιν ἀλλήλους, ὅταν παρα-
96 γενόμενοι τυπτομένοις παραβοηθῶσιν· οἱ δὲ παι-
δεύοντες καὶ ἰατρεύοντες καὶ διδάσκοντες ἀγαθόν
τι, οὗτοι δὲ ταῖς ἐπιστήμαις εὐεργετοῦσιν· ὅταν
δ' εἰσέλθωσιν εἰς δικαστήριον ἄλλος ὑπὲρ ἄλλου
βοηθὸς καὶ λόγον τινὰ ἐπιεικῆ ὑπὲρ αὐτοῦ εἴπῃ,
οὗτος δὴ λόγῳ εὐεργετεῖ. τῆς ἄρα εὐεργεσίας ἡ
μέν ἐστι διὰ χρημάτων, ἡ δὲ διὰ σωμάτων, ἡ δὲ
διὰ ἐπιστημῶν, τετάρτη διὰ λόγων.

Διαιρεῖται τὸ τέλος τῶν πραγμάτων εἰς τέτταρα
εἴδη· ἐν μὲν κατὰ νόμον τέλος τὰ πράγματα λαμβάνει, ὅταν ψήφισμα γένηται καὶ τοῦθ' ὁ νόμος
τελέσῃ· κατὰ φύσιν δὲ τέλος τὰ πράγματα λαμβάνει, ἥ τε ἡμέρα καὶ ὁ ἐνιαυτὸς καὶ αἱ ὧραι.
κατὰ τέχνην δὲ τέλος τὰ πράγματα λαμβάνει,
οἷον ἡ οἰκοδομική· οἰκίαν γάρ τις ἐπιτελεῖ· καὶ ἡ
97 ναυπηγική· πλοῖα γάρ. κατὰ τύχην δὲ γίνεται τοῖς
πράγμασι τέλος, ὅταν ἄλλως καὶ μὴ ὡς ὑπο-
λαμβάνει τις ἀποβαίνῃ. τοῦ τέλους ἄρα τῶν πραγμάτων τὸ μὲν κατὰ νόμον, τὸ δὲ κατὰ φύσιν, τὸ
δὲ κατὰ τέχνην, τὸ δὲ κατὰ τύχην ἐστίν.

Ἡ δύναμις διαιρεῖται εἰς τέτταρα εἴδη· ἐν μὲν
ὃ δυνάμεθα τῇ διανοίᾳ, λογίζεσθαι καὶ ὑπονοεῖν

discourse must be made suitable to the audience as being elderly men; whereas in addressing juniors the discourse must be suitable to young men. The proper time of speaking is neither too soon nor too late; otherwise you will miss the mark and not speak with success.

Of conferring benefits there are four divisions. For it takes place either by pecuniary aid or by personal service, by means of knowledge or of speech. Pecuniary aid is given when one assists a man in need, so that he is relieved from all anxiety on the score of money. Personal service is given when men come up to those who are being beaten and rescue them. Those who train or heal, or who teach something valuable, confer benefit by means of knowledge. But when men enter a law-court and one appears as advocate for another and delivers an effective speech on his behalf, he is benefiting him by speech. Thus benefits are conferred by means either of money or of personal service, or of knowledge, or of speech.

There are four ways in which things are completed and brought to an end. The first is by legal enactment, when a decree is passed and this decree is confirmed by law. The second is in the course of nature, as the day, the year and the seasons are completed. The third is by the rules of art, say the builder's art, for so a house is completed; and so it is with shipbuilding, whereby vessels are completed. Fourthly, matters are brought to an end by chance or accident, when they turn out otherwise than is expected. Thus the completion of things is due either to law, or to nature, or to art, or to chance.

Of power or ability there are four divisions. First, whatever we can do with the mind, namely calculate

ἕτερον δὲ τῷ σώματι, οἷον πορεύεσθαι καὶ διδόναι
καὶ λαμβάνειν καὶ τὰ τοιαῦτα· τρίτον ὃ δυνάμεθα
πλήθει στρατιωτῶν καὶ χρημάτων, ὅθεν καλεῖται
πολλὴν δύναμιν ἔχων βασιλεύς· τετάρτη δὲ διαίρεσις
δυνάμεως πάσχειν καὶ εὖ ποιεῖν καὶ κακῶς· οἷον
ἀρρωστεῖν καὶ παιδεύεσθαι δυνάμεθα καὶ ὑγιεῖς
γίνεσθαι καὶ πάντα τὰ τοιαῦτα. τῆς ἄρα δυνάμεως
ἡ μέν ἐστιν ἐν διανοίᾳ, ἡ δ' ἐν τῷ σώματι, ἡ δ'
ἐν στρατοπέδῳ καὶ χρήμασιν, ἡ δ' ἐν τῷ ποιεῖν
καὶ πάσχειν.

98 Τῆς φιλανθρωπίας ἐστὶν εἴδη τρία· ἓν μὲν διὰ
τῆς προσηγορίας γινόμενον, οἷον ἐν οἷς τινες τὸν
ἐντυχόντα πάντα προσαγορεύουσι καὶ τὴν δεξιὰν
ἐμβάλλοντες χαιρετίζουσιν. ἄλλο εἶδος, ὅταν τις
βοηθητικὸς ᾖ παντὶ τῷ ἀτυχοῦντι. ἕτερον εἶδός
ἐστι τῆς φιλανθρωπίας, ἐν ᾧ τινες φιλοδειπνισταί
εἰσι. τῆς ἄρα φιλανθρωπίας τὸ μέν ἐστι διὰ τοῦ
προσαγορεύειν, τὸ δὲ διὰ τοῦ εὐεργετεῖν, τὸ δὲ διὰ
τοῦ ἑστιᾶν καὶ φιλοσυνουσιάζειν.

Ἡ εὐδαιμονία διαιρεῖται εἰς πέντε μέρη· ἡ μὲν
γὰρ αὐτῆς ἐστιν εὐβουλία, ἕτερον δὲ εὐαισθησία
καὶ ὑγίεια τοῦ σώματος, τρίτον εὐτυχία ἐν ταῖς
πράξεσι, τέταρτον εὐδοξία παρὰ τοῖς ἀνθρώποις,
πέμπτον εὐπορία χρημάτων καὶ τῶν εἰς τὸν βίον
99 χρησίμων. ἡ μὲν εὐβουλία γίνεται ἐκ παιδείας
καὶ ἐκ τοῦ πολλῶν ἔμπειρον γενέσθαι· ἡ δὲ εὐαισθησία ἐκ τῶν τοῦ σώματος μερῶν, οἷον ἐάν τις
ὀφθαλμοῖς ὁρᾷ καὶ τοῖς ὠσὶν ἀκούῃ καὶ τῇ ῥινὶ καὶ
τῷ στόματι αἰσθάνηται ὧν δεῖ αἰσθάνεσθαι· τὸ δὴ
τοιοῦτον εὐαισθησία. ἡ δὲ εὐτυχία, ὅταν ἐφ' ἃ
σκοπεῖ πράξῃ κατ' ὀρθὸν ἃ δεῖ πράττειν τὸν σπου-

or anticipate ; next, whatever we can effect with the body, for instance, marching, giving, taking and the like. Thirdly, whatever we can do by a multitude of soldiers or a plentiful supply of money ; hence a king is said to have great power. The fourth division of power or influence is doing, or being done by, well or ill ; thus we can become ill or be educated, be restored to health and the like. Power, then, is either in the mind, or the body, or in armies and resources, or in acting and being acted upon.

Philanthropy is of three kinds. One is by way of salutations, as when certain people address every one they meet and, stretching out their hand, give him a hearty greeting ; another mode is seen when one is given to assisting every one in distress ; another mode of philanthropy is that which makes certain people fond of giving dinners. Thus philanthropy is shown either by a courteous address, or by conferring benefits, or by hospitality and the promotion of social intercourse.

Welfare or happiness includes five parts. One part of it is good counsel, a second soundness of the senses and bodily health, a third success in one's undertakings, a fourth a reputation with one's fellow-men, a fifth ample means in money and in whatever else subserves the end of life. Now deliberating well is a result of education and of having experience of many things. Soundness of the senses depends upon the bodily organs : I mean, if one sees with his eyes, hears with his ears, and perceives with his nostrils and his mouth the appropriate objects, then such a condition is soundness of the senses. Success is attained when a man does what he aims at in the right way, as becomes a good man.

δαῖον. εὐδοξία δ' ἐστὶν ὅταν τις εὖ ἀκούῃ· εὐπορία
δ' ἐστὶν ὅταν τις πρὸς τὰς ἐν τῷ βίῳ χρήσεις
οὕτως ἔχῃ ὥστε καὶ φίλους εὖ ποιῆσαι καὶ φιλο-
τίμως καὶ εὐπόρως ἀπολειτουργῆσαι. ᾧ δὲ ὑπ-
άρχει ταῦτα πάντα, οὗτός ἐστιν εὐδαίμων τελέως.
τῆς ἄρα εὐδαιμονίας ἐστὶ τὸ μὲν εὐβουλία, τὸ δὲ
εὐαισθησία καὶ ὑγίεια τοῦ σώματος, τὸ δὲ εὐτυχία,
τὸ δὲ εὐδοξία, τὸ δὲ εὐπορία.

100 Αἱ τέχναι εἰς τρία διαιροῦνται· ἡ μὲν πρώτη, ἡ
δὲ δευτέρα, ἡ δὲ τρίτη. πρώτη μὲν οὖν ἡ μεταλ-
λευτικὴ καὶ ὑλοτομική· παρασκευαστικαὶ γάρ εἰσιν.
ἡ δὲ χαλκευτικὴ καὶ ἡ τεκτονικὴ μετασχημα-
τιστικαί εἰσιν· ἐκ μὲν γὰρ τοῦ σιδήρου ἡ χαλκευτικὴ
ὅπλα ποιεῖ, ἡ δὲ τεκτονικὴ ἐκ τῶν ξύλων αὐλοὺς
καὶ λύρας. ἡ δὲ χρηστική, οἷον ἱππικὴ τοῖς
χαλινοῖς χρῆται, ἡ πολεμικὴ τοῖς ὅπλοις, ἡ μουσικὴ
τοῖς αὐλοῖς καὶ τῇ λύρᾳ. τῆς τέχνης ἄρα τρία
εἴδη ἐστί· τὸ μέν τι πρῶτον, τὸ δέ τι δεύτερον,
τὸ δέ τι τρίτον.

101 Τὸ ἀγαθὸν εἰς τέτταρα γένη διαιρεῖται· ὧν ἓν
μὲν λέγομεν εἶναι τὸν τὴν ἀρετὴν ἔχοντα ἰδίᾳ
ἀγαθόν· ἄλλο δὲ αὐτὴν τὴν ἀρετὴν καὶ τὴν δικαιοσύνην λέγομεν ἀγαθὸν εἶναι· τρίτον δέ, οἷον σιτία
καὶ γυμνάσια τὰ πρόσφορα καὶ φάρμακα· τέταρτον
δέ φαμεν εἶναι ἀγαθόν, οἷον αὐλητικὴν καὶ ὑποκριτικὴν καὶ τὰ τοιαῦτα. ἀγαθοῦ ἄρα τέτταρα
εἴδη ἐστί· τὸ μὲν τὸ τὴν ἀρετὴν ἔχειν, ἕτερον δὲ
αὐτὴ ἡ ἀρετή, τρίτον δὲ σιτία καὶ γυμνάσια τὰ
ὠφέλιμα· τέταρτον δὲ αὐλητικὴν καὶ ὑποκριτικὴν
102 καὶ ποιητικὴν ἀγαθὸν λέγομεν εἶναι. τῶν ὄντων
τὰ μέν ἐστι κακά, τὰ δὲ ἀγαθά, τὰ δὲ οὐδέτερα.
τούτων κακὰ μὲν ταῦτα λέγομεν, τὰ δυνάμενα

A man has a good reputation when he is well spoken
of. A man has ample means when he is so equipped
for the needs of life that he can afford to benefit his
friends and discharge his public services with lavish
display. If a man has all these things, he is completely happy. Thus of welfare or happiness one
part is good counsel, another soundness of senses
and bodily health, a third success, a fourth a good
reputation, a fifth ample means.

There are three divisions of the arts and crafts.
The first division consists of mining and forestry,
which are productive arts. The second includes
the smith's and carpenter's arts which transform
material; for the smith makes weapons out of iron,
and the carpenter transforms timber into flutes and
lyres. The third division is that which uses what is
thus made, as horsemanship employs bridles, the art
of war employs weapons, and music flutes and the
lyre. Thus of art there are three several species,
those above-mentioned in the first, second and third
place.

Good is divided into four kinds. One is the possessor of virtue, whom we affirm to be individually
good. Another is virtue itself and justice; these
we affirm to be good. A third includes such things
as food, suitable exercises and drugs. The fourth
kind which we affirm to be good includes the arts of
flute-playing, acting and the like. Thus there are
four kinds of good: the possession of virtue; virtue
itself; thirdly, food and beneficial exercises; lastly,
flute-playing, acting, and the poetic art. Whatever
is is either evil or good or indifferent. We call that
evil which is capable of invariably doing harm; for

βλάπτειν ἀεί, οἷον ἀκρισίαν καὶ ἀφροσύνην καὶ
ἀδικίαν καὶ τὰ τοιαῦτα· τὰ δὲ τούτοις ἐναντία
ἀγαθά ἐστι. τὰ δὲ ἐνίοτε μὲν ὠφελεῖν, ἐνίοτε δὲ
βλάπτειν—οἷον τὸ περιπατεῖν καὶ τὸ καθῆσθαι
καὶ ἐσθίειν—‹ἢ› ὅλως μήτε ὠφελῆσαι μήτε βλάψαι
δυνάμενα, ταῦτα γοῦν οὔτε ἀγαθὰ οὔτε κακά ἐστι.
τῶν ἄρα ὄντων τὰ μὲν ἀγαθά, τὰ δὲ κακά, τὰ δ'
οὐδέτερα τούτων.

103 Εὐνομία διαιρεῖται εἰς τρία· ἓν μέν, ἐὰν ὦσιν οἱ
νόμοι σπουδαῖοι, εὐνομίαν φαμὲν εἶναι· ἕτερον δέ,
ἐὰν τοῖς κειμένοις νόμοις ἐμμένωσιν οἱ πολῖται,
καὶ τοῦτό φαμεν εὐνομίαν εἶναι· τρίτον δέ, ἐὰν
μὴ ὄντων τῶν νόμων κατὰ ἔθη καὶ ἐπιτηδεύματα
χρηστῶς πολιτεύωνται, καὶ τοῦτο εὐνομίαν προσ-
αγορεύομεν· τῆς εὐνομίας ἄρα ἓν μέν ἐστι νόμους
σπουδαίους εἶναι· ἄλλο δέ, ἐὰν τοῖς οὖσι νόμοις
ἐμμένωσι· τρίτον δέ, ἐὰν ἔθεσι καὶ ἐπιτηδεύμασι
χρηστοῖς πολιτεύωνται.

Διαιρεῖται ἡ ἀνομία εἰς τρία· ὧν ἓν μέν ἐστιν,
ἐὰν ὦσιν οἱ νόμοι μοχθηροὶ καὶ πρὸς ξένους καὶ
104 πρὸς πολίτας· ἕτερον δέ, ἐὰν τοῖς ὑπάρχουσι μὴ
πείθωνται· ἄλλο δέ, ἐὰν ὅλως μηδεὶς ᾖ νόμος.
τῆς ἄρα ἀνομίας ἓν μέν ἐστι τὸ μοχθηροὺς εἶναι
τοὺς νόμους· ἄλλο δέ, ἐὰν τοῖς οὖσι μὴ πείθωνται·
τρίτον δέ, ἐὰν μηδεὶς ᾖ νόμος.

Τὰ ἐναντία διαιρεῖται εἰς τρία· οἷον ἀγαθὰ κακοῖς
ἐναντία φαμὲν εἶναι, ὡς τὴν δικαιοσύνην τῇ ἀδικίᾳ
καὶ τὴν φρόνησιν τῇ ἀφροσύνῃ καὶ τὰ τοιαῦτα.
κακὰ δὲ κακοῖς ἐναντία ἐστίν, οἷον ἡ ἀσωτία τῇ
ἀνελευθερίᾳ καὶ τὸ ἀδίκως στρεβλοῦσθαι τῷ
δικαίως στρεβλοῦσθαι· καὶ τὰ τοιαῦτα κακὰ κακοῖς
ἐναντία ἐστί. τὸ δὲ βαρὺ τῷ κούφῳ καὶ τὸ ταχὺ

instance, bad judgement and folly and injustice and the like. The contraries of these things are good. But the things which can sometimes benefit and sometimes harm, such as walking and sitting and eating, or which can neither do any benefit nor harm at all, these are things indifferent, neither good nor evil. Thus all things whatever are either good, or evil, or neither good nor evil.

Good order in the state falls under three heads. First, if the laws are good, we say that there is good government. Secondly, if the citizens obey the established laws, we also call this good government. Thirdly, if, without the aid of laws, the people manage their affairs well under the guidance of customs and institutions, we call this again good government. Thus three forms of good government may exist, (1) when the laws are good, (2) when the existing laws are obeyed, (3) when the people live under salutary customs and institutions.

Disorder in a state has three forms. The first arises when the laws affecting citizens and strangers are alike bad, the second when the existing laws are not obeyed, and the third when there is no law at all. Thus the state is badly governed when the laws are bad or not obeyed, or lastly, when there is no law.

Contraries are divided into three species. For instance, we say that goods are contrary to evils, as justice to injustice, wisdom to folly, and the like. Again, evils are contrary to evils, prodigality is contrary to niggardliness, and to be unjustly tortured is the contrary of being justly tortured, and so with similar evils. Again, heavy is the contrary of light,

τῷ βραδεῖ καὶ τὸ μέλαν τῷ λευκῷ ὡς οὐδέτερα
105 οὐδετέροις ἐναντία ἐστίν. τῶν ἐναντίων ἄρα τὰ
μὲν ὡς ἀγαθὰ κακοῖς ἐναντία ἐστί· τὰ δὲ ὡς κακὰ
κακοῖς· τὰ δὲ ὡς οὐδετέροις οὐδέτερα.

Τῶν ἀγαθῶν γένη ἐστὶ τρία· τὰ μὲν γάρ ἐστιν
ἑκτά, τὰ δὲ μεθεκτά, τὰ δὲ ὑπαρκτά. τὰ μὲν
οὖν ἑκτά ἐστιν, ὅσα ἐνδέχεται ἔχειν, οἷον ἡ δικαιοσύνη καὶ ἡ ὑγίεια· μεθεκτὰ δέ, ὅσα ἔχειν μὲν
μὴ ἐνδέχεται, μετασχεῖν δὲ αὐτῶν ἐνδέχεται·
οἷον αὐτὸ τὸ ἀγαθὸν ἔχειν μὲν οὐκ ἐνδέχεται,
μετασχεῖν δὲ αὐτοῦ ἐνδέχεται. ὑπαρκτὰ δέ, ὅσα
μήτε μετασχεῖν μήτε σχεῖν ἐνδέχεται, ὑπάρχειν
δὲ δεῖ· οἷον τὸ σπουδαῖον εἶναι <καὶ> τὸ δίκαιον
εἶναι ἀγαθόν ἐστι· καὶ ταῦτα οὔτε σχεῖν οὔτε
μετασχεῖν ἐστιν, ἀλλ’ ὑπάρχειν δεῖ [σπουδαῖον
εἶναι καὶ δίκαιον εἶναι]. τῶν ἀγαθῶν ἄρα τὰ μέν
ἐστιν ἑκτά, τὰ δὲ μεθεκτά, τὰ δὲ ὑπαρκτά.

106 Ἡ συμβουλία διαιρεῖται εἰς τρία· ἔστι γὰρ
αὐτῆς ἓν μὲν ἐκ τῶν παροιχομένων χρόνων λαμ-
βανόμενον, ἓν δὲ ἐκ τῶν μελλόντων, ἓν δὲ ἐκ τῶν
ἐνεστώτων. τὰ μὲν οὖν ἐκ τῶν παροιχομένων
παραδείγματα, οἷον τί ἔπαθον Λακεδαιμόνιοι πι-
στεύσαντες· τὰ δ’ ἐκ τῶν παρόντων, οἷον ἀποφαίνειν
τείχη ἀσθενῆ, δειλοὺς ἀνθρώπους, σῖτον ὀλίγον·
τὰ δ’ ἐκ τῶν μελλόντων, οἷον ταῖς ὑπονοίαις μὴ
ἀδικεῖν τὰς πρεσβείας, ὅπως μὴ ἄδοξος ἡ Ἑλλὰς
γένηται. τῆς ἄρα συμβουλίας τὰ μέν ἐστιν ἐκ
τῶν παροιχομένων, τὰ δ’ ἐκ τῶν παρόντων, τὰ
δ’ ἐκ τῶν μελλόντων.

quick of slow, black of white, and these pairs are contraries, while they are neither good nor evil. Thus, of contraries, some are opposed as goods to evils, others as evils to evils, and others, as things which are neither good nor evil, are opposed to one another.

There are three kinds of goods, those which can be exclusively possessed, those which can be shared with others, and those which simply exist. To the first division, namely, those which can be exclusively possessed, belong such things as justice and health. To the next belong all those which, though they cannot be exclusively possessed, can be shared with others. Thus we cannot possess the absolute good, but we can participate in it. The third division includes those goods the existence of which is necessary, though we can neither possess them exclusively nor participate in them. The mere existence of worth and justice is a good; and these things cannot be shared or had in exclusive possession, but must simply exist. Of goods, then, some are possessed exclusively, some shared, and others merely subsist.

Counsel is divided under three heads. One is taken from past time, one from the future, and the third from the present. That from past time consists of examples; for instance, what the Lacedaemonians suffered through trusting others. Counsel drawn from the present is to show, for instance, that the walls are weak, the men cowards, and the supplies running short. Counsel from the future is, for instance, to urge that we should not wrong the embassies by suspicions, lest the fair fame of Hellas be stained. Thus counsel is derived from the past, the present and the future.

107 Ἡ φωνὴ διαιρεῖται εἰς δύο· ἓν μὲν αὐτῆς ἐστιν
ἔμψυχον, ἓν δὲ ἄψυχον. ἔμψυχον μὲν ἡ τῶν ζῴων
φωνή, ἄψυχον δὲ φθόγγοι καὶ ἦχοι. τῆς τοῦ
ἐμψύχου φωνῆς ἡ μέν ἐστιν ἐγγράμματος, ἡ δὲ
ἀγράμματος. ἐγγράμματος μὲν ἡ τῶν ἀνθρώπων,
ἀγράμματος δὲ ἡ τῶν ζῴων. τῆς ἄρα φωνῆς ἡ
μὲν ἔμψυχος, ἡ δὲ ἄψυχος.

Τῶν ὄντων ἐστὶ τὰ μὲν μεριστά, τὰ δὲ ἀμέριστα.
τούτων δὲ τῶν μεριστῶν τὰ μὲν ὁμοιομερῆ, τὰ
δὲ ἀνομοιομερῆ. ἀμερῆ μὲν οὖν ἐστιν ὅσα μὴ ἔχει
διαίρεσιν μηδὲ ἔκ τινος σύγκειται, οἷον ἥ τε μονὰς
καὶ ἡ στιγμὴ καὶ ὁ φθόγγος· μεριστὰ δὲ ὅσα ἔκ
τινος σύγκειται, οἷον αἵ τε συλλαβαὶ καὶ συμ-
108 φωνίαι καὶ ζῷα καὶ ὕδωρ καὶ χρυσός. ὁμοιομερῆ
ὅσα ἐξ ὁμοίων σύγκειται καὶ μηδὲν διαφέρει τὸ
ὅλον τοῦ μέρους εἰ μὴ τῷ πλήθει, οἷον τὸ ὕδωρ
καὶ τὸ χρυσίον καὶ πᾶν τὸ χυτὸν καὶ τὸ τοιοῦτον.
ἀνομοιομερῆ δὲ ὅσα ἐξ ἀνομοίων μερῶν σύγκειται,
οἷον οἰκία καὶ τὰ τοιαῦτα. τῶν ὄντων ἄρα τὰ μέν
ἐστι μεριστά, τὰ δὲ ἀμερῆ· τῶν δὲ μεριστῶν τὰ
μὲν ὁμοιομερῆ, τὰ δὲ ἀνομοιομερῆ.

Τῶν ὄντων τὰ μέν ἐστι καθ᾽ ἑαυτά, τὰ δὲ πρός
τι λέγεται. τὰ μὲν οὖν καθ᾽ ἑαυτὰ λεγόμενά ἐστιν
ὅσα ἐν τῇ ἑρμηνείᾳ μηδενὸς προσδεῖται· ταῦτα δ᾽
ἂν εἴη οἷον ἄνθρωπος, ἵππος καὶ τἆλλα ζῷα.
109 τούτων γὰρ οὐδὲν δι᾽ ἑρμηνείας χωρεῖ. τῶν δὲ
πρός τι λεγομένων ὅσα προσδεῖταί τινος ἑρμηνείας,
οἷον τὸ μεῖζόν τινος καὶ τὸ θᾶττόν τινος καὶ τὸ
κάλλιον καὶ τὰ τοιαῦτα· τό τε γὰρ μεῖζον ἐλάτ-
τονός ἐστι μεῖζον καὶ τὸ θᾶττόν τινός ἐστι <θᾶττον>.

Vocal sound falls into two divisions according as it is animate or inanimate. The voice of living things is animate sound; notes of instruments and noises are inanimate. And of the animate voice part is articulate, part inarticulate, that of men being articulate speech, that of the animals inarticulate. Thus vocal sound is either animate or inanimate.

Whatever exists is either divisible or indivisible. Of divisible things some are divisible into similar and others into dissimilar parts. Those things are indivisible which cannot be divided and are not compounded of elements, for example, the unit, the point and the musical note; whereas those which have constituent parts, for instance, syllables, concords in music, animals, water, gold, are divisible. If they are composed of similar parts, so that the whole does not differ from the part except in bulk, as water, gold and all that is fusible, and the like, then they are termed homogeneous. But whatever is composed of dissimilar parts, as a house and the like, is termed heterogeneous. Thus all things whatever are either divisible or indivisible, and of those which are divisible some are homogeneous, others heterogeneous in their parts.

Of existing things some are absolute and some are called relative. Things said to exist absolutely are those which need nothing else to explain them, as man, horse, and all other animals. For none of these gains by explanation. To those which are called relative belong all which stand in need of some explanation, as that which is greater than something or quicker than something, or more beautiful and the like. For the greater implies a less, and the quicker is quicker than something. Thus existing

τῶν ὄντων ἄρα τὰ μὲν αὐτὰ καθ' αὑτὰ λέγεται,
τὰ δὲ πρός τι. ὧδε καὶ τὰ πρῶτα διῄρει κατὰ τὸν
'Αριστοτέλην.

Γέγονε δὲ καὶ ἄλλος Πλάτων φιλόσοφος 'Ρόδιος,
μαθητὴς Παναιτίου, καθά φησι Σέλευκος ὁ
γραμματικὸς ἐν πρώτῳ Περὶ φιλοσοφίας· καὶ
ἄλλος, περιπατητικός, μαθητὴς 'Αριστοτέλους·
καὶ ἕτερος Πραξιφάνους· καὶ ὁ τῆς ἀρχαίας
κωμῳδίας ποιητής.

things are either absolute or relative. And in this way, according to Aristotle, Plato used to divide the primary conceptions also.

There was also another man named Plato, a philosopher of Rhodes, a pupil of Panaetius, as is stated by Seleucus the grammarian in his first book *On Philosophy*; another a Peripatetic and pupil of Aristotle; and another who was a pupil of Praxiphanes; and lastly, there was Plato, the poet of the Old Comedy.

Δ

Κεφ. α'. ΣΠΕΥΣΙΠΠΟΣ

1 Τὰ μὲν περὶ Πλάτωνος τοσαῦτα ἦν ἐς τὸ δυνατὸν ἡμῖν συναγαγεῖν, φιλοπόνως διειλήσασι τὰ λεγόμενα περὶ τἀνδρός. διεδέξατο δ' αὐτὸν Σπεύσιππος Εὐρυμέδοντος Ἀθηναῖος, τῶν μὲν δήμων Μυρρινούσιος, υἱὸς δὲ τῆς ἀδελφῆς αὐτοῦ Πωτώνης. καὶ ἐσχολάρχησεν ἔτη ὀκτώ, ἀρξάμενος ἀπὸ τῆς ὀγδόης καὶ ἑκατοστῆς Ὀλυμπιάδος· Χαρίτων τ' ἀγάλματ' ἀνέθηκεν ἐν τῷ μουσείῳ τῷ ὑπὸ Πλάτωνος ἐν Ἀκαδημείᾳ ἱδρυθέντι. καὶ ἔμεινε μὲν ἐπὶ τῶν αὐτῶν Πλάτωνι δογμάτων· οὐ μὴν τό γ' ἦθος διέμεινε τοιοῦτος. καὶ γὰρ ὀργίλος καὶ ἡδονῶν ἥττων ἦν. φασὶ γοῦν αὐτὸν ὑπὸ θυμοῦ τὸ κυνίδιον εἰς τὸ φρέαρ ῥῖψαι καὶ ὑφ' ἡδονῆς ἐλθεῖν εἰς Μακεδονίαν ἐπὶ τὸν Κασάνδρου γάμον.

2 Ἐλέγοντο δὲ αὐτοῦ καὶ αἱ Πλάτωνος ἀκούειν μαθήτριαι, Λασθένειά τε ἡ Μαντινικὴ καὶ Ἀξιοθέα ἡ Φλιασία. ὅτε καὶ Διονύσιος πρὸς αὐτὸν γράφων τωθαστικῶς φησι· " καὶ ἐκ τῆς Ἀρκαδικῆς σου μαθητρίας ἔστι καταμαθεῖν τὴν σοφίαν. καὶ Πλάτων μὲν ἀτελεῖς φόρων τοὺς παρ' αὐτὸν φοιτῶντας

ᵃ 348–344 B.C.

BOOK IV

Chapter 1. SPEUSIPPUS (*circa* 407–339 B.C.)
(Head of the Academy, 347–339 B.C.)

THE foregoing is the best account of Plato that we were able to compile after a diligent examination of the authorities. He was succeeded by Speusippus, an Athenian and son of Eurymedon, who belonged to the deme of Myrrhinus, and was the son of Plato's sister Potone. He was head of the school for eight years beginning in the 108th Olympiad.[a] He set up statues of the Graces in the shrine of the Muses erected by Plato in the Academy. He adhered faithfully to Plato's doctrines. In character, however, he was unlike him, being prone to anger and easily overcome by pleasures. At any rate there is a story that in a fit of passion he flung his favourite dog into the well, and that pleasure was the sole motive for his journey to Macedonia to be present at the wedding-feast of Casander.

It was said that among those who attended his lectures were the two women who had been pupils of Plato, Lasthenia of Mantinea and Axiothea of Phlius. And at the time Dionysius in a letter says derisively, " We may judge of your wisdom by the Arcadian girl who is your pupil. And, whereas Plato exempted from fees all who came to him, you

ἐποίει· σὺ δὲ δασμολογεῖς καὶ παρ' ἑκόντων καὶ ἀκόντων λαμβάνεις." οὗτος πρῶτος, καθά φησι Διόδωρος ἐν 'Απομνημονευμάτων πρώτῳ, ἐν τοῖς μαθήμασιν ἐθεάσατο τὸ κοινὸν καὶ συνῳκείωσε καθόσον ἦν δυνατὸν ἀλλήλοις· καὶ πρῶτος παρὰ 'Ισοκράτους τὰ καλούμενα ἀπόρρητα ἐξήνεγκεν, ὥς φησι Καινεύς. καὶ πρῶτος εὗρεν ᾧ τὰ φορμία τῶν φρυγάνων εὔογκα ποιοῦσιν.

"Ἤδη δὲ ὑπὸ παραλύσεως καὶ τὸ σῶμα διέφθαρτο, καὶ πρὸς Ξενοκράτην διεπέμπετο παρακαλῶν αὐτὸν ἐλθεῖν καὶ τὴν σχολὴν διαδέξασθαι. φασὶ δὲ αὐτὸν ἐπ' ἀμαξίου φερόμενον εἰς τὴν 'Ακαδημείαν συναντῆσαι Διογένει καὶ Χαῖρε εἰπεῖν· τὸν δὲ φάναι, "ἀλλὰ μὴ σύ γε, ὅστις ὑπομένεις ζῆν τοιοῦτος ὤν." καὶ τέλος ὑπὸ ἀθυμίας ἑκὼν τὸν βίον μετήλλαξε γηραιὸς ὤν. καὶ ἔστιν ἡμῶν εἰς αὐτόν·

ἀλλ' εἰ μὴ Σπεύσιππον ἐμάνθανον ὧδε θανεῖσθαι,
οὐκ ἄν ἔπεισέ μέ τις τόδε λέξαι·
ὡς ἦν οὐχὶ Πλάτωνι πρὸς αἵματος· οὐ γὰρ ἀθυμῶν
κάτθανεν ἄν διά τι σφόδρα μικρόν.

Πλούταρχος δέ φησιν ἐν τῷ Λυσάνδρου βίῳ καὶ Σύλλα φθειρσὶν ἐκζέσαι αὐτόν. ἦν δὲ καὶ τὸ σῶμα διακεχυμένος, ὥς φησι Τιμόθεος ἐν τῷ Περὶ βίων. οὗτος, φησί, πρὸς τὸν ἐρῶντα πλούσιον ἀμόρφου ἔφη, "τί δέ σοι δεῖ τούτου; ἐγὼ γάρ σοι δέκα ταλάντων εὐμορφοτέραν[1] εὑρήσω."

---

[1] εὐμορφοτέραν] fort. ἀμορφοτέρον H. Richards.

---

[a] Romance seems to have been busy with the life of Speusippus. Athenaeus, vii. 279 E, quotes from the same forged letter of Dionysius to Speusippus bringing similar charges.

levy tribute on them and collect it whether they will or no." [a] According to Diodorus in the first book of his *Memorabilia*, Speusippus was the first to discern the common element in all studies and to bring them into connexion with each other so far as that was possible. And according to Caeneus he was the first to divulge what Isocrates called the secrets of his art, and the first to devise the means by which fagots of firewood are rendered portable.

When he was already crippled by paralysis, he sent a message to Xenocrates entreating him to come and take over the charge of the school.[b] They say that, as he was being conveyed to the Academy in a tiny carriage, he met and saluted Diogenes, who replied, " Nay, if you can endure to live in such a plight as this, I decline to return your greeting." At last in old age he became so despondent that he put an end to his life. Here follows my epigram upon him [c] :

Had I not learnt that Speusippus would die thus, no one would have persuaded me to say that he was surely not of Plato's blood : for else he would never have died in despair for a trivial cause.

Plutarch in the Lives of Lysander and Sulla makes his malady to have been " morbus pedicularis." [d] That his body wasted away is affirmed by Timotheus in his book *On Lives*. Speusippus, he says, meeting a rich man who was in love with one who was no beauty, said to him, " Why, pray, are you in such sore need of him ? For ten talents I will find you a more handsome bride."

---

[b] The most trustworthy account of what happened when Xenocrates was elected is furnished by *Index Academicus*, pp. 38 *sq.* ed. Mekler.

[c] *Anth. Pal.* viii. 101. [d] *Cf. supra*, iii. 40.

Καταλέλοιπε δὲ πάμπλειστα ὑπομνήματα καὶ διαλόγους πλείονας, ἐν οἷς καὶ

Ἀρίστιππον τὸν Κυρηναῖον.
Περὶ πλούτου αʹ.
Περὶ ἡδονῆς αʹ.
Περὶ δικαιοσύνης αʹ.
Περὶ φιλοσοφίας αʹ.
Περὶ φιλίας αʹ.
Περὶ θεῶν αʹ.
Φιλόσοφος αʹ.
Πρὸς Κέφαλον αʹ.
Κέφαλος αʹ.
Κλεινόμαχος ἢ Λυσίας αʹ.
Πολίτης αʹ.
Περὶ ψυχῆς αʹ.
Πρὸς Γρύλλον αʹ.
5 Ἀρίστιππος αʹ.
Τεχνῶν ἔλεγχος αʹ.
Ὑπομνηματικοὶ διάλογοι.
Τεχνικὸν αʹ.
Διάλογοι τῶν περὶ τὴν πραγματείαν ὁμοίων αʹ βʹ γʹ
      δʹ εʹ ϛʹ ζʹ ηʹ θʹ ιʹ.
Διαιρέσεις καὶ πρὸς τὰ ὅμοια ὑποθέσεις.
Περὶ γενῶν καὶ εἰδῶν παραδειγμάτων.
Πρὸς τὸν Ἀμάρτυρον.
Πλάτωνος ἐγκώμιον.
Ἐπιστολαὶ πρὸς Δίωνα, Διονύσιον, Φίλιππον.
Περὶ νομοθεσίας.
Μαθηματικός.
Μανδρόβολος.
Λυσίας.
Ὅροι.
Τάξεις ὑπομνημάτων.

He has left behind a vast store of memoirs and numerous dialogues, among them :

Aristippus the Cyrenaic.
On Wealth, one book.
On Pleasure, one book.
On Justice,
On Philosophy,
On Friendship,
On the Gods,
The Philosopher,
A Reply to Cephalus,
Cephalus,
Clinomachus or Lysias,
The Citizen,
Of the Soul,
A Reply to Gryllus,
Aristippus,
Criticism of the Arts, each in one book.
Memoirs, in the form of dialogues.
Treatise on System, in one book.
Dialogues on the Resemblances in Science, in ten books.
Divisions and Hypotheses relating to the Resemblances.
On Typical Genera and Species.
A Reply to the Anonymous Work.
Eulogy of Plato.
Epistles to Dion, Dionysius and Philip.
On Legislation.
The Mathematician.
Mandrobolus.
Lysias.
Definitions.
Arrangements of Commentaries.

DIOGENES LAERTIUS

Στίχοι τρεῖς καὶ τετρακισμύριοι τεσσαρακόσιοι
ἑβδομήκοντα πέντε. πρὸς τοῦτον γράφει καὶ
Τιμωνίδης[1] τὰς ἱστορίας, ἐν αἷς κατέταξε τὰς
πράξεις Δίωνός τε καὶ Βίωνος.[2] φησὶ δὲ καὶ Φαβωρῖνος ἐν δευτέρῳ Ἀπομνημονευμάτων ὡς Ἀριστοτέλης αὐτοῦ τὰ βιβλία τριῶν ταλάντων ὠνήσατο.

Γέγονε Σπεύσιππος καὶ ἕτερος, ἰατρὸς Ἡρο-
φίλειος Ἀλεξανδρεύς.

Κεφ. β'. ΞΕΝΟΚΡΑΤΗΣ

6 Ξενοκράτης Ἀγαθήνορος Χαλκηδόνιος· οὗτος ἐκ
νέου Πλάτωνος ἤκουσεν, ἀλλὰ καὶ εἰς Σικελίαν
αὐτῷ συναπεδήμησεν. ἦν δὲ τὴν φύσιν νωθρός,
ὥστε λέγειν τὸν Πλάτωνα συγκρίνοντα αὐτὸν
Ἀριστοτέλει, " τῷ μὲν μύωπος δεῖ, τῷ δὲ χαλινοῦ."
καὶ " ἐφ' οἷον ἵππον οἷον ὄνον ἀλείφω." σεμνὸς
δὲ τά τ' ἄλλα Ξενοκράτης καὶ σκυθρωπὸς ἀεί,
ὥστε αὐτῷ λέγειν συνεχὲς τὸν Πλάτωνα, " Ξενό-
κρατες, θῦε ταῖς Χάρισι." διῆγέ τ' ἐν Ἀκαδημείᾳ
τὰ πλεῖστα· καὶ εἴ ποτε μέλλοι εἰς ἄστυ ἀνιέναι,
φασὶ τοὺς θορυβώδεις πάντας καὶ προυνίκους
7 ὑποστέλλειν αὐτοῦ τῇ παρόδῳ. καί ποτε καὶ
Φρύνην τὴν ἑταίραν ἐθελῆσαι πειρᾶσαι αὐτόν, καὶ
δῆθεν διωκομένην ὑπό τινων καταφυγεῖν εἰς τὸ
οἰκίδιον. τὸν δὲ ἕνεκα τοῦ ἀνθρωπίνου εἰσδέξασθαι, καὶ ἑνὸς ὄντος κλινιδίου δεομένῃ μετα-
δοῦναι τῆς κατακλίσεως· καὶ τέλος πολλὰ ἐκλιπα-

---

[1] Τιμωνίδης] Σιμωνίδης vulg.: sed cf. Plut. *Vit. Dion.*
35 et 31.
[2] τε καὶ Βίωνος secl. Mueller, *F.H.G.* ii. 83. Βίωνος] fort.
Διονυσίου.

---

[a] Nothing is known of any such Bion having taken part

They comprise in all 43,475 lines. To him Timon-
ides addresses his narrative in which he related the
achievements of Dion and Bion.[a] Favorinus also in
the second book of his *Memorabilia* relates that
Aristotle purchased the works of Speusippus for three
talents.

There was another Speusippus, a physician of
Alexandria, of the school of Herophilus.

CHAPTER 2. XENOCRATES (396–314 B.C.)
(Head of the Academy 339–314 B.C.)

Xenocrates, the son of Agathenor, was a native of
Chalcedon. He was a pupil of Plato from his earliest
youth ; moreover he accompanied him on his journey
to Sicily. He was naturally slow and clumsy. Hence
Plato, comparing him to Aristotle, said, " The one
needed a spur, the other a bridle." And again,
" See what an ass I am training and what a horse
he has to run against." However, Xenocrates was
in all besides dignified and grave of demeanour,
which made Plato say to him continually, " Xenocrates, sacrifice to the Graces." He spent most of
his time in the Academy ; and whenever he was going
to betake himself to the city, it is said that all the
noisy rabble and hired porters made way for him as
he passed. And that once the notorious Phryne
tried to make his acquaintance and, as if she were
being chased by some people, took refuge under his
roof ; that he admitted her out of ordinary humanity
and, there being but one small couch in the room,
permitted her to share it with him, and at last, after

in the expedition of Dion against Syracuse. There may be
an error in the text arising from dittography.

ρουσαν ἄπρακτον ἀναστῆναι. λέγειν τε πρὸς τοὺς
πυνθανομένους ὡς οὐκ ἀπ᾽ ἀνδρός, ἀλλ᾽ ἀπ᾽
ἀνδριάντος ἀνασταίη. ἔνιοι δὲ Λαΐδα φασὶ παρα-
κατακλῖναι αὐτῷ τοὺς μαθητάς· τὸν δὲ οὕτως εἶναι
ἐγκρατῆ, ὥστε καὶ τομὰς καὶ καύσεις πολλάκις
ὑπομεῖναι περὶ τὸ αἰδοῖον. ἦν δὲ καὶ ἀξιόπιστος
σφόδρα, ὥστε μὴ ἐξὸν ἀνώμοτον μαρτυρεῖν, τούτῳ
8 μόνῳ συνεχώρουν Ἀθηναῖοι. καὶ δὴ καὶ αὐταρκέ-
στατος ἦν. Ἀλεξάνδρου γοῦν ποτὲ συχνὸν ἀργύριον
ἀποστείλαντος αὐτῷ, τρισχιλίας Ἀττικὰς ἀφελὼν
τὸ λοιπὸν ἀπέπεμψεν, εἰπὼν ἐκείνῳ πλειόνων δεῖν
πλείονας τρέφοντι. ἀλλὰ καὶ ⟨τὸ⟩ ὑπ᾽ Ἀντιπάτρου
πεμφθὲν μὴ προσέσθαι, ὥς φησι Μυρωνιανὸς ἐν
Ὁμοίοις. καὶ χρυσῷ στεφάνῳ τιμηθέντα ἐπάθλῳ
πολυποσίας τοῖς Χουσὶ παρὰ Διονυσίῳ ἐξιόντα
θεῖναι πρὸς τὸν ἱδρυμένον Ἑρμῆν, ἔνθαπερ τιθέναι
καὶ τοὺς ἀνθινοὺς εἰώθει. λόγος δὲ αὐτὸν μετὰ καὶ
ἄλλων πεμφθῆναι πρεσβευτὴν πρὸς Φίλιππον· καὶ
τοὺς μὲν δώροις μαλθασσομένους καὶ εἰς τὰς
κλήσεις συνιέναι καὶ τῷ Φιλίππῳ λαλεῖν· τὸν δὲ
μηδέτερον τούτων ποιεῖν. οὔτε γὰρ ὁ Φίλιππος
9 αὐτὸν προσίετο διὰ τοῦτο. ὅθεν ἐλθόντας τοὺς
πρέσβεις εἰς τὰς Ἀθήνας φάσκειν ὡς μάτην αὐτοῖς
Ξενοκράτης συνεληλύθοι· καὶ τοὺς ἑτοίμους εἶναι
ζημιοῦν αὐτόν. μαθόντας δὲ παρ᾽ αὐτοῦ ὡς νῦν
καὶ μᾶλλον φροντιστέον εἴη τῆς πόλεως αὐτοῖς
(τοὺς μὲν γὰρ ᾔδει δωροδοκήσαντας ὁ Φίλιππος,

many importunities, she retired without success,
telling those who inquired that he whom she quitted
was not a man but a statue. Another version of the
story is that his pupils induced Laïs to invade his
couch ; and that so great was his endurance that he
many times submitted to amputation and cautery.
His words were entirely worthy of credit, so much
so that, although it was illegal for witnesses to give
evidence unsworn, the Athenians allowed Xenocrates
alone to do so. Furthermore, he was extremely
independent ; at all events, when Alexander sent
him a large sum of money, he took three thousand
Attic drachmas and sent back the rest to Alexander,
whose needs, he said, were greater than his own,
because he had a greater number of people to keep.
Again, he would not accept the present sent him by
Antipater, as Myronianus attests in his *Parallels*.
And when he had been honoured at the court of
Dionysius with a golden crown as the prize for his
prowess in drinking at the Feast of Pitchers, he went
out and placed it on the statue of Hermes just as
he had been accustomed to place there garlands of
flowers. There is a story that, when he was sent,
along with others also, on an embassy to Philip, his
colleagues, being bribed, accepted Philip's invitations to feasts and talked with him. Xenocrates
did neither the one nor the other. Indeed on this
account Philip declined to see him. Hence, when
the envoys returned to Athens, they complained
that Xenocrates had accompanied them without
rendering any service. Thereupon the people were
ready to fine him. But when he told them that
now more than ever they ought to consider the
interests of the state—" for," said he, " Philip knew

DIOGENES LAERTIUS

ἐμὲ δὲ μηδενὶ λόγῳ ὑπαξόμενος) φασὶ διπλασίως
αὐτὸν τιμῆσαι. καὶ τὸν Φίλιππον δὲ λέγειν
ὕστερον ὡς μόνος εἴη Ξενοκράτης τῶν πρὸς αὐτὸν
ἀφιγμένων ἀδωροδόκητος. ἀλλὰ καὶ πρεσβεύων
πρὸς Ἀντίπατρον περὶ αἰχμαλώτων Ἀθηναίων
κατὰ τὸν Λαμιακὸν πόλεμον, καὶ κληθεὶς ἐπὶ
δεῖπνον πρὸς αὐτὸν προηνέγκατο ταυτί·

ὦ Κίρκη, τίς γάρ κεν ἀνήρ, ὃς ἐναίσιμος εἴη,
πρὶν τλαίη πάσσασθαι ἐδητύος ἠδὲ ποτῆτος,
πρὶν λύσασθ᾽ ἑτάρους καὶ ἐν ὀφθαλμοῖσιν ἰδέσθαι;

καὶ τὸν ἀποδεξάμενον τὴν εὐστοχίαν εὐθὺς ἀφεῖναι.
10 Στρουθίου δέ ποτε διωκομένου ὑπὸ ἱέρακος καὶ
εἰσπηδήσαντος εἰς τοὺς κόλπους αὐτοῦ, καταψήσας
μεθῆκεν, εἰπὼν τὸν ἱκέτην δεῖν μὴ ἐκδιδόναι.
σκωπτόμενος ὑπὸ Βίωνος οὐκ ἔφη αὐτῷ ἀπο-
κρινεῖσθαι· μηδὲ γὰρ τὴν τραγῳδίαν ὑπὸ τῆς
κωμῳδίας σκωπτομένην ἀποκρίσεως ἀξιοῦν. πρὸς
δὲ τὸν μήτε μουσικὴν μήτε γεωμετρίαν μήτε
ἀστρονομίαν μεμαθηκότα, βουλόμενον δὲ παρ᾽
αὐτὸν φοιτᾶν, "πορεύου," ἔφη· "λαβὰς γὰρ οὐκ
ἔχεις φιλοσοφίας." οἱ δὲ τοῦτό φασιν εἰπεῖν,
"παρ᾽ ἐμοὶ γὰρ πόκος οὐ κνάπτεται."
11 Εἰπόντος δὲ Διονυσίου πρὸς Πλάτωνα ὡς
ἀφαιρήσεται αὐτοῦ τὸν τράχηλον, παρὼν οὗτος καὶ
δείξας τὸν ἴδιον, "οὐκ ἄν γε," ἔφη, "τὶς πρότερον
τούτου." φασὶ καὶ Ἀντιπάτρου ποτὲ ἐλθόντος
εἰς Ἀθήνας καὶ ἀσπασαμένου αὐτόν, μὴ πρότερον
ἀντιπροσαγορεῦσαι πρὶν ἢ τὸν λόγον ὃν ἔλεγε
διαπεράνασθαι. ἀτυφότατος δὲ ὢν πολλάκις τῆς

that the others had accepted his bribes, but that he would never win me over "—then the people paid him double honours. And afterwards Philip said that, of all who had arrived at his court, Xenocrates was the only man whom he could not bribe. Moreover, when he went as envoy to Antipater to plead for Athenians taken prisoners in the Lamian war,[a] being invited to dine with Antipater, he quoted to him the following lines [b] :

O Circe ! what righteous man would have the heart to taste meat and drink ere he had redeemed his company and beheld them face to face ?

and so pleased Antipater with his ready wit that he at once released them.

When a little sparrow was pursued by a hawk and rushed into his bosom, he stroked it and let it go, declaring that a suppliant must not be betrayed. When bantered by Bion, he said he would make no reply. For neither, said he, does tragedy deign to answer the banter of comedy. To some one who had never learnt either music or geometry or astronomy, but nevertheless wished to attend his lectures, Xenocrates said, " Go your ways, for you offer philosophy nothing to lay hold of." Others report him as saying, " It is not to me that you come for the carding of a fleece."

When Dionysius told Plato that he would lose his head, Xenocrates, who was present, pointed to his own and added, " No man shall touch it till he cut off mine." They say too that, when Antipater came to Athens and greeted him, he did not address him in return until he had finished what he was saying. He was singularly free from pride ; more than once

[a] 322 B.C.   [b] Hom. *Od.* x. 383-5.

ἡμέρας ἑαυτῷ ἐμελέτα, καὶ ὥραν μίαν, φασὶν, ἀπένεμε σιωπῇ.

Καὶ πλεῖστα ὅσα καταλέλοιπε συγγράμματα καὶ ἔπη καὶ παραινέσεις, ἅ ἐστι ταῦτα·

Περὶ φύσεως α´ β´ γ´ δ´ ε´ ϛ´.
Περὶ σοφίας ϛ´.
Περὶ πλούτου α´.
Ἀρκὰς α´.
Περὶ τοῦ ἀορίστου α´.
Περὶ τοῦ παιδίου α´.
Περὶ ἐγκρατείας α´.
Περὶ τοῦ ὠφελίμου α´.
Περὶ τοῦ ἐλευθέρου α´.
Περὶ θανάτου α´.
Περὶ ἑκουσίου α´.
Περὶ φιλίας α´ β´.
Περὶ ἐπιεικείας α´.
Περὶ τοῦ ἐναντίου α´ β´.
Περὶ εὐδαιμονίας α´ β´.
Περὶ τοῦ γράφειν α´.
Περὶ μνήμης α´.
Περὶ τοῦ ψεύδους α´.
Καλλικλῆς α´.
Περὶ φρονήσεως α´ β´.
Οἰκονομικὸς α´.
Περὶ σωφροσύνης α´.
Περὶ δυνάμεως νόμου α´.
Περὶ πολιτείας α´.
Περὶ ὁσιότητος α´.
Ὅτι παραδοτὴ ἡ ἀρετὴ α´.
Περὶ τοῦ ὄντος α´.
Περὶ εἱμαρμένης α´.

12

a day he would retire into himself, and he assigned, it is said, a whole hour to silence.

He left a very large number of treatises, poems and addresses, of which I append a list :

On Nature, six books.
On Wisdom, six books.
On Wealth, one book.
The Arcadian, one book.
On the Indeterminate, one book.
On the Child, one book.
On Continence, one book.
On Utility, one book.
On Freedom, one book.
On Death, one book.[a]
On the Voluntary, one book.
On Friendship, two books.
On Equity, one book.
On that which is Contrary, two books.
On Happiness, two books.
On Writing, one book.
On Memory, one book.
On Falsehood, one book.
Callicles, one book.
On Prudence, two books.
The Householder, one book.
On Temperance, one book.
On the Influence of Law, one book.
On the State, one book.
On Holiness, one book.
That Virtue can be taught, one book.
On Being, one book.
On Fate, one book.

[a] Supposed by Marsilius Ficinus to be the extant dialogue *Axiochus* attributed to Plato (*cf. supra*, iii. 62).

Περὶ παθῶν α.
Περὶ βίων α'.
Περὶ ὁμονοίας α'
Περὶ μαθητῶν α' β'.
Περὶ δικαιοσύνης α'.
Περὶ ἀρετῆς α' β'.
Περὶ εἰδῶν α'.
Περὶ ἡδονῆς α' β'.
Περὶ βίου α'.
Περὶ ἀνδρείας α'.
Περὶ τοῦ ἑνὸς α'.
Περὶ ἰδεῶν α'.
13 Περὶ τέχνης α'.
Περὶ θεῶν α' β'.
Περὶ ψυχῆς α' β'.
Περὶ ἐπιστήμης α'.
Πολιτικὸς α'.
Περὶ ἐπιστημοσύνης α'.
Περὶ φιλοσοφίας α'.
Περὶ τῶν Παρμενίδου α'.
Ἀρχέδημος ἢ περὶ δικαιοσύνης α'.
Περὶ τἀγαθοῦ α'.
Τῶν περὶ τὴν διάνοιαν α' β' γ' δ' ε' ϛ' ζ' η'.
Λύσις τῶν περὶ τοὺς λόγους ι'.
Φυσικῆς ἀκροάσεως α' β' γ' δ' ε' ϛ'.
Κεφάλαιον α'.
Περὶ γενῶν καὶ εἰδῶν α'.
Πυθαγόρεια α'.
Λύσεις α' β'.
Διαιρέσεις η'.
Θέσεων βιβλία κμγ'.
Τῆς περὶ τὸ διαλέγεσθαι πραγματείας βιβλία
    ιδμαβψμ'.

On the Emotions, one book.
On Modes of Life, one book.
On Concord, one book.
On Students, two books.
On Justice, one book.
On Virtue, two books.
On Forms, one book.
On Pleasure, two books.
On Life, one book.
On Bravery, one book.
On the One, one book.
On Ideas, one book.
On Art, one book.
On the Gods, two books.
On the Soul, two books.
On Science, one book.
The Statesman, one book.
On Cognition, one book.
On Philosophy, one book.
On the Writings of Parmenides, one book.
Archedemus or Concerning Justice, one book.
On the Good, one book.
Things relating to the Understanding, eight
 books.
Solution of Logical Problems, ten books.
Physical Lectures, six books.
Summary, one book.
On Genera and Species, one book.
Things Pythagorean, one book.
Solutions, two books.
Divisions, eight books.
Theses, in twenty books, 30,000 lines.
The Study of Dialectic, in fourteen books, 12,740
 lines.

Μετὰ τοῦτο βιβλία ιε΄ καὶ ἄλλα βιβλία ις΄ περὶ
    μαθημάτων τῶν περὶ τὴν λέξιν.
Λογιστικῶν βιβλία θ΄.
Τῶν περὶ τὰ μαθήματα βιβλία ς΄.
Τῶν περὶ τὴν διάνοιαν ἄλλα βιβλία δύο.
Περὶ γεωμετρῶν βιβλία ε΄.
Ὑπομνημάτων α΄.
Ἐναντίων α΄.
Περὶ ἀριθμῶν α΄.
Ἀριθμῶν θεωρία α΄.
Περὶ διαστημάτων α΄.
Τῶν περὶ ἀστρολογίαν ς΄.
14 Στοιχεῖα πρὸς Ἀλέξανδρον περὶ βασιλείας δ΄.
Πρὸς Ἀρύβαν.
Πρὸς Ἡφαιστίωνα.
Περὶ γεωμετρίας α΄ β΄.
    Στίχοι μκβδσλθ΄.

Ἀθηναῖοι δ᾽ ὅμως αὐτὸν ὄντα τοιοῦτον ἐπί-
πρασκόν ποτε, τὸ μετοίκιον ἀπονοῦντα θεῖναι. καὶ
αὐτὸν ὠνεῖται Δημήτριος ὁ Φαληρεὺς καὶ ἑκάτερον
ἀποκατέστησε· Ξενοκράτει μὲν τὴν ἐλευθερίαν,
Ἀθηναίοις δὲ τὸ μετοίκιον. τοῦτό φησι Μυρωνιανὸς ὁ Ἀμαστριανὸς ἐν τῷ πρώτῳ τῶν Ἱστορικῶν
Ὁμοίων κεφαλαίων. διεδέξατο δὲ Σπεύσιππον
καὶ ἀφηγήσατο τῆς σχολῆς πέντε καὶ εἴκοσιν ἔτη
ἐπὶ Λυσιμαχίδου ἀρξάμενος κατὰ τὸ δεύτερον
ἔτος τῆς δεκάτης καὶ ἑκατοστῆς Ὀλυμπιάδος.
ἐτελεύτα δὲ νυκτὸς λεκάνῃ προσπταίσας, ἔτος
ἤδη γεγονὼς δεύτερον καὶ ὀγδοηκοστόν.
15   Φαμὲν δὲ καὶ εἰς αὐτὸν οὑτωσί·

After this come fifteen books, and then sixteen
  books of Studies relating to Style.
Nine books on Ratiocination.
Six books concerned with Mathematics.
Two other books entitled Things relating to the
  Intellect.
On Geometers, five books.
Commentaries, one book.
Contraries, one book.
On Numbers, one book.
Theory of Numbers, one book.
On Dimensions, one book.
On Astronomy, six books.
Elementary Principles of Monarchy, in four books,
  dedicated to Alexander.
To Arybas.
To Hephaestion.
On Geometry, two books.
These works comprise in all 224,239 lines.

Such was his character, and yet, when he was
unable to pay the tax levied on resident aliens, the
Athenians put him up for sale. And Demetrius of
Phalerum purchased him, thereby making twofold
restitution, to Xenocrates of his liberty, and to
the Athenians of their tax. This we learn from
Myronianus of Amastris in the first book of his
Chapters on Historical Parallels. He succeeded
Speusippus and was head of the school for twenty-five
years from the archonship of Lysimachides, beginning
in the second year of the 110th Olympiad.[a] He died
in his 82nd year from the effects of a fall over some
utensil in the night.

Upon him I have expressed myself as follows [b]:

[a] 339–338 B.C.   [b] *Anth. Pal.* vii. 102.

χαλκῇ προσκόψας λεκάνῃ ποτὲ καὶ τὸ μέτωπον
πλήξας ἴαχεν ὦ σύντονον, εἶτ᾽ ἔθανεν,
ὁ πάντα πάντῃ Ξενοκράτης ἀνὴρ γεγώς.

Γεγόνασι δὲ καὶ ἄλλοι Ξενοκράτεις ἕξ· ὅ τε
τακτικὸς ἀρχαῖος σφόδρα ✻ ✻ καὶ ὁ συγγενὴς ἅμα
καὶ πολίτης τῷ προειρημένῳ φιλοσόφῳ· φέρεται
δὲ αὐτοῦ λόγος Ἀρσινοητικός, γεγραμμένος περὶ
Ἀρσινόης ἀποθανούσης. τέταρτος φιλόσοφος, ἐλε-
γείαν γεγραφὼς οὐκ ἐπιτυχῶς. ἴδιον δέ· ποιηταὶ
μὲν γὰρ ἐπιβαλλόμενοι πεζογραφεῖν ἐπιτυγχάνουσι·
πεζογράφοι δὲ ἐπιτιθέμενοι ποιητικῇ πταίουσι· τῷ
δῆλον τὸ μὲν φύσεως εἶναι, τὸ δὲ τέχνης ἔργον.
πέμπτος ἀνδριαντοποιός· ἕκτος ᾄσματα γεγραφώς,
ὥς φησιν Ἀριστόξενος.

Κεφ. γ´. ΠΟΛΕΜΩΝ

16 Πολέμων Φιλοστράτου μὲν ἦν υἱός, Ἀθηναῖος
τῶν δήμων Οἴηθεν. νέος δ᾽ ὢν ἀκόλαστός τε καὶ
διακεχυμένος ἦν οὕτως, ὥστε καὶ περιφέρειν
ἀργύριον πρὸς τὰς ἑτοίμους λύσεις τῶν ἐπιθυμιῶν·
ἀλλὰ καὶ ἐν τοῖς στενωποῖς διέκρυπτεν. καὶ ἐν
Ἀκαδημείᾳ πρὸς κίονί τινι τριώβολον εὑρέθη
προσπεπλασμένον αὐτοῦ διὰ [τὴν] ὁμοίαν τῇ
προειρημένῃ πρόφασιν. καί ποτε συνθέμενος τοῖς
νέοις μεθύων καὶ ἐστεφανωμένος εἰς τὴν Ξενοκράτους ᾖξε σχολήν· ὁ δὲ οὐδὲν διατραπεὶς εἶρε
τὸν λόγον ὁμοίως· ἦν δὲ περὶ σωφροσύνης. ἄκουον
δὴ τὸ μειράκιον κατ᾽ ὀλίγον ἐθηράθη καὶ οὕτως

---

[a] In the enumeration of the first three one has accidentally
dropped out.
[b] Cf. Lucian's account of his follies (Bis accusatus, 16),

Xenocrates, that type of perfect manliness, stumbled over a vessel of bronze and broke his head, and, with a loud cry, expired.

There have been six other men named Xenocrates: (1) a tactician in very ancient times; (2) the kinsman and fellow-citizen of the philosopher: a speech by him is extant entitled the Arsinoëtic, treating of a certain deceased Arsinoë *a*; (4) a philosopher and not very successful writer of elegies; it is a remarkable fact that poets succeed when they undertake to write prose, but prose-writers who essay poetry come to grief; whereby it is clear that the one is a gift of nature and the other of art; (5) a sculptor; (6) a writer of songs mentioned by Aristoxenus.

Chapter 3. POLEMO
(Head of the Academy from 314 to *c.* 276 b.c.)

Polemo, the son of Philostratus, was an Athenian who belonged to the deme of Oea. In his youth he was so profligate and dissipated that he actually carried about with him money to procure the immediate gratification of his desires, and would even keep sums concealed in lanes and alleys.*b* Even in the Academy a piece of three obols was found close to a pillar, where he had buried it for the same purpose. And one day, by agreement with his young friends, he burst into the school of Xenocrates quite drunk, with a garland on his head. Xenocrates, however, without being at all disturbed, went on with his discourse as before, the subject being temperance. The lad, as he listened, by degrees was taken in the toils. He became so industrious

the more piquant because put into the mouth of Academy pleading against Carouse, Μέθη.

ἐγένετο φιλόπονος ὡς ὑπερβάλλεσθαι τοὺς ἄλλους
καὶ αὐτὸς διαδέξασθαι τὴν σχολήν, ἀρξάμενος ἀπὸ
τῆς ἕκτης καὶ δεκάτης καὶ ἑκατοστῆς Ὀλυμπιάδος.

17   Φησὶ δὲ Ἀντίγονος ὁ Καρύστιος ἐν τοῖς Βίοις τὸν
πατέρα αὐτοῦ πρῶτόν τε εἶναι τῶν πολιτῶν καὶ
ἁρματοτροφῆσαι. φυγεῖν δὲ τὸν Πολέμωνα καὶ
δίκην κακώσεως ὑπὸ τῆς γυναικός, ὡς μειρακίοις
συνόντα. τοσοῦτον δὲ ἐπιτεῖναι τὸ ἦθος ἀρξά-
μενον φιλοσοφεῖν, ὥστ' ἐπὶ ταὐτοῦ σχήματος τῆς
μορφῆς πάντοτε μένειν. ἀλλὰ καὶ τὴν φωνὴν
ἀναλλοίωτος ἦν· διὸ καὶ θηραθῆναι Κράντορα ὑπ'
αὐτοῦ. κυνὸς γοῦν λυττῶντος [καὶ] τὴν ἰγνύαν
διασπάσαντος μόνον μὴ ὠχριᾶσαι· καὶ ταραχῆς
γενομένης ἐπὶ τῆς πόλεως πυθομένων τὸ γεγονὸς
ἄτρεπτον μεῖναι. ἔν τε τοῖς θεάτροις ἀσυμπαθέ-

18 στατος ἦν. Νικοστράτου γοῦν ποτε τοῦ ἐπικαλου-
μένου Κλυταιμνήστρα ἀναγινώσκοντός τι τοῦ
ποιητοῦ αὐτῷ τε καὶ Κράτητι, τὸν μὲν συνδια-
τίθεσθαι, τὸν δ' ἴσα καὶ μὴ ἀκοῦσαι. καὶ ὅλως ἦν
τοιοῦτος οἷόν φησι Μελάνθιος ὁ ζωγράφος ἐν τοῖς
Περὶ ζωγραφικῆς· φησὶ γὰρ δεῖν αὐθάδειάν τινα
καὶ σκληρότητα τοῖς ἔργοις ἐπιτρέχειν, ὁμοίως δὲ
κἀν τοῖς ἤθεσιν. ἔφασκε δὲ ὁ Πολέμων δεῖν ἐν
τοῖς πράγμασι γυμνάζεσθαι καὶ μὴ ἐν τοῖς δια-
λεκτικοῖς θεωρήμασι, καθάπερ ἁρμονικόν τι τέχνιον
καταπιόντα καὶ μὴ μελετήσαντα, ὡς κατὰ μὲν τὴν
ἐρώτησιν θαυμάζεσθαι, κατὰ δὲ τὴν διάθεσιν
ἑαυτοῖς μάχεσθαι.

---

as to surpass all the other scholars, and rose to be himself head of the school in the 116th Olympiad.[a]

Antigonus of Carystus in his *Biographies* says that his father was foremost among the citizens and kept horses to compete in the chariot-race ; that Polemo himself had been defendant in an action brought by his wife, who charged him with cruelty owing to the irregularities of his life ; but that, from the time when he began to study philosophy, he acquired such strength of character as always to maintain the same unruffled calm of demeanour. Nay more, he never lost control of his voice. This in fact accounts for the fascination which he exercised over Crantor.[b] Certain it is that, when a mad dog bit him in the back of his thigh, he did not even turn pale, but remained undisturbed by all the clamour which arose in the city at the news of what had happened. In the theatre too he was singularly unmoved. For instance, Nicostratus, who was nicknamed Clytemnestra, was once reading to him and Crates something from Homer; and, while Crates was deeply affected, he was no more moved than if he had not heard him. Altogether he was a man such as Melanthius the painter describes in his work *On Painting*. There he says that a certain wilfulness and stubbornness should be stamped on works of art, and that the same holds good of character. Polemo used to say that we should exercise ourselves with facts and not with mere logical speculations, which leave us, like a man who has got by heart some paltry handbook on harmony but never practised, able, indeed, to win admiration for skill in asking questions, but utterly at variance with ourselves in the ordering of our lives.

Ἦν οὖν ἀσόλοικός τις καὶ γενναῖος, παρητημέ-
νος ἅ φησιν Ἀριστοφάνης περὶ Εὐριπίδου, " ὀξωτὰ
19 καὶ σιλφιωτά," ἅπερ, ὡς ὁ αὐτός φησι,

καταπυγοσύνη ταῦτ' ἐστὶ πρὸς κρέας μέγα.

ἀλλὰ μὴν οὐδὲ καθίζων ἔλεγε πρὸς τὰς θέσεις,
φασί, περιπατῶν δὲ ἐπεχείρει. διὰ δὴ οὖν τὸ
φιλογενναῖον ἐτιμᾶτο ἐν τῇ πόλει. οὐ μὴν ἀλλὰ
καὶ ἐκπεπατηκὼς ἦν διατρίβων ἐν τῷ κήπῳ, παρ'
ὃν οἱ μαθηταὶ μικρὰ καλύβια ποιησάμενοι κατῴκουν
πλησίον τοῦ μουσείου καὶ τῆς ἐξέδρας. ἐῴκει δὴ ὁ
Πολέμων κατὰ πάντα ἐζηλωκέναι τὸν Ξενοκράτην·
καὶ ἐρασθῆναι αὐτοῦ φησιν Ἀρίστιππος ἐν τῷ
τετάρτῳ Περὶ παλαιᾶς τρυφῆς. ἀεὶ γοῦν ἐμέμνητο
αὐτοῦ, τήν τ' ἀκακίαν καὶ τὸν αὐχμὸν ἐνεδέδυτο
τἀνδρὸς καὶ τὸ βάρος οἱονεὶ τῆς Δωριστὶ ἁρμονίας.
20 ἦν δὲ καὶ φιλοσοφοκλῆς, καὶ μάλιστα ἐν ἐκείνοις
ὅπου κατὰ τὸν κωμικὸν τὰ ποιήματα αὐτῷ

κύων τις ἐδόκει συμποιεῖν Μολοττικός,

καὶ ἔνθα ἦν κατὰ τὸν Φρύνιχον

οὐ γλύξις οὐδ' ὑπόχυτος, ἀλλὰ Πράμνιος.

ἔλεγεν οὖν τὸν μὲν Ὅμηρον ἐπικὸν εἶναι Σοφοκλέα,
τὸν δὲ Σοφοκλέα Ὅμηρον τραγικόν.

Ἐτελεύτησε δὲ γηραιὸς ἤδη ὑπὸ φθίσεως, ἱκανὰ
συγγράμματα καταλιπών. καὶ ἔστιν ἡμῶν εἰς
αὐτόν·

οὐκ ἀΐεις; Πολέμωνα κεκεύθαμεν, ὃν θέτο τῇδε
ἀρρωστίη, τὸ δεινὸν ἀνθρώποις πάθος.

---

a Frag. 180 Dind.
b Cf. supra, i. § 112 note.

He was, then, refined and generous, and would beg
to be excused, in the words of Aristophanes about
Euripides, the " acid, pungent style," which, as the
same author says, is "strong seasoning for meat when
it is high." [a] Further, he would not, they say, even
sit down to deal with the themes of his pupils, but
would argue walking up and down. It was, then,
for his love of what is noble that he was honoured
in the state. Nevertheless would he withdraw from
society [b] and confine himself to the Garden of the
Academy, while close by his scholars made themselves little huts and lived not far from the shrine of
the Muses and the lecture-hall. It would seem that
in all respects Polemo emulated Xenocrates. And
Aristippus in the fourth book of his work *On the
Luxury of the Ancients* affirms him to have been his
favourite. Certainly he always kept his predecessor
before his mind and, like him, wore that simple
austere dignity which is proper to the Dorian mode.
He loved Sophocles, particularly in those passages
where it seemed as if, in the phrase of the comic
poet,

> A stout Molossian mastiff lent him aid,

and where the poet was, in the words of Phrynichus,[c]

> Nor must, nor blended vintage, but true Pramnian.

Thus he would call Homer the Sophocles of epic, and
Sophocles the Homer of tragedy

He died at an advanced age of gradual decay,
leaving behind him a considerable number of works.
I have composed the following epigram upon him [d]:

> Dost thou not hear? We have buried Polemo, laid here
> by that fatal scourge of wasted strength. Yet not Polemo,

[c] Meineke, *C.G.F.* ii. 605.
[d] *Anth. Plan.* ii. 380.

οὐ μᾶλλον Πολέμωνα, τὸ σῶμα δέ· τοῦτο γὰρ
αὐτὸς
βαίνων ἐς ἄστρα διάβορον θῆκεν χαμαί.

Κεφ. δ΄. ΚΡΑΤΗΣ

21 Κράτης πατρὸς μὲν ἦν Ἀντιγένους ‹Ἀθηναῖος›,
Θριάσιος δὲ τῶν δήμων, ἀκροατὴς ἅμα καὶ ἐρώμενος Πολέμωνος· ἀλλὰ καὶ διεδέξατο τὴν σχολὴν
αὐτοῦ. καὶ οὕτως ἀλλήλω ἐφιλείτην ὥστε καὶ
ζῶντε οὐ μόνον τῶν αὐτῶν ἤστην ἐπιτηδευμάτων,
ἀλλὰ καὶ μέχρι σχεδὸν ἀναπνοῆς ἐξωμοιώθην
ἀλλήλοιν καὶ θανόντε τῆς αὐτῆς ταφῆς ἐκοινωνείτην.
ὅθεν Ἀνταγόρας εἰς ἄμφω τοῦτον ἐποίησε τὸν
τρόπον·

> μνήματι τῷδε Κράτητα θεουδέα καὶ Πολέμωνα
> ἔννεπε κρύπτεσθαι, ξεῖνε, παρερχόμενος,
> ἄνδρας ὁμοφροσύνῃ μεγαλήτορας, ὧν ἄπο μῦθος
> ἱερὸς ἤισσεν δαιμονίου στόματος,
> καὶ βίοτος καθαρὸς σοφίας ἐπὶ θεῖον ἐκόσμει
> αἰῶν’ ἀστρέπτοις δόγμασι πειθόμενος.

22 ἔνθεν καὶ Ἀρκεσίλαον μετελθόντα παρὰ Θεοφράστου πρὸς αὐτοὺς λέγειν ὡς εἶεν θεοί τινες ἢ λείψανα
τῶν ἐκ τοῦ χρυσοῦ γένους. καὶ γὰρ ἤστην οὐ
φιλοδημώδεε· ἀλλ’ οἷον Διονυσόδωρόν ποτέ φασι
τὸν αὐλητὴν εἰπεῖν, σεμνυνόμενον ἐπὶ τῷ μηδένα
τῶν κρουμάτων αὐτοῦ μήτ’ ἐπὶ τριήρους μήτ’ ἐπὶ
κρήνης ἀκηκοέναι, καθάπερ Ἰσμηνίου. συσσίτιον
δέ φησιν αὐτῷ ὁ Ἀντίγονος εἶναι παρὰ Κράντορι,
ὁμονόως συμβιούντων τούτων τε καὶ Ἀρκεσίλαου.
τὴν δὲ οἴκησιν Ἀρκεσίλαον μὲν ἔχειν μετὰ Κράντορος, Πολέμωνα δὲ σὺν Κράτητι μετὰ Λυσι-

but merely his body, which on his way to the stars he left to moulder in the ground.

Chapter 4. CRATES (of Athens)
(Head of the Academy in third century B.C.)

Crates, whose father was Antigenes, was an Athenian belonging to the deme of Thria. He was a pupil and at the same time a favourite of Polemo, whom he succeeded in the headship of the school. The two were so much attached to each other that they not only shared the same pursuits in life but grew more and more alike to their latest breath, and, dying, shared the same tomb. Hence Antagoras, writing of both, employed this figure *a* :

Passing stranger, say that in this tomb rest godlike Crates and Polemo, men magnanimous in concord, from whose inspired lips flowed sacred speech, and whose pure life of wisdom, in accordance with unswerving tenets, decked them for a bright immortality.

Hence Arcesilaus, who had quitted Theophrastus and gone over to their school, said of them that they were gods or a remnant of the Golden Age. They did not side with the popular party, but were such as Dionysodorus the flute-player is said to have claimed to be, when he boasted that no one ever heard his melodies, as those of Ismenias were heard, either on shipboard or at the fountain. According to Antigonus, their common table was in the house of Crantor ; and these two and Arcesilaus lived in harmony together. Arcesilaus and Crantor shared the same house, while Polemo and Crates lived with

* *Anth. Pal.* vii. 103.

κλέους τινὸς τῶν πολιτῶν. ἦν δέ, φησίν, ἐρώμενος,
Κράτης μέν, ὡς προείρηται, Πολέμωνος· Ἀρκεσίλαος δὲ Κράντορος.

23 Τελευτῶν δὲ ὁ Κράτης, καθά φησιν Ἀπολλόδωρος ἐν τρίτῳ τῶν Χρονικῶν, ἀπέλιπε βιβλία τὰ
μὲν φιλοσοφούμενα, τὰ δὲ περὶ κωμῳδίας, τὰ δὲ
λόγους δημηγορικοὺς καὶ πρεσβευτικούς. ἀλλὰ
καὶ μαθητὰς ἐλλογίμους· ὧν Ἀρκεσίλαον περὶ οὗ
λέξομεν—διήκουσε γὰρ καὶ τούτου—καὶ Βίωνα τὸν
Βορυσθενίτην, ὕστερον δὲ Θεοδώρειον ἀπὸ τῆς
αἱρέσεως ἐπικαλούμενον, περὶ οὗ καὶ αὐτοῦ λέξομεν
ἐχομένως Ἀρκεσιλάου.

Γεγόνασι δὲ Κράτητες δέκα· πρῶτος ὁ τῆς
ἀρχαίας κωμῳδίας ποιητής, δεύτερος ῥήτωρ Τραλ-
λιανὸς Ἰσοκράτειος, τρίτος ταφρωρύχος Ἀλεξάνδρῳ συνών, τέταρτος ὁ κύων περὶ οὗ λέξομεν,
πέμπτος φιλόσοφος περιπατητικός, ἕκτος Ἀκα-
δημαϊκὸς ὁ προειρημένος, ἕβδομος Μαλώτης γραμματικός, ὄγδοος γεωμετρικὰ γεγραφώς, ἔνατος
ἐπιγραμμάτων ποιητής, δέκατος Ταρσεὺς φιλόσοφος
Ἀκαδημαϊκός.

Κεφ. ε'. ΚΡΑΝΤΩΡ

24 Κράντωρ Σολεὺς θαυμαζόμενος ἐν τῇ ἑαυτοῦ
πατρίδι ἀπῆρεν εἰς Ἀθήνας καὶ Ξενοκράτους διήκουσε Πολέμωνι συσχολάζων. καὶ κατέλιπεν ὑπομνήματα εἰς μυριάδας στίχων τρεῖς, ὧν τινά
τινες Ἀρκεσιλάῳ προσάπτουσι. φασὶ δὲ αὐτὸν
ἐρωτηθέντα τίνι θηραθείη ὑπὸ Πολέμωνος, εἰπεῖν
400

Lysicles, one of the citizens. Crates, as already stated, was the favourite of Polemo and Arcesilaus of Crantor.

According to Apollodorus in the third book of his *Chronology*, Crates at his death left behind him works, some of a philosophical kind, others on comedy, others again speeches delivered in the assembly or when he was envoy. He also left distinguished pupils ; among them Arcesilaus, of whom we shall speak presently—for he was also a pupil of Crates ; another was Bion of Borysthenes, who was afterwards known as the Theodorean, from the school which he joined ; of him too we shall have occasion to speak next after Arcesilaus.

There have been ten men who bore the name of Crates : (1) the poet of the Old Comedy ; (2) a rhetorician of Tralles, a pupil of Isocrates ; (3) a sapper and miner who accompanied Alexander ; (4) the Cynic, of whom more hereafter ; (5) a Peripatetic philosopher ; (6) the Academic philosopher described above ; (7) a grammarian of Malos ; (8) the author of a geometrical work ; (9) a composer of epigrams ; (10) an Academic philosopher of Tarsus.

Chapter 5. CRANTOR

(Perhaps about 340–290 b.c.)

Crantor of Soli, though he was much esteemed in his native country, left it for Athens and attended the lectures of Xenocrates at the same time as Polemo. He left memoirs extending to 30,000 lines, some of which are by some critics attributed to Arcesilaus. He is said to have been asked what it was in Polemo that attracted him, and to have

τῷ μήτ' ὀξύτερον μήτε βαρύτερον ἀκοῦσαι φθεγγομένου. οὗτος νοσήσας εἰς τὸ 'Ασκληπιεῖον ἀνεχώρησε κἀκεῖ περιεπάτει· οἱ δὲ πανταχόθεν προσῄεσαν αὐτῷ, νομίζοντες οὐ διὰ νόσον, ἀλλὰ βούλεσθαι αὐτόθι σχολὴν συστήσασθαι. ὧν ἦν καὶ 'Αρκεσίλαος θέλων ὑπ' αὐτοῦ συστῆναι Πολέμωνι, καίπερ ἐρῶντος, ὡς ἐν τῷ περὶ 'Αρκεσιλάου
25 λέξομεν. ἀλλὰ καὶ αὐτὸν ὑγιάναντα διακούειν Πολέμωνος, ἐφ' ᾧ καὶ μάλιστα θαυμασθῆναι. λέγεται δὲ καὶ τὴν οὐσίαν καταλιπεῖν 'Αρκεσιλάῳ, ταλάντων οὖσαν δυοκαίδεκα. καὶ ἐρωτηθέντα πρὸς αὐτοῦ ποῦ βούλεται ταφῆναι, εἰπεῖν·

ἐν γῆς φίλης μυχοῖσι κρυφθῆναι καλόν.

λέγεται δὲ καὶ ποιήματα γράψαι καὶ ἐν τῇ πατρίδι ἐν τῷ τῆς 'Αθηνᾶς ἱερῷ σφραγισάμενος αὐτὰ θεῖναι. καί φησι Θεαίτητος ὁ ποιητὴς περὶ αὐτοῦ οὑτωσί·

ἥνδανεν ἀνθρώποις, ὁ δ' ἐπὶ πλέον ἥνδανε
    Μούσαις
Κράντωρ, καὶ γήρως ἤλυθεν οὔτι πρόσω.
γῆ, σὺ δὲ τεθνηῶτα τὸν ἱερὸν ἄνδρ' ὑπόδεξαι·
ἠρέμα καὶ κεῖθι ζῴη ἐν εὐθενίῃ.

26 'Εθαύμαζε δὲ ὁ Κράντωρ πάντων δὴ μᾶλλον
"Ομηρον καὶ Εὐριπίδην, λέγων ἐργῶδες εἶναι ἐν τῷ κυρίῳ τραγικῶς ἅμα καὶ συμπαθῶς γράψαι. καὶ προεφέρετο τὸν στίχον τὸν ἐκ τοῦ Βελλεροφόντου·

οἴμοι· τί δ' οἴμοι; θνητά τοι πεπόνθαμεν.

λέγεται δὲ καὶ 'Ανταγόρα τοῦ ποιητοῦ ὡς Κράντορος εἰς "Ερωτα πεποιημένα φέρεσθαι ταυτί·

ᵃ Nauck, T.G.F.², Adesp. 281.   ᵇ Anth. Plan. ii. 28.

replied, " The fact that I never heard him raise or lower his voice in speaking." He happened to fall ill, and retired to the temple of Asclepius, where he proceeded to walk about. At once people flocked round him in the belief that he had retired thither, not on account of illness, but in order to open a school. Among them was Arcesilaus, who wished to be introduced by his means to Polemo, notwithstanding the affection which united the two, as will be related in the Life of Arcesilaus. However, when he recovered, he continued to attend Polemo's lectures, and for this he was universally praised. He is also said to have left Arcesilaus his property, to the value of twelve talents. And when asked by him where he wished to be buried, he answered [a] :

Sweet in some nook of native soil to rest.

It is also said that he wrote poems and deposited them under seal in the temple of Athena in his native place. And Theaetetus the poet writes thus of him [b] :

Pleasing to men, more pleasing to the Muses, lived Crantor, and never saw old age. Receive, O earth, the hallowed dead ; gently may he live and thrive even in the world below.

Crantor admired Homer and Euripides above all other poets ; it is hard, he said, at once to write tragedy and to stir the emotions in the language of everyday life. And he would quote the line from the story of Bellerophon [c] :

Alas ! But why Alas ? We have suffered the lot of mortals.

And it is said that there are extant [d] these lines of the poet Antagoras, spoken by Crantor on Love :

[a] Nauck, *T.G.F.*[2], *Eur.* 300.   [d] *Anth. Plan.* iii. 60.

ἐν δοιῇ μοι θυμός, ἐπεὶ γένος ἀμφίσβητον,
ἤ σε θεῶν τὸν πρῶτον ἀειγενέων, Ἔρος, εἴπω,
τῶν ὅσσους Ἔρεβός τε πάλαι βασίλειά τε παῖδας
γείνατο Νὺξ πελάγεσσιν ὑπ' εὐρέος Ὠκεανοῖο·
27   ἤ σέ γε Κύπριδος υἷα περίφρονος, ἠέ σε Γαίης,
ἤ Ἀνέμων· τοῖος σὺ κακὰ φρονέων ἀλάλησαι
ἀνθρώποις ἠδ' ἐσθλά· τὸ καὶ σέο σῶμα δίφυιον.

Ἦν δὲ καὶ δεινὸς ὀνοματοποιῆσαι. τραγῳδὸν
γοῦν ἀπελέκητον εἶπεν ἔχειν φωνὴν καὶ φλοιοῦ
μεστήν· καί τινος ποιητοῦ σκίφης μεστοὺς εἶναι
τοὺς στίχους· καὶ τὰς Θεοφράστου θέσεις ὀστρέῳ
γεγράφθαι. θαυμάζεται δὲ αὐτοῦ βιβλίον μάλιστα
τὸ Περὶ πένθους. καὶ κατέστρεψε πρὸ Πολέμωνος καὶ Κράτητος, ὑδρωπικῇ διαθέσει νοσήσας.
καὶ ἔστιν εἰς αὐτὸν ἡμῶν·

ἐπέκλυσε καὶ σέ, Κράντορ, ἡ νόσων κακίστη,
χοὖτω μέλαν κατῆλθες Πλουτέως ἄβυσσον.
καὶ σὺ μὲν ἐκεῖθι χαίρεις, σῶν λόγων δὲ χήρη
ἕστηκεν Ἀκαδήμεια καὶ Σόλοι, πατρίς σευ.

Κεφ. ϛʹ.   ΑΡΚΕΣΙΛΑΟΣ

28   Ἀρκεσίλαος Σεύθου ([ἢ Σκύθου], ὡς Ἀπολλόδωρος ἐν τρίτῳ Χρονικῶν), Πιτάνης τῆς Αἰολίδος.
οὗτός ἐστιν ὁ τῆς μέσης Ἀκαδημείας κατάρξας,
πρῶτος ἐπισχὼν τὰς ἀποφάσεις διὰ τὰς ἐναντιό-
τητας τῶν λόγων. πρῶτος δὲ καὶ εἰς ἑκάτερον
ἐπεχείρησε, καὶ πρῶτος τὸν λόγον ἐκίνησε τὸν ὑπὸ
Πλάτωνος παραδεδομένον καὶ ἐποίησε δι' ἐρωτήσεως καὶ ἀποκρίσεως ἐριστικώτερον. παρέβαλε δὲ

---

* "Legimus omnes Crantoris, veteris Academici, de

My mind is in doubt, since thy birth is disputed, whether I am to call thee, Love, the first of the immortal gods, the eldest of all the children whom old Erebus and queenly Night brought to birth in the depths beneath wide Ocean ; or art thou the child of wise Cypris, or of Earth, or of the Winds ? So many are the goods and ills thou devisest for men in thy wanderings. Therefore hast thou a body of double form.

He was also clever at inventing terms. For instance, he said of a tragic player's voice that it was unpolished and unpeeled. And of a certain poet that his verses abounded in miserliness. And that the disquisitions of Theophrastus were written with an oyster-shell. His most highly esteemed work is the treatise *On Grief*.[a] He died before Polemo and Crates, his end being hastened by dropsy. I have composed upon him the following epigram [b] :

The worst of maladies overwhelmed you, Crantor, and thus did you descend the black abyss of Pluto. While you fare well even in the world below, the Academy and your country of Soli are bereft of your discourses.

Chapter 6. ARCESILAUS (c. 318–242 b.c.)

Arcesilaus, the son of Seuthes, according to Apollodorus in the third book of his *Chronology*, came from Pitane in Aeolis. With him begins the Middle Academy ; he was the first to suspend his judgement owing to the contradictions of opposing arguments. He was also the first to argue on both sides of a question, and the first to meddle with the system handed down by Plato and, by means of question and answer, to make it more closely resemble eristic.

luctu ; est enim non magnus, verum aureolus et, ut Tuberoni Panaetius praecipit, ad verbum ediscendus libellus " (Cic. *Ac. Pr.* ii. 44).   [b] *Anth. Plan.* ii. 381.

Κράντορι τοῦτον τὸν τρόπον. τέταρτος ἀδελφὸς ἦν
ὧν εἶχε δύο μὲν ὁμοπατρίους, δύο δὲ ὁμομητρίους·
καὶ τῶν μὲν ὁμομητρίων πρεσβύτερον Πυλάδην,
τῶν δὲ ὁμοπατρίων Μοιρέαν, ὃς ἦν αὐτῷ ἐπίτροπος.
29 ἤκουσε δὲ κατ' ἀρχὰς μὲν Αὐτολύκου τοῦ μαθη-
ματικοῦ πολίτου τυγχάνοντος, πρὶν ἀπαίρειν εἰς
Ἀθήνας, μεθ' οὗ καὶ εἰς Σάρδεις ἀπεδήμησεν·
ἔπειτα Ξάνθου τοῦ Ἀθηναίου μουσικοῦ· μεθ' ὃν
Θεοφράστου διήκουσεν. ἔπειτα μετῆλθεν εἰς Ἀκαδημείαν πρὸς Κράντορα· Μοιρέας μὲν γὰρ ὁ προειρημένος ἀδελφὸς ἦγεν αὐτὸν ἐπὶ ῥητορικήν· ὁ
δὲ φιλοσοφίας ἤρα, καὶ αὐτοῦ Κράντωρ ἐρωτικῶς
διατεθεὶς ἐπύθετο τὰ ἐξ Ἀνδρομέδας Εὐριπίδου
προενεγκάμενος·

ὦ παρθέν', εἰ σώσαιμί σ', εἴσει μοι χάριν;

καὶ ὃς τὰ ἑχόμενα·

ἄγου μ', ὦ ξέν', εἴτε δμωΐδ' ἐθέλεις εἴτ' ἄλοχον.

30 ἐκ τούτου συνήστην ἀλλήλοιν· ἵνα καὶ τὸν Θεόφραστον κνιζόμενόν φασιν εἰπεῖν ὡς εὐφυὴς καὶ
εὐεπιχείρητος ἀπεληλυθὼς τῆς διατριβῆς εἴη νεανίσκος. καὶ γὰρ ἐν τοῖς λόγοις ἐμβριθέστατος καὶ
φιλογράμματος ἱκανῶς γενόμενος ἥπτετο καὶ ποιητικῆς. καὶ αὐτοῦ φέρεται ἐπίγραμμα εἰς Ἄτταλον
ἔχον οὕτω·

Πέργαμος οὐχ ὅπλοις κλεινὴ μόνον, ἀλλὰ καὶ
    ἵπποις
πολλάκις αὐδᾶται Πῖσαν ἀνὰ ζαθέην.
εἰ δὲ τὸν ἐκ Διόθεν θεμιτὸν θνατῷ νόον εἰπεῖν,
ἔσσεται εἰσαῦτις πολλὸν ἀοιδοτέρη.

He came across Crantor in this way. He was the
youngest of four brothers, two of them being his
brothers by the same father, and two by the same
mother. Of the last two Pylades was the elder, and
of the former two Moereas, and Moereas was his
guardian. At first, before he left Pitane for Athens,
he was a pupil of the mathematician Autolycus, his
fellow-countryman, and with him he also travelled
to Sardis. Next he studied under Xanthus, the
musician, of Athens ; then he was a pupil of Theophrastus. Lastly, he crossed over to the Academy
and joined Crantor. For while his brother Moereas,
who has already been mentioned, wanted to make
him a rhetorician, he was himself devoted to philosophy, and Crantor, being enamoured of him, cited
the line from the *Andromeda* of Euripides [a] :

O maiden, if I save thee, wilt thou be grateful to me ?

and was answered with the next line [b] :

Take me, stranger, whether for maidservant or for wife.

After that they lived together. Whereupon Theophrastus, nettled at his loss, is said to have remarked,
" What a quick-witted and ready pupil has left my
school ! " For, besides being most effective in argument and decidedly fond of writing books, he also
took up poetry. And there is extant an epigram of
his upon Attalus which runs thus [c] :

Pergamos, not famous in arms alone, is often celebrated
for its steeds in divine Pisa. And if a mortal may make
bold to utter the will of heaven, it will be much more sung
by bards in days to come.

          [a] Nauck, *T.G.F.*[2], *Eur.* 129.
  [b] *Ib.* 132.   [c] *Anth. Plan.* iii. 56.

ἀλλὰ καὶ εἰς Μηνόδωρον τὸν Εὐγάμου ἑνὸς τῶν
συσχολαστῶν ἐρώμενον·

31 τηλοῦ μὲν Φρυγίη, τηλοῦ δ᾽ ἱερὴ Θυάτειρα·
ὦ Μηνόδωρε, σὴ πατρίς, Καδανάδη.
ἀλλὰ γὰρ εἰς Ἀχέροντα τὸν οὐ φατὸν ἶσα κέλευθα,
ὡς αἶνος ἀνδρῶν, πάντοθεν μετρεύμενα.
σῆμα δέ τοι τόδ᾽ ἔρεξεν ἀριφραδὲς Εὔγαμος, ᾧ σὺ
πολλῶν πενεστέων ἦσθα προσφιλέστατος.

Ἀπεδέχετο δὲ πάντων μᾶλλον Ὅμηρον, οὗ καὶ
εἰς ὕπνον ἰὼν πάντως τι ἀνεγίνωσκεν, ἀλλὰ καὶ
ὄρθρου λέγων ἐπὶ τὸν ἐρώμενον ἀπιέναι ὁπότε
βούλοιτο ἀναγνῶναι. τόν τε Πίνδαρον ἔφασκε
δεινὸν εἶναι φωνῆς ἐμπλῆσαι καὶ ὀνομάτων καὶ
ῥημάτων εὐπορίαν παρασχεῖν. Ἴωνα δὲ καὶ ἐχαρα-
κτήριζε νέος ὤν.

32 Διήκουσε δὲ καὶ Ἱππονίκου τοῦ γεωμέτρου· ὃν
καὶ ἔσκωψε τὰ μὲν ἄλλα νωθρὸν ὄντα καὶ χασμώδη,
ἐν δὲ τῇ τέχνῃ τεθεωρημένον, εἰπὼν τὴν γεωμετρίαν
αὐτοῦ χάσκοντος εἰς τὸ στόμα ἐμπτῆναι. τοῦτον
καὶ παρακόψαντα ἀναλαβὼν οἴκοι ἐς τοσοῦτον
ἐθεράπευσεν, ἐς ὅσον ἀποκαταστῆσαι. Κράτητος
δὲ ἐκλιπόντος κατέσχε τὴν σχολήν, ἐκχωρήσαντος
αὐτῷ Σωκρατίδου τινός. διὰ δὲ τὸ περὶ πάντων
ἐπέχειν οὐδὲ βιβλίον, φασί τινες, συνέγραψεν· οἱ
δέ, ὅτι ἐφωράθη ⟨Κράντορος⟩ τινὰ διορθῶν, ἅ φασιν
οἱ μὲν ἐκδοῦναι, οἱ δὲ κατακαῦσαι. ἐῴκει δὴ
θαυμάζειν καὶ τὸν Πλάτωνα καὶ τὰ βιβλία ἐκέ-
33 κτητο αὐτοῦ. ἀλλὰ καὶ τὸν Πύρρωνα κατά τινας
ἐζηλώκει καὶ τῆς διαλεκτικῆς εἴχετο καὶ τῶν

---

[a] *Anth. Plan.* ii. 382.
[b] If this be so, the study of the poet Ion (§ 31) must have remained unpublished.

And again upon Menodorus, the favourite of Eugamus, one of his fellow-students [a] :

Far, far away are Phrygia and sacred Thyatira, thy native land, Menodorus, son of Cadanus. But to unspeakable Acheron the ways are equal, from whatever place they be measured, as the proverb saith. To thee Eugamus raised this far-seen monument, for thou wert dearest to him of all who for him toiled.

He esteemed Homer above all the poets and would always read a passage from him before going to sleep. And in the morning he would say, whenever he wanted to read Homer, that he would pay a visit to his dear love. Pindar too he declared matchless for imparting fullness of diction and for affording a copious store of words and phrases. And in his youth he made a special study of Ion.

He also attended the lectures of the geometer Hipponicus, at whom he pointed a jest as one who was in all besides a listless, yawning sluggard but yet proficient in his subject. " Geometry," he said, " must have flown into his mouth while it was agape." When this man's mind gave way, Arcesilaus took him to his house and nursed him until he was completely restored. He took over the school on the death of Crates, a certain Socratides having retired in his favour. According to some, one result of his suspending judgement on all matters was that he never so much as wrote a book.[b] Others relate that he was caught revising some works of Crantor, which according to some he published, according to others he burnt. He would seem to have held Plato in admiration, and he possessed a copy of his works. Some represent him as emulous of Pyrrho as well. He was devoted to dialectic and adopted the methods

409

Ἐρετρικῶν ἥπτετο λόγων, ὅθεν καὶ ἐλέγετο ἐπ'
αὐτοῦ ὑπ' Ἀρίστωνος·

πρόσθε Πλάτων, ὄπιθεν Πύρρων, μέσσος Διόδωρος.

καὶ ὁ Τίμων ἐπ' αὐτοῦ φησιν οὕτως·

τῇ γὰρ ἔχων Μενεδήμου ὑπὸ στέρνοισι μόλιβδον
θεύσεται ἢ Πύρρωνα τὸ πᾶν κρέας ἢ Διόδωρον.

καὶ διαλιπὼν αὐτὸν ποιεῖ λέγοντα·

νήξομαι εἰς Πύρρωνα καὶ εἰς σκολιὸν Διόδωρον.

Ἦν δὲ καὶ ἀξιωματικώτατος καὶ συνηγμένος
καὶ ἐν τῇ λαλιᾷ διαστατικὸς τῶν ὀνομάτων, ἐπι-
34 κόπτης θ' ἱκανῶς καὶ παρρησιαστής· διὸ καὶ πάλιν
ὁ Τίμων οὑτωσὶ περὶ αὐτοῦ·

καὶ * νόον αἰμυλίοις[1] ἐπιπλήξεσιν ἐγκαταμιγνύς.

ὅθεν καὶ πρὸς τὸν θρασύτερον διαλεγόμενον νεανίσκον, "οὐ λήψεταί τις," ἔφη, "τοῦτον ἀστραγάλῳ;"
πρὸς δὲ τὸν αἰτίαν ἔχοντα περαίνεσθαι, ὡς ἀν-
ήνεγκεν αὐτῷ ὅτι οὐ δοκεῖ ἕτερον ἑτέρου μεῖζον
εἶναι, ἠρώτησεν εἰ οὐδὲ τὸ δεκαδάκτυλον τοῦ ἑξα-
δακτύλου. Ἥμονος δέ τινος Χίου ἀειδοῦς ὄντος
καὶ ὑπολαμβάνοντος εἶναι καλοῦ καὶ ἐν χλανίσιν
ἀεὶ ἀναστρεφομένου εἰπόντος ὅτι οὐ δοκεῖ αὐτῷ
⟨ὁ⟩ σοφὸς ἐρασθήσεσθαι, ἔφη, πότερον οὐδ' ἐὰν
οὕτω καλὸς ᾖ τις ὥσπερ σὺ οὐδ' ἐὰν οὕτω καλὰ
ἱμάτια ἔχῃ; ἐπεὶ δὲ καὶ παρακίναιδος ὢν ὡς εἰς
βαρὺν τὸν Ἀρκεσίλαον ἔφη·

[1] καὶ νέον μη λησῃς vulg.: νόον Casaubon: αἰμυλίοις Wilam.:
παίγνιον αἰμυλίως (inter alia) Wachs.

---

* A parody of Homer, Il. vi. 181 : a chimaera has a lion's
front, a dragon's tail, and the body of a goat.

of argument introduced by the Eretrian school. On account of this Ariston said of him :

> Plato the head of him, Pyrrho the tail, midway Diodorus.[c]

And Timon speaks of him thus [b] :

> Having the lead of Menedemus at his heart, he will run either to that mass of flesh, Pyrrho, or to Diodorus.

And a little farther on he introduces him as saying :

> I shall swim to Pyrrho and to crooked Diodorus.

He was highly axiomatic and concise, and in his discourse fond of distinguishing the meaning of terms. He was satirical enough, and outspoken. This is why Timon speaks of him again as follows :

> And mixing sound sense with wily cavils.[c]

Hence, when a young man talked more boldly than was becoming, Arcesilaus exclaimed, " Will no one beat him at a game of knuckle-bone ? " Again, when some one of immodest life denied that one thing seemed to him greater than another, he rejoined, "Then six inches and ten inches are all the same to you ? " There was a certain Hemon, a Chian, who, though ugly, fancied himself to be handsome, and always went about in fine clothes. He having propounded as his opinion that the wise man will never fall in love, Arcesilaus replied, " What, not with one so handsome as you and so handsomely dressed ? " And when one of loose life, to imply that Arcesilaus was arrogant, addressed him thus [d] :

---

[b] *Cf.* Hom. *Od.* v. 346.

[c] Or possibly with Wachsmuth : " mixing jest in wily fashion (αἱμυλίως) with abuse."

[d] Nauck, *T.G.F.²*, *Adesp.* 282.

85 ἔξεστ' ἐρωτᾶν πότνιά σ' ἢ σιγὴν ἔχω;
ὑπολαβὼν ἔφη·

γύναι, τί μοι τραχεῖα κοὐκ εἰθισμένως
λαλεῖς;

στωμύλου δὲ ἀγεννοῦς πράγματα αὐτῷ παρέχοντος
ἔφη·

ἀκόλασθ' ὁμιλεῖν γίγνεται δούλων τέκνα.

ἄλλου δὲ πολλὰ φλυαροῦντος οὐδὲ τίτθης αὐτὸν
χαλεπῆς τετυχηκέναι ἔφη· τισὶ δὲ οὐδὲ ἀπεκρίνετο.
πρὸς δὲ τὸν δανειστικὸν καὶ φιλόλογον εἰπόντα τι
ἀγνοεῖν, ἔφη·

λήθουσι γάρ τοι κἀνέμων διέξοδοι
θήλειαν ὄρνιν, πλὴν ὅταν τόκος παρῇ.

ἔστι δὲ ταῦτα ἐκ τοῦ Οἰνομάου τοῦ Σοφοκλέους.

86 Πρὸς Ἀλεξίνειόν τινα διαλεκτικὸν μὴ δυνάμενον
κατ' ἀξίαν τῶν Ἀλεξίνου τι διηγήσασθαι τὸ
Φιλοξένῳ πρὸς τοὺς πλινθιακοὺς πραχθὲν εἶπεν·
ἐκεῖνος γὰρ τὰ αὑτοῦ κακῶς ᾄδοντας τούτους
καταλαβὼν αὐτὸς τὰς πλίνθους αὐτῶν συνεπάτησεν,
εἰπών, " ὡς ὑμεῖς τὰ ἐμὰ διαφθείρετε, οὕτω κἀγὼ
τὰ ὑμέτερα." ἤχθετο οὖν δὴ τοῖς μὴ καθ' ὥραν
τὰ μαθήματα ἀνειληφόσι. φυσικῶς δέ πως ἐν τῷ
διαλέγεσθαι ἐχρῆτο τῷ Φημ' ἐγώ, καί, Οὐ συγ-
καταθήσεται τούτοις ὁ δεῖνα, εἰπὼν τοὔνομα· ὁ

---

[a] Nauck, *T.G.F.*[2], *Adesp.* 283 : *cf.* Wilam. *Antiq. v.
Kar.* p. 74.
[b] Nauck, *T.G.F.*[2], Eur. 976.
[c] Nauck, *T.G.F.*[2], Soph. 436.
[d] " Men pay little heed to obvious facts except when their
own interests are concerned." So A. C. Pearson, *ad loc.*,

> Queen, may I speak, or must I silence keep?

his reply was [a]:

> Woman, why talk so harshly, not as thou art wont?

When some talkative person of no family caused him considerable trouble, he cited the line [b]:

> Right ill to live with are the sons of slaves.

Of another who talked much nonsense he said that he could not have had even a nurse to scold him. And some persons he would not so much as answer. To a money-lending student, upon his confessing ignorance of something or other, Arcesilaus replied with two lines from the *Oenomaus* of Sophocles [c]:

> Be sure the hen-bird knows not from what quarter the wind blows until she looks for a new brood in the nest. [d]

A certain dialectic, a follower of Alexinus, was unable to repeat properly some argument of his teacher, whereupon Arcesilaus reminded him of the story of Philoxenus and the brickmakers. He found them singing some of his melodies out of tune ; so he retaliated by trampling on the bricks they were making, saying, " If you spoil my work, I'll spoil yours." He was, moreover, genuinely annoyed with any who took up their studies too late. By some natural impulse he was betrayed into using such phrases as " I assert," and " So-and-so " (mentioning the name) " will not assent to this." [e] And this trait

Soph. *Fragments*, 477 (vol. ii. p. 130), who takes διέξοδοι in the more specific sense : " passage of the winds (through her body)," the reference being to the old fable of the wind-egg (Aristoph. *Aves*, 695, Aristot. *Hist. An.* vi. 2, 560 a 6). To the usurer τόκος would suggest interest on loans.

[e] The use of these phrases was inconsistent with the suspension of judgement professed by Arcesilaus.

καὶ πολλοὶ τῶν μαθητῶν ἐζήλουν ⟨ὡς⟩ καὶ τὴν
ῥητορείαν καὶ πᾶν τὸ σχῆμα.

37 Ἦν δὲ καὶ εὑρεσιλογώτατος ἀπαντῆσαι εὐστόχως
καὶ ἐπὶ τὸ προκείμενον ἀνενεγκεῖν τὴν περίοδον
τῶν λόγων καὶ ἅπαντι συναρμόσασθαι καιρῷ.
πειστικός τε ὑπὲρ πάνθ' ὁντινοῦν· παρὸ καὶ πλείους
πρὸς αὐτὸν ἀπήντων εἰς τὴν σχολὴν καίπερ
ὑπ' ὀξύτητος αὐτοῦ ἐπιπληττόμενοι. ἀλλ' ἔφερον
ἡδέως· καὶ γὰρ ἦν ἀγαθὸς σφόδρα καὶ ἐλπίδων
ὑποπιμπλὰς τοὺς ἀκούοντας. ἔν τε τῷ βίῳ
κοινωνικώτατος ἐγένετο καὶ εὐεργετῆσαι πρόχειρος
ἦν καὶ λαθεῖν τὴν χάριν ἀτυφότατος. εἰσελθὼν
γοῦν ποτὲ πρὸς Κτησίβιον νοσοῦντα καὶ ἰδὼν
ἀπορίᾳ θλιβόμενον, κρύφα βαλάντιον ὑπέθηκε τῷ
προσκεφαλαίῳ· καὶ ὃς εὑρών, " Ἀρκεσιλάου," φησί,
" τὸ παίγνιον." ἀλλὰ καὶ ἄλλοτε χιλίας ἀπέστειλεν.

38 Ἀρχίαν τε τὸν Ἀρκάδα Εὐμένει συστήσας
πολλῆς ἐποίησε τυχεῖν τῆς ἀξίας. ἐλευθέριός τε
ὢν καὶ ἀφιλαργυρώτατος εἰς τὰς ἀργυρικὰς δείξεις
ἀπήντα πρῶτος, καὶ ἐπὶ τὴν Ἀρχεκράτους καὶ
Καλλικράτους τὰς χρυσιαίας παντὸς ἔσπευδε
μᾶλλον. συχνοῖς τε ἐπήρκει καὶ συνηράνιζε· καὶ
ποτέ τινος ἀργυρώματα λαβόντος εἰς ὑποδοχὴν
φίλων καὶ ἀποστεροῦντος οὐκ ἀπήτησεν οὐδὲ
προσεποιήθη. οἱ δέ φασιν ἐπίτηδες χρῆσαι καὶ
ἀποδιδόντος, ἐπεὶ πένης ἦν, χαρίσασθαι. ἦν μὲν
οὖν αὐτῷ καὶ ἐν Πιτάνῃ περιουσία, ἀφ' ἧς ἀπέστειλεν αὐτῷ Πυλάδης ὁ ἀδελφός. ἀλλὰ καὶ

many of his pupils imitated, as they did also his style of speaking and his whole address.

Very fertile in invention, he could meet objection acutely or bring the course of discussion back to the point at issue, and fit it to every occasion. In persuasiveness he had no equal, and this all the more drew pupils to the school, although they were in terror of his pungent wit. But they willingly put up with that ; for his goodness was extraordinary, and he inspired his pupils with hopes. He showed the greatest generosity in private life, being ever ready to confer benefits, yet most modestly anxious to conceal the favour. For instance, he once called upon Ctesibius when he was ill and, seeing in what straits he was, quietly put a purse under his pillow. He, when he found it, said, " This is the joke of Arcesilaus." Moreover, on another occasion, he sent him 1000 drachmas.

Again, by introducing Archias the Arcadian to Eumenes, he caused him to be advanced to great dignity. And, as he was very liberal, caring very little for money, so he was the first to attend performances where seats were paid for, and he was above all eager to go to those of Archecrates and Callicrates, for which the fee was a gold piece. And he helped many people and collected subscriptions for them. Some one once borrowed his silver plate in order to entertain friends and never brought it back, but Arcesilaus did not ask him for it and pretended it had not been borrowed. Another version of the story is that he lent it on purpose, and, when it was returned, made the borrower a present of it because he was poor. He had property in Pitane from which his brother Pylades sent him supplies. Furthermore, Eumenes,

ἐχορήγει αὐτῷ πολλὰ Εὐμένης ὁ τοῦ Φιλεταίρου·
διὸ καὶ τούτῳ μόνῳ τῶν ἄλλων βασιλέων προσ-
εφώνει.

39 Πολλῶν δὲ καὶ τὸν Ἀντίγονον θεραπευόντων
καὶ ὁπότε ἥκοι ἀπαντώντων αὐτὸς ἡσύχαζε, μὴ
βουλόμενος προεμπίπτειν εἰς γνῶσιν. φίλος τε
ἦν μάλιστα Ἱεροκλεῖ τῷ τὴν Μουνιχίαν ἔχοντι
καὶ τὸν Πειραιᾶ· ἔν τε ταῖς ἑορταῖς κατῄει πρὸς
αὐτὸν ἑκάστοτε. καὶ δὴ καὶ πολλὰ ἐκείνου συμ-
πείθοντος ὥστ᾽ ἀσπάσασθαι τὸν Ἀντίγονον, οὐκ
ἐπείσθη, ἀλλ᾽ ἕως πυλῶν ἐλθὼν ἀνέστρεψε. μετά
τε τὴν Ἀντιγόνου ναυμαχίαν πολλῶν προσιόντων
καὶ ἐπιστόλια παρακλητικὰ γραφόντων αὐτὸς
ἐσιώπησεν. ἀλλ᾽ οὖν ὅμως ὑπὲρ τῆς πατρίδος
ἐπρέσβευσεν εἰς Δημητριάδα πρὸς Ἀντίγονον καὶ
οὐκ ἐπέτυχε. τὸ πᾶν δὴ διέτριβεν ἐν τῇ Ἀκαδημείᾳ
τὸν πολιτισμὸν ἐκτοπίζων.

40 Καί ποτε δὴ καὶ Ἀθήνησιν ἐν τῷ Πειραιεῖ πρὸς
τὰς θέσεις λέγων ἐχρόνισεν, οἰκείως ἔχων πρὸς
Ἱεροκλέα· ἐφ᾽ ᾧ καὶ πρός τινων διεβάλλετο.
πολυτελὴς δὲ ἄγαν ὤν—καὶ τί γὰρ ἄλλο ἢ ἕτερος
Ἀρίστιππος;—ἐπὶ τὰ δεῖπνα πρὸς τοὺς ὁμοιο-
τρόπους μέν, πλὴν ἀλλ᾽ ἀπήντα. καὶ Θεοδότῃ τε
καὶ Φίλᾳ ταῖς Ἠλείαις ἑταίραις συνῴκει φανερῶς
καὶ πρὸς τοὺς διασύροντας προεφέρετο τὰς Ἀριστίππου χρείας. φιλομειράκιός τε ἦν καὶ κατα-
φερής· ὅθεν οἱ περὶ Ἀρίστωνα τὸν Χῖον στωικοὶ

---

[a] The reference may be to one of the naval victories gained
by Antigonus over the Egyptian fleet towards the end of
his reign, at Cos and again at Andros. See W. W. Tarn,
Antigonus Gonatas, pp. 378, 461-6.

[b] It has been suggested that the sense would be improved

the son of Philetaerus, furnished him with large sums, and for this reason Eumenes was the only one of the contemporary kings to whom he dedicated any of his works.

And whereas many persons courted Antigonus and went to meet him whenever he came to Athens, Arcesilaus remained at home, not wishing to thrust himself upon his acquaintance. He was on the best of terms with Hierocles, the commandant in Munichia and Piraeus, and at every festival would go down to see him. And though Hierocles joined in urging him to pay his respects to Antigonus, he was not prevailed upon, but, after going as far as the gates, turned back. And after the battle at sea,[a] when many went to Antigonus or wrote him flattering letters, he held his peace. However, on behalf of his native city, he did go to Demetrias as envoy to Antigonus, but failed in his mission. He spent his time wholly in the Academy, shunning politics.

Once indeed, when at Athens, he stopped too long in the Piraeus, discussing themes, out of friendship for Hierocles, and for this he was censured by certain persons.[b] He was very lavish, in short another Aristippus, and he was fond of dining well, but only with those who shared his tastes. He lived openly with Theodete and Phila, the Elean courtesans, and to those who censured him he quoted the maxims of Aristippus. He was also fond of boys and very susceptible. Hence he was accused by Ariston of

if Ἀθήνησι were transposed to come between τὸν and πολιτισμόν, adding καὶ πρὸς τὰς θέσεις λέγων after πολιτισμὸν ἐκτοπίζων instead of after Πειραιεῖ. This account seems in some respects to confirm the impression conveyed by the sentence a little higher up, beginning πολλῶν δὲ καὶ τὸν Ἀντίγονον . . . ἑκάστοτε.

ἐπεκάλουν αὐτῷ, φθορέα τῶν νέων καὶ κιναιδο-
41 λόγον καὶ θρασὺν ἀποκαλοῦντες. καὶ γὰρ δὴ καὶ
Δημητρίου τοῦ πλεύσαντος εἰς Κυρήνην ἐπὶ πλέον
ἐρασθῆναι λέγεται, καὶ Κλεοχάρους τοῦ Μυρλεανοῦ·
ἐφ' ᾧ καὶ πρὸς τοὺς κωμάσαντας εἰπεῖν αὐτὸς μὲν
θέλειν ἀνοῖξαι, ἐκεῖνον δὲ διακωλύειν. τούτου δὲ
ἤρων καὶ Δημοχάρης ὁ Λάχητος καὶ Πυθοκλῆς ὁ
τοῦ Βουγέλου· οὓς καταλαβὼν ὑπ' ἀνεξικακίας
παραχωρεῖν ἔφη. διὰ ταῦτα δὴ οὖν ἔδακνόν τε
αὐτὸν οἱ προειρημένοι καὶ ἐπέσκωπτον ὡς φίλοχλον
καὶ φιλόδοξον· μάλιστα δὲ ἐπετίθεντο αὐτῷ οἱ
περὶ Ἱερώνυμον τὸν Περιπατητικόν,[a] ὁπότε συνάγοι
τοὺς φίλους εἰς τὴν Ἀλκυονέως τοῦ Ἀντιγόνου
υἱοῦ ἡμέραν, εἰς ἣν ἱκανὰ χρήματα ἀπέστελλεν
42 Ἀντίγονος πρὸς ἀπόλαυσιν. ἔνθα καὶ παραιτού-
μενος ἑκάστοτε τὰς ἐπικυλικείους ἐξηγήσεις πρὸς
Ἀριδείκην προτείνοντά τι θεώρημα καὶ ἀξιοῦντα
εἰς αὐτὸ λέγειν εἶπεν, "ἀλλ' αὐτὸ τοῦτο μάλιστα
φιλοσοφίας ἴδιον, τὸ τὸν καιρὸν ἑκάστων ἐπίστασθαι." εἰς δὲ τὸ διαβαλλόμενον αὐτοῦ φίλοχλον καὶ Τίμων τά τ' ἄλλα φησίν, ἀτὰρ δὴ καὶ
τοῦτον τὸν τρόπον·

ὣς εἰπὼν ὄχλοιο περίστασιν εἰσκατέδυνεν.
οἱ δέ μιν ἠΰτε γλαῦκα πέρι σπίζαι τερατοῦντο
ἠλέματον δεικνύντες, ὁθούνεκεν ὀχλοάρεσκος.
οὐ μέγα πρῆγμα, τάλας· τί πλατύνεαι ἠλίθιος ὥς;

Οὐ μὴν ἀλλ' οὕτως ἄτυφος ἦν ὥστε τοῖς μα-

---

[a] οἱ περὶ Ἱερώνυμον τὸν Περιπατητικόν is said by Stephanus
to be a marginal gloss. The reading of the mss. is παρὰ
Ἱερωνύμῳ τῷ Π.
[b] Cf. infra, v. 59.

Chios, the Stoic, and his followers, who called him a corrupter of youth and a shameless teacher of immorality. He is said to have been particularly enamoured of Demetrius who sailed to Cyrene, and of Cleochares of Myrlea ; of him the story is told that, when a band of revellers came to the door, he told them that for his part he was willing to admit them but that Cleochares would not let him. This same youth had amongst his admirers Demochares the son of Laches, and Pythocles the son of Bugelus, and once when Arcesilaus had caught them, with great forbearance he ordered them off. For all this he was assailed and ridiculed by the critics above-mentioned, as a friend of the mob who courted popularity. The most virulent attacks were made upon him in the circle of Hieronymus the Peripatetic,[a] whenever he collected his friends to keep the birth-day of Halcyoneus, son of Antigonus, an occasion for which Antigonus used to send large sums of money to be spent in merrymaking. There he had always shunned discussion over the wine ; and when Aridices, proposing a certain question, requested him to speak upon it, he replied, "The peculiar province of philosophy is just this, to know that there is a time for all things." As to the charge brought against him that he was the friend of the mob, Timon, among many other things, has the following [b] :

So saying, he plunged into the surrounding crowd. And they were amazed at him, like chaffinches about an owl, pointing him out as vain, because he was a flatterer of the mob. And why, insignificant thing that you are, do you puff yourself out like a simpleton ? [c]

And yet for all that he was modest enough to

[c] Frag. 34 D. *Cf.* the rhythm, Hom. *Il.* i. 326 and iv. 482.

θηταῖς παρῄνει καὶ ἄλλων ἀκούειν. καί τινος Χίου νεανίσκου μὴ εὐαρεστουμένου τῇ διατριβῇ αὐτοῦ, ἀλλ' Ἱερωνύμου τοῦ προειρημένου, αὐτὸς ἀπαγαγὼν συνέστησε τῷ φιλοσόφῳ, παραινέσας εὐτακτεῖν.

43 Χάριεν δ' αὐτοῦ φέρεται κἀκεῖνο· πρὸς τὸν πυθόμενον διὰ τί ἐκ μὲν τῶν ἄλλων μεταβαίνουσιν εἰς τὴν Ἐπικούρειον, ἐκ δὲ τῶν Ἐπικουρείων οὐδέποτε, ἔφη, '' ἐκ μὲν γὰρ ἀνδρῶν γάλλοι γίνονται, ἐκ δὲ γάλλων ἄνδρες οὐ γίνονται.''

Λοιπὸν δὲ πρὸς τῷ τέλει γενόμενος ἅπαντα καταλέλοιπε Πυλάδῃ τἀδελφῷ τὰ αὐτοῦ, ἀνθ' ὧν ἐς Χῖον αὐτὸν προήγαγε τὸν Μοιρέαν λανθάνων, κἀκεῖθεν εἰς Ἀθήνας ἀπήγαγε. περιὼν δὲ οὔτε γύναιον ἐπηγάγετο οὔτ' ἐπαιδοποιήσατο. τρεῖς τε διαθήκας ποιησάμενος ἔθετο τὴν μὲν ἐν Ἐρετρίᾳ πρὸς Ἀμφίκριτον, τὴν δ' Ἀθήνησι παρά τινας τῶν φίλων, τὴν δὲ τρίτην ἀπέστειλεν εἰς οἶκον πρὸς Θαυμασίαν ἕνα τινὰ τῶν ἀναγκαίων, ἀξιώσας διατηρῆσαι· πρὸς ὃν καὶ γράφει ταυτί·

'' Ἀρκεσίλαος Θαυμασίᾳ χαίρειν.

44 '' Δέδωκα Διογένει διαθήκας ἐμαυτοῦ κομίσαι πρὸς σέ· διὰ γὰρ τὸ πολλάκις ἀρρωστεῖν καὶ τὸ σῶμα ἀσθενῶς ἔχειν ἔδοξέ μοι διαθέσθαι, ἵν' εἴ τι γένοιτο ἀλλοῖον, μήτι σὲ ἠδικηκὼς ἀπίω τὸν εἰς ἔμ' ἐκτενῶς οὕτω πεφιλοτιμημένον. καὶ ἀξιοπιστότατος δ' εἶ τῶν ἐνθάδε σύ μοι τηρῶν αὐτὰς διά τε τὴν ἡλικίαν καὶ τὴν πρὸς ἡμᾶς οἰκειότητα. πειρῶ οὖν, μεμνημένος διότι σοι πίστιν τὴν ἀναγκαιοτάτην παρακατατίθεμαι, δίκαιος ἡμῖν εἶναι,

recommend his pupils to hear other philosophers. And when a certain youth from Chios was not well pleased with his lectures and preferred those of the above-mentioned Hieronymus, Arcesilaus himself took him and introduced him to that philosopher, with an injunction to behave well.

Another pleasant story told of him is this. Some one had inquired why it was that pupils from all the other schools went over to Epicurus, but converts were never made from the Epicureans : " Because men may become eunuchs, but a eunuch never becomes a man," was his answer.

At last, being near his end, he left all his property to his brother Pylades, because, unknown to Moereas, he had taken him to Chios and thence brought him to Athens. In all his life he never married nor had any children. He made three wills : the first he left at Eretria in the charge of Amphicritus, the second at Athens in the charge of certain friends, while the third he dispatched to his home to Thaumasias, one of his relatives, with the request that he would keep it safe. To this man he also wrote as follows :

" Arcesilaus to Thaumasias greeting.

" I have given Diogenes my will to be conveyed to you. For, owing to my frequent illnesses and the weak state of my body, I decided to make a will, in order that, if anything untoward should happen, you, who have been so devotedly attached to me, should not suffer by my decease. You are the most deserving of all those in this place to be entrusted with the will, on the score both of age and of relationship to me. Remember then that I have reposed the most absolute confidence in you, and strive to

ὅπως ὅσον ἐπὶ σοὶ τὰ κατ᾽ ἐμὲ εὐσχημόνως ᾖ μοι
διῳκημένα. κεῖνται δὲ ᾽Αθήνησιν αὗται παρά
τισι τῶν γνωρίμων καὶ ἐν ᾽Ερετρίᾳ παρ᾽ ᾽Αμφι-
κρίτῳ.᾽᾽

᾽Ετελεύτησε δέ, ὥς φησιν ῞Ερμιππος, ἄκρατον
ἐμφορηθεὶς πολὺν καὶ παρακόψας, ἤδη γεγονὼς
ἔτος πέμπτον καὶ ἑβδομηκοστόν, ἀποδεχθεὶς πρὸς
᾽Αθηναίων ὡς οὐδείς.

45 ῎Εστι καὶ εἰς τοῦτον ἡμῶν·

᾽Αρκεσίλαε, τί μοι τόσον οἶνον ἄκρητον ἀφειδῶς
ἔσπασας, ὥστε φρενῶν ἐκτὸς ὄλισθες ἑῶν;
οἰκτείρω σ᾽ οὐ τόσσον ἐπεὶ θάνες, ἀλλ᾽ ὅτι Μούσας
ὕβρισας οὐ μετρίῃ χρησάμενος κύλικι.

Γεγόνασι δὲ καὶ ἄλλοι τρεῖς ᾽Αρκεσίλαοι· ποιητὴς
ἀρχαίας κωμῳδίας, ἄλλος ἐλεγείας, ἕτερος ἀγαλ-
ματοποιός· εἰς ὃν καὶ Σιμωνίδης ἐποίησεν ἐπίγραμμα τουτί·

᾽Αρτέμιδος τόδ᾽ ἄγαλμα, διηκόσιαι δ᾽ ἄρ᾽ ὁ μισθὸς
δραχμαὶ ταὶ Πάριαι, τῶν ἐπίσημα τράγος.
ἀσκητὸς δ᾽ ἐποίησεν ᾽Αθηναίης παλάμῃσιν
ἄξιος ᾽Αρκεσίλας υἱὸς ᾽Αριστοδίκου.

῾Ο δὲ προειρημένος φιλόσοφος, καθά φησιν
᾽Απολλόδωρος ἐν Χρονικοῖς, ἤκμαζε περὶ τὴν
εἰκοστὴν καὶ ἑκατοστὴν ᾽Ολυμπιάδα.

Κεφ. ζ΄. ΒΙΩΝ

46 Βίων τὸ μὲν γένος ἦν Βορυσθενίτης, ὧντινων δὲ
γονέων καὶ ἀφ᾽ οἵων πραγμάτων ἦξεν ἐπὶ φιλο-

deal justly by me, in order that, so far as you are concerned, the provisions I have made may be carried out with fitting dignity. A copy is deposited at Athens with some of my acquaintance, and another in Eretria with Amphicritus."

He died, according to Hermippus, through drinking too freely of unmixed wine which affected his reason ; he was already seventy-five and regarded by the Athenians with unparalleled good-will.

I have written upon him as follows [a] :

Why, pray, Arcesilaus, didst thou quaff so unsparingly unmixed wine as to go out of thy mind ? I pity thee not so much for thy death as because thou didst insult the Muses by immoderate potations.

Three other men have borne the name of Arcesilaus : a poet of the Old Comedy, another poet who wrote elegies, and a sculptor besides, on whom Simonides composed this epigram [b] :

This is a statue of Artemis and its cost two hundred Parian drachmas, which bear a goat for their device. It was made by Arcesilaus, the worthy son of Aristodicus, well practised in the arts of Athena.

According to Apollodorus in his *Chronology*, the philosopher described in the foregoing flourished about the 120th Olympiad.[c]

CHAPTER 7. BION (third century B.C.)

Bion was by birth a citizen of Borysthenes [Olbia] ; who his parents were, and what his circumstances before he took to philosophy, he himself told

---

[a] *Anth. Pal.* vii. 104.
[b] *Anth. Plan.* iii. 9.   [c] 300–296 B.C.

DIOGENES LAERTIUS

σοφίαν, αὐτὸς Ἀντιγόνῳ διασαφεῖ. ἐρομένου γὰρ αὐτὸν

τίς πόθεν εἶς ἀνδρῶν; πόθι τοι πόλις ἠδὲ τοκῆες;

αἰσθόμενος ὅτι προδιαβέβληται, φησὶ πρὸς αὐτόν· '' ἐμοὶ ὁ πατὴρ μὲν ἦν ἀπελεύθερος, τῷ ἀγκῶνι ἀπομυσσόμενος—διεδήλου δὲ τὸν ταριχέμπορον— γένος Βορυσθενίτης, ἔχων οὐ πρόσωπον, ἀλλὰ συγγραφὴν ἐπὶ τοῦ προσώπου, τῆς τοῦ δεσπότου πικρίας σύμβολον· μήτηρ δὲ οἵαν ὁ τοιοῦτος ἂν γήμαι, ἀπ᾽ οἰκήματος. ἔπειτα ὁ πατὴρ παρα- τελωνησάμενός τι πανοίκιος ἐπράθη μεθ᾽ ἡμῶν. καί με ἀγοράζει τις ῥήτωρ νεώτερον ὄντα καὶ εὔχαριν· ὃς καὶ ἀποθνήσκων κατέλιπέ μοι πάντα.
47 κἀγὼ κατακαύσας αὐτοῦ τὰ συγγράμματα καὶ πάντα συγχύσας Ἀθήναζε ἦλθον καὶ ἐφιλοσόφησα.

ταύτης τοι γενεῆς τε καὶ αἵματος εὔχομαι εἶναι.

ταῦτά ἐστι τὰ κατ᾽ ἐμέ. ὥστε παυσάσθωσαν Περσαῖός τε καὶ Φιλωνίδης ἱστοροῦντες αὐτά· σκόπει δέ με ἐξ ἐμαυτοῦ.''

Καὶ ἦν ὡς ἀληθῶς ὁ Βίων τὰ μὲν ἄλλα πολύ- τροπος καὶ σοφιστὴς ποικίλος καὶ πλείστας ἀφ- ορμὰς δεδωκὼς τοῖς βουλομένοις καθιππάζεσθαι φιλοσοφίας· ἔν τισι δὲ καὶ πομπικὸς καὶ ἀπολαῦσαι τύφου δυνάμενος. πλεῖστά τε καταλέλοιπεν ὑπο- μνήματα, ἀλλὰ καὶ ἀποφθέγματα χρειώδη πραγ- ματείαν περιέχοντα. οἷον ὀνειδιζόμενος ἐπὶ τῷ μὴ θηρᾶσαι μειράκιον,'' οὐχ οἷόν τε,'' εἶπεν, '' ἁπαλὸν
48 τυρὸν ἀγκίστρῳ ἐπισπᾶσθαι.'' ἐρωτηθείς ποτε

Antigonus in plain terms. For, when Antigonus
inquired :

Who among men, and whence, are you ? What is your
city and your parents ?[a]

he, knowing that he had already been maligned to
the king, replied, " My father was a freedman, who
wiped his nose on his sleeve "—meaning that he
was a dealer in salt fish—" a native of Borysthenes,
with no face to show, but only the writing on his
face, a token of his master's severity. My mother
was such as a man like my father would marry, from
a brothel. Afterwards my father, who had cheated
the revenue in some way, was sold with all his
family. And I, then a not ungraceful youngster,
was bought by a certain rhetorician, who on his
death left me all he had. And I burnt his books,
scraped everything together, came to Athens and
turned philosopher.

This is the stock and this the blood from which I boast
to have sprung.[b]

Such is my story. It is high time, then, that Persaeus
and Philonides left off recounting it. Judge me by
myself."

In truth Bion was in other respects a shifty
character, a subtle sophist, and one who had given
the enemies of philosophy many an occasion to
blaspheme, while in certain respects he was even
pompous and able to indulge in arrogance. He left
very many memoirs, and also sayings of useful
application. For example, when he was reproached
for not paying court to a youth, his excuse was,
" You can't get hold of a soft cheese with a hook."
Being once asked who suffers most from anxiety, he

τίς μᾶλλον ἀγωνιᾷ, ἔφη, " ὁ τὰ μέγιστα βουλόμενος εὐημερεῖν." ἐρωτηθεὶς εἰ γήμαι—ἀναφέρεται γὰρ καὶ εἰς τοῦτον—ἔφη, " ἐὰν μὲν γήμῃς
αἰσχράν, ἕξεις ποινήν· ἂν δὲ καλήν, ἕξεις κοινήν."
τὸ γῆρας ἔλεγεν ὅρμον εἶναι τῶν κακῶν· εἰς αὐτὸ
γοῦν πάντα καταφεύγειν. τὴν δόξαν ⟨ἀρ⟩ετῶν¹
μητέρα εἶναι· τὸ κάλλος ἀλλότριον ἀγαθόν· τὸν
πλοῦτον νεῦρα πραγμάτων. πρὸς τὸν τὰ χωρία
κατεδηδοκότα, " τὸν μὲν Ἀμφιάραον," ἔφη, " ἡ
γῆ κατέπιε, σὺ δὲ τὴν γῆν." μέγα κακὸν τὸ μὴ
δύνασθαι φέρειν κακόν. κατεγίνωσκε δὲ καὶ τῶν
τοὺς ἀνθρώπους κατακαόντων μὲν ὡς ἀναισθήτους,
49 παρακαόντων δὲ ὡς αἰσθανομένους. ἔλεγε δὲ
συνεχὲς ὅτι αἱρετώτερόν ἐστι τὴν ὥραν ἄλλῳ
χαρίζεσθαι ἢ ἀλλοτρίας ἀποδρέπεσθαι· καὶ γὰρ
εἰς σῶμα βλάπτεσθαι καὶ εἰς ψυχήν. διέβαλε δὲ
καὶ τὸν Σωκράτην, λέγων ὡς εἰ μὲν εἶχεν Ἀλκιβιάδου χρείαν καὶ ἀπείχετο, μάταιος ἦν· εἰ δὲ μὴ
εἶχεν, οὐδὲν ἐποίει παράδοξον. εὔκολον ἔφασκε
τὴν εἰς ᾅδου ὁδόν· καταμύοντας γοῦν ἀπιέναι. τὸν
Ἀλκιβιάδην μεμφόμενος ἔλεγεν ὡς νέος μὲν ὢν
τοὺς ἄνδρας ἀπαγάγοι τῶν γυναικῶν, νεανίσκος
δὲ γενόμενος τὰς γυναῖκας τῶν ἀνδρῶν. ἐν
Ῥόδῳ τὰ ῥητορικὰ διασκούντων τῶν Ἀθηναίων
τὰ φιλοσοφούμενα ἐδίδασκε· πρὸς οὖν τὸν αἰτιασάμενον ἔφη, " πυροὺς ἐκόμισα καὶ κριθὰς πι-
πράσκω;"
50 Ἔλεγε δὲ τοὺς ἐν ᾅδου μᾶλλον ἂν κολάζεσθαι
εἰ ὁλοκλήροις καὶ μὴ τετρημένοις ἀγγείοις ὑδρο-

---

¹ ⟨ἀρ⟩ετῶν corr. H. Richards, ἐτῶν vulg.

replied, " He who is ambitious of the greatest prosperity." Being consulted by some one as to whether
he should marry—for this story is also told of Bion—
he made answer, " If the wife you marry be ugly,
she will be your bane ; if beautiful, you will not
keep her to yourself." [a] He called old age the
harbour of all ills ; at least they all take refuge
there. Renown he called the mother of virtues ;
beauty another's good ; wealth the sinews of success.
To some one who had devoured his patrimony he
said, " The earth swallowed Amphiaraus, but you
have swallowed your land." To be unable to bear
an ill is itself a great ill. He used to condemn those
who burnt men alive as if they could not feel, and
yet cauterized them as if they could. He used
repeatedly to say that to grant favours to another
was preferable to enjoying the favours of others.
For the latter means ruin to both body and soul.
He even abused Socrates, declaring that, if he felt
desire for Alcibiades and abstained, he was a fool ; if he
did not, his conduct was in no way remarkable. The
road to Hades, he used to say, was easy to travel ;
at any rate men passed away with their eyes shut.
He said in censure of Alcibiades that in his boyhood
he drew away the husbands from their wives, and as
a young man the wives from their husbands. When
the Athenians were absorbed in the practice of
rhetoric, he taught philosophy at Rhodes. To some
one who found fault with him for this he replied,
" How can I sell barley when what I brought to
market is wheat ? "

He used to say that those in Hades would be
more severely punished if the vessels in which they
drew water were whole instead of being pierced with

φόρουν. πρὸς τὸν ἀδολέσχην λιπαροῦντα αὐτῷ
συλλαβέσθαι, " τὸ ἱκανόν σοι ποιήσω," φησίν, " ἐὰν
παρακλήτους πέμψῃς καὶ αὐτὸς μὴ ἔλθῃς." πλέων
μετὰ πονηρῶν λῃσταῖς περιέπεσε· τῶν δέ, " ἀπολώ-
λαμεν," εἰπόντων, " ἐὰν γνωσθῶμεν," " ἐγὼ δέ
γε," φησίν, " ἐὰν μὴ γνωσθῶ." τὴν οἴησιν ἔλεγε
προκοπῆς ἐγκοπήν. πρὸς τὸν μικρολόγον πλούσιον,
" οὐχ οὗτος," ἔφη, " τὴν οὐσίαν κέκτηται, ἀλλ᾽ ἡ
οὐσία τοῦτον." ἔλεγε τοὺς μικρολόγους τῶν μὲν
ὑπαρχόντων ὡς ἰδίων ἐπιμελεῖσθαι, ὡς δ᾽ ἐξ
ἀλλοτρίων μηδὲν ὠφελεῖσθαι. τῇ μὲν ἀνδρείᾳ
νέους ὄντας ἔφη χρῆσθαι, τῇ δὲ φρονήσει γηράσκον-
51 τας ἀκμάζειν. τοσοῦτον διαφέρειν τὴν φρόνησιν
τῶν ἄλλων ἀρετῶν, ὅσον τὴν ὅρασιν τῶν ἄλλων
αἰσθήσεων. μὴ δεῖν ἔφασκεν ὀνειδίζειν τὸ γῆρας,
εἰς ὅ, ἔφη, πάντες εὐχόμεθα ἐλθεῖν. πρὸς τὸν
βάσκανον ἐσκυθρωπακότα, " οὐκ οἶδα," ἔφη,
" πότερον σοὶ κακὸν γέγονεν ἢ ἄλλῳ ἀγαθόν." τὴν
δυσγένειαν πονηρὸν ἔλεγεν εἶναι σύνοικον τῇ
παρρησίᾳ·

δουλοῖ γὰρ ἄνδρα, κἂν θρασύσπλαγχνός τις ᾖ.

τοὺς φίλους ὁποῖοι ἂν ὦσι συντηρεῖν, ἵνα μὴ
δοκοίημεν πονηροῖς κεχρῆσθαι ἢ χρηστοὺς παρ-
ῃτῆσθαι.

Οὗτος τὴν ἀρχὴν μὲν παρῃτεῖτο τὰ Ἀκαδημαϊκά,
καθ᾽ ὃν χρόνον ἤκουε Κράτητος· εἶτ᾽ ἐπανείλετο
τὴν κυνικὴν ἀγωγήν, λαβὼν τρίβωνα καὶ πήραν.
52 καὶ τί γὰρ ἄλλο μετεσκεύασεν αὐτὸν πρὸς

---

[a] Eur. *Hipp.* 424.
[b] *i.e.* he had his doubts. Reiske, however, by his con-

428

holes. To an importunate talker who wanted his
help he said, " I will satisfy your demand, if you will
only get others to plead your cause and stay away
yourself." On a voyage in bad company he fell in
with pirates. When his companions said, " We are
lost if we are discovered," " And I too," he replied,
" unless I am discovered." Conceit he styled a
hindrance to progress. Referring to a wealthy miser
he said, " He has not acquired a fortune ; the fortune
has acquired him." Misers, he said, took care of
property as if it belonged to them, but derived no
more benefit from it than if it belonged to others.
" When we are young," said he, " we are courageous,
but it is only in old age that prudence is at its height."
Prudence, he said, excels the other virtues as much
as sight excels the other senses. He used to say
that we ought not to heap reproaches on old age,
seeing that, as he said, we all hope to reach it. To
a slanderer who showed a grave face his words were,
" I don't know whether you have met with ill luck,
or your neighbour with good." He used to say that
low birth made a bad partner for free speech, for—

> It cows a man, however bold his heart.[a]

We ought, he remarked, to watch our friends and
see what manner of men they are, in order that we
may not be thought to associate with the bad or to
decline the friendship of the good.

Bion at the outset used to deprecate the Academic
doctrines,[b] even at the time when he was a pupil of
Crates. Then he adopted the Cynic discipline,
donning cloak and wallet. For little else was needed
to convert him to the doctrine of entire insensibility.

jecture προύρητο gives the statement a totally different turn,
viz. that Bion *had* at the outset *preferred* the Academy.

ἀπάθειαν; ἔπειτα ἐπὶ τὰ Θεοδώρεια μετῆλθε
διακούσας Θεοδώρου τοῦ ἀθέου κατὰ πᾶν εἶδος
λόγου σοφιστεύοντος· μεθ' ὃν Θεοφράστου διήκουσε
τοῦ περιπατητικοῦ. ἦν δὲ καὶ θεατρικὸς καὶ
πολὺς ἐν τῷ γελοίως διαφορῆσαι, φορτικοῖς ὀνόμασι κατὰ τῶν πραγμάτων χρώμενος. διὰ δὴ
οὖν τὸ παντὶ εἴδει λόγου κεκρᾶσθαί φασι λέγειν
ἐπ' αὐτοῦ τὸν Ἐρατοσθένην, ὡς πρῶτος Βίων τὴν
φιλοσοφίαν ἀνθινὰ ἐνέδυσεν. εὐφυὴς γὰρ ἦν καὶ
παρῳδῆσαι· οἷά ἐστιν αὐτοῦ καὶ ταῦτα·

ὦ πέπον Ἀρχύτα, ψαλληγενές, ὀλβιότυφε,
τῆς ὑπάτης ἔριδος πάντων ἐμπειρότατ' ἀνδρῶν.

53 καὶ ὅλως καὶ μουσικὴν καὶ γεωμετρίαν διέπαιζεν.
ἦν δὲ πολυτελής· καὶ διὰ τοῦτο πόλιν ἐκ πόλεως
ἤμειβεν, ἐνίοτε καὶ φαντασίαν ἐπιτεχνώμενος. ἐν
γοῦν Ῥόδῳ τοὺς ναύτας ἔπεισε σχολαστικὰς
ἐσθῆτας ἀναλαβεῖν καὶ ἀκολουθῆσαι αὐτῷ· σὺν
οἷς εἰσβάλλων εἰς τὸ γυμνάσιον περίβλεπτος ἦν.
εἰώθει τε νεανίσκων τινῶν υἱοθεσίας ποιεῖσθαι εἰς
τὸ ἀποχρῆσθαι αὐτοῖς ἔς τε τὰς ἡδονὰς καὶ ὥστε
φυλάττεσθαι ὑπ' εὐνοίας αὐτῶν· ἀλλὰ καὶ φίλαυτος
ἦν ἰσχυρῶς καὶ πολὺς ἐγκείμενος τῷ Κοινὰ τὰ
φίλων. παρ' ὃ καὶ οὐδεὶς μαθητὴς αὐτοῦ ἐπιγράφεται, τοσούτων αὐτῷ σχολασάντων· καίτοι
54 τινὰς εἰς ἀναισχυντίαν προῆγεν. ὁ γοῦν Βητίων
εἷς τῶν συνήθων αὐτῷ πρὸς Μενέδημόν ποτε
λέγεται εἰπεῖν, "ἐγώ τοι, ὦ Μενέδημε, νύκτωρ
συνδέομαι Βίωνι καὶ οὐδὲν ἄτοπον δοκῶ μοι

• Cf. Hom. Il. iii. 182 ὦ μάκαρ Ἀτρεΐδη, μοιρηγενές,
ὀλβιόδαιμον. The address πάντων ἐκπαγλότατ' ἀνδρῶν occurs
in Il. i. 146 and xviii. 170.
ᵇ See, however, supra, 49.

Next he went over to Theodorean views, after he had heard the lectures of Theodorus the Atheist, who used every kind of sophistical argument. And after Theodorus he attended the lectures of Theophrastus the Peripatetic. He was fond of display and great at cutting up anything with a jest, using vulgar names for things. Because he employed every style of speech in combination, Eratosthenes, we hear, said of him that he was the first to deck philosophy with bright-flowered robes. He was clever also at parody. Here is a specimen of his style :

O gentle Archytas, musician-born, blessed in thine own conceit, most skilled of men to stir the bass of strife.[a]

And in general he made sport of music and geometry. He lived extravagantly, and for this reason he would move from one city to another, sometimes contriving to make a great show. Thus at Rhodes he persuaded the sailors to put on students' garb and follow in his train. And when, attended by them, he made his way into the gymnasium, all eyes were fixed on him. It was his custom also to adopt certain young men for the gratification of his appetite and in order that he might be protected by their goodwill.[b] He was extremely selfish and insisted strongly on the maxim that " friends share in common." And hence it came about that he is not credited with a single disciple, out of all the crowds who attended his lectures. And yet there were some who followed his lead in shamelessness. For instance, Betion, one of his intimates, is said once to have addressed Menedemus in these words: " For my part, Menedemus, I pass the night with Bion, and I don't think I am any the worse for it." In

πεπονθέναι.'' πολλὰ δὲ καὶ ἀθεώτερον προεφέρετο
τοῖς ὁμιλοῦσι, τοῦτο Θεοδώρειον ἀπολαύσας. καὶ
ὕστερόν ποτε ἐμπεσὼν εἰς νόσον, ὡς ἔφασκον οἱ
ἐν Χαλκίδι—αὐτόθι γὰρ καὶ κατέστρεψε—περίαπτα
λαβεῖν ἐπείσθη καὶ μεταγινώσκειν ἐφ᾽ οἷς ἐπλημ-
μέλησεν εἰς τὸ θεῖον. ἀπορίᾳ δὲ καὶ τῶν νοσο-
κομούντων δεινῶς διετίθετο, ἕως ᾽Αντίγονος αὐτῷ
δύο θεράποντας ἀπέστειλε. καὶ ἠκολούθει γε
αὑτὸς[1] ἐν φορείῳ, καθά φησι Φαβωρῖνος ἐν Παντοδαπῇ ἱστορίᾳ.

᾽Αλλὰ καὶ ὡς κατέστρεψε καὶ ἡμεῖς αὐτὸν οὕτως
ᾐτιασάμεθα·

55 Βίωνα, τὸν Βορυσθένης ἔφυσε γῆ Σκύθισσα,
λέγειν ἀκούομεν θεοὺς ὡς οὐδέν εἰσιν ὄντως.
κεἰ μὲν τὸ δόγμα τοῦτ᾽ ἔχων ἔμιμνεν, ἦν ἂν εἰκὸς
λέγειν, φρονεῖν ὅπως δοκεῖ· κακῶς μέν, ἀλλ᾽ ἔδοξε.
νῦν δ᾽ ἐς νόσον πεσὼν μακρὴν καὶ μὴ θάνῃ δεδοικὼς
ὁ μὴ θεοὺς εἶναι λέγων, ὁ νηὸν οὐδὲ βλέψας,

56 ὁ πολλὰ χλευάσας βροτούς, ὅσοι θεοῖς ἔθυον,
οὐ μοῦνον ἐσχάρης ὕπερ βωμῶν τε καὶ τραπέζης
κνίσῃ, λίπει, θυλήμασιν θεῶν ἔδαισε ῥῖνας·
οὐδ᾽ εἶπε μοῦνον, ῞Ηλιτον, σύγγνωτε τοῖς πρίν· ἀλλὰ
καὶ γραῖ δῶκεν εὐμαρῶς τράχηλον εἰς ἐπῳδὴν
καὶ σκυτίσιν βραχίονας πεπεισμένως ἔδησε·

57 ῥάμνον τε καὶ κλάδον δάφνης ὑπὲρ θύρην ἔθηκεν,
ἅπαντα μᾶλλον ἢ θανεῖν ἕτοιμος ὢν ὑπουργεῖν.
μωρὸς δ᾽ ὃς ἤθελέν τινος μισθοῦ τὸ θεῖον εἶναι,
ὡς τῶν θεῶν ὄντων ὅταν Βίων θέλῃ νομίζειν.
τοιγὰρ μάτην φρονῶν, ὅτ᾽ ἦν ἅπας ὁ λέμφος ἄνθραξ,
τὴν χεῖρα τείνας ὧδέ πως, Χαῖρ᾽, εἶπε, χαῖρε,
Πλουτεῦ.

---

[1] αὐτῷ codd.: corr. Reiske.

his familiar talk he would often vehemently assail belief in the gods, a taste which he had derived from Theodorus. Afterwards, when he fell ill (so it was said by the people of Chalcis where he died), he was persuaded to wear an amulet and to repent of his offences against religion. And even for want of nurses he was in a sad plight, until Antigonus sent him two servants. And it is stated by Favorinus in his *Miscellaneous History* that the king himself followed in a litter.

Even so he died, and in these lines [a] I have taken him to task :

We hear that Bion, to whom the Scythian land of Bory-sthenes gave birth, denied that the gods really exist. Had he persisted in holding this opinion, it would have been right to say, " He thinks as he pleases : wrongly, to be sure, but still he does think so." But in fact, when he fell ill of a lingering disease and feared death, he who denied the exist-ence of the gods, and would not even look at a temple, who often mocked at mortals for sacrificing to deities, not only over hearth and high altars and table, with sweet savour and fat and incense did he gladden the nostrils of the gods ; nor was he content to say " I have sinned, forgive the past," but he cheerfully allowed an old woman to put a charm round his neck, and in full faith bound his arms with leather and placed the rhamnus and the laurel-branch over the door, being ready to submit to anything sooner than die. Fool for wishing that the divine favour might be purchased at a certain price, as if the gods existed just when Bion chose to recognize them! It was then with vain wisdom that, when the driveller was all ashes, he stretched out his hand and said " Hail, Pluto, hail ! "

[a] *Anth. Plan.* v. 37.

58 Γεγόνασι δὲ Βίωνες δέκα· πρῶτος ὁ Φερεκύδῃ τῷ Συρίῳ συνακμάσας, οὗ φέρεται βιβλία δύο Ἰάδι· ἔστι δὲ Προκοννήσιος. δεύτερος Συρακόσιος, τέχνας ῥητορικὰς γεγραφώς· τρίτος αὐτὸς οὗτος· τέταρτος Δημοκρίτειος καὶ μαθηματικός, Ἀβδη· ρίτης, Ἀτθίδι γεγραφὼς καὶ Ἰάδι· οὗτος πρῶτος εἶπεν εἶναί τινας οἰκήσεις ἔνθα γίνεσθαι ἐξ μηνῶν τὴν νύκτα καὶ ἐξ τὴν ἡμέραν. πέμπτος Σολεύς, Αἰθιοπικὰ γεγραφώς· ἕκτος ῥητορικός, οὗ φέρεται ἐννέα βιβλία Μουσῶν ἐπιγραφόμενα· ἕβδομος μελικὸς ποιητής· ὄγδοος Μιλήσιος ἀνδριαντο- ποιός, οὗ μέμνηται καὶ Πολέμων· ἔνατος ποιητὴς τραγῳδίας τῶν Ταρσικῶν λεγομένων· δέκατος ἀγαλματοποιὸς Κλαζομένιος ἢ Χῖος, οὗ μέμνη- ται καὶ Ἱππῶναξ.

Κεφ. η΄. ΛΑΚΥΔΗΣ

59 Λακύδης Ἀλεξάνδρου Κυρηναῖος. οὗτός ἐστιν ὁ τῆς νέας Ἀκαδημείας κατάρξας καὶ Ἀρκεσίλαον διαδεξάμενος, ἀνὴρ σεμνότατος καὶ οὐκ ὀλίγους ἐσχηκὼς ζηλωτάς· φιλόπονός τε ἐκ νέου καὶ πένης μέν, εὔχαρις δ᾽ ἄλλως καὶ εὐόμιλος. τοῦτόν φασι καὶ περὶ οἰκονομίαν γλυκύτατα ἐσχηκέναι· ἐπειδὴ γάρ τι προέλοι τοῦ ταμιείου, σφραγισάμενος πάλιν εἴσω τὸν δακτύλιον διὰ τῆς ὀπῆς ἐρρίπτει, ὡς μηδέποτ᾽ αὐτοῦ περιαιρεθείη τι καὶ βασταχθείη τῶν ἀποκειμένων. μαθόντα δὴ τοῦτο τὰ θερά- πόντια ἀπεσφράγιζε καὶ ὅσα ἐβούλετο ἐβάσταζεν· ἔπειτα τὸν δακτύλιον τὸν αὐτὸν τρόπον διὰ τῆς

---

[a] Possibly Pytheas of Massilia in his " Northern Voyage " had had experience of Arctic winters and summers.

Ten men have borne the name of Bion : (1) the contemporary of Pherecydes of Syria, to whom are assigned two books in the Ionic dialect ; he was of Proconnesus ; (2) a Syracusan, who wrote rhetorical handbooks ; (3) our philosopher ; (4) a follower of Democritus and mathematician of Abdera, who wrote both in Attic and in Ionic : he was the first to affirm that there are places where the night lasts for six months and the day for six months *a* ; (5) a native of Soli, who wrote a work on Aethiopia ; (6) a rhetorician, the author of nine books called after the Muses ; (7) a lyric poet ; (8) a Milesian sculptor, mentioned by Polemo ; (9) a tragic poet, one of the poets of Tarsus, as they are called ; (10) a sculptor of Clazomenae or Chios, mentioned by Hipponax.

CHAPTER 8. LACYDES

(Head of the Academy c. 242–216 B.C.)

Lacydes, son of Alexander, was a native of Cyrene He was the founder of the New Academy and the successor of Arcesilaus : a man of very serious character who found numerous admirers ; industrious from his youth up and, though poor, of pleasant manners and pleasant conversation. A most amusing story is told of his housekeeping. Whenever he brought anything out of the store-room, he would seal the door up again and throw his signet-ring inside through the opening, to ensure that nothing laid up there should be stolen or carried off. So soon, then, as his rogues of servants got to know this, they broke the seal and carried off what they pleased, afterwards throwing the ring in the same way through

ὀπῆς ἐνίει εἰς τὴν στοάν· καὶ τοῦτο ποιοῦντα οὐδέ
ποτ' ἐφωράθη.

60 Ὁ γοῦν Λακύδης ἐσχόλαζεν ἐν Ἀκαδημείᾳ ἐν
τῷ κατασκευασθέντι κήπῳ ὑπὸ Ἀττάλου τοῦ
βασιλέως, καὶ Λακύδειον ἀπ' αὐτοῦ προσηγορεύετο.
καὶ μόνος τῶν ἀπ' αἰῶνος ζῶν παρέδωκε τὴν
σχολὴν Τηλεκλεῖ καὶ Εὐάνδρῳ τοῖς Φωκαεῦσι.
παρὰ δ' Εὐάνδρου διεδέξατο Ἡγησίνους Περ-
γαμηνός, ἀφ' οὗ Καρνεάδης. χάριεν δ' εἰς τὸν
Λακύδην ἀναφέρεται· Ἀττάλου γὰρ αὐτὸν μετα-
πεμπομένου φασὶν εἰπεῖν τὰς εἰκόνας πόρρωθεν
δεῖν θεωρεῖσθαι. ὀψὲ δὲ αὐτῷ γεωμετροῦντι
λέγει τις, '' εἶτα νῦν καιρός; '' ⟨καὶ ὅς·⟩ '' εἶτα
μηδὲ νῦν; ''

61 Ἐτελεύτησε δὲ σχολαρχεῖν ἀρξάμενος τῷ τετάρτῳ ἔτει τῆς τετάρτης καὶ τριακοστῆς καὶ
ἑκατοστῆς Ὀλυμπιάδος, τῆς σχολῆς ἀφηγησάμενος ἓξ πρὸς τοῖς εἴκοσιν ἔτη· ἡ τελευτὴ δὲ
αὐτῷ παράλυσις ἐκ πολυποσίας. καὶ αὐτῷ προσ-
επαίξαμεν ἡμεῖς οὑτωσί·

καὶ σέο, Λακύδη, φάτιν ἔκλυον ὡς ἄρα καὶ σὲ
Βάκχος ἑλὼν Ἀΐδῃ ποσσὶν ἔσυρεν[1] ἄκροις.
ἦ σαφὲς ἦν, Διόνυσος ὅταν πολὺς ἐς δέμας ἔλθῃ,
λῦσε μέλη· διὸ δὴ μήτι Λυαῖος ἔφυ;

Κεφ. θ'. ΚΑΡΝΕΑΔΗΣ

62 Καρνεάδης Ἐπικώμου ἢ Φιλοκώμου, ὡς Ἀλέξανδρος ἐν Διαδοχαῖς, Κυρηναῖος. οὗτος τὰ τῶν

---

[1] σὲ . . . Βάκχος . . . ἔσυρεν Cobet: σὺ . . . βάκχον . . .
ἔσυρες codd. nisi quod Anth. Pal. vii. 105 βάκχου scriptum sit.

436

the opening into the store-room. Nor were they ever detected in this.

Lacydes used to lecture in the Academy, in the garden which had been laid out by King Attalus, and from him it derived its name of Lacydeum. He did what none of his predecessors had ever done ; in his lifetime he handed over the school to Telecles and Evander, both of Phocaea. Evander was succeeded by Hegesinus of Pergamum, and he again by Carneades. A good saying is attributed to Lacydes. When Attalus sent for him, he is said to have remarked that statues are best seen from a distance. He studied geometry late, and some one said to him, " Is this a proper time ? " To which he replied, " Nay, is it not even yet the proper time ? "

He assumed the headship of the school in the fourth year of the 134th Olympiad,[a] and at his death he had been head for twenty-six years. His end was a palsy brought on by drinking too freely. And here is a quip of my own upon the fact[b] :

Of thee too, O Lacydes, I have heard a tale, that Bacchus seized thee and dragged thee on tip-toe[c] to the underworld. Nay, was it not clear that when the wine-god comes in force into the frame, he loosens our limbs? Perhaps this is why he gets his name of the Loosener.

Chapter 9. CARNEADES (*c.* 213–129 B.C.)

Carneades, the son of Epicomus or (according to Alexander in his *Successions of Philosophers*) of Philocomus, was a native of Cyrene. He studied

---

[a] July 241–June 240 B.C.   [b] *Anth. Pal.* vii. 105.
[c] Or " with trailing toes." The vases show bodies carried in the arms or flung over the shoulders with the toes just touching the ground.

Στωικῶν βιβλία ἀναγνοὺς ἐπιμελῶς ‹ καὶ μάλιστα › τὰ Χρυσίππου, ἐπιεικῶς αὐτοῖς ἀντέλεγε καὶ εὐημέρει τοσοῦτον, ὥστε ἐκεῖνο ἐπιλέγειν·

εἰ μὴ γὰρ ἦν Χρύσιππος, οὐκ ἂν ἦν ἐγώ.

φιλόπονος δ᾽ ἄνθρωπος γέγονεν εἰ καί τις ἄλλος, ἐν μὲν τοῖς φυσικοῖς ἧττον φερόμενος, ἐν δὲ τοῖς ἠθικοῖς μᾶλλον. ὅθεν καὶ ἐκόμα καὶ ἔτρεφεν ὄνυχας ἀσχολίᾳ τῇ περὶ τοὺς λόγους. τοσοῦτον δ᾽ ἴσχυσεν ἐν φιλοσοφίᾳ, ὥστε καὶ τοὺς ῥήτορας ἀπολύσαντας ἐκ τῶν σχολῶν παρ᾽ αὐτὸν ἰέναι καὶ αὐτοῦ ἀκούειν.

63 Ἦν δὲ καὶ μεγαλοφωνότατος, ὥστε τὸν γυμνασίαρχον προσπέμψαι αὐτῷ μὴ οὕτω βοᾶν· τὸν δὲ εἰπεῖν, " καὶ δὸς μέτρον φωνῆς." ἔνθεν εὐστόχως ἑλόντα ἀμείψασθαι· φάναι γάρ, " μέτρον ἔχεις τοὺς ἀκούοντας." δεινῶς τ᾽ ἦν ἐπιπληκτικὸς καὶ ἐν ταῖς ζητήσεσι δύσμαχος· τά τε δεῖπνα λοιπὸν παρῃτεῖτο διὰ τὰς προειρημένας αἰτίας. οὗτός ποτε Μέντορος τοῦ Βιθυνοῦ μαθητοῦ ὄντος καὶ παρ᾽ αὐτὸν ἐλθόντος εἰς τὴν διατριβήν, ὡς ἐπείρα αὐτοῦ τὴν παλλακὴν ὁ Μέντωρ, καθά φησι Φαβωρῖνος ἐν Παντοδαπῇ ἱστορίᾳ, μεταξὺ λέγων παρῴδησεν εἰς αὐτόν·

64 πωλεῖταί τις δεῦρο γέρων ἅλιος νημερτής,
    Μέντορι εἰδόμενος ἠμὲν δέμας ἠδὲ καὶ αὐδήν·
    τοῦτον σχολῆς τῆσδ᾽ ἐκκεκηρῦχθαι λέγω·

καὶ ὃς ἀναστὰς ἔφη·

438

carefully the writings of the Stoics and particularly those of Chrysippus, and by combating these successfully he became so famous that he would often say :

Without Chrysippus where should I have been ?

The man's industry was unparalleled, although in physics he was not so strong as in ethics. Hence he would let his hair and nails grow long from intense devotion to study. Such was his predominance in philosophy that even the rhetoricians would dismiss their classes and repair to him to hear him lecture.

His voice was extremely powerful, so that the keeper of the gymnasium sent to him and requested him not to shout so loud. To which he replied, " Then give me something by which to regulate my voice." Thereupon by a happy hit the man replied in the words, " You have a regulator in your audience." His talent for criticizing opponents was remarkable, and he was a formidable controversialist. And for the reasons already given he further declined invitations to dine out. One of his pupils was Mentor the Bithynian, who tried to ingratiate himself with a concubine of Carneades ; so on one occasion (according to Favorinus in his *Miscellaneous History*), when Mentor came to lecture, Carneades in the course of his remarks let fall these lines by way of parody at his expense :

Hither comes an old man of the sea, infallible, like to Mentor in person and in voice.[a] Him I proclaim to have been banished from this school.

Thereupon the other got up and replied :

[a] Carneades applies two lines from the *Odyssey*, namely iv. 384 and (with a change to the masculine participle) ii. 268 or 401.

οἱ μὲν ἐκήρυσσον, τοὶ δ' ἠγείροντο μάλ' ὦκα.

Δειλότερον δέ πως δοκεῖ περὶ τὴν τελευτὴν
ἀνεστράφθαι, ὅτε συνεχὲς ἔλεγεν, "ἡ συστήσασα
φύσις καὶ διαλύσει." μαθών τε 'Αντίπατρον φάρμακον πιόντα ἀποθανεῖν, παρωρμήθη πρὸς τὸ
εὐθαρσὲς τῆς ἀπαλλαγῆς καί φησι, "δότε οὖν
κἀμοί·" τῶν δὲ εἰπόντων, "τί;" "οἰνόμελι"
εἶπεν. τελευτῶντος δ' αὐτοῦ φασιν ἔκλειψιν
γενέσθαι σελήνης, συμπάθειαν, ὡς ἂν εἴποι τις,
αἰνιττομένου τοῦ μεθ' ἥλιον καλλίστου τῶν ἄστρων.

65 Φησὶ δὲ 'Απολλόδωρος ἐν Χρονικοῖς ἀπελθεῖν
αὐτὸν ἐξ ἀνθρώπων ἔτει τετάρτῳ τῆς δευτέρας
καὶ ἑξηκοστῆς καὶ ἑκατοστῆς 'Ολυμπιάδος, βιώ-
σαντα ἔτη πέντε πρὸς τοῖς ὀγδοήκοντα. φέρονται
δ' αὐτοῦ ἐπιστολαὶ πρὸς 'Αριαράθην τὸν Καππα-
δοκίας βασιλέα. τὰ δὲ λοιπὰ αὐτοῦ οἱ μαθηταὶ
συνέγραψαν· αὐτὸς δὲ κατέλιπεν οὐδέν. ἔστι καὶ
εἰς τοῦτον ἡμῶν τῷ λογαοιδικῷ μέτρῳ [καὶ 'Αρχε-
βουλείῳ]·

τί με Καρνεάδην, τί με, Μοῦσα, θέλεις ἐλέγχειν;
ἀμαθὴς γὰρ ὃς οὔτι κάτοιδεν ὅπως δεδοίκει
τὸ θανεῖν· ὅτε καὶ φθισικήν ποτ' ἔχων κακίστην
νόσον, οὐκ ἔθελεν λύσιν ἰσχέμεν· ἀλλ' ἀκούσας
ὅτι φάρμακον 'Αντίπατρός τι πιὼν ἀπέσβη,
66 "δότε τοίνυν," ἔφησε, "τί κἀμὲ πιεῖν." "τί μέντοι;
τί;" "δότ' οἰνόμελι." σφόδρα τ' εἶχε πρόχειρα
ταυτί·
"φύσις ἡ συνέχουσά με καὶ διαλύσεται δή."
ὁ μὲν οὐδὲν ἔλασσον ἔβη κατὰ γῆς, ἐνῆν δὲ
τὰ πλέω κακὰ κέρδε' ἔχοντα μολεῖν ἐς ᾅδου.

Λέγεται καὶ τὰς ὄψεις νυκτὸς ὑποχυθῆναι καὶ

Those on their part made proclamation, and these speedily assembled.[a]

He seems to have shown some want of courage in the face of death, repeating often the words, " Nature which framed this whole will also destroy it." When he learnt that Antipater committed suicide by drinking a potion, he was greatly moved by the constancy with which he met his end, and exclaimed, " Give it then to me also." And when those about him asked " What ? " " A honeyed draught," said he. At the time he died the moon is said to have been eclipsed, and one might well say that the brightest luminary in heaven next to the sun thereby gave token of her sympathy.

According to Apollodorus in his *Chronology*, he departed this life in the fourth year of the 162nd Olympiad [b] at the age of eighty-five years. Letters of his to Ariarathes, king of Cappadocia, are extant. Everything else was compiled by his pupils ; he himself left nothing in writing. I have written upon him in logaoedic metre as follows [c] :

Why, Muse, oh why wouldst thou have me censure Carneades ? For he is ignorant who knoweth not how he feared death. When wasting away with the worst of diseases, he would not find release. But when he heard that Antipater's life was quenched by drinking a potion, " Give me too," he cried, " a draught to drink." " What ? pray what ? " " Give me a draught of honeyed wine." He had often on his lips the words, " Nature which holds this frame together will surely dissolve it." None the less he too went down to the grave, and he might have got there sooner by cutting short his tale of woes.

It is said that his eyes went blind at night without

[a] Hom. *Il.* ii. 52.
[b] 129–128 B.C.
[c] *Anth. Plan.* v. 39.

ἀγνοεῖν· κελεῦσαί τε τὸν παῖδα λύχνον ἅψαι· εἰσκο-
μίσαντος δὲ καὶ εἰπόντος, " κεκόμικα," " οὐκοῦν,"
εἰπεῖν, " σὺ ἀναγίνωσκε."

Τούτου πολλοὶ μὲν καὶ ἄλλοι γεγόνασι μαθηταί,
ἐλλογιμώτατος δὲ Κλειτόμαχος· περὶ οὗ καὶ
λεκτέον.

Γέγονε μέντοι καὶ ἄλλος Καρνεάδης, ἐλεγείας
ποιητὴς ψυχρός.

Κεφ. ι΄. ΚΛΕΙΤΟΜΑΧΟΣ

67 Κλειτόμαχος Καρχηδόνιος. οὗτος ἐκαλεῖτο μὲν
Ἀσδρούβας καὶ τῇ ἰδίᾳ φωνῇ κατὰ τὴν πατρίδα
ἐφιλοσόφει. ἐλθὼν δ᾽ εἰς Ἀθήνας ἤδη τετταράκοντ᾽
ἔτη γεγονὼς ἤκουσε Καρνεάδου· κἀκεῖνος ἀπο-
δεξάμενος αὐτοῦ τὸ φιλόπονον γράμματά τ᾽ ἐποίησε
μαθεῖν καὶ συνήσκει τὸν ἄνδρα. ὁ δὲ εἰς τοσοῦτον
ἤλασεν ἐπιμελείας, ὥστε ὑπὲρ τὰ τετρακόσια
βιβλία συνέγραψε. καὶ διεδέξατο τὸν Καρνεάδην
καὶ τὰ αὐτοῦ μάλιστα διὰ τῶν συγγραμμάτων
ἐφώτισεν. ἀνὴρ ἐν ταῖς τρισὶν αἱρέσεσι διαπρέψας,
ἔν τε τῇ Ἀκαδημαϊκῇ καὶ περιπατητικῇ καὶ στωικῇ.

Καθόλου δὲ τοὺς Ἀκαδημαϊκοὺς ὁ Τίμων οὕτω
διασύρει·

οὐδ᾽ Ἀκαδημιακῶν πλατυρημοσύνης ἀναλίστου.

Ἡμεῖς δὲ τοὺς Ἀκαδημαϊκοὺς τοὺς ἀπὸ Πλάτωνος διεληλυθότες ἔλθωμεν ἐπὶ τοὺς ἀπὸ Πλάτωνος περιπατητικούς, ὧν ἦρξεν Ἀριστοτέλης.

his knowing it, and he ordered the slave to light the lamp.   The latter brought it and said, " Here it is." " Then," said Carneades, " read."

He had many other disciples, but the most illustrious of them all was Clitomachus, of whom we have next to speak.

There was another Carneades, a frigid elegiac poet.

Chapter 10.   CLITOMACHUS
(Head of the Academy from 129 b.c.)

Clitomachus was a Carthaginian, his real name being Hasdrubal, and he taught philosophy at Carthage in his native tongue.   He had reached his fortieth year when he went to Athens and became a pupil of Carneades.   And Carneades, recognizing his industry, caused him to be educated and took part in training him.   And to such lengths did his diligence go that he composed more than four hundred treatises.   He succeeded Carneades in the headship of the school, and by his writings did much to elucidate his opinions.   He was eminently well acquainted with the three sects—the Academy, the Peripatetics, and the Stoics.

The Academics in general are assailed by Timon in the line :

The prolixity of the Academics unseasoned by salt.

Having thus reviewed the Academics who derived from Plato, we will now pass on to the Peripatetics, who also derived from Plato.   They begin with Aristotle.

E

Κεφ. α΄. ΑΡΙΣΤΟΤΕΛΗΣ

1 Ἀριστοτέλης Νικομάχου καὶ Φαιστίδος Σταγειρίτης. ὁ δὲ Νικόμαχος ἦν ἀπὸ Νικομάχου τοῦ
Μαχάονος τοῦ Ἀσκληπιοῦ, καθά φησιν Ἕρμιππος
ἐν τῷ Περὶ Ἀριστοτέλους· καὶ συνεβίω Ἀμύντᾳ τῷ
Μακεδόνων βασιλεῖ ἰατροῦ καὶ φίλου χρείᾳ. οὗτος
γνησιώτατος τῶν Πλάτωνος μαθητῶν, τραυλὸς
τὴν φωνήν, ὥς φησι Τιμόθεος ὁ Ἀθηναῖος ἐν τῷ
Περὶ βίων· ἀλλὰ καὶ ἰσχνοσκελής, φασίν, ἦν καὶ
μικρόμματος ἐσθῆτί τ' ἐπισήμῳ χρώμενος καὶ
δακτυλίοις καὶ κουρᾷ. ἔσχε δὲ καὶ υἱὸν Νικόμαχον
ἐξ Ἑρπυλλίδος τῆς παλλακῆς, ὥς φησι Τίμαιος.[1]

2 Ἀπέστη δὲ Πλάτωνος ἔτι περιόντος· ὥστε φασὶν
ἐκεῖνον εἰπεῖν, "Ἀριστοτέλης ἡμᾶς ἀπελάκτισε,
καθαπερεὶ τὰ πωλάρια γεννηθέντα τὴν μητέρα."
φησὶ δ' Ἕρμιππος ἐν τοῖς Βίοις ὅτι πρεσβεύοντος
αὐτοῦ πρὸς Φίλιππον ὑπὲρ Ἀθηναίων σχολάρχης
ἐγένετο τῆς ἐν Ἀκαδημείᾳ σχολῆς Ξενοκράτης·
ἐλθόντα δὴ αὐτὸν καὶ θεασάμενον ὑπ' ἄλλῳ τὴν
σχολήν, ἑλέσθαι περίπατον τὸν ἐν Λυκείῳ καὶ

---

[1] codd. Τιμόθεος repeated from above.

BOOK V

Chapter 1. ARISTOTLE (384–322 B.C.)

Aristotle, son of Nicomachus and Phaestis, was
a native of Stagira. His father, Nicomachus, as
Hermippus relates in his book *On Aristotle*, traced
his descent from Nicomachus who was the son of
Machaon and grandson of Asclepius ; and he resided
with Amyntas, the king of Macedon, in the capacity
of physician and friend. Aristotle was Plato's most
genuine disciple ; he spoke with a lisp, as we learn
from Timotheus the Athenian in his book *On Lives* ;
further, his calves were slender (so they say), his
eyes small, and he was conspicuous by his attire, his
rings, and the cut of his hair. According to
Timaeus, he had a son by Herpyllis, his concubine,
who was also called Nicomachus.

He seceded from the Academy while Plato was
still alive. Hence the remark attributed to the
latter : " Aristotle spurns me, as colts kick out at
the mother who bore them." [a] Hermippus in his
Lives mentions that he was absent as Athenian
envoy at the court of Philip when Xenocrates became
head of the Academy, and that on his return, when
he saw the school under a new head, he made choice
of a public walk in the Lyceum where he would walk

* *Cf.* Aelian, *V.H.* iv. 9.

μέχρι μὲν ἀλείμματος[1] ἀνακάμπτοντα τοῖς μαθηταῖς
συμφιλοσοφεῖν· ὅθεν περιπατητικὸν προσαγορευθῆ-
ναι. οἱ δ', ὅτι ἐκ νόσου περιπατοῦντι Ἀλεξάνδρῳ
συμπαρὼν διελέγετο ἄττα.

3 Ἐπειδὴ δὲ πλείους ἐγένοντο ἤδη, καὶ ἐκάθισεν
εἰπών·

αἰσχρὸν σιωπᾶν, Ξενοκράτην δ' ἐᾶν λέγειν.

καὶ πρὸς θέσιν συνεγύμναζε τοὺς μαθητάς, ἅμα καὶ
ῥητορικῶς ἐπασκῶν. ἔπειτα μέντοι ἀπῆρε πρὸς
Ἑρμίαν τὸν εὐνοῦχον, Ἀταρνέως ὄντα τύραννον·
ὃν οἱ μέν φασι παιδικὰ γενέσθαι αὐτοῦ, οἱ δὲ καὶ
κηδεῦσαι αὐτῷ δόντα τὴν θυγατέρα ἢ ἀδελφιδῆν, ὥς
φησι Δημήτριος ὁ Μάγνης ἐν τοῖς Περὶ ὁμωνύμων
ποιητῶν τε καὶ συγγραφέων· ὃς καὶ δοῦλον Εὐβούλου φησὶ γενέσθαι τὸν Ἑρμίαν, γένει Βιθυνὸν ὄντα
καὶ τὸν δεσπότην ἀνελόντα. Ἀρίστιππος δ' ἐν τῷ
πρώτῳ[2] Περὶ παλαιᾶς τρυφῆς φησιν ἐρασθῆναι τὸν
4 Ἀριστοτέλην παλλακίδος τοῦ Ἑρμίου. τοῦ δὲ
συγχωρήσαντος ἔγημέ τ' αὐτὴν καὶ ἔθυεν ὑπερχαίρων τῷ γυναίῳ, ὡς Ἀθηναῖοι τῇ Ἐλευσινίᾳ
Δήμητρι· τῷ τε Ἑρμίᾳ παιᾶνα ἔγραψεν, ὃς ἔνδον
γέγραπται. ἐντεῦθέν τε γενέσθαι ἐν Μακεδονίᾳ
παρὰ Φιλίππῳ καὶ λαβεῖν μαθητὴν παρ' αὐτοῦ τὸν
υἱὸν Ἀλέξανδρον, καὶ αἰτῆσαι ἀναστῆσαι αὐτοῦ τὴν
πατρίδα κατασκαφεῖσαν ὑπὸ Φιλίππου καὶ τυχεῖν·

---

[1] ἀλείμματος. Bywater puts this between daggers.
[2] πρώτῳ] τετάρτῳ Wilamowitz.

---

* Eur. *Philoct.* Frag. 785 Dind., 796 Nauck[2].
† Most authorities put Isocrates here in place of Xenocrates.
‡ This story comes ultimately from Lyco the Pythagorean;
cf. Aristocles. *Cf.* Euseb. *Praep. Ev.* xv. 2 § 5 φησὶ γὰρ

up and down discussing philosophy with his pupils until it was time to rub themselves with oil. Hence the name " Peripatetic." But others say that it was given to him because, when Alexander was recovering from an illness and taking daily walks, Aristotle joined him and talked with him on certain matters.

In time the circle about him grew larger ; he then sat down to lecture, remarking [a] :

It were base to keep silence and let Xenocrates [b] speak.

He also taught his pupils to discourse upon a set theme, besides practising them in oratory. Afterwards, however, he departed to Hermias the eunuch, who was tyrant of Atarneus, and there is one story that he was on very affectionate terms with Hermias ; according to another, Hermias bound him by ties of kinship, giving him his daughter or his niece in marriage, and so Demetrius of Magnesia narrates in his work on *Poets and Writers of the Same Name.* The same author tells us that Hermias had been the slave of Eubulus, and that he was of Bithynian origin and had murdered his master. Aristippus in his first book *On the Luxury of the Ancients* says that Aristotle fell in love with a concubine of Hermias, and married her with his consent, and in an excess of delight sacrificed to a weak woman as the Athenians did to Demeter of Eleusis [c] ; and that he composed a paean in honour of Hermias, which is given below ; next that he stayed in Macedonia at Philip's court and received from him his son Alexander as his pupil ; that he petitioned Alexander to restore his native city which had been destroyed by Philip and obtained his

θύειν 'Αριστοτέλην θυσίαν τετελευτηκυία τῇ γυναικὶ τοιαύτην ὁποίαν 'Αθηναῖοι τῇ Δήμητρι. This version is irreconcilable with ὑπερχαίρων in D. L.

οἷς καὶ νόμους θεῖναι. ἀλλὰ καὶ ἐν τῇ σχολῇ
νομοθετεῖν μιμούμενον Ξενοκράτην, ὥστε κατὰ
δέκα ἡμέρας ἄρχοντα ποιεῖν. ἐπειδὴ δ' ἐδόκει
ἐπιεικῶς αὐτῷ συγγεγενῆσθαι Ἀλεξάνδρῳ, ἀπῆρεν
εἰς Ἀθήνας, συστήσας αὐτῷ τὸν συγγενῆ Καλλι-
5 σθένην τὸν Ὀλύνθιον· ὃν καὶ παρρησιαστικώτερον
λαλοῦντα τῷ βασιλεῖ καὶ μὴ πειθόμενον αὐτῷ φασιν
ἐπιπλήξαντα εἰπεῖν·

ὠκύμορος δή μοι, τέκος, ἔσσεαι, οἷ' ἀγορεύεις.[α]

καὶ δὴ καὶ ἐγένετο. δόξας γὰρ Ἑρμολάῳ συμ-
μετεσχηκέναι τῆς εἰς Ἀλέξανδρον ἐπιβουλῆς ἐν
σιδηρᾷ περιήγετο γαλεάγρᾳ, φθειριῶν καὶ ἀ-
κόμιστος· καὶ τέλος λέοντι παραβληθείς, οὕτω κατέστρεψεν.

Ὁ δ' οὖν Ἀριστοτέλης ἐλθὼν εἰς τὰς Ἀθήνας
καὶ τρία πρὸς τοῖς δέκα τῆς σχολῆς ἀφηγησάμενος
ἔτη ὑπεξῆλθεν εἰς Χαλκίδα, Εὐρυμέδοντος αὐτὸν
τοῦ ἱεροφάντου δίκην ἀσεβείας γραψαμένου, ἢ
Δημοφίλου, ὥς φησι Φαβωρῖνος ἐν Παντοδαπῇ
ἱστορίᾳ, ἐπειδήπερ τὸν ὕμνον ἐποίησεν εἰς τὸν
6 προειρημένον Ἑρμίαν, ἀλλὰ καὶ ἐπίγραμμα ἐπὶ
τοῦ ἐν Δελφοῖς ἀνδριάντος τοιοῦτον·[β]

τόνδε ποτ' οὐχ ὁσίως παραβὰς μακάρων θέμιν
    ἁγνὴν
ἔκτεινεν Περσῶν τοξοφόρων βασιλεύς,
οὐ φανερῶς λόγχῃ φονίοις ἐν ἀγῶσι κρατήσας,
ἀλλ' ἀνδρὸς πίστει χρησάμενος δολίου.

Ἐνταῦθα δὴ πιὼν ἀκόνιτον ἐτελεύτησεν, ὡς

[α] Hom. Il. xviii. 95.
[β] As in ii. 78, iii. 19 and v. 77, Favorinus is curious to
state the names of the accusers of philosophers put upon trial.

request ; and that he also drew up a code of laws for the inhabitants. We learn further that, following the example of Xenocrates, he made it a rule in his school that every ten days a new president should be appointed. When he thought that he had stayed long enough with Alexander, he departed to Athens, having first presented to Alexander his kinsman Callisthenes of Olynthus. But when Callisthenes talked with too much freedom to the king and disregarded his own advice, Aristotle is said to have rebuked him by citing the line [a] :

Short-lived, I ween, wilt thou be, my child, by what thou sayest.

And so indeed it fell out. For he, being suspected of complicity in the plot of Hermolaus against the life of Alexander, was confined in an iron cage and carried about until he became infested with vermin through lack of proper attention ; and finally he was thrown to a lion and so met his end.

To return to Aristotle : he came to Athens, was head of his school for thirteen years, and then withdrew to Chalcis because he was indicted for impiety by Eurymedon the hierophant, or, according to Favorinus [b] in his *Miscellaneous History*, by Demophilus, the ground of the charge being the hymn he composed to the aforesaid Hermias, as well as the following inscription for his statue at Delphi [c] :

This man in violation of the hallowed law of the immortals was unrighteously slain by the king of the bow-bearing Persians, who overcame him, not openly with a spear in murderous combat, but by treachery with the aid of one in whom he trusted.

At Chalcis he died, according to Eumelus in the

[c] *Anth. Plan.* iii. 48.

φησιν Εὔμηλος ἐν τῇ πέμπτῃ τῶν Ἱστοριῶν, βιοὺς
ἔτη ἑβδομήκοντα. ὁ δ᾽ αὐτός φησιν αὐτὸν καὶ
Πλάτωνι τριακοντούτην συστῆναι, διαπίπτων· βε-
βίωκε γὰρ τρία μὲν πρὸς τοῖς ἑξήκοντα, Πλάτωνι
δὲ ἑπτακαιδεκέτης συνέστη.

Ὁ δὲ ὕμνος ἔχει τοῦτον τὸν τρόπον·

7 ἀρετά, πολύμοχθε γένει βροτείῳ,
θήραμα κάλλιστον βίῳ,
σᾶς πέρι, παρθένε, μορφᾶς
καὶ θανεῖν ζαλωτὸς ἐν Ἑλλάδι πότμος
καὶ πόνους τλῆναι μαλεροὺς ἀκάμαντας·
τοῖον ἐπὶ φρένα βάλλεις
κάρτος ἀθάνατον χρυσοῦ τε κρεῖσσον
καὶ γονέων μαλακαυγήτοιό θ᾽ ὕπνου.
σεῦ δ᾽ ἕνεχ᾽ οὐκ Διὸς Ἡρακλέης Λήδας τε κοῦροι
πόλλ᾽ ἀνέτλασαν ἔργοις
σὰν ἀγρεύοντες δύναμιν.

8 σοῖς δὲ πόθοις Ἀχιλεὺς
Αἴας τ᾽ Ἀΐδαο δόμους ἦλθον·
σᾶς δ᾽ ἕνεκεν φιλίου μορφᾶς καὶ Ἀταρνέος
ἔντροφος ἀελίου χήρωσεν αὐγάς.
τοιγὰρ ἀοίδιμος ἔργοις, ἀθάνατόν τε μιν αὐξή-
σουσι Μοῦσαι
Μναμοσύνας θύγατρες, Διὸς ξενίου σέβας αὔ-
ξουσαι φιλίας τε γέρας βεβαίου.

Ἔστι δ᾽ οὖν καὶ εἰς τοῦτον ἡμῶν οὕτως ἔχον·

Εὐρυμέδων ποτ᾽ ἔμελλεν Ἀριστοτέλην ἀσεβείας
γράψασθαι Δηοῦς μύστιδος ὢν πρόπολος,
ἀλλὰ πιὼν ἀκόνιτον ὑπέκφυγε· τοῦτ᾽ ἀκονιτὶ
ἦν ἄρα νικῆσαι συκοφάσεις ἀδίκους.

fifth book of his *Histories*, by drinking aconite, at the age of seventy. The same authority makes him thirty years old when he came to Plato ; but here he is mistaken. For Aristotle lived to be sixty-three, and he was seventeen when he became Plato's pupil.

The hymn in question runs as follows :

O virtue, toilsome for the generation of mortals to achieve, the fairest prize that life can win, for thy beauty, O virgin, it were a doom glorious in Hellas even to die and to endure fierce, untiring labours. Such courage dost thou implant in the mind, imperishable, better than gold, dearer than parents or soft-eyed sleep. For thy sake Heracles, son of Zeus, and the sons of Leda endured much in the tasks whereby they pursued thy might. And yearning after thee came Achilles and Ajax to the house of Hades, and for the sake of thy dear form the nursling of Atarneus too was bereft of the light of the sun. Therefore shall his deeds be sung, and the Muses, the daughters of Memory, shall make him immortal, exalting the majesty of Zeus, guardian of strangers, and the grace of lasting friendship.

There is, too, something of my own upon the philosopher which I will quote [a] :

Eurymedon, the priest of Deo's mysteries, was once about to indict Aristotle for impiety, but he, by a draught of poison, escaped prosecution. This then was an easy way of vanquishing unjust calumnies.

* *Anth. Pal.* vii. 107.

9 Τοῦτον πρῶτον Φαβωρῖνος ἐν Παντοδαπῇ ἱστορίᾳ λόγον δικανικὸν ὑπὲρ ἑαυτοῦ συγγράψαι φησὶν ἐπ' αὐτῇ ταύτῃ τῇ δίκῃ καὶ λέγειν ὡς Ἀθήνησιν

ὄγχνη ἐπ' ὄγχνῃ γηράσκει, σῦκον δ' ἐπὶ σύκῳ.

Φησὶ δ' Ἀπολλόδωρος ἐν Χρονικοῖς γεννηθῆναι μὲν αὐτὸν τῷ πρώτῳ ἔτει τῆς ἐνάτης καὶ ἐνενηκοστῆς Ὀλυμπιάδος, παραβαλεῖν δὲ Πλάτωνι καὶ διατρῖψαι παρ' αὐτῷ εἴκοσιν ἔτη, ἑπτακαιδεκέτην συστάντα· καὶ εἴς τε Μυτιλήνην ἐλθεῖν ἐπ' ἄρχοντος Εὐβούλου τῷ τετάρτῳ ἔτει τῆς ὀγδόης καὶ ἑκατοστῆς Ὀλυμπιάδος. Πλάτωνος δὲ τελευτήσαντος τῷ πρώτῳ ἔτει ἐπὶ Θεοφίλου, πρὸς Ἑρμίαν ἀπᾶραι 10 καὶ μεῖναι ἔτη τρία· ἐπὶ Πυθοδότου δ' ἐλθεῖν πρὸς Φίλιππον τῷ δευτέρῳ ἔτει τῆς ἐνάτης καὶ ἑκατοστῆς Ὀλυμπιάδος, Ἀλεξάνδρου πεντεκαίδεκα ἔτη ἤδη γεγονότος. εἰς δ' Ἀθήνας ἀφικέσθαι τῷ δευτέρῳ ἔτει τῆς ἑνδεκάτης καὶ ἑκατοστῆς Ὀλυμπιάδος καὶ ἐν Λυκείῳ σχολάσαι ἔτη τρία πρὸς τοῖς δέκα, εἶτ' ἀπᾶραι εἰς Χαλκίδα τῷ τρίτῳ ἔτει τῆς τετάρτης καὶ δεκάτης καὶ ἑκατοστῆς Ὀλυμπιάδος, καὶ τελευτῆσαι ἐτῶν τριῶν που καὶ ἑξήκοντα νόσῳ, ὅτε καὶ Δημοσθένην καταστρέψαι ἐν Καλαυρείᾳ, ἐπὶ Φιλοκλέους. λέγεται δὲ διὰ τὴν Καλλισθένους πρὸς Ἀλέξανδρον σύστασιν προσκροῦσαι τῷ βασιλεῖ· κἀκεῖνον ἐπὶ τῷ τοῦτον λυπῆσαι Ἀναξιμένην μὲν αὐξῆσαι, πέμψαι δὲ καὶ Ξενοκράτει δῶρα.

11 Ἀπέσκωψε δ' εἰς αὐτὸν ἐπίγραμμα καὶ Θεό-

---

[a] Hom. Od. vii. 120.

[b] There must have been a chapter in Favorinus dealing with "inventions."

[c] 384–383 B.C.　　　[d] 345–344 B.C.　　　[e] 347–346 B.C.

Favorinus in his *Miscellaneous History* affirms that Aristotle was the first to compose a forensic speech in his own defence written for this very suit; and he cites him as saying that at Athens [a]

Pear upon pear grows old and fig upon fig. [b]

According to Apollodorus in his *Chronology* he was born in the first year of the 99th Olympiad. [c] He attached himself to Plato and resided with him twenty years, having become his pupil at the age of seventeen. He went to Mitylene in the archonship of Eubulus in the fourth year of the 108th Olympiad. [d] When Plato died in the first year of that Olympiad, [e] during the archonship of Theophilus, he went to Hermias and stayed with him three years. In the archonship of Pythodotus, in the second year of the 109th Olympiad, [f] he went to the court of Philip, Alexander being then in his fifteenth year. His arrival at Athens was in the second year of the 111th Olympiad, [g] and he lectured in the Lyceum for thirteen years; then he retired to Chalcis in the third year of the 114th Olympiad [h] and died a natural death, at the age of about sixty-three, in the archonship of Philocles, in the same year in which Demosthenes died at Calauria. It is said that he incurred the king's displeasure because he had introduced Callisthenes to him, and that Alexander, in order to cause him annoyance, honoured Anaximenes [i] and sent presents to Xenocrates.

Theocritus of Chios, according to Ambryon in his

---

[f] 342–341 B.C.   [g] 335–334 B.C.   [h] 322–321 B.C.
[i] No doubt Anaximenes of Lampsacus (*cf. supra*, ii. § 3), to whom is attributed the *Rhetorica ad Alexandrum*, which has come down to us in the Aristotelian Corpus.

κριτος ὁ Χῖος, οὑτωσὶ ποιήσας, ὥς φησιν Ἀμβρύων ἐν τῷ Περὶ Θεοκρίτου·

Ἑρμίου εὐνούχου ἠδ' Εὐβούλου ἅμα δούλου
σῆμα κενὸν κενόφρων τεῦξεν Ἀριστοτέλης,
‹ὃς διὰ τὴν ἀκρατῆ γαστρὸς φύσιν εἵλετο ναίειν,
ἀντ' Ἀκαδημείας, Βορβόρου ἐν προχοαῖς›[1].

ἀλλὰ καὶ Τίμων αὐτοῦ καθήψατο εἰπών·

οὐδ' ἄρ' Ἀριστοτέλους εἰκαιοσύνης ἀλεγεινῆς.

Καὶ οὗτος μὲν ὁ βίος τοῦ φιλοσόφου. ἡμεῖς δὲ καὶ διαθήκαις αὐτοῦ περιετύχομεν, οὕτω πως ἐχούσαις·

" Ἔσται μὲν εὖ· ἐὰν δέ τι συμβαίνῃ, τάδε διέθετο Ἀριστοτέλης· ἐπίτροπον μὲν εἶναι πάντων καὶ διὰ
12 παντὸς Ἀντίπατρον· ἕως δ' ἂν Νικάνωρ καταλάβῃ, ἐπιμελεῖσθαι Ἀριστομένην, Τίμαρχον, Ἵππαρχον, Διοτέλην, Θεόφραστον, ἐὰν βούληται καὶ ἐνδέχηται αὐτῷ, τῶν τε παιδίων καὶ Ἑρπυλλίδος καὶ τῶν καταλελειμμένων. καὶ ὅταν ὥρα ᾖ τῇ παιδί, ἐκδίδοσθαι αὐτὴν Νικάνορι· ἐὰν δὲ τῇ παιδὶ συμβῇ τι—ὃ μὴ γένοιτο οὐδὲ ἔσται—πρὸ τοῦ γήμασθαι ἢ ἐπειδὰν γήμηται, μήπω παιδίων ὄντων, Νικάνωρ κύριος ἔστω καὶ περὶ τοῦ παιδίου καὶ περὶ τῶν ἄλλων διοικεῖν ἀξίως καὶ αὐτοῦ καὶ ἡμῶν. ἐπιμελείσθω δὲ Νικάνωρ καὶ τῆς παιδὸς καὶ τοῦ παιδὸς Νικομάχου, ὅπως ἂν ἀξιοῖ τὰ περὶ αὐτῶν[2], ὡς καὶ πατὴρ ὢν καὶ ἀδελφός. ἐὰν δέ τι πρότερον συμβῇ Νικάνορι—ὃ μὴ γένοιτο—ἢ πρὸ τοῦ λαβεῖν τὴν

---

[1] addunt editores ex Plutarcho et Eusebio.
[2] αὐτῶν codd.: αὐτὼ Reiske.

book *On Theocritus,* ridiculed him in an epigram which runs as follows [a] :

> To Hermias the eunuch, the slave withal of Eubulus, an empty monument was raised by empty-witted Aristotle, who by constraint of a lawless appetite chose to dwell at the mouth of the Borborus [muddy stream] rather than in the Academy.

Timon again attacked him in the line [b] :

> No, nor yet Aristotle's painful futility.[c]

Such then was the life of the philosopher. I have also come across his will, which is worded thus :

" All will be well ; but, in case anything should happen, Aristotle has made these dispositions. Antipater is to be executor in all matters and in general ; but, until Nicanor shall arrive, Aristomenes, Timarchus, Hipparchus, Dioteles and (if he consent and if circumstances permit him) Theophrastus shall take charge as well of Herpyllis and the children as of the property. And when the girl shall be grown up she shall be given in marriage to Nicanor ; but if anything happen to the girl (which heaven forbid and no such thing will happen) before her marriage, or when she is married but before there are children, Nicanor shall have full powers, both with regard to the child and with regard to everything else, to administer in a manner worthy both of himself and of us. Nicanor shall take charge of the girl and of the boy Nicomachus as he shall think fit in all that concerns them as if he were father and brother. And if anything should happen to Nicanor (which heaven forbid !) either before he marries the girl, or

---

[a] *Anth. Plan.* ii. 46.   [b] Frag. 36 D.
[c] *Cf.* Hom. *Il.* xxiii. 701.

παῖδα ἢ ἐπειδὰν λάβῃ, μήπω παιδίων ὄντων, ἐὰν
13 μέν τι ἐκεῖνος τάξῃ, ταῦτα κύρια ἔστω· ἐὰν δὲ
βούληται Θεόφραστος εἶναι μετὰ τῆς παιδός,
καθάπερ πρὸς Νικάνορα· εἰ δὲ μή, τοὺς ἐπιτρόπους
βουλευομένους μετ' Ἀντιπάτρου καὶ περὶ τῆς
παιδὸς καὶ περὶ τοῦ παιδίου διοικεῖν ὅπως ἂν
αὐτοῖς δοκῇ ἄριστα εἶναι. ἐπιμελεῖσθαι δὲ τοὺς
ἐπιτρόπους καὶ Νικάνορα μνησθέντας ἐμοῦ καὶ
Ἑρπυλλίδος, ὅτι σπουδαία περὶ ἐμὲ ἐγένετο, τῶν
τε ἄλλων καὶ ἐὰν βούληται ἄνδρα λαμβάνειν, ὅπως
μὴ ἀναξίῳ ἡμῶν δοθῇ. δοῦναι δ' αὐτῇ πρὸς τοῖς
πρότερον δεδομένοις καὶ ἀργυρίου τάλαντον ἐκ τῶν
καταλελειμμένων καὶ θεραπαίνας τρεῖς, ⟨ἃς⟩ ἂν
βούληται, καὶ τὴν παιδίσκην ἣν ἔχει καὶ παῖδα τὸν
14 Πυρραῖον· καὶ ἐὰν μὲν ἐν Χαλκίδι βούληται οἰκεῖν,
τὸν ξενῶνα τὸν πρὸς τῷ κήπῳ· ἐὰν δὲ ἐν Σταγείροις,
τὴν πατρῴαν οἰκίαν. ὁποτέραν δ' ἂν τούτων
βούληται, κατασκευάσαι τοὺς ἐπιτρόπους σκεύεσιν
οἷς ἂν δοκῇ κάκείνοις καλῶς ἔχειν καὶ Ἑρπυλλίδι
ἱκανῶς. ἐπιμελείσθω δὲ Νικάνωρ καὶ Μύρμηκος
τοῦ παιδίου, ὅπως ἂν ἀξίως ἡμῶν τοῖς ἰδίοις
ἐπικομισθῇ σὺν τοῖς ὑπάρχουσιν ἃ εἰλήφαμεν αὐτοῦ.
εἶναι δὲ καὶ Ἀμβρακίδα ἐλευθέραν καὶ δοῦναι
αὐτῇ, ὅταν ἡ παῖς ἐκδοθῇ, πεντακοσίας δραχμὰς
καὶ τὴν παιδίσκην ἣν ἔχει. δοῦναι δὲ καὶ Θαλῇ
πρὸς τῇ παιδίσκῃ ἣν ἔχει, τῇ ὠνηθείσῃ, χιλίας
15 δραχμὰς καὶ παιδίσκην· καὶ Σίμωνι χωρὶς τοῦ
πρότερον ἀργυρίου αὐτῷ ⟨δοθέντος⟩ εἰς παῖδ'
ἄλλον, ἢ παῖδα πρίασθαι ἢ ἀργύριον ἐπιδοῦναι.
Τύχωνα δ' ἐλεύθερον εἶναι, ὅταν ἡ παῖς ἐκδοθῇ,
καὶ Φίλωνα καὶ Ὀλύμπιον καὶ τὸ παιδίον αὐτοῦ.

when he has married her but before there are children, any arrangements that he may make shall be valid. And if Theophrastus is willing to live with her, < he shall have > the same rights as Nicanor. Otherwise the executors in consultation with Antipater shall administer as regards the daughter and the boy as seems to them to be best. The executors and Nicanor, in memory of me and of the steady affection which Herpyllis has borne towards me, shall take care of her in every other respect and, if she desires to be married, shall see that she be given to one not unworthy ; and besides what she has already received they shall give her a talent of silver out of the estate and three handmaids whomsoever she shall choose besides the maid she has at present and the man-servant Pyrrhaeus ; and if she chooses to remain at Chalcis, the lodge by the garden, if in Stagira, my father's house. Whichever of these two houses she chooses, the executors shall furnish with such furniture as they think proper and as Herpyllis herself may approve. Nicanor shall take charge of the boy Myrmex, that he be taken to his own friends in a manner worthy of me with the property of his which we received. Ambracis shall be given her freedom, and on my daughter's marriage shall receive 500 drachmas and the maid whom she now has. And to Thale shall be given, in addition to the maid whom she has and who was bought, a thousand drachmas and a maid. And Simon, in addition to the money before paid to him towards another servant, shall either have a servant purchased for him or receive a further sum of money. And Tycho, Philo, Olympius and his child shall have their freedom when my daughter is married. None of

μὴ πωλεῖν δὲ τῶν παίδων μηδένα τῶν ἐμὲ θεραπευόντων, ἀλλὰ χρῆσθαι αὐτοῖς· ὅταν δ' ἐν ἡλικίᾳ
γένωνται, ἐλευθέρους ἀφεῖναι κατ' ἀξίαν. ἐπιμελεῖσθαι δὲ καὶ τῶν ἐκδεδομένων εἰκόνων παρὰ
Γρυλλίωνα, ὅπως ἐπιτελεσθεῖσαι ἀνατεθῶσιν, ἥ τε
Νικάνορος καὶ ἡ Προξένου, ἣν διενοούμην ἐκδοῦναι,
καὶ ἡ τῆς μητρὸς τῆς Νικάνορος· καὶ τὴν Ἀρι-
μνήστου τὴν πεποιημένην ἀναθεῖναι, ὅπως μνημεῖον
16 αὐτοῦ ᾖ, ἐπειδὴ ἄπαις ἐτελεύτησε· καὶ <τὴν> τῆς
μητρὸς τῆς ἡμετέρας τῇ Δήμητρι ἀναθεῖναι εἰς
Νεμέαν ἢ ὅπου ἂν δοκῇ. ὅπου δ' ἂν ποιῶνται τὴν
ταφήν, ἐνταῦθα καὶ τὰ Πυθιάδος ὀστᾶ ἀνελόντας
θεῖναι, ὥσπερ αὐτὴ προσέταξεν· ἀναθεῖναι δὲ καὶ
Νικάνορα σωθέντα, ἣν εὐχὴν ὑπὲρ αὐτοῦ ηὐξάμην,
ζῷα λίθινα τετραπήχη Διὶ σωτῆρι καὶ Ἀθηνᾷ σω-
τείρᾳ ἐν Σταγείροις."

Τοῦτον ἴσχουσιν αὐτῷ αἱ διαθῆκαι τὸν τρόπον.
λέγεται δὲ καὶ λοπάδας αὐτοῦ πλείστας εὑρῆσθαι·
καὶ Λύκωνα λέγειν ὡς ἐν πυέλῳ θερμοῦ ἐλαίου
λούοιτο καὶ τοὔλαιον διαπωλοῖτο. ἔνιοι δὲ καὶ
ἀσκίον θερμοῦ ἐλαίου ἐπιτιθέναι αὐτὸν τῷ στο-
μάχῳ φασί· καὶ ὁπότε κοιμῷτο, σφαῖραν χαλκῆν
βάλλεσθαι αὐτῷ εἰς τὴν χεῖρα λεκάνης ὑποκειμένης,
ἵν' ἐκπεσούσης τῆς σφαίρας εἰς τὴν λεκάνην ὑπὸ
τοῦ ψόφου ἐξέγροιτο.

ᵃ The last clause was curiously misunderstood by three
eminent authorities on Aristotle, namely Grant, Grote and
Zeller, who took ζῷα τετραπήχη to mean " four animal
figures," instead of " figures four cubits high " ; see *Journ.
of Phil.* vol. xxxii. 303. The article " Verify your quotations," although modestly followed by two asterisks, was
written, I believe, by the late Ingram Bywater, then one of
the editors of the journal. This concession by Aristotle to
the popular faith (for the statues from their size seem those

the servants who waited upon me shall be sold but they shall continue to be employed ; and when they arrive at the proper age they shall have their freedom if they deserve it. My executors shall see to it, when the images which Gryllion has been commissioned to execute are finished, that they be set up, namely that of Nicanor, that of Proxenus, which it was my intention to have executed, and that of Nicanor's mother ; also they shall set up the bust which has been executed of Arimnestus, to be a memorial of him seeing that he died childless, and shall dedicate my mother's statue to Demeter at Nemea or wherever they think best. And wherever they bury me, there the bones of Pythias shall be laid, in accordance with her own instructions. And to commemorate Nicanor's safe return, as I vowed on his behalf, they shall set up in Stagira stone statues of life size to Zeus and Athena the Saviours."[a]

Such is the tenor of Aristotle's will. It is said that a very large number of dishes belonging to him were found, and that Lyco mentioned his bathing in a bath of warm oil and then selling the oil. Some relate that he placed a skin of warm oil on his stomach, and that, when he went to sleep, a bronze ball was placed in his hand with a vessel under it, in order that, when the ball dropped from his hand into the vessel, he might be waked up by the sound.[b]

of deities) some critics regard with suspicion, because they see in it a resemblance to the last words of Socrates (Plato, *Phaedo*, 118). Accordingly they are disposed to doubt the genuineness of the will. But see C. G. Bruns, *Kl. Schrift.* ii. 192 *sqq.* ; H. Diels, *Philos. Aufsätze*, 231 *sqq.* ; B. Laum, *Stiftungen in der griech. u. röm. Antike.*

[b] Next come (*a*) the sayings of Aristotle (§§ 17-21) ; (*b*) the catalogue of his writings (§§ 21-27) ; (*c*) his tenets (§§ 28-34).

17 Ἀναφέρεται δ' εἰς αὐτὸν καὶ ἀποφθέγματα
κάλλιστα ταυτί. ἐρωτηθεὶς τί περιγίνεται κέρδος
τοῖς ψευδομένοις, " ὅταν," ἔφη, " λέγωσιν ἀληθῆ,
μὴ πιστεύεσθαι." ὀνειδιζόμενός ποτε ὅτι πονηρῷ
ἀνθρώπῳ ἐλεημοσύνην ἔδωκεν, " οὐ τὸν τρόπον,"
εἶπεν, " ἀλλὰ τὸν ἄνθρωπον ἠλέησα." συνεχὲς
εἰώθει λέγειν πρός τε τοὺς φίλους καὶ τοὺς φοιτῶντας αὐτῷ, ἔνθα ἂν καὶ ὅπου διατρίβων ἔτυχεν, ὡς
ἡ μὲν ὅρασις ἀπὸ τοῦ περιέχοντος [ἀέρος] λαμβάνει
τὸ φῶς, ἡ δὲ ψυχὴ ἀπὸ τῶν μαθημάτων. πολλάκις
δὲ καὶ ἀποτεινόμενος τοὺς Ἀθηναίους ἔφασκεν
εὑρηκέναι πυροὺς καὶ νόμους· ἀλλὰ πυροῖς μὲν
χρῆσθαι, νόμοις δὲ μή.

18 Τῆς παιδείας ἔφη τὰς μὲν ῥίζας εἶναι πικράς,
τὸν δὲ καρπὸν γλυκύν. ἐρωτηθεὶς τί γηράσκει
ταχύ, " χάρις," ἔφη. ἐρωτηθεὶς τί ἐστιν ἐλπίς,
" ἐγρηγορότος," εἶπεν, " ἐνύπνιον." Διογένους
ἰσχάδ' αὐτῷ διδόντος νοήσας ὅτι, εἰ μὴ λάβοι,
χρείαν εἴη μεμελετηκώς, λαβὼν ἔφη Διογένην μετὰ
τῆς χρείας καὶ τὴν ἰσχάδα ἀπολωλεκέναι· πάλιν
τε διδόντος λαβὼν καὶ μετεωρίσας ὡς τὰ παιδία
εἰπών τε " μέγας Διογένης," ἀπέδωκεν αὐτῷ.
τριῶν ἔφη δεῖν παιδείᾳ, φύσεως, μαθήσεως,
ἀσκήσεως. ἀκούσας ὑπό τινος λοιδορεῖσθαι,
" ἀπόντα με," ἔφη, " καὶ μαστιγούτω." τὸ κάλλος παντὸς ἔλεγεν ἐπιστολίου συστατικώτερον.
19 οἱ δὲ οὕτω[1] μὲν Διογένην φασὶν ὁρίσασθαι,
αὐτὸν δὲ θεοῦ[2] δῶρον εἰπεῖν εὐμορφίαν[3]· Σωκράτην

---

[1] οὕτω Byw.: τοῦτο codd.
[2] θεοῦ Cobet : τοῦτο L : om. cett. codd.
[3] εὐμορφίαν Casaub.: εὐμορφίας codd.

[a] Cf. infra, § 21.

Some exceedingly happy sayings are attributed to him, which I proceed to quote. To the question, " What do people gain by telling lies ? " his answer was, " Just this, that when they speak the truth they are not believed." Being once reproached for giving alms to a bad man, he rejoined, " It was the man and not his character that I pitied." [a] He used constantly to say to his friends and pupils, whenever or wherever he happened to be lecturing, " As sight takes in light from the surrounding air, so does the soul from mathematics." Frequently and at some length he would say that the Athenians were the discoverers of wheat and of laws ; but, though they used wheat, they had no use for laws.

" The roots of education," he said, " are bitter, but the fruit is sweet." Being asked, " What is it that soon grows old ? " he answered, " Gratitude." He was asked to define hope, and he replied, " It is a waking dream." When Diogenes offered him dried figs, he saw that he had prepared something caustic to say if he did not take them ; so he took them and said Diogenes had lost his figs and his jest into the bargain. And on another occasion he took them when they were offered, lifted them up aloft, as you do babies, and returned them with the exclamation, " Great is Diogenes." Three things he declared to be indispensable for education : natural endowment, study, and constant practice. On hearing that some one abused him, he rejoined, " He may even scourge me so it be in my absence." Beauty he declared to be a greater recommendation than any letter of introduction. Others attribute this definition to Diogenes ; Aristotle, they say, defined good looks as the gift of god, Socrates as a short-lived reign,

δὲ ὀλιγοχρόνιον τυραννίδα· Πλάτωνα προτέρημα
φύσεως· Θεόφραστον σιωπῶσαν ἀπάτην· Θεό-
κριτον ἐλεφαντίνην ζημίαν· Καρνεάδην ἀδορυ-
φόρητον βασιλείαν. ἐρωτηθεὶς τίνι διαφέρουσιν οἱ
πεπαιδευμένοι τῶν ἀπαιδεύτων, " ὅσῳ," εἶπεν, " οἱ
ζῶντες τῶν τεθνεώτων." τὴν παιδείαν ἔλεγεν
ἐν μὲν ταῖς εὐτυχίαις εἶναι κόσμον, ἐν δὲ ταῖς
ἀτυχίαις καταφυγήν. τῶν γονέων τοὺς παιδεύ-
σαντας ἐντιμοτέρους εἶναι τῶν μόνον γεννησάντων·
τοὺς μὲν γὰρ τὸ ζῆν, τοὺς δὲ τὸ καλῶς ζῆν παρα-
σχέσθαι. πρὸς τὸν καυχώμενον ὡς ἀπὸ μεγάλης
πόλεως εἴη, " οὐ τοῦτο," ἔφη, " δεῖ σκοπεῖν, ἀλλ'
20 ὅστις μεγάλης πατρίδος ἄξιός ἐστιν." ἐρωτηθεὶς
τί ἐστι φίλος, ἔφη, " μία ψυχὴ δύο σώμασιν ἐν-
οικοῦσα." τῶν ἀνθρώπων ἔλεγε τοὺς μὲν οὕτω
φείδεσθαι ὡς ἀεὶ ζησομένους, τοὺς δὲ οὕτως
ἀναλίσκειν ὡς αὐτίκα τεθνηξομένους. πρὸς τὸν
πυθόμενον διὰ τί τοῖς καλοῖς πολὺν χρόνον ὁμι-
λοῦμεν, " τυφλοῦ," ἔφη, " τὸ ἐρώτημα." ἐρωτηθεὶς τί ποτ' αὐτῷ περιγέγονεν ἐκ φιλοσοφίας,
ἔφη, " τὸ ἀνεπιτάκτως ποιεῖν ἅ τινες διὰ τὸν ἀπὸ
τῶν νόμων φόβον ποιοῦσιν." ἐρωτηθεὶς πῶς ἂν
προκόπτοιεν οἱ μαθηταί, ἔφη, " ἐὰν τοὺς προ-
έχοντας διώκοντες τοὺς ὑστεροῦντας μὴ ἀναμένωσι."
πρὸς τὸν εἰπόντα ἀδολέσχην, ἐπειδὴ αὐτοῦ πολλὰ
κατήντλησε, " μήτι σου κατεφλυάρησα;" " μὰ
21 Δί'," εἶπεν· " οὐ γάρ σοι προσεῖχον." πρὸς τὸν
αἰτιασάμενον ὡς εἴη μὴ ἀγαθῷ ἔρανον δεδωκώς—

---

[a] *Cf. supra*, i. § 69, ii. § 69.
[b] Cicero ascribed a similar reply to Xenocrates : " ut id sua
sponte facerent, quod cogerentur facere legibus " (Cic. *De rep.*
i. § 3).

Plato as natural superiority, Theophrastus as a mute
deception, Theocritus as an evil in an ivory setting,
Carneades as a monarchy that needs no bodyguard.
Being asked how the educated differ from the uneducated, " As much," he said, " as the living from
the dead." [a] He used to declare education to be an
ornament in prosperity and a refuge in adversity.
Teachers who educated children deserved, he said,
more honour than parents who merely gave them
birth ; for bare life is furnished by the one, the
other ensures a good life. To one who boasted that
he belonged to a great city his reply was, " That is
not the point to consider, but who it is that is worthy
of a great country." To the query, " What is a
friend ? " his reply was, " A single soul dwelling in
two bodies." Mankind, he used to say, were divided
into those who were as thrifty as if they would live
for ever, and those who were as extravagant as if
they were going to die the next day. When some one
inquired why we spend much time with the beautiful,
" That," he said, " is a blind man's question." When
asked what advantage he had ever gained from
philosophy, he replied, " This, that I do without
being ordered what some are constrained to do by
their fear of the law." [b] The question being put,
how can students make progress, he replied, " By
pressing hard on those in front and not waiting for
those behind." To the chatterbox who poured out
a flood of talk upon him and then inquired, " Have
I bored you to death with my chatter ? " he replied,
" No, indeed ; for I was not attending to you."
When some one accused him of having given a sub-
scription to a dishonest man—for the story is also

φέρεται γὰρ καὶ οὕτως—" οὐ τῷ ἀνθρώπῳ,"
φησίν, " ἔδωκα, ἀλλὰ τῷ ἀνθρωπίνῳ." ἐρωτηθεὶς
πῶς ἂν τοῖς φίλοις προσφεροίμεθα, ἔφη, " ὡς ἂν
εὐξαίμεθα αὐτοὺς ἡμῖν προσφέρεσθαι." τὴν δικαιοσύνην ἔφη ἀρετὴν ψυχῆς διανεμητικὴν τοῦ
κατ' ἀξίαν. κάλλιστον ἐφόδιον τῷ γήρᾳ τὴν
παιδείαν ἔλεγε. φησὶ δὲ Φαβωρῖνος ἐν τῷ δευτέρῳ
τῶν Ἀπομνημονευμάτων ὡς ἑκάστοτε λέγοι, " ᾧ
φίλοι, οὐδεὶς φίλος "· ἀλλὰ καὶ ἐν τῷ ἑβδόμῳ τῶν
Ἠθικῶν ἐστι. καὶ ταῦτα μὲν εἰς αὐτὸν ἀναφέρεται.

Συνέγραψε δὲ πάμπλειστα βιβλία, ἅπερ ἀκό-
λουθον ἡγησάμην ὑπογράψαι διὰ τὴν περὶ πάντας
λόγους τἀνδρὸς ἀρετήν·

22 Περὶ δικαιοσύνης α' β' γ' δ'.
Περὶ ποιητῶν α' β' γ'.
Περὶ φιλοσοφίας α' β' γ'.
Περὶ πολιτικοῦ α' β'.
Περὶ ῥητορικῆς ἢ Γρῦλος α'.
Νήρινθος α'.
Σοφιστὴς α'.
Μενέξενος α'.
Ἐρωτικὸς α'.
Συμπόσιον α'.
Περὶ πλούτου α'.
Προτρεπτικὸς α'.
Περὶ ψυχῆς α'.
Περὶ εὐχῆς α'.
Περὶ εὐγενείας α'.

---

^a Cf. supra, § 17.
^b E.E. vii. 12, 1245 b 20 ; N.E. ix. 10. 6, 1171 a 15-17.
^c This is one of three catalogues which we have of the
Aristotelian writings. Hesychius furnishes one, appended

told in this form [a]—" It was not the man," said he,
" that I assisted, but humanity." To the question
how we should behave to friends, he answered, " As
we should wish them to behave to us." Justice he
defined as a virtue of soul which distributes according
to merit. Education he declared to be the best
provision for old age. Favorinus in the second book
of his *Memorabilia* mentions as one of his habitual
sayings that " He who has friends can have no true
friend." Further, this is found in the seventh book
of the *Ethics*.[b] These then are the sayings attributed
to him.

His writings are very numerous and, considering
the man's all-round excellence, I deemed it in-
cumbent on me to catalogue them[c] :

Of Justice, four books.
On Poets, three books.
On Philosophy, three books.
Of the Statesman, two books.
On Rhetoric, or Grylus, one book.
Nerinthus, one book.
The Sophist, one book.
Menexenus, one book.
Concerning Love, one book.
Symposium, one book.
Of Wealth, one book.
Exhortation to Philosophy, one book.
Of the Soul, one book.
Of Prayer, one book.
On Noble Birth, one book.

to his Life of Aristotle ; see V. Rose's edition of the Fragments, p. 9 *seq.* Another by Ptolemy the philosopher, of
which the Greek original has perished, is preserved in Arabic ;
see V. Rose, Frag. p. 18 *seq.*

Περὶ ἡδονῆς α΄.

'Αλέξανδρος ἢ ὑπὲρ ἀποίκων α΄.

Περὶ βασιλείας α΄.

Περὶ παιδείας α΄.

Περὶ τἀγαθοῦ α΄ β΄ γ΄.

Τὰ ἐκ τῶν νόμων Πλάτωνος α΄ β΄ γ΄.

Τὰ ἐκ τῆς πολιτείας α΄ β΄.

Περὶ οἰκονομίας α΄.

Περὶ φιλίας α΄.

Περὶ τοῦ πάσχειν ἢ πεπονθέναι α΄.

Περὶ ἐπιστημῶν α΄.

Περὶ ἐριστικῶν α΄ β΄.

Λύσεις ἐριστικαὶ δ΄.

Διαιρέσεις σοφιστικαὶ δ΄.

Περὶ ἐναντίων α΄.

Περὶ εἰδῶν καὶ γενῶν α΄.

Περὶ ἰδίων α΄.

23 Ὑπομνήματα ἐπιχειρηματικὰ γ΄.

Προτάσεις περὶ ἀρετῆς α΄ β΄.

'Ενστάσεις α΄.

Περὶ τῶν ποσαχῶς λεγομένων ἢ κατὰ πρόσθεσιν α΄.

Περὶ παθῶν <ἢ περὶ> ὀργῆς α΄.

'Ηθικῶν α΄ β΄ γ΄ δ΄ ε΄.

Περὶ στοιχείων α΄ β΄ γ΄.

Περὶ ἐπιστήμης α΄.

Περὶ ἀρχῆς α΄.

Διαιρέσεις ιζ΄.

Διαιρετικὸν[1] α΄.

<Περὶ> ἐρωτήσεως καὶ ἀποκρίσεως α΄ β΄.

Περὶ κινήσεως α΄.

Προτάσεις α΄.

Προτάσεις ἐριστικαὶ α΄.

---

[1] διαιρετικὸν Rose: -ῶν codd.

On Pleasure, one book.
Alexander, or a Plea for Colonies, one book.
On Kingship, one book.
On Education, one book.
Of the Good, three books.
Extracts from Plato's Laws, three books.
Extracts from the Republic, two books.
Of Household Management, one book.
Of Friendship, one book.
On being or having been affected, one book.
Of Sciences, one book.
On Controversial Questions, two books.
Solutions of Controversial Questions, four books.
Sophistical Divisions, four books.
On Contraries, one book.
On Genera and Species, one book.
On Essential Attributes, one book.
Three note-books on Arguments for Purposes of
    Refutation.
Propositions concerning Virtue, two books.
Objections, one book.
On the Various Meanings of Terms or Expressions
    where a Determinant is added, one book.
Of Passions or of Anger, one book.
Five books of Ethics.
On Elements, three books.
Of Science, one book.
Of Logical Principle, one book.
Logical Divisions, seventeen books.
Concerning Division, one book.
On Dialectical Questioning and Answering, two books.
Of Motion, one book.
Propositions, one book.
Controversial Propositions, one book.

Συλλογισμοὶ αʹ.
Προτέρων ἀναλυτικῶν αʹ βʹ γʹ δʹ εʹ ϛʹ ζʹ ηʹ.
Ἀναλυτικῶν ὑστέρων μεγάλων αʹ βʹ
Περὶ προβλημάτων αʹ.
Μεθοδικὰ αʹ βʹ γʹ δʹ εʹ ϛʹ ζʹ ηʹ.
Περὶ τοῦ βελτίονος αʹ.
Περὶ τῆς ἰδέας αʹ.
Ὅροι πρὸ τῶν τοπικῶν αʹ βʹ γʹ δʹ εʹ ϛʹ ζʹ.
Συλλογισμῶν αʹ βʹ.
24 Συλλογιστικὸν καὶ ὅροι αʹ.
Περὶ τοῦ αἱρετοῦ καὶ τοῦ συμβεβηκότος αʹ.
Τὰ πρὸ τῶν τόπων αʹ.
Τοπικῶν πρὸς τοὺς ὅρους αʹ βʹ.
Πάθη αʹ.
Διαιρετικὸν αʹ.
Μαθηματικὸν αʹ.
Ὁρισμοὶ ιγʹ.
Ἐπιχειρημάτων αʹ βʹ.
Περὶ ἡδονῆς αʹ.
Προτάσεις αʹ.
Περὶ ἑκουσίου αʹ.
Περὶ καλοῦ αʹ.
Θέσεις ἐπιχειρηματικαὶ κεʹ.
Θέσεις ἐρωτικαὶ δʹ.
Θέσεις φιλικαὶ βʹ.
Θέσεις περὶ ψυχῆς αʹ.
Πολιτικὰ[1] βʹ.
Πολιτικῆς ἀκροάσεως ὡς ἡ Θεοφράστου αʹ βʹ γʹ δʹ εʹ
    ϛʹ ζʹ ηʹ.
Περὶ δικαίων αʹ βʹ.
Τεχνῶν συναγωγὴ αʹ βʹ.
Τέχνης ῥητορικῆς αʹ βʹ.
Τέχνη αʹ.

----

[1] ⟨Θέσεις⟩ πολιτικα⟨ὶ⟩ Rose: Πολιτικὰ codd.

Syllogisms, one book.
Eight books of Prior Analytics.
Two books of Greater Posterior Analytics.
Of Problems, one book.
Eight books of Methodics.
Of the Greater Good, one book.
On the Idea, one book.
Definitions prefixed to the Topics, seven books.
Two books of Syllogisms.
Concerning Syllogism with Definitions, one book.
Of the Desirable and the Contingent, one book.
Preface to Commonplaces, one book.
Two books of Topics criticizing the Definitions.
Affections or Qualities, one book.
Concerning Logical Division, one book.
Concerning Mathematics, one book.
Definitions, thirteen books.
Two books of Refutations.
Of Pleasure, one book.
Propositions, one book.
On the Voluntary, one book.
On the Beautiful, one book.
Theses for Refutation, twenty-five books.
Theses concerning Love, four books.
Theses concerning Friendship, two books.
Theses concerning the Soul, one book.
Politics, two books.
Eight books of a course of lectures on Politics like
     that of Theophrastus.
Of Just Actions, two books.
A Collection of Arts [that is, Handbooks], two
     books.
Two books of the Art of Rhetoric.
Art, a Handbook, one book.

Αλλης τεχνῶν συναγωγῆς α' β'.
Μεθοδικὸν α'.
Τέχνης τῆς Θεοδέκτου συναγωγὴ α'.
Πραγματεία τέχνης ποιητικῆς α' β'.
Ἐνθυμήματα ῥητορικὰ α'.
Περὶ μεγέθους α'.
Ἐνθυμημάτων διαιρέσεις α'.
Περὶ λέξεως α' β'.
Περὶ συμβουλίας α'.
25 Συναγωγῆς α' β'.
Περὶ φύσεως α' β' γ'.
Φυσικὸν α'.
Περὶ τῆς Ἀρχυτείου φιλοσοφίας α' β' γ'.
Περὶ τῆς Σπευσίππου καὶ Ξενοκράτους α'.
Τὰ ἐκ τοῦ Τιμαίου καὶ τῶν Ἀρχυτείων α'.
Πρὸς τὰ Μελίσσου α'.
Πρὸς τὰ Ἀλκμαίωνος α'.
Πρὸς τοὺς Πυθαγορείους α'.
Πρὸς τὰ Γοργίου α'.
Πρὸς τὰ Ξενοφάνους α'.
Πρὸς τὰ Ζήνωνος α'.
Περὶ τῶν Πυθαγορείων α'.
Περὶ ζῴων α' β' γ' δ' ε' ϛ' ζ' η' θ'.
Ἀνατομῶν α' β' γ' δ' ε' ϛ' ζ' η'.
Ἐκλογὴ ἀνατομῶν α'.
Ὑπὲρ τῶν συνθέτων ζῴων α'.
Ὑπὲρ τῶν μυθολογουμένων ζῴων α'.
Ὑπὲρ τοῦ μὴ γεννᾶν α'.
Περὶ φυτῶν α' β'.
Φυσιογνωμονικὸν α'.

---

[a] Περὶ μεγέθους, between two books on Enthymemes, must be on Degree, the topic of μᾶλλον καὶ ἧττον (§ 60). " Degree " is Cope's term (see his *Introduction to Aristotle's Rhetoric*, p. 129, where he cites Aristotle's own distinctions in *Rhetoric*, ii. cc. 18, 19).

Another Collection of Handbooks, two books.
Concerning Method, one book.
Compendium of the " Art " of Theodectes, one book.
A Treatise on the Art of Poetry, two books.
Rhetorical Enthymemes, one book.
Of Degree,ᵃ one book.
Divisions of Enthymemes, one book.
On Diction, two books.
Of Taking Counsel, one book.
A Collection or Compendium, two books.
On Nature, three books.
Concerning Nature, one book.
On the Philosophy of Archytas, three books.
On the Philosophy of Speusippus and Xenocrates, one book.
Extracts from the *Timaeus* and from the Works of Archytas, one book.
A Reply to the Writings of Melissus, one book.
A Reply to the Writings of Alcmaeon, one book.
A Reply to the Pythagoreans, one book.
A Reply to the Writings of Gorgias, one book.
A Reply to the Writings of Xenophanes, one book.
A Reply to the Writings of Zeno, one book.
On the Pythagoreans, one book.
On Animals, nine books.
Eight books of Dissections.
A selection of Dissections, one book.
On Composite Animals, one book.
On the Animals of Fable, one book.
On Sterility, one book.
On Plants, two books.
Concerning Physiognomy, one book.

Ἰατρικὰ β'.
Περὶ μονάδος α'.
26 Σημεῖα χειμώνων α'.
Ἀστρονομικὸν α'.
Ὀπτικὸν α'.
Περὶ κινήσεως α'.
Περὶ μουσικῆς α'.
Μνημονικὸν α'.
Ἀπορημάτων Ὁμηρικῶν α' β' γ' δ' ε' ϛ'.
Ποιητικὰ α'.
Φυσικῶν κατὰ στοιχεῖον λη'.
Ἐπιτεθεαμένων προβλημάτων α' β'.
Ἐγκυκλίων α' β'.
Μηχανικὸν α'.
Προβλήματα ἐκ τῶν Δημοκρίτου β'.
Περὶ τῆς λίθου α'.
Παραβολαὶ α'.
Ἄτακτα ιβ'.
Ἐξηγημένα κατὰ γένος ιδ'.
Δικαιώματα α'.
Ὀλυμπιονῖκαι α'.
Πυθιονῖκαι <α'.
Περὶ> μουσικῆς α'.
Πυθικὸς α'.
Πυθιονικῶν ἔλεγχος α'.
Νῖκαι Διονυσιακαὶ α'.
Περὶ τραγῳδιῶν α'.
Διδασκαλίαι α'.
Παροιμίαι α'.
Νόμοι συσσιτικοὶ[1] α'.
Νόμων α' β' γ' δ'.
Κατηγοριῶν α'.

---

[1] νομὸς συστατικὸς codd.: corr. Rose.

Two books concerning Medicine.

On the Unit, one book.

Prognostics of Storms, one book.

Concerning Astronomy, one book.

Concerning Optics, one book.

On Motion, one book.

On Music, one book.

Concerning Memory, one book.

Six books of Homeric Problems.

Poetics, one book.

Thirty - eight books of Physics according to the lettering.

Two books of Problems which have been examined.

Two books of Routine Instruction.

Mechanics, one book.

Problems taken from the works of Democritus, two books.

On the Magnet, one book.

Analogies, one book.

Miscellaneous Notes, twelve books.

Descriptions of Genera, fourteen books.

Claims advanced, one book.

Victors at Olympia, one book.

Victors at the Pythian Games, one book.

On Music, one book.

Concerning Delphi, one book.

Criticism of the List of Pythian Victors, one book.

Dramatic Victories at the Dionysia, one book.

Of Tragedies, one book.

Dramatic Records, one book.

Proverbs, one book.

Laws of the Mess-table, one book.

Four books of Laws.

Categories, one book.

Περὶ ἑρμηνείας αʹ.

27 Πολιτεῖαι πόλεων δυοῖν δεούσαιν ρξʹ <κοιναὶ> καὶ
ἴδιαι, δημοκρατικαί, ὀλιγαρχικαί, ἀριστοκρατικαὶ
καὶ τυραννικαί.

Ἐπιστολαὶ πρὸς Φίλιππον.

Σηλυμβρίων ἐπιστολαί.

Πρὸς Ἀλέξανδρον ἐπιστολαὶ δʹ.

Πρὸς Ἀντίπατρον θʹ.

Πρὸς Μέντορα αʹ.

Πρὸς Ἀρίστωνα αʹ.

Πρὸς Ὀλυμπιάδα αʹ.

Πρὸς Ἡφαιστίωνα αʹ.

Πρὸς Θεμισταγόραν αʹ.

Πρὸς Φιλόξενον αʹ.

Πρὸς Δημόκριτον αʹ.

Ἔπη ὧν ἀρχή, Ἁγνὲ θεῶν πρέσβισθ' ἑκατηβόλε.

Ἐλεγεῖα ὧν ἀρχή, Καλλιτέκνου μητρὸς θύγατερ.

Γίνονται αἱ πᾶσαι μυριάδες στίχων τέτταρες
καὶ τετταράκοντα πρὸς τοῖς πεντακισχιλίοις καὶ
διακοσίοις ἑβδομήκοντα.

28 Καὶ τοσαῦτα μὲν αὐτῷ πεπραγμάτευται βιβλία.
βούλεται δὲ ἐν αὐτοῖς τάδε· διττὸν εἶναι τὸν κατὰ
φιλοσοφίαν λόγον, τὸν μὲν πρακτικόν, τὸν δὲ
θεωρητικόν· καὶ τοῦ πρακτικοῦ τόν τε ἠθικὸν καὶ
πολιτικόν, οὗ τά τε περὶ πόλιν καὶ τὰ περὶ οἶκον
ὑπογεγράφθαι· τοῦ δὲ θεωρητικοῦ τόν τε φυσικὸν
καὶ λογικόν, οὗ τὸ λογικὸν οὐχ ὁλομερῶς, ἀλλ'
ὡς ὄργανον προσηκριβωμένον. καὶ τούτου διττοὺς
ὑποθέμενος σκοποὺς τό τε πιθανὸν καὶ τὸ ἀληθὲς
διεσάφησε. δύο δὲ πρὸς ἑκάτερον δυνάμεσιν ἐχρή-
σατο, διαλεκτικῇ μὲν καὶ ῥητορικῇ πρὸς τὸ πιθα-

De Interpretatione, one book.
Constitutions of 158 Cities, in general and in parti-
    cular, democratic, oligarchic, aristocratic, tyran-
    nical.
Letters to Philip.
Letters of Selymbrians.
Letters to Alexander, four books.
Letters to Antipater, nine books.
To Mentor, one book.
To Ariston, one book.
To Olympias, one book.
To Hephaestion, one book.
To Themistagoras, one book.
To Philoxenus, one book.
In reply to Democritus, one book.
Verses beginning Ἁγνὲ θεῶν πρέσβισθ' ἐκατηβόλε
    (" Holy One and Chiefest of Gods, far-darting ").
Elegiac verses beginning Καλλιτέκνου μητρὸς θύγατερ
    (" Daughter of a Mother blessed with fair
    offspring ").

In all 445,270 lines.
Such is the number of the works written by him.
And in them he puts forward the following views.
There are two divisions of philosophy, the practical
and the theoretical. The practical part includes
ethics and politics, and in the latter not only the
doctrine of the state but also that of the household
is sketched. The theoretical part includes physics
and logic, although logic is not an independent
science, but is elaborated as an instrument to the
rest of science. And he clearly laid down that it
has a twofold aim, probability and truth. For each
of these he employed two faculties, dialectic and
rhetoric where probability is aimed at, analytic and

νόν, ἀναλυτικῇ δὲ καὶ φιλοσοφίᾳ πρὸς τὸ ἀληθές·
οὐδὲν ὑπολειπόμενος οὔτε τῶν πρὸς εὕρεσιν, οὔτε
29 τῶν πρὸς κρίσιν, οὔτε μὴν τῶν πρὸς χρῆσιν. πρὸς
μὲν οὖν τὴν εὕρεσιν τά τε Τοπικὰ καὶ Μεθοδικὰ
παρέδωκε προτάσεων πλῆθος, ἐξ ὧν πρὸς τὰ
προβλήματα πιθανῶν ἐπιχειρημάτων οἷόν τε εὐ-
πορεῖν· πρὸς δὲ τὴν κρίσιν τὰ Ἀναλυτικὰ πρότερα
καὶ ὕστερα. διὰ μὲν οὖν τῶν προτέρων τὰ λήμματα κρίνεται, διὰ δὲ τῶν ὑστέρων ἡ συναγωγὴ
ἐξετάζεται. πρὸς δὲ τὴν χρῆσιν τά τε ἀγωνιστικὰ
καὶ τὰ περὶ ἐρωτήσεως [ἐριστικά τε] καὶ σοφιστι-
κῶν ἐλέγχων τε καὶ συλλογισμῶν καὶ τῶν ὁμοίων
τούτοις. κριτήριον δὲ τῆς ἀληθείας τῶν μὲν κατὰ
φαντασίαν ἐνεργημάτων τὴν αἴσθησιν ἀπεφήνατο·
τῶν δὲ ἠθικῶν, τῶν περὶ πόλιν καὶ περὶ οἶκον καὶ
περὶ νόμους τὸν νοῦν.

30   Τέλος δὲ ἓν ἐξέθετο χρῆσιν ἀρετῆς ἐν βίῳ τελείῳ.
ἔφη δὲ καὶ τὴν εὐδαιμονίαν συμπλήρωμα ἐκ τριῶν
ἀγαθῶν εἶναι· τῶν περὶ ψυχήν, ἃ δὴ καὶ πρῶτα τῇ
δυνάμει καλεῖ· ἐκ δευτέρων δὲ τῶν περὶ σῶμα,
ὑγιείας καὶ ἰσχύος καὶ κάλλους καὶ τῶν παρα-
πλησίων· ἐκ τρίτων δὲ τῶν ἐκτός, πλούτου καὶ
εὐγενείας καὶ δόξης καὶ τῶν ὁμοίων. τήν τε
ἀρετὴν μὴ εἶναι αὐτάρκη πρὸς εὐδαιμονίαν· προσδεῖσθαι γὰρ τῶν τε περὶ σῶμα καὶ τῶν ἐκτὸς
ἀγαθῶν, ὡς κακοδαιμονήσοντος τοῦ σοφοῦ, κἂν
ἐν πόνοις ᾖ κἂν ἐν πενίᾳ καὶ τοῖς ὁμοίοις. τὴν
μέντοι κακίαν αὐτάρκη πρὸς κακοδαιμονίαν, κἂν
ὅτι μάλιστα παρῇ αὐτῇ τὰ ἐκτὸς ἀγαθὰ καὶ τὰ
31 περὶ σῶμα. τάς τ' ἀρετὰς ἔφη μὴ ἀντακολουθεῖν·
ἐνδέχεσθαι γὰρ φρόνιμόν τινα καὶ ὁμοίως δίκαιον

philosophy where the end is truth; he neglects
nothing which makes either for discovery or for
judgement or for utility. As making for discovery
he left in the *Topics* and *Methodics* a number of
propositions, whereby the student can be well sup-
plied with probable arguments for the solution of
problems. As an aid to judgement he left the *Prior*
and *Posterior Analytics*. By the Prior Analytics the
premisses are judged, by the Posterior the process of
inference is tested. For practical use there are the
precepts on controversy and the works dealing with
question and answer, with sophistical fallacies,
syllogisms and the like. The test of truth which he
put forward was sensation in the sphere of objects
actually presented, but in the sphere of morals
dealing with the state, the household and the laws,
it was reason.

The one ethical end he held to be the exercise
of virtue in a completed life. And happiness he
maintained to be made up of goods of three sorts:
goods of the soul, which indeed he designates as
of the highest value; in the second place bodily
goods, health and strength, beauty and the like;
and thirdly external goods, such as wealth, good
birth, reputation and the like. And he regarded
virtue as not of itself sufficient to ensure happiness;
bodily goods and external goods were also necessary,
for the wise man would be miserable if he lived in
the midst of pains, poverty, and similar circumstances.
Vice, however, is sufficient in itself to secure misery,
even if it be ever so abundantly furnished with
corporeal and external goods. He held that the
virtues are not mutually interdependent. For a man
might be prudent, or again just, and at the same

ὄντα ἀκόλαστον καὶ ἀκρατῆ εἶναι. ἔφη δὲ τὸν
σοφὸν ἀπαθῆ μὲν μὴ εἶναι, μετριοπαθῆ δέ.

Τήν τε φιλίαν ὡρίζετο ἰσότητα εὐνοίας ἀντι-
στρόφου· ταύτης δὲ τὴν μὲν εἶναι συγγενικήν, τὴν
δὲ ἐρωτικήν, τὴν δὲ ξενικήν. εἶναι δὲ καὶ τὸν
ἔρωτα μὴ μόνον συνουσίας, ἀλλὰ καὶ φιλοσοφίας.
καὶ ἐρασθήσεσθαι δὲ τὸν σοφὸν καὶ πολιτεύσεσθαι,
γαμήσειν τε μὴν καὶ βασιλεῖ συμβιώσεσθαι. βίων
τε τριῶν ὄντων, θεωρητικοῦ, πρακτικοῦ, ἡδονικοῦ,
τὸν θεωρητικὸν προέκρινεν. εὔχρηστα δὲ καὶ τὰ
ἐγκύκλια μαθήματα πρὸς ἀρετῆς ἀνάληψιν.

82 Ἔν τε τοῖς φυσικοῖς αἰτιολογικώτατος πάντων
ἐγένετο μάλιστα, ὥστε καὶ περὶ τῶν ἐλαχίστων
τὰς αἰτίας ἀποδιδόναι· διόπερ καὶ οὐκ ὀλίγα βιβλία
συνέγραψε φυσικῶν ὑπομνημάτων. τὸν δὲ θεὸν
ἀσώματον ἀπέφαινε, καθὰ καὶ ὁ Πλάτων. διατείνειν δὲ αὐτοῦ τὴν πρόνοιαν μέχρι τῶν οὐρανίων
καὶ εἶναι ἀκίνητον αὐτόν· τὰ δ' ἐπίγεια κατὰ τὴν
πρὸς ταῦτα συμπάθειαν οἰκονομεῖσθαι. εἶναι δὲ
παρὰ τὰ τέτταρα στοιχεῖα καὶ ἄλλο πέμπτον, ἐξ
οὗ τὰ αἰθέρια συνεστάναι. ἀλλοίαν δ' αὐτοῦ τὴν
κίνησιν εἶναι· κυκλοφορητικὴν γάρ. καὶ τὴν ψυχὴν
δὲ ἀσώματον, ἐντελέχειαν οὖσαν τὴν πρώτην
σώματος [γὰρ] φυσικοῦ καὶ ὀργανικοῦ δυνάμει
33 ζωὴν ἔχοντος. λέγει δ' ἐντελέχειαν, ἧς ἐστιν
εἶδός τι ἀσώματον· διττὴ δ' ἐστὶν αὕτη κατ' αὐτόν.[1]

---

[1] διττὴ . . . αὐτὸν ante λέγει δ' vulg.

ᵃ *Cf. supra*, iii. 81. and Aristotle, *Rhet.* ii. 4 § 28, 1381 b 33
ᵇ *De anima*, ii. 1, 412 a 27.

time profligate and unable to control his passions. He said too that the wise man was not exempt from all passions, but indulged them in moderation.

He defined friendship as an equality of reciprocal good-will, including under the term as one species the friendship of kinsmen, as another that of lovers, and as a third that of host and guest.[a] The end of love was not merely intercourse but also philosophy. According to him the wise man would fall in love and take part in politics; furthermore he would marry and reside at a king's court. Of three kinds of life, the contemplative, the practical, and the pleasure-loving life, he gave the preference to the contemplative. He held that the studies which make up the ordinary education are of service for the attainment of virtue.

In the sphere of natural science he surpassed all other philosophers in the investigation of causes, so that even the most insignificant phenomena were explained by him. Hence the unusual number of scientific notebooks which he compiled. Like Plato he held that God was incorporeal; that his providence extended to the heavenly bodies, that he is unmoved, and that earthly events are regulated by their affinity with them (the heavenly bodies). Besides the four elements he held that there is a fifth, of which the celestial bodies are composed. Its motion is of a different kind from that of the other elements, being circular. Further, he maintained the soul to be incorporeal, defining it as the first entelechy [i.e. realization] of a natural organic body potentially possessed of life.[b] By the term realization he means that which has an incorporeal form. This realization, according to him, is twofold.

ἡ μὲν κατὰ δύναμιν, ὡς ἐν τῷ κηρῷ ὁ Ἑρμῆς
ἐπιτηδειότητα ἔχοντι ἐπιδέξασθαι τοὺς χαρακτῆρας, καὶ ὁ ἐν τῷ χαλκῷ ἀνδριάς· καθ' ἕξιν δὲ
λέγεται ἐντελέχεια ἡ τοῦ συντετελεσμένου Ἑρμοῦ
ἢ ἀνδριάντος. σώματος δὲ φυσικοῦ, ἐπεὶ τῶν
σωμάτων τὰ μέν ἐστι χειρόκμητα, ὡς τὰ ὑπὸ
τεχνιτῶν γινόμενα, οἷον πύργος, πλοῖον· τὰ δὲ ὑπὸ
φύσεως, ὡς φυτὰ καὶ τὰ τῶν ζῴων. ὀργανικοῦ
δὲ εἶπε, τουτέστι πρός τι κατεσκευασμένου, ὡς ἡ
ὄρασις πρὸς τὸ ὁρᾶν καὶ ἡ ἀκοὴ πρὸς τὸ ἀκούειν·
δυνάμει δὲ ζωὴν ἔχοντος, οἷον ἐν ἑαυτῷ.

34 Τὸ δυνάμει δὲ διττόν, ἢ καθ' ἕξιν ἢ κατ' ἐνέρ-
γειαν· κατ' ἐνέργειαν μέν, ὡς ὁ ἐγρηγορὼς λέγεται
ψυχὴν ἔχειν· καθ' ἕξιν δ', ὡς ὁ καθεύδων. ἵν' οὖν
καὶ οὗτος ὑποπίπτῃ, τὸ δυνάμει προσέθηκε.

Πολλὰ δὲ καὶ ἄλλα περὶ πολλῶν ἀπεφήνατο,
ἅπερ μακρὸν ἂν εἴη καταριθμεῖσθαι. τοῖς γὰρ
ὅλοις φιλοπονώτατος ἐγένετο καὶ εὑρετικώτατος,
ὡς δῆλον ἐκ τῶν προγεγραμμένων συγγραμμάτων,
ἃ τὸν ἀριθμὸν ἐγγὺς ἥκει τῶν τετρακοσίων, τὰ ὅσα
γε ἀναμφίλεκτα· πολλὰ γὰρ καὶ ἄλλα εἰς αὐτὸν
ἀναφέρεται συγγράμματ' αὐτοῦ καὶ ἀποφθέγματα,
ἀγράφου φωνῆς εὐστοχήματα.

35 Γεγόνασι δὲ Ἀριστοτέλεις ὀκτώ· πρῶτος αὐτὸς
οὗτος· δεύτερος ὁ πολιτευσάμενος Ἀθήνησιν· οὗ
καὶ δικανικοὶ φέρονται λόγοι χαρίεντες· τρίτος
περὶ Ἰλιάδος πεπραγματευμένος· τέταρτος Σι-
κελιώτης ῥήτωρ, πρὸς τὸν Ἰσοκράτους Πανη-
γυρικὸν ἀντιγεγραφώς· πέμπτος ὁ ἐπικληθεὶς
Μῦθος, Αἰσχίνου τοῦ Σωκρατικοῦ γνώριμος· ἕκτος

---

a Probably this is the Aristotle who appears in Plato's
dialogue *Parmenides.*

Either it is potential, as that of Hermes in the wax, provided the wax be adapted to receive the proper mouldings, or as that of the statue implicit in the bronze; or again it is determinate, which is the case with the completed figure of Hermes or the finished statue. The soul is the realization " of a natural body," since bodies may be divided into (a) artificial bodies made by the hands of craftsmen, as a tower or a ship, and (b) natural bodies which are the work of nature, such as plants and the bodies of animals. And when he said " organic " he meant constructed as means to an end, as sight is adapted for seeing and the ear for hearing. Of a body " potentially possessed of life," that is, in itself.

There are two senses of " potential," one answering to a formed state and the other to its exercise in act. In the latter sense of the term he who is awake is said to have soul, in the former he who is asleep. It was then in order to include the sleeper that Aristotle added the word " potential."

He held many other opinions on a variety of subjects which it would be tedious to enumerate. For altogether his industry and invention were remarkable, as is shown by the catalogue of his writings given above, which come to nearly 400 in number, *i.e.* counting those only the genuineness of which is not disputed. For many other written works and pointed oral sayings are attributed to him.

There were in all eight Aristotles: (1) our philosopher himself; (2) an Athenian statesman,[a] the author of graceful forensic speeches; (3) a scholar who commented on the *Iliad*; (4) a Sicilian rhetorician, who wrote a reply to the Panegyric of Isocrates; (5) a disciple of Aeschines the Socratic philosopher,

Κυρηναῖος, γεγραφὼς περὶ ποιητικῆς· ἕβδομος παιδοτρίβης, οὗ μέμνηται Ἀριστόξενος ἐν τῷ Πλάτωνος βίῳ· ὄγδοος, γραμματικὸς ἄσημος, οὗ φέρεται τέχνη περὶ πλεονασμοῦ.

Τοῦ δὴ Σταγειρίτου γεγόνασι μὲν πολλοὶ γνώριμοι, διαφέρων δὲ μάλιστα Θεόφραστος, περὶ οὗ λεκτέον.

Κεφ. β΄. ΘΕΟΦΡΑΣΤΟΣ

36 Θεόφραστος Μελάντα Ἐρέσιος κναφέως υἱός, ὥς φησιν Ἀθηνόδωρος ἐν ὀγδόῃ Περιπάτων. οὗτος πρῶτον μὲν ἤκουσεν Ἀλκίππου τοῦ πολίτου ἐν τῇ πατρίδι, εἶτ' ἀκούσας Πλάτωνος μετέστη πρὸς Ἀριστοτέλην· κἀκείνου εἰς Χαλκίδα ὑποχωρήσαντος αὐτὸς διεδέξατο τὴν σχολὴν Ὀλυμπιάδι τετάρτῃ καὶ δεκάτῃ καὶ ἑκατοστῇ. φέρεται δ' αὐτοῦ καὶ δοῦλος φιλόσοφος ὄνομα Πομπύλος, καθά φησι Μυρωνιανὸς Ἀμαστριανὸς ἐν τῷ πρώτῳ τῶν Ὁμοίων ἱστορικῶν κεφαλαίων. ὁ δὲ Θεόφραστος γέγονεν ἀνὴρ συνετώτατος καὶ φιλοπονώτατος καί, καθά φησι Παμφίλη ἐν τῷ τριακοστῷ δευτέρῳ τῶν Ὑπομνημάτων, διδάσκαλος 37 Μενάνδρου τοῦ κωμικοῦ· ἄλλως τε καὶ εὐεργετικὸς[1] καὶ φιλόλογος. Κάσανδρος γοῦν αὐτὸν ἀπεδέχετο καὶ Πτολεμαῖος ἔπεμψεν ἐπ' αὐτόν· τοσοῦτον δ' ἀποδοχῆς ἠξιοῦτο παρ' Ἀθηναίοις, ὥστ' Ἀγνωνίδης τολμήσας ἀσεβείας αὐτὸν γράψασθαι, μικροῦ καὶ προσῶφλεν. ἀπήντων τ' εἰς τὴν διατριβὴν αὐτοῦ μαθηταὶ πρὸς δισχιλίους. οὗτος τά τ'

[1] ἐνεργητικὸς R.

surnamed Myth ; (6) a native of Cyrene, who wrote upon the art of poetry ; (7) a trainer of boys, mentioned by Aristoxenus in his *Life of Plato* ; (8) an obscure grammarian, whose handbook *On Redundancy* is still extant.

Aristotle of Stagira had many disciples ; the most distinguished was Theophrastus, of whom we have next to speak.

CHAPTER 2. THEOPHRASTUS (*c.* 370–286 B.C.)
(Head of the School from 323 B.C.)

Theophrastus was a native of Eresus, the son of Melantes, a fuller, as stated by Athenodorus in the eighth book of his *Walks*. He first heard his countryman Alcippus lecture in his native town and afterwards he heard Plato, whom he left for Aristotle. And when the latter withdrew to Chalcis he took over the school himself in the 114th Olympiad.[a] A slave of his named Pompylus is also said to have been a philosopher, according to Myronianus of Amastris in the first book of his *Historical Parallels*. Theophrastus was a man of remarkable intelligence and industry and, as Pamphila says in the thirty-second book of her *Memorabilia*, he taught Menander the comic poet. Furthermore, he was ever ready to do a kindness and fond of discussion. Casander certainly granted him audience and Ptolemy made overtures to him. And so highly was he valued at Athens that, when Agnonides ventured to prosecute him for impiety, the prosecutor himself narrowly escaped punishment. About 2000 pupils used to attend his lectures. In a letter to Phanias the

[a] 323 B.C.

ἀλλὰ καὶ περὶ δικαστηρίου[1] τοιαῦτα διείλεκται ἐν
τῇ πρὸς Φανίαν τὸν περιπατητικὸν ἐπιστολῇ· " οὐ
γὰρ ὅτι πανήγυριν, ἀλλ' οὐδὲ συνέδριον ῥᾴδιον,
οἷόν τις βούλεται, λαβεῖν· αἱ δ' ἀναγνώσεις ποιοῦσιν
ἐπανορθώσεις· τὸ δ' ἀναβάλλεσθαι πάντα καὶ
ἀμελεῖν οὐκέτι φέρουσιν αἱ ἡλικίαι." ἐν ταύτῃ τῇ
ἐπιστολῇ σχολαστικὸν ὠνόμακε.

38   Τοιοῦτος δ' ὤν, ὅμως ἀπεδήμησε πρὸς ὀλίγον
καὶ οὗτος καὶ πάντες οἱ λοιποὶ φιλόσοφοι, Σοφοκλέους τοῦ Ἀμφικλείδου νόμον εἰσενεγκόντος,
μηδένα τῶν φιλοσόφων σχολῆς ἀφηγεῖσθαι, ἂν
μὴ τῇ βουλῇ καὶ τῷ δήμῳ δόξῃ· εἰ δὲ μή, θάνατον
εἶναι τὴν ζημίαν. ἀλλ' αὖθις ἐπανῆλθον εἰς νέωτα,
Φίλωνος τὸν Σοφοκλέα γραψαμένου παρανόμων.
ὅτε καὶ τὸν νόμον μὲν ἄκυρον ἐποίησαν Ἀθηναῖοι,
τὸν δὲ Σοφοκλέα πέντε ταλάντοις ἐζημίωσαν
κάθοδόν τε τοῖς φιλοσόφοις ἐψηφίσαντο, ἵνα καὶ
Θεόφραστος κατέλθοι καὶ ἐν τοῖς ὁμοίοις εἴη.
τοῦτον Τύρταμον λεγόμενον Θεόφραστον διὰ τὸ
τῆς φράσεως θεσπέσιον Ἀριστοτέλης μετωνόμα-
39   σεν· οὗ καὶ τοῦ υἱέος Νικομάχου φησὶν ἐρωτικῶς
διατεθῆναι, καίπερ ὄντα διδάσκαλον, Ἀρίστιππος
ἐν τετάρτῳ Περὶ παλαιᾶς τρυφῆς. λέγεται δ' ἐπ'
αὐτοῦ τε καὶ Καλλισθένους τὸ ὅμοιον εἰπεῖν
Ἀριστοτέλην, ὅπερ Πλάτωνα, καθὰ προείρηται,
φασὶν εἰπεῖν ἐπί τε Ξενοκράτους καὶ αὐτοῦ τούτου·
φάναι γάρ, τοῦ μὲν Θεοφράστου καθ' ὑπερβολὴν

_____

[1] δικαστηρίου] διδασκαλίου Wyse; cf. Plut. Mor. 1108 E:
διδακτηρίου Apelt.

_____

[a] In the extract from the letter Theophrastus seems to be
considering the best means of preparing for publication what
he has to say, possibly in lecture, before the large class
which, as we have just been informed, sometimes numbered

Peripatetic, among other topics, he speaks of a tribunal as follows [a] : " To get a public or even a select circle such as one desires is not easy. If an author reads his work, he must re-write it. Always to shirk revision and ignore criticism is a course which the present generation of pupils will no longer tolerate." And in this letter he has called some one " pedant."

Although his reputation stood so high, nevertheless for a short time he had to leave the country with all the other philosophers, when Sophocles the son of Amphiclides proposed a law that no philosopher should preside over a school except by permission of the Senate and the people, under penalty of death. The next year, however, the philosophers returned, as Philo had prosecuted Sophocles for making an illegal proposal. Whereupon the Athenians repealed the law, fined Sophocles five talents, and voted the recall of the philosophers, in order that Theophrastus also might return and live there as before. He bore the name of Tyrtamus, and it was Aristotle who re-named him Theophrastus on account of his graceful style. And Aristippus, in his fourth book *On the Luxury of the Ancients*, asserts that he was enamoured of Aristotle's son Nicomachus, although he was his teacher. It is said that Aristotle applied to him and Callisthenes what Plato had said of Xenocrates and himself (as already related), namely, that the one needed a bridle and the other a goad ; for Theophrastus interpreted all his meaning with

2000. It is difficult to see how this topic can have been worked into a letter on the law courts as such, and there is much to be said for Mr. Wyse's emendation διδασκαλίου. If this be accepted, the whole letter would be about means or subjects of instruction in lecture.

ὀξύτητος πᾶν τὸ νοηθὲν ἐξερμηνεύοντος, τοῦ δὲ
νωθροῦ τὴν φύσιν ὑπάρχοντος, ὡς τῷ μὲν χαλινοῦ
δέοι, τῷ δὲ κέντρου. λέγεται δ᾽ αὐτὸν καὶ ἴδιον
κῆπον σχεῖν μετὰ τὴν Ἀριστοτέλους τελευτήν,
Δημητρίου τοῦ Φαληρέως, ὃς ἦν καὶ γνώριμος
αὐτῷ, τοῦτο συμπράξαντος. φέρεται δ᾽ αὐτοῦ
ἀποφθέγματα ταυτὶ χρειώδη· θᾶττον ἔφη πιστεύειν
40 δεῖν ἵππῳ ἀχαλίνῳ ἢ λόγῳ ἀσυντάκτῳ. πρὸς δὲ
τὸν ἐν τῷ συμποσίῳ σιωπῶντα τὸ ὅλον ἔφη, '' εἰ
μὲν ἀμαθὴς εἶ, φρονίμως ποιεῖς, εἰ δὲ πεπαίδευσαι,
ἀφρόνως.'' συνεχές τε ἔλεγε πολυτελὲς ἀνάλωμα
εἶναι τὸν χρόνον.

Ἐτελεύτα δὴ γηραιός, βιοὺς ἔτη πέντε καὶ
ὀγδοήκοντα, ἐπειδήπερ ὀλίγον ἀνῆκε τῶν πόνων.
καὶ ἔστιν ἡμῶν εἰς αὐτόν·

οὐκ ἄρα τοῦτο μάταιον ἔπος μερόπων τινὶ λέχθη,
ῥήγνυσθαι σοφίης τόξον ἀνιέμενον·
δὴ γὰρ καὶ Θεόφραστος ἕως ἐπόνει μὲν ἄπηρος
ἦν δέμας, εἶτ᾽ ἀνεθεὶς κάτθανε πηρομελής.

Φασὶ δ᾽ αὐτὸν ἐρωτηθέντα ὑπὸ τῶν μαθητῶν εἴ
τι ἐπισκήπτει, εἰπεῖν, '' ἐπισκήπτειν μὲν ἔχειν
οὐδέν, πλὴν ὅτι πολλὰ τῶν ἡδέων ὁ βίος διὰ τὴν
41 δόξαν καταλαζονεύεται. ἡμεῖς γὰρ ὁπότ᾽ ἀρχό-
μεθα ζῆν, τότ᾽ ἀποθνήσκομεν. οὐδὲν οὖν ἀλυσι-
τελέστερόν ἐστι φιλοδοξίας. ἀλλ᾽ εὐτυχεῖτε καὶ
ἤτοι τὸν λόγον ἄφετε—πολὺς γὰρ ὁ πόνος—ἢ
καλῶς αὐτοῦ πρόστητε· μεγάλη γὰρ ἡ δόξα. τὸ
δὲ κενὸν τοῦ βίου πλέον τοῦ συμφέροντος. ἀλλ᾽
ἐμοὶ μὲν οὐκέτ᾽ ἐκποιεῖ βουλεύεσθαι τί πρακτέον,
ὑμεῖς δ᾽ ἐπισκέψασθε τί ποιητέον.'' ταῦτα, φασίν,

an excess of cleverness, whereas the other was naturally backward. He is said to have become the owner of a garden of his own after Aristotle's death, through the intervention of his friend Demetrius of Phalerum. There are pithy sayings of his in circulation as follows : " An unbridled horse," he said, " ought to be trusted sooner than a badly-arranged discourse." To some one who never opened his lips at a banquet he remarked : " Yours is a wise course for an ignoramus, but in an educated man it is sheer folly." He used constantly to say that in our expenditure the item that costs most is time.

He died at the age of eighty-five, not long after he had relinquished his labours. My verses upon him are these [a] :

Not in vain was the word spoken to one of human kind,
" Slacken the bow of wisdom and it breaks." Of a truth, so long as Theophrastus laboured he was sound of limb, but when released from toil his limbs failed him and he died.

It is said that his disciples asked him if he had any last message for them, to which he replied : " Nothing else but this, that many of the pleasures which life boasts are but in the seeming. For when we are just beginning to live, lo ! we die. Nothing then is so unprofitable as the love of glory. Farewell, and may you be happy. Either drop my doctrine, which involves a world of labour, or stand forth its worthy champions, for you will win great glory. Life holds more disappointment than advantage. But, as I can no longer discuss what we ought to do, do you go on with the inquiry into right conduct."

[a] *Anth. Pal* vii. 110.

εἰπὼν ἀπέπνευσε· καὶ αὐτόν, ὡς ὁ λόγος, Ἀθηναῖοι
πανδημεὶ παρέπεμψαν ποσί, τὸν ἄνδρα τιμήσαντες.
Φαβωρῖνος δέ φησι γηράσαντα αὐτὸν ἐν φορείῳ
περιφέρεσθαι· καὶ τοῦτο λέγειν Ἕρμιππον, παρα-
τιθέμενον ἱστορεῖν Ἀρκεσίλαον τὸν Πιταναῖον
ἐν οἷς ἔφασκε πρὸς Λακύδην τὸν Κυρηναῖον.

42   Καταλέλοιπε δὲ βιβλία καὶ αὐτὸς ὅτι μάλιστα
πάμπλειστα, ἃ καὶ αὐτὰ ἄξιον ἡγησάμην ὑπογράψαι
διὰ τὸ πάσης ἀρετῆς πεπληρῶσθαι. ἔστι δὲ τάδε·

Ἀναλυτικῶν προτέρων α' β' γ'.
Ἀναλυτικῶν ὑστέρων α' β' γ' δ' ε' ϛ' ζ'.
Περὶ ἀναλύσεως συλλογισμῶν α'.
Ἀναλυτικῶν ἐπιτομὴ α'.
Ἀνηγμένων τόπων α' β'.
Ἀγωνιστικὸν τῆς περὶ τοὺς ἐρωτικοὺς λόγους θεωρίας
Περὶ αἰσθήσεων α'.
Πρὸς Ἀναξαγόραν α'.
Περὶ τῶν Ἀναξαγόρου α'.
Περὶ τῶν Ἀναξιμένους α'.
Περὶ τῶν Ἀρχελάου α'.
Περὶ ἁλῶν, νίτρου, στυπτηρίας α'.
Περὶ τῶν λιθουμένων α' β'.
Περὶ τῶν ἀτόμων γραμμῶν α'.
Ἀκροάσεως α' β'.
Περὶ ἀνέμων α'.
Ἀρετῶν διαφοραὶ α'.
Περὶ βασιλείας α'.
Περὶ παιδείας βασιλέως α'.
Περὶ βίων α' β' γ'.
43 Περὶ γήρως α'.
Περὶ τῆς Δημοκρίτου ἀστρολογίας α'.

ᵃ *Cf.* a similar statement about Bion, also attributed to
Favorinus.

With these words, they say, he breathed his last. And according to the story all the Athenians, out of respect for the man, escorted his bier on foot. And Favorinus tells that he had in his old age to be carried about in a litter [a]; and this he says on the authority of Hermippus, whose account is taken from a remark of Arcesilaus of Pitane to Lacydes of Cyrene.

He too has left a very large number of writings. I think it right to catalogue them also because they abound in excellence of every kind. They are as follows :

Three books of Prior Analytics.
Seven books of Posterior Analytics.
On the Analysis of Syllogisms, one book.
Epitome of Analytics, one book.
Two books of Classified Topics.
Polemical discussion on the Theory of Eristic Argument.
Of the Senses, one book.
A Reply to Anaxagoras, one book.
On the Writings of Anaxagoras, one book.
On the Writings of Anaximenes, one book.
On the Writings of Archelaus, one book.
Of Salt, Nitre and Alum, one book.
Of Petrifactions, two books.
On Indivisible Lines, one book.
Two books of Lectures.
Of the Winds, one book.
Characteristics of Virtues, one book.
Of Kingship, one book.
Of the Education of Kings, one book.
Of Various Schemes of Life, three books.
Of Old Age, one book.
On the Astronomy of Democritus, one book.

Τῆς μεταρσιολεσχίας α΄.
Περὶ τῶν εἰδώλων α΄.
Περὶ χυμῶν, χρῶν, σαρκῶν α΄.
Περὶ τοῦ διακόσμου α΄.
Περὶ τῶν ἀνθρώπων α΄.
Τῶν Διογένους συναγωγὴ α΄.
Διορισμῶν α΄ β΄ γ΄.
Ἐρωτικὸς α΄.
Ἄλλο περὶ ἔρωτος α΄.
Περὶ εὐδαιμονίας α΄.
Περὶ εἰδῶν α΄ β΄.
Περὶ ἐπιλήψεως α΄.
Περὶ ἐνθουσιασμοῦ α΄.
Περὶ Ἐμπεδοκλέους α΄.
Ἐπιχειρημάτων α΄ β΄ γ΄ δ΄ ε΄ ς΄ ζ΄ η΄ θ΄ ι΄ ια΄ ιβ΄
    ιγ΄ ιδ΄ ιε΄ ις΄ ιζ΄ ιη΄.
Ἐνστάσεων α΄ β΄ γ΄.
Περὶ ἑκουσίου α΄.
Ἐπιτομὴ τῆς Πλάτωνος Πολιτείας α΄ β΄.
Περὶ ἑτεροφωνίας ζῴων τῶν ὁμογενῶν α΄.
Περὶ τῶν ἀθρόων φαινομένων α΄.
Περὶ δακέτων καὶ βλητικῶν α΄.
Περὶ τῶν ζῴων ὅσα λέγεται φθονεῖν ι΄.
Περὶ τῶν ἐν ξηρῷ διαμενόντων α΄.
14 Περὶ τῶν τὰς χρόας μεταβαλλόντων ι΄.
Περὶ τῶν φωλευόντων α΄.
Περὶ ζῴων α΄ β΄ γ΄ δ΄ ε΄ ς΄ ζ΄.
Περὶ ἡδονῆς ὡς Ἀριστοτέλης α΄.
Περὶ ἡδονῆς ἄλλο α΄.
Θέσεις κδ΄.
Περὶ θερμοῦ καὶ ψυχροῦ α΄.
Περὶ ἰλίγγων καὶ σκοτώσεων α΄.
Περὶ ἰδρώτων α΄.

On Meteorology, one book.
On Visual Images or Emanations, one book.
On Flavours, Colours and Flesh, one book.
Of the Order of the World, one book.
Of Mankind, one book.
Compendium of the Writings of Diogenes, one book.
Three books of Definitions.
Concerning Love, one book.
Another Treatise on Love, one book.
Of Happiness, one book.
On Species or Forms, two books.
On Epilepsy, one book.
On Frenzy, one book.
Concerning Empedocles, one book.
Eighteen books of Refutative Arguments.
Three books of Polemical Objections.
Of the Voluntary, one book.
Epitome of Plato's Republic, two books.
On the Diversity of Sounds uttered by Animals of
    the same Species, one book.
Of Sudden Appearances, one book.
Of Animals which bite or gore, one book.
Of Animals reputed to be spiteful, one book.
Of the Animals which are confined to Dry Land, one
    book.
Of those which change their Colours, one book.
Of Animals that burrow, one book.
Of Animals, seven books.
Of Pleasure according to Aristotle, one book.
Another treatise on Pleasure, one book.
Theses, twenty-four books.
On Hot and Cold, one book.
On Vertigo and Dizziness, one book.
On Sweating Sickness, one book.

Περὶ καταφάσεως καὶ ἀποφάσεως αʹ.
Καλλισθένης ἢ περὶ πένθους αʹ.
Περὶ κόπων α.
Περὶ κινήσεως αʹ βʹ γʹ.
Περὶ λίθων αʹ.
Περὶ λοιμῶν αʹ.
Περὶ λιποψυχίας αʹ.
Μεγαρικὸς αʹ.
Περὶ μελαγχολίας αʹ.
Περὶ μετάλλων αʹ βʹ.
Περὶ μέλιτος αʹ.
Περὶ τῶν Μητροδώρου συναγωγῆς αʹ.
Μεταρσιολογικῶν αʹ βʹ.
Περὶ μέθης αʹ.
Νόμων κατὰ στοιχεῖον κδʹ.
Νόμων ἐπιτομῆς αʹ βʹ γʹ δʹ εʹ ϛʹ ζʹ ηʹ θʹ ιʹ.
45 Πρὸς τοὺς ὁρισμοὺς αʹ.
Περὶ ὀδμῶν αʹ.
Περὶ οἴνου καὶ ἐλαίου.
Πρώτων προτάσεων αʹ βʹ γʹ δʹ εʹ ϛʹ ζʹ ηʹ θʹ ιʹ ιαʹ
ιβʹ ιγʹ ιδʹ ιεʹ ιϛʹ ιζʹ ιηʹ.
Νομοθετῶν αʹ βʹ γʹ.
Πολιτικῶν αʹ βʹ γʹ δʹ εʹ ϛʹ.
Πολιτικὸν πρὸς τοὺς καιροὺς αʹ βʹ γʹ δʹ.
Πολιτικῶν ἐθῶν αʹ βʹ γʹ δʹ.
Περὶ τῆς ἀρίστης πολιτείας αʹ.
Προβλημάτων συναγωγῆς αʹ βʹ γʹ δʹ εʹ.
Περὶ παροιμιῶν αʹ.
Περὶ πήξεων καὶ τήξεων αʹ.
Περὶ πυρὸς αʹ βʹ.
Περὶ πνευμάτων αʹ.
Περὶ παραλύσεως αʹ.

On Affirmation and Negation, one book.
Callisthenes, or On Bereavement, one book.
On Fatigues, one book.
On Motion, three books.
On Precious Stones, one book.
On Pestilences, one book.
On Fainting, one book.
Megarian Treatise, one book.
Of Melancholy, one book.
On Mines, two books.
On Honey, one book.
Compendium on the Doctrines of Metrodorus, one book.
Two books of Meteorology.
On Intoxication, one book.
Twenty-four books of Laws distinguished by the letters of the alphabet.
Ten books of an Epitome of Laws.
Remarks upon Definitions, one book.
On Smells, one book.
On Wine and Oil.
Introduction to Propositions, eighteen books.
Of Legislators, three books.
Of Politics, six books.
A Political Treatise dealing with important Crises, four books.
Of Social Customs, four books.
Of the Best Constitution, one book.
A Collection of Problems, five books.
On Proverbs, one book.
On Coagulation and Liquefaction, one book.
On Fire, two books.
On Winds, one book.
Of Paralysis, one book.

Περὶ πνιγμοῦ αʹ
Περὶ παραφροσυνης αʹ.
Περὶ παθῶν αʹ.
Περὶ σημείων αʹ.
Σοφισμάτων αʹ βʹ.
Περὶ συλλογισμῶν λύσεως αʹ.
Τοπικῶν αʹ βʹ.
Περὶ τιμωρίας αʹ βʹ.
Περὶ τριχῶν αʹ.
Περὶ τυραννίδος αʹ.
Περὶ ὕδατος αʹ βʹ γʹ.
Περὶ ὕπνου καὶ ἐνυπνίων αʹ.
Περὶ φιλίας αʹ βʹ γʹ.
Περὶ φιλοτιμίας αʹ βʹ.
16 Περὶ φύσεως αʹ βʹ γʹ
Περὶ φυσικῶν αʹ βʹ γʹ δʹ εʹ ςʹ ζʹ ηʹ θʹ ιʹ ιαʹ ιβʹ ιγʹ
    ιδʹ ιεʹ ιςʹ ιζʹ ιηʹ.
Περὶ φυσικῶν ἐπιτομῆς αʹ βʹ.
Φυσικῶν αʹ βʹ γʹ δʹ εʹ ςʹ ζʹ ηʹ.
Πρὸς τοὺς φυσικοὺς αʹ.
Περὶ φυτικῶν ἱστοριῶν αʹ βʹ γʹ δʹ εʹ ςʹ ζʹ ηʹ θʹ ιʹ.
Φυτικῶν αἰτιῶν αʹ βʹ γʹ δʹ εʹ ςʹ ζʹ ηʹ
Περὶ χυλῶν αʹ βʹ γʹ δʹ εʹ.
Περὶ ψεύδους ἡδονῆς αʹ.
Περὶ ψυχῆς θέσις μία.
Περὶ τῶν ἀτέχνων πίστεων αʹ.
Περὶ τῶν ἁπλῶν διαπορημάτων αʹ.
Ἁρμονικῶν αʹ.
Περὶ ἀρετῆς αʹ.
Ἀφορμαὶ ἢ ἐναντιώσεις αʹ.
Περὶ ἀποφάσεως αʹ.
Περι γνώμης αʹ.
Περὶ γελοίου αʹ.
Δειλινῶν αʹ βʹ.

Of Suffocation, one book.
Of Mental Derangement, one book.
On the Passions, one book.
On Symptoms, one book.
Two books of Sophisms.
On the solution of Syllogisms, one book.
Two books of Topics.
Of Punishment, two books.
On Hair, one book.
Of Tyranny, one book.
On Water, three books.
On Sleep and Dreams, one book.
Of Friendship, three books.
Of Ambition, two books.
On Nature, three books.
On Physics, eighteen books.
An Epitome of Physics, two books.
Eight books of Physics.
A Reply to the Physical Philosophers, one book
Of Botanical Researches, ten books.
Of Botanical Causes, eight books.
On Juices, five books.
Of False Pleasure, one book.
One Dissertation on the Soul.
On Unscientific Proofs, one book.
On Simple Problems, one book.
Harmonics, one book.
Of Virtue, one book.
Materials for Argument, or Contrarieties, one
    book.
On Negation, one book.
On Judgement, one book.
Of the Ludicrous, one book.
Afternoon Essays, two books.

Διαιρέσεις α' β'.
Περὶ τῶν διαφορῶν α'.
Περὶ τῶν ἀδικημάτων α'.
Περὶ διαβολῆς α'.
Περὶ ἐπαίνου α'.
Περὶ ἐμπειρίας α'.
Ἐπιστολῶν α' β' γ'.
Περὶ τῶν αὐτομάτων ζῴων α'.
Περὶ ἐκκρίσεως α'.
47 Ἐγκώμια θεῶν α'.
Περὶ ἑορτῶν α'.
Περὶ εὐτυχίας α'.
Περὶ ἐνθυμημάτων α'.
Περὶ εὑρημάτων α' β'.
Ἠθικῶν σχολῶν α'.
Ἠθικοὶ χαρακτῆρες α'.
Περὶ θορύβου α'.
Περὶ ἱστορίας α'.
Περὶ κρίσεως συλλογισμῶν α'.
Περὶ κολακείας α'.
Περὶ θαλάττης α'.
Πρὸς Κάσανδρον περὶ βασιλείας α'.
Περὶ κωμῳδίας α'.
[Περὶ μέτρων α'].
Περὶ λέξεως α'.
Λόγων συναγωγὴ α'.
Λύσεις α'.
Περὶ μουσικῆς α' β' γ'.
Περὶ μέτρων α'.
Μεγακλῆς α'.
Περὶ νόμων α'.
Περὶ παρανόμων α'.
Τῶν Ξενοκράτους συναγωγῆς α'.

Divisions, two books.
On Differences, one book.
On Crimes, one book.
On Calumny, one book.
Of Praise, one book.
Of Experience, one book.
Three books of Letters.
On Animals produced spontaneously, one book.
Of Secretion, one book.
Panegyrics on the Gods, one book.
On Festivals, one book.
Of Good Fortune, one book.
On Enthymemes, one book.
Of Discoveries, two books.
Lectures on Ethics, one book.
Character Sketches, one book.
On Tumult or Riot, one book.
On Research, one book.
On Judging of Syllogisms, one book.
Of Flattery, one book.
Of the Sea, one book.
To Casander on Kingship, one book.
Of Comedy, one book.
[Of Metres, one book.]
Of Diction, one book.
A Compendium of Arguments, one book.
Solutions, one book.
On Music, three books.
On Measures, one book.
Megacles, one book.
On Laws, one book.
On Illegalities, one book.
A Compendium of the Writings of Xenocrates, one
    book.

Ὁμιλητικὸς α΄.

Περὶ ὅρκου α΄.

Παραγγέλματα ῥητορικῆς α΄.

Περὶ πλούτου α΄.

Περὶ ποιητικῆς α΄.

Προβλήματα πολιτικά, ἠθικά, φυσικά, ἐρωτικὰ α΄.

48 Προοιμίων α΄.

Προβλημάτων συναγωγῆς α΄.

Περὶ τῶν προβλημάτων φυσικῶν α΄.

Περὶ παραδείγματος α΄.

Περὶ προθέσεως καὶ διηγήματος α΄.

Περὶ ποιητικῆς ἄλλο α΄.

Περὶ τῶν σοφῶν α΄.

Περὶ συμβουλῆς α΄.

Περὶ σολοικισμῶν α΄.

Περὶ τέχνης ῥητορικῆς α΄.

Περὶ τεχνῶν ῥητορικῶν εἴδη ιζ΄.

Περὶ ὑποκρίσεως α΄.

Ὑπομνημάτων Ἀριστοτελικῶν ἢ Θεοφραστείων α΄ β΄
γ΄ δ΄ ε΄ ϛ΄.

Φυσικῶν δοξῶν α΄ β΄ γ΄ δ΄ ε΄ ϛ΄ ζ΄ η΄ θ΄ ι΄ ια΄ ιβ΄
ιγ΄ ιδ΄ ιε΄ ιϛ΄.

Φυσικῶν [δοξῶν] ἐπιτομῆς α΄.

Περὶ χάριτος α΄.

[Χαρακτῆρες ἠθικοί.]

Περὶ ψεύδους καὶ ἀληθοῦς α΄.

Τῶν περὶ τὸ θεῖον ἱστορίας α΄ β΄ γ΄ δ΄ ε΄ ϛ΄.

Περὶ θεῶν α΄ β΄ γ΄.

Ἱστορικῶν γεωμετρικῶν α΄ β΄ γ΄ δ΄.

49 Ἐπιτομῶν Ἀριστοτέλους περὶ ζῴων α΄ β΄ γ΄ δ΄ ε΄ ϛ΄.

Ἐπιχειρημάτων α΄ β΄.

Θέσεις γ΄.

Περὶ βασιλείας α΄ β΄.

Περὶ αἰτιῶν α΄.

Concerning Conversation, one book.
On Taking an Oath, one book.
Rhetorical Precepts, one book.
Of Wealth, one book.
On the Art of Poetry, one book.
Problems in Politics, Ethics, Physics, and in the Art
    of Love, one book.
Preludes, one book.
A Collection of Problems, one book.
On Physical Problems, one book.
On Example, one book.
On Introduction and Narrative, one book.
Another tract on the Art of Poetry, one book.
Of the Wise, one book.
On Consultation, one book.
On Solecisms, one book.
On the Art of Rhetoric, one book.
The Special Commonplaces of the Treatises on
    Rhetoric, seventeen books.
On Acting, one book.
Lecture Notes of Aristotle or Theophrastus, six books.
Sixteen books of Physical Opinions.
Epitome of Physical Opinions, one book.
On Gratitude, one book.
[Character Sketches, one book.]
On Truth and Falsehood, one book.
The History of Theological Inquiry, six books.
Of the Gods, three books.
Geometrical Researches, four books.
Epitomes of Aristotle's work on Animals, six books.
Two books of Refutative Arguments.
Theses, three books.
Of Kingship, two books.
Of Causes, one book.

Περὶ Δημοκρίτου αʹ.
[Περὶ διαβολῆς αʹ.]
Περὶ γενέσεως αʹ.
Περὶ ζῴων φρονήσεως καὶ ἤθους αʹ.
Περὶ κινήσεως αʹ βʹ.
Περὶ ὄψεως αʹ βʹ γʹ δʹ.
Πρὸς ὅρους αʹ βʹ.
Περὶ τοῦ δεδόσθαι αʹ.
Περὶ μείζονος καὶ ἐλάττονος αʹ.
Περὶ τῶν μουσικῶν αʹ.
Περὶ τῆς θείας εὐδαιμονίας αʹ.
Πρὸς τοὺς ἐξ Ἀκαδημείας αʹ.
Προτρεπτικὸς αʹ.
Πῶς ἂν ἄριστα πόλεις οἰκοῖντο αʹ.
Τὰ ὑπομνήματα αʹ.
Περὶ ῥύακος τοῦ ἐν Σικελίᾳ αʹ.
Περὶ τῶν ὁμολογουμένων αʹ.
[Περὶ τῶν προβλημάτων φυσικῶν αʹ.
Τίνες οἱ τρόποι τοῦ ἐπίστασθαι αʹ.
Περὶ τοῦ ψευδομένου αʹ βʹ γʹ.
50 Τὰ πρὸ τῶν τόπων αʹ.
Πρὸς Αἰσχύλον αʹ.
Ἀστρολογικῆς ἱστορίας αʹ βʹ γʹ δʹ εʹ ϛʹ.
Ἀριθμητικῶν ἱστοριῶν περὶ αὐξήσεως αʹ.
Ἀκίχαρος αʹ.
Περὶ δικανικῶν λόγων αʹ.
[Περὶ διαβολῆς αʹ.]
Ἐπιστολαὶ αἱ ἐπὶ τῷ Ἀστυκρέοντι, Φανίᾳ, Νικάνορι.
Περὶ εὐσεβείας αʹ.
Εὐϊάδος αʹ.
Περὶ καιρῶν αʹ βʹ.
Περὶ οἰκείων λόγων αʹ.

On Democritus, one book.
[Of Calumny, one book.]
Of Becoming, one book.
Of the Intelligence and Character of Animals, one
    book.
On Motion, two books.
On Vision, four books.
Relating to Definitions, two books.
On Data, one book.
On Greater and Less, one book.
On the Musicians, one book.
Of the Happiness of the Gods, one book.
A Reply to the Academics, one book.
Exhortation to Philosophy, one book.
How States can best be governed, one book.
Lecture-Notes, one book.
On the Eruption in Sicily, one book.
On Things generally admitted, one book.
[On Problems in Physics, one book.]
What are the methods of attaining Knowledge, one
    book.
On the Fallacy known as the Liar, three books.
Prolegomena to Topics, one book.
Relating to Aeschylus, one book.
Astronomical Research, six books.
Arithmetical Researches on Growth, one book.
Acicharus, one book.
On Forensic Speeches, one book.
[Of Calumny, one book.]
Correspondence with Astycreon, Phanias and Nicanor.
Of Piety, one book.
Evias, one book.
On Times of Crisis, two books.
On Relevant Arguments, one book.

Περὶ παίδων ἀγωγῆς αʹ.
Ἄλλο διάφορον ἅ.
Περὶ παιδείας ἢ περὶ ἀρετῶν ἢ περὶ σωφροσύνης αʹ.
[Προτρεπτικὸς αʹ.]
Περὶ ἀριθμῶν αʹ.
Ὁριστικὰ περὶ λέξεως συλλογισμῶν αʹ.
Περὶ οὐρανοῦ αʹ.
Πολιτικοῦ αʹ βʹ.
Περὶ φύσεως.
Περὶ καρπῶν.
Περὶ ζώων.

Ἃ γίνονται στίχων Μʹ κʹ γʹ Β ωʹ ηʹ· τοσαῦτα
μὲν οὖν καὶ τῷδε τὰ βιβλία·

51 Εὗρον δ' αὐτοῦ καὶ διαθήκας τοῦτον ἐχούσας τὸν
τρόπον·

" Ἔσται μὲν εὖ· ἐὰν δέ τι συμβῇ, τάδε δια-
τίθεμαι· τὰ μὲν οἴκοι ὑπάρχοντα πάντα δίδωμι
Μελάντῃ καὶ Παγκρέοντι τοῖς υἱοῖς Λέοντος.
ἀπὸ δὲ τῶν παρ' Ἱππάρχου συμβεβλημένων τάδε
μοι βούλομαι γενέσθαι· πρῶτον μὲν τὰ περὶ τὸ
μουσεῖον καὶ τὰς θεὰς συντελεσθῆναι κἄν τι ἄλλο
ἰσχύῃ περὶ αὐτὰς ἐπικοσμηθῆναι πρὸς τὸ κάλλιον·
ἔπειτα τὴν Ἀριστοτέλους εἰκόνα τεθῆναι εἰς τὸ
ἱερὸν καὶ τὰ λοιπὰ ἀναθήματα ὅσα πρότερον
ὑπῆρχεν ἐν τῷ ἱερῷ· εἶτα τὸ στῳίδιον οἰκοδομη-
θῆναι τὸ πρὸς τῷ μουσείῳ μὴ χεῖρον ἢ πρότερον·

---

[a] *i.e.* at Eresus.

[b] Mentioned below, §§ 53, 54, 55, 66. We infer that he
had been acting as trustee not only for Theophrastus but
for the School, which in the eye of the law was a religious
foundation.

[c] Evidently the Museum had suffered in some recent
political troubles, perhaps the second siege of Athens by

On the Education of Children, one book.
Another treatise with the same title, one book.
Of Education or of the Virtues or of Temperance, one book.
[An Exhortation to Philosophy, one book.]
On Numbers, one book.
Definitions concerning the Diction of Syllogisms, one book.
Of the Heavens, one book.
Concerning Politics, two books.
On Nature.
On Fruits.
On Animals.

In all 232,808 lines. So much for his writings.

I have also come across his will, couched in the following terms :

" All will be well ; but in case anything should happen, I make these dispositions. I give and bequeath all my property at home *a* to Melantes and Pancreon, the sons of Leon. It is my wish that out of the trust funds at the disposal of Hipparchus *b* the following appropriations should be made. First, they should be applied to finish the rebuilding of the Museum with the statues of the goddesses, and to add any improvements which seem practicable to beautify them.*c* Secondly, to replace in the temple the bust of Aristotle with the rest of the dedicated offerings which formerly were in the temple. Next, to rebuild the small cloister adjoining the Museum

Demetrius Poliorcetes, 296-294 B.C. Plut. *Demetr.* 33, 34; Paus. i. 25. 8. There was, however, a serious disturbance when Athens revolted from Macedon, 289-287, for which see Plut. *Demetr.* 46, and Paus. i. 25. 2; 26. 1 f. This latter event is nearer to the death of Theophrastus in Ol. 123.

ἀναθεῖναι δὲ καὶ τοὺς πίνακας, ἐν οἷς αἱ τῆς γῆς
52 περίοδοί εἰσιν, εἰς τὴν κάτω στοάν· ἐπισκευασθῆναι
δὲ καὶ τὸν βωμόν, ὅπως ἔχῃ τὸ τέλειον καὶ τὸ
εὔσχημον. βούλομαι δὲ καὶ τὴν Νικομάχου εἰκόνα
συντελεσθῆναι ἴσην. τὸ μὲν τῆς πλάσεως ἔχει
Πραξιτέλης, τὸ δ' ἄλλο ἀνάλωμα ἀπὸ τούτου
γενέσθω. σταθῆναι δὲ ὅπου ἂν δοκῇ τοῖς καὶ τῶν
ἄλλων ἐπιμελουμένοις τῶν ἐν τῇ διαθήκῃ γεγραμμένων. καὶ τὰ μὲν περὶ τὸ ἱερὸν καὶ τὰ ἀναθήματα
τοῦτον ἐχέτω τὸν τρόπον. τὸ δὲ χωρίον τὸ ἐν
Σταγείροις ἡμῖν ὑπάρχον δίδωμι Καλλίνῳ· τὰ δὲ
βιβλία πάντα Νηλεῖ. τὸν δὲ κῆπον καὶ τὸν περίπατον καὶ τὰς οἰκίας τὰς πρὸς τῷ κήπῳ πάσας
δίδωμι τῶν γεγραμμένων φίλων ἀεὶ τοῖς βουλομένοις συσχολάζειν καὶ συμφιλοσοφεῖν ἐν αὐταῖς,
53 ἐπειδήπερ οὐ δυνατὸν πᾶσιν ἀνθρώποις ἀεὶ ἐπι-
δημεῖν, μήτ' ἐξαλλοτριοῦσι μήτ' ἐξιδιαζομένου μη-
δενός, ἀλλ' ὡς ἂν ἱερὸν κοινῇ κεκτημένοις, καὶ τὰ
πρὸς ἀλλήλους οἰκείως καὶ φιλικῶς χρωμένοις,
ὥσπερ προσῆκον καὶ δίκαιον. ἔστωσαν δὲ οἱ
κοινωνοῦντες Ἵππαρχος, Νηλεύς, Στράτων, Καλλῖνος, Δημότιμος, Δημάρατος, Καλλισθένης, Μελάν-
της, Παγκρέων, Νίκιππος. ἐξεῖναι δὲ βουλομένῳ
φιλοσοφεῖν καὶ Ἀριστοτέλει τῷ Μητροδώρου καὶ
Πυθιάδος υἱῷ καὶ μετέχειν τούτων· καὶ αὐτοῦ
πᾶσαν ἐπιμέλειαν ποιεῖσθαι τοὺς πρεσβυτάτους,
ὅπως ὅτι μάλιστα προαχθῇ κατὰ φιλοσοφίαν.
θάψαι δὲ καὶ ἡμᾶς ὅπου ἂν δοκῇ μάλιστα ἁρμόττον

_____
ᵃ Cf. iv. § 70.

at least as handsomely as before, and to replace in
the lower cloister the tablets containing maps of the
countries traversed by explorers. Further, to repair
the altar so that it may be perfect and elegant. It
is also my wish that the statue of Nicomachus should
be completed of life size. The price agreed upon
for the making of the statue itself has been paid to
Praxiteles, but the rest of the cost should be defrayed
from the source above mentioned. The statue should
be set up in whatever place seems desirable to the
executors entrusted with carrying out my other
testamentary dispositions. Let all that concerns the
temple and the offerings set up be arranged in this
manner. The estate at Stagira belonging to me I
give and bequeath to Callinus. The whole of my
library I give to Neleus. The garden and the walk
and the houses adjoining the garden, all and sundry,
I give and bequeath to such of my friends herein-
after named as may wish to study literature and
philosophy there in common,[a] since it is not possible
for all men to be always in residence, on condition
that no one alienates the property or devotes it to
his private use, but so that they hold it like a temple
in joint possession and live, as is right and proper,
on terms of familiarity and friendship. Let the
community consist of Hipparchus, Neleus, Strato,
Callinus, Demotimus, Demaratus, Callisthenes,
Melantes, Pancreon, Nicippus. Aristotle, the son
of Metrodorus and Pythias, shall also have the right
to study and associate with them if he so desire.
And the oldest of them shall pay every attention to
him, in order to ensure for him the utmost pro-
ficiency in philosophy. Let me be buried in any
spot in the garden which seems most suitable,

εἶναι τοῦ κήπου, μηδὲν περίεργον μήτε περὶ τὴν
54 ταφὴν μήτε περὶ τὸ μνημεῖον ποιοῦντας. ὅπως
δὲ συνείρηται, μετὰ τὰ περὶ ἡμᾶς συμβάντα, τὰ
περὶ τὸ ἱερὸν καὶ τὸ μνημεῖον καὶ τὸν κῆπον καὶ
τὸν περίπατον θεραπευόμενα συνεπιμελεῖσθαι καὶ
Πομπύλον τούτων ἐποικοῦντα αὐτὸν καὶ τὴν τῶν
ἄλλων ἐπιμέλειαν ποιούμενον ἥν καὶ πρότερον·
τῆς δὲ λυσιτελείας ἐπιμελεῖσθαι αὐτοὺς τοὺς
ἔχοντας ταῦτα. Πομπύλῳ δὲ καὶ Θρέπτῃ πάλαι
ἐλευθέροις οὖσι καὶ ἡμῖν πολλὴν χρείαν παρεσχη-
μένοις, εἴ τι πρότερον ἔχουσι παρ' ἡμῶν καὶ εἴ τι
αὐτοὶ ἐκτήσαντο καὶ ἃ νῦν παρ' Ἱππάρχου αὐτοῖς
συντέταχα, δισχιλίας δραχμάς, ἀσφαλῶς οἶμαι δεῖν
αὐτοῖς ὑπάρχειν ταῦτα, καθάπερ καὶ αὐτὸς[1] δι-
ελέχθην Μελάντῃ καὶ Παγκρέοντι πλεονάκις καὶ
πάντα μοι συγκατετίθεντο. δίδωμι δ' αὐτοῖς καὶ
55 Σωματάλην τὴν παιδίσκην. τῶν δὲ παίδων Μό-
λωνα μὲν καὶ Τίμωνα καὶ Παρμένοντα ἤδη ἐλευθέρους ἀφίημι· Μανῆν δὲ καὶ Καλλίαν παραμείναντας
ἔτη τέτταρα ἐν τῷ κήπῳ καὶ συνεργασαμένους καὶ
ἀναμαρτήτους γενομένους ἀφίημι ἐλευθέρους. τῶν
δὲ οἰκηματικῶν σκευῶν ἀποδιδόντας Πομπύλῳ ὅσ'
ἂν δοκῇ τοῖς ἐπιμεληταῖς καλῶς ἔχειν, τὰ λοιπὰ
ἐξαργυρίσαι. δίδωμι δὲ καὶ Καρίωνα Δημο-
τίμῳ, Δόνακα δὲ Νηλεῖ· Εὔβοιον δ'· ἀποδόσθαι.
δότω δ' Ἵππαρχος Καλλίνῳ τρισχιλίας δραχμάς·
Μελάντῃ δὲ καὶ Παγκρέοντι εἰ μὲν μὴ ἑωρῶμεν
Ἵππαρχον καὶ ἡμῖν πρότερον χρείαν παρεσχημένον
καὶ νῦν ἐν τοῖς ἰδίοις μάλα νεναυαγηκότα, προσετά-
ξαμεν ἂν μετὰ Μελάντου καὶ Παγκρέοντος ἐξάγειν
56 αὐτά. ἐπειδὴ δὲ οὔτ' ἐκείνοις ἑώρων ῥᾴδιον ὄντα

[1] αὐτοῖς codd. : corr. Reiske.

without unnecessary outlay upon my funeral or upon my monument. And according to previous agreement let the charge of attending, after my decease, to the temple and the monument and the garden and the walk be shared by Pompylus in person, living close by as he does, and exercising the same supervision over all other matters as before ; and those who hold the property shall watch over his interests. Pompylus and Threpta have long been emancipated and have done me much service ; and I think that 2000 drachmas certainly ought to belong to them from previous payments made to them by me, from their own earnings, and my present bequest to them to be paid by Hipparchus, as I stated many times in conversation with Melantes and Pancreon themselves, who agreed with me. I give and bequeath to them the maidservant Somatale. And of my slaves I at once emancipate Molon and Timon and Parmeno ; to Manes and Callias I give their freedom on condition that they stay four years in the garden and work there together and that their conduct is free from blame. Of my household furniture let so much as the executors think right be given to Pompylus and let the rest be sold. I also devise Carion to Demotimus, and Donax to Neleus. But Euboeus must be sold. Let Hipparchus pay to Callinus 3000 drachmas. And if I had not seen that Hipparchus had done great service to Melantes and Pancreon and formerly to me, and that now in his private affairs he has made shipwreck, I would have appointed him jointly with Melantes and Pancreon to carry out my wishes. But, since I saw that it

συνοικονομεῖν λυσιτελέστερόν τ' αὐτοῖς ὑπελάμ-
βανον εἶναι τεταγμένον τι λαβεῖν παρὰ Ἱππάρχου,
δότω Ἵππαρχος Μελάντῃ καὶ Παγκρέοντι, ἑκατέρῳ
τάλαντον· διδόναι δ' Ἵππαρχον καὶ τοῖς ἐπιμεληταῖς
εἰς τὰ ἀναλώματα τὰ ἐν τῇ διαθήκῃ γεγραμμένα
κατὰ τοὺς ἑκάστου καιροὺς τῶν δαπανημάτων.
οἰκονομήσαντα δὲ ταῦτα Ἵππαρχον ἀπηλλάχθαι τῶν
συμβολαίων τῶν πρὸς ἐμὲ πάντων· καὶ εἴ τι ἐπὶ
τοῦ ἐμοῦ ὀνόματος συμβέβληκεν Ἵππαρχος ἐν
Χαλκίδι, Ἱππάρχου τοῦτό ἐστιν. ἐπιμεληταὶ δὲ
ἔστωσαν τῶν ἐν τῇ διαθήκῃ γεγραμμένων Ἵππαρχος,
Νηλεύς, Στράτων, Καλλῖνος, Δημότιμος, Καλλι-
57 σθένης, Κτήσαρχος. αἱ διαθῆκαι κεῖνται ἀντίγραφα
τῷ Θεοφράστου δακτυλίῳ σεσημασμέναι, μία μὲν
παρὰ Ἡγησίᾳ Ἱππάρχου· μάρτυρες Κάλλιππος
Παλληνεύς, Φιλόμηλος Εὐωνυμεύς, Λύσανδρος
Ὑβάδης, Φίλων Ἀλωπεκῆθεν. τὴν δ' ἑτέραν ἔχει
Ὀλυμπιόδωρος· μάρτυρες δ' οἱ αὐτοί. τὴν δ'
ἑτέραν[1] ἔλαβεν Ἀδείμαντος, ἀπήνεγκε δὲ Ἀνδρο-
σθένης ὁ υἱός· μάρτυρες Ἀρίμνηστος Κλεοβούλου,
Λυσίστρατος Φείδωνος Θάσιος, Στράτων Ἀρκεσιλάου Λαμψακηνός, Θήσιππος Θησίππου ἐκ Κερα-
μέων, Διοσκουρίδης Διονυσίου Ἐπικηφίσιος."

Ὧδ' ἔχουσιν αὐτῷ καὶ αἱ διαθῆκαι.

Ἀκοῦσαι δ' αὐτοῦ καὶ Ἐρασίστρατον τὸν ἰατρόν
εἰσιν οἳ λέγουσι· καὶ εἰκός.

Κεφ. γ΄. ΣΤΡΑΤΩΝ

58 Διεδέξατο δ' αὐτοῦ τὴν σχολὴν Στράτων Ἀρκεσι-

---

[1] τρίτην R.

was not easy for them to share the management with him, and I thought it more advantageous for them to receive a fixed sum from Hipparchus, let Hipparchus pay Melantes and Pancreon one talent each and let Hipparchus provide funds for the executors to defray the expenses set down in the will, as each disbursement falls due. And when Hipparchus shall have carried out all these injunctions, he shall be released in full from his liabilities to me. And any advance that he has made in Chalcis in my name belongs to him alone. Let Hipparchus, Neleus, Strato, Callinus, Demotimus, Callisthenes and Ctesarchus be executors to carry out the terms of the will. One copy of the will, sealed with the signet-ring of Theophrastus, is deposited with Hegesias, the son of Hipparchus, the witnesses being Callippus of Pallene, Philomelus of Euonymaea, Lysander of Hyba, and Philo of Alopece. Olympiodorus has another copy, the witnesses being the same. The third copy was received by Adeimantus, the bearer being Androsthenes junior; and the witnesses are Arimnestus the son of Cleobulus, Lysistratus the son of Pheidon of Thasos, Strato the son of Arcesilaus of Lampsacus, Thesippus the son of Thesippus of Cerameis, and Dioscurides the son of Dionysius of Epicephisia."

Such is the tenor of his will.

There are some who say that Erasistratus the physician was also a pupil of his, and it is not improbable.

CHAPTER 3. STRATO
(Head of the School 286–268 B.C.)

His successor in the school was Strato, the son of

λάου Λαμψακηνός, οὗ καὶ ἐν ταῖς διαθήκαις ἐμνημό-
νευσεν· ἀνὴρ ἐλλογιμώτατος καὶ φυσικὸς ἐπικληθεὶς ἀπὸ τοῦ περὶ τὴν θεωρίαν ταύτην παρ' ὁντινοῦν
ἐπιμελέστατα διατετριφέναι. ἀλλὰ καὶ καθηγήσατο Πτολεμαίου τοῦ Φιλαδέλφου καὶ ἔλαβε, φασί,
παρ' αὐτοῦ τάλαντα ὀγδοήκοντα· σχολαρχεῖν δέ,
καθά φησιν Ἀπολλόδωρος ἐν Χρονικοῖς, ἤρξατο
τῇ τρίτῃ καὶ εἰκοστῇ καὶ ἑκατοστῇ Ὀλυμπιάδι,
τῆς σχολῆς ἀφηγησάμενος ἔτη ὀκτωκαίδεκα.

59   Φέρεται δ' αὐτοῦ βιβλία

Περὶ βασιλείας τρία.
Περὶ δικαιοσύνης τρία.
Περὶ τἀγαθοῦ γ'.
Περὶ θεῶν γ'.
Περὶ ἀρχῶν γ'.
Περὶ βίων.
Περὶ εὐδαιμονίας.
Περὶ βασιλέως φιλοσόφου.
Περὶ ἀνδρείας.
Περὶ τοῦ κενοῦ.
Περὶ τοῦ οὐρανοῦ.
Περὶ τοῦ πνεύματος.
Περὶ φύσεως ἀνθρωπίνης.
Περὶ ζωογονίας.
Περὶ μίξεως.
Περὶ ὕπνου.
Περὶ ἐνυπνίων.
Περὶ ὄψεως.
Περὶ αἰσθήσεως.
Περὶ ἡδονῆς.
Περὶ χρωμάτων.
Περὶ νόσων.

Arcesilaus, a native of Lampsacus, whom he mentioned in his will; a distinguished man who is generally known as " the physicist," because more than anyone else he devoted himself to the most careful study of nature. Moreover, he taught Ptolemy Philadelphus and received, it is said, 80 talents from him. According to Apollodorus in his *Chronology* he became head of the school in the 123rd Olympiad,[a] and continued to preside over it for eighteen years.

There are extant of his works :

Of Kingship, three books.
Of Justice, three books.
Of the Good, three books.
Of the Gods, three books.
On First Principles, three books.
On Various Modes of Life.
Of Happiness.
On the Philosopher-King.
Of Courage.
On the Void.
On the Heaven.
On the Wind.
Of Human Nature.
On the Breeding of Animals.
Of Mixture.
Of Sleep.
Of Dreams.
Of Vision.
Of Sensation.
Of Pleasure.
On Colours.
Of Diseases.

Περὶ κρίσεων.

Περὶ δυνάμεων.

Περὶ τῶν μεταλλικῶν μηχανημάτων.

Περὶ λιμοῦ[1] καὶ σκοτώσεων.

Περὶ κούφου καὶ βαρέος.

Περὶ ἐνθουσιασμοῦ.

Περὶ χρόνου.

Περὶ τροφῆς καὶ αὐξήσεως.

Περὶ τῶν ἀπορουμένων ζῴων.

Περὶ τῶν μυθολογουμένων ζῴων.

Περὶ αἰτιῶν.

Λύσεις ἀπορουμένων.

Τόπων προοίμια.

Περὶ τοῦ συμβεβηκότος.

60 Περὶ τοῦ ὅρου.

Περὶ τοῦ μᾶλλον καὶ ἧττον.

Περὶ ἀδίκου.

Περὶ τοῦ προτέρου καὶ ὑστέρου

Περὶ τοῦ προτέρου γένους.

Περὶ τοῦ ἰδίου.

Περὶ τοῦ μέλλοντος.

Εὑρημάτων ἔλεγχοι δύο.

Ὑπομνήματα, ἃ δισταζεται.

Ἐπιστολαὶ ὧν ἡ ἀρχή· "Στράτων Ἀρσινόῃ εὖ
πράττειν."

Τοῦτόν φασιν οὕτω γενέσθαι λεπτὸν ὡς ἀναι-
σθήτως τελευτῆσαι. καὶ ἔστιν ἡμῶν εἰς αὐτὸν
οὕτως ἔχον·

λεπτὸς ἀνὴρ δέμας ἦν, εἴ μοι προσέχεις, ἀπὸ
χρισμῶν.[2]

Στράτωνα τοῦτόν φημί σοι

---

[1] λιμοῦ] ἰλίγγου Reiske.

[2] προσέχῃς ἀπόχρη μοι Stadtmüller.

Of the Crises in Diseases.
On Faculties.
On Mining Machinery.
Of Starvation and Dizziness.
On the Attributes Light and Heavy.
Of Enthusiasm or Ecstasy.
On Time.
On Growth and Nutrition.
On Animals the existence of which is questioned.
On Animals in Folk-lore or Fable.
Of Causes.
Solutions of Difficulties.
Introduction to Topics.
Of Accident.
Of Definition.
On difference of Degree.
Of Injustice.
Of the logically Prior and Posterior.
Of the Genus of the Prior.
Of the Property or Essential Attribute.
Of the Future.
Examinations of Discoveries, in two books.
Lecture-notes, the genuineness of which is doubted.
Letters beginning " Strato to Arsinoë greeting."

Strato is said to have grown so thin that he felt
nothing when his end came. And I have written
some lines upon him as follows [a] :

A thin, spare man in body, take my word for it, owing
to his use of unguents,[b] was this Strato, I at least affirm, to

[a] *Anth. Pal.* vii. 111.
[b] Or " if you attend to me, I am content," according to
the alternative reading.

Λάμψακος ὅν ποτ' ἔφυσεν· ἀεὶ δὲ νόσοισι παλαίων
θνῆσκει λαθών, οὐδ' ἤσθετο.

61 Γεγόνασι δὲ Στράτωνες ὀκτώ· πρῶτος Ἰσοκράτους ἀκροατής· δεύτερος αὐτὸς οὗτος· τρίτος ἰατρός,
μαθητὴς Ἐρασιστράτου, ὡς δέ τινες, τρόφιμος·
τέταρτος ἱστορικός, Φιλίππου καὶ Περσέως τῶν
Ῥωμαίοις πολεμησάντων γεγραφὼς πράξεις· * *
ἕκτος ποιητὴς ἐπιγραμμάτων· ἕβδομος ἰατρὸς
ἀρχαῖος, ὡς Ἀριστοτέλης φησίν· ὄγδοος περιπατητικός, βεβιωκὼς ἐν Ἀλεξανδρείᾳ.

Τοῦ δ' οὖν φυσικοῦ φέρονται καὶ διαθῆκαι τοῦτον
ἔχουσαι τὸν τρόπον·

"Τάδε διατίθεμαι, ἐάν τι πάσχω· τὰ μὲν οἴκοι
καταλείπω πάντα Λαμπυρίωνι καὶ Ἀρκεσιλάῳ.
ἀπὸ δὲ τοῦ Ἀθήνησιν ὑπάρχοντός μοι ἀργυρίου
πρῶτον μὲν οἱ ἐπιμεληταὶ τὰ περὶ τὴν ἐκφορὰν
ἐπιμεληθήτωσαν καὶ ὅσα νομίζεται μετὰ τὴν
ἐκφοράν, μηδὲν μήτε περίεργον ποιοῦντες μήτ'
62 ἀνελεύθερον. ἐπιμεληταὶ δὲ ἔστωσαν τῶν κατὰ
τὴν διαθήκην οἵδε· Ὀλύμπιχος, Ἀριστείδης, Μνη-
σιγένης, Ἱπποκράτης, Ἐπικράτης, Γοργύλος, Διοκλῆς, Λύκων, Ἀθάνης. καταλείπω δὲ τὴν μὲν
διατριβὴν Λύκωνι, ἐπειδὴ τῶν ἄλλων οἱ μέν εἰσι
πρεσβύτεροι, οἱ δὲ ἄσχολοι. καλῶς δ' ἂν ποιοῖεν
καὶ οἱ λοιποὶ συγκατασκευάζοντες τούτῳ. καταλείπω δ' αὐτῷ καὶ τὰ βιβλία πάντα, πλὴν ὧν αὐτοὶ
γεγράφαμεν, καὶ τὰ σκεύη πάντα κατὰ τὸ συσσίτιον
καὶ τὰ στρώματα καὶ τὰ ποτήρια. δότωσαν δὲ οἱ
ἐπιμεληταὶ Ἐπικράτει πεντακοσίας δραχμὰς καὶ
63 τῶν παίδων ἕνα ὃν ἂν δοκῇ Ἀρκεσιλάῳ. καὶ
πρῶτον μὲν Λαμπυρίων καὶ Ἀρκεσίλαος ἀράσθω-

whom Lampsacus gave birth. For ever wrestling with
diseases, he died unawares or ever he felt the hand of death.

There have been eight men who bore the name of
Strato: (1) a pupil of Isocrates; (2) our subject;
(3) a physician, a disciple, or, as some say, a foster-
child, of Erasistratus; (4) a historian, who treated
of the struggle of Philip and Perseus against the
Romans; (5) * *; (6) a poet who wrote epigrams;
(7) a physician who lived in ancient times, mentioned
by Aristotle; (8) a Peripatetic philosopher who lived
in Alexandria.

But to return to Strato the physicist. His will is
also extant and it runs as follows:

" In case anything should happen to me I make
these dispositions. All the goods in my house I
give and bequeath to Lampyrio and Arcesilaus.
From the money belonging to me in Athens, in the
first place my executors shall provide for my funeral
and for all that custom requires to be done after the
funeral, without extravagance on the one hand or
meanness on the other. The executors of this my
will shall be Olympichus, Aristides, Mnesigenes,
Hippocrates, Epicrates, Gorgylus, Diocles, Lyco,
Athanes. I leave the school to Lyco, since of the
rest some are too old and others too busy. But it
would be well if the others would co-operate with him.
I also give and bequeath to him all my books, except
those of which I am the author, and all the furniture
in the dining-hall, the cushions and the drinking-cups.
The trustees shall give Epicrates 500 drachmas and
one of the servants whom Arcesilaus shall approve.
And in the first place Lampyrio and Arcesilaus shall

σαν τὰς συνθήκας ἃς ἔθετο Δάϊππος ὑπὲρ Ἱραίου·
καὶ μηδὲν ὀφειλέτω μήτε Λαμπυρίωνι μήτε τοῖς
Λαμπυρίωνος κληρονόμοις, ἀλλ' ἀπηλλάχθω παντὸς
τοῦ συμβολαίου. δότωσαν δ' αὐτῷ καὶ οἱ ἐπιμεληταὶ ἀργυρίου δραχμὰς πεντακοσίας καὶ τῶν
παίδων ἕνα ὃν ἂν δοκιμάζῃ Ἀρκεσίλαος, ὅπως
ἂν πολλὰ συμπεπονηκὼς ἡμῖν καὶ παρεσχημένος
χρείας ἔχῃ βίον ἱκανὸν καὶ εὐσχήμονα. ἀφίημι δὲ
καὶ Διόφαντον ἐλεύθερον καὶ Διοκλέα καὶ Ἄβουν·
Σιμίαν δὲ ἀποδίδωμι Ἀρκεσιλάῳ. ἀφίημι δὲ καὶ
Δρόμωνα ἐλεύθερον. ἐπειδὰν δὲ παραγένηται
Ἀρκεσίλαος, λογισάσθω Ἵραιος μετ' Ὀλυμπίχου
καὶ Ἐπικράτους καὶ τῶν ἄλλων ἐπιμελητῶν τὸ
γεγονὸς ἀνάλωμα εἰς τὴν ἐκφορὰν καὶ τἆλλα τὰ
64 νομιζόμενα. τὸ δὲ περιὸν ἀργύριον κομισάσθω
Ἀρκεσίλαος παρ' Ὀλυμπίχου, μηδὲν ἐνοχλῶν
αὐτὸν κατὰ τοὺς καιροὺς καὶ τοὺς χρόνους· ἀράσθω
δὲ καὶ τὰς συνθήκας Ἀρκεσίλαος ἃς ἔθετο Στράτων
πρὸς Ὀλύμπιχον καὶ Ἀμεινίαν, τὰς κειμένας
παρὰ Φιλοκράτει Τισαμενοῦ. τὰ δὲ περὶ τὸ
μνημεῖον ποιείτωσαν ὡς ἂν δοκῇ Ἀρκεσιλάῳ καὶ
Ὀλυμπίχῳ καὶ Λύκωνι."

Καὶ αἵδε μέν εἰσιν αἱ φερόμεναι αὐτοῦ διαθῆκαι,
καθά που συνήγαγε καὶ Ἀρίστων ὁ Κεῖος.[1] αὐτὸς
δὲ ὁ Στράτων ἀνὴρ γέγονε, καθὰ καὶ ἄνω δεδή-
λωται, πολλῆς τῆς ἀποδοχῆς ἄξιος, διαπρέψας ἐν
παντὶ λόγων εἴδει καὶ μάλιστά γε ἐν τῷ καλουμένῳ

[1] οἰκεῖος vulg.: corr. Zeller.

---

[a] πολλῆς τῆς ἀποδοχῆς ἄξιος. This phrase might be taken
as Diogenes Laertius's defence for his inclusion of the Life of
Strato. According to the scheme of i. 14, 15, the Peripatetics

cancel the agreement which Daïppus made on behalf of Iraeus. And he shall not owe anything either to Lampyrio or to Lampyrio's heirs, but shall have a full discharge from the whole transaction. Next, the executors shall give him 500 drachmas in money and one of the servants whom Arcesilaus shall approve, so that, in return for all the toil he has shared with me and all the services he has rendered me, he may have the means to maintain himself respectably. Further, I emancipate Diophantus, Diocles and Abus; and Simias I make over to Arcesilaus. I also emancipate Dromo. As soon as Arcesilaus has arrived, Iraeus shall, with Olympichus, Epicrates, and the other executors, prepare an account of the money expended upon the funeral and the other customary charges. Whatever money remains over, Arcesilaus shall take over from Olympichus, without however pressing him as to times and seasons. Arcesilaus shall also cancel the agreement made by Strato with Olympichus and Ameinias and deposited with Philocrates the son of Tisamenus. With regard to my monument they shall make it as Arcesilaus, Olympichus and Lyco shall approve."

Such are the terms of his extant will, according to the Collection of Ariston of Ceos. Strato himself, however, was, as stated above, a man entitled to full approbation,[a] since he excelled in every branch of learning, and most of all in that which is styled

ended with Theophrastus, whose successors were often held to be vastly inferior, and unworthy to rank beside him; see Cicero, *De Fin.* v. §§ 12, 13; Strabo xiii. 609. The latter alleges as the reason for this decline the well-known story that the school was deprived of Aristotle's library, which had been carried away to Scepsis.

φυσικῷ, ὅπερ εἶδος ἀρχαιότερόν τε καὶ σπουδαιότερον.

Κεφ. δ΄. ΛΥΚΩΝ

65 Τοῦτον διεδέξατο Λύκων Ἀστυάνακτος Τρωαδεύς, φραστικὸς ἀνὴρ καὶ περὶ παίδων ἀγωγὴν ἄκρως συντεταγμένος.[1] ἔφασκε γὰρ δεῖν παρεζεῦχθαι τοῖς παισὶ τὴν αἰδῶ καὶ φιλοτιμίαν ὡς τοῖς ἵπποις μύωπα καὶ χαλινόν. τὸ δ᾽ ἐκφραστικὸν αὐτοῦ καὶ περιγεγονὸς ἐν τῇ ἑρμηνείᾳ φαίνεται κἀνθένδε· φησὶ γὰρ τοῦτον τὸν τρόπον ἐπὶ παρθένου πενιχρᾶς· " βαρὺ γὰρ φορτίον πατρὶ κόρη διὰ σπάνιν προικὸς ἐκτρέχουσα τὸν ἀκμαῖον τῆς ἡλικίας καιρόν." διὸ δὴ καὶ φασιν Ἀντίγονον ἐπ᾽ αὐτοῦ τοῦτο εἰπεῖν, ὡς οὐκ ἦν ὥσπερ μήλου τὴν εὐωδίαν καὶ χάριν ἄλλοθί που μετενεγκεῖν, ἀλλ᾽ ἐπ᾽ αὐτοῦ τοῦ ἀνθρώπου καθάπερ ἐπὶ τοῦ δένδρου τῶν λεγομένων 66 ἕκαστον ἔδει θεωρεῖσθαι. τοῦτο δὲ ὅτι ἐν μὲν τῷ λέγειν γλυκύτατος ἦν· παρὸ καί τινες τὸ γάμμα αὐτοῦ τῷ ὀνόματι προσετίθεσαν. ἐν δὲ τῷ γράφειν ἀνόμοιος αὐτῷ. ἀμέλει γοῦν καὶ ἐπὶ τῶν μεταγινωσκόντων ἐπειδὴ μὴ ἔμαθον ὅτε καιρὸς καὶ εὐχομένων τοῦτον ἐκαλλιλέκτει τὸν τρόπον· ἔλεγεν " αὐτῶν κατηγορεῖν, ἀδυνάτῳ μηνύοντας εὐχῇ μετάνοιαν ἀργίας ἀδιορθώτου." τούς τε βουλευμένους οὐκ ὀρθῶς διαπίπτειν ἔφασκε τῷ λογισμῷ, οἱονεὶ στρεβλῷ κανόνι βασανίζοντας εὐθεῖαν φύσιν ἢ πρόσωπον ὕδατι κλυδαττομένῳ ἢ κατόπτρῳ διεστραμμένῳ. καὶ ἐπὶ μὲν τὸν ἐν τῇ ἀγορᾷ στέφανον πολλοὺς ἀπιέναι, ἐπὶ δὲ τὸν Ὀλυμπίασιν

[1] συντεταμένος R.

"physics," a branch of philosophy more ancient and important than the others.

CHAPTER 4.   LYCO (299–225 B.C.)

Strato's successor was Lyco, the son of Astyanax of Troas, a master of expression and of the foremost rank in the education of boys. For he used to say that modesty and love of honour were as necessary an equipment for boys as spur and bridle for horses. His eloquence and sonorousness of diction appear from the following fact; he speaks of a penniless maiden as follows: " A grievous burden to a father is a girl, when for lack of a dowry she runs past the flower of her age." Hence the remark which Antigonus is said to have made about him, that it was not possible to transfer elsewhere the fragrance and charm of the apple, but each separate expression must be contemplated in the speaker himself as every single apple is on the tree. This was because Lyco's voice was exceedingly sweet, so that some persons altered his name to Glyco, by prefixing a G. But in writing he fell off sadly. For instance, those who regretted their neglect to learn when they had the opportunity and wished they had done so he would hit off neatly as follows, remarking that " they were their own accusers, betraying, by vain regret, repentance for an incorrigible laziness." Those who deliberated wrongly he used to say were out in their calculations, as if they had used a crooked rule to test something straight, or looked at the reflection of a face in troubled water or a distorting mirror. Again, " Many go in search of the garland of the market-place; few or none seek

519

ἢ ὀλίγους ἢ οὐδένα. πολλάκις τε πολλὰ συμβουλεύσας Ἀθηναίοις, τὰ μέγιστα αὐτοὺς ὠφέλησεν.
67 Ἦν δὲ καὶ καθαρώτατος τὴν στολήν, ὡς ἀνυπερ-
βλήτῳ χρῆσθαι μαλακότητι ἱματίων, καθά φησιν
Ἕρμιππος. ἀλλὰ καὶ γυμναστικώτατος ἐγένετο
καὶ εὐέκτης τὸ σῶμα τήν τε πᾶσαν σχέσιν ἀθλη-
τικὴν ἐπιφαίνων, ὠτοθλαδίας καὶ ἐμπινὴς ὤν,
καθά φησιν Ἀντίγονος ὁ Καρύστιος· διὰ τοῦτο
δὲ καὶ παλαῖσαι λέγεται τά τ' ἐν τῇ πατρίδι Ἰλίεια
καὶ σφαιρίσαι. ὡς οὐκ ἄλλος τ' ἦν φίλος τοῖς
περὶ Εὐμένην καὶ Ἄτταλον, οἳ καὶ πλεῖστα
ἐπεχορήγουν αὐτῷ. ἐπειράθη δ' αὐτὸν σχεῖν καὶ
68 Ἀντίοχος, ἀλλ' οὐκ ἔτυχεν. οὕτω δ' ἦν ἐχθρὸς
Ἱερωνύμῳ τῷ περιπατητικῷ, ὡς μόνος μὴ ἀπαντᾶν
πρὸς αὐτὸν εἰς τὴν ἐτήσιον ἡμέραν, περὶ ἧς ἐν τῷ
Ἀρκεσιλάου βίῳ διειλέγμεθα.

Ἀφηγήσατο δὲ τῆς σχολῆς ἔτη τέτταρα πρὸς
τοῖς τετταράκοντα, Στράτωνος αὐτὸν ἐν ταῖς
διαθήκαις καταλιπόντος κατὰ τὴν ἑβδόμην καὶ
εἰκοστὴν καὶ ἑκατοστὴν Ὀλυμπιάδα. οὐ μὴν
ἀλλὰ καὶ Πανθοίδου διήκουσε τοῦ διαλεκτικοῦ.
ἐτελεύτησε δὲ γεγονὼς ἔτος τέταρτον καὶ ἑβδομηκοστόν, νόσῳ ποδαγρικῇ καταπονηθείς. καὶ ἔστιν
ἡμῶν εἰς αὐτόν·

οὐ μὰ τόν, οὐδὲ Λύκωνα παρήσομεν, ὅττι ποδαλγὴς
κάτθανε· θαυμάζω τοῦτο μάλιστα δ' ἐγώ,
τὴν οὕτως ἀΐδαο μακρὴν ὁδὸν εἰ πρὶν ὁ ποσσὶν
ἀλλοτρίοις βαδίσας ἔδραμε νυκτὶ μιῇ.

69 Γεγόνασι δὲ καὶ ἄλλοι Λύκωνες· πρῶτος
Πυθαγορικός, δεύτερος αὐτὸς οὗτος, τρίτος ἐπῶν
ποιητής, τέταρτος ἐπιγραμμάτων ποιητής.

the crown at Olympia." He often gave the Athenians advice on various subjects and thus conferred on them the greatest benefits.

In his dress he was most immaculate, so that the clothes he wore were unsurpassed for the softness of the material, according to Hermippus. Furthermore, he was well practised in gymnastics and kept himself in condition, displaying all an athlete's habit of body, with battered ears and skin begrimed with oil, so we are told by Antigonus of Carystus. Hence it is said that he not only wrestled but played the game of ball common in his birthplace of Ilium. He was esteemed beyond all other philosophers by Eumenes and Attalus, who also did him very great service. Antiochus too tried to get hold of him, but without success. He was so hostile to Hieronymus the Peripatetic that he alone declined to meet him on the anniversary which we have mentioned in the Life of Arcesilaus.[a]

He presided over the school forty-four years after Strato had bequeathed it to him by his will in the 127th Olympiad.[b] Not but what he also attended the lectures of the logician Panthoides. He died at the age of seventy-four after severe sufferings from gout. This is my epitaph upon him [c] :

Nor, I swear! will I pass over Lyco either, for all that he died of the gout. But this it is which amazes me the most, if he who formerly could walk only with the feet of others, did in a single night traverse the long, long road to Hades.

Other men have borne the name of Lyco : (1) a Pythagorean, (2) our present subject, (3) an epic poet, (4) a poet who wrote epigrams.

[a] iv. 41.
[b] 274–270 B.C.
[c] *Anth. Pal.* vii. 112.

Τοῦ δὲ **φιλοσόφου** καὶ διαθήκαις περιετύχομεν ταῖσδε·

" Τάδε διατίθεμαι περὶ τῶν κατ' ἐμαυτόν, ἐὰν μὴ δυνηθῶ τὴν ἀρρωστίαν ταύτην ὑπενεγκεῖν· τὰ μὲν ἐν οἴκῳ πάντα δίδωμι τοῖς ἀδελφοῖς Ἀστυάνακτι καὶ Λύκωνι. καὶ οἶμαι δεῖν ἀποδοθῆναι ἀπὸ τούτων ὅσα κατακέχρημαι Ἀθήνησι παρά τινος ἔχων ἢ ἐκπεπραχώς· καὶ ἃ ἂν εἰς τὴν ἐκφορὰν 70 ἀναλωθῇ καὶ εἰς τἆλλα τὰ νομιζόμενα. τὰ δ' ἐν ἄστει καὶ ἐν Αἰγίνῃ δίδωμι Λύκωνι διὰ τὸ καὶ τοὔνομα φέρειν ἡμῶν καὶ συνδιατετριφέναι πλείω χρόνον ἀρεστῶς πάνυ, καθάπερ δίκαιον ἦν τὸν υἱοῦ τάξιν ἐσχηκότα. τὸν δὲ περίπατον καταλείπω τῶν γνωρίμων τοῖς βουλομένοις, Βούλωνι, Καλλίνῳ, Ἀρίστωνι, Ἀμφίωνι, Λύκωνι, Πύθωνι, Ἀριστομάχῳ, Ἡρακλείῳ, Λυκομήδει, Λύκωνι τῷ ἀδελφιδῷ. προστησάσθωσαν δ' αὐτοὶ ὃν ἂν ὑπολαμβάνωσι διαμενεῖν ἐπὶ τοῦ πράγματος καὶ συναύξειν μάλιστα δυνήσεσθαι. συγκατασκευαζέτωσαν δὲ καὶ οἱ λοιποὶ γνώριμοι κἀμοῦ καὶ τοῦ τόπου χάριν. περὶ δὲ τῆς ἐκφορᾶς καὶ καύσεως ἐπιμεληθήτωσαν Βούλων καὶ Καλλῖνος μετὰ τῶν συνήθων, ὅπως 71 μήτ' ἀνελεύθερος γένηται μήτε περίεργος. τῶν δ' ἐν Αἰγίνῃ μοι γενομένων μορίων μετὰ τὴν ἐμὴν ἀπόλυσιν καταχωρισάτω Λύκων τοῖς νεανίσκοις εἰς ἐλαιοχρηστίαν, ὅπως κἀμοῦ καὶ τοῦ τιμήσαντος ἐμὲ μνήμη γένηται διὰ τῆς χρείας αὕτη ἡ προσήκουσα. καὶ ἀνδριάντα ἡμῶν ἀναθέτω· τὸν δὲ τόπον, ὅπως ἁρμόττων ᾖ τῆς καταστάσεως, ἐπιβλεψάτω καὶ συμπραγματευθήτω Διόφαντος καὶ Ἡρακλείδης Δημητρίου. ἀπὸ δὲ τῶν ἐν ἄστει Λύκων ἀποδότω πᾶσι παρ' ὧν τι προείληφα

I have also come across this philosopher's will. It is this :

"These are my dispositions concerning my property, in case I should be unable to sustain my present ailment. All the goods in my house I give to my brothers Astyanax and Lyco, and from this source should, I think, be paid all the money I have laid out at Athens, whether by borrowing or by purchase, as well as all the cost of my funeral and the other customary charges. But my property in town and at Aegina I give to Lyco because he bears the same name with me, and has resided for a long time with me to my entire satisfaction, as became one whom I treated as my son. I leave the Peripatus to such of my friends as choose to make use of it, to Bulo, Callinus, Ariston, Amphion, Lyco, Pytho, Aristomachus, Heracleus, Lycomedes, and my nephew Lyco. They shall put over it any such person as in their opinion will persevere in the work of the school and will be most capable of extending it. And all my other friends should co-operate for love of me and of the spot. Bulo and Callinus, together with their colleagues, shall provide for my funeral and cremation, so as to avoid meanness on the one hand and extravagance on the other. After my decease Lyco shall make over, for the use of the young men, the oil from the olive-trees belonging to me in Aegina for the due commemoration—so long as they use it—of myself and the benefactor who did me honour. He shall also set up my statue, and shall choose a convenient site where it shall be erected, with the assistance of Diophantus and Heraclides the son of Demetrius. From my property in town Lyco shall repay all from whom I have

μετὰ τὴν ἀποδημίαν τὴν ἐκείνου. παρεχέσθωσαν
δὲ Βούλων καὶ Καλλῖνος καὶ ἃ ἂν εἰς τὴν ἐκφορὰν
ἀναλωθῇ καὶ τἄλλα τὰ νομιζόμενα. κομισάσθωσαν
δὲ ταῦτ᾽ ἀπὸ τῶν ἐν οἴκῳ κοινῇ καταλειπομένων
72 ἀμφοτέροις ὑπ᾽ ἐμοῦ. τιμησάτωσαν δὲ καὶ τοὺς
ἰατροὺς Πασίθεμιν καὶ Μηδίαν, ἀξίους ὄντας καὶ
διὰ τὴν ἐπιμέλειαν τὴν περὶ ἐμὲ καὶ τὴν τέχνην
καὶ μείζονος ἔτι τιμῆς. δίδωμι δὲ τῷ Καλλίνου
παιδίῳ Θηρικλείων ζεῦγος, καὶ τῇ γυναικὶ αὐτοῦ
Ῥοδιακῶν ζεῦγος, ψιλοτάπιδα, ἀμφίταπιν, περίστρωμα, προσκεφάλαια δύο τὰ βέλτιστα τῶν
καταλειπομένων· ὡς ἂν ἐφ᾽ ὅσον ἀνήκει πρὸς
τιμήν, καὶ τούτων φανῶμεν μὴ ἀμνήμονες ὄντες.
περὶ δὲ τῶν θεραπευόντων ἐμαυτὸν οὕτως ἐξάγω·
Δημητρίῳ μὲν ἐλευθέρῳ πάλαι ὄντι ἀφίημι τὰ
λύτρα καὶ δίδωμι πέντε μνᾶς καὶ ἱμάτιον καὶ
χιτῶνα, ἵνα πολλὰ πεπονηκὼς μετ᾽ ἐμοῦ βίον
εὐσχήμονα ἔχῃ. Κρίτωνι δὲ Χαλκηδονίῳ, καὶ
τούτῳ τὰ λύτρα ἀφίημι καὶ δίδωμι τέτταρας
μνᾶς. καὶ τὸν Μίκρον ἀφίημι ἐλεύθερον· καὶ
θρεψάτω Λύκων αὐτὸν καὶ παιδευσάτω ἀπὸ τοῦ
73 νῦν χρόνου ἐξ ἔτη. καὶ Χάρητα ἀφίημι ἐλεύθερον·
καὶ θρεψάτω Λύκων αὐτόν. καὶ δύο μνᾶς αὐτῷ
δίδωμι καὶ τἀμὰ βιβλία τὰ ἀνεγνωσμένα· τὰ δ᾽
ἀνέκδοτα Καλλίνῳ ὅπως ἐπιμελῶς αὐτὰ ἐκδῷ.
δίδωμι δὲ καὶ Σύρῳ ἐλευθέρῳ ὄντι τέτταρας μνᾶς
καὶ τὴν Μηνοδώραν δίδωμι· καὶ εἴ τί μοι ὀφείλει,
ἀφίημι αὐτῷ. καὶ Ἱλαρᾷ πέντε μνᾶς καὶ ἀμφίταπιν
καὶ δύο προσκεφάλαια καὶ περίστρωμα καὶ κλίνην
ἣν ἂν βούληται. ἀφίημι δ᾽ ἐλευθέραν καὶ τὴν
τοῦ Μίκρου μητέρα καὶ Νοήμονα καὶ Δίωνα καὶ
Θέωνα καὶ Εὐφράνορα καὶ Ἑρμείαν. καὶ Ἀγά-

borrowed anything after his departure. Bulo and
Callinus shall provide the sums expended upon my
funeral and other customary charges. These sums
they shall recover from the moneys in the house
bequeathed by me to them both in common. They
shall also remunerate the physicians Pasithemis and
Medias who for their attention to me and their skill
deserve far higher reward. I bequeath to the child
of Callinus a pair of Thericlean cups, and to his wife
a pair of Rhodian vessels, a smooth carpet, a rug with
nap on both sides, a sofa cover and two cushions the
best that are left, that, so far as I have the means
of recompensing them, I may prove not ungrateful.
With regard to the servants who have waited upon
me, my wishes are as follows. To Demetrius I
remit the purchase-money for the freedom which he
has long enjoyed, and bequeath to him five minas
and a suit of clothes to ensure him a decent maintenance, in return for all the toil he has borne with me.
To Crito of Chalcedon I also remit the purchase-
money for his freedom and bequeath to him four
minas. And Micrus I emancipate ; and Lyco shall
keep him and educate him for the next six years.
And Chares I emancipate, and Lyco shall maintain
him, and I bequeath him two minas and my published
writings, while those which have not been given to
the world I entrust to Callinus, that he may carefully
edit them. To Syrus who has been set free I give
four minas and Menodora, and I remit to him any
debt he owes me. And to Hilara I give five minas
and a double-napped rug, two cushions, a sofa-cover
and a bed, whichever she prefers. I also set free the
mother of Micrus as well as Noëmon, Dion, Theon,
Euphranor and Hermias. Agathon should be set

θωνα δύο ἔτη παραμείναντα ἀφεῖσθαι ἐλεύθερον·
καὶ τοὺς φορεαφόρους Ὠφελίωνα καὶ Ποσει-
74 δώνιον τέτταρα ἔτη παραμείναντας. δίδωμι δὲ
καὶ Δημητρίῳ καὶ Κρίτωνι καὶ Σύρῳ κλίνην
ἑκάστῳ καὶ στρώματα τῶν καταλειπομένων ἃ
ἂν φαίνηται Λύκωνι καλῶς ἔχειν. ταῦτ' ἔστω
αὐτοῖς ἀποδείξασιν ὀρθῶς ἐφ' ὧν ἕκαστοι τεταγ-
μένοι εἰσί. περὶ δὲ τῆς ταφῆς ἐάν τ' αὐτοῦ
βούληται Λύκων θάπτειν, ἐάν τ' ἐν οἴκῳ, οὕτω
ποιείτω. πέπεισμαι γὰρ αὐτὸν οὐδὲν ἧττον ἐμοῦ
συνορᾶν τὸ εὔσχημον. ταῦτα δὲ πάντα οἰκο-
νομήσαντι κυρία ἔστω ἡ δόσις τῶν ἐνταῦθα. μάρτυρες Καλλῖνος Ἑρμιονεύς, Ἀρίστων Κεῖος, Εὐ-
φρόνιος Παιανιεύς.''

Οὕτω μέντοι αὐτῷ συνετῶς τὰ πάντα πράττοντι
τά τε περὶ παιδείαν καὶ πάντας λόγους, οὐδὲν
ἧττον καὶ τὰ τῶν διαθηκῶν τρόπον τινὰ καὶ σφόδρα
ἐπιμελῶς τε καὶ οἰκονομικῶς ἴσχει· ὥστε κἀνταῦθα
ζηλωτέος.

Κεφ. ε'. ΔΗΜΗΤΡΙΟΣ

75 Δημήτριος Φανοστράτου Φαληρεύς. οὗτος ἤκουσε μὲν Θεοφράστου· δημηγορῶν δὲ παρ' Ἀθηναίοις
τῆς πόλεως ἐξηγήσατο ἔτη δέκα, καὶ εἰκόνων
ἠξιώθη χαλκῶν ἑξήκοντα πρὸς ταῖς τριακοσίαις,
ὧν αἱ πλείους ἐφ' ἵππων ἦσαν καὶ ἁρμάτων καὶ
συνωρίδων, συντελεσθεῖσαι ἐν οὐδὲ τριακοσίαις
ἡμέραις· τοσοῦτον ἐσπουδάσθη. ἄρξασθαι δ' αὐτὸν
τῆς πολιτείας φησὶ Δημήτριος ὁ Μάγνης ἐν τοῖς

free after two years, and the litter-bearers Ophelio and Posidonius after four years' further service. To Demetrius, to Crito and to Syrus I give a bed apiece and such bed-furniture out of my estate as Lyco shall think proper. These shall be given them for properly performing their appointed tasks. As regards my burial, let Lyco bury me here if he chooses, or if he prefers to bury me at home let him do so, for I am persuaded that his regard for propriety is not less than my own. When he has managed all these things, he can dispose of the property there, and such disposition shall be binding. Witnesses are Callinus of Hermione, Ariston of Ceos, Euphronius of Paeania."

Thus while his shrewdness is seen in all his actions, in his teaching and in all his studies, in some ways his will is no less remarkable for carefulness and wise management, so that in this respect also he is to be admired

Chapter 5. DEMETRIUS (perhaps 350–280 b.c.; supreme in Athens 318–307 b.c.)

Demetrius, the son of Phanostratus, was a native of Phalerum. He was a pupil of Theophrastus, but by his speeches in the Athenian assembly he held the chief power in the State for ten years and was decreed 360 bronze statues, most of them representing him either on horseback or else driving a chariot or a pair of horses. And these statues were completed in less than 300 days, so much was he esteemed. He entered politics, says Demetrius of Magnesia in his work on *Men of the Same Name*,

Ὁμωνύμοις, ὁπότε φυγὼν Ἀλέξανδρον εἰς Ἀθήνας ἧκεν Ἅρπαλος. πολλὰ δὲ καὶ κάλλιστα τῇ πατρίδι ἐπολιτεύσατο. καὶ γὰρ προσόδοις καὶ κατα-σκευαῖς ηὔξησε τὴν πόλιν, καίπερ οὐκ εὐγενὴς ὤν.

76 ἦν γὰρ ἐκ τῆς Κόνωνος οἰκίας, ὡς Φαβωρῖνος ἐν πρώτῳ τῶν Ἀπομνημονευμάτων φησίν, ἀλλ' ἀστῇ καὶ εὐγενεῖ συνῴκει Λαμίᾳ τῇ ἐρωμένῃ, καθάπερ ὁ αὐτὸς ἐν τῷ πρώτῳ φησίν· ἀλλὰ καὶ ὑπὸ Κλέωνος πεπονθέναι ἐν τῷ δευτέρῳ ἱστορεῖ. Δίδυμος δ' ἐν Συμποσιακοῖς καὶ Χαριτοβλέφαρον καὶ Λαμπιτὼ καλεῖσθαι αὐτόν φησιν ἀπό τινος[1] ἑταίρας. λέγεται δ' ἀποβαλόντα αὐτὸν τὰς ὄψεις ἐν Ἀλεξανδρείᾳ, κομίσασθαι αὖθις παρὰ τοῦ Σαράπιδος· ὅθεν καὶ τοὺς παιᾶνας ποιῆσαι τοὺς μέχρι νῦν ᾀδομένους.

Σφόδρα δὲ λαμπρὸς ὢν παρὰ τοῖς Ἀθηναίοις, ὅμως ἐπεσκοτήθη καὶ αὐτὸς ὑπὸ τοῦ τὰ πάντα

77 διεσθίοντος φθόνου. ἐπιβουλευθεὶς γὰρ ὑπό τινων δίκην θανάτου οὐ παρὼν ὦφλεν. οὐ μὴν ἐκυρίευσαν τοῦ σώματος αὐτοῦ, ἀλλὰ τὸν ἰὸν ἀπήρυγον εἰς τὸν χαλκόν, κατασπάσαντες αὐτοῦ τὰς εἰκόνας καὶ τὰς μὲν ἀποδόμενοι, τὰς δὲ βυθίσαντες, τὰς δὲ κατακόψαντες εἰς ἀμίδας· λέγεται γὰρ καὶ τοῦτο. μία δὲ μόνη σώζεται ἐν ἀκροπόλει. Φαβω-ρῖνος δέ φησιν ἐν Παντοδαπῇ ἱστορίᾳ τοῦτο ποιῆσαι τοὺς Ἀθηναίους Δημητρίου κελεύσαντος τοῦ

[1] ⟨ἀντὶ⟩ Schwartz.

---

[a] 324 B.C.

[b] The first sentence is paralleled by Aelian, *Var. Hist.* **xii.** 43 Δημήτριον δὲ τὸν Φαληρέα οἰκότριβα γενέσθαι λέγουσιν ἐκ τῆς οἰκίας τῆς Τιμοθέου καὶ Κόνωνος. The insertion of this reference to the family of Conon has had the effect of

when Harpalus, fleeing from Alexander,[a] came to Athens. As a statesman he rendered his country many splendid services. For he enriched the city with revenues and buildings, though he was not of noble birth. For he was one of Conon's household servants,[b] according to Favorinus in the first book of his *Memorabilia*; yet Lamia, with whom he lived, was a citizen of noble family, as Favorinus also states in his first book. Further, in his second book Favorinus alleges that he suffered violence from Cleon, while Didymus in his *Table-talk* relates how a certain courtesan nicknamed him Charito-Blepharos (" having the eyelids of the Graces "), and Lampito (" of shining eyes "). He is said to have lost his sight when in Alexandria and to have recovered it by the gift of Sarapis ; whereupon he composed the paeans which are sung to this day.

For all his popularity with the Athenians he nevertheless suffered eclipse through all-devouring envy. Having been indicted by some persons on a capital charge, he let judgement go by default ; and, when his accusers could not get hold of his person, they disgorged their venom on the bronze of his statues. These they tore down from their pedestals ; some were sold, some cast into the sea, and others were even, it is said, broken up to make bedroom-utensils. Only one is preserved in the Acropolis. In his *Miscellaneous History* Favorinus tells us that the Athenians did this at the bidding of King Demetrius.

separating two clauses which ought to be closely joined : καίπερ οὐκ εὐγενής ὤν (the last words of § 75) and ἀστῇ καὶ εὐγενεῖ (in § 76). Hesychius in Suidas emphasizes the beauty of Demetrius. In a modern book the statement that, according to Favorinus, Demetrius was in Conon's family would find a more suitable place in a footnote.

βασιλέως. ἀλλὰ καὶ τῷ ἔτει τῆς ἀρχῆς αὐτοῦ
ἐπέγραψαν ἀνομίας, ὡς Φαβωρῖνος.

78 Φησὶ δ᾽ αὐτὸν Ἕρμιππος μετὰ τὸν Κασάνδρου
θάνατον φοβηθέντα Ἀντίγονον παρὰ Πτολεμαῖον
ἐλθεῖν τὸν Σωτῆρα· κἀκεῖ χρόνον ἱκανὸν διατρίβοντα
συμβουλεύειν τῷ Πτολεμαίῳ πρὸς τοῖς ἄλλοις καὶ
τὴν βασιλείαν τοῖς ἐξ Εὐρυδίκης περιθεῖναι παισί.
τοῦ δὲ οὐ πεισθέντος, ἀλλὰ παραδόντος τὸ διάδημα
τῷ ἐκ Βερενίκης, μετὰ τὴν ἐκείνου τελευτὴν
ἀξιωθῆναι πρὸς τούτου παραφυλάττεσθαι ἐν τῇ
χώρᾳ μέχρι τι δόξει περὶ αὐτοῦ. ἐνταῦθα ἀθυ-
μότερον διῆγε· καί πως ὑπνώττων ὑπ᾽ ἀσπίδος
τὴν χεῖρα δηχθεὶς τὸν βίον μεθῆκε. καὶ τέθαπται
ἐν τῷ Βουσιρίτῃ νομῷ πλησίον Διοσπόλεως.

79 Καὶ αὐτῷ ἐπεγράψαμεν ἡμεῖς·

ἀνεῖλεν ἀσπὶς τὸν σοφὸν Δημήτριον
ἰὸν ἔχουσα πολὺν
ἄσμηκτον, οὐ στίλβουσα φῶς ἀπ᾽ ὀμμάτων,
ἀλλ᾽ ἀΐδην μέλανα.

Ἡρακλείδης δ᾽ ἐν τῇ ἐπιτομῇ τῶν Σωτίωνος
Διαδοχῶν τῷ Φιλαδέλφῳ τὴν βασιλείαν θέλειν
ἐκχωρῆσαι τὸν Πτολεμαῖον· τὸν δ᾽ ἀποτρέπειν
φάσκοντα, " ἂν ἄλλῳ δῷς, σὺ οὐχ ἕξεις." ὁπηνίκα
δ᾽ ἐσυκοφαντεῖτο ἐν ταῖς Ἀθήναις—μανθάνω γὰρ
καὶ τοῦτο—Μένανδρος ὁ κωμικὸς παρ᾽ ὀλίγον
ἦλθε κριθῆναι δι᾽ οὐδὲν ἄλλο ἢ ὅτι φίλος ἦν αὐτῷ·
ἀλλ᾽ αὐτὸν παρῃτήσατο Τελεσφόρος ὁ ἀνεψιὸς τοῦ
Δημητρίου.

80 Πλήθει δὲ βιβλίων καὶ ἀριθμῷ στίχων σχεδὸν
ἅπαντας παρελήλακε τοὺς κατ᾽ αὐτὸν περιπατητικούς, εὐπαίδευτος ὢν καὶ πολύπειρος παρ᾽

And in the official list the year in which he was archon was styled " the year of lawlessness," according to this same Favorinus.

Hermippus tells us that upon the death of Casander, being in fear of Antigonus, he fled to Ptolemy Soter. There he spent a considerable time and advised Ptolemy, among other things, to invest with sovereign power his children by Eurydice. To this Ptolemy would not agree, but bestowed the diadem on his son by Berenice, who, after Ptolemy's death, thought fit to detain Demetrius as a prisoner in the country until some decision should be taken concerning him. There he lived in great dejection, and somehow, in his sleep, received an asp-bite on the hand which proved fatal. He is buried in the district of Busiris near Diospolis.

Here are my lines upon him [a] :

A venomous asp was the death of the wise Demetrius, an asp withal of sticky venom, darting, not light from its eyes, but black death.

Heraclides in his epitome of Sotion's *Successions of Philosophers* says that Ptolemy himself wished to transmit the kingdom to Philadelphus, but that Demetrius tried to dissuade him, saying, " If you give it to another, you will not have it yourself." At the time when he was being continually attacked in Athens, Menander, the Comic poet, as I have also learnt, was very nearly brought to trial for no other cause than that he was a friend of Demetrius. However, Telesphorus, the nephew of Demetrius, begged him off.

In the number of his works and their total length in lines he has surpassed almost all contemporary Peripatetics. For in learning and versatility he has

[a] *Anth. Pal.* vii. 113.

ὁντινοῦν· ὧν ἐστι τὰ μὲν ἱστορικά, τὰ δὲ πολιτικά,
τὰ δὲ περὶ ποιητῶν, τὰ δὲ ῥητορικά, δημηγοριῶν
τε καὶ πρεσβειῶν, ἀλλὰ μὴν καὶ λόγων Αἰσωπείων
συναγωγαὶ καὶ ἄλλα πλείω. ἔστι δὲ τὰ

Περὶ τῆς Ἀθήνησι νομοθεσίας α′ β′ γ′ δ′ ε′.
Περὶ τῶν Ἀθήνησι πολιτειῶν α′ β′.
Περὶ δημαγωγίας α′ β′.
Περὶ πολιτικῶν α′ β′.
Περὶ νόμων α′.
Περὶ ῥητορικῆς α′ β′.
Στρατηγικῶν α′ β′.
81 Περὶ Ἰλιάδος α′ β′.
Περὶ Ὀδυσσείας α′ β′ γ′ δ′.
Πτολεμαῖος α′.
Ἐρωτικὸς α′.
Φαιδώνδας α′.
Μαίδων α′.
Κλέων α′.
Σωκράτης α′.
Ἀρταξέρξης α′.
Ὁμηρικὸς α′.
Ἀριστείδης α′.
Ἀριστόμαχος α′.
Προτρεπτικὸς α′.
Ὑπὲρ τῆς πολιτείας α′.
Περὶ τῆς δεκαετίας α′.
Περὶ τῶν Ἰώνων α′.
Πρεσβευτικὸς α′.
Περὶ πίστεως α′.
Περὶ χάριτος α′.
Περὶ τύχης α′.

no equal. Some of these works are historical and others political ; there are some dealing with poets, others with rhetoric. Then there are public speeches and reports of embassies, besides collections of Aesop's fables and much else. He wrote :

Of Legislation at Athens, five books.
Of the Constitutions of Athens, two books.
Of Statesmanship, two books.
On Politics, two books.
Of Laws, one book.
On Rhetoric, two books.
On Military Matters, two books.
On the Iliad, two books.
On the Odyssey, four books.

And the following works, each in one book :

Ptolemy.
Concerning Love.
Phaedondas.
Maedon.
Cleon.
Socrates.
Artaxerxes.
Concerning Homer.
Aristides.
Aristomachus.
An Exhortation to Philosophy.
Of the Constitution.
On the ten years of his own Supremacy.
Of the Ionians.
Concerning Embassies.
Of Belief.
Of Favour.
Of Fortune.

Περὶ μεγαλοψυχίας αʹ.
Περὶ γάμου αʹ.
Περὶ τοῦ δοκοῦ αʹ.
Περὶ εἰρήνης αʹ.
Περὶ νόμων αʹ.
Περὶ ἐπιτηδευμάτων αʹ.
Περὶ καιροῦ αʹ.
Διονύσιος αʹ.
Χαλκιδικὸς αʹ.
Ἀθηναίων καταδρομὴ αʹ.
Περὶ Ἀντιφάνους αʹ.
Προοίμιον ἱστορικὸν αʹ.
Ἐπιστολαὶ αʹ.
Ἐκκλησία ἔνορκος αʹ.
Περὶ γήρως αʹ.
Δίκαια αʹ.
Αἰσωπείων αʹ.
Χρειῶν αʹ.

82 Χαρακτὴρ δὲ φιλόσοφος, εὐτονίᾳ ῥητορικῇ καὶ δυνάμει κεκραμένος. οὗτος ἀκούσας ὅτι τὰς εἰκόνας αὐτοῦ κατέστρεψαν Ἀθηναῖοι, " ἀλλ᾽ οὐ τὴν ἀρετήν," ἔφη, " δι᾽ ἣν ἐκείνας ἀνέστησαν." ἔλεγε μικρὸν μὲν εἶναι μέρος τὰς ὀφρῦς, ὅλῳ δ᾽ ἐπισκοτῆσαι τῷ βίῳ δύνασθαι. οὐ μόνον τὸν πλοῦτον ἔφη τυφλόν, ἀλλὰ καὶ τὴν ὁδηγοῦσαν αὐτὸν τύχην. ὅσον ἐν πολέμῳ δύνασθαι σίδηρον, τοσοῦτον ἐν πολιτείᾳ ἰσχύειν λόγον. ἰδών ποτε νεανίσκον ἄσωτον, " ἰδού," ἔφη, " τετράγωνος Ἑρμῆς ἔχων σύρμα,[1] κοιλίαν, αἰδοῖον, πώγωνα." τῶν τετυ-

---

[1] σύρμα] στόμα Reiske : στῦμα deleto αἰδοῖον D. S. Robertson.

Of Magnanimity.
Of Marriage.
Of the Beam in the Sky.[a]
Of Peace.
On Laws.
On Customs.
Of Opportunity.
Dionysius.
Concerning Chalcis.
A Denunciation of the Athenians.
On Antiphanes.
Historical Introduction.
Letters.
A Sworn Assembly.
Of Old Age.
Rights.
Aesop's Fables.
Anecdotes.

His style is philosophical, with an admixture of rhetorical vigour and force. When he heard that the Athenians had destroyed his statues, "That they may do," said he, "but the merits which caused them to be erected they cannot destroy." He used to say that the eyebrows formed but a small part of the face, and yet they can darken the whole of life by the scorn they express. Again, he said that not only was Plutus blind, but his guide, Fortune, as well ; that all that steel could achieve in war was won in politics by eloquence. On seeing a young dandy, "There," quoth he, "is a four-square Hermes for you, with trailing robe, belly, beard and

---

[a] "Of the Beam in the Sky." Some render this "Of Opinion," but the word used in this sense is δόκησις : cf. Schäf. Schol. Par. Ap. Rh. ii. 1088.

φωμένων ἀνδρῶν ἔφη τὸ μὲν ὕψος δεῖν περιαιρεῖν,
τὸ δὲ φρόνημα καταλείπειν. τοὺς νέους ἔφη δεῖν
ἐπὶ μὲν τῆς οἰκίας τοὺς γονέας αἰδεῖσθαι, ἐν δὲ
ταῖς ὁδοῖς τοὺς ἀπαντῶντας, ἐν δὲ ταῖς ἐρημίαις
83 ἑαυτούς. τοὺς φίλους ἐπὶ μὲν τὰ ἀγαθὰ παρακα-
λουμένους ἀπιέναι, ἐπὶ δὲ τὰς συμφορὰς αὐτομάτους.
τοσαῦτα καὶ εἰς τοῦτον ἀναφέρεσθαι δοκεῖ.

Γεγόνασι δὲ Δημήτριοι ἀξιόλογοι εἴκοσι· πρῶτος
Χαλκηδόνιος, ῥήτωρ καὶ Θρασυμάχου πρεσβύ-
τερος· δεύτερος αὐτὸς οὗτος· τρίτος Βυζάντιος,
περιπατητικός· τέταρτος καλούμενος Γραφικὸς
καὶ σαφὴς διηγήσασθαι· ἦν δὲ ὁ αὐτὸς καὶ ζω-
γράφος· πέμπτος Ἀσπένδιος, μαθητὴς Ἀπολ-
λωνίου τοῦ Σολέως· ἕκτος Καλλατιανός, ὁ γεγραφὼς περὶ Ἀσίας καὶ Εὐρώπης εἴκοσι βίβλους·
ἕβδομος Βυζάντιος, ἐν τρισκαίδεκα βιβλίοις γεγραφὼς τὴν Γαλατῶν διάβασιν ἐξ Εὐρώπης εἰς
Ἀσίαν καὶ ἐν ἄλλοις ὀκτὼ τὰ περὶ Ἀντίοχον καὶ
Πτολεμαῖον καὶ τὴν τῆς Λιβύης ὑπ' αὐτῶν δι-
84 οίκησιν· ὄγδοος ὁ διατρίψας ἐν Ἀλεξανδρείᾳ σοφιστής, τέχνας γεγραφὼς ῥητορικάς· ἔνατος Ἀδρα-
μυττηνὸς γραμματικός, ἐπικληθεὶς Ἰξίων διὰ τὸ
ἀδικῆσαί τι δοκεῖν περὶ τὴν Ἥραν· δέκατος
Κυρηναῖος, γραμματικός, ὁ ἐπικληθεὶς Στάμνος,
ἀνὴρ ἀξιόλογος· ἑνδέκατος Σκήψιος, πλούσιος
καὶ εὐγενὴς ἄνθρωπος καὶ φιλόλογος ἄκρως·
οὗτος καὶ Μητρόδωρον προεβίβασε τὸν πολίτην.
δωδέκατος γραμματικὸς Ἐρυθραῖος, πολιτογρα-

---

[a] Since Herms at Athens show neither drapery nor belly,
but archaic hair, this saying would seem either to be in-
correctly reported or to need a fresh interpretation. It has
been suggested that a long lock pendent over the shoulder
may lurk under σύοια (cf. Anth. Pal. v. 12. 2 σύρμα μένει

all." [a] When men are haughty and arrogant, he declared we should cut down their tall stature and leave them their spirit unimpaired. Children should honour their parents at home, out-of-doors everyone they meet, and in solitude themselves. In prosperity friends do not leave you unless desired, whereas in adversity they stay away of their own accord. All these sayings seem to be set down to his credit.

There have been twenty noteworthy men called Demetrius : (1) a rhetorician of Chalcedon, older than Thrasymachus ; (2) the subject of this notice ; (3) a Peripatetic of Byzantium ; (4) one called the graphic writer, clear in narrative ; he was also a painter ; (5) a native of Aspendus, a pupil of Apollonius of Soli ; (6) a native of Callatis, who wrote a geography of Asia and Europe in twenty books ; (7) a Byzantine, who wrote a history of the migration of the Gauls from Europe into Asia in thirteen books, and another work in eight books dealing with Antiochus and Ptolemy and their settlement of Libya ; (8) the sophist who lived at Alexandria, author of handbooks of rhetoric ; (9) a grammarian of Adramyttium, surnamed Ixion because he was thought to be unjust to Hera ; (10) a grammarian of Cyrene, surnamed Wine-jar, an eminent man ; (11) a native of Scepsis, a man of wealth and good birth, ardently devoted to learning ; he was also the means of bringing his countryman Metrodorus into prominence ; (12) a grammarian of Erythrae enrolled as a citizen of

πλοκάμων, and Ael. *Var. Hist.* xii. 14 τὴν μὲν γὰρ κόμην ἀνασεσύρθαι), or that a Herm might sometimes have been made by cutting down a larger, draped, statue ; or perhaps on festal days Herms were decked with robes. In Stobaeus, *Flor.* iv. 68, Philip is credited with a sneer to the same effect on Athenians at large.

DIOGENES LAERTIUS

φηθεὶς ἐν τῇ Μνῷ· τρισκαιδέκατος Βιθυνὸς Διφίλου
τοῦ στωϊκοῦ υἱός, μαθητὴς δὲ Παναιτίου τοῦ
85 Ῥοδίου· τεσσαρεσκαιδέκατος ῥήτωρ Σμυρναῖος.
καὶ οὗτοι μὲν λογικοί. ποιηταὶ δὲ πρῶτος ἀρχαίαν
κωμῳδίαν πεποιηκώς· δεύτερος ἐπῶν ποιητής,
οὗ μόνα σώζεται πρὸς τοὺς φθονεροὺς εἰρημένα
τάδε·

ζωὸν ἀτιμήσαντες ἀποφθίμενον ποθέουσι·
καί ποθ' ὑπὲρ τύμβοιο καὶ ἀπνόου εἰδώλοιο
ἄστεα νεῖκος ἐπῆλθεν, ἔριν δ' ἐστήσατο λαός.

τρίτος Ταρσικὸς σατυρογράφος· τέταρτος ἰάμβους
γεγραφώς, πικρὸς ἀνήρ· πέμπτος ἀνδριαντοποιός,
οὗ μέμνηται Πολέμων· ἕκτος Ἐρυθραῖος, ποικιλο-
γράφος ἄνθρωπος, ὃς καὶ ἱστορικὰ καὶ ῥητορικὰ
πεποίηκε βιβλία.

Κεφ. ς'. ΗΡΑΚΛΕΙΔΗΣ

86 Ἡρακλείδης Εὐθύφρονος Ἡρακλεώτης τοῦ Πόν-
του, ἀνὴρ πλούσιος. Ἀθήνησι δὲ παρέβαλε πρῶτον
μὲν Σπευσίππῳ· ἀλλὰ καὶ τῶν Πυθαγορείων
διήκουσε καὶ τὰ Πλάτωνος ἐζηλώκει· καὶ ὕστερον
ἤκουσεν Ἀριστοτέλους, ὥς φησι Σωτίων ἐν Διαδοχαῖς. οὗτος ἐσθῆτί τε μαλακῇ ἐχρῆτο καὶ ὑπέρ-
ογκος ἦν τὸ σῶμα, ὥστ' αὐτὸν ὑπὸ τῶν Ἀττικῶν
μὴ Ποντικὸν ἀλλὰ Πομπικὸν καλεῖσθαι. πρᾶός
τ' ἦν τὸ βλέμμα καὶ ϲεμνός. φέρεται δ' αὐτοῦ
συγγράμματα κάλλιστά τε καὶ ἄριστα· διάλογοι,
ὧν ἠθικὰ μὲν

ᵃ That Heraclides was a member of the Academy is
established beyond all doubt by the fact that he was a
candidate for the headship of the School on the death of

Mnos ; (13) a Bithynian, son of Diphilus the Stoic and pupil of Panaetius of Rhodes ; (14) a rhetorician of Smyrna. The foregoing were prose authors. Of poets bearing this name the first belonged to the Old Comedy ; the second was an epic poet whose lines to the envious alone survive :

> While he lives they scorn the man whom they regret when he is gone ; yet, some day, for the honour of his tomb and lifeless image, contention seizes cities and the people set up strife ;

the third of Tarsus, writer of satires ; the fourth, a writer of lampoons, in a bitter style ; the fifth, a sculptor mentioned by Polemo ; the sixth, of Erythrae, a versatile man, who also wrote historical and rhetorical works.

Chapter 6. HERACLIDES (*floruit* 360 B.C.)

Heraclides, son of Euthyphro, born at Heraclea in the Pontus, was a wealthy man. At Athens he first attached himself to Speusippus. He also attended the lectures of the Pythagoreans and admired the writings of Plato. Last of all he became a pupil of Aristotle, as Sotion says in his *Successions of Philosophers.*[a] He wore fine soft clothes, and he was extremely corpulent, which made the Athenians call him Pompicus rather than Ponticus. He was mild and dignified of aspect. Works by him survive of great beauty and excellence. There are ethical dialogues :

Speusippus : *Index Acad.* p. 38 Mekler. However, not only does Diogenes Laertius make him, on Sotion's authority, a pupil of Aristotle, but Aëtius also seems, iii. 2. 5, to associate him with the Peripatetics (καθάπερ ἀμέλει πάντες οἱ Περιπατητικοί).

Περὶ δικαιοσύνης γ΄.
Ἐν δὲ περὶ σωφροσύνης
Περί τ' εὐσεβείας ε΄ καὶ
Περὶ ἀνδρείας α΄.
Κοινῶς τε περὶ ἀρετῆς α΄ καὶ ἄλλο.
Περὶ εὐδαιμονίας α΄.
87 Περὶ τῆς ἀρχῆς α΄ καὶ
Νόμων α΄ καὶ τῶν συγγενῶν τούτοις.
Περὶ ὀνομάτων α΄.
Συνθῆκαι α΄.
Ἀκούσιος α΄.
Ἐρωτικὸς καὶ Κλεινίας α΄.

Φυσικὰ δὲ

Περὶ νοῦ.
Περὶ ψυχῆς καὶ κατ' ἰδίαν περὶ ψυχῆς καὶ
Περὶ φύσεως καὶ
Περὶ εἰδώλων.
Πρὸς Δημόκριτον.
Περὶ τῶν ἐν οὐρανῷ α΄.
Περὶ τῶν ἐν ᾄδου.
Περὶ βίων α΄ β΄.
Αἰτίαι περὶ νόσων α΄.
Περὶ τἀγαθοῦ α΄.
Πρὸς τὰ Ζήνωνος α΄.
Πρὸς τὰ Μήτρωνος α΄.

Γραμματικὰ δὲ

Περὶ τῆς Ὁμήρου καὶ Ἡσιόδου ἡλικίας α΄ β΄.
Περὶ Ἀρχιλόχου καὶ Ὁμήρου α΄ β΄.

Καὶ μουσικὰ δὲ

Περὶ τῶν παρ' Εὐριπίδῃ καὶ Σοφοκλεῖ α΄ β΄ γ΄.

Of Justice, three books.
Of Temperance, one book.
Of Piety, five books.
Of Courage, one book.
Of Virtue in general, one book.
A second with the same title.
Of Happiness, one book.
Of Government, one book.
On Laws, one book, and on subjects kindred to these.
Of Names, one book.
Agreements, one book.
On the Involuntary, one book.
Concerning Love, and Clinias, one book.

Others are physical treatises:

Of Reason.
Of the Soul, and a separate treatise with the same
    title.
Of Nature.
Of Images.
Against Democritus.
Of Celestial Phenomena, one book
Of Things in the Under-world.
On Various Ways of Life, two books.
The Causes of Diseases, one book.
Of the Good, one book.
Against Zeno's Doctrines, one book.
A Reply to Metron's Doctrines, one book.

To grammar and criticism belong:

Of the Age of Homer and Hesiod, two books
Of Archilochus and Homer, two books.

Of a literary nature are:

A work on passages in Euripides and Sophocles,
    three books.

Περὶ μουσικῆς α' β'.

88 Λύσεων Ὁμηρικῶν α' β'.

Θεωρηματικὸν α'.

Περὶ τῶν τριῶν τραγῳδοποιῶν **α'**.

Χαρακτῆρες α'.

Περὶ ποιητικῆς καὶ τῶν ποιητῶν α'.

Περὶ στοχασμοῦ α'.

Προοπτικὸν α'.

Ἡρακλείτου ἐξηγήσεις δ'.

Πρὸς τὸν Δημόκριτον ἐξηγήσεις **α'**.

Λύσεων ἐριστικῶν α' β'.

Ἀξίωμα α'.

Περὶ εἰδῶν **α'**.

Λύσεις α'.

Ὑποθῆκαι α'.

Πρὸς Διονύσιον **α'**.

Ῥητορικὰ δὲ

Περὶ τοῦ ῥητορεύειν ἢ Πρωταγόρας.

Ἱστορικά·

Περὶ τῶν Πυθαγορείων καὶ

Περὶ εὑρημάτων.

Τούτων τὰ μὲν κωμικῶς πέπλακεν, ὡς τὸ Περὶ ἡδονῆς καὶ Περὶ σωφροσύνης· τὰ δὲ τραγικῶς, ὡς τὸ Περὶ τῶν καθ᾽ ᾅδην καὶ τὸ Περὶ εὐσεβείας καὶ τὸ Περὶ ἐξουσίας.

89 Ἔστι δ᾽ αὐτῷ καὶ μεσότης τις ὁμιλητικὴ φιλοσόφων τε καὶ στρατηγικῶν καὶ πολιτικῶν ἀνδρῶν πρὸς ἀλλήλους διαλεγομένων. ἀλλὰ καὶ γεωμετρικά ἐστιν αὐτοῦ καὶ διαλεκτικά. ἄλλως τ᾽ ἐν ἅπασι ποικίλος τε καὶ διηρμένος τὴν λέξιν ἐστὶ καὶ ψυχαγωγεῖν ἱκανῶς δυνάμενος.

On Music, two books.
Solutions of Homeric Problems, two books.
Of Theorems, one book.
On the Three Tragic Poets, one book.
Characters, one book.
Of Poetry and Poets, one book.
Of Conjecture, one book.
Concerning Prevision, one book.
Expositions of Heraclitus, four books.
Expositions in Reply to Democritus, one book.
Solutions of Eristic Problems, two books.
Logical Proposition, one book.
Of Species, one book.
Solutions, one book.
Admonitions, one book.
A Reply to Dionysius, one book.

To rhetoric belongs :

Of Public Speaking, or Protagoras.

To history :

On the Pythagoreans.
Of Discoveries.

Some of these works are in the style of comedy, for instance the tracts On Pleasure and On Temperance ; others in the style of tragedy, as the books entitled Of those in Hades, Of Piety, and Of Authority.

Again, he has a sort of intermediate style of conversation which he employs when philosophers, generals and statesmen converse with each other. Furthermore, he wrote geometrical and dialectical works, and is, besides, everywhere versatile and lofty in diction, and a great adept at charming the reader's mind.

Δοκεῖ δὲ καὶ τὴν πατρίδα τυραννουμένην ἐλευθερῶσαι, τὸν μόναρχον κτείνας, ὥς φησι Δημήτριος
ὁ Μάγνης ἐν Ὁμωνύμοις. ὃς καὶ τοιόνδε ἱστορεῖ
περὶ αὐτοῦ· " θρέψαι αὐτὸν δράκοντα ἐκ νέου καὶ
αὐξηθέντα, ἐπειδὴ τελευτᾶν ἔμελλε, κελεῦσαί τινι
τῶν πιστῶν αὐτοῦ τὸ σῶμα κατακρύψαι, τὸν
δὲ δράκοντα ἐπὶ τῆς κλίνης θεῖναι, ἵνα δόξειεν
90 εἰς θεοὺς μεταβεβηκέναι. ἐγένετο δὲ πάντα.
καὶ μεταξὺ παραπεμπόντων Ἡρακλείδην τῶν
πολιτῶν καὶ εὐφημούντων, ὁ δράκων ἀκούσας
τῆς ἐπιβοῆς ἐξέδυ τῶν ἱματίων καὶ διετάραξε
τοὺς πλείστους. ὕστερον μέντοι ἐξεκαλύφθη πάντα
καὶ ὤφθη Ἡρακλείδης οὐχ οἷος ἐδόκει, ἀλλ᾽
οἷος ἦν."

Καὶ ἔστιν ἡμῶν εἰς αὐτὸν οὕτως ἔχον·

ἤθελες ἀνθρώποισι λιπεῖν φάτιν, Ἡρακλείδη,
ὡς ῥα θανὼν ἐγένου ζωὸς ἅπασι[1] δράκων.
ἀλλὰ διεψεύσθης, σεσοφισμένε· δὴ γὰρ ὁ μὲν θὴρ
ἦε δράκων, σὺ δὲ θήρ, οὐ σοφὸς ὤν, ἑάλως.

ταῦτα δέ φησι καὶ Ἱππόβοτος.

91 Ἕρμιππος δὲ λιμοῦ κατασχόντος τὴν χώραν
φησὶν αἰτεῖν τοὺς Ἡρακλεώτας τὴν Πυθίαν λύσιν.
τὸν δὲ Ἡρακλείδην διαφθεῖραι χρήμασι τούς τε
θεωροὺς καὶ τὴν προειρημένην, ὥστ᾽ ἀνειπεῖν ἀπ-
αλλαγήσεσθαι τοῦ κακοῦ, εἰ ζῶν μὲν Ἡρακλείδης
ὁ Εὐθύφρονος χρυσῷ στεφάνῳ στεφανωθείη πρὸς
αὐτῶν, ἀποθανὼν δὲ ὡς ἥρως τιμῷτο. ἐκομίσθη
ὁ δῆθεν χρησμὸς καὶ οὐδὲν ὤναντο οἱ πλάσαντες
αὐτόν. αὐτίκα γὰρ ἐν τῷ θεάτρῳ στεφανούμενος

[1] ἅπασι] ἄπαρτι Reiske.

It seems that he delivered his native city from
oppressions by assassinating its ruler, as is stated
in his work on *Men of the Same Name* by Demetrius
of Magnesia, who also tells the following story about
him : " As a boy, and when he grew up, he kept a
pet snake, and, being at the point of death, he ordered
a trusted attendant to conceal the corpse but to
place the snake on his bier, that he might seem to
have departed to the gods. All this was done. But
while the citizens were in the very midst of the
procession and were loud in his praise, the snake,
hearing the uproar, popped up out of the shroud,
creating widespread confusion. Subsequently, however, all was revealed, and they saw Heraclides, not
as he appeared, but as he really was."

I have written of him as follows [a] :

You wished, Heraclides, to leave to all mankind a reputation that after death you lived as a snake.[b] But you were
deceived, you sophist, for the snake was really a brute beast,
and you were detected as more of a beast than a sage.

Hippobotus too has this tale.

Hermippus relates that, when their territory was
visited by famine, the people of Heraclea besought
the Pythian priestess for relief, but Heraclides bribed
the sacred envoys as well as the aforesaid priestess
to reply that they would be rid of the calamity if
Heraclides, the son of Euthyphro, were crowned with
a crown of gold in his lifetime and after his death
received heroic honours. The pretended oracle was
brought home, but its forgers got nothing by it.
For directly Heraclides was crowned in the theatre,

[a] *Anth. Pal.* vii. 104.
[b] Or, reading ἄπαρτι for ἄπασι, " wished to leave a report
behind you that immediately after death you became a
living snake."

ὁ Ἡρακλείδης ἀπόπληκτος ἐγένετο, οἵ τε θεωροὶ
καταλευσθέντες διεφθάρησαν. ἀλλὰ καὶ ἡ Πυθία
τὴν αὐτὴν ὥραν κατιοῦσα ἐς τὸ ἄδυτον καὶ ἐπι-
στᾶσα ἑνὶ τῶν δρακόντων δηχθεῖσα παραχρῆμα
ἀπέπνευσε. καὶ τὰ μὲν περὶ τὸν θάνατον αὐτοῦ
τοσαῦτα.

92 Φησὶ δ᾽ Ἀριστόξενος ὁ μουσικὸς καὶ τραγῳδίας
αὐτὸν ποιεῖν καὶ Θέσπιδος αὐτὰς ἐπιγράφειν.
Χαμαιλέων τε τὰ παρ᾽ ἑαυτοῦ φησι κλέψαντα αὐτὸν
τὰ περὶ Ἡσιόδου καὶ Ὁμήρου γράψαι· ἀλλὰ καὶ
Αὐτόδωρος ὁ Ἐπικούρειος ἐπιτιμᾷ αὐτῷ, τοῖς περὶ
δικαιοσύνης ἀντιλέγων. ἔτι καὶ Διονύσιος ὁ Μετα-
θέμενος (ἢ Σπίνθαρος, ὡς ἔνιοι) γράψας τὸν Παρ-
θενοπαῖον ἐπέγραψε Σοφοκλέους. ὁ δὲ πιστεύσας
εἴς τι τῶν ἰδίων συγγραμμάτων ἐχρῆτο μαρτυρίοις
93 ὡς Σοφοκλέους. αἰσθόμενος δ᾽ ὁ Διονύσιος ἐμή-
νυσεν αὐτῷ τὸ γεγονός· τοῦ δ᾽ ἀρνουμένου καὶ
ἀπιστοῦντος ἐπέστειλεν ἰδεῖν τὴν παραστιχίδα· καὶ
εἶχε Πάγκαλος. οὗτος δ᾽ ἦν ἐρώμενος Διονυσίου·
ὡς δ᾽ ἔτι ἀπιστῶν ἔλεγε κατὰ τὴν τύχην ἐνδέχεσθαι
οὕτως ἔχειν, πάλιν ἀντεπέστειλεν ὁ Διονύσιος ὅτι
" καὶ ταῦτα εὑρήσεις·

A. γέρων πίθηκος οὐχ ἁλίσκεται πάγῃ·
B. ἁλίσκεται μέν, μετὰ χρόνον δ᾽ ἁλίσκεται."

καὶ πρὸς τούτοις· " Ἡρακλείδης γράμματα οὐκ ἐπί-
σταται οὐδ᾽ ᾐσχύνθη."

Γεγόνασι δ᾽ Ἡρακλεῖδαι τεσσαρεσκαίδεκα· πρῶτος αὐτὸς οὗτος· δεύτερος πολίτης αὐτοῦ, πυρρίχας
94 καὶ φλυαρίας συντεταγμένος· τρίτος Κυμαῖος,

---

[a] We should say, " An old bird is not caught with chaff."
[b] Von Arnim's emendation (ὁ δὲ) gives a different turn to

he was seized with apoplexy, whereupon the envoys to the oracle were stoned to death. Moreover, at the very same time the Pythian priestess, after she had gone down to the shrine and taken her seat, was bitten by one of the snakes and died instantly. Such are the tales told about his death.

Aristoxenus the musician asserts that Heraclides also composed tragedies, inscribing upon them the name of Thespis. Chamaeleon complains that Heraclides' treatise on the works of Homer and Hesiod was plagiarized from his own. Furthermore, Autodorus the Epicurean criticizes him in a polemic against his tract Of Justice. Again, Dionysius the Renegade, or, as some people call him, the " Spark," when he wrote the Parthenopaeus, entitled it a play of Sophocles ; and Heraclides, such was his credulity, in one of his own works drew upon this forged play as Sophoclean evidence. Dionysius, on perceiving this, confessed what he had done ; and, when the other denied the fact and would not believe him, called his attention to the acrostic which gave the name of Pancalus, of whom Dionysius was very fond. Heraclides was still unconvinced. Such a thing, he said, might very well happen by chance. To this Dionysius, " You will also find these lines :

A. An old monkey is not caught by a trap.[a]
B. Oh yes, he's caught at last, but it takes time."

And this besides : " Heraclides is ignorant of letters and not ashamed of his ignorance."[b]

Fourteen persons have borne the name of Heraclides : (1) the subject of this notice ; (2) a fellow-citizen of his, author of Pyrrhic verses and tales ;

the story, viz. " And this besides: 'Heraclides is ignorant of letters.' This made Heraclides blush."

γεγραφὼς Περσικὰ ἐν πέντε βιβλίοις· τέταρτος
Κυμαῖος, ῥήτωρ τέχνας γεγραφώς· πέμπτος Καλ-
λατιανὸς ἢ Ἀλεξανδρεύς, γεγραφὼς τὴν Διαδοχὴν
ἐν ἓξ βιβλίοις καὶ Λεμβευτικὸν λόγον, ὅθεν καὶ
Λέμβος ἐκαλεῖτο· ἕκτος Ἀλεξανδρεύς, γεγραφὼς
τὰ Περσικὰ ἰδιώματα· ἕβδομος διαλεκτικὸς Βαργυ-
ληΐτης, κατ' Ἐπικούρου γεγραφώς· ὄγδοος ἰατρὸς
τῶν ἀπὸ Ἱκεσίου· ἔνατος ἰατρὸς Ταραντῖνος, ἐμ-
πειρικός· δέκατος ποιητικός, παραινέσεις γεγραφώς·
ἑνδέκατος ἀνδριαντοποιὸς Φωκαεύς· δωδέκατος
ἐπιγραμμάτων ποιητὴς λιγυρός· τρισκαιδέκατος
Μάγνης, Μιθραδατικὰ γεγραφώς· τεσσαρεσκαι
δέκατος ἀστρολογούμενα συγγεγραφώς.

(3) a native of Cyme, who wrote of Persia in five books; (4) another native of Cyme, who wrote rhetorical textbooks; (5) of Callatis or Alexandria, author of the *Succession of Philosophers* in six books and a work entitled *Lembeuticus*, from which he got the surname of Lembus (a fast boat or scout); (6) an Alexandrian who wrote on the Persian national character; (7) a dialectician of Bargylis, who wrote against Epicurus; (8) a physician of the school of Hicesius; (9) another physician of Tarentum, an empiric; (10) a poet who was the author of admonitions; (11) a sculptor of Phocaea; (12) a Ligurian poet, author of epigrams; (13) Heraclides of Magnesia, who wrote a history of Mithradates; (14) the compiler of an Astronomy.